The Law of Carriage of Goods by Sea

Arun Kasi

The Law of Carriage of Goods by Sea

Springer

Arun Kasi
Arun Kasi & Co
Kuala Lumpur, Malaysia

ISBN 978-981-33-6792-0 ISBN 978-981-33-6793-7 (eBook)
https://doi.org/10.1007/978-981-33-6793-7

This Springer imprint is published by the registered company Springer Nature Singapore Pte Ltd.
The registered company address is: 152 Beach Road, #21-01/04 Gateway East, Singapore 189721, Singapore

This book is dedicated to my dear parents, Mr. Kasi Arunachalam Chettiar and Mdm. Manomani Kupusamy, only by blessings, guidance and teachings of whom I am today where I am and have intellectually produced what I have.

Preface

This book covers the law and practice of international trade, bills of lading and charterparties. It also outlines sea waybills and ship's delivery orders. It is written, primarily, with maritime law practitioners, students and academicians in mind. It will also be a useful guide to sea carriers, forwarding agents, marine insurers, international trade financiers, arbitrators, etc. The book includes analytical and critical commentary on numerous cases and presents alternative possible arguments which law practitioners will find to be of immediate use for their cases. Cases, and commentary on them, are used as an illustration to develop a clear understanding of the underlying principles.

The book is primarily based on the English law. However, it makes extensive reference to cases from Singapore and Malaysia. In addition to the Singaporean and Malaysian laws, Indian statutes, namely Contract Act and Evidence Act, have been amply referred to. These are, in effect, the codification of the English law on these subjects and model statutes adopted in many Commonwealth jurisdictions. These references make the book quite relevant to Commonwealth jurisdictions as well as dealing with cases before the English courts and arbitrations where the applicable law is that of the Commonwealth jurisdictions.

The book is up to date with material available as at 30 April 2021.

Kuala Lumpur, Malaysia
April 2021

Arun Kasi

Acknowledgements

My thanks are due to Baltic and International Maritime Council (BIMCO) and Association of Ship Brokers & Agents (USA) Inc (ASBA) for giving permission to reproduce clauses from their standard forms of shipping contracts. The Hague-Rules of 1924, the Hague-Visby Rules of 1968, the Hague-Visby Rules of 1968 as amended by the Protocol of 1979 and the Convention on Limitation of Liability for Maritime Claims of 1976 as amended by the Protocol of 1996 further amended in 2012, all copyrighted by the United Nations, are reproduced, in part or full, with the permission of the United Nations. The UK Crown copyrighted materials are reproduced by Open Government Licence v 3.0. I am indebted to Sweet & Maxwell, Lexis Nexis and Commonwealth Lawyers Association for giving me permission to include matters that, substantially, I had previously written for their journals as articles.

Should any copyright holder have been inadvertently overlooked in my seeking permission, my apologies for the same and I will make the necessary arrangement at the earliest opportunity. I cannot miss out, in my acknowledgements, all the authors and publishers of the materials referred to in the References for making the knowledge contained therein available.

Acknowledgments

List of Cases

Ace Imports Pty Ltd v Companhia de Navegacao Lloyd Brasileiro (The Esmeralda 1) [1988] 1 Lloyd's Rep 206 192

Action Navigation Inc v Bottiglieri di Navigation SpA (The Kitsa) [2005] EWHC 177 (Comm) 453

Action SA v Britannic Shipping Corpn Ltd (The Aegis Britannic) [1987] 1 Lloyd's Rep 119 414

Actis Co Ltd v Sanko Steamship Co Ltd (The Aquacharm) (CA) [1982] 1 All ER 390 485

Actis Co Ltd v Sanko Steamship Co Ltd (The Aquacharm) (HC) [1980] 2 Lloyd's Rep 237 .... 380, 481

Adamastos Shipping Co Ltd v Anglo-Saxon Petroleum Co Ltd [1959] AC 133 .... 114, 287, 383

Aegean Sea Traders Corpn v Repsol Petroleo SA (The Aegean Sea) [1998] 2 Lloyd's Rep 39 .... 57, 463

Aegnoussiotis Shipping Corpn of Monrovia v A/S Kristian Jebsens Rederi of Bergen (The Aegnoussiotis) [1977] 1 Lloyd's Rep 268 416

Afovos Shipping Co SA v Pagnan and Lli (The Afovos) [1983] 1 All ER 449 475

Agios Stylianous Compania Naviera SA v Maritime Associates International Ltd Lagos (The Agios Stylianos) [1975] 1 Lloyd's Rep 426 434

AIC Limited v Marine Pilot Limited (The Archimidis) [2008] EWCA Civ 175 .... 401, 458

Aktieselskabet de Danske Sukkerfabrikker v Bajamar Compania Naviera SA (The Torenia) [1983] 2 Lloyd's Rep 210 .... 217, 281

Albacora SRL v Westcott & Laurance Line Ltd (The Maltasian) [1966] 2 Lloyd's Rep 53 .... 132, 285, 288, 308, 312, 318

Aldebaran Compania Maritime SA, Panama v Aussenhandel AG Zurich (The Darrah) [1977] AC 157 434

Alder v Dickson [1955] 1 QB 158 .... 168, 169

Alfred C Toepfer Schiffahrtsgesellschaft Gmbh v Tossa Marine Co Ltd. *See* Tossa Marine Co Ltd v Alfred C Toepfer Schiffahrtsgesellschaft Gmbh (The Derby) [1985] 2 Lloyd's Rep 325

Alize 1954 and another v Allianz Elementar Versicherungs AG and others (The GMA CGM Libra) [2020] EWCA Civ 293 . 208

Allison v Bristol Marine Insurance Co (1876) 1 App Cas 209 ... 406, 415

Almas Shipping Corp of Monrovia v Mantovani (The Dione) [1975] 1 Lloyd's Rep 114 490

Amixco Asia Pte Ltd v Bank Negara Indonesia [1992] 1 SLR 703 145

Andre & Cie SA v Orient Shipping Rotterdam BV (The Laconian Confidence) [1997] 1 Lloyd's Rep 139 483

Angara Maritime Ltd v Oceanconnect UK Ltd [2010] EWHC 619 384

Antariksa Logistics Pte Ltd and others v McTrans Cargo (S) Pte Ltd [2012] SGHC 154 157

Aries Tanker Corpn v Total Transport Ltd (The Aries) [1977] 1 All ER 398 .... 333, 375, 406, 407

Armar Shipping Co Ltd v Caisse Algérienne d'Assurance et de Réassurance (The Armar) [1981] 1 All ER 498 262

Armement Adolf Deppe v John Robinson & Co Ltd [1917] 2 KB 204 .... 386, 388

Armour & Co Ltd v Leopold Walford (London) Ltd [1921] 3 KB 473 .... 71, 122

Arthur Guinness, Son & Co (Dublin) Ltd v The Freshfield (Owners) (The Lady Gwendolen) [1965] P 294 299

Asfar v Blundell [1896] 1 QB 123 .... 403, 406, 409

Atkins International HA v Islamic Republic of Iran Shipping Lines (The APJ Priti) [1987] 2 Lloyd's Rep 37 458

Atlantic Oil Carriers Ltd v British Petroleum Co Ltd (The Atlantic Duchess) [1957] 2 Lloyd's Rep 55 132

Attica Sea Carriers Corpn v Ferrostaal Poseidon Bulk Reederei GmbH (The Puerto Buitrago) [1976] 1 Lloyd's Rep 250 490

Awilco A/S v Fulvia SpA di Navigazione (The Chikuma) [1981] 1 All ER 652 469

Balian & Sons v Joly, Victoria & Co (1890) 6 TLR 345 236

Bandung Shipping Pte Ltd v Keppel Tatlee Bank Ltd [2003] 1 SLR 295 .... 24, 65

Bangkok Bank Limited v Wiel Brothers Cotton Inc [1977] 2 MLJ 134 34

Bank Line v Capel (Arthur) & Co [1919] AC 435 .... 387, 392, 394

Barber v Meyerstein (1870) LR 4 HL 317 .... 24, 30, 40, 44, 51, 54, 143, 147, 154

Batis Maritime Corporation v Petroleos Del Mediterraneo SA (The Batis) [1990] 1 Lloyd's Rep 345 402

Baumwoll Manufactur von Carl Scheibler v Furness [1893] AC 868 111

Beam Technology (MFG) Pte Ltd v Standard Chartered Bank [2003] 1 SLR 597 .... 98, 99

Belships v Canadian Forest Products Ltd (1999) 45 Lloyd's Alert Service 379

Ben Shipping Co (Pte) Ltd v An-Board Bainne (The C Joyce) [1986] 2 Lloyd's Rep 285 382

Bhojwani & Anor v Chung Khiaw Bank Ltd [1990] 1 SLR 128 .. 96

Biccard v Shepherd (1861) 14 Moo PCC 471 216

Black v Rose (1864) 2 Moo PCCNS 277 403

Blue Anchor Line Ltd v Alfred C Toepfer International GmbH (The Union Amsterdam) [1982] 2 Lloyd's Rep 432 ..... 442, 445

Bolam v Friern Hospital Management Committee [1957] 2 All ER 118 347

Bolitho v City and Hackney Health Authority [1998] AC 232 ... 347

Bolivinter Oil v Manhattan Bank [1984] 1 All ER 351 98

Borealis AB (formerly Borealis Petrokemi AB and Statoil Petrokemi AB) v Stargas Ltd (The Berge Sisar) [2001] UKHL 17 .... 67, 68

Borneo Co (M) Sdn Bhd v Penang Port Commission [1975] 2 MLJ 204 183

Bouillon v Lupton (1863) 15 CBNS 113 216

Boukadoura Maritime Corpn v Marocaine de l'Industrie et du Raffinage SA (The Boukadoura) [1989] 1 Lloyd's Rep 393 ... 455
Brandt v Liverpool, Brazil and River Plate Steam Navigation Co Ltd [1924] 1 KB 575, [1923] All ER Rep 656 123
Brass v Maitland (1856) 26 LJ QB 49 .... 361, 362
Brefka & Hehnke GmbH & Co KG v Navire Shipping Co Ltd (The Saga Explorer) [2012] EWHC 3124 (Comm) 194
Brierly v Kendall (1852) 17 QB 937 156
Brown & Co Ltd v Harrison, Hourani v Harrison (1927) 96 LJKB 1025 285
Brown Boveri (Australia) Pty Limited v Baltic Shipping Company (The Nadezhda Krupskaya) [1989] 1 Lloyd's Rep 518 349
Brown Jenkinson & Co Ltd v Percy-Dalton (London) Ltd [1957] 2 QB 621 349
Brown v Gaudet (Cargo ex Argos) (1873) LR 5 PC 134 403
Browner International Ltd v Monarch Shipping Co Ltd (The European Enterprise) [1989] 2 Lloyd's Rep 185 .... 256, 298
BSkyB Ltd v HP Enterprise Services UK Ltd [2010] EWHC 86 (TCC) 141, 200
Bulk Transport Group Shipping Co Ltd v Seacrystal Shipping Ltd (The Kyzikos) [1989] AC 1264 .... 430, 433
Bunge SA v Adm Do Brasil Ltd (The Darya Radhe) [2009] EWHC 845 (Comm) 363
Bunge y Born Ltda Sociedad Anonima Commercial Financiera y Industrial of Buenos Aires v HA Brightman & Co [1925] AC 799 441
C Czarnikow Ltd v Koufos (The Heron II) [1969] 1 AC 350 357
C Groom Ltd v Barbar [1915] 1 KB 316 .... 82, 83, 182
Calcutta Steamship Co Ltd v Andrew Weir & Co [1910] 1 KB 759 .... 69, 119
Caltex Refining Co Pty Ltd v BHP Transport Ltd (The Iron Gippsland) [1994]1 Lloyd's Rep 335 296
Canadian and Dominion Sugar Co Ltd v Canadian National (West Indies) Steamship Ltd [1947] AC 46 196
Caparo Industries plc v Dickman [1990] 2 AC 605 199
Captain v Far Eastern Shipping Co [1979] 1 Lloyd's Rep 595 ... 254, 314
Carboex SA v Louis Dreyfus Commodities Suisse SA [2011] EWHC 1165 (Comm) 434

Caresse Navigation Ltd v Zurich Assurances MAROC (The Channel Ranger) [2014] EWCA Civ 1366 .... 115, 116

Cargo ex Argos. *See* Brown v Gaudet (Cargo ex Argos) (1873) LR 5 PC 134

Carlill v Carbolic Smoke Ball Company [1892] EWCA Civ 1 ... 32, 65, 87

Cascade Shipping Inc v Eka Jaya Agencies (Pte) Ltd [1993] 1 SLR 980 .... 105, 420

Castleton Commodities Shipping Co Pte Ltd v Silver Rock Investments (The Clipper Monarch) [2015] EWHC 2584 (Comm) 418

Century Textiles and Industry Ltd v Tomoe Shipping Co (Singapore) Pte Ltd (The Aditya Vaibhav) [1991] 1 Lloyd's Rep 573 470

Ceval Alimentos SA v Agrimpex Trading Co Ltd (The Northern Progress) (No. 2) [1996] 2 Lloyd's Rep 81, 88

Chabbra Corporation Pte Ltd v Jag Shakti (Owners) (The Jag Shakti) [1986] 1 MLJ 197 .... 59, 144, 146, 158

Chan Cheng Kum v Wah Tat Bank [1971] 1 Lloyd's Rep 439 ... 33, 38, 51, 52, 149, 250

Chandris v Isbrandtsen-Moller Co Inc [1951] 1 KB 240 456

Charles Goodfellow Lumber Sales Ltd v Verreault, Hovington and Verreault Navigation Inc [1971] 1 Lloyd's Rep 185 304

Charles Robert Leader and Henrietta Ada Leader v Duffey and Amyatt Edmond Ray [1888] 13 App Cas 294 81

Cheikh Boutros Selim El-Khoury and Others v Ceylon Shipping Lines Ltd (The Madeleine) [1967] 2 Lloyd's Rep 224 .. 387

China National Foreign Trade Transportation Corporation v Evlogia Shipping Co SA of Panama (The Mihalios Xilas) [1979] 2 All ER 1044 473

China Ocean Shipping Co (Owners of Xingcheng) v Andros (Owners of The Andros) [1987] 1 WLR 1213 106

China Offshore Oil (Singapore) International Pte Ltd v Giant Shipping Ltd (The Posidon) [2001] 1 Lloyd's Rep 697 403

China Steel Corporation & Anor v The Owners of Virginia Rhea (The Virginia Thea) [1985] 2 MLJ 1 339

China Steel Corporation v Pan Asia Shipyard & Engineering Co (Pte) Ltd [1988] 1 SLR 458 182

China-Pacific SA v Food Corpn of India (The Winson) [1982] AC 939 476

Chiswell Shipping Ltd and Liberian Jaguar Transports Inc v National Iranian Tanker Co (The World Symphony and The World Renown) [1992] 2 Lloyd's Rep 115 495
Cho Yang Shipping Co Ltd v Coral (UK) Ltd [1997] 2 Lloyd's Rep 641 .... 105, 413
Chong Fui Shipping & Forwarding Sdn Bhd v Steel Industries (Sabah) Sdn Bhd [2016] 5 MLJ 46 341
Christensen v Hindustan Steel [1971] 1 Lloyd's Rep 395 427
Cia Portorafti Commerciale SA v Ultramar Panama Inc (The Captain Gregos) [1990] 1 Lloyd's Rep 310 265
Ciampa and Others v British India Steam Navigation Co Ltd [1915] 2 KB 774 .... 208, 224
Classic Maritime Inc v Limbungan Makmur Sdn Bhd [2019] EWCA Civ 1102 382
Clea Shipping Corporation v Bulk Oil International Ltd (The Alaskan Trader) (No. 2) [1983] 2 Lloyd's Rep 645 492
Cobelfret NV v Cyclades Shipping Co Ltd (The Linardos) [1994] 1 Lloyd's Rep 28 428
Cohn v Davidson (1877) 2 QBD 455 215
Colchester BC v Smith [1991] Ch 448 185
Cole v Shallet (1682) 3 Lev 41 234
Colgate-Palmolive (Asia) Ltd v Swedish East Asia Co Ltd [1967] 1 MLJ 115 .... 109, 337
Colonial Bank v European Grain & Shipping Ltd (The Dominique) [1989] 1 Lloyd's Rep 431 406
Compania Comercial y Naviera San Martin SA v China National Foreign Trade Transportation Corporation (The Constanza M) (HC) [1980] 1 Lloyd's Rep 505 412
Compania Comercial y Naviera San Martin SA v China National Foreign Trade Transportation Corporation (The Constanza M) (CA) [1981] 2 Lloyd's Rep 147 117
Compania de Naviera Nedelka SA of Panama v Tradax International SA of Panama City RP (The Tres Flores) [1974] QB 264 386
Compania Naviera General SA v Kerametal Ltd (The Lorna I) [1983] 1 Lloyd's Rep 373 .... 392, 406, 409
Compania Naviera Maropan SA v Bowaters Lloyd Pulp and Paper Mills Ltd (The Stork) [1955] 2 QB 68 459

Compania Sud American Vapores v MS ER Hamburg Schiffarhtsgesellschaft mbH & Co KG [2006] EWHC 483 (Comm) 500
Compania Sud Americana de Vapores v Shipmair BV (The Teno) [1977] 2 Lloyd's Rep 289 470
Comptoir d'Achat et de Vente du Boerenbond Belge S/A v Luis de Ridder Ltda (The Julia) [1949] AC 293 .... 33, 41, 80, 85
Connolly Shaw Ltd v Nordenfjeldske Steamship Co (1934) 49 Ll L Rep 183 231
Continental Fertilizer Co Ltd v Pionier Shipping CV (The Pionier) [1995] 1 Lloyd's Rep 223 341
Continental Pacific Shipping Ltd v Deemand Shipping Co Ltd (The Lendoudis Evangelos II) [1997] 1 Lloyd's Rep 404 491
Cosco Bulk Carrier Co Ltd v Team-Up Owning Co Ltd (The Saldanha) [2010] EWHC 1340 (Comm) 482
Cox, Patterson & Co v Bruce & Co (1886) 18 QBD 147 196
Credit Agricole Indosuez v Generale bank and Seco Steel Trading Inc and Considar Inc (No. 2) 92
Cremer v General Carriers SA (The Dona Mari) [1973] 2 Lloyd's Rep 366 185
CSSA Chartering and Shipping Services SA v Mitsui OSK Lines Ltd (The Pacific Voyager) [2018] All ER (D) 32 (Nov) 390
Cunard Steamship Co Ltd v Buerger [1927] AC 1 227
D'Amico Shipping Italia SpA v Endofa DMCC [2016] EWHC 2223 (Comm) 404
Daewoo Heavy Industries Ltd v Klipriver Shipping Ltd (The Kapitan Petko Voivoda) [2003] EWCA Civ 451 .... 240, 241, 348
Dahl v Nelson, Donkin & Co (1881) 6 App Cas 38 410
Dainford Navigation Inc v PDVSA Petroleo SA (The Moscow Stars) [2017] EWHC 2150 (Comm) 418, 419
Dairy Containers Ltd v Tasman Orient Line CV (The Tasman Discoverer) [2002] 1 Lloyd's Rep 528 247
Dakin v Oxley (1864) 15 CBNS 646 406
Dalwood Marine Co v Nordana Line A/S (The Elbrus) [2009] EWHC 3394 (Comm) 493
Daval Aciers d'Usinor et de Sacilor v Armare Srl (The Nerano) [1994] 2 Lloyd's Rep 50 116
Davidson v Gwynne (1810) 1 Camp 376 234
Davies v Elsby Brothers Ltd [1960] 3 All ER 672 .... 334, 337

Davis v Garrett (1830) 6 Bing 716 .... 226, 276
Deep Sea Maritime Ltd v Monjasa A/S (The Alhani) [2018] EWHC 1495 (Comm) 170, 330, 332, 340
Dera Commercial Estate v Derya Inc (The Sur) [2019] 1 All ER 1147 237
Deutsche Ruckversicherung AG v Walbrook Insurance Co Ltd & Ors [1995] 1 Lloyd's Rep 153 98
DGC Commodities Corp v Sea Metropolitan SA (The Andra) [2012] EWHC 1984 (Comm) 445
Diamond Alkali Export Corp v Fl Bourgeois [1921] 3 KB 443 .. 37
Dias Cia Naviera SA v Louis Dreyfus Corpn (The Dias) [1978] 1 All ER 724 445
Dommett v Beckford (1833) 5 B & Ad 521 413
Dong Yuan Hang Trading Pte Ltd v Sunko (Singapore) Co Pte Ltd [1994] 3 SLR 603 82
Donoghue v Stevenson [1932] AC 562 .... 49, 139
Dow Chemical (Nederland) BV v BP Tanker Co Ltd (The Vorras) [1983] 1 Lloyd's Rep 579 425
Dow-Europe v Novoklav Inc [1988] 1 Lloyd's Rep 206 459
Dr V Thuraisingam v Sanmarkanganapathy [2015] 8 CLJ 248 ... 347
Dry Bulk Handy Holding Inc and Another v Fayette International Holdings Ltd and Another (The Bulk Chile) [2013] EWCA Civ 184 .... 420, 476
Dunlop v Lambert (1839) 6 Cl & F 600 .... 153, 176
Duthie v Hilton (1868) 4 CP 138 409
Dwarkanath Raimohan Chaudhuri and Another v The Rivers Steam Navigation Company Limited [1917] UKPC 108 .... 131, 315
East West Corp v Dampskibsselskabet AF, 1912 [2003] EWCA Civ 174 .... 65, 66, 67, 134
Eastern Mediterranean Maritime (Liechtenstein) Ltd v Unimarine SA (The Marika M) [1981] 2 Lloyd's Rep 622 ...... 481, 488
Edward Owen Edward Owen Engineering Ltd v Barclays Bank International Ltd [1978] 1 All ER 976 98
Edwinton Commercial Corp v Tsavliris Russ (Worldwide Salvage and Towage) Ltd (The Sea Angel) [2007] EWCA Civ 547 395

Effort Shipping Co Ltd v Linden Management SA (The Giannis NK) [1998] AC 605 .... 289, 364, 365, 366, 367
Egon Oldendorff v Libera Corpn (No 2) [1996] 1 Lloyd's Rep 380 397
El Greco (Australia) Pty Ltd v Mediterranean Shipping Co SA [2004] 2 Lloyd's Rep 537 359
Elder Dempster Lines v Ishag (The Lycaon) [1983] 2 Lloyd's Rep 548 38
Elder, Dempster & Co Ltd v Paterson, Zochonis & Co, Griffiths Lewis Steam Navigation Co v Paterson, Zochonis & Co Ltd [1923] 1 KB 420 .... 121, 136, 168, 224
Eleni Shipping Ltd v Transgrain Shipping BV (The Eleni P) [2019] EWHC 910 (Comm) 486
Ellis Shipping Corporation v Voest Alpine Intertrading (The Lefthero) [1991] 2 Lloyd's Rep 599 402
Elof Hansson v Hamel and Horley [1922] 2 AC 36 88
Emeraldian Ltd Partnership v Wellmix Shipping Ltd (The Vine) [2010] EWHC 1411 (Comm) 459
Empire Distributors v United States Lines [1987] AMC 455 223
Empire Meat Co Ltd v Patrick Empire Meat Co Ltd [1939] 2 All ER 85 162
ENE Kos 1 Ltd v Petroleo Brasileiro SA (No 2) (The Kos) [2012] UKSC 17 476
Enichem Anic SpA and Others v Ampelos Shipping Co Ltd (The Delfini) [1990] 1 Ll L Rep 252 .... 33, 61, 154
Enka Insaat Ve Sanayi AS v OOO Insurance Company Chubb [2020] UKSC 38 397
Equitable Trust Co of New York v Dawson Partners Ltd [1926] 27 LI L Rep 49 93
Euro-Asian Oil SA (formerly Euro-Asian Oil AG) v Credit Suisse AG and Another [2018] EWCA Civ 1720 80
Evergreen Marine Corp v Aldgate Warehouse (Wholesale) Ltd [2003] EWHC 667 (Comm) 106
Evryalos Maritime Ltd v China Pacific Insurance Co Ltd (The Michael S) [2001] All ER (D) 325 (Dec) 56
Exercise Shipping Co Ltd v Bay Maritime Lines Ltd (The Fantasy) [1992] 1 Lloyd's Rep 235 .... 378, 380

FA Tamplin Steamship Co Ltd v Anglo-Mexican Petroleum Products Co Ltd [1916] 2 AC 397 395

Farenco Shipping Co Ltd v Daebo Shipping Co Ltd (Dampskibsselskabet Norden A/S, third party) (Deiulemar Shipping SpA, fourth party) (The Bremen Max) [2009] 1 All ER (Comm) 423 465

FC Bradley & Sons Ltd v Federal Steam Navigation Co Ltd (1927) 27 Ll L Rep 395 .... 211, 245

Federal Bulker Federal Bulker Carriers Inc v C Itoh & Co Ltd (The Federal Bulker) [1989] 1 Lloyd's Rep 103 .... 113, 115

Federal Commerce and Navigation Co Ltd v Tradax Export SA (The Maratha Envoy) [1978] AC 1 432

Federal Commerce and Navigation Ltd v Molena Alpha Inc and others (The Nanfri, The Benfri, The Lorfri) [1979] AC 757 .. 454, 470, 477, 478

Feoso (Singapore) Pte Ltd v Faith Maritime Co Ltd (The Daphne L) [2003] SGCA 34 .... 117, 418, 433

Fercometal SARL v Mediterranean Shipping Co SA (The Simona) [1989] AC 788 387

Fetim BV v Oceanspeed Shipping Ltd (The Flecha) [1999] 1 Lloyd's Rep 612 108

Filikos Shipping Corpn of Monrovia v Shipmair BV (The Filikos) [1983] 1 Lloyd's Rep 9 499

Finagra (UK) Ltd v OT Africa Line Ltd [1998] 2 Lloyd's Rep 622 247

Fiumana Società di Navigazione v Bunge & Co Ltd [1930] 2 KB 47 218

Fletcher (W & R) (New Zealand) v Sigurd Haavik A/S (The Vikfrost) [1980] 1 Lloyd's Rep 560 111

Forestships International Ltd v Armonia Shipping and Finance Corporation (The Ira) [1995] 1 Lloyd's Rep 103 488

Fort Sterling Ltd and Another v South Atlantic Cargo Shipping NV and Others (The Finnrose) [1994] 1 Lloyd's Rep 559 340

Frank Hammond Pty Ltd v Huddard Parker Ltd and the Australian Shipping Board [1956] VLR 496 353

Freeman v Taylor (1831) 8 Bing 124 .... 205, 390

Freight Connect (S) Pte Ltd v Paragon Shipping Pte Ltd [2015] SGCA 37 .... 372, 426, 430, 434, 435

Fulton Shipping Inc of Panama v Globalia Business Travel SAU (formerly TravelPlan SAU) of Spain (The New Flamenco) [2017] UKSC 43 493

Fyffes Group Ltd. And Caribbean Gold Ltd v Reefer Express Lines Pty Ltd and Reefkrit Shipping Inc (The Kriti Rex) [1996] 2 Lloyd's Rep 171 214

Galaxy Energy International Ltd v Novorossiysk Shipping Co (The Petr Schmidt) [1997] 1 Lloyd's Rep 284 493

Gard Marine and Energy Ltd v China National Chartering Co Ltd (The Ocean Victory) [2017] UKSC 35 .... 300, 460, 462

Gem Shipping Co of Monrovia v Babanaft (Lebanon) SARL (The Fontevivo) [1975] 1 Lloyd's Rep 339 442

General and Finance Facilities Ltd v Cooks Cars (Romford) Ltd [1963] 2 All ER 314 .... 154, 156, 157

General Feeds Inc v Burnham Shipping Corpn (The Amphion) [1991] 2 Lloyd's Rep 101 .... 132, 363

Geogas SA v Trammo Gas Ltd (The Baleares) [1993] 1 Lloyd's Rep 215 391

Gerani Compania Naviera SA v General Organisation for Supply Goods (The Demosthenes V) (No. 1) [1982] 1 Lloyd's Rep 275 389

Gesellschaft Burgerlichen Rechts and Others v Stockholms Rederiaktiebolag Svea [1967] 1 QB 588 381

Gian Singh & Co Ltd v Banque De L'Indochine [1972-1974] 1 SLR 28 93

Gill & Duffus SA v Berger & Co Inc [1984] AC 382 89

Glebe Island Terminals Pty Ltd v Continental Seagram Pty Ltd (The Antwerpen) [1994] 1 Lloyd's Rep 213 163

Glencore Energy UK Ltd & Anor v Freeport Holdings Ltd (The Lady M) [2019] EWCA Civ 388 .... 290, 294, 298, 299, 301, 310, 382

Glencore Grain Ltd v Flacker Shipping Ltd (The Happy Day) [2002] EWCA Civ 1068 429

Glencore Grain Ltd v Goldbeam Shipping Inc (The Mass Glory) [2002] EWHC 27 (Comm) 430

Global Process Systems Inc v Syarikat Takaful Malaysia Bhd (The Cendor Mopu) [2011] UKSC 5 309

Globalink Transportation and Logistics Worldwide LLP v DHL Project & Chartering Limited [2019] EWHC 225 (Comm) 333
Glory Wealth Shipping Pte Limited v North China Shipping Limited (The North Prince) [2010] EWHC 1692 (Comm) 494
Glyn Mills Currie & Co v The East and West India Dock Co (1882) 7 App Cas 591 .... 33, 164
Glynn v Margetson & Co [1893] AC 351 .... 5, 161, 226, 231, 233, 234
Golden Strait Corporation v Nippon Yusen Kubishka Kaisha (The Golden Victory) [2007] UKHL 12 492
Goldman v Thai Airways International Ltd [1983] 1 WLR 1186 360
Goodwin, Ferreira & Co Ltd v Lamport & Holt Lines Ltd (1929) 34 Ll L Rep 192 310
Gosse Millerd Ltd v Canadian Government Merchant Marine Ltd (The Canadian Highlander) [1929] AC 223 295
Goulandris Brothers Ltd v B Goldman & Sons Ltd [1957] 3 WLR 596 213
Government of Ceylon v Societe Franco-Tunisienne D'armement-Tunis (The Massalia) (No. 2) [1960] 2 Lloyd's Rep 352 434
Grampian Steamship Co Ltd v Carver & Co (1893) 9 TLR 210 .. 388
Grand Champion Tankers Ltd v Norpipe A/S (The Marion) [1984] AC 563 299
Granit SA v Benship International Inc [1994] 1 Lloyd's Rep 526 372
Grant & Co v Coverdale, Todd & Co (1884) 9 App Cas 470 440
Grant v Norway (1851) 10 CB 665 184
Gray v Carr (1871) LR 6 QB 522 .... 114, 116
Great China Metal Industries Co Ltd v Malaysian International Shipping Corporation Berhad (The Bunga Seroja) [1999] 1 Lloyd's Rep 512 304
Great Indian Peninsula Rly v Turnbull (1885) 5 Asp MLC 465 .. 407
Greatship (India) Ltd v Oceanografia SA de CV (The Greatship Dhriti) [2012] EWHC 3468 (Comm) 478
Guan Bee & Co v Palembang Shipping Co Ltd [1969] 1 MLJ 90 276

Guinomar of Conakry and Another v Samsung Fire & Marine Insurance Co Ltd (The Kamsar Voyager) [2002] 2 Lloyd's Rep 57 214

Habas Sinai Ve Tibbi Gazlar Istihsal v VSC Steel Co Ltd [2013] EWHC 4071 (Comm) 397

Hadley v Baxendale (1854) 9 Ex D 341 358

Hain Steamship Co Ltd v Tate & Lyle Ltd (1936) 41 Com Cas 350 .... 234, 236

Hamilton, Fraser & Co v Pandorf & Co (1885) 16 QBD 629 244

Hang Fung Shipping and Trading Co Ltd v Mullion & Co Ltd [1966] 1 Lloyd's Rep 511 221

Hansen-Tangens Rederi III A/S v Total Transport Corpn (The Sagona) [1984] 1 Lloyd's Rep 194 463

Hedley Byrne & Co Ltd v Heller & Partners Ltd [1964] AC 465 . 199

Hellenic Steel Co v Svolamar Shipping Co Ltd (The Komninos S) [1991] 1 Lloyd's Rep 370 260

Henderson v Merrett [1995] 2 AC 145 .... 141, 200

Henriksens Rederi A/S V Thz Rolimpex (The Brede) [1973] 2 Lloyd's Rep 333 406

Henry Smith & Co v Bedouin Steam Navigation Co Ltd [1896] AC 70 191

Hingston v Wendt (1876) 1 QB 367 415

Hiort v London and North Western Railway Co (1870) 4 Ex D 188 144

Hogarth Shipping Co Ltd v Blyth, Greene, Jourdain & Co Ltd [1917] 2 KB 534 113

Hogarth v Alexander Miller Bros & Co (The Westfalia) [1891] AC 48 489

Hogarth v Walker [1899] 2 QB 401 222

Homburg Houtimport BV v Agrosin Private Ltd (The Starsin) [2003] UKHL 12 .... 49, 108, 136, 140, 171, 172, 247, 318

Hong Kong Fir Shipping Co Ltd v Kawasaki Kisen Kaisha Ltd [1962] 2 QB 26 .... 209, 220, 479

Hopper v Burness (1876) 1 CPD 137 402

Houlden & Co Ltd and Others v SS Red Jacket and American Export Lines Ltd. *See* The Red Jacket [1978] 1 Lloyd's Rep 300 427

Houlder v General SN Co (1862) 3 F&F 170 427
Houlder v Weir [1905] 2 QB 267 443
Howard v Shepherd (1850) 9 CB 297 29
HSBC Bank Malaysia Bhd v Dharani Sugars & Chemical Ltd and another appeal [2011] 1 MLJ 52 94
Hudson v Ede (1868) LR 2 QB 566 .... 426, 441
Hunter v Prinsep (1808) 10 East 378 .... 402, 409
Hurlocke and Saunderson v Collett (1539) Select Pleas, vol I, pp. 88-89 26
Huyton SA v Inter Operators SA (The Stainless Emperor) [1994] 1 Lloyd's Rep 298 435
Hyundai Merchant Marine Co Ltd v Furness Withy (Australia) Pty (The Doric Pride) [2006] EWCA Civ 599 .... 482, 484
Hyundai Merchant Marine Co Ltd v Gesuri Chartering Co Ltd (The Peonia) [1991] 1 Lloyd's Rep 100 .... 494, 496
Idaho D/S A/S v Peninsular and Oriental Steam Navigation Co (The Strathnewton) [1983] 1 Lloyd's Rep 219 383
IMT Shipping and Chartering GmbH v Changsung Shipping Company Limited (The Zenovia) [2009] EWHC 739 (Comm) ... 491
In re Nos 55 & 57, Holmes Road, Kentish Town [1958] 2 All ER 311 335
Inca Compania Naviera SA and Commercial and Maritime Enterprises Evanghelos P Nomikos SA v Mofinol Inc (The President Brand) [1967] 2 Lloyd's Rep 338 436
India Steamship Co v Louis Dreyfus Sugar Ltd (The Indian Reliance) [1997] 1 Lloyd's Rep 52 413
Indian Oil Corporation v Vanol Inc [1991] 2 Lloyd's Rep 634 ... 172
Indian Overseas Bank v United Coconut Oil Mills Inc [1993] 1 SLR 141 95
Industrie Chimiche Italia Centrale SpA v Nea Ninemia Shipping Co SA (The Emmanuel C) [1983] 1 Lloyd's Rep 310 .. 244, 303
Interfoto Picture Library Ltd v Stiletto Visual Programmes Ltd [1989] QB 433 .... 81, 144
International Packers London Ltd v Ocean Steam Ship Co Ltd [1955] 2 Lloyd's Rep 218 209
Internationale Guano en Superphosphaat-Werken v Robert Macandrew & Co [1909] 2 KB 360 .... 234, 236
Inverkip SS Co v Bunge [1917] 2 KB 193 444

Ionian Navigation Company Inc v Atlantic Shipping Company SA (The Loucas N) [1971] 1 Lloyd's Rep 215 434
Irish Shipping Ltd v Commercial Union Assurance Co plc (The Irish Rowan) [1991] 2 QB 206 177
Irrawaddy Flotilla Co v Bugwandas (1891) 18 IA 121 129
Islander Shipping Enterprises SA v Empresa Maritima Del Estado SA (The Khian Sea) [1979] 1 Lloyd's Rep 545 462
Ismail v Polish Ocean Lines (The Ciechocinek) [1976] QB 893 307
Itex Itagrani Export SA v Care Shipping Corp (The Cebu) (No. 2) [1990] 2 Lloyd's Rep 316 422
Itoh & Co Ltd v Atlantska Plovidba (The Gundulić) [1981] 2 Lloyd's Rep 418 .... 214, 221
J Glynn & Sons Ltd v Consorzio Approvvigionamenti Fra Meccanici Ed Affini (1920) 4 Ll L Rep 183 388
J Lauritzen AS v Wijsmuller BV (The Super Servant Two) [1990] 1 Lloyd's Rep 1 394
James Buchanan & Co Ltd v Babco Forwarding and Shipping (UK) Ltd [1978] AC 141 289
James Morrison & Co Ltd v Shah, Savill and Albion Co Ltd [1916] 2 KB 783 234
JH Rayner & Co Ltd v Hambro's Bank Ltd [1943] KB 37 97
Jindal Iron and Steel Co Ltd v Islamic Solidarity Shipping Co Jordan Inc (The Jordan II) [2004] UKHL 49 .... 212, 278, 283, 284
Johnson Matthey & Co Ltd v Constantine Terminals Ltd [1976] 2 Lloyd's Rep 215 137
Jones v European & General Express Co Ltd (1920) 4 Ll L Rep 127 40
Joseph Thorley Ltd v Orchis Steamship Co Ltd [1907] 1 KB 660 234
Joseph Travers & Sons Ltd v Cooper [1915] 1 KB 73, [1914-15] All ER Rep 104 317
K Line PTE Ltd v Priminds Shipping (HK) Co Ltd (The Eternal Bliss) [2020] EWHC 2373 (Comm) 446
K Lokumal & Sons (London) Ltd v Lotte Shipping Co Pte Ltd (The August Leonhardt) 336
Kamilla Hans-Peter Eckhoff KG v AC Oerssleff's EFTF A/B (The Kamilla) [2006] EWHC 509 498
Karsales v Wallis [1956] EWCA Civ 4 233

Ke Mohamed Sultan Maricar v The Prudential Assurance Co Ltd [1941] 1 MLJ 20 .... 15, 16

Kenya Railways v Antares Co Pte Ltd (The Antares) [1987] 1 Lloyd's Rep 424 .... 238, 343

KH Enterprise v Pioneer Container (The Pioneer Container) [1994] 2 AC 324 .... 126, 136, 139

Kiramas Sdn Bhd v Federal Land Development Authority [1991] 2 MLJ 1998 98

Kirchner v Venus (1859) 12 Moo PC 361 415

Kish v Taylor [1912] AC 604 .... 218, 229, 230

KMA Abdul Rahim & Anor v Owners of Lexa Maersk & Ors [1954] 2 QB 402 254

Kodros Shipping Corp v Empresa Cubana de Fletes (The Evia) (No. 2) [1983] 1 AC 736

Kopitoff v Wilson [1874-80] All ER Rep 609 .... 207, 211

Koufos v C Czarnikow Ltd (The Heron II) [1969] 1 AC 350 386

Krall v Burnett (1877) 25 WR 305 405

Kuo International Oil Co Ltd v Daisy Shipping Co Ltd (The Yamatogawa) [1990] 2 Lloyd's Rep 39 280

Kuok Ling Timber Industries Sdn Bhd v The Owners of and Other Persons Interested in the Vessel MV Thonfullin (The MV Thonfullin) [2000] 2 MLJ 615 .... 304, 305

Kuwait Airways Corpn v Iraqi Airways Co (Nos. 4 and 5) (HL) [2002] UKHL 19 .... 145, 158

Kuwait Airways Corpn v Iraqi Airways Co (Nos. 4 and 5) (CA) [2001] 3 WLR 1117 144

Kuwait Maritime Transport Co v Rickmers Linie KG (The Danah) [1993] 1 Lloyd's Rep 351 .... 378, 380

Kuwait Petroleum Corpn v I and D Oil Carriers Ltd (The Houda) [1994] 2 Lloyd's Rep 541 .... 450, 463

Kwan Sun Ming v Chak Chee Hing [1965] 1 MLJ 236 305

Kwantung Provincial Bank v Osaka Shoshen Kaisha [1967] 2 Lloyd's Rep 82 191

Kyokuyo Co Ltd v AP Møller-Maersk A/S (trading as 'Maersk Line') (The Maersk Tangier) [2018] EWCA Civ 778 359

Laemthong International Lines Co Ltd v Artis (The Laemthong Glory) (No 2) [2005] EWCA Civ 519 464

Lansat Shipping Co Ltd v Glencore Grain BV (The Paragon) [2009] EWCA Civ 855 496

Leduc v Ward (1888) 20 QBD 475 .... 36, 56, 112, 121, 234, 235

Leeds Shipping Co Ltd v Société Française Bunge (The Eastern City) [1958] 2 Lloyd's Rep 127 .... 461, 462

Leesh River Tea Co Ltd v British India Steam Navigation Co Ltd (The Chyebassa) [1967] 2 QB 250 311

Leigh and Sillivan Ltd v Aliakmon Shipping Co Ltd (The Aliakmon) (HC) [1983] 1 Lloyd's Rep 203 124

Leigh and Sillavan Ltd v Aliakmon Shipping Co Ltd (The Aliakmon) (HL) [1986] AC 785 .... 86, 126, 140

Lensen Shipping Ltd v Anglo-Soviet Co (1935) 52 Ll L Rep 141 481

Leon Corporation v Atlantic Lines and Navigation Co Inc (The Leon) [1985] 2 Lloyd's Rep 470 470

Leonis Steamship Company Limited v Rank Limited [1908] 1 KB 499 .... 388, 424

Lickbarrow v Mason (1794) 5 TR 683 .... 6, 28, 39, 51, 54

Liver Alkali Co v Johnson (1874) LR 9 Ex 338 235

Losinjska Plovidba v Transco Overseas Ltd (The Orjula) [1995] 2 Lloyd's Rep 395 141

Lotus Cars Ltd v Southampton Cargo Handling plc and Others (The Rigoletto) [2000] 2 All ER (Comm) 705 171

Lyon v Mells (1804) 5 East 428 .... 206, 214, 274

Lyric Shipping Inc v Intermetals Ltd (The Al Taha) [1990] 2 Lloyd's Rep 117 230

M Golodetz & Co Inc v Czarnikow-Rionda Co Inc (The Galatia) [1980] 1 All ER 501 181

MacAndrew v Chapple (1866) LR 1 CP 643 390

Macieo Shipping Ltd v Clipper Shipping Lines Ltd (The Clipper Sao Luis) [2000] 1 Lloyd's Rep 645 500

MacWilliam (JI) Co Inc v Mediterranean Shipping Co SA (The Rafaela S) [2005] UKHL 11 .... 24, 25, 51, 75, 120, 127, 251, 254

Maintop Shipping Co Ltd v Bulkindo Lines Pte Ltd (The Marinicki) [2003] EWHC 1894 (Admlty) 462

Malas (Hamzeh) & Sons v British Imex Industries Ltd [1958] 2 QB 127 87

Malayan Banking Bhd v Punjab National Bank [2018] MLJU 1716 .... 42, 43, 91
Manbre Saccharine Co v Corn Products Co [1919] 1 KB 198 ... 52, 53, 182
Manchester Trust Ltd v Furness Withy & Co Ltd [1895] 2 QB 539 111
Manifest Shipping & Co Ltd v Uni-Polaris Insurance Co Ltd and La Reunion Europeene (The Star Sea) [1995] 1 Lloyd's Rep 651 209
Mansel Oil Ltd v Troon Storage Tankers SA (The Ailsa Craig) [2009] EWCA Civ 425 386
Marbienes Compania Naviera SA v Ferrostaal AG (The Democritos) [1976] 2 Lloyd's Rep 149 .... 386, 390
Marbig Rexel Pty Ltd and Another v ABC Container Line NV (The TNT Express) [1912] 2 Lloyd's Rep 636 363
Marc Rich & Co AG v Bishop Rock Marine Co Ltd (The Nicholas H) [1996] AC 211 .... 140, 266
Mardorf Peach & Co Ltd v Attica Sea Carriers Corpn of Liberia (The Laconia) [1977] AC 850 .... 469, 473
Maredelanto Compania Naviera SA v Bergbau-Handel GmbH (The Mihalis Angelos) [1970] EWCA Civ 4 387
Marfani & Co Ltd v Midland Bank Ltd [1968] 1 WLR 956 145
Margaronis Navigation Agency Ltd v Henry W Peabody & Co of London Ltd (The Vrontados) (HC) [1965] 1 QB 300 426
Margaronis Navigation Agency Ltd v Henry W Peabody & Co of London Ltd (The Vrontados) (CA) [1965] 2 QB 430 401
Maritime National Fish Ltd v Ocean Trawlers Ltd [1935] AC 524 394
Markt & Co Ltd v Knight Steamship Co Ltd [1910] 2 KB 1021 . 176
Mash & Murrell Ltd v Joseph I Emanuel Ltd [1961] 2 Lloyd's Rep 326 85
Maxine Footwear Co Ltd v Canadian Government Merchant Marine Ltd [1959] AC 589 .... 204, 271, 282, 287, 301, 303, 307
Mayhew Foods Ltd v Overseas Containers Ltd [1984] 1 Lloyd's Rep 317 .... 48, 255, 258, 314
MB Pyramid Sound NV v Briese Schiffahrts GmbH and Co KG MS Sina and Latvian Shipping Assoc Ltd (The Ines) [1995] 2 Lloyd's Rep 144 .... 103, 105, 162

McCarren & Co Ltd v Humber International Transport Ltd and Truckline Ferries (Poole) Ltd (The Vechscroon) [1982] 1 Lloyd's Rep 301 256

McFadden & Co v Blue Star Line [1905] 1 KB 697 .... 211, 214, 215, 216, 219

Mediterranean Freight Services Ltd v BP Oil International Ltd (The Fiona) [1994] 2 Lloyd's Rep 506 .... 588, 636

Mediterranean Salvage & Towage Ltd v Seamar Trading & Commerce Inc (The Reborn) [2008] EWHC 1875 (Comm) 458

Mediterranean Shipping Co SA v Trafigura Beheer BV and Another (The MSC Amsterdam) [2007] EWCA Civ 794 .... 159, 255, 259, 331, 348

Meredith Jones (A) & Co Ltd v Vangemar Shipping Co Ltd (The Apostolis) [1996] 1 Lloyd's Rep 475 297

Metall Market OOO v Vitorio Shipping Co Ltd (The Lehmann Timber) [2013] EWCA Civ 650 419

Mewah-Oils Sdn Bhd v Lushing Traders Pte Ltd [2018] 5 CLJ 185 .... 143, 151, 153

Midland Silicones Ltd v Scruttons Ltd [1962] AC 446 168

Minerva Navigation Inc v Oceana Shipping AG (The Athena) [2013] EWCA Civ 1723 488

Ministry of Food v Reardon Smith Line Ltd [1951] 2 Lloyd's Rep 265 277

Minmetals South-East Asia Corp Pte Ltd v Nakhoda Logistics Sdn Bhd [2019] 3 CLJ 19 .... 42, 43, 51, 109, 110, 143, 159, 330, 331

Miramar Maritime Corpn v Holborn Oil Trading Ltd (The Miramar) [1984] AC 676 .... 117, 416

Mitchell v Ede (1840) 11 Ad & El 888 25

Mitchell, Cotts & Co v Steel Bros & Co Ltd [1916] 2 KB 610 363

Mitsui & Co Ltd v Flota Mercante Grancolombiana SA (The Ciudad de Pasto and The Ciudad de Neiva) [1989] 1 All ER 951 at 957 153

Mitsui & Co Ltd v Novorossiysk Shipping Co (The Gudermes) (HC) [1991] 1 Lloyd's Rep 456 141

Mitsui & Co Ltd v Novorossiysk Shipping Co (The Gudermes) (CA) [1993] 1 Lloyd's Rep 311 124

Mitsui OSK. Lines Ltd v Garnac Grain Co Inc (The Myrtos) [1984] 2 Lloyd's Rep 449 390

Moel Tryvan Ship Co Ltd v Andrew Weir & Co [1910] 2 KB 844 387
Moerland (Arnt J) K/S v Kuwait Petroleum Corpn (The Fjordaas) [1988] 2 All ER 714 435
Molthes Rederi Aktieselskabet v Ellerman's Wilson Line Ltd [1927] 1 KB 710 107
Monarch Steamship Co Ltd v A/B Karlshamns Oljefabriker [1949] AC 196 . . . . . . 220, 229
Monroe Brothers Ltd v Ryan [1935] 2 KB 28 390
Montedison SpA v Icroma SpA (The Caspian Sea) [1979] 3 All ER 378 . . . . . . 403, 409
Montrod v Frandkotter Fleischvertriebs GmbH [2002] CLC 446 98
More OG Romsdal Fylkesbatar AS v The demise charters of the Ship Jotunheim [2005] 1 Lloyd's Rep 181 473
Motis Exports (No. 2) (2001) Admiralty Court, 2 Feb 2001 61
Motis Exports Ltd v Dampskibsselskabet AF 1912 Aktieselskab and Aktieselskabet Dampskibsselskabet Svendborg [2000] 1 All ER (Comm) 91 . . . . . . 33, 161, 164
Motor Oil Hellas (Corinth) Refineries SA v Shipping Corpn of India (The Kanchenjunga) [1990] 1 Lloyd's Rep 391 459
MSC Mediterranean Shipping Co SA v Alianca Bay Shipping Co Ltd (The Argonaut) [1985] 2 Lloyd's Rep 216 500
MSC Mediterranean Shipping Company SA v Glencore International AG [2017] EWCA Civ 365 . . . . . . 34, 164
Murphy v Brentwood District Council [1990] 2 All ER 908 141
Murugesan v Krishnasamy & Anor [1958] MLJ 92 162
National Jaya (Pte) Ltd v Hong Tat Marine Shipping Pte Ltd [1979] 2 MLJ 6 . . . . . . 253, 282
National Petroleum Co v Athelviscount (Owners) (The Athelviscount) (1934) 48 Ll L Repl 164 196
National Shipping Co of Saudi Arabia v BP Oil Supply Co (The Abqaiq) [2011] EWCA Civ 1127 446
Navalmar UK Ltd v Kale Maden Hammaddeler Sanayi Ve Ticart AS (The Arundel Castle) [2017] EWHC 116 (Comm) 432
Navig8 Chemicals Pool Inc v Glencore Agriculture BV (The Songa Winds) [2018] All ER (D) 115 (Aug) 465
Navrom v Callitsis Ship Management SA (The Radauti) [1988] 2 Lloyd's Rep 416 441

Nea Agrex SA v Baltic Shipping Co Ltd and Intershipping Charter Co (The Agios Lazaros) [1976] QB 933 .... 343, 377

Nelson Pine Industries Ltd v Seatrans New Zealand Ltd (The Pembroke) [1995] 2 Lloyd's Rep 290 298

Neptune Orient Lines Ltd v JVC (UK) Ltd (The Chevalier Roze) [1983] 2 Lloyd's Rep 438 175

Nereide SpA di Navigazione v Bulk Oil International (The Laura Prima) [1982] 1 Lloyd's Rep 1 .... 436, 437

New Chinese Antimony Co Ltd v Ocean Steamship Co Ltd [1917] 2 KB 664 190

New Zealand Shipping Co Ltd v AM Satterthwaite (The Eurymedon) [1975] AC 154, [1974] 1 All ER 1015 321

Newa Line v Erechthion Shipping Co SA [1987] 2 Lloyd's Rep 180 452

Newsom v Thornton (1806) 6 East 17 28

Ngo Chew Hong Edible Oil Pte Ltd v Scindia Steam Navigation Co Ltd (The Jalamohan) [1988] 1 Lloyd's Rep 443 .. 404, 413

Nippon Yusen Kaisha v International Import and Export Co Ltd (The Elbe Maru) [1978] 1 Lloyd's Rep 206 .... 174, 175

Nippon Yusen Kaisha v Marocaine de L'Industrie du Raffinage (The Tsukuba Maru) [1979] 1 Lloyd's Rep 459 445

Nisshin Shipping Co Ltd v Cleaves & Co Ltd [2003] EWHC 2602 (Comm) 167

Noble Resources Ltd v Cavalier Shipping Corpn (The Atlas) [1996] 1 Lloyd's Rep 642, [1996] CLC 1148 191

Noemijulia Steamship Co Ltd v Minister of Food (1950) 84 Ll L Rep 354 388

Nolisement (Owners) v Bunge and Born [1916-17] All ER Rep 734 447

Noranda Inc v Barton (Time Charter) Ltd (The Marinor) [1996] 1 Lloyd's Rep 301 328

North River Freighters Ltd v HE President of India [1956] 1 QB 333 434

Northern Shipping Co v Deutsche Seereederei GmbH and Others (The Kapitan Sakharov) [2000] 2 Lloyd's Rep 255 ...... 208, 280, 365

Northumbrian Shipping Company Limited v Timm And Son Limited [1939] AC 397 216

Notara v Henderson (1872) LR 7 QB 225 .... 241, 283

Novologistics SARL v Five Ocean Corp (The Merida) [2009] EWHC 3046 (Comm) 430

Nugent v Smith (1876) 1 CPD 423 .... 235, 309

NYK Bulkship (Atlantic) NV v Cargill International SA (The Global Santosh) [2016] UKSC 20 482

OBG Ltd and another v Allan and others Douglas and others v Hello! Ltd and others (No. 3) Mainstream Properties Ltd v Young [2008] 1 AC 1 157

Ocean Glory Compania Naviera SA v A/S PV Christensen (The Loanna) [1985] 2 Lloyd's Rep 164 480

Ocean Pride Maritime Ltd Partnership v Qingdao Ocean Shipping Co (The Northgate) [2007] EWHC 2796 (Comm) 429

Ocean Projects Inc v Ultratech Pte Ltd [1994] 2 SLR 369 ...... 36, 110, 402, 416

Ocean Tramp Tankers Corpn v V/O Sovfracht (The Eugenia) [1964] 2 QB 226 .... 653, 684

Oceanfocus Shipping Ltd v Hyundai Merchant Marine Co Ltd (The Hawk) [1999] 1 Lloyd's Rep 176 456

Official Assignee of Madras v Mercantile Bank of India Ltd [1935] AC 53 .... 34, 35, 52, 53, 250

OK Petroleum AB v Vitol Energy SA [1995] 2 Lloyd's Rep 160 81

Oldendorff (E L) & Co GmbH v Tradax Export SA (The Johanna Oldendorff) [1974] AC 479 .... 431, 436

Oldendorff GmbH & Co KG v Sea Powerful II Special Maritime Enterprises (The Zagora) [2016] EWHC 3212 464

Olivine Electronics Pte Ltd v Seabridge Transport Pte Ltd [1995] 3 SLR 143 147

Onego Shipping & Chartering BV v JSC Arcadia Shipping (The Socol 3) [2010] EWHC 777 379

Oricon Waren-Handels GmbH v Intergraan NV [1967] 2 Lloyd's Rep 82 190

Oriental Maritime Pte Ltd v Ministry of Food, Government of the People's Republic of Bangladesh (The Silva Plana, Bahamastars and Magic Sky) [1989] 2 Lloyd's Rep 371 715

Oriental Steamship v Tylor [1893] 2 QB 518 405

OT Africa Line Ltd v Hijazy and Others (The Kribi) [2001] 1 Lloyd's Rep 76 56

Overseas Transportation Co v Mineralimportexport (The Sinoe) [1971] 1 Lloyd's Rep 514 443

Owneast Shipping Ltd v Qatar Navigation QSC [2010] EWHC 1663 (Comm) 471, 475

Owners of cargo lately laden on board ship or vessel Makedonia v Makedonia (Owners) (The Makedonia) [1962] P 190 .... 214, 217, 272, 273

Owners of Cargo Lately Laden on Board the Ship or Vessel Thomaseverett v Owners of and Other Persons Interested in the Ship or Vessel Thomaseverett (The Thomaseverett) [1992] 2 SLR 1068 616

Owners of Cargo lately on board River Gurara v Nigerian National Shipping Line Ltd (The River Gurara) [1998] 1 Lloyd's Rep 225 .... 290, 359

Owners of Cargo on Board The Merak v The Merak (Owners) (The Merak) [1965] P 223 115

Owners of Cargo on The Maori King v Hughes (The Maori King) [1895] 2 QB 550 .... 221, 243, 275

Owners of the ship or vessel 'Kota Bakti' v Douglas Fraser & Sons (London) Ltd (The Kota Bakti) [1993] 1 SLR 849 .... 125, 134

P Odernamall & Co v American President Lines Ltd and Penang Harbour Board (No 1) [1956] 1 MLJ 6 320

Pacific Electric Wire & Cable Co Ltd & Anor v Neptune Orient Lines Ltd & Ors [1993] SLR(R) 102 .... 15, 16

Pacol Ltd and Others v Trade Lines Ltd and R/I Sif IV (The Henrik Sif) [1982] 1 Lloyd's Rep 456 335

Pagnan SpA v Tradax Ocean Transportation SA [1987] 2 Lloyd's Rep 342 81

Panoutsos v Raymond Hadley Corpn of New York [1917] 2 KB 437 89

Papera Traders Co Ltd v Hyundai Merchant Marine Co Ltd (The Eurasian Dream) (No.1) [2002] EWHC 118 .... 386, 497

Parbulk II A/S Heritage Maritime SA (The Mahakam) [2011] EWHC 2917 (Comm) 473

Parker Distributors (Singapore) Pte Ltd v A/S D/S Svenborg & Anor [1982-1983] 1 SLR 153 348

Parsons Corp v CV Scheepvaartonderneming (Happy Ranger) [2002] EWHC Civ 649 .... 278, 322

Parsons v New Zealand Shipping [1901] 1 QB 548 185

Partenreederei M/S Heidberg v Grosvenor Grain and Feed Co Ltd (The Heidberg) [1994] 2 Lloyd's Rep 287 115

Paterson Steamship Ltd v Canadian Co-operative Wheat Producers [1934] AC 538 135
Patten v Thompson (1816) 5 M & S 350 29
Paynter v James (1867) LR 2 CP 348 403
Pearl Carriers Inc v Japan Line Ltd (The Chemical Venture) [1993] 1 Lloyd's Rep 508 .... 458, 459, 463
Peekay Intermark Ltd v ANZ Banking Group Ltd [2006] EWCA Civ 386 185
Peninsular & Oriental Steam Navigation Co Ltd & Ors v Rambler Cycle Co Ltd [1964] 30 MLJ 443 .... 170, 331
Penta Shipping (K/S) A/S v Ethiopian Shipping Lines Corpn (The Saga Cob) [1991] 2 Lloyd's Rep 398 798
Pentonville Shipping Ltd v Transfield Shipping Inc (The Johnny K) [2006] EWHC 134 (Comm) 403
Petrofina SA of Brussels v Compagnia Italiana Trasporto Olii Minerali of Genoa (1937) 53 TLR 650, (1937) 57 Ll L Rep 247 225
Petroleo Brasileiro SA v Kriti Akti Shipping Co SA (The Kriti Akti) [2004] EWCA Civ 116 .... 479, 491, 495
Petroships Pte Ltd of Singapore v Petec Trading and Investment Co of Vietnam and Ors (The Petro Ranger) [2001] EWHC 418 (Comm) 306
Phelps, James & Co v Hill [1891] 1 QB 604 229
Phillips Petroleum Co v Cabaneli Naviera SA (The Theodegmon) [1990] 1 Lloyd's Rep 52 .... 383, 398, 438, 441, 492, 497, 499
Photo Production Ltd v Securicor Transport Ltd [1980] AC 827 .... 5, 160, 234, 236, 237
Playing Cards (Malaysia) Sdn Bhd v China Mutual Navigation Co Ltd [1980] 2 MLJ 182 .... 36, 56, 243
Port Jackson Stevedoring Pty Ltd v Salmond & Spraggon (Australia) Pty Ltd (The New York Star) [1981] 1 WLR 138, [1980-84] LRC (Comm) 105 .... 170, 331, 332
Port Swettenham Authority v The Borneo Co (Malaysia) Sdn Bhd [1975] 2 MLJ 80 .... 127, 131
Port Swettenham Authority v Tw Wu and Company (M) Sdn Bhd [1978] 2 MLJ 137 .... 128, 315

President of India v Metcalfe Shipping Co Ltd (The Dunelmia) [1970] 1 QB 289 .... 68, 119, 123, 187, 376
Primera Maritime (Hellas) Ltd v Jiangsu Eastern Heavy Industry Co Ltd [2013] EWHC 3066 (Comm) 473, 477
Primetrade AG v Ythan Ltd (The Ythan) [2005] EWHC 2399 (Comm) [1980] AC 827 .... 41, 60, 68, 151, 154
Procter & Gamble Philippine Manufacturing Corpn v Kurt A Becher GmbH & Co KG [1988] 2 Lloyd's Rep 21 199
Product Star Shipping Ltd (The Product Star) (No. 2) [1993] 1 Lloyd's Rep 397 461
Provender v Wood (1630) Hetley 30 .... 62, 166
PS Chellaram & Co Ltd v China Ocean Shipping Co (The Zhi Jiang Kou) [1991] 1 Lloyd's Rep 493 .... 331, 332
Pteroti Cia Nav SA v National Coal Board [1958] 1 QB 469 430
Punjab National Bank v Malayan Banking Berhad [2020] 1 LNS 232 .... 42, 43, 52, 92, 110, 143, 151, 153, 159, 163, 331, 350, 352
Pyrene Co Ltd v Scindia Navigation Co Ltd [1954] 2 QB 402 .... 29, 30, 48, 70, 71, 106, 121, 122, 127, 141, 143, 160, 190, 200, 242, 254, 265, 271, 284, 330
Queensland National Bank v Peninsular and Oriental Steam Navigation Co [1898] 1 QB 567 222
RA Lister & Co Ltd v EG Thomson (Shipping) Ltd (The Benarty) (No. 2) [1985] QB 325 325
Ramdas Vithaldasm Durba v Amerchand (1916) 85 LJPC 214 38
Raymond Burke v Mersey Docks and Harbour Board [1986] 1 Lloyd's Rep 155 171
RD Harbottle (Mercantile) Ltd v National Westminster Bank [1977] 2 All ER 862 98
Re Ropner Shipping Co Ltd & Cleeves Wester Valley Anthracite Colliers Ltd [1927] 1 KB 879 443

Reardon Smith Line Ltd v Ministry of Agriculture, Fisheries and Food [1963] AC 691 .... 425, 442
Reardon Smith Lines Ltd v Black Sea and Baltic General Insurance Co Ltd (The Indian City) [1939] AC 562 227
Reardon-Smith Line v Australian Wheat Board (The Houston City) [1956] AC 266 462
Redgrave v Hurd (1881) 20 Ch D 1 185
Reeve v Palmer (1858) 5 CBNS 84 317
Renton (GH) & Co Ltd v Palmyra Trading Corpn of Panama [1957] AC 149 232
Rey Banano Del Pacifico CA and Others v Transportes Navieros Ecuatorianos and Another (The Isla Fernandina) [2000] 2 Lloyd's Rep 15 214
Rheinoel GmbH v Huron Liberian Co (The Concordia C) [1985] 2 Lloyd's Rep 55 493
Rich (Marc) & Co Ltd v Tourloti Cia Naviera SA (The Kalliopi A) [1988] 2 Lloyd's Rep 101 445
Richardson v Mellish (1824) 2 Bing 252 162
Rimpacific Navigation Inc v Daehan Shipbuilding Co [2011] EWHC 2618 (Comm) 493
Rio Tinto v Seed Shipping (1926) 23 LI L Rep 316 .... 227, 234, 235
Ritchie v Atkinson (1808) 10 East 295 403
Riverstone Meat Co Pty Ltd v Lancashire Shipping Co Ltd (The Muncaster Castle) [1961] AC 807 278
Robertson v French [1803-13] All ER Rep 350 231
Robinson v Knights (1873) LR 8 CP 465 405
Rodocanachi, Sons & Co v Milburn Bros (1886) 18 QBD 67 .... 68, 119, 376
Roelandts v Harison (1854) 23 LJ Ex 169 404
Rolimpex (Ch E) Ltd v Avra Shipping Co Ltd (The Angeliki) [1973] 2 Lloyd's Rep 226 343
Ronex Properties Ltd v John Laing Construction Ltd [1983] 1 QB 398 333
Rosenthal v Alderton & Sons Ltd [1946] KB 374 157
Rotherfield Steamship Co Ltd v Tweedie, Reid & Co (1897) 2 Com Cas 84 401
Royal Exchange Shipping Co Ltd v Dixon (1886) 12 App Cas 11 .... 240, 267
Ruapehu (Owners) v R and H Green and Silley Weir Ltd (The Ruapehu) (1925) 21 Ll L Rep 310 559

Sabarudin bin Othman & Anor v Malayan Banking Bhd and another appeal [2018] MLJU 304 346
Samuel, Samuel & Co v West Hartlepool Steam Navigation Co (1907) 12 Com Cas 203 107
Sanders Bros v Maclean & Co (1883) 11 QBD 327 30
Santa Martha Baay Scheepvaart and Handelsmaatschappij NV v Scanbulk A/S (The Rijn) [1981] 2 Lloyd's Rep 267 481
Santiren Shipping Ltd v Unimarine SA (The Chrysovalandou Dyo) [1981] 1 All ER 340 .... 417, 469, 470, 471
Sarathi Co v Owners of Vishva Prathiba [1980] 2 MLJ 265 350
Sarawak Electricity Supply Corp v MS Shipping Sdn Bhd [2000] 5 MLJ 721 .... 38, 53, 281, 282
Scancarriers A/S v Aotearoa International Ltd (The Barranduna and Tarago) [1985] 2 Lloyd's Rep 419 123
Scaramanga & Co v Stamp and Another (1880) 5 CPD 295 .... 226, 227, 228
Schelde Delta Shipping BV v Astarte Shipping Ltd (The Pamela) [1995] 2 Lloyd's Rep 249 .... 470, 471, 474, 475, 476
Scipion Active Trading Fund v Vallis Group Ltd (formerly Vallis Commodities Ltd) [2020] EWHC 795 (Comm) 126
Scotson v Pegg (1861) 6 H & N 295 170
Scottish & Newcastle Int Ltd v Othon Ghalanos Ltd [2008] UKHL 11 82
Sea Master Shipping Inc v Arab Bank (Switzerland) Ltd [2018] EWHC 1902 55
Sea Tank Shipping AS (formerly known as Tank Invest AS) v Vinnlustodin HF and Another (The Aqasia) [2018] EWCA Civ 276 327
Seals (LD) NV v Mitsui Osk Lines Ltd (The Darya Tara) [1997] 1 Lloyd's Rep 42 .... 454, 471
Seatrade Group NV v Hakan Agro DMCC (The Aconcagua Bay) [2018] EWHC 654 (Comm) 436
Sebor (Sarawak) Trading Sdn Bhd & Anor v Syarikat Cheap Hin Toy Manufacture Sdn Bhd [2003] 2 MLJ 486 .... 163, 350, 353
Serena Navigation Ltd v Dera Commercial Establishment (The Limnos) [2008] EWHC 1036 (Comm) 357
Sewell v Burdick (The Zoe) (1884) 10 App Case 74 451
Sheffield Corp v Barclays [1905] AC 392 451

Shell International Petroleum Co Ltd v Seabridge Shipping (The Metula) [1978] 2 Lloyd's Rep 5 400

Shipping Corp of India Ltd v Gamlen Chemical Co (A/Asia) Pty Ltd 147 CLR 142 538

Shipping Corpn of India Ltd v Nsb Niederelbe Schiffahrtsgesellschaft Mbh & Co (The Black Falcon) [1991] 1 Lloyd's Rep 77 495

Shipping Developments Corpn v v/o Sojuzneftexport (The Delian Spirit) [1972] 1 QB 103 436

Shun Cheong Steam Navigation Co Ltd v Wo Fong Trading Co [1979] 2 MLJ 254 .... 241, 341, 345, 349

SIAT di Dal Ferro v Tradax Overseas SA [1980] 1 Lloyd's Rep 53 92

Sib International SRL v Metallgesellschaft Corporation (The Noel Bay) [1989] 1 Lloyd's Rep 361 493

Sideridraulic Systems SpA v BBC Chartering & Logistic GmbH & Co KG (The BBC Greenland) [2011] EWHC 3106 (Comm) 259

Sidermar SpA v Apollo Corporation (The Apollo) [1978] 1 Lloyd's Rep 200 485

Sig Bergesen DY & Co and Others V Mobil Shipping and Transportation Co (The Berge Sund) [1993] 2 Lloyd's Rep 453 .. 453, 484

Silver and Layton v Ocean Steamship Co Ltd [1930] 1 KB 416 .. 105, 307, 309, 318

Skibs A/S Trolla And Skibs A/S Tautra v United Enterprises & Shipping (Pte) Ltd (The Tarva) [1973] 2 Lloyd's Rep 385 406

Skibsaktieselskapet Snefonn, Skibsaksjeselskapet Bergehus and Sig Bergesen DY & Co v Kawasaki Kisen Kaisha Ltd (The Berge Tasta) [1975] 1 Lloyd's Rep 422 841

Skips A/S Nordheim v Syrian Petroleum Co Ltd (The Varenna) [1984] QB 599 .... 114, 115

SL Sethia Liners Ltd v Naviagro Maritime Corpn (The Kostas Melas) [1981] 1 Lloyd's Rep 18 471

Smith Hill & Co v Pyman Bell & Co [1891] 1 QB 742 405

Smith, Hogg v Black Sea and Baltic General Insurance [1940] AC 997 .... 218, 230, 283

Snia Societa di Navigazione Industria e Commercio v Suzuki & Co (1924) 29 Com Cas 284 214

Sociedad Financiera De Bienes Raices Sa v Agrimpex Hungarian Trading Company for Agricultural Products [Appeal in The Aello] [1961] AC 135 437

Societe De Distribution De Toutes Merchandises En Cote D'Ivoire (t/a "SDTM-CI") v Continental Lines NV (The Sea Mirror) [2015] EWHC 1747 (Comm) 284

Sofial SA v Ove Skou Rederi (The Helle Skou) [1976] 2 Lloyd's Rep 205 429

Somes v British Empire Shipping Co (1858) El Bl & El 353 724

Sonicare International Ltd v East Anglia Freight Terminal Ltd [1997] 2 Lloyd's Rep 48 .... 126, 137

Soon Hua Seng Co Ltd v Glencore Grain Ltd [1996] 1 Lloyd's Rep 398 85

Soproma SpA v Marine and Animal By-Products Corp [1966] 1 Lloyd's Rep 367 89

Spar Shipping AS v Grand China Logistics Holding (Group) Co Ltd [2016] EWCA Civ 982 .... 471, 472

Spectra International plc v Hayesoak Ltd [1997] 1 Lloyd's Rep 153 .... 125, 145

SS Ardennes (Cargo Owners) v SS Ardennes (Owners) [1951] 1 KB 55 .... 86, 112, 121

SS Athamas (Owners) v Dig Vijay Cement Co Ltd (The Athamas) [1963] 1 Lloyd's Rep 287 410

St Enoch Shiping v Phosphate Mining [1916] 2 KB 624 402

Stag Line Ltd v Board of Trade [1950] 2 KB 194 402

Stag Line Ltd v Foscolo, Mango & Co Ltd[1932] AC 328 ...... 229, 230, 238, 289, 300

Standard Chartered Bank Malaysia Bhd v Duli Yang Maha Mulia Tuanku Ja'Afar Ibni Almarhum Tuanku Abdul Rahman, Yang Di Pertuan Besar Negeri Sembilan Darul Khusus [2009] 4 MLJ 1 87

Standard Chartered Bank v Boomland Development Sdn Bhd & Ors [1997] MLJU 19 68

Standard Chartered Bank v Dorchester LNG (2) Ltd (The Erin Schulte) [2014] EWCA Civ 1382 .... 135, 139

Standard Chartered Bank v Pakistan National Shipping Corp (No 2) [2000] 1 All ER (Comm) 1 198

Standard Oil Co of New York v Clan Line Steamers Ltd [1924] AC 100 209

Star Reefers Pool Inc v JFC Group Co Ltd [2011] EWHC 2204 (Comm) 493
Steamship Heathfield Co v Rodenacher (1986) 2 Com Cas 55 ... 401
Steel v State Line Steamship Co (1877) 3 App Cas 72 214
Steelwood Carriers Inc of Monrovia, Liberia v Evimeria Cia Naviera SA of Panama (The Agios Giorgis) [1976] 2 Lloyd's Rep 192 416
Stevens v Bromley & Sons [1919] 2 KB 722 402
Stolt Tankers v Landmark [2002] 1 Lloyd's Rep 786 .... 424, 443
Stora Enso Oyj v Port of Dundee [2006] CSOH 40 80
STX Pan Ocean Co Ltd v Ugland Bulk Transport AS (The Livanita) [2007] All ER (D) 43 (Jun), [2007] EWHC 1317 (Comm) 458
Successors of Moine Comte & Co Ltd v East Asiatic Co Ltd [1954] MLJ 113 320
Suck AG v Glencore International AG [2011] EWHC 1361 (Comm) 433
Sucre Export SA v Northern Shipping Ltd (The Sormovskiy 3068) [1994] 2 Lloyd's Rep 266 .... 147, 163, 463
Suisse Atlantique Société d'Armement Maritime SA v Rotterdamsche Kolen Centrale NV [1967] 1 AC 361 375
Sun Shipping Co Ltd v Watson & Youell Shipping Agency Ltd (1926) 24 Ll L Rep 28 389
Sunbeam Shipping Co Ltd v President of India (The Atlantic Sunbeam) [1973] 1 Lloyd's Rep 482 437
Sunlight Mercantile Pte Ltd and Another v Ever Lucky Shipping Co Ltd [2003] SGCA 47 .... 213, 243, 379
Sunrise Maritime Inc v Uvisco Ltd (The Hector) [1998] 2 Lloyd's Rep 287 .... 108, 112
Surrey Shipping Co Ltd v Compagnie Continentale (France) SA (The Shackleford) [1978] 1 WLR 1080 428
Svenska Traktor Aktiebolget v Maritime Agencies (Southampton) Ltd [1953] 2 QB 295 457
Swiss Bank Corp v Lloyds Bank Ltd [1979] Ch 548 385
Sze Hai Tong Bank Ltd v Rambler Cycle Co Ltd [1959] AC 576 .... 5, 69, 146, 160
TA Shipping Ltd v Comet Shipping Ltd (The Agamemnon) [1998] 1 Lloyd's Rep 675 439

Tank Shipping AS (formerly known as Tank Invest AS) v Vinnlustodin HF and Another (The Aqasia) [2018] EWCA Civ 276 .... 327, 351, 359

Tasman Orient Line CV v New Zealand China Clays (The Tasman Pioneer) [2010] NZSC 37 .... 522, 530, 533

Tattersall v National Steamship Co (1884) 12 QBD 297 211

Telfair Shipping Corporation v Athos Shipping Co SA, Solidor Shipping Co Ltd, Horizon Finance Corporation and AN Cominos (The Athos) [1983] 1 Lloyd's Rep 127 473

Telfair Shipping Corporation v Inersea Carriers SA (The Caroline P) [1985] 1 WLR 553 455

Tenax Steamship Co Ltd v Reinante Transoceania Navegacion SA (The Brimnes) [1975] QB 929 473

The Abqaiq. *See* National Shipping Co of Saudi Arabia v BP Oil Supply Co (The Abqaiq) [2011] EWCA Civ 1127

The Achilleas. *See* Transfield Inc v Mercator Shipping Inc (The Achilleas) [2008] UKHL 28

The Aconcagua Bay. *See* Seatrade Group NV v Hakan Agro DMCC (The Aconcagua Bay) [2018] EWHC 654 (Comm)

The Aditya Vaibhav. *See* Century Textiles and Industry Ltd v Tomoe Shipping Co (Singapore) Pte Ltd (The Aditya Vaibhav) [1991] 1 Lloyd's Rep 573

The Aegean Sea [1998] 2 Lloyd's Rep 39 57

The Aegis Britannic. *See* Action SA v Britannic Shipping Corpn Ltd (The Aegis Britannic) [1987] 1 Lloyd's Rep 119

The Aegis Spirit [1977] 1 Lloyd's Rep 93 .... 223, 352

The Aegnoussiotis. *See* Aegnoussiotis Shipping Corpn of Monrovia v A/S Kristian Jebsens Rederi of Bergen (The Aegnoussiotis) [1977] 1 Lloyd's Rep 268

The Afovos. *See* Afovos Shipping Co SA v Pagnan and Lli (The Afovos) [1983] 1 All ER 449

The Agamemnon. *See* TA Shipping Ltd v Comet Shipping Ltd (The Agamemnon) [1998] 1 Lloyd's Rep 675

The Agios Giorgis. *See* Steelwood Carriers Inc of Monrovia, Liberia v Evimeria Cia Naviera SA of Panama (The Agios Giorgis) [1976] 2 Lloyd's Rep 192

The Agios Lazaros. *See* Nea Agrex SA v Baltic Shipping Co Ltd and Intershipping Charter Co (The Agios Lazaros) [1976] QB 933

The Agios Stylianos. *See* Agios Stylianous Compania Naviera SA v Maritime Associates International Ltd Lagos (The Agios Stylianos) [1975] 1 Lloyd's Rep 426

The Ailsa Craig. *See* Mansel Oil Ltd v Troon Storage Tankers SA (The Ailsa Craig) [2009] EWCA Civ 425
The Al Taha. *See* Lyric Shipping Inc v Intermetals Ltd (The Al Taha) [1990] 2 Lloyd's Rep 117
The Alamosa. *See* United States Shipping Board v Bunge y Born Ltda Sociedad (The Alamosa) (1925) 42 TLR 174
The Alaskan Trader. *See* Clea Shipping Corporation v Bulk Oil International Ltd (The Alaskan Trader) (No. 2) [1983] 2 Lloyd's Rep 645
The Alev. *See* Vantage Navigation Corp v Suhail and Saud Bahvan Building Materials (The Alev) [1989] 1 Lloyd's Rep 138
The Alhani. *See* Deep Sea Maritime Ltd v Monjasa A/S (The Alhani) [2018] EWHC 1495 (Comm)
The American Accord. *See* United City Merchants (Investments) Ltd and Others v Royal Bank of Canada and Others (The American Accord) [1983] 1 AC 168
The American Astronaut [1978–1979] 1 SLR 187 .... 32, 192
The Amphion. *See* General Feeds Inc v Burnham Shipping Corpn (The Amphion) [1991] 2 Lloyd's Rep 101
The Amstelslot. *See* Union of India v NV Reederij Amsterdam (The Amstelslot) [1963] 2 Lloyd's Rep 223
The Andra. *See* DGC Commodities Corp v Sea Metropolitan SA (The Andra) [2012] EWHC 1984 (Comm)
The Andrewe (1544) Select Pleas, vol. I, p. 126 27
The Angeliki. *See* Rolimpex (Ch E) Ltd v Avra Shipping Co Ltd (The Angeliki) [1973] 2 Lloyd's Rep 226
The Antares. *See* Kenya Railways v Antares Co Pte Ltd (The Antares) [1987] 1 Lloyd's Rep 424
The Antigoni [1991] 1 Lloyd's Rep 209 .... 280, 311
The Antwerpen. *See* Glebe Island Terminals Pty Ltd v Continental Seagram Pty Ltd (The Antwerpen) [1994] 1 Lloyd's Rep 213
The APJ Priti. *See* Atkins International HA v Islamic Republic of Iran Shipping Lines (The APJ Priti) [1987] 2 Lloyd's Rep 37
The Apollo. *See* Sidermar SpA v Apollo Corporation (The Apollo) [1978] 1 Lloyd's Rep 200
The Aqasia. *See* Sea Tank Shipping AS (formerly known as Tank Invest AS) v Vinnlustodin HF and Another (The Aqasia) [2018] EWCA Civ 276
The Aramis (HC) [1987] 2 Lloyd's Rep 58 327
The Aramis (CA) [1989] 1 Lloyd's Rep 213 124

The Archimidis. *See* AIC Limited v Marine Pilot Limited (The Archimidis) [2008] EWCA Civ 175
The Ardennes. *See* SS Ardennes (Cargo Owners) v SS Ardennes (Owners) [1951] 1 KB 55
The Argonaut. *See* MSC Mediterranean Shipping Co SA v Alianca Bay Shipping Co Ltd (The Argonaut) [1985] 2 Lloyd's Rep 216
The Aries. *See* Aries Tanker Corpn v Total Transport Ltd (The Aries) [1977] 1 WLR 185
The Arktis Sky [2000] 1 SLR 57 162
The Armar. *See* Armar Shipping Co Ltd v Caisse Algérienne d'Assurance et de Réassurance (The Armar) [1981] 1 All ER 498
The Arpad [1934] All ER Rep 326 .... 158, 358
The Arundel Castle. *See* Navalmar UK Ltd v Kale Maden Hammaddeler Sanayi Ve Ticart AS (The Arundel Castle) [2017] EWHC 116 (Comm)
The Asia Star [2007] SGCA 17 .... 222, 243
The Athamas. *See* SS Athamas (Owners) v Dig Vijay Cement Co Ltd (The Athamas) [1963] 1 Lloyd's Rep 287
The Athanasia Comninos and Georges Chr Lemos [1990] 1 Lloyd's Rep 277 .... 132, 361, 363, 453, 456
The Athelviscount. *See* National Petroleum Co v Athelviscount (Owners) (The Athelviscount) (1934) 48 Ll L Repl 164
The Athena. *See* Minerva Navigation Inc v Oceana Shipping AG (The Athena) [2013] EWCA Civ 1723
The Athos. *See* Telfair Shipping Corporation v Athos Shipping Co SA, Solidor Shipping Co Ltd, Horizon Finance Corporation and AN Cominos (The Athos) [1983] 1 Lloyd's Rep 127
The Atlantic Duchess. *See* Atlantic Oil Carriers Ltd v British Petroleum Co Ltd (The Atlantic Duchess) [1957] 2 Lloyd's Rep 55
The Atlantic Sunbeam. *See* Sunbeam Shipping Co Ltd v President of India (The Atlantic Sunbeam) [1973] 1 Lloyd's Rep 482
The Atlas. *See* Noble Resources Ltd v Cavalier Shipping Corpn (The Atlas) [1996] 1 Lloyd's Rep 642, [1996] CLC 1148
The Atrice. *See* Vinmar International Ltd v Theresa Navigation SA (The Atrice) [2001] 2 All ER (Comm) 243

The August Leonhardt. *See* K Lokumal & Sons (London) Ltd v Lotte Shipping Co Pte Ltd (The August Leonhardt)
The Baleares. *See* Geogas SA v Trammo Gas Ltd (The Baleares) [1993] 1 Lloyd's Rep 215
The Barranduna and Tarago. *See* Scancarriers A/S v Aotearoa International Ltd (The Barranduna and Tarago) [1985] 2 Lloyd's Rep 419
The Batis. *See* Batis Maritime Corporation v Petroleos Del Mediterraneo SA (The Batis) [1990] 1 Lloyd's Rep 345
The BBC Greenland. *See* Sideridraulic Systems SpA v BBC Chartering & Logistic GmbH & Co KG (The BBC Greenland) [2011] EWHC 3106 (Comm)
The Benarty. *See* RA Lister & Co Ltd v EG Thomsom (Shipping) Ltd (The Benarty) (No. 2) [1985] QB 325
The Berge Sisar. *See* Borealis AB (formerly Borealis Petrokemi AB and Statoil Petrokemi AB) v Stargas Ltd (The Berge Sisar) [2001] UKHL 17
The Berge Sund. *See* Sig Bergesen DY & Co and Others V Mobil Shipping and Transportation Co (The Berge Sund) [1993] 2 Lloyd's Rep 453
The Berge Tasta. *See* Skibsaktieselskapet Snefonn, Skibsaksjeselskapet Bergehus and Sig Bergesen DY & Co v Kawasaki Kisen Kaisha Ltd (The Berge Tasta) [1975] 1 Lloyd's Rep 422
The Berkshire [1974] 1 Lloyd's Rep 185 104
The Black Falcon. *See* Shipping Corpn of India Ltd v Nsb Niederelbe Schiffahrtsgesellschaft Mbh & Co (The Black Falcon) [1991] 1 Lloyd's Rep 77
The Boukadoura. *See* Boukadoura Maritime Corpn v Marocaine de l'Industrie et du Raffinage SA (The Boukadoura) [1989] 1 Lloyd's Rep 393
The Brede. *See* Henriksens Rederi A/S V Thz Rolimpex (The Brede) [1973] 2 Lloyd's Rep 333
The Bremen Max. *See* Farenco Shipping Co Ltd v Daebo Shipping Co Ltd (Dampskibsselskabet Norden A/S, third party) (Deiulemar Shipping SpA, fourth party) (The Bremen Max) [2009] 1 All ER (Comm) 423
The Brimnes. *See* Tenax Steamship Co Ltd v Reinante Transoceania Navegacion SA (The Brimnes) [1975] QB 929
The Bulk Chile. *See* Dry Bulk Handy Holding Inc and Another v Fayette International Holdings Ltd and Another (The Bulk Chile) [2013] EWCA Civ 184

The Bunga Seroja. *See* Great China Metal Industries Co Ltd v Malaysian International Shipping Corporation Berhad (The Bunga Seroja) [1999] 1 Lloyd's Rep 512
The C Joyce. *See* Ben Shipping Co (Pte) Ltd v An-Board Bainne (The C Joyce) [1986] 2 Lloyd's Rep 285
The Canadian Highlander. *See* Gosse Millerd Ltd v Canadian Government Merchant Marine Ltd (The Canadian Highlander) [1929] AC 223
The Captain Gregos. *See* Cia Portorafti Commerciale SA v Ultramar Panama Inc (The Captain Gregos) [1990] 1 Lloyd's Rep 310
The Caroline P. *See* Telfair Shipping Corporation v Inersea Carriers SA (The Caroline P) [1985] 1 WLR 553
The Caspian Sea. *See* Montedison SpA v Icroma SpA (The Caspian Sea) [1979] 3 All ER 378
The Cebu. *See* Itex Itagrani Export SA v Care Shipping Corp (The Cebu) (No. 2) [1990] 2 Lloyd's Rep 316
The Cendor Mopu. *See* Global Process Systems Inc v Syarikat Takaful Malaysia Bhd (The Cendor Mopu) [2011] UKSC 5
The Chanda. *See* Wibau Maschinenfabric Hartman SA and Another v Mackinnon Mackenzie & Co (The Chanda) [1989] 2 Lloyd's Rep 494
The Channel Ranger. *See* Caresse Navigation Ltd v Zurich Assurances MAROC (The Channel Ranger) [2014] EWCA Civ 1366
The Chemical Venture. *See* Pearl Carriers Inc v Japan Line Ltd (The Chemical Venture) [1993] 1 Lloyd's Rep 508
The Cherry and Others [2003] 1 SLR 471 .... 146, 148, 149
The Chevalier Roze. *See* Neptune Orient Lines Ltd v JVC (UK) Ltd (The Chevalier Roze) [1983] 2 Lloyd's Rep 438
The Chikuma. *See* Awilco A/S v Fulvia SpA di Navigazione (The Chikuma) [1981] 1 All ER 652
The Christel Vinnen [1924] P 208 219
The Chrysovalandou Dyo. *See* Santiren Shipping Ltd v Unimarine SA (The Chrysovalandou Dyo) [1981] 1 All ER 340
The Chyebassa. *See* Leesh River Tea Co Ltd v British India Steam Navigation Co Ltd (The Chyebassa) [1967] 2 QB 250
The Ciechocinek. *See* Ismail v Polish Ocean Lines (The Ciechocinek) [1976] QB 893
The Clipper Monarch. *See* Castleton Commodities Shipping Co Pte Ltd v Silver Rock Investments (The Clipper Monarch) [2015] EWHC 2584 (Comm)

The Clipper Sao Luis. *See* Macieo Shipping Ltd v Clipper Shipping Lines Ltd (The Clipper Sao Luis) [2000] 1 Lloyd's Rep 645
The Concordia C. *See* Rheinoel GmbH v Huron Liberian Co (The Concordia C) [1985] 2 Lloyd's Rep 55
The Dagny Skou [1980-1981] 1 SLR 200 296
The Danah. *See* Kuwait Maritime Transport Co v Rickmers Linie KG (The Danah) [1993] 1 Lloyd's Rep 351
The Daphne L. *See* Feoso (Singapore) Pte Ltd v Faith Maritime Co Ltd (The Daphne L) [2003] SGCA 34
The Darrah. *See* Aldebaran Compania Maritime SA, Panama v Aussenhandel AG Zurich (The Darrah) [1977] AC 157
The Darya Radhe. *See* Bunge SA v Adm Do Brasil Ltd (The Darya Radhe) [2009] EWHC 845 (Comm)
The Darya Tara. *See* Seals (LD) NV v Mitsui Osk Lines Ltd (The Darya Tara) [1997] 1 Lloyd's Rep 42
The David Agmashenebeli (cargo owners) v The David Agmashenebeli (owners) [2002] EWHC 104 (Admlty) 142
The Delfini. *See* Enichem Anic SpA and Others v Ampelos Shipping Co Ltd (The Delfini) [1990] 1 Ll L Rep 252
The Delian Spirit. *See* Shipping Developments Corpn v v/o Sojuzneftexport (The Delian Spirit) [1972] 1 QB 103
The Democritos. *See* Marbienes Compania Naviera SA v Ferrostaal AG (The Democritos) [1976] 2 Lloyd's Rep 149
The Demosthenes V. *See* Gerani Compania Naviera SA v General Organisation for Supply Goods (The Demosthenes V) (No. 1) [1982] 1 Lloyd's Rep 275
The Derby. *See* Tossa Marine Co Ltd v Alfred C Toepfer Schiffahrtsgesellschaft Gmbh (The Derby) [1985] 2 Lloyd's Rep 325
The Dias. *See* Dias Cia Naviera SA v Louis Dreyfus Corpn (The Dias) [1978] 1 All ER 724
The Dione. *See* Almas Shipping Corp of Monrovia v Mantovani (The Dione) [1975] 1 Lloyd's Rep 114
The Dolphina [2012] 1 Lloyd's Rep 304 59
The Dominique. *See* Colonial Bank v European Grain & Shipping Ltd (The Dominique) [1989] 1 Lloyd's Rep 431
The Dona Mari. *See* Cremer v General Carriers SA (The Dona Mari) [1973] 2 Lloyd's Rep 366
The Doric Pride. *See* Hyundai Merchant Marine Co Ltd v Furness Withy (Australia) Pty (The Doric Pride) [2006] EWCA Civ 599
The Dunelmia. *See* President of India v Metcalfe Shipping Co Ltd (The Dunelmia) [1970] 1 QB 289

The Eagle Valencia [2010] EWCA Civ 713 .... 440, 446
The Eastern City. *See* Leeds Shipping Co Ltd v Société Française Bunge (The Eastern City) [1958] 2 Lloyd's Rep 127
The Elbe Maru. *See* Nippon Yusen Kaisha v International Import and Export Co Ltd (The Elbe Maru) [1978] 1 Lloyd's Rep 206
The Elbrus. *See* Dalwood Marine Co v Nordana Line A/S (The Elbrus) [2009] EWHC 3394 (Comm)
The Eleni P. *See* Eleni Shipping Ltd v Transgrain Shipping BV (The Eleni P) [2019] EWHC 910 (Comm)
The Emmanuel C. *See* Industrie Chimiche Italia Centrale SpA v Nea Ninemia Shipping Co SA (The Emmanuel C) [1983] 1 Lloyd's Rep 310
The Endurance 1 [1999] 1 SLR 661 .... 816, 819
The Epar [1985] 2 MLJ 3 .... 246, 262
The Epic [2000] 3 SLR 735 .... 147, 463
The Epsilon Rosa. *See* Welex AG v Rosa Maritime Ltd (The Epsilon Rosa) [2002] EWHC 762 (Comm)
The Erin Schulte. *See* Standard Chartered Bank v Dorchester LNG (2) Ltd (The Erin Schulte) [2014] EWCA Civ 1382
The Esmeralda 1. *See* Ace Imports Pty Ltd v Companhia de Navegacao Lloyd Brasileiro (The Esmeralda 1) [1988] 1 Lloyd's Rep 206
The Eternal Bliss. *See* K Line PTE Ltd v Priminds Shipping (HK) Co Ltd (The Eternal Bliss) [2020] EWHC 2373 (Comm)
The Eternity. *See* The Petroleum Oil and Gas Corporation of South Africa (Pty) Ltd v Fr8 Singapore Pte Ltd (The Eternity) [2009] 1 Lloyd's Rep 107
The Eugenia. *See* Ocean Tramp Tankers Corpn v V/O Sovfracht (The Eugenia) [1964] 2 QB 226
The Eurasian Dream. *See* Papera Traders Co Ltd v Hyundai Merchant Marine Co Ltd (The Eurasian Dream) (No. 1) [2002] EWHC 118
The Europa [1908] P 84 219
The European Enterprise. *See* Browner International Ltd v Monarch Shipping Co Ltd (The European Enterprise) [1989] 2 Lloyd's Rep 185
The Eurus. *See* Total Transport Corporation v Arcadia Petroleum Ltd (The Eurus) [1996] 2 Lloyd's Rep 408
The Eurymedon. *See* New Zealand Shipping Co Ltd v AM Satterthwaite (The Eurymedon) [1975] AC 154, [1974] 1 All ER 1015

The Evaggelos Theta. *See* Vardinoyannis v The Egyptian General Petroleum Corporation (The Evaggelos Theta) [1971] 2 Lloyd's Rep 200
The Evia. *See* Kodros Shipping Corp v Empresa Cubana de Fletes (The Evia) (No. 2) [1983] 1 AC 736
The Exeter Carrier Case (1743) 2 Ld Raym 867 415
The Fantasy. *See* Exercise Shipping Co Ltd v Bay Maritime Lines Ltd (The Fantasy) [1992] 1 Lloyd's Rep 235
The Federal Bulker. *See* Federal Bulker Federal Bulker Carriers Inc v C Itoh & Co Ltd (The Federal Bulker) [1989] 1 Lloyd's Rep 103
The Fehmarn [1958] 1 All ER 333 .... 246, 262
The Filikos. *See* Filikos Shipping Corpn of Monrovia v Shipmair BV (The Filikos) [1983] 1 Lloyd's Rep 9
The Finnrose. *See* Fort Sterling Ltd and Another v South Atlantic Cargo Shipping NV and Others (The Finnrose) [1994] 1 Lloyd's Rep 559
The Fiona. *See* Mediterranean Freight Services Ltd v BP Oil International Ltd (The Fiona) [1994] 2 Lloyd's Rep 506
The Fjordaas. *See* Moerland (Arnt J) K/S v Kuwait Petroleum Corpn (The Fjordaas) [1988] 2 All ER 714
The Flecha. *See* Fetim BV v Oceanspeed Shipping Ltd (The Flecha) [1999] 1 Lloyd's Rep 612
The Fontevivo. *See* Gem Shipping Co of Monrovia v Babanaft (Lebanon) SARL (The Fontevivo) [1975] 1 Lloyd's Rep 339
The Fortune Plum. *See* White Rosebay Shipping SA v Hong Kong Chain Glory Shipping Ltd (The Fortune Plum) [2013] EWHC 1355 (Comm)
The Forum Craftsman [1985] 1 Lloyd's Rep 291 138
The Front Commander. *See* Tidebrook Maritime Corp v Vitol SA of Geneva (The Front Commander) [2006] 2 Lloyd's Rep 251
The Future Express [1993] 2 Lloyd's Rep 542 127
The Galam (Cargo ex) (1863) Brown & Lush 167 .... 411, 415
The Galatia. *See* M Golodetz & Co Inc v Czarnikow-Rionda Co Inc (The Galatia) [1980] 1 All ER 501
The Garden City [1982] 2 Lloyd's Rep 382 298
The George of Legh (1544) Select Pleas, vol II, p. 61 27
The Giannis NK. See Effort Shipping Co Ltd v Linden Management SA (The Giannis NK) [1998] AC 605
The Glendarroch [1894] P 226 .... 245, 316
The Glenfruin (1885) 10 PD 103 214

The Global Santosh. *See* NYK Bulkship (Atlantic) NV v Cargill International SA (The Global Santosh) [2016] UKSC 20
The GMA CGM Libra. *See* Alize 1954 and another v Allianz Elementar Versicherungs AG and others (The GMA CGM Libra) [2020] EWCA Civ 293
The Golden Victory. *See* Golden Strait Corporation v Nippon Yusen Kubishka Kaisha (The Golden Victory) [2007] UKHL 12
The Greatship Dhriti. *See* Greatship (India) Ltd v Oceanografia SA de CV (The Greatship Dhriti) [2012] EWHC 3468 (Comm)
The Gregos. *See* Torvald Klaveness A/S V Arni Maritime Corporation (The Gregos) [1995] 1 Lloyd's Rep 1
The Gundulic. *See* Itoh & Co Ltd v Atlantska Plovidba (The Gundulic) [1981] 2 Lloyd's Rep 418
The Happy Day. *See* Glencore Grain Ltd v Flacker Shipping Ltd (The Happy Day) [2002] EWCA Civ 1068
The Happy Ranger. *See* Parsons Corp v CV Scheepvaartonderneming (Happy Ranger) [2002] EWHC Civ 649
The Havhelt [1993] 1 Lloyd's Rep 523 340
The Hawk. *See* Oceanfocus Shipping Ltd v Hyundai Merchant Marine Co Ltd (The Hawk) [1999] 1 Lloyd's Rep 176
The Hector. *See* Sunrise Maritime Inc v Uvisco Ltd (The Hector) [1998] 2 Lloyd's Rep 287
The Heidberg. *See* Partenreederei M/S Heidberg v Grosvenor Grain and Feed Co Ltd (The Heidberg) [1994] 2 Lloyd's Rep 287
The Helenus and Motagua [1982] 2 Lloyd's Rep 261 454
The Helle Skou. *See* Sofial SA v Ove Skou Rederi (The Helle Skou) [1976] 2 Lloyd's Rep 205
The Hellenic Dolphin [1978] 2 Lloyd's Rep 336 .... 277, 279, 419
The Henrik Sif. *See* Pacol Ltd and Others v Trade Lines Ltd and R/I Sif IV (The Henrik Sif) [1982] 1 Lloyd's Rep 456
The Heron II. *See* C Czarnikow Ltd v Koufos (The Heron II) [1969] 1 AC 350, See Koufos v C Czarnikow Ltd (The Heron II) [1969] 1 AC 350
The Hill Harmony. *See* Whistler International Ltd v Kawasaki Kisen Kaisha Ltd (The Hill Harmony) [2001] 1 Lloyd's Rep 147
The Hollandia [1983] 1 AC 565 .... 10, 246, 249

The Houda. *See* Kuwait Petroleum Corpn v I & D Oil Carriers Ltd (The Houda) [1994] 2 Lloyd's Rep 541
The Houston City. *See* Reardon-Smith Line v Australian Wheat Board (The Houston City) [1956] AC 266
The Imvros. *See* Transocean Liners Reederei GmbH v Euxine Shipping Co Ltd (The Imvros) [1999] 1 All ER (Comm) 724, See Transocean Liners Reederei GmbH v Euxine Shipping Co Ltd (The Imvros) [1999] 1 Lloyd's Rep 848
The Indian City. *See* Reardon Smith Lines Ltd v Black Sea and Baltic General Insurance Co Ltd (The Indian City) [1939] AC 562
The Indian Reliance. *See* India Steamship Co v Louis Dreyfus Sugar Ltd (The Indian Reliance) [1997] 1 Lloyd's Rep 52
The Ines. *See* MB Pyramid Sound NV v Briese Schiffahrts GmbH and Co KG MS Sina and Latvian Shipping Assoc Ltd (The Ines) [1995] 2 Lloyd's Rep 144
The Ion. *See* Unicoopjapan and Marubeni-Iida Company Ltd v Ion Shipping Company (The Ion) [1971] 1 Lloyd's Rep 541
The Ira. *See* Forestships International Ltd v Armonia Shipping and Finance Corporation (The Ira) [1995] 1 Lloyd's Rep 103
The Irish Rowan. *See* Irish Shipping Ltd v Commercial Union Assurance Co plc (The Irish Rowan) [1991] 2 QB 206
The Iron Gippsland. *See* Caltex Refining Co Pty Ltd v BHP Transport Ltd (The Iron Gippsland) [1994]1 Lloyd's Rep 335
The Isla Fernandina. *See* Rey Banano Del Pacifico CA and Others v Transportes Navieros Ecuatorianos and Another (The Isla Fernandina) [2000] 2 Lloyd's Rep 15
The Island Archon. *See* Triad Shipping Co v Stellar Chartering & Brokerage Inc (The Island Archon) [1995] 1 All ER 595
The Jag Shakti. *See* Chabbra Corporation Pte Ltd v Jag Shakti (Owners) (The Jag Shakti) [1986] 1 MLJ 197
The Jalamohan. *See* Ngo Chew Hong Edible Oil Pte Ltd v Scindia Steam Navigation Co Ltd (The Jalamohan) [1988] 1 Lloyd's Rep 443
The Jay Bola. *See* Zalnalabdin Payabi and Baker Rasti Lari v Armstel Shipping Corporation and Panthai Shipping Ltd (The Jay Bola) [1992] 2 Lloyd's Rep 62
The Jian He [2000] 1 SLR 8 .... 33, 164, 170
The Johanna Oldendorff. *See* Oldendorff (E L) & Co GmbH v Tradax Export SA (The Johanna Oldendorff) [1974] AC 479

The John Evangelist (1544) Select Pleas 26, 27
The Johnny K. *See* Pentonville Shipping Ltd v Transfield Shipping Inc (The Johnny K) [2006] EWHC 134 (Comm)
The Jordan II. *See* Jindal Iron and Steel Co Ltd v Islamic Solidarity Shipping Co Jordan Inc (The Jordan II) [2004] UKHL 49
The Julia. *See* Comptoir d'Achat et de Vente du Boerenbond Belge S/A v Luis de Ridder Ltda (The Julia) [1949] AC 293
The Kalliopi A. *See* Rich (Marc) & Co Ltd v Tourloti Cia Naviera SA (The Kalliopi A) [1988] 2 Lloyd's Rep 101
The Kamilla. *See* Kamilla Hans-Peter Eckhoff KG v AC Oerssleff's EFTF A/B (The Kamilla) [2006] EWHC 509
The Kamsar Voyager. *See* Guinomar of Conakry and Another v Samsung Fire & Marine Insurance Co Ltd (The Kamsar Voyager) [2002] 2 Lloyd's Rep 57
The Kanchenjunga. *See* Motor Oil Hellas (Corinth) Refineries SA v Shipping Corpn of India (The Kanchenjunga) [1990] 1 Lloyd's Rep 391
The Kapitan Petko Voivoda. *See* Daewoo Heavy Industries Ltd v Klipriver Shipping Ltd (The Kapitan Petko Voivoda) [2003] EWCA Civ 451
The Kapitan Sakharov. *See* Northern Shipping Co v Deutsche Seereederei GmbH and Others (The Kapitan Sakharov) [2000] 2 Lloyd's Rep 255
The Karin Vatis. *See* Vagres Compania Maritima SA v Nissho-Iwai American Corporation (The Karin Vatis) [1988] 2 Lloyd's Rep 330
The Khian Sea. *See* Islander Shipping Enterprises SA v Empresa Maritima Del Estado SA (The Khian Sea) [1979] 1 Lloyd's Rep 545
The Kildare.. *See* Zodiac Maritime Agencies Limited v Fortescue Metals Group Limited (The Kildare) [2010] EWHC 903
The Kitsa. *See* Action Navigation Inc v Bottiglieri di Navigation SpA (The Kitsa) [2005] EWHC 177 (Comm)
The Komninos S. *See* Hellenic Steel Co v Svolamar Shipping Co Ltd (The Komninos S) [1991] 1 Lloyd's Rep 370
The Kos. *See* ENE Kos 1 Ltd v Petroleo Brasileiro SA (No 2) (The Kos) [2012] UKSC 17
The Kostas Melas. *See* SL Sethia Liners Ltd v Naviagro Maritime Corpn (The Kostas Melas) [1981] 1 Lloyd's Rep 18
The Kota Bakti. *See* Owners of the ship or vessel 'Kota Bakti' v Douglas Fraser & Sons (London) Ltd (The Kota Bakti) [1993] 1 SLR 849

The Kota Pahlawan [1982-1983] 1 SLR 88 338
The Kribi. *See* OT Africa Line Ltd v Hijazy and Others (The Kribi) [2001] 1 Lloyd's Rep 76
The Kriti Akti. *See* Petroleo Brasileiro SA v Kriti Akti Shipping Co SA (The Kriti Akti) [2004] EWCA Civ 116, See Petroleo Brasileiro SA v Kriti Akti Shipping Co SA (The Kriti Akti) [2004] EWCA Civ 116
The Kriti Rex. *See* Fyffes Group Ltd. And Caribbean Gold Ltd v Reefer Express Lines Pty Ltd and Reefkrit Shipping Inc (The Kriti Rex) [1996] 2 Lloyd's Rep 171
The Kusu Island [1989] 1 SLR 119 339
The Kyzikos. *See* Bulk Transport Group Shipping Co Ltd v Seacrystal Shipping Ltd (The Kyzikos) [1989] AC 1264
The Laconia. *See* Mardorf Peach & Co Ltd v Attica Sea Carriers Corpn of Liberia (The Laconia) [1977] AC 850
The Laconian Confidence. *See* Andre & Cie SA v Orient Shipping Rotterdam BV (The Laconian Confidence) [1997] 1 Lloyd's Rep 139
The Lady Gwendolen. *See* Arthur Guinness, Son & Co (Dublin) Ltd v The Freshfield (Owners) (The Lady Gwendolen) [1965] P 294
The Lady M. *See* Glencore Energy UK Ltd & Anor v Freeport Holdings Ltd (The Lady M) [2019] EWCA Civ 388
The Laemthong Glory. *See* Laemthong International Lines Co Ltd v Artis (The Laemthong Glory) (No 2) [2005] EWCA Civ 519
The Laura Prima. *See* Nereide SpA di Navigazione v Bulk Oil International (The Laura Prima) [1982] 1 Lloyd's Rep 1
The Lefthero. *See* Ellis Shipping Corporation v Voest Alpine Intertrading (The Lefthero) [1991] 2 Lloyd's Rep 599
The Lehmann Timber. *See* Metall Market OOO v Vitorio Shipping Co Ltd (The Lehmann Timber) [2013] EWCA Civ 650
The Lendoudis Evangelos II. *See* Continental Pacific Shipping Ltd v Deemand Shipping Co Ltd (The Lendoudis Evangelos II) [1997] 1 Lloyd's Rep 404
The Leni. *See* Transworld Oil (USA) Inc v Minos Compania Naviera SA (The Leni) [1992] 2 Lloyd's Rep 48
The Leon. *See* Leon Corporation v Atlantic Lines and Navigation Co Inc (The Leon) [1985] 2 Lloyd's Rep 470
The Li Hai. *See* Western Bulk Carriers K/S v Li hai Maritime Inc (The Li Hai) [2005] EWHC 735 (Comm)
The Limnos. *See* Serena Navigation Ltd v Dera Commercial Establishment (The Limnos) [2008] EWHC 1036 (Comm)

The Linardos. *See* Cobelfret NV v Cyclades Shipping Co Ltd (The Linardos) [1994] 1 Lloyd's Rep 28
The Livanita. *See* STX Pan Ocean Co Ltd v Ugland Bulk Transport AS (The Livanita) [2007] All ER (D) 43 (Jun), [2007] EWHC 1317 (Comm)
The Loanna. *See* Ocean Glory Compania Naviera SA v A/S PV Christensen (The Loanna) [1985] 2 Lloyd's Rep 164
The London Explorer. *See* Timber Shipping Co SA v London & Overseas Freighters Ltd (The London Explorer) [1972] AC 1
The Lorna I *See* Compania Naviera General SA v Kerametal Ltd (The Lorna I) [1983] 1 Lloyd's Rep 373
The Loucas N. *See* Ionian Navigation Company Inc v Atlantic Shipping Company SA (The Loucas N) [1971] 1 Lloyd's Rep 215
The Lucille. *See* Uni-Ocean Lines Pte Ltd v C-Trade SA (The Lucille) [1984] 1 Lloyd's Rep 387
The Lung Yung & Thai Yung, Owners & Ors v Sadit Timber Sdn Bhd & Ors [1984] 1 MLJ 29 .... 170, 331
The Lutetian. *See* Tradax Export SA v Dorada Compania Naviera SA (The Lutetian) [1982] 2 Lloyd's Rep 140
The Lycaon. *See* Elder Dempster Lines v Ishag (The Lycaon) [1983] 2 Lloyd's Rep 548
The Madeleine. *See* Cheikh Boutros Selim El-Khoury and Others v Ceylon Shipping Lines Ltd (The Madeleine) [1967] 2 Lloyd's Rep 224
The Maersk Tangier. *See* Kyokuyo Co Ltd v AP Møller-Maersk A/S (trading as 'Maersk Line') (The Maersk Tangier) [2018] EWCA Civ 778
The Mahakam. *See* Parbulk II A/S Heritage Maritime SA (The Mahakam) [2011] EWHC 2917 (Comm)
The Maheno [1977] 1 Lloyd's Rep 81 .... 40, 47
The Mahkutai [1996] AC 650 172
The Makedonia *See* Owners of cargo lately laden on board ship or vessel Makedonia v Makedonia (Owners) (The Makedonia) [1962] P 190
The Maltasian. *See* Albacora SRL v Westcott & Laurance Line Ltd (The Maltasian) [1966] 2 Lloyd's Rep 53
The Maratha Envoy. *See* Federal Commerce and Navigation Co Ltd v Tradax Export SA (The Maratha Envoy) [1978] AC 1
The Marielle Bolten. *See* Whitsea Shipping and Trading Corp v El Paso Rio Clara Ltda (The Marielle Bolten) [2009] EWHC 2552 (Comm)

The Marika M. *See* Eastern Mediterranean Maritime (Liechtenstein) Ltd v Unimarine SA (The Marika M) [1981] 2 Lloyd's Rep 622
The Marinicki. *See* Maintop Shipping Co Ltd v Bulkindo Lines Pte Ltd (The Marinicki) [2003] EWHC 1894 (Admlty)
The Marinor. *See* Noranda Inc v Barton (Time Charter) Ltd (The Marinor) [1996] 1 Lloyd's Rep 301
The Marion. *See* Grand Champion Tankers Ltd v Norpipe A/S (The Marion) [1984] AC 563
The Mary (1541) Select Pleas, vol. 1, p. 112 . . . . 26, 27
The Mass Glory. *See* Glencore Grain Ltd v Goldbeam Shipping Inc (The Mass Glory) [2002] EWHC 27 (Comm)
The Massalia. *See* Government of Ceylon v Societe Franco-Tunisienne D'armement-Tunis (The Massalia) (No. 2) [1960] 2 Lloyd's Rep 352
The Merak. *See* Owners of Cargo on Board The Merak v The Merak (Owners) (The Merak)
The Merida. *See* Novologistics SARL v Five Ocean Corp (The Merida) [2009] EWHC 3046 (Comm)
The Metula. *See* Shell International Petroleum Co Ltd v Seabridge Shipping (The Metula) [1978] 2 Lloyd's Rep 5
The Michael S. *See* Evryalos Maritime Ltd v China Pacific Insurance Co Ltd (The Michael S) [2001] All ER (D) 325 (Dec)
The Mihalios Xilas. *See* China National Foreign Trade Transportation Corporation v Evlogia Shipping Co SA of Panama (The Mihalios Xilas) [1979] 2 All ER 1044
The Mihalis Angelos. *See* Maredelanto Compania Naviera SA v Bergbau-Handel GmbH (The Mihalis Angelos) [1970] EWCA Civ 4
The Miramar. *See* Miramar Maritime Corpn v Holborn Oil Trading Ltd (The Miramar) [1984] AC 676
The Moscow Stars. *See* Dainford Navigation Inc v PDVSA Petroleo SA (The Moscow Stars) [2017] EWHC 2150 (Comm)
The MSC Amsterdam. *See* Mediterranean Shipping Co SA v Trafigura Beheer BV and Another (The MSC Amsterdam) [2007] EWCA Civ 794
The Muncaster Castle. *See* Riverstone Meat Co Pty Ltd v Lancashire Shipping Co Ltd (The Muncaster Castle) [1961] AC 807
The MV Kantang. *See* Zuellig (Gold Coin Mills) v MV Antoly (Owners) (The MV Kantang) [1971] 1 MLJ 183

The MV Thonfullin. *See* Kuok Ling Timber Industries Sdn Bhd v The Owners of and Other Persons Interested in the Vessel MV Thonfullin (The MV Thonfullin) [2000] 2 MLJ 615
The Myrtos. *See* Mitsui OSK. Lines Ltd v Garnac Grain Co Inc (The Myrtos) [1984] 2 Lloyd's Rep 449
The Nadezhda Krupskaya. *See* Brown Boveri (Australia) Pty Limited v Baltic Shipping Company (The Nadezhda Krupskaya) [1989] 1 Lloyd's Rep 518
The Nanfri, The Benfri, The Lorfri. *See* Federal Commerce and Navigation Ltd v Molena Alpha Inc and others (The Nanfri, The Benfri, The Lorfri) [1979] AC 757
The Nea Tyhi [1982] 1 Lloyd's Rep 606 112
The Nerano. *See* Daval Aciers d'Usinor et de Sacilor v Armare Srl (The Nerano) [1994] 2 Lloyd's Rep 50
The New Flamenco. *See* Fulton Shipping Inc of Panama v Globalia Business Travel SAU (formerly TravelPlan SAU) of Spain (The New Flamenco) [2017] UKSC 43
The New York Star. *See* Port Jackson Stevedoring Pty Ltd v Salmond & Spraggon (Australia) Pty Ltd (The New York Star) [1981] 1 WLR 138, [1980-84] LRC (Comm) 105
The Nicholas H. *See* Marc Rich & Co AG v Bishop Rock Marine Co Ltd (The Nicholas H) [1996] AC 211
The Noel Bay. *See* Sib International SRL v Metallgesellschaft Corporation (The Noel Bay) [1989] 1 Lloyd's Rep 361
The Nordglimt [1987] 2 Lloyd's Rep 470 340
The North Prince. *See* Glory Wealth Shipping Pte Limited v North China Shipping Limited (The North Prince) [2010] EWHC 1692 (Comm)
The Northern Progress. *See* Ceval Alimentos SA v Agrimpex Trading Co Ltd (The Northern Progress) (No. 2) [1996] 2 Lloyd's Rep
The Northgate. *See* Ocean Pride Maritime Ltd Partnership v Qingdao Ocean Shipping Co (The Northgate) [2007] EWHC 2796 (Comm)
The Ocean Victory. *See* Gard Marine and Energy Ltd v China National Chartering Co Ltd (The Ocean Victory) [2017] UKSC 35
The Orjula. *See* Losinjska Plovidba v Transco Overseas Ltd (The Orjula) [1995] 2 Lloyd's Rep 395
The Pacific Voyager. *See* CSSA Chartering and Shipping Services SA v Mitsui OSK Lines Ltd (The Pacific Voyager) [2018] All ER (D) 32 (Nov)
The Pacific Wisdom [1998] 3 SLR 705 .... 102, 337

The Pamela. *See* Schelde Delta Shipping BV v Astarte Shipping Ltd (The Pamela) [1995] 2 Lloyd's Rep 249
The Paragon. *See* Lansat Shipping Co Ltd v Glencore Grain BV (The Paragon) [2009] EWCA Civ 855
The Pembroke. *See* Nelson Pine Industries Ltd v Seatrans New Zealand Ltd (The Pembroke) [1995] 2 Lloyd's Rep 290
The Peonia. *See* Hyundai Merchant Marine Co Ltd v Gesuri Chartering Co Ltd (The Peonia) [1991] 1 Lloyd's Rep 100
The Peter der Grosse (1875) 1 PD 414 .... 192, 195
The Petr Schmidt. *See* Galaxy Energy International Ltd v Novorossiysk Shipping Co (The Petr Schmidt) [1997] 1 Lloyd's Rep 284
The Petro Ranger. *See* Petroships Pte Ltd of Singapore v Petec Trading and Investment Co of Vietnam and Ors (The Petro Ranger) [2001] EWHC 418 (Comm)
The Petroleum Oil and Gas Corporation of South Africa (Pty) Ltd v Fr8 Singapore Pte Ltd (The Eternity) [2009] 1 Lloyd's Rep 107 .... 296, 446
The Pioneer Container. *See* KH Enterprise v Pioneer Container (The Pioneer Container) [1994] 2 AC 324
The Pionier. *See* Continental Fertilizer Co Ltd v Pionier Shipping CV (The Pionier) [1995] 1 Lloyd's Rep 223
The Port Russel. *See* Trafigura Beheer BV v Ravennavi SpA (The Port Russel) [2013] EWHC 490 (Comm)
The Posidon. *See* China Offshore Oil (Singapore) International Pte Ltd v Giant Shipping Ltd (The Posidon) [2001] 1 Lloyd's Rep 697
The President Brand. *See* Inca Compania Naviera SA and Commercial and Maritime Enterprises Evanghelos P Nomikos SA v Mofinol Inc (The President Brand) [1967] 2 Lloyd's Rep 338
The Pride of Donegal [2002] EWHC 24 214
The Product Star. *See* Product Star Shipping Ltd (The Product Star) (No. 2) [1993] 1 Lloyd's Rep 397
The Puerto Buitrago. *See* Attica Sea Carriers Corpn v Ferrostaal Poseidon Bulk Reederei GmbH (The Puerto Buitrago) [1976] 1 Lloyd's Rep 250
The Radauti. *See* Navrom v Callitsis Ship Management SA (The Radauti) [1988] 2 Lloyd's Rep 416
The Radnor [1955] 2 Lloyd's Rep 668 435
The Rafaela S. *See* MacWilliam (JI) Co Inc v Mediterranean Shipping Co SA (The Rafaela S) [2005] UKHL 11
The Rainbow Spring [2003] SGCA 31 372

The Reborn. *See* Mediterranean Salvage & Towage Ltd v Seamar Trading & Commerce Inc (The Reborn) [2008] EWHC 1875 (Comm)
The Red Jacket [1978] 1 Lloyd's Rep 300 223
The Rigoletto. *See* Lotus Cars Ltd v Southampton Cargo Handling plc and Others (The Rigoletto) [2000] 2 All ER (Comm) 705
The Rijn. *See* Santa Martha Baay Scheepvaart and Handelsmaatschappij NV v Scanbulk A/S (The Rijn) [1981] 2 Lloyd's Rep 267
The River Gurara [1997] 4 All ER 498 351
The River Ngada [2003] LMLN 13 Sept 2001 80
The Roachbank. *See* Venezolana (CA) de Navegacion SA v Bank Line Ltd (The Roachbank) [1987] 2 Lloyd's Rep 498
The Rosa S [1988] 2 Lloyd's Rep 574 349
The Ruapehu. *See* Ruapehu (Owners) v R and H Green and Silley Weir Ltd (The Ruapehu) (1925) 21 Ll L Rep 310
The Sabrewing. *See* Waterfront Shipping Company Ltd V Trafigura AG (The Sabrewing) [2007] EWHC 2482 (Comm)
The Saga Cob. *See* Penta Shipping (K/S) A/S v Ethiopian Shipping Lines Corpn (The Saga Cob) [1991] 2 Lloyd's Rep 398
The Saga Explorer. *See* Brefka & Hehnke GmbH & Co KG v Navire Shipping Co Ltd (The Saga Explorer) [2012] EWHC 3124 (Comm)
The Sagona. *See* Hansen-Tangens Rederi III A/S v Total Transport Corpn (The Sagona) [1984] 1 Lloyd's Rep 194
The Saldanha. *See* Cosco Bulk Carrier Co Ltd v Team-Up Owning Co Ltd (The Saldanha) [2010] EWHC 1340 (Comm)
The Saudi Crown [1986] 1 Lloyd's Rep 261 366
The Sea Angel. *See* Edwinton Commercial Corp v Tsavliris Russ (Worldwide Salvage and Towage) Ltd (The Sea Angel) [2007] EWCA Civ 547
The Sea Mirror. *See* Societe De Distribution De Toutes Merchandises En Cote D'Ivoire (t/a "SDTM-CI") v Continental Lines NV (The Sea Mirror) [2015] EWHC 1747 (Comm)
The Shackleford. *See* Surrey Shipping Co Ltd v Compagnie Continentale (France) SA (The Shackleford) [1978] 1 WLR 1080
The Ship "Marlborough Hill" v Alex Cowan and Sons Limited, and Others [1921] 1 AC 444 38

The Silva Plana, Bahamastars and Magic Sky. *See* Oriental Maritime Pte Ltd v Ministry of Food, Government of the People's Republic of Bangladesh (The Silva Plana, Bahamastars and Magic Sky) [1989] 2 Lloyd's Rep 371
The Simona. *See* Fercometal SARL v Mediterranean Shipping Co SA (The Simona) [1989] AC 788
The Sinoe. *See* Overseas Transportation Co v Mineralimportexport (The Sinoe) [1971] 1 Lloyd's Rep 514
The Skarp [1935] P 134 .... 184, 196
The Socol 3. *See* Onego Shipping & Chartering BV v JSC Arcadia Shipping (The Socol 3) [2010] EWHC 777
The Songa Winds. *See* Navig8 Chemicals Pool Inc v Glencore Agriculture BV (The Songa Winds) [2018] All ER (D) 115 (Aug)
The Sonia. *See* Trafigura Beheer BV v Golden Stavraetos Maritime Inc (The Sonia) [2003] EWCA Civ 664
The Sormovskiy 3068. *See* Sucre Export SA v Northern Shipping Ltd (The Sormovskiy 3068) [1994] 2 Lloyd's Rep 266
The Spiros C. *See* Tradigrain SA and Others v King Diamond Marine Ltd (The Spiros C) [2000] 2 Lloyd's Rep 319, See Tradigrain SA and Others v King Diamond Marine Ltd (The Spiros C) [2000] All ER (D) 979
The Stainless Emperor. *See* Huyton SA v Inter Operators SA (The Stainless Emperor) [1994] 1 Lloyd's Rep 298
The Star Sea. *See* Manifest Shipping & Co Ltd v Uni-Polaris Insurance Co Ltd and La Reunion Europeene (The Star Sea) [1995] 1 Lloyd's Rep 651
The Starsin. *See* Homburg Houtimport BV v Agrosin Private Ltd (The Starsin) [2003] UKHL 12
The Stettin (1889) 14 PD 142 .... 60, 146
The Stolt Loyalty [1993] 2 Lloyd's Rep 281 336
The Stork. *See* Compania Naviera Maropan SA v Bowaters Lloyd Pulp and Paper Mills Ltd (The Stork) [1955] 2 QB 68
The Stranna [1938] P 69 244
The Strathnewton *See* D/S A/S Idaho v Peninsular and Oriental Steam Navigation Co (The Strathnewton) [1983] 1 Lloyd's Rep 219
The Super Servant Two. *See* J Lauritzen AS v Wijsmuller BV (The Super Servant Two) [1990] 1 Lloyd's Rep 1
The Superior Pescadores. *See* Yemgas Fzco v Superior Pescadores SA Panama (The Superior Pescadores) [2016] EWCA Civ 101

The Sur. *See* Dera Commercial Estate v Derya Inc (The Sur) [2019] 1 All ER 1147
The Tarva. *See* Skibs A/S Trolla And Skibs A/S Tautra v United Enterprises & Shipping (Pte) Ltd (The Tarva) [1973] 2 Lloyd's Rep 385
The Tasman Discoverer. *See* Dairy Containers Ltd v Tasman Orient Line CV (The Tasman Discoverer) [2002] 1 Lloyd's Rep 528
The Teno. *See* Compania Sud Americana de Vapores v Shipmair BV (The Teno) [1977] 2 Lloyd's Rep 289
The TFL Prosperity. *See* Tor Line AB v Alltrans Group of Canada (The TFL Prosperity) [1984] 1 Lloyd's Rep 123
The Theodegmon. *See* Phillips Petroleum Co v Cabaneli Naviera SA (The Theodegmon) [1990] 1 Lloyd's Rep 52
The Thomas (1538) Select Pleas, vol I, p. 61 27
The Thomaseverett. *See* Owners of Cargo Lately Laden on Board the Ship or Vessel Thomaseverett v Owners of and Other Persons Interested in the Ship or Vessel Thomaseverett (The Thomaseverett) [1992] 2 SLR 1068
The Thorsa [1916] P 257, 116 LT 300 224
The Tilia Gorthon [1985] 1 Ll Rep 552 304
The Timna. *See* Zim Israel Navigation Co Ltd v Tradax Export SA (The Timna) [1971] 2 Lloyd's Rep 91
The TNT Express. *See* Marbig Rexel Pty Ltd and Another v ABC Container Line NV (The TNT Express) [1912] 2 Lloyd's Rep 636
The Toledo [1995] 1 Lloyd's Rep 40 .... 277, 278
The Torenia. *See* Aktieselskabet de Danske Sukkerfabrikker v Bajamar Compania Naviera SA (The Torenia) [1983] 2 Lloyd's Rep 210
The Tres Flores. *See* Compania de Naviera Nedelka SA of Panama v Tradax International SA of Panama City RP (The Tres Flores) [1974] QB 264
The TS Singapore. *See* TS Lines Ltd v Delphis NV (The TS Singapore) [2009] EWHC 678
The Tsukuba Maru. *See* Nippon Yusen Kaisha v Marocaine de L'Industrie du Raffinage (The Tsukuba Maru) [1979] 1 Lloyd's Rep 459
The Union Amsterdam. *See* Blue Anchor Line Ltd v Alfred C Toepfer International GmbH (The Union Amsterdam) [1982] 2 Lloyd's Rep 432
The Vechscroon. *See* McCarren & Co Ltd v Humber International Transport Ltd and Truckline Ferries (Poole) Ltd (The Vechscroon) [1982] 1 Lloyd's Rep 301

The Vikfrost. *See* Fletcher (W & R) (New Zealand) v Sigurd Haavik A/S (The Vikfrost). [1980] 1 Lloyd's Rep 560
The Vine. *See* Emeraldian Ltd Partnership v Wellmix Shipping Ltd (The Vine) [2010] EWHC 1411 (Comm)
The Virginia Thea. *See* China Steel Corporation & Anor v The Owners of Virginia Rhea (The Virginia Thea) [1985] 2 MLJ 1
The Visurgis [1999] 1 Lloyd's Rep 218 380
The Vorras. *See* Dow Chemical (Nederland) BV v BP Tanker Co Ltd (The Vorras) [1983] 1 Lloyd's Rep 579
The Vortigern [1899] P 140 .... 207, 214, 215
The Western Moscow. *See* Western Bulk Shipowning III A/S v Carbofer Maritime Trading ApS (The Western Moscow) [2012] EWHC 1224 (Comm)
The Westfalia. *See* Hogarth v Alexander Miller Bros & Co (The Westfalia) [1891] AC 48
The While Angel (1577) Select Pleas 27
The Winson. *See* China-Pacific SA v Food Corpn of India (The Winson) [1982] AC 939
The World Symphony and The World Renown. *See* Chiswell Shipping Ltd and Liberian Jaguar Transports Inc v National Iranian Tanker Co (The World Symphony and The World Renown) [1992] 2 Lloyd's Rep 115
The Xantho. *See* Thomas Wilson, Sons & Co v Owners of the Cargo per The Xantho (The Xantho) (1887) 12 App Cas 503
The Xingcheng and The Andros. *See* China Ocean Shipping Co (Owners of Xingcheng) v Andros (Owners of The Andros) [1987] 1 WLR 1213
The Xingcheng v The Andros [1988] LRC (Comm) 139 346
The Yamatogawa. *See* Kuo International Oil Co Ltd v Daisy Shipping Co Ltd (The Yamatogawa) [1990] 2 Lloyd's Rep 39
The Yangtze Xing Hua. *See* Transgrain Shipping (Singapore) Pte Ltd v Yangtze Navigation (Hong Kong) Co Ltd (The Yangtze Xing Hua) [2016] EWHC 3132
The Ythan. *See* Primetrade AG v Ythan Ltd (The Ythan) [2005] EWHC 2399 (Comm)
The Yue You 902 [2019] SGHC 106 60
The Zagora. *See* Oldendorff GmbH & Co KG v Sea Powerful II Special Maritime Enterprises (The Zagora) [2016] EWHC 3212

The Zenovia. *See* IMT Shipping and Chartering GmbH v Changsung Shipping Company Limited (The Zenovia) [2009] EWHC 739 (Comm)
The Zhi Jiang Kou. *See* PS Chellaram & Co Ltd v China Ocean Shipping Co (The Zhi Jiang Kou) [1991] 1 Lloyd's Rep 493
The Zoe. *See* Sewell v Burdick (The Zoe) (1884) 10 App Case 74
Thomas v Harrowing Steamship Co [1913] 2 KB 171 .... 400, 409
Thomas Wilson, Sons & Co v Owners of the Cargo per The Xantho (The Xantho) (1887) 12 App Cas 503 244
Thomas Young and Sons Ltd v Hobson and Partners [1949] 65 TLR 365 83
Thompson v Dominy (1845) 14 M & W 403 88
Thorman v Burt, Boulton & Co (1886) 54 LT 349 184
Thornton v Shoe Lane Parking [1971] 2 WLR 585 .... 81, 114
Tidebrook Maritime Corp v Vitol SA of Geneva (The Front Commander) [2006] 2 Lloyd's Rep 251 .... 439, 440
Timber Shipping Co SA v London & Overseas Freighters Ltd (The London Explorer) [1972] AC 1 494
Tithes Dental & Photo Supply Sdn Bhd v Empresa Lineas Maritimes Argentinas & Ors [1977] 2 MLJ 13 128
Tokio Marine & Fire Insurance Co Ltd v Relta Steamship Co [1970] 2 Lloyd's Rep 91 194
Tor Line AB v Alltrans Group of Canada (The TFL Prosperity) [1984] 1 Lloyd's Rep 123 381
Torvald Klaveness A/S V Arni Maritime Corporation (The Gregos) [1995] 1 Lloyd's Rep 1 495
Tossa Marine Co Ltd v Alfred C Toepfer Schiffahrtsgesellschaft Gmbh (The Derby) [1985] 2 Lloyd's Rep 325 208
Total Transport Corporation v Arcadia Petroleum Ltd (The Eurus) [1996] 2 Lloyd's Rep 408 426
Tradax Export SA v Dorada Compania Naviera SA (The Lutetian) [1982] 2 Lloyd's Rep 140 471
Tradigrain SA and Others v King Diamond Marine Ltd (The Spiros C) [2000] All ER (D) 979 .... 62, 111, 412, 420
Trafigura Beheer BV v Golden Stavraetos Maritime Inc (The Sonia) [2003] EWCA Civ 664 330

Trafigura Beheer BV v Ravennavi SpA (The Port Russel) [2013] EWHC 490 (Comm) 440
Transco plc v United Utilities Water plc [2005] EWHC 2784, [2005] All ER (D) 281 (Oct) 157
Transfield Inc v Mercator Shipping Inc (The Achilleas) [2008] UKHL 28 496
Transgrain Shipping (Singapore) Pte Ltd v Yangtze Navigation (Hong Kong) Co Ltd (The Yangtze Xing Hua) [2016] EWHC 3132 498
Transgrain Shipping BV v Global Transporte Oceanico SA (The Mexico 1) (HC) [1988] 2 Lloyd's Rep 149 372
Transgrain Shipping BV v Global Transporte Oceanico SA (The Mexico 1) (CA) [1990] 1 Lloyd's Rep 507 ..... 429, 438
Transocean Liners Reederei GmbH v Euxine Shipping Co Ltd (The Imvros) [1999] 1 All ER (Comm) 724 ..... 213, 379, 499
Transworld Oil (USA) Inc v Minos Compania Naviera SA (The Leni) [1992] 2 Lloyd's Rep 48 ..... 336, 342
Triad Shipping Co v Stellar Chartering & Brokerage Inc (The Island Archon) [1995] 1 All ER 595 ..... 382, 451, 453
Tropwood AG of Zug v Jade Enterprises Ltd (The Tropwind) (No. 2) [1982] 1 Lloyd's Rep 232 476
Tropwood AG v Jade Enterprises Ltd (The Tropwind) (No.1) [1977] 1 Lloyd's Rep 397 473
TS Lines Ltd v Delphis NV (The TS Singapore) [2009] EWHC 678 480
Tsakiroglou & Co Ltd v Noblee Thorl GmbH [1962] AC 93 394
TW Thomas & Co Ltd v Portsea Steamship Co Ltd [1912] AC 1 115
UCO Bank v Golden Shore Transportation Pte Ltd [2005] SGCA 42 58
Unicoopjapan and Marubeni-Iida Company Ltd v Ion Shipping Company (The Ion) [1971] 1 Lloyd's Rep 541 ..... 341, 342
Uni-Ocean Lines Pte Ltd v C-Trade SA (The Lucille) [1984] 1 Lloyd's Rep 387 460
Union of India v NV Reederij Amsterdam (The Amstelslot) [1963] 2 Lloyd's Rep 223 279
United City Merchants (Investments) Ltd and Others v Royal Bank of Canada and Others (The American Accord) [1983] 1 AC 168 99

United States Shipping Board v Bunge y Born Ltda Sociedad (The Alamosa) (1925) 42 TLR 174 234
Universal Cargo Carriers Corp v Citati [1957] 2 QB 401 .... 391, 444
Vagres Compania Maritima SA v Nissho-Iwai American Corporation (The Karin Vatis) [1988] 2 Lloyd's Rep 330 .... 404, 407
Vantage Navigation Corp v Suhail and Saud Bahvan Building Materials (The Alev) [1989] 1 Lloyd's Rep 138 476
Vardinoyannis v The Egyptian General Petroleum Corporation (The Evaggelos Theta) [1971] 2 Lloyd's Rep 200 ... 460
Vaughan v Campbell, Heatley & Co (1855) 2 TLR 33 389
Vaynar Suppiah & Sons v KMA Abdul Rahim & Anor [1972-1974] 1 SLR 239 312
Venezolana (CA) de Navegacion SA v Bank Line Ltd (The Roachbank) [1987] 2 Lloyd's Rep 498 485
Victoria Laundry (Windsor) Ltd v Newman Industries Ltd [1949] 2 KB 528 358
Vinmar International Ltd v Theresa Navigation SA (The Atrice) [2001] 2 All ER (Comm) 243 .... 214, 220, 225
Vita Foods Products Inc v Unus Shipping Co Ltd [1939] AC 277 .... 9, 246, 248
Vitachem (M) Sdn Bhd v Ing Hua Fu Marine Line Sdn Bhd [2014] 6 MLJ 566 258 132
Vogemann v Zanzibar [1902] 7 Com Cas 254 838 488
Volcafe Ltd and others v Compania Sud Americana De Vapores SA (t/a CSAV) [2018] UKSC 61 .... 132, 235, 245, 275, 288, 289, 290, 298, 303, 305, 308, 312, 313
Voss v APL Co Pte Ltd [2003] 3 LRC 632 .... 75, 251
Wah Tat Bank Ltd & Ors v Chan Cheng Kum [1975] 1 MLJ 97 .. 291
Waterfront Shipping Company Ltd V Trafigura AG (The Sabrewing) [2007] EWHC 2482 (Comm) 446
Wehner v Dene Steam Shipping Co [1905] 2 KB 92 .... 107, 412
Weir v Union Steamship [1900] AC 525 452
Welex AG v Rosa Maritime Ltd (The Epsilon Rosa) [2002] EWHC 762 (Comm) 415
Welsh Development Agency (Holdings) Ltd v Modern Injection Mouldings Ltd [1986] Lexis Citation 1535 118

Western Bulk Carriers K/S v Li Hai Maritime Inc (The Li Hai) [2005] EWHC 735 (Comm) 470, 471, 474
Western Bulk Shipowning III A/S v Carbofer Maritime Trading ApS (The Western Moscow) [2012] EWHC 1224 (Comm) 421, 422
Whistler International Ltd v Kawasaki Kisen Kaisha Ltd (The Hill Harmony) [2001] 1 Lloyd's Rep 147 .... 293, 294, 452
White Rosebay Shipping SA v Hong Kong Chain Glory Shipping Ltd (The Fortune Plum) [2013] EWHC 1355 (Comm) 473, 477
Whitsea Shipping and Trading Corp v El Paso Rio Clara Ltda (The Marielle Bolten) [2009] EWHC 2552 (Comm) 174
Whittam v WJ Daniel & Co Ltd [1961] 3 All ER 796 590
Wibau Maschinenfabric Hartman SA and Another v Mackinnon Mackenzie & Co (The Chanda) [1989] 2 Lloyd's Rep 494 .... 240, 241
William Alenxander & Sons v Aktieselskabet Dampskibet Hansa [1920] AC 88 443
Williams & Co v Canton Insurance [1901] AC 462 408
Wilson & Coventry Ltd v Otto Thoresen Linie [1910] 2 KB 405 444
WJ Tatem Ltd v Gamboa [1939] 1 KB 132 685
Wolff v Trinity Logistics USA Inc [2018] EWCA Civ 2765 ..... 59, 75, 146
Yemgas Fzco v Superior Pescadores SA Panama (The Superior Pescadores) [2016] EWCA Civ 101 377
Yeo Goon Nyoh and another v Ocean Steamship Co Ltd [1965–1967] SLR(R) 783 320
Zalnalabdin Payabi and Baker Rasti Lari v Armstel Shipping Corporation and Panthai Shipping Ltd (The Jay Bola) [1992] 2 Lloyd's Rep 62 .... 334, 337
Zim Israel Navigation Co Ltd v Tradax Export SA (The Timna) [1971] 2 Lloyd's Rep 91 448
Zodiac Maritime Agencies Limited v Fortescue Metals Group Limited (The Kildare) [2010] EWHC 903 492
Zuellig (Gold Coin Mills) v MV Antoly (Owners) (The MV Kantang) [1971] 1 MLJ 183 .... 284, 301

Table of Legislation, Rules, Conventions and Model Laws

UK

Arbitration Act 1996 .... 8, 13, 18, 342, 343, 344, 371, 373, 396, 418, 446
Bills of Lading Act 1855 .... 6, 11, 16, 29, 38, 55, 61, 67, 101, 106, 120, 126, 367, 416, 539, 559
Carriage of Goods by Sea Act 1924 .... 8, 14, 214, 248, 276, 289, 320, 377, 541
Carriage of Goods by Sea Act 1971 .... 8, 10, 12, 14, 18, 44, 51, 71, 75, 96, 214, 245, 249, 276, 301, 302, 337, 342, 355, 356, 377, 549
Carriage of Goods by Sea Act 1992 .... 3, 6, 13, 16, 21, 30, 31, 38, 41, 53, 54, 55, 57, 58, 59, 61, 62, 66, 67, 73, 74, 76, 77, 101, 106, 120, 126, 137, 148, 165, 167, 176, 179, 187, 197, 366, 367, 416, 519
Contracts (Rights of Third Parties) Act 1999 .... 12, 13, 17, 55, 102, 165, 166, 174, 175, 266, 421, 464
CPR 14, 18, 183, 313, 314, 322, 336, 337, 345, 396, 417, 422
Limitation Act 1980 .... 337, 346
Merchant Shipping Act 1955 .... 228, 301, 322, 324, 325
Merchant Shipping Act 1995 (Amendment) Order 2016 322

Sale of Goods Act 1979 .... 12, 13, 17, 34, 78, 79, 84, 85, 86, 88, 153, 155, 384

Senior Courts Act 1981 .... 13, 18, 19, 37, 40, 286, 306, 341, 373

Unfair Contract Terms Act 1977 .... 17, 137, 168, 245

US

Carriage of Goods by Sea Act 1936 .... 8, 193, 287, 296, 349, 378, 445, 565

Singapore

Singapore Arbitration Act 343, 344

Singapore International Arbitration Act 13, 343, 344, 396, 418

Singapore Bills of Lading Act 38, 60, 62, 67, 73, 148, 182, 367

Singapore Carriage of Goods by Sea (Singapore Currency Equivalents) Order 71

Singapore Carriage of Goods by Sea Act 75, 245, 248, 257, 258, 264, 338

Singapore Contracts (Rights of Third Parties) Act 464

Singapore Interpretation Act 343

Singapore Limitation Act 343, 346

Singapore Merchant Shipping Act 323, 324

Singapore Rules of Court 338, 339, 345

Singapore Sale of Goods Act 13, 88

Singapore Unfair Contract Terms Act 13

Malaysia

Arbitration Act 2005 .... 78, 421, 422, 473, 495

Carriage of Goods by Sea (Amendment) Act 2020 .... 78, 94, 335, 344, 397

Carriage of Goods by Sea Act 1950 78

Contracts Act 1950 .... 11, 78

Courts of Judicature Act 1964 78

Evidence Act 1950 78

Interpretation Acts 1948 and 1967 .... 11, 78

Limitation Act 1952 78

Merchant Shipping (Applied Subsidiary Legislation) Regulations 1961 .... 23, 79

Merchant Shipping (Implementation of Conventions Relating to Carriage of Goods by Sea and to Liability of Shipowners and Others) Regulations 1960 .... 23, 79
Merchant Shipping Ordinance 1952 79
Rules of Court 2012 79
Sale of Goods Act 1957 79

India

Contract Act 1872 .... 11, 79
Evidence Act 1987 79

International Conventions

2012 Amendments to Protocol of 1996 to amend the Convention on Limitation of Liability for Maritime Claims 1976 79
Convention on Limitation of Liability for Maritime Claim of 1976 79
Hague Rules 6, 15, 18, 20, 79
Hague-Visby Rules 6, 12, 13, 15, 16, 17, 18, 20
Hague-Visby Rules (as amended by SDR Protocol) ... 79
International Convention relating to the Limitation of the Liability of Owners of Sea-Going Ships of 1957 ... 79
Protocol of 1996 to amend the Convention on Limitation of Liability for Maritime Claims 1976 79
Vienna Convention on the Law of Treaties 79

Model Laws

UNCITRAL Model Law on Electronic Commerce of 1996 79
UNCITRAL Model Law on Electronic Transferable Records of 2017 80
UNCITRAL Model Law on International Commercial Arbitration 1985, amended in 2006 80

About This Book

This book, written in three parts, covers the basics of the international trade, financing and the legal framework related to the law of carriage of goods by sea, elaborates on bills of lading in depth and sea waybills and ship's delivery orders in brief and charterparties in depth. While the book is based on the English law, cases and materials from other jurisdictions, particularly Singapore, Malaysia, India, the USA, and Australia are brought in to provide an international perspective. The practical analyses, commentary and critiques of cases would be a useful guide for practitioners in developing case arguments. Although written with practitioners, academicians and students in mind, the book will also serve as a useful guide for sea carriers, freight forwarders, international traders, financiers, etc. as the complex subject is presented in reader-friendly and easy to grasp manner.

Contents

Part I Introduction and International Trade

1	**Introduction and Legal Framework**		3
	1.1	Introduction	3
	1.2	Preliminaries	4
		1.2.1 Terms of Carriage-Contract	4
		1.2.2 Transferability of Bills of Lading	6
		1.2.3 Payment Mechanism in International Trade	7
	1.3	Legal Framework	7
		1.3.1 Hague/Hague-Visby Rules, etc.	7
		1.3.2 Transferability of Bills of Lading	11
		1.3.3 Bailment, Conversion, Negligence and Evidence	11
		1.3.4 Contact Law and Third-Party Rights	12
		1.3.5 Sale of Goods Act	12
		1.3.6 Legal Framework in Singapore and Malaysia	12
	1.4	Cargo Claims: A Glimpse	18
2	**Shipping Documents**		21
	2.1	Introduction	21
	2.2	Bill of Lading	22
		2.2.1 Common Terminologies	23
		2.2.2 History of Bill of Lading	25
		2.2.3 Characteristics and Functions of Bill of Lading	30
		2.2.4 Shipped Bill v. Received for Shipment Bill	36
		2.2.5 Bill of Lading Issued by NVOCs	40
		2.2.6 Bill of Lading Issued by Time-Charterers	45
		2.2.7 Through Bill of Lading	46
		2.2.8 Document of Title v. Document of Possession	51
		2.2.9 Negotiability v. Transferability	53
		2.2.10 Transferability of Bills of Lading	54
		2.2.11 Period of Responsibility Under Bill of Lading	68

2.2.12 Contract on Terms of the Would-Be Bill Even Before Issuance of Bill ... 70
2.2.13 Application of International Conventions to Carriage Contracts ... 70
2.2.14 Electronic Bills of Lading ... 71
2.3 Sea Waybill ... 73
2.4 Ship's Delivery Order ... 76

3 International Trade ... 79
3.1 Introduction ... 79
3.2 Shipment Terms ... 80
3.2.1 Classical Shipment Terms: fob, c&f, and cif ... 81
3.2.2 Variants of Fob Term ... 82
3.2.3 Incoterms: FOB, CFR, CIF, E Terms, D Terms ... 83
3.3 Passing of Risk ... 84
3.4 Passing of Property ... 86
3.5 Letter of Credit ... 86
3.5.1 The Mechanism of Payment Through Letters of Credit ... 86
3.5.2 Fraud Exception to Autonomy of Letters of Credit ... 96

Part II Bills of Lading

4 Cargo Claims: Legal Bases ... 101
4.1 Introduction ... 101
4.2 Contract-Action ... 102
4.2.1 Direct Contract ... 103
4.2.2 Statutory Contract ... 120
4.2.3 Contract by Agency Principle ... 121
4.2.4 Implied Contract ... 122
4.3 Bailment-Action ... 125
4.3.1 Bailment-Action Only for Bailor Against Head or Sub-Bailee ... 126
4.3.2 Burden of Proof in England and Wales ... 127
4.3.3 Burden of Proof in Commonwealth Countries with Evidence Act and Contract Act ... 128
4.3.4 Burden of Proof in Commonwealth Countries with Evidence Act but not Contract Act ... 133
4.3.5 Utility of Bailment-Action in Carriage of Goods by Sea ... 134
4.3.6 Terms of Bailment in Carriage of Goods by Sea ... 136
4.4 Tort-Action: Negligence ... 139
4.4.1 Negligence Action in General ... 139
4.4.2 Limitations to Negligence Action in Carriage of Goods by Sea ... 140

4.4.3 Rule Against Recovery of Economic Loss in Negligence-Action ... 141
4.4.4 Negligence Action Subject to Contractual Limitations ... 141
4.4.5 Action in Negligence Versus Action in Bailment ... 142
4.5 Conversion (Tort)/Non-delivery (Contract) ... 143
4.5.1 Non-delivery v. Misdelivery ... 143
4.5.2 Misdelivery ... 146
4.5.3 Assessment of Damages for Misdelivery/Non-delivery ... 158
4.5.4 Excluding or Limiting Liability for Misdelivery/Non-delivery ... 160
4.5.5 Spent Bills ... 164

5 Protection and Action for Third Parties ... 165
5.1 Introduction ... 165
5.2 Contracts (Rights of Third Parties) Act 1999 ... 166
5.3 Himalaya Clause ... 168
5.3.1 Himalaya Clauses Recognised ... 168
5.3.2 Event within Responsibility Period of Carrier ... 170
5.3.3 Third-Party Dealing with Shipper on Third Party's Own Terms ... 171
5.3.4 Himalaya Protection to Shipowner Limited to Rules Threshold ... 171
5.3.5 Jurisdiction and Choice of Law Clauses ... 172
5.4 Circular Indemnity Clause ... 173
5.4.1 Utilities of Circular Indemnity Clause ... 174
5.4.2 Limitations to Effectiveness of Circular Indemnity Clause ... 175
5.4.3 Pure Indemnity Claim ... 175
5.5 Suit for Benefit of Another ... 175
5.6 Representative Action ... 176

6 Proof of Damages: Presumptions and Estoppels ... 179
6.1 Introduction ... 179
6.2 Preliminaries ... 180
6.2.1 Claused and Clean Bill ... 181
6.2.2 Three Levels of Evidentiary Value of Representations ... 181
6.3 Sources of Presumptions and Estoppels ... 182
6.3.1 Estoppels at Common Law ... 184
6.3.2 Presumptions Under Hague Rules (Prima Facie Evidence) ... 185
6.3.3 Presumptions Under Hague-Visby Rules (Conclusive Evidence) ... 186

6.3.4 Presumptions Under COGSA 1992 Section 4 (Conclusive Evidence) 187
6.4 Role of Presumptions in Proof of Transit-Damage 188
6.4.1 Why is Time of Damage Crucial? 188
6.4.2 Role of Presumptions in Proof of Damages During Carriage 189
6.4.3 Period of Carriage Under Hague or Hague-Visby Rules 189
6.5 Popular Clausings 190
6.5.1 'Quantity or Weight Not Known' Clausing 190
6.5.2 'Contents not Known' Clausing 192
6.5.3 'Said to Contain' Clausing 192
6.5.4 'Condition not Known' Clausing 194
6.5.5 'Retla' Clausing 194
6.6 'Apparent Good Order and Condition' Statement 195
6.6.1 Condition Different from Quality 195
6.6.2 Specific Clausing to Limit 'Apparent Good Order and Condition' 196
6.7 Shipper's Indemnity 197
6.8 Other Actions for Misstatements in Bill of Lading 197
6.8.1 Action for Tort of Deceit 198
6.8.2 Action for Tort of Negligent Misstatement 199
6.8.3 Action Under Section 2(1) of UK Misrepresentation Act 1967 200
6.8.4 Tort or Misrepresentation Act Action Subject to Hague or Hague-Visby Limitations? 200
6.8.5 Action Under Contract Act 1950 in Malaysia 201

7 Implied Terms and Exclusion Clauses 203
7.1 Introduction 203
7.2 Common Law Implied Terms 204
7.2.1 Relationship Between Common Law and the Rules 205
7.2.2 Relationship Between Seaworthiness and Cargoworthiness 206
7.2.3 Seaworthiness 206
7.2.4 Cargoworthiness 221
7.2.5 Deviation 225
7.2.6 Quasi-deviation (Carriage on Deck) 240
7.2.7 Obligation to Take Reasonable Care of Cargo 241
7.3 Exclusion Clauses 242
7.3.1 'Perils of the Sea' Exception 244
7.3.2 Excluding Liability for 'Negligence' 244
7.3.3 Burden of Proof 245

8 Hague/Hague-Visby Rules: Application ... 247
8.1 Introduction ... 247
8.2 Significance of Distinction Between Statutory and Contractual Application ... 248
8.3 Conflict Between Terms of Bill and the Rules ... 249
8.4 Statutory Application of the Rules ... 249
8.4.1 Criteria for Application of the Rules ... 251
8.4.2 Circumventing Rules by Choice of Law and Jurisdiction Clauses ... 262
8.5 Article IV*bis* of Hague-Visby Rules ... 266
8.5.1 Article IV*bis*(1) ... 267
8.5.2 Article IV*bis*(2) ... 267
8.5.3 Article IV*bis*(3) ... 268
8.5.4 Article IV*bis*(4) ... 269
8.6 Interpretation ... 269

9 Hague/Hague-Visby Rules: Carriers' Obligation and Defences ... 271
9.1 Introduction ... 271
9.2 Articles III(1) and IV(1) ... 272
9.2.1 Operation of Doctrine of Stages Under the Rules Regime ... 275
9.2.2 Due Diligence and Burden of Proof ... 279
9.2.3 Article IV(2) Defences not Apply to Article III(1) Obligations ... 284
9.3 Articles III(2) ... 285
9.3.1 Free-In and Free-Out ... 286
9.3.2 Properly and Carefully ... 287
9.3.3 Non-Delegable Nature of Duty ... 287
9.4 Article IV(2) Defences ... 287
9.4.1 Initial Observation ... 288
9.4.2 Article IV(2)(a) and (b) ... 294
9.4.3 Article IV(2)(c)-(q) ... 304
9.5 Article III(2) and IV(2): Burden of Proof ... 313
9.5.1 Volcafe v CSAV [2018] UKSC 61 ... 315
9.5.2 Application of Volcafe in Malaysia and Singapore ... 320

10 Hague/Hague-Visby Rules: Carriers' Liability and Time Limitations ... 323
10.1 Introduction ... 323
10.2 Tonnage Limitation Preserved ... 324
10.3 Comparison Between Schemes in the Rules: A Glimpse ... 328
10.4 Article III(6) and III(6)*bis*: Time Limitation ... 329
10.4.1 Article III(6) ... 330
10.4.2 Article III(6)bis ... 347

10.5 Article IV(5): Liability-Limitation ... 349
10.5.1 Hague Rules ... 349
10.5.2 Hague-Visby Rules ... 355
10.6 Loss of Protection in Case of Deviation ... 362

11 Shipper's Obligation for Dangerous Goods ... 363
11.1 Introduction ... 363
11.2 Duty Under Common Law ... 364
11.3 Duty Under Article IV(6) ... 366
11.3.1 Part 1 of Article IV(6) ... 367
11.3.2 Part 2 of Article IV(6) ... 367
11.3.3 Article IV(3) Defence to Shipper ... 368
11.4 Transfer of Shipper's Liability to Bill of Lading Holder ... 369

Part III Charterparties

12 Charterparty: Introduction ... 373
12.1 Introduction ... 373
12.2 Types of Charterparty ... 375
12.2.1 Demise Charter ... 375
12.2.2 Time Charter ... 375
12.2.3 Voyage Charter ... 376
12.2.4 Trip Charter and Importance of Classification ... 377
12.2.5 Standard Forms of Charterparty ... 378
12.3 Some Common Terms in Charterparties ... 378
12.3.1 Clause Paramount ... 379
12.3.2 Allocation of Risk in Deck Cargo ... 380
12.3.3 Exceptions Clauses ... 383
12.3.4 Construction of Competing Clauses ... 385
12.4 Title to Bunkers ... 385
12.5 Sale of Ship While Serving Charter ... 386
12.6 Cancelling Date and Approach Voyage ... 387
12.6.1 Cancelling Date ... 387
12.6.2 Approach Voyage ... 391
12.7 Frustration ... 394
12.7.1 Consequences of Frustration ... 394
12.7.2 Self-induced Frustration ... 396
12.7.3 Judging Frustration ... 396
12.8 Dispute Resolution ... 398

13 Voyage Charter: Freight and Lien ... 401
13.1 Introduction ... 401
13.2 Freight v. Hire ... 402
13.3 Bases of Freight Calculation ... 402
13.4 Earning of Freight ... 405
13.4.1 Concept of Freight Earned and No Set-Off ... 405

13.4.2 Freight Payable Upon Delivery 409
13.4.3 Case of Cargo Ex Galam/Voyage Interrupted by Charterer 413
13.4.4 Applicability of Principles to Bills of Lading 414
13.5 Obligation of B/L Holder to Pay Charter-Freight 414
13.6 'Cesser' Clause 415
13.7 Lien 416
13.7.1 Conditions for Lien: Contractual Link/Completion of Carriage 418
13.7.2 Manner of Exercising Lien and Sale of Cargo 419
13.7.3 Lien on Sub-freight 422
13.7.4 Lien on Sub-hire 424

14 Voyage Charter: Laytime and Demurrage 425
14.1 Introduction 425
14.2 Laytime Definitions 426
14.2.1 Calculation of Laytime 426
14.2.2 Weather Day and Working Day Qualifications 427
14.3 Charterer's Obligations 428
14.4 Starting of Laytime 429
14.4.1 Notice of Readiness 429
14.4.2 Arrived Ship 432
14.4.3 Ready to Load/Discharge 440
14.4.4 Pre-conditions for Notice 440
14.4.5 Manner and Timing of Issuance of Notice 441
14.5 Suspension of Laytime 442
14.5.1 Laytime Exceptions 442
14.5.2 Loss of Laytime Attributable to Shipowner 444
14.6 Termination and Demurrage 445
14.6.1 Termination 445
14.6.2 Demurrage 446
14.6.3 Detention Distinguished from Demurrage 449

15 Time Charter: Orders and Indemnity 451
15.1 Introduction 451
15.2 Legitimate v. Illegitimate Orders 452
15.3 Breach v. Indemnity Claims 452
15.4 Limitations to Indemnity Claim 454
15.4.1 Employment V Navigation Orders 454
15.4.2 Proximate Causation 454
15.4.3 Voluntarily Assumed Risk 455
15.5 Common Types of Order 456
15.5.1 Orders About Issuing Bills of Lading 456
15.5.2 Orders About Cargoes to Be Loaded 458
15.5.3 Orders About Ports to Call 459

15.5.4 Orders for Delivery Against Indemnity-Undertaking 465

16 Time Charter: Withdrawal, Off-Hire and Redelivery 469
16.1 Introduction 469
16.2 Termination and Withdrawal 470
16.2.1 Obligation to Pay Hire 470
16.2.2 Termination 473
16.2.3 Withdrawal 474
16.2.4 Suspending Performance 479
16.3 Off-Hire 481
16.3.1 Triggering Event 482
16.3.2 Calculating 'Off-Hire' Period 489
16.4 Redelivery 491
16.4.1 Redelivery Window 492
16.4.2 Early Redelivery 494
16.4.3 Late Redelivery 496

17 Time Charter: Apportionment of Cargo-Claims Liability 499
17.1 Introduction 499
17.2 Inter-Club Agreement 499
17.3 No Special Clauses Relating to Cargo Claims 501

Appendix A: Hague Rules of 1924 503

Appendix B: Hague-Visby Rules of 1968 511

Appendix C: Hague-Visby Rules amended by SDR Protocol of 1979 521

Appendix D: Hague Rules, Hague-Visby Rules, Hague-Visby Rules as amended by SDR Protocol (Compared) 531

Appendix E: Bills of Lading Act 1855 (UK) 541

Appendix F: Carriage of Goods by Sea Act 1924 (UK) 543

Appendix G: Carriage of Goods by Sea Act 1971 (UK) 551

Appendix H: Carriage of Goods by Sea Act 1992 (UK) 561

Appendix I: Carriage of Goods by Sea Act 1936 (US) 567

Index 575

About the Author

Arun Kasi is a barrister specialising in maritime law. He undertakes court matters as well as work as arbitrator and arbitration counsel under the terms of London Maritime Arbitrators Association (LMAA) and Singapore Chamber of Maritime Arbitration (SCMA). He holds a doctorate degree in maritime law. He graduated with his law degree when he was 19 years old and has been working in the field since then. To date, over a span of three decades, he has authored six books and about 50 articles.

Abbreviations

Art.	Article
ASBA	Association of Ship Brokers & Agents (USA), Inc
B/L	Bill of lading
BIMCO	Baltic and International Maritime Council
Bolreo	Bills of Lading in Europe
c&f	Cost and freight
CA	Court of Appeal
CFR	Cost and Freight (defined by Incoterms)
cif	Cost, insurance and freight
CIF	Cost, Insurance and Freight (defined by Incoterms)
CJ	Chief Justice
cl.	Clause
CLS	Collecte Localisation Satellites
CMI	Comité Maritime International
COGSA 1992	UK Carriage of Goods by Sea Act 1992
CPR	Civil Procedure Rules (of England and Wales, 1998)
DAP	Delivered at Place (defined by Incoterms)
DAT	Delivered at Terminal (defined by Incoterms in pre-2020 versions)
DDP	Delivered Duty Paid (defined by Incoterms)
DPU	Delivered at Place Unloaded (defined by Incoterms 2020)
eg.	Exempli gratia (for example)
ETA	Estimated time of arrival
etc.	Et cetera
EXW	Ex Works (defined by Incoterms)
FC	Federal Court
FCL	Full container load
FFA	Free fatty acid
fiost	Free in, out, stowed and trimmed
fob	Free on board
FOB	Free on Board (defined by Incoterms)

FOSFA	Federation of Oils, Seeds and Fact Association
GAFT	Grain and Feed Trade Association
HC	High Court
i.e.	Id est (that is)
IACS	International Association of Classification Societies
ICA	Inter-club Agreement
ICC	International Chamber of Commerce
IG	International Group
IMDG Code	CodeInternational Maritime Dangerous Goods Code
IMF	International Monetary Fund
IMO	International Maritime Organisation
ISM Code	International Safety Management Code
ISPS Code	International Ship and Port Facility Security Code
ITF	International Transport Workers' Federation
J	Justice
LCL	Less than a container load
LJ	Lord Justice
LMAA	London Maritime Arbitrators Association
Model Law	UNCITRAL Model Law on International Commercial Arbitration 1985, amended in 2006
MSC	Maritime Security Committee (of IMO)
MY	Malaysia
N. Ireland	Northern Ireland
NODISP	No disposal
NOR	Notice of Readiness
NVOC	Non-vehicle owning carrier
NYPE	New York Produce Exchange
NZ	New Zealand
P&I	Protection and Indemnity
reg.	Regulation
RM	Ringgit Malaysia (Malaysian currency)
s.	Section
Sabah Regulations	Merchant Shipping (Applied Subsidiary Legislation) Regulations 1961
Sarawak Regulations	Merchant Shipping (Implementation of Conventions Relating to Carriage of Goods by Sea and to Liability of Shipowners and Others) Regulations 1960
SC	Supreme Court
SDR	Special Drawing Rights
SEADOCS	Seaman Documents Manager
SG	Singapore
SGD	Singapore Dollars
SITPRO	SITPRO Limited, formerly known as Simpler Trade Procedures Board
SMA	Singapore Chamber of Maritime Arbitration

SMA	Society of Maritime Arbitrators (New York)
SOLAS	International Convention for the Safety of Life at Sea of 1974 (as amended)
SWIFT	Society for Worldwide Interbank Financial Telecommunication
UCP	Uniform Customs and Practice for Documentary Credits, made by ICC
UK	United Kingdom
UNCITRAL	United Nations Commission on International Trade Law
UNCTAD	United Nations Conference on Trade and Development
US	United States
USA	United States of America
USD	United States Dollars
wibon	Whether in berth or not
wipon	Whether in port or not

Part I
Introduction and International Trade

Chapter 1
Introduction and Legal Framework

This chapter introduces the legal framework relevant to carriage of goods by sea. In that course, it briefly introduces the background to and development of the laws regulating the terms of contracts of carriage of goods by sea and transferability of bills of lading, and the payment mechanism in international trade, namely, letters of credit. It then sets out the legal framework relating to carriage of goods by sea. This includes an introduction to the international conventions (particularly, Hague and Hague-Visby Rules), legislations providing for transfer of contractual rights in bills of lading (including the UK Carriage of Goods by Sea Act 1992), common law concept of transferability of constructive possession of goods attached to the bill of lading, laws relating to bailment, conversion, negligence, and evidence, laws concerning contract law and third-party rights, and legislations dealing with sale of goods. A note about the legal framework in Singapore and Malaysia, with some reference to Commonwealth countries in general is included. This is followed by a glimpse of cargo claims in a practical context, which is covered at depth in the subsequent chapters.

1.1 Introduction

Carriage of good by sea is regulated by a legal framework that comprises domestic and international laws. It involves international trade and law, hence the need for the domestic laws to align with certain international conventions to maintain uniformity internationally. International laws, ratified domestically, largely control the terms of the contract of carriage. At the outset, this is necessary to protect the interests of the shipper who may not have a choice otherwise to accept any term imposed by the carrier. The control measures are balanced by giving the carrier a limitation of liability and certain defences beyond what would otherwise be available. Such balancing is necessary to keep the cost of sea-carriage affordable. Apart from these matters, there are peculiar aspects involved in international trade and carriage of

A. Kasi, *The Law of Carriage of Goods by Sea*,
https://doi.org/10.1007/978-981-33-6793-7_1

goods by sea such as the sale of goods in transit accompanied by transfer of the bill of lading, often commercially abbreviated as 'B/L', and the need for a special payment mechanism, usually by letter of credit, between the seller and the buyer situated in different jurisdictions.

Terms of contract of carriage and transfer of bills of lading are directly related to the subject of contract of carriage. Payment mechanism relates more directly to the sale and purchase contract between the seller and the buyer, i.e. international trade.

In this chapter, each of the above said three subjects, namely terms of the carriage-contract, transfer of bills of lading and payment mechanism, is briefly addressed in turn below as preliminaries. That is followed by an analysis of the legal framework, which includes the international conventions, the legislations regarding the transferability of contractual rights in bills of lading, transferability of possessory rights at common law, the common law bailment-obligation of the carriers, the common law liability of the carriers in torts of conversion and negligence at common law. That is further followed by a glimpse over cargo claims, which are dealt with in detail in later chapters.[1]

In the next chapter, a detailed introduction to shipping documents with a focus on bills of lading is undertaken. Then, the following chapter deals with the aspects of international trade, namely, the shipping terms used in the international trade, the concepts of passing of risk and the property that has a bearing on cargo claims, and letters of credit.

1.2 Preliminaries

Here is introduced the three preliminary matters, namely, terms of contract of carriage, transferability of contractual rights and possessory rights in bills of lading and payment mechanism in international trade.

1.2.1 Terms of Carriage-Contract

Before 1924, carriers enjoyed the full freedom to contract on terms agreed by the parties.[2] They took this opportunity to include broad exclusion clauses that will go to the root of the contract. This was particularly so as the shippers, commercially, had limited bargaining power against the carriers. In response to this, courts had to come out with judicial ingenuity to curb the effect of such clauses as a matter of construction. The courts went to the extent of developing a doctrine called 'fundamental breach' to strike down exclusion clauses that exempt the carriers from liability

[1] See Chaps. 4 through 10.

[2] Subject only to restrictions, like rule against illegality, generally applicable to contracts.

when they fail to do the very thing they agreed to do[3] such as the delivery to the right person at the destination port. However, this particular development of 'fundamental breach' did not long last[4] and the courts came back to the 'construction' mechanism to control the exclusion clauses, however, influenced by the doctrine of 'fundamental breach'.[5]

To mitigate the problems causes by the wide contractual freedom, the international community came out with a convention in 1924, called the Hague Rules,[6] to strike a balance between the two interests, by imposing minimum threshold obligations on the carrier and at the same time limiting the liability of the carrier and affording some special defences to the carrier. This was a welcome matter as it promoted uniformity and a balance between the carrier and cargo interests. Many countries ratified it and enacted it as their domestic law.

However, soon after that, the shortfalls in the Rules were showing out. Shortfalls were not only in the concept of the Rules but also in their drafting. However, amending the convention was not an easy thing as it could result in loss of uniformity when not all the contracting states ratify the amendment, as it happens with most of the international conventions. However, some amendments to the conventions came about in 1968 and the amended convention was called the Hague-Visby Rules.[7] Some, but not all, of the contracting states to the Hague Rules ratified this. A further amendment came about in 1979, particularly to introduce the Special Drawing Rights (SDR) Protocol.[8] Again, some, but not all, of the Hague-Visby contracting states ratified this.

One thing that must be noticed about all the three Hague group of conventions is that their master framework is the same and the various shortfalls were not addressed by any amendments within the framework. Hence, the international community came out with two entirely new sets of rules, respectively the Hamburg Rules in 1978[9] and the Rotterdam Rules in 2009.[10] The generally accepted view is that the Hague group of rules has many shortfalls and that these later conventions are better formulated and drafted. However, neither of these later conventions gained widespread adoption,

---

[3] *Glynn v Margetson & Co* [1893] AC 351, [1891–4] All ER Rep 693 (UK HL).

[4] *Photo Production Ltd v Securicor Transport Ltd* [1980] AC 827, [1980] 1 All ER 556, [1980] 2 WLR 283, [1980] 1 Lloyd's Rep 545 (UK HL).

[5] *Sze Hai Tong Bank Ltd v Rambler Cycle Co Ltd* [1959] AC 576, [1959] 2 Lloyd's Rep 114, [1959] 3 All ER 182 [1959] 3 WLR 214 (PC on appeal from Singapore).

[6] The International Convention for the Unification of Certain Rules of Law relating to Bills of Lading of 1924.

[7] The International Convention for the Unification of Certain Rules of Law relating to Bills of Lading of 1924, amended by Brussels Protocol of 1968.

[8] 'Protocol amending the International Convention for the Unification of Certain Rules of Law relating to Bills of Lading of 25 August 1924, as amended by the Protocol of 23 February 1968' (made in 1979).

[9] United Nations Convention on the Carriage of Goods by Sea, 1978.

[10] United Nations Convention on Contracts for the International Carriage of Goods Wholly or Partly by Sea.

although a few countries ratified one or the other of them.[11] The reasons for the failure of these two rules to go far are twofold. First, uniformity will be lost if they were not widely ratified. Second, starting a new regime of rules will mean the loss of the wealth of precedents gained in relation to the Hague group of rules. The reluctance of the international community to go for a change can colloquially be said to be because of the 'fear of the unknown' or 'known devil is better than the unknown angel'.

1.2.2 Transferability of Bills of Lading

The question of transferability contractual rights and possessory rights in bills of lading has not been addressed by any of the international conventions. The need was not there as there were already an established trade practice and custom that had found their way into the law.

The custom was that a bearer-bill[12] may be transferred by mere delivery and an order-bill by indorsement and delivery.[13] The obligation of the carrier was to deliver the goods to the holder of the bill against presentation of the bills. The *bill* performed the function of a *goods-token* (i.e. immediate right to possession/constructive possession) at common law.[14] Added to it, in 1855, the UK enacted the Bills of Lading Act 1855 which transferred the *contractual rights* under the bill of lading to the transferee of the bill.[15]

It must be borne in mind that the two types of transferability are different from one another. One is transfer of the possessory rights over the goods attached to the bill (i.e. constructive possession) and the other is transfer of the contractual rights in the bill.

The bill represents the possession of the goods. As the goods are in the hands of the shipowner, it represents the *constructive possession*, i.e. the right to claim delivery from the carrier. In other words, the bill is a *document of possessory right* and the transfer of it is the *constructive delivery* of the goods. It can be said 'the delivery of the bill is the delivery of the goods'. Transfer of constructive possession has always been and is regulated by the common law.

That is different from transfer of the contractual rights, effected by legislation such as the 1855 Act now repealed and replaced with the UK Carriage of Goods by Sea Act 1992.[16] The 1992 Act provides a more sophisticated scheme of transferability

---

[11] In the case of the Hamburg Rules, more than 30 countries have ratified it, mostly African countries. In the case of the Rotterdam Rules, more than 20 countries have signed it including a few European countries and the USA, but only a few African countries and Spain have ratified it.

[12] A bill of lading that confers the right to claim delivery from the shipowner on the bearer of the bill.

[13] Like negotiable instruments.

[14] *Lickbarrow v Mason* (1794) 5 TR 683, 101 ER 380 (EW HC).

[15] Now been repealed and replaced with the UK Carriage of Goods by Sea Act 1992.

[16] Applicable to the whole of the UK.

of contractual rights and additionally covers other types of shipping documents, namely, sea waybill and ship's delivery order. A popular shortfall in the 1855 Act was that it required the *property in the goods* to pass for the contractual rights under the bill to pass. This meant that a bank taking the bill as a *pledgee* would not have the contractual rights transferred to it. The said requirement is no longer there in the 1992 Act.

1.2.3 Payment Mechanism in International Trade

Payment mechanism in international trade has not presented problems like those relating to the terms of the carriage contract. The reason is that the mode of payment will often be by letter of credit and the banks will be at the centre of the system of payment by letters of credit. They have voluntarily developed quite safe mechanisms and practice concerning this. Almost invariably, the banks have adopted the standard contract terms drawn by the International Chamber of Commerce (ICC) known as the Uniform Customs and Practice for Documentary Credits (UCP). This is a standard form, meant for voluntary adoption by the banks when issuing a letter of credit. The UCP standard forms were first available as early as 1933 and have since then been updated based on industry experience. The latest version of it is UCP 600 made in 2007.

As this is well self-regulated, there has been no need for legislative intervention, whilst there is a wealth of judicial precedents on this subject. The regular laws of contract in the respective countries will apply and cater for this.

1.3 Legal Framework

The legal frameworks regulating the shipping documents particularly bills of lading, cargo claims, third-party rights, sale of goods and evidence are visited in this sub-chapter.

1.3.1 Hague/Hague-Visby Rules, etc.

The terms of bills of lading from the commencement of the loading to the completion of discharge are usually regulated by an international that is given effect to by the domestic legislation. Through this mechanism, the conventions also largely control cargo claims in respect of matters that happened during the said period. Different jurisdictions have ratified different conventions. Some have not ratified any convention but have domestically enacted laws that are largely in line with one of the conventions, e.g. the USA.[17] The available conventions, insofar as bills of lading are concerned, are Hague Rules, Hague-Visby Rules (without SDR Protocol), Hague-Visby Rules as amended by SDR Protocol, Hamburg Rules and Rotterdam Rules.

The most popular ones are the Hague group of Rules.[18] Currently, the Hague Rules is in force in about 61 countries, the Hague-Visby Rules without SDR Protocol is in force in about 7 countries, and the Hague-Visby Rules as amended by SDR Protocol in about 24 countries. At present, the UK have ratified the Hague-Visby Rules as amended by SDR Protocol.[19] Countries that have ratified and enacted the Hague-Visby Rules without the SDR Protocol include Singapore, while countries like Malaysia still remain with the Hague Rules.

Although the UK has, at present, adopted the Hague-Visby Rules as amended by SDR Protocol, questions pertaining to the two previous versions of the Rules frequently arise before English arbitral tribunals and courts. This is because the law applicable to the bill of lading in question may be a law of some other country that has subscribed to one of the two previous Rules. Another reason is that, where the Rules do not statutorily apply, the shipping document in question, e.g. a charterparty, may voluntarily incorporate one of the three Rules.[20] This is more so as the shipping document may have a London arbitration clause, as it quite frequently happens in the case of charterparties, and an appeal or application may lie from the arbitration to the English court.[21]

Accordingly, all the three Rules are studied at depth in this work. Cases from Singapore and Malaysia are included. They will serve as examples of application of the Hague-Visby Rules (pre SDR Protocol) and Hague Rules, respectively. They also serve as added examples of application of the English law principles on this subject as both these Commonwealth jurisdictions have generally largely adopted the English law.

The background to the Hague group of Rules is that by a convention in 1924, a set of rules called the Hague Rules was born out. The UK signed the convention in 1924 itself[22] and gave effect to it by the UK Carriage of Goods by Sea Act 1924.[23] Section 1 of the Act read as follows:

> Subject to the provisions of this Act, the Rules shall have effect in relation to and in connexion with the carriage of goods by sea in ships carrying goods from any port in Great Britain or Northern Ireland to any other port whether in or outside Great Britain or Northern Ireland.

---

[17] The US Carriage of Goods by Sea Act 1936.

[18] The Hague group of rules are in place in about 97 countries.

[19] By the 1979 amendment to the UK Carriage of Goods by Sea Act 1971.

[20] Such incorporation clause is called 'clause paramount'.

[21] Sections 67–71 of the UK Arbitration Act 1996.

[22] Any convention does not have legal effect until it is given effect to by law enacted for that purpose.

[23] Now repealed and replaced with the UK Carriage of Goods by Sea Act 1971.

In addition to that, the Act contained a provision, in Section 3, requiring the fact of application of the Rules to be declared in the bill of lading. The Section 3 read as follows:

> Every bill of lading or similar document of title issued in Great Britain or Northern Ireland which contains or is evidence of any contract *to which the rules apply*, shall contain an express statement that it is to have effect subject to the provisions of the said rules as applied by this Act. [emphasis added]

However, if the clause paramount is missed, it has no impact on the statutory application of the Rules. This point was emphasised by the Privy Council in *Vita Foods Products Inc v Unus Shipping Co Ltd*[24] as follows:

> [T]he omission of what is called the clause paramount does not make the bills of lading illegal documents, in whole or in part, either within Newfoundland or outside it. Section 3 is in their Lordships' judgment directory. It is not obligatory, nor does failure to comply with its terms nullify the contract contained in the bill of lading. This, in their Lordships' judgment, is the true construction of the statute, having regard to its scope and its purpose and to the inconvenience which would follow from any other conclusion.

It was similarly said by the Malaysian High Court, when dealing with Malaysian Carriage of Goods by Sea Act 1950, which is materially identical to the UK 1924 Act, in the case of *Sarawak Electricity Supply Corp v MS Shipping Sdn Bhd*,[25] where the High Court expressed:

> [T]he shipping order is as good as a document of tile ... This is notwithstanding the absence of an endorsement on the shipping order that it is subject to the Hague Rules because the failure to comply with reg [or s] 4[26] did not render the shipping order an illegal document or render the contract of carriage illegal.

Subsequently, a protocol amending the Hague Rules was made in 1968,[27] which again the UK signed in 1968 itself and enacted it into law by the Carriage of Goods Act 1971, repealing the predecessor 1924 Act. The amended set of Rules is called the Hague-Visby Rules. These Rules made themselves applicable when (a) a bill is issued in a contracting state, (b) the shipment is from a contracting state or (c) the bill makes a provision for the application of the Rules.[28] The 1971 Act accorded the Rules the force of law by Section 1(2), subject to some exceptions,[29] and it was applicable for all shipments from a UK port (to whichever port in the world) by Section 1(3). The Act is in force now. The Sections 1(2) and (3) reads as follows:

---

[24] [1939] AC 277 at 295, [1939] UKPC 7 (PC on appeal from Nova Scotia).

[25] [2000] 5 MLJ 721 (MY HC in Sarawak).

[26] Section 4 of the Malaysian 1950 Act is equivalent to Section 3 of the UK 1924 Act.

[27] Protocol to amend the International Convention for the Unification of Certain Rules of Law relating to Bills of Lading signed at Brussels on 25 August 1924.

[28] Article X.

[29] In case of deck cargo or live animals.

> (2) The provisions of the Rules, as set out in the Schedule to this Act, shall have the force of law.
>
> (3) Without prejudice to subsection (2) above, the said provisions shall have effect (and have the force of law) in relation to and in connection with the carriage of goods by sea in ships where the port of shipment is a port in the United Kingdom, whether or not the carriage is between ports in two different States within the meaning of Article X of the Rules.

There is no longer the 'clause paramount requirement' in the 1971 Act. It was no longer necessary as the Hague-Visby Rules made themselves applicable also when a bill is issued in any contracting state.

Many of the signatories to the Hague Rules did not sign the Hague-Visby Rules. Thus, many countries, like Malaysia, are still under the Hague Rules only. Those countries that still remain with the Hague Rules usually have an Act similar to the 1924 Act, e.g. Malaysia.

One of the key differences between the 1924 Rules and the 1968 Rules is that under the former a carrier's liability was limited per package or unit, called package limitation. Under the latter, the carrier's liability is limited by package or gross weight, whichever is higher.[30] The liability-limitation in the 1924 Act did not cover bulk cargo, but the 1968 Rules cover this, hence more favourable to the carrier in this respect. The latter limits the liability based on package or gross weight, whichever is higher, hence more favourable to the cargo interest in this respect. However, the liability limit under the later Rules, whether based on package or gross weight, can be less than that under the former Rules, hence possibly more favourable to the cargo claimant in this respect. In totality, when the two Rules are compared, there are pros and cons on both sides and whom they benefit may differ from case to case. It is not uncommon for carriers, in any given case, to argue to be within the Rules that will better favour them.[31]

Thereafter, a second amending protocol was made in 1979.[32] This made some further amendments to the Hague-Visby Rules of 1968 particularly relating to units of compensation and by fixing the liability limit by reference to SDR. This amendment came to be known as the 'SDR Protocol'.[33] The UK signed this protocol in 1979 itself and brought the amendments into effect by amending the Carriage of Goods by Sea Act 1971.[34] Again, not all those signatories to the Hague-Visby Rules signed this amending protocol. For example, Singapore did not sign this, but enacted a scheme of its own liability-limitation and unit of compensation.

Whether it is the Hague or Hague-Visby Rules, they apply compulsorily only for the sea voyage from the commencement of loading to the end of discharge.[35]

---

[30] Article 5(a).

[31] E.g. *The Hollandia* [1983] 1 AC 565, [1982] 3 All ER 1141, [1982] 3 WLR 1111, [1983] 1 Lloyd's Rep 1 (UK HL).

[32] Protocol amending the International Convention for the Unification of Certain Rules of Law relating to Bills of Lading, 25 August 1924 as amended by the Protocol 23 February 1968.

[33] Article 5.

[34] The amendments were made by Merchant Shipping Act 1981.

[35] Article I(e) read together with Article 2 of the Hague/Hague-Visby Rules.

However, there is nothing to stop the parties from contractually extending the application of the Rules to the period outside the convention-period. It is common for bills of lading to declare that one of these Rules shall apply when the carrier receives the goods before shipment on board the ship such as into warehouse or after discharge from the ship into a terminal warehouse. The terms of the Rules, when it applies statutorily, may not be ousted or modified by the parties to render the terms of the carriage contract more favourable to the carrier, but ousting and modification is not barred when the application of the Rules is by contractual incorporation only.[36] Where there exists a charterparty, the bill of lading may incorporate by reference the terms of the charterparty.[37] When the Rules are incorporated into a charterparty or a bill of lading voluntarily, the clause thus incorporating is called 'clause paramount'.

1.3.2 Transferability of Bills of Lading

In the UK, Carriage of Goods by Sea 1992 Act, in force now, regulates transferability of contractual rights in bills of lading, having repealed its predecessor, the Bills of Lading Act 1855. One of the key differences between the 1855 Act and the 1992 Act is that, under the former Act, the contractual rights under the bill would be transferred to the transferee only if the property too passed with the transfer of the bill. Hence, a bank taking a pledge of the bill was at a disadvantage as it would not secure the contractual rights under the bill because there would be no intention to transfer the property to the bank. This shortfall was made good in the 1992 Act and the test now rather is whether the transferee is the lawful holder of the bill.

Transferability of the right to possession (i.e. constructive possession/possessory rights) is not regulated by the statute. But it is regulated by the common law.

1.3.3 Bailment, Conversion, Negligence and Evidence

In England and Wales, the law of bailment is provided for by the common law. The laws of conversion and negligence are largely regulated by the common law. The law of evidence is largely regulated by the common law.

[36] Article III(8) of the Hague-Visby Rules.

[37] A popular standard form of bill of lading incorporating charterparty terms is BIMCO CONGENBILL 2016. 'BIMCO' is the abbreviation for Baltic and International Maritime Council.

1.3.4 Contact Law and Third-Party Rights

The substantive law of contract, in England and Wales, is provided for by the common law. The doctrine of privity of contract at common law bars a third party from taking action on a contract even if the contract conferred a benefit on the third party. In Great Britain, the position has been statutorily modified in certain circumstances by the Contracts (Rights of Third Parties) Act 1999.

1.3.5 Sale of Goods Act

The UK Sale of Goods Act 1979 makes certain provisions relating to the sale of goods. The relevant sections of the Act are Sections 16, 17(1), 18, 20(1) 20(2) 20(3), 20A, 20B and 32(2).

Section 16 imposes a general requirement that for property to pass the goods must be ascertained. Section 17(1) provides that the property will pass when intended to pass. Section 18 sets out a few rules for ascertaining the intention. Section 20(1) provides that risk passes with the property, unless otherwise agreed. Sections 20A and 20B facilitate passing of property in an unascertained portion of a bulk cargo, by way of exception to Section 16. Section 32(2) provides that delivery to the carrier would be deemed delivery to the buyer in certain circumstances.

1.3.6 Legal Framework in Singapore and Malaysia

Here is introduced the legal framework in Singapore and Malaysia, in turn, below.

1.3.6.1 Singapore

Singapore has ratified and enacted the Hague-Visby Rules (without SDR Protocol) by the Carriage of Goods by Sea Act. In place of the SDR protocol, Singapore has come out with its own scheme of liability limitation scheme by the Carriage of Goods by Sea (Singapore Currency Equivalents) Order. Sections 2 and 3(1)–(7) of the Singapore Act is materially similar to Section 1 of the UK Carriage of Goods by Sea Act 1971 and gives effect to the Hague-Visby Rules (without SDR Protocol) as at 1968 annexed as the Schedule to the Act. Section 3(8) of the Singapore Act additionally allows the Minister to modify the scheme of liability limitation in Article IV(5) of the Rules. By this authority, the Minister has modified the scheme of liability limitation by para 2 of the Carriage of Goods by Sea (Singapore Currency Equivalents) Order, which reads as follows:

> 2. For the purposes of paragraph 5 of Article IV of the Rules and of Article IV bis of the Rules set out in the Schedule to the Act, $1,563.65 cents and $4.69 cents are hereby specified as the amounts which shall be taken as equivalent to 10,000 gold francs and 30 gold francs, respectively. [underlining added]

Section 4 of the Singapore Act is materially identical to Section 3 of the UK 1971 Act and abolishes any *absolute* warranty of seaworthiness by implied term.

Transfer of contractual rights under bill of lading is provided for in Singapore by the Bills of Lading Act. The Singapore Act is materially identical to the UK Carriage of Goods by Sea Act 1992 with the same section numbering. The transferability of constructive possession associated with the bill of lading, with transfer of the bill, is not regulated by any statute and is regulated by common law, as in England and Wales.

The law of evidence is codified in Singapore by Evidence Act, modelled on the Indian Evidence Act 1872, with difference in section numbering in some parts. The Indian Act model, adopted in many Commonwealth countries, is largely a codification of the English common law. The law relating to negligence is largely regulated by common law in Singapore, as in England and Wales.

In Singapore, contract law is regulated by the common law, as in England and Wales. In Singapore, the law relating to specific reliefs is regulated by the common law/equitable principles, as in England and Wales. Same is true of the laws of agency and bailment.

Singapore has a Contracts (Rights of Third Parties) Act, which is materially identical to the UK Contracts (Rights of Third Parties) Act 1999. Sections 2–9 of the Singapore Act correspond, respectively, with Sections 1–8 of the UK 1999 Act.

Singapore Sale of Goods Act is materially identical to the UK Sale of Goods Act 1979 with the same section numbering.[38] Singapore Unfair Contract Terms Act is materially identical the UK Unfair Contract Terms Act 1979 with the same section numbering.[39] Singapore has a Misrepresentation Act, which is materially identical to the UK Misrepresentation Act 1967 with the same section numbering.[40] Sections 3 and 4 of the Singapore High Court (Admiralty Jurisdiction) Act is materially similar to Sections 20 and 21 of the UK Senior Courts Act 1981.

Singapore International Arbitration Act is modelled on the UNCITRAL[41] Model Law 1985 (amended in 2006)[42] and is significantly different from the UK Arbitration Act 1996. The civil procedure in Singapore is provided for by the Rules of Court, which are divided by 'Orders' and 'rules'. The Rules are materially identical to the Malaysian Rules of Court 2012 with the same Orders and rules numbering. A

---

[38] Save that there is no equivalent in the Singapore Act to Section 63 of the UK 1979 Act and the Section 63 of the Singapore Act corresponds with Section 64 of the UK 1979 Act.

[39] Save that Section 30 of the Singapore Act corresponds with Sections 31 and 32 of the UK 1977 Act.

[40] Save that Sections 4 and 5 of the Singapore Act corresponds with Sections 5 and 6 of the UA 1967 Act.

[41] United Nations Commission on International Trade Law.

[42] UNCITRAL Model Law on International Commercial Arbitration 1985, amended in 2006.

short description of some of the Orders that are referred to in this work follows. Order 17 makes provision for interpleader proceedings. Order 20 makes provision for amendment to documents including pleadings (called 'statements of case' in the Civil Procedure Rules (CPR) of England and Wales). Order 69 makes provision for arbitration proceedings. Order 70 makes provision for admiralty proceedings.

All the references made in this work to the UK provisions, which have a correspondingly similar provision in Singapore, are applicable in the Singapore context.

1.3.6.2 Malaysia

Malaysia has ratified and enacted the Hague Rules. For Peninsular Malaysia this is done by the Carriage of Goods by Sea Act 1950. This Act is materially similar to the now repealed UK Carriage of Goods by Sea Act 1924.[43] Section 2 of the Malaysian 1950 Act is materially identical to Section 1 of the UK 1924 Act and gives effect to the Hague Rules, which is annexed as the First Schedule to the Malaysian Act, for shipments from any Malaysian port. Section 3 of the Malaysian 1950 Act is materially identical to Section 2 of the UK 1924 Act and abolishes any *absolute* warranty of seaworthiness by implied term. Section 4 of the Malaysian 1950 Act is materially identical to Section 3 of the UK 1924 Act and requires a clause paramount statement in any bill of lading issued in Malaysia. Although application of the Malaysian 1950 Act is limited, by Section 1(2), Peninsular Malaysia only, which includes the federal territory of Kuala Lumpur and Putrajaya,[44] Section 2 of the Act gives effect to the Hague Rules to any shipment out of Malaysia, which comprises Peninsular Malaysia, East Malaysia and the federal territory of Labuan, and Section 4 of the Act requires a clause paramount in any bill of lading issued in Malaysia. Despite this, by virtue of the limitation in Section 1(2), the Act appears to apply only to Peninsular Malaysia.

For East Malaysia, i.e. the states of Sarawak and Sabah, the states have come out with respective regulations giving effect to the Hague Rules. In Sarawak, this is done by Merchant Shipping (Implementation of Conventions Relating to Carriage of Goods by Sea and to Liability of Shipowners and Others) Regulations 1960 (1960 Sarawak Regulations).[45] The regulations 2–6 of the Regulations materially mirror Sections 2–6 of the Malaysian 1950 Act, except that reg 7 modifies the £100 limitation in Article IV(5) of the Hague Rules to MYR850.[46] In Sabah, effect to the Hague Rules is given by Merchant Shipping (Applied Subsidiary Legislation) Regulations 1961

---

[43] Repealed and replaced with the UK Carriage of Goods by Sea Act 1971.

[44] By definition of 'Peninsular Malaysia' in Section 3 of Malaysian Interpretation Acts 1948 and 1967.

[45] Under the authority in Section 277 of Merchant Shipping Ordinance 1960 (Ord 2/1960) [Sarawak].

[46] For a discussion of validity of the MYR850 limit, see Arun Kasi, 'The Dancing Liability-Limit in Hague Rules and Validity of MYR850 Limit for East Malaysia', *Malaysian Law Journal*, [2021] 1 MLJ cxciv where this discussion first appeared. See also Chap. 10.3.1.

(1961 Sabah Regulations) through regulation 3(1) incorporating by reference the 1960 Sarawak Regulations.[47]

However, none of these Regulations or the Malaysian 1950 Act applies to Labuan, since it was severed from Sabah and made a federal territory of Malaysia situated outside Peninsular Malaysia in 1984[48] (the 'Labuan lacuna').[49] A consideration must be made, at this point, whether Sections 3(1)(b) and (c) and 5(2) of the Malaysian Civil Law Act 1956 will bring home any Rules for Labuan. The Sections 3 and 5 of the Malaysian Civil Law Act 1956 will import the English laws, where there is no Malaysian enaction on the subject in question. Section 3(1)(a) imports English common law, rules of equity and statutes of general application as at 1951[50] for Labuan. Section 3(2)(b) similarly imports the English laws as at 1949[51] for Sarawak. In somewhat conflict with this, Section 5(2) imports commercial laws of England including the law of the sea at the current time.[52] While Section 3(1) will import the English laws as at 1949/1951, Section 5(2) will import the current English laws in commercial matters for the states of Penang, Malacca, Sabah and Sarawak. The conflict can be easily resolved by the rule of interpretation, *lex specialis derogat legi general*.[53] As Section 5(2) is a specific provision, it will prevail over Section 3(1) that makes a general provision. However, the Section 5(2) will not apply to Labuan because Labuan is no longer part of the state of Sabah since 1984, unless 'Sabah' in 5(2), is interpreted by judicial manipulation to include Labuan, by reference to the time that the sections was enacted,[54] when Labuan was part of Sabah and thus the true intent of the Act. Notably, Section 17A of the Malaysian Interpretations Act 1948 and 1967 require statutes to be interpreted purposively. If such an interpretation is adopted, then Section 5(2) will apply to Labuan and thereby import the UK 1971 Act, thus the Hague-Visby Rules as amended by SDR Protocol.

Having said the above, the Carriage of Goods by Sea (Amendment) Act 2020 has now been passed to amend the 1950 Act, expected to come into force in July 2021. This will bring two amendments. One is to extend the application of the Rules and the Act to all sea carriage documents, that will include sea waybills and ship's

---

[47] Under the authority in Sections 277 and 278 of Merchant Shipping Ordinance 1960 (No 11/1960) [Sabah].

[48] 16 April 1984.

[49] For a detailed discussion of the 'Labuan lacuna', see Arun Kasi, 'The 'Labuan Lacuna': Hague or Hague-Visby Rules for Labuan?', *Malaysian Law Journal*, [2020] 6 MLJ cxxxi , where this subject first appeared.

[50] 1 December 1951.

[51] 12 December 1949.

[52] *Ke Mohamed Sultan Maricar v The Prudential Assurance Co Ltd* [1941] 1 MLJ 20 (SG HC). In this case, Singapore High Court interpreted a similar section (the then Section 5(1) of the Singapore Civil Law Act) to refer to the English laws of current time when a matter comes before the court. In *Pacific Electric Wire & Cable Co Ltd & Anor v Neptune Orient Lines Ltd & Ors* [1993] SLR(R) 102 (SG HC), the Singapore High Court utilised the said provision to import English laws relating to bills of lading.

[53] 'The specific governs over the general'.

[54] As it is now.

delivery orders. Another is to allow the Minister to amend the Rules included in the schedule to the Act by an order published in the *Gazette*. The Explanatory Notes to the bill states that the objective of the second amendment is to enable the Hague-Visby Rules (as amended by SDR Protocol) to be implemented in Malaysia. This bill, if and when enacted, will have no impact on the Labuan lacuna.

Coming to transfer of contractual rights in the bill of lading, there is no statute in Malaysia regulating it or equivalent to the UK Bills of Lading Act 1855 or the UK Carriage of Goods by Sea Act 1992. For Peninsular Malaysia, except for the states of Penang and Malacca, Section 5(1) of the Malaysian Civil Law Act imports the English laws of commerce including the law of the sea as at 1957.[55] This will bring home the UK 1855 Act. For the states of Penang, Malacca, Sabah and Sarawak, Section 5(2) of the Malaysian Civil Law Act imports the English laws of commerce including the law of the sea as at current time.[56] Accordingly, the UK 1855 Act will apply for Peninsular Malaysia save for Penang and Malacca, and the UK 1992 Act will apply for Penang, Malacca, Sabah and Sarawak.[57] Labuan is left in lacuna again, unless judicial manipulation is employed to interpret 'Sabah' to include Labuan by reference to the time the section was enacted[58] and its true intent.

The transferability of constructive possession associated with the bill of lading, with the transfer of the bill, is not regulated by any statute. Section 3(1)(a) imports the English common law as at 1956[59] for Peninsular Malaysia where there is no written law in Malaysia on a subject. Section 3(1)(b) similarly imports the English law as at 1951[60] for Sabah[61] and Section 3(1)(c) imports the English law as at 1949 for Sarawak. Hence, the English common law around 1950 will apply in Malaysia (save for Labuan, unless 'Sabah' is interpreted to include Labuan by judicial manipulation). The English law on this subject around 1950 is materially the same as it is now. The same is the position as regards the law of negligence in Malaysia.

The law of evidence is codified in Malaysia by Evidence Act 1950, modelled on the Indian Evidence Act 1872, with same section numbering. The Indian Act model, adopted in many Commonwealth countries, is largely a codification of the English common law.

---

[55] 7 April 1957.

[56] *Ke Mohamed Sultan Maricar v The Prudential Assurance Co Ltd* [1941] 1 MLJ 20 (SG HC). In this case, Singapore High Court interpreted a similar section (the then Section 5(1) of the Singapore Civil Law Act) to refer to the English laws of current time when a matter comes before the court. In *Pacific Electric Wire & Cable Co Ltd & Anor v Neptune Orient Lines Ltd & Ors* [1993] SLR(R) 102 (SG HC), the Singapore High Court utilised the said provision to import English laws relating to bills of lading.

[57] See Arun Kasi, 'UK Bills of Lading Act 1855 or Carriage of Goods by Sea Act 1992 for Penang, Malacca, Sabah and Sarawak?', *Malaysian Law Journal*, [2020] 5 MLJ cxxxiv, where a detailed discussion of this subject first appeared.

[58] As it is now.

[59] 7 April 1956.

[60] 1 December 1951.

[61] 12 December 1949.

In Malaysia, contract law is codified by Contracts Act 1950 modelled on the Indian Contract Act 1872 with some difference in section numbering. The Indian Act model, adopted in many Commonwealth countries, is largely a codification of the English common law. The areas of laws covered by the Indian Act is more than those covered by the Malaysian Act. The Malaysian Act covers Contracts, Agency,[62] Bailment,[63] etc., which are again largely codification of the English common laws on these subjects. There is no statute in Malaysia like the UK Misrepresentation Act 1974, but Section 18 of the Malaysian Contracts Act defines 'misrepresentation' and Section 19 provides for the consequences of the misrepresentation. In Malaysia, there is also a Specific Relief Act 1950, modelled on the Indian Specific Relief Act 1872, which is again largely a codification of the English common law on this subject.

Malaysia has no statute equivalent to the UK Contracts (Rights of Third Parties) Act 1999. Nor does the Malaysian Contracts Act 1950 has any provisions equivalent to those in the UK 1999 Act.[64] Hence, the doctrine of privity of contract is applicable in Malaysia without any such exception as in the UK 1999 Act. However, the doctrine of privity of contract, where applicable, is no bar to an action in Malaysia by a third party if he is indeed the principal of the contracting party, even if the agency is undisclosed.[65]

Malaysian Sale of Goods Act 1957 is quite substantially similar to the UK Sale of Goods Act 1979 with some difference in section number. However, there is no sections equivalent to Sections 20A and 20B of the UK 1979 Act, which facilitate passing of property in an unascertained portion of a bulk cargo. Similarly, there is no equivalent provision to Section 18 of the UK 1979 Act (rules for ascertaining the intention as to passing of property). Sections 18, 19, 26 and 29 of the Malaysian 1957 Act is materially identical to the UK 1999 Act Sections 16 (property may not pass when goods not ascertained), 17 (property pass when intended to pass), 20 (risk passes with property unless otherwise agreed), and 32 (delivery to carrier deemed to be delivered to the buyer in certain circumstances).

There is no statute of general application in Malaysia equivalent to the UK Unfair Contract Terms Act 1977. Nor does the Malaysian Contracts Act 1950 includes any such provision.[66] The Malaysian High Court in *Standard Chartered Bank v Boomland Development Sdn Bhd & Ors*[67] refused to allow the UK 1977 Act to be imported through the Section 5(2) Malaysian Civil Law Act 1956 route with no sustainable reason stated. However, a valid reason would have been that this is not an area where there is no written law, because the Malaysian Contracts Act 1950 is there.

---

[62] Part X, as in the Indian 1872 Act.

[63] Part IX, as in the Indian 1872 Act.

[64] The same is true of the Indian Contract Act 1872.

[65] Malaysian Contracts 1950—Sections 179, 183, 184 and 185. Indian Contracts Act 1872—Sections 226, 230, 231 and 232.

[66] The same is true in the case of the Indian Contract Act 1872.

[67] [1997] MLJU 19 (MY HC).

There is no admiralty statute in Malaysia, but Section 24(b) of the Malaysian Courts of Judicature Act 1964 imports the admiralty laws of England. Hence, Sections 20 and 21 of the UK Senior Courts Act 1981 applies in Malaysia.

Malaysian Arbitration Act is modelled on the UNCITRAL[68] Model Law 1985 (amended in 2006)[69] and is significantly different from the UK Arbitration Act 1996. The civil procedure in Malaysia is provided for by the Rules of Court 2012, which are divided by 'Orders' and 'rules'. The Rules are materially identical to the Singapore Rules of Court 2012 with the same Orders and rules numbering. A short description of some of the Orders that are referred to in this work follows. Order 17 makes provision for interpleader proceedings. Order 20 makes provision for amendment to documents including pleadings (called 'statements of case' in the Civil Procedure Rules (CPR) of England and Wales). Order 69 makes provision for arbitration proceedings. Order 70 makes provision for admiralty proceedings.

All the references made in this work to the UK provisions, which have a correspondingly similar provision in Malaysia, are applicable in the Malaysian context.

1.4 Cargo Claims: A Glimpse

The subject of cargo claims is dealt with in detail later.[70] Below is a glimpse of it. Cargo claims will usually be brought by the bill of lading holder, which may be the end-buyer or even a bank. A cargo claim may also be brought by other parties such as the seller where the seller retained the risk after shipment until delivery.

The cargo claim will usually be made against the carrier. However, it may be brought against others involved in the carriage such as the shipowner where the cargo was carried under a time-charterer's bill. It may even be brought against independent contractors engaged by the shipowner such as stevedores. The cause of action can be in contract.[71] It may also be in negligence,[72] conversion[73] or bailment.[74]

Once liability is established, the question of assessment and quantum of damages arises.[75] Any such quantum will be subject to any liability-limitation that the carrier is statutorily entitled to.[76] The Hague and Hague-Visby Rules, whichever applies to

[68] United Nations Commission on International Trade Law.

[69] UNCITRAL Model Law on International Commercial Arbitration 1985, amended in 2006.

[70] See Chaps. 4 through 10.

[71] Contract by bill of lading.

[72] A tort.

[73] A tort.

[74] A *sui generis*.

[75] Canvassed in Chap. 10.

[76] Under Article IV(5) of the Hague or Hague-Visby Rules, whichever is applicable. In cases to which the UK law applies, the Hague-Visby Rules have the force of law under Section 1(2) of the UK Carriage of Goods by Sea Act 1971.

a particular case, play an important role in defining liabilities of the carrier and the limits to it.[77] They also provide various defences to the carrier.[78]

The cargo insurers may pay and settle the end-consignee. If so, the insurer may bring the action in the name of the end-consignee by virtue of subrogation. The action will usually be defended by the Protection and Indemnity (P&I) Club that has insured the shipowner or demise charterer for liabilities. However, the P&I Club will not cover in certain events such as deviation in the route of the ship, misdelivery and issuance of a clean bill when the cargo as received was damaged.

A cargo claimant may want to find a way to sue the shipowner, contractually or non-contractually, so that the ship may be arrested.[79] This is because, once the ship is arrested, normally the P&I Club, who is the liability insurer for the shipowner or demise charterer, will give an undertaking to settle any award or judgement made against the shipowner or demise charterer. In the absence of such an undertaking, there is no assurance that the claimant will be able to recover any award or judgement sum from the P&I Club. This is because the P&I Club, under the usual terms of its cover issued to the shipowners or demise charterers, will not be liable to pay any award or judgement sum until the shipowner or demise charter has first settled the same to the claimant. Accordingly, if the shipowner is unable to settle the claim, then the claimant will have no avenue, in the absence of the undertaking, of claiming directly from the P&I Club. The same is true if the shipowner or demise charterer becomes insolvent or dissolved and thus does not settle the claim.

It must be noted that the UK Third Parties (Rights against Insurers) Act 2010[80] is of no help to the claimant. This is because, although Sections 1, 2 and 6 of the Act transfers the right of the insured onto the claimant in the event of insolvency or dissolution of the insured, Sections 9(1) and 9(5) read together with Section 9(6), renders the transfer nugatory in the case of marine insurance for non-compliance with the condition that the insured must first pay the claimant (except in claims for personal injury and death). However, arguably, a tricky way of overcoming this is by Section 9(2) that provides that the claimant may himself satisfy the condition. Hence, if the claimant pays itself on behalf of the insured, then the condition of payment would be satisfied. But the difficulty with this is that it is illogical to say that one pays himself, and such a result would defeat the purpose of Section 9.

---

[77] Canvassed in Chap. 10.

[78] Article IV.

[79] See Sections 20 and 21 of the UK Senior Courts Act 1981.

[80] Materially identical to Singapore Third Parties (Rights against Insurers) Act. There is no similar Act in Malaysia.

Chapter 2
Shipping Documents

This chapter introduces the three types of shipping documents: bills of lading, sea waybills and ship's delivery orders. It analyses bills of lading in fine detail. This includes setting out the common terminologies used in connection with bills of lading, a millennium's history briefly and development of laws since *Lickbarrow v Mason* in 1974 to Carriage of Goods by Sea Act 1992 to rightly understand the law in its current state and be clear of misconceptions. The three functions of the bill of lading, namely, receipt, undertaking to deliver and constructive possession, and evidence of contract of carriage, are clearly set out. The differences between 'received for shipment' bill and 'shipped' bill are dealt with. The choice of words between 'document of title' and 'document of constructive possession', and 'negotiability' and 'transferability', are considered. The commercial problems and legal issues with house or combined transport bills issued by non-vehicle owning carriers like freight forwarders, and their transferability, are critically examined. Bills issued by time-charterers and through bills are considered. Then considered is transferability of bills of lading, period of carrier's responsibility, effect of would-be terms of the carriage-contract, and application of international conventions. Then, a note about electronic bills of lading.

2.1 Introduction

'Shipping documents' may refer to more than one type of document used in shipping business. Broadly, there are two types of documents relating to shipping. One is a document that *acknowledges shipment or the receipt of the goods* by the carrier. The documents falling under this category are bills of lading, sea waybills and ship's delivery orders. Another type is a document that does not make such an acknowledgement, like a charterparty, which is only an *agreement* related to shipping. The better approach is to confine 'shipping documents' to the former category, as the latter is not a document by which any shipment or receipt of goods for shipment

A. Kasi, *The Law of Carriage of Goods by Sea*,
https://doi.org/10.1007/978-981-33-6793-7_2

is acknowledged. But if a broad approach is taken, then all these documents can be called 'shipping contracts'. In this work, references to 'shipping document' are confined to the former type. This chapter analyses each of the shipping documents, namely, bill of lading, sea waybill and ship's delivery order.

2.2 Bill of Lading

Bill of lading is a core document in international trade and the most widely used shipping document. In domestic trade, the seller may deliver the cargo to the buyer against payment. However, this is not practical in an international trade where the seller and the buyer may be situated in different jurisdictions.

Hence, a system of completing the sale by documents developed. This, in its simplest version, means that the seller will load the cargo into a ship. The shipowner will issue a bill of lading to the seller. The bill of lading will acknowledge receipt by the shipowner of the cargo in apparent good order and condition. The bill of lading will also constitute the shipowner's undertaking to deliver the cargo to the holder of the bill of lading. The seller will pass this bill to the buyer in exchange for payment. The sale and purchase transaction is completed at this point. The payment is, thus, made before the buyer receives or even sees the cargo, but a report by an independent inspection agency[1] at the point of shipment is a common requirement for payment. If the cargo, as loaded onto the ship, differs from that described in the bill of lading and also the contract between the seller and the buyer, then the buyer will have a claim against both the seller and the shipowner. The claim against the seller will be for breach of the sale and purchase contract. The claim against the shipowner will be for issuing an inaccurate bill of lading, which the buyer relied on to pay the seller. If the cargo was loaded onto the ship in the right condition as stated in the bill of lading but was subsequently damaged whilst in transit on board the ship, the buyer's claim will be against the shipowner only but not the seller.

Upon shipment of the cargo, the shipowner will issue a bill of lading, usually in a set of three original copies, to the consignor. The bill of lading will set out the goods received by the shipowner, their quantity and apparent condition. The bill of lading will also set out the terms of the contract of carriage and freight payment information such as 'freight prepaid' or 'freight collect' upon arrival. The consignor may indorse and transfer the bill to any other person, usually, the buyer. Upon such indorsement and transfer, the rights under the bill of lading are taken over by the transferee, so that the transferee may present the bill to the shipowner at the destination port and claim the goods, subject to the terms of the bill of lading. In the event the goods are not delivered as they should be, the transferee may take action against the shipowner.

---

[1] E.g. SGS.

Some of the popular standard forms of the bill of lading are CONLINEBILL[2] and CONGENBILL[3] made by the Baltic and International Maritime Council (BIMCO).

The primary characteristics and functions of the bill of lading are, in general, that (i) it acknowledges the receipt by the shipowner of the goods in a certain quantity and apparent condition; (ii) it is an undertaking by the shipowner to deliver the goods at the destination port to the person presenting the bill of lading to the shipowner (thus passing the constructive possession of the goods to the holder of the bill); and (iii) it records the terms of the contract of carriage. These second function necessarily entail its transferability, also called 'negotiability',[4] from one holder of the bill to another.

In this sub-chapter, some common terminologies used in connection with bills lading are visited below. That is followed by a brief history of the bill lading, the characteristics and functions of the bill of lading. Then, a few issues concerning bills of lading are analysed. They will include the question of effectiveness of 'received for shipment' bill as opposed to 'shipped bill', the status of bills issued by non-vehicle owning carriers (NVOCs) and charterers, the status of through bills, the qualified meaning of 'document of title' in the context of bill of lading which is indeed a document of constructive possession, the choice of word between 'negotiable' and 'transferable' when describing a bill of lading, the period of responsibility under the bill, and the terms of the carriage-contract before the bill is issued. Thereafter, the extent of regulation by the applicable international convention of the terms of the bill is visited, followed a short discussion of unsuccessful attempts made to introduce electronic bills of lading.

2.2.1 Common Terminologies

In the law of carriage of goods by sea, 'shipper' refers to the one who entered into the contract for carriage with the carrier. It may be the seller or the buyer. This is different from 'consignor'. Usually, the seller will be the consignor, the person delivers the cargo to the ship.

Based on the description of 'consignee' in a bill of lading, the bill can be classified into one of three types. One is an 'order bill', which is the most common one. Another is 'bearer bill'. The other is 'straight bill'.

In an order bill, the consignee will be stated as 'to order' (or less popularly 'to assigns') of the shipper or to order' of a named consignee such as "To order of ABC Limited". If the consignee is stated merely as 'to order' only without specifying whose order it is made to, then that will mean 'to order' of the shipper. It will be a bearer bill when the consignee is stated as 'to bearer'. It will be a straight bill

[2] The latest version is BIMCO CONLINEBILL 2016. This is meant to be a liner bill of lading.

[3] The latest version is BIMCO CONGENBILL 2016. This format is for use with charterparty.

[4] The difference between the two words, and the controversy over which is the right word, is discussed later in Chap. 2.2.9.

when the consignee is a named party without any 'to order' addition, such as "ABC Limited".

Order bills and bearer bills are, generally, transferable. In the case of a straight bill, it may only be transferred once from the consignor to the consignee,[5] and thereafter no transfer from the consignee is allowed.[6] In the case of bearer bills, they are transferred by mere delivery without any indorsement. Bearer bills are not so popular because of the risk that they may fall into wrong hands, although banks may require them for ease of transfer from one hand to another.

An order bill can be transferred by the current 'to order' party to any other through indorsement at the back of the bill. The party in whose favour the bill is so indorsed is also called 'indorsee'. There are two types of indorsement. One is a special indorsement, also called an indorsement in full. Another is a general indorsement, also called an indorsement in blank.

In the case of a special indorsement, the party named as the consignee with 'to order' addition will sign and stamp the bill with the name of a new consignee, which may again be 'to order' of the new consignee or be straight to the new consignee. If the indorsement is to order of the new consignee, the bill may similarly be further indorsed by the new consignee, and so forth, down a line of subsequent consignees. If the indorsement is straight to the new consignee without 'to order' addition, no further indorsement will be possible by the new consignee and the bill from that point takes the characteristics of a straight bill. In the case of an indorsement in blank, the bill turns into a bearer bill from that point onward. But it may be converted back as an order bill, if the bearer is indorsed in full, from that point onward.[7]

It must be noted that no attornment by the carrier is necessary for the indorsement. An 'attornment' is the consent of the party bound by a right held by another against the consenting party for assignment of the said right to a new party. However, no such attornment, or even notice to the carrier, is necessary in the case of bills of lading to give effect to, and bind the carrier on, an indorsement of the bill of lading to a new consignee. This is a speciality of bills of lading.[8]

The person who will ordinarily first get hold of the bill from the carrier is the consignor. The consignor will normally pass it on to the consignee, whether it is made 'to order' of the consignee or 'straight' to the consignee, in exchange for payment. Usually, the exchange is facilitated by banks.[9] The person at any time

---

5 *MacWilliam (JI) Co Inc v Mediterranean Shipping Co SA (The Rafaela S)* [2005] UKHL 11, [2005] 2 AC 423, [2005] 2 All ER 86, [2005] 2 WLR 554, [2005] 1 All ER (Comm) 393, [2005] 1 Lloyd's Rep 347 (UK HL).

6 *The River Ngada* [2003] Lloyd's Maritime Law Newsletter 13 Sept 2001 (EW HC): any purported transfer from the consignee to any other person will be invalid.

7 *Bandung Shipping Pte Ltd v Keppel Tatlee Bank Ltd* [2003] 1 SLR 295 (SG CA).

8 *Barber v Meyerstein* (1870) LR 4 HL 317, [1861–73] All ER Rep Ext 1810 (UK HL), speech of Lord Hatherley: "When they have arrived at the docks, until they are delivered to some person who has the right to them, the bill of lading still remains the only symbol that can be dealt with by way of assignment, mortgage, or otherwise." Other similar and equivalent document of title too can transfer the rights under the document to the transferee, discussed later in this chapter.

9 Discussed later in this chapter.

holding the bill by the lawful process outlined above is called a 'lawful holder' of the bill.

In the event the intended buyer, whichever be the type of bill, does not pay or becomes insolvent, the consignor may indorse it to any other party if it is a bill to the order of the consignor. If the 'to order' party is other than the consignor, then the consignor will have to surrender the bill to the carrier to change the description of the consignee. This is so even if the bill was a 'straight bill' because the straight consignee does not get any right on the bill merely because he is named as consignee until he gets hold of the bill from the consignor.[10]

As long as the consignor has not parted with the bill, the constructive control or constructive possession[11] of the cargo will still be with the consignor. Thus the consignor will be able to give instructions to the carrier to change the name of the consignee in the bill, by surrendering the bill in exchange for a new one.[12] The constructive control or constructive possession is with the lawful holder of the bill at any time.

Any lawful holder of the bill may request the carrier to change the name of the shipper or consignee in the bill by surrendering the old bill in exchange for a new one. This happens when a buyer wants to sell over the cargo while in transit but does not want the new buyer to know the identity of the shipper. Such a bill is commercially called a 'switch' bill of lading. Similarly, in the case of bulk cargo, the lawful holder of a bill may request the carrier, by the surrender of the bill to the carrier, to issue ship's delivery orders in favour of more than one consignee, splitting the bulk cargo among those consignees.

2.2.2 *History of Bill of Lading*

International trade via carriage of goods by sea began to develop in the 10th or 11th century. By then, a practice of properly recording the goods shipped by a *ship's register* maintained by a *ship's mate* developed. Such practice even became a legal requirement in some places, for instance, Ordonnance Maritime of Tirani of 1063, in force then at the Italian town of Tirani, requiring shipowners to have a *clerk* to record the shipments of goods.[13]

By the 13th or 14th century, the practice was to ensure that the record was on board the ship. This corresponds with the current practice of keeping a copy of the bill of lading on board the ship. During that era, the shipper was usually the consignor

[10] See *MacWilliam (JI) Co Inc v Mediterranean Shipping Co SA (The Rafaela S)* [2005] UKHL 11, [2005] 2 AC 423, [2005] 2 All ER 86, [2005] 2 WLR 554, [2005] 1 All ER (Comm) 393, [2005] 1 Lloyd's Rep 347 (UK HL).

[11] Discussed later in this chapter.

[12] *Mitchell v Ede* (1840) 11 Ad & El 888.

[13] See Bennett, '*The History and Present Position of the Bill of Lading*', UK, Cambridge, 1914, p. 7.

and travelled with his goods in the ship to sell or deliver them at the destination port. Correspondingly, the Hague group of Rules until now does not properly separate the shipper from the consignor.[14]

The practice of the shipper going with the goods vanished over time, hence the need for the shippers to ask the shipowner for some proof of shipment for the shipper to forward the same to the shipper's correspondent at the destination port, who may be the consignee. The initial practice was for the shipowners to give a copy of the ship's register.

It appears that the shipowners issued the record of shipment addressed to the world at large and delivered to the shipper and it was in the form of an undertaking to deliver the goods to the order of the consignee. Such a document[15] issued in 1390 read[16] as follows:

> 1390, the 25th day of June. Know all men that [name of shipper or his agent] shipped [description of goods] … which things must be delivered at [port of discharge name] to [consignee name], and **by order of the said [consignee name]** who shall deliver all things to [his agent], and I [ship's mate name] shall deliver all his goods at [name of a place] and for the better caution I affix my mark so. …
>
> [Ship's mate name] mate of the ship of [ship's name]. [emphasis added]

The above resembled the current bill of lading functions of receipt and, in some way, undertaking. However, the characteristic of 'transferability' was not there. Although the document said that the shipowner would deliver the goods to the order of the consignee, that did not mean that the bill could be transferred by endorsement or that the shipowner gave that undertaking to anyone other than the shipper. Very importantly, the document did not say that the goods would be delivered against the presentation of the document, hence it could not have value as a document conferring constructive possession on the holder of the bill.

The function of 'contract' was not there. At that time, the need for this was not there because the contract was in a different document, namely, a charterparty between the shipowner and every shipper.[17] As the receipt was not intended to be transferable, there was no reason to state the contractual terms as part of the receipt. By the 16th century, there seems to be some evidence of the bills incorporating the terms of the charterparty into the bill, thus stuffing the function of 'contract' into the bill.[18]

---

[14] See Article 1 definition of 'carrier' that deals with description of 'shipper' and Article III(3) that assumes, albeit without basis in the current marketplace, that the shipper must be the consignor (which may not in actual fact be so, particularly in a pure fob contract).

[15] Bensa, '*The Early History of Bills of Lading*', UK, Caimo & C, 1925, p. 7.

[16] Translated.

[17] Malynes, '*Consuetudo, vel Lex Mercantoria*', UK, Adam Islip-Anno Dom, 1622: "No ship should be freighted without a Charterpartie …".

[18] See *Hurlocke and Saunderson v Collett* (1539) Select Pleas, vol I, pp. 88–89; *The Mary* (1541) Select Pleas, vol. 1, p. 112; *The John Evangelist* (1544) Select Pleas, vol. I, p. 126; *The While Angel* (1577) Select Pleas, vol II, pp. 59–60.

By the 17th century, the phrase 'bill of lading' came to appear[19] with a commercial practice of treating it as somewhat transferable.[20] A bill issued in the 18th century[21] was as below:

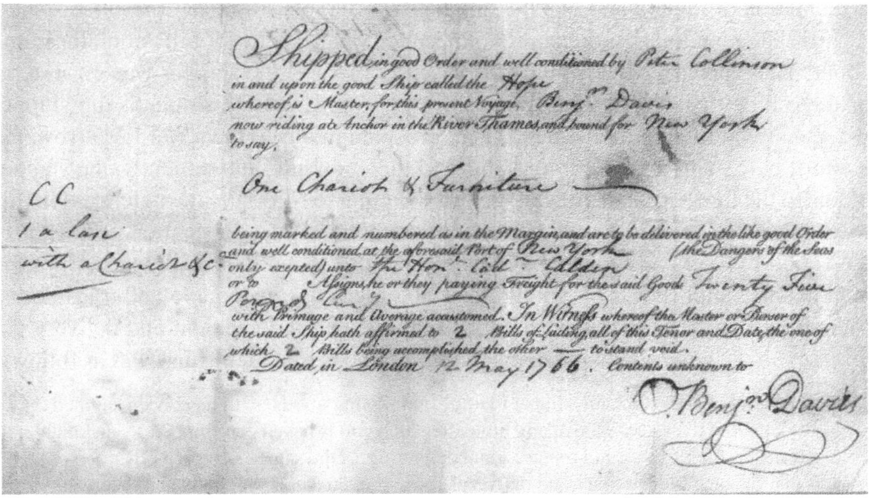
Shipped in good Order and well conditioned by Peter Collinson in and upon the good Ship called the Hope whereof is Master, for this present Voyage, Benj.n Davis now riding at Anchor in the River Thames, and bound for New York to say,

One Chariot & Furniture

CC 1 a case with a Chariot &c.

being marked and numbered as in the Margin, and are to be delivered in the like good Order and well conditioned at the aforesaid Port of New York (the Dangers of the Seas only excepted) unto the Hon. Cadr. Colden or to Assigns, he or they paying Freight for the said Goods Twenty Five Pounds Curr.y with Primage and Average accustomed. In Witness whereof the Master or Purser of the said Ship hath affirmed to 2 Bills of Lading, all of this Tenor and Date, the one of which 2 Bills being accomplished, the other — to stand void.
Dated in London 12 May 1766. Contents unknown to

Benj.n Davis

The above bill dated in 1766 read as follows:

Shipped in good Order and well conditioned by [shipper name] in and upon the good Ship called the [ship name] whereof is the Master, for this present Voyage, [master name] now riding at Anchor in the [load port name] and bound for [discharge port name] to say

[description of goods]

being marked and numbered as in the margin and **are to be delivered** in the like good Order and well conditioned at the aforesaid Port of [port of discharge name] **(the Dangers of the Seas only excepted) unto the [consignee name] or to the Assigns**, he or **they paying Freight for the said Goods [freight amount] with Primage and Average Accustomed.** In Witness whereof the Master or Purser of the said Ship has affirmed to [number of bills issued] Bills of Lading, all of this Tenor and Date, the one of which [number of bills issued] Bills being **accomplished the other to stand void.**

Dated in [place of issue] [date: 12 May 1766]. Contents unknown to [master name]

[Signed by the master]

[emphasis added]

---

[19] See Malynes, '*Consuetudo, vel Lex Mercantoria*', UK, Adam Islip-Anno Dom, 1622: "… Bills of lading do declare what goods are laden, and bindeth the Master to deliver them well conditioned to the place of discharge, according to the contents of the Charterpartie, binding himself, his ship, tackle, and furniture of it, for the performance thereof".

[20] See *The Thomas* (1538) Select Pleas, vol I, p. 61; *The Mary* (1541) Select Pleas, vol. 1, p. 112; *The John Evangelist* (1544) Select Pleas, vol. I, p. 126; *The While Angel* (1577) Select Pleas, vol II, pp. 59–60; *The George of Legh* (1544) Select Pleas, vol II, p. 61; *The Andrewe* (1544) Select Pleas, vol. I, p. 126.

[21] Source: Cadwallader Colden Papers, 1677–1832, Box 7.

The portions rendered in bold above in some way embedded the essence of the three basic functions of the bill of lading, namely, receipt, undertaking to deliver and terms of the carriage contract. The words "one … being accomplished the other to stand void" seemed to evidence the intention that the goods were deliverable only upon presentation of the bill and that the bill was transferable from one to another.

In 1794, a landmark judicial pronouncement on the status of bills of lading came about. That was in *Lickbarrow v Mason*.[22] In this case, the shipper was given a set of three bills of lading, made 'unto order or assigns' of the shipper. The shipper indorsed two of them to Freeman. Then, Freeman indorsed them to Lickbarrow, the plaintiff here, who took them for value and in good faith. Subsequently, the shipper indorsed the third original copy of the bill of lading to Mason,[23] the defendant in this case. Mason successfully took delivery of the goods at the destination port. Hence, the action by Lickbarrow against Mason. The jury found that by the custom of the merchants a shipped bill of lading made 'to order' was negotiable and transferable by indorsement. The jury further found that by such indorsement and delivery the *property in the goods* is passed to the indorsee. The verdict of the jury was as follows:

> [B]y custom of the merchants, bills of lading, expressing goods … to have been shipped … to be delivered to order … are at any time after such goods have been shipped … negotiable and transferable … by … indorsing … and delivering … the same … to such other person… and that by such indorsement and delivery … the property in such goods hath been, and is transferred and passed to such other person …

Upon the verdict, the court held accordingly. It followed that the court held that Lickbarrow became the owner of the goods when the bill was transferred to him by Freeman for value and in good faith, and hence the subsequent transfer by the shipper to Mason was ineffective to pass any ownership unto Mason. Thus, the English High Court found in favour of Lickbarrow against Mason in trover.[24]

From this, it has come to be said that a bill of lading is a 'document of title'. However, there was some want of clarity as to whether the finding was that a bill of lading was a document of title in general or that in the context of the case the bill of lading passed title to Lickbarrow, by the intention of the parties.

About a decade later in 1806, the English Court of King's Bench in *Newsom v Thornton*[25] took the position that the delivery of the bill of lading was as good as the delivery of the goods, but that does not pass any more title than that intended. In this case, the bill of lading was indorsed to a factor, authorised only to sell. However, the factor pledged the bill as security for a loan. The question was whether the title had passed by the indorsement and delivery of the bill to the factor. The court answered this question in the negative and distinguished *Lickbarrow v Mason* on grounds that in *Lickbarrow v Mason* the delivery of the bill was by the vendor to the vendee upon

---

[22] (1794) 5 TR 683, 101 ER 380 (EW HC).

[23] The reason for this was that Freeman did not pay and the shipper came to know that Freeman had become a bankrupt.

[24] Conversion.

[25] (1806) 6 East 17 (EW Court of King's Bench).

a sale and purchase transaction and the parties intended that the property would be passed with the delivery of the bill. Accordingly, the court somewhat recognised the bill of lading a document conferring constructive possession rather than as a document of title.

A decade after that, in 1816, the English Court of King's Bench decided *Patten v Thompson*.[26] In this case, a vendor indorsed and delivered the bill of lading to the vendee. The vendee indorsed and delivered the bill of lading to the vendee's factor. The vendor was unpaid and the vendee had become insolvent. The vendee's factor collected the goods from the ship. Hence, the action by the vendor against the vendee's factor in trover.[27] The court found for the vendor because there was no intention to pass any property to the vendee's factor, unlike in the case of *Lickbarrow v Mason*. The court did not recognise, contrary to *Newton v Thornton*, the holder of the bill as being entitled to possession of the goods, in which even there would have been no trover.

These cases were only about if some sort of property or constructive possession of the goods were passed to the transferee of the bill of lading. They were not about whether the contractual rights under the bill of lading were passed to the transferee. By the mid of 19th century, the question of transfer of contractual rights under the bill of lading arose in such cases as *Thompson v Dominy*[28] and *Howard v Shepherd*.[29] The courts answered the question in the negative, whilst taking the position that although an indorsement and delivery of the bill would transfer some right in the goods to the transferee but not the contractual rights under the bill of lading. The courts were ready to recognise that a chose in action, such as a contractual right, was only recognised at the common law to be transferred to the indorsee in the case of bills of exchange.[30]

This led to the passing of the UK Bills of Lading Act 1855, that, by Section 1, transferred the contractual rights to the transferee of the bill. However, the shortfall in the Act was that it additionally required the property in the goods to pass as a condition for the contractual rights to pass. This did not answer the question as to, or in any way deal with, the immediate right of the holder of the bill to possession and standing to take action in conversion (also called 'trover').[31] A conversion-action was[32] left to be regulated by common law, which action when taken against the shipowner will be subject to any contractual defences and exceptions available to the shipowner.[33] But the Act resolved one thing. It gave the comfort to the *buyer*, to whom the bill had been indorsed and delivered and the property had been passed to,

[26] (1816) 5 M & S 350, 105 ER 1079 (EW Court of King's Bench).

[27] Conversion.

[28] (1845) 14 M & W 403 (EW Court of Exchequer Chambers).

[29] (1850) 9 CB 297 (EW Court of Common Pleas).

[30] E.g. cheques and promissory notes.

[31] A tort.

[32] And is largely.

[33] See *Pyrene Co Ltd v Scindia Navigation Co Ltd* [1954] 2 QB 402, [1954] 2 All ER 158, [1954] 2 WLR 1005, [1954] 1 Lloyd's Rep 321 (EW HC).

to take contractual action against the shipowner for non-delivery, damage to goods, loss of goods, etc., as if the buyer was the shipper, thus breaking the 'privity of contract' barrier.

Returning to the question of whether the bill is a document of title or one conferring constructive possession, in 1870, the House of Lords in *Barber v Meyerstein*[34] recognised that it was the "symbol of the goods, and its delivery to be a delivery of them" and was the "key to the warehouse", hence it is a document giving constructive possession. Subsequently, by the end of the 19th century, this principle was upheld in a few high authorities as *Sanders Bros v Maclean & Co*[35] and *The Zoe.*[36]

Then came the UK Carriage of Goods by Sea Act 1992, repealing and replacing the 1855 Act and provided an improved scheme of transfer of contractual rights by indorsement and delivery in the case of 'order bills' and by delivery in the case of 'bearer bills'. Again, this was not related to the common law actions in conversion by the holder of the bill within the *Barber v Meyerstein* principle but only about the contractual action.

Hence, at all times, there are two different schemes of actions available to the holder when a bill is indorsed and transferred to him. One at the common law, in conversion,[37] under the *Barber v Meyerstein* principle. The other under the 1992 Act in contract. The action in tort, however, will be subject to any contractual limitations.[38]

2.2.3 Characteristics and Functions of Bill of Lading

The three characteristics and functions of the bill of lading are dealt with in this sub-chapter. First, the 'receipt' function. Second, the 'constructive possession' function which is necessarily connected to the concept of transferability (as a token representing the goods) at the common law and which arises from the unilateral undertaking of the carrier to deliver the goods to anyone who duly presents the token.[39] Third, the 'evidence of contract' function, the enhanced value of which was achieved only when the statute was introduced to transfer the contractual rights under the bill of lading to the transferee of the bill.

---

[34] (1870) LR 4 HL 317 (UK HL).

[35] (1883) 11 QBD 327 (EW CA).

[36] *Sewell v Burdick (The Zoe)* (1884) 10 App Case 74 (UK HL).

[37] A tort.

[38] See *Pyrene Co Ltd v Scindia Navigation Co Ltd* [1954] 2 QB 402, [1954] 2 All ER 158, [1954] 2 WLR 1005, [1954] 1 Lloyd's Rep 321 (EW HC).

[39] The bill of lading.

2.2.3.1 'Receipt'

The most and classical basic characteristic of the bill of lading is that it acknowledges receipt of the cargo by the carrier.[40] The details of the receipt will include a description of the cargo, the quantity received and the apparent condition at the time of receipt or shipment. Traditionally, the receipt function was related to the time of shipment (i.e. 'shipped' bill), although the practice has grown now whereby it is related to the time of receipt of the goods before shipment (i.e. 'received for shipment' bill).

Other than acknowledging receipt, the bill of lading will also state the name of the vessel, the port of loading, the port of discharge, name of the shipper, description of the consignee, the party to notify on arrival, date shipped on board,[41] shipper's declared value (if any), number of original bills of lading issued in respect of the shipment. It will be signed by the carrier or on behalf of the carrier by the master[42] or agent.

The receipt statement is binding on the carrier as between the carrier and the lawful holder of the bill so that the carrier will not be allowed to adduce evidence to rebut it.[43] It has been described as a 'negotiable receipt'.[44] However, as between the carrier and the consignor, the bill of lading will only serve as *prima facie* evidence of the description, quantity and condition of the cargo, so that the carrier can adduce evidence to rebut it.[45] A shipped bill of lading will usually be issued, or as such annotated, based on 'mate's receipt' which is the ship record of cargo loaded onto the ship.

It will ordinarily state that the cargo was received in 'apparent good order and condition (unless otherwise stated herein)'. If no adverse condition is recorded, it is called a 'clean' bill of lading. If any adverse condition is recorded, then it will be a 'claused' bill of lading.

Receipt Function Restricted in Case of Containerised Cargo

In the case of containerised cargo, some special considerations are there. Containerised cargoes are shipped as full container load (FCL) or less than container load (LCL).

When a consignor ships FCL and the consignee receives it as FCL, the consignment is called FCL/FCL. When the consignor ships FCL and a few consignees receive portions of it as LCL, it is called FCL/LCL. When a consignor ships LCL and the consignee receives it as LCL, that is called LCL/LCL. It is also possible

---

[40] Article 1(a) of the Hague/Hague-Visby Rules defines carrier to include "the owner or charterer who enters into a contract of carriage with a shipper."

[41] Date of loading on board the ship.

[42] Captain.

[43] Section 4 of the UK Carriage of Goods by Sea Act 1992. See Article IV of the Hague-Visby Rules. Under the common law, this will be by way of estoppel against the carrier.

[44] *Kuwait Petroleum Corpn v I & D Oil Carriers Ltd (The Houda)* [1994] 2 Lloyd's Rep 541 at 553 (EW CA), speech of Leggatt LJ.

[45] See Article IV of the Hague-Visby Rules.

for a consignment to be LCL/FCL when multiple consignors fill a container to be delivered to a single consignee.

In the case of FCL consignment, it is common for the carrier to send a container to the consignor's warehouse for the consignor to 'stuff' the cargo.[46] The consignor may also seal the container after stuffing. Upon discharge, the carrier will send the container to the consignee's warehouse. These consignments are called 'house to house' or 'door to door' consignments. It is another variant of consignment when the carrier receives and delivers the container at respective container depots in loading and discharge places. Another variant of the consignment is 'pier to pier' or 'port to port', in which the carrier receives the stuffed container at the loading port and delivers it at the discharge port.

Some other variants of consignments such as 'house to pier container' or 'shipper's load, stowage and count', whether noted in connection with FCL or LCL, all mean that the container was stuffed and sealed by the shipper.[47] Whichever of the above variants is used, the carrier will usually have no means of verifying the cargo stuffed into the container. In such cases, the carrier will issue a bill of lading that will state "said to contain" above the cargo description.

This is not a true receipt of cargo but rather only of the container. In the event the cargo is found damaged on arrival, the burden will be on the consignee to prove the condition that the cargo was in when stuffed if the consignee desires to make a claim against the carrier.[48] This will be an insurmountable burden in most cases. However, in such cases, an action may better lie against the seller.

In the case of LCL consignment, the carrier may receive the cargo for stuffing into the container. In such a case, the carrier will issue a bill of lading that will acknowledge receipt of cargo without 'said to contain' reservation, as the carrier can verify the description, quantity and apparent condition of the cargo.

Sea waybills are quite commonly used in case of containerised cargo, which is unlikely to be sold in transit. The receipt in the sea waybills will still usually be with the reservation 'said to contain' in FCL consignments. Hence, the insurmountable burden will fall on the consignee if he desires to take action against the carrier rather than the seller.

2.2.3.2 'Undertaking to Deliver'—'Constructive Possession' and 'Transferability'

By issuing the bill of lading, the carrier gives an open undertaking that it will deliver the goods at the destination port against presentation of the bill as per the terms of the bill. At common law, this can be equated with a unilateral offer, as that recognised in *Carlill v Carbolic Smoke Ball Company*,[49] which may be accepted by any person

[46] Containers commonly belong to the carrier. However, they may belong to the consignor or shipper.

[47] *The American Astronaut* [1978–1979] 1 SLR 187 (SG CA).

[48] *The American Astronaut* [1978–1979] 1 SLR 187 (SG CA).

[49] [1892] EWCA Civ 1, [1893] 1 QB 256, [1891–94] All ER Rep 127 (EW CA).

taking the bill in good faith. This 'undertaking' element is linked to two functions. One, the conferment on the holder of the bill the immediate right to possession of the goods from the carrier pursuant to the terms of the bill of lading, i.e. 'constructive possession' or 'possessory right'. The other, the transferability of the bill.

'Constructive Possession' Function

The immediate right to possession has been described in many ways for easy visualisation. It has been described as the 'key to the warehouse',[50] where the warehouse is the ship and the key is the bill of lading. Delivery of the bill has been described as 'symbolic delivery of the goods'.[51] The significance of the immediate right to possession is that the person entitled to it, i.e. the holder of the bill, can bring an action in conversion against the carrier in the event of misdelivery.[52] The classical case on this is *Barber v Meyerstein*.[53] The simplest way to understand the function of 'constructive possession' is to visualise it as the token that a safe-keeping counter in a supermarket will give in return for customer's belongings left there. The supermarket will return the belongings to anyone presenting the token. The token represents the belongings physically, irrespective of who the owner of the belongings legally is. That is 'constructive possession'. The 'holder' here refers to one to whom the carrier issued the bill and any other to whom the bill has been indorsed and delivered in the case of an order bill, or delivered in the case of a bearer bill, or the consignee to whom the bill has been transferred in the case of a straight bill.

A bill is normally issued in a set of three originals. All that is required for the carrier to deliver the cargo is the surrender of one of them.[54] Upon such delivery, the bill becomes 'spent' and no longer good to claim delivery. The carrier is not liable to any other person subsequently presenting any other originals of the bill as long as the carrier had no notice of any want of title in the party who first presented the bill.[55] However, a carrier will be strictly liable for misdelivery in conversion if he delivers against a forged bill,[56] even if there was no means of the carrier knowing it was a forged bill.[57]

---

[50] *Enichem Anic SpA and Others v Ampelos Shipping Co Ltd (The Delfini)* [1990] 1 Ll L Rep 252 at 268 (EW CA), speech of Mustill LJ: "It is a symbol of constructive possession of the goods which (unlike many such symbols) can transfer constructive possession by endorsement and transfer; it is a transferable 'key to the warehouse'."

[51] *Comptoir d'Achat et de Vente du Boerenbond Belge S/A v Luis de Ridder Ltda (The Julia)* [1949] AC 293, [1949] 1 All ER 269 (UK HL); *Chan Cheng Kum v Wah Tat Bank* [1971] 1 Lloyd's Rep 439, [1971] 1 MLJ 177 (PC on appeal from Singapore).

[52] Delivery to the wrong party, which will constitute misdelivery and conversion.

[53] (1870) LR 4 HL 317 (UK HL), discussed above under the heading 'History of Bill of Lading'.

[54] *Motis Exports Ltd v Dampskibsselskabet AF 1912 Aktieselskab and Aktieselskabet Dampskibsselskabet Svendborg* [2000] 1 All ER (Comm) 91, [2000] 1 Lloyd's Rep 211, [1999] All ER (D) 1490 (EW CA).

[55] *Glyn Mills Currie & Co v The East and West India Dock Co* (1882) 7 App Cas 591, [1881–5] All ER Rep 674 (UK HL).

[56] *The Jian He* [2000] 1 SLR 8 (SG CA).

[57] *Motis Exports Ltd v Dampskibsselskabet AF 1912 Aktieselskab and Aktieselskabet Dampskibsselskabet Svendborg* [2000] 1 All ER (Comm) 91, [2000] 1 Lloyd's Rep 211, [1999] All ER (D)

The holder of the bill need not necessarily be the owner of the cargo. A buyer may commonly pledge the bill to a bank that finances the purchase. In such a case, the bill will be indorsed to the order of the bank. It is not uncommon for a bill to be issued to the order of the bank. The bank, in such cases, as the lawful holder, will have the constructive possession, although the ownership, as per the intention of the parties, can be with the buyer.[58] The bank will, in the exercise of the right to constructive possession, collect and sell the cargo or sell the bill of lading if the buyer defaults in payment to the bank or becomes insolvent. Hence, the possessory rights take precedence over the proprietary rights in the case of bills of lading.

The fact that the bill of lading passes constructive possession facilitates it to be pledged and financing. In *Official Assignee of Madras v Mercantile Bank of India Ltd*,[59] a buyer pledged railway receipts of groundnuts in transit to its bank. The practice was that the bank would, upon arrival of the goods, indorse and return the receipts to the buyer on certain terms to enable the latter to present the receipts to the railway for collection of the goods. While the goods were in transit, the buyer became insolvent and all its assets became vested in the insolvency administrator.[60] The insolvency administrator claimed entitlement to the goods, and when they were sold by order of the court so that they will be divisible among the creditors. The bank claimed its priority interest over the goods and later the proceeds, as the pledgee or equitable chargee. The Privy Council held that the railway receipts were documents of title (in the sense that it conferred the possessory right on the holder of the receipts).[61] The bank was pledgee and equitable chargee of the goods. The insolvency administrator merely stood in the borrower's shoes and was bound by the pledge and equitable charge for value. The goods were not assets divisible among creditors, as they were pledged to the bank. The insolvency administrator was not entitled to the proceeds.

The Federal Court in Malaysia dealt with a similar situation in an interim application but arrived at a contrary decision in *Bangkok Bank Limited v Wiel Brothers Cotton Inc*.[62] In this case, the bank was holding the bill of lading issued to its order. A third party secured a judgment against the buyer and obtained an injunction to freeze the assets of the buyer, namely the cargo under the bill still in transit at that time, to satisfy the judgment debt. The bank applied for leave[63] to intervene in the injunction proceedings with a view to an order to enable the bank to present the bill

---

1490 (EW CA). The same is true when a carrier delivers against a stolen pin code: *MSC Mediterranean Shipping Company SA v Glencore International AG* [2017] EWCA Civ 365, [2017] 2 All ER (Comm) 881, [2017] 2 Lloyd's Rep 186, [2017] All ER (D) 02 (Jun) (EW CA).

[58] Ownership is transferred only as intended: Section 17 of the UK Sale of Goods Act 1979.

[59] [1935] AC 53, 104 LJPC 1, 40 Com Cas 143, 4 LDAB 462, [1934] All ER Rep 237, 152 LT 170 (PC on appeal from India).

[60] Known as 'official assignee'.

[61] By specific reference to the *then* Section 178 of the Indian Contracts Act 1872, which provided "A person who is in possession of any goods, or of any bill of lading order for delivery, or any other document of title to goods, may make a valid pledge of such goods, or documents ...".

[62] [1977] 2 MLJ 134 (MY FC).

[63] Permission.

and collect the cargo. The High Court refused to allow the bank to present the bill and receive the cargo (unless the bank furnishes a bank guarantee for a certain amount). It directed the bank to file interpleader proceedings, with the bank as the plaintiff[64] and the third party as the defendant. The bank did not furnish the bank guarantee and appealed to the Federal Court. In the meantime, goods were sold by the sheriff and proceeds deposited into the court. The Federal Court upheld the decision, whilst by that time the goods were already sold by the sheriff and hence that part of the order was spent. This decision will not be welcomed, as it undermines the function of the bill of lading as a document conferring the right to possession, the ability of the holder of the bill to pledge it and trade certainty related to bills of lading. When ordering interpleader proceedings, the court did not sufficiently consider the bank's own interest in the goods as the financier, as opposed to any interest of the third party and the buyer, as well as the bank's immediate right to the goods. The court also did not sufficiently consider that the goods were pledged to the bank and the interest of any judgment creditor over the assets of the buyer was subject to the bank's interest in these goods as a pledgee and equitable chargee for value. It is dubious whether this decision represents the right law.[65] The decision of the Privy Council in *Official Assignee of Madras v Mercantile Bank of India Ltd* is to be preferred to this. The function of 'constructive possession' has somewhat confusingly has been labelled as 'document of title'.

'Transferability' Function

The function of 'transferability' function is dealt with later in this chapter. It is also called the function of 'negotiability'. There is some controversy over the choice of terminology, which is also dealt with later in this chapter.

2.2.3.3 Evidence of Contract of Carriage and Its Transferability

In addition to being a document of receipt and a transferable document conferring the constructive possession on the holder of the bill of lading, it also serves as the evidence of a contract of carriage. Usually, the standard terms of the contract will be set out in small-sized print at the back of the bill.

A question that arose in connection with the contract was whether its terms could be relied on by a transferee of the bill. This question arose because the holder is not privy to the contract, on the face of it, and hence will be barred by the doctrine of 'privity of contract'. However, after the case of *Carlill v Carbolic Smoke Ball*

---

[64] Claimant.

[65] In some way, there was not much choice of substance to the Federal Court, since the essential part of the High Court order as to entitlement of the bank to possession of the goods were already spent and the proceeds of sale was safe in the court. This might have induced the Federal Court to maintain the interim order made by the High Court even if it was not rightly made. The option of applying for summary judgement was always open to the bank once the interpleader proceedings have commenced.

Company,[66] where the concept of the unilateral contract was recognised, this question should have become a non-issue by the end of the 19th century. The concept has been codified in many Commonwealth countries, including Malaysia,[67] that has Contract Act modelled on the Indian Contract Act 1872.[68] The bill of lading, by intention, is an offer by the carrier to be bound by its terms to anyone who purchases or otherwise deals with the underlying goods and receives the bill in due course by indorsement or otherwise legally recognised methods such as the delivery of the bill in the case of a bearer will. Accordingly, within the *Carlill v Carbolic* principle, it will constitute the agreement between the carrier and the holder of the bill in good faith, i.e. transferability.

Although it is said to be the contract of carriage, that statement is not so accurate as far as the shipper is concerned since the actual contract between the shipper and carrier would have been concluded before the bill of lading came into existence.[69] However, it is the contract of carriage as far as any subsequent transferee of the bill is concerned.

The terms of the contract, evidenced in the bill of lading, are irrebuttable in the case of action between the carrier and a transferee of the bill in good faith, as parol evidence of any other agreement between the shipper and the carrier is not allowed.[70] However, such parol evidence may be allowed when the action is between the shipper and the carrier, in which case, the evidentiary value of the contractual terms in the bill is only *prima facie*.

2.2.4 Shipped Bill v. Received for Shipment Bill

The bill of lading will be marked as a 'shipped' bill[71] if the cargo has been loaded onto the ship. If the cargo was received by the carrier before loading onto the ship such as when received into the warehouse of the carrier, then it will be marked as a 'received for shipment' bill of lading. Once the cargo is loaded onto the ship, it will be annotated 'shipped' so that it will become a 'shipped' bill of lading from that point onward. If cargo is received under a 'received for shipment' bill but not shipped as agreed in the bill, the carrier will be liable to any transferee of the bill for the breach of contract, although the bill does not become a 'shipped' bill.[72]

---

[66] [1892] EWCA Civ 1, [1893] 1 QB 256, [1891–94] All ER Rep 127 (EW CA).

[67] Malaysian Contracts Act 1950.

[68] Section 8. In Malaysia, by the same numbered section in the Malaysian Contracts Act 1950.

[69] See *SS Ardennes (Cargo Owners) v SS Ardennes (Owners)* [1951] 1 KB 55, [1950] 2 All ER 517 (EW HC).

[70] See *Leduc v Ward* (1888) 20 QBD 475, [1886–90] All ER Rep 266 (EW CA).

[71] A shipowner's shipped bill was referred to as 'on board ocean bill of lading' in the contract of carriage in *Ocean Projects Inc v Ultratech Pte Ltd* [1994] 2 SLR 369 (SG CA).

[72] *Playing Cards (Malaysia) Sdn Bhd v China Mutual Navigation Co Ltd* [1980] 2 MLJ 182 (MY FC).

Ordinarily, it is a condition, even if not expressed, in international trade contracts, that the bill of lading must be a shipped and clean one to be good for payment by the buyer or the buyer's bank. In *Diamond Alkali Export Corp v Fl Bourgeois*[73] decided in 1921, it was held that a 'received for shipment' bill was not a good tender under a cif contract.[74] UCP[75] 600[76] requires that a bill of lading must be a 'shipped' one for payment under a letter of credit.

The reason for rejecting 'received for shipment' bill, even if issued by the shipowner or demise charterer, lies in that, if the goods are subsequently never shipped or damaged or lost before shipment, the claim will only be *in personam* against the issuer of the bill, i.e. the contractual carrier, as the UK Senior Courts Act 1981 Section 21(4) requirement that the claim must be *in connection with the ship* for an *in rem* action under Section 20(2)(e) - (r) would not be satisfied. Conversely, when it is a 'shipped' bill, issued by the shipowner or demise charterer, the claim can be *in rem* against the ship, as the ship will be liable to answer for any loss of or damage to goods carried in her by Section 20(2)(g) of the 1981 Act. For this, the ship can be arrested, in which case, usually the Protection and Indemnity (P&I) Club will give an undertaking to pay any award of damages in return for the release of the ship.[77] Accordingly, a 'shipped' bill (issued by the shipowner or demise charterer) is backed by a security, in the sense of the ship, for loss of or damage to the goods. The security function was said in the early 17th century by Malynes[78] as follows:

> … Bills of lading do declare what goods are laden, and bindeth the Master to deliver them well conditioned to the place of discharge, according to the contents of the Charterpartie, *binding himself, his ship*, tackle, and furniture of it, *for the performance thereof*. [emphasis added]

As buyers pay money the strength of the bill as opposed to physical delivery of the goods in the hands of the shipowner, this security was conventionally considered to be an essential element that a bill of lading should encompass. The term 'bill of lading' itself denotes that the goods have been 'laden' (i.e. loaded) on board the ship.

In contrast to the conventional position taken in *The Diamond Alkali*, to some extent, the 'received for shipment' bill of lading is recognised in law now. The Hague and Hague-Visby Rules[79] recognise a 'received for shipment' bill. Section 1(2)(b)

---

[73] [1921] 3 KB 443, [1921] All ER Rep 283 (EW HC).

[74] This does not affect the 'received for shipment' bill being a negotiable document—discussed later in this chapter.

[75] Almost invariably, the banks have adopted standard contract terms drawn by the International Chamber of Commerce (ICC) known as Uniform Customs and Practice for Documentary Credits (UCP) in issuing letters of credit. This is a standard form, meant for voluntary adoption.

[76] UCP 600, Article 20(ii).

[77] Section 20(2)(g) of the UK Superior Courts Act 1981.

[78] See Malynes, '*Consuetudo, vel Lex Mercantoria*', UK, Adam Islip-Anno Dom, 1622: "… Bills of lading do declare what goods are laden, and bindeth the Master to deliver them well conditioned to the place of discharge, according to the contents of the Charterpartie, binding himself, his ship, tackle, and furniture of it, for the performance thereof."

[79] Article III(7).

of the UK Carriage of Goods by Sea Act 1992 seems to assume that a 'received for shipment' bill of lading is a negotiable document.[80] Section 1(2)(a) of the Acts limits the application of Section 1(2)(b) to bills that are transferable by indorsement or, in the case of a bearer bill, by delivery without indorsement. This refers back to the question of negotiability of the bill at common law. Section 1(2) reads[81] as follows:

> References in this Act to a bill of lading—
>
> (a) do not include references to a document which is incapable of transfer either by indorsement or, as a bearer bill, by delivery without indorsement; but
>
> (b) subject to that, do include references to a received for shipment bill of lading.

The Privy Council in *The Marlborough Hill*[82] held that a 'received for shipment' bill was a bill of lading within the meaning of the UK Bills of Lading Act 1855.[83] Based on this, the English High Court in *The Lycaon*[84] considered such a bill to be a transferable document. In this case, the carrier first issued a 'received for shipment' bill and subsequently issued a 'shipped' bill without first securing the return of the former bill. The carrier did not opt to convert the former bill into a 'shipped' bill simply by an annotation. Subsequently, with two bills in circulation, the carrier did not deliver the cargo to any of the claimants and return-carried them to the port of loading and claimed the costs of the return carriage in an interpleader action. The court refused the claim as the carrier was at fault in allowing two bills to be in circulation.

In *Chan Cheng Kum v Wah Tat Bank*,[85] the Privy Council hearing an appeal from Singapore in 1971, recognised the trade custom to hold a mate's receipt to be transferable. A similar decision was reached by the Malaysian High Court in *Sarawak Electricity Supply Corp v MS Shipping Sdn Bhd*,[86] where the court found a 'shipping order' to be a document at that time in that locality because it was used in the ordinary course of business 'over a period of time as proof of the control or possession of the cargo and authorising the possessor to receive the goods represented by the shipping order'. In coming to this conclusion, the court approved a passage from *Ramdas Vithaldasm Durba v Amerchand (S) & Co; Ramdas Vithaldas Durbar v Chhaganlal Pitamber*,[87] where it was said as follows:

---

[80] See Section 1(2)(a) and (b).

[81] And the Singapore Bills of Lading Act.

[82] *The Ship "Marlborough Hill" v Alex Cowan and Sons Limited, and Others* [1921] 1 AC 444 (PC on appeal from NSW).

[83] Predecessor to the UK Carriage of Goods by Sea Act 1992, that rendered bills of lading negotiable. This point was decided with the result, in that case, that it was the effect of the 'received for shipment' bill under UK Admiralty Court Act 1861.

[84] *Elder Dempster Lines v Ishag (The Lycaon)* [1983] 2 Lloyd's Rep 548 (EW HC).

[85] [1971] 1 Lloyd's Rep 439, [1971] 1 MLJ 177 (PC on appeal from Singapore).

[86] [2000] 5 MLJ 721 (MY HC in Sarawak).

[87] (1916) 85 LJPC 214 at 215.

> [W]henever any doubt arises as to whether a particular document is a 'document showing title' or a document of title' to goods ... the test is whether the document in question is used in the ordinary course of business as proof of the possession or control of goods, or authorising or purporting to authorise, either by endorsement or by delivery, the possessor of the document to transfer or receive the goods thereby represented.

Recognition of shipped bills of lading as a transferable document at common law itself traces back to trade custom to that effect.[88] Interestingly, Lord Devlin, in a lecture paper,[89] observed the relationship between the merchant's commercial practice and commercial law as follows:

> The law merchant ... were designed to give ... simple justice according to the custom of merchants. By the 17th century it was established that the custom of merchants was part of the common law. Such custom is after all no more than a rule which merchants informally make for their own conduct and in theory therefore commercial law ought to be a reflection of the constantly changing ideas of conduct which merchants may have.

In the case of 'received for shipment' bills, they have gained a commercial status as a document representing the possession of the goods and as transferable. It must be observed that the question of whether the goods have been laden does not affect the basic functions of the bill, namely as a receipt, document conferring constructive possession and evidence of contact of carriage. Notably, it does not affect the 'constructive possession' function because the carrier has the 'actual possession' and has given an undertaking to deliver to the holder of the bill. Hence, what is affected in the case of a 'received for shipment' bill is the security, by the ship, for loss of or damage to the goods. Accordingly, conceptually, 'received for shipment' bills are not derogative of the basic functions of the bill of lading and should be treated as such. A 19th-century author on maritime law, Robert Desty,[90] emphasised these two functions, namely, the 'actual possession' and 'undertaking', as the core elements of transferability of the bill of lading in the following words:

> When goods have been set apart in the hands of a third person, who has undertaken to deliver them to the consignee, and the latter has advanced or accepted upon the faith of such arrangement, a special property vests in the consignee. There is a mixed possession, actual possession in the carrier, and an implied possession in the owner. There is a mixed possession, actual possession in the carrier, and an implied possession in the owner.

However, the question of whether it is a good tender under a contract is one of construction in each case, which must be guided by the intention of parties and trade usage whilst it will not be good tender when the payment is by letter of credit subject to UCP 600.[91]

---

[88] *Lickbarrow v Mason* (1794) 5 TR 683, 101 ER 380 (EW HC).

[89] Devlin, 'The Relationship between Commercial Law and Commercial Practice', *The Modern Law Review*, vol. 14, no. 3, July 1951.

[90] Robert Desty, '*Manual of the Law relating to Shipping and Admiralty*', (San Francisco, Section Whitney, 1879), chap. X.

[91] UCP 600, Article 20(a)(ii).

2.2.5 *Bill of Lading Issued by NVOCs*

Conventionally, a bill was only issued by a shipowner or a disponent shipowner (i.e. demise charterer). In either case, the ship will be liable *in rem* to answer any cargo claim for any claim for loss of or damage to goods carried in the ship.[92] However, over the last century, a commercial practice developed whereby non-vehicle owning carriers (NVOCs), such as freight forwarders, have been issuing sea carriage documents labelled 'bill of lading'. They may be styled as 'house' bill of lading. A 'combined transport' bill of lading may also be one issued by an NVOC. It may not be apparent on the face of the bill whether it is an NVOC's bill and a perusal of the bill may be required to determine this. There are both legal and commercial issues with NVOC's bills.

The NVOC, having issued its bill to the shipper, will in turn make respective carriage contract with the actual carrier.[93] A ground of objection to such bills, even if annotated 'shipped',[94] is that the contractual carrier has never acquired physical possession of the cargo and hence cannot give constructive possession to the lawful holder of the bill.

Spectra International plc v Hayesoak Ltd,[95] decided by the English County Court, supports the proposition that one may become the bailee of cargo without taking physical possession of the cargo, as long as he is able to instruct the one having physical possession. However, this will not accurately relate to the question of whether a bill issued by NVOC is a document of entitlement to possession and thus transferable. Similarly, through bills in which the principal carrier may be an NVOC in respect of some legs of the sea voyage have been recognised by UCP 600[96] for payment.

Some argue that these NVOC's bills have at least commercially achieved the status of negotiability. This argument does not have merit as it will be a legal impossibility for NVOC's bills to achieve any true status as a bill of lading. This is because the NVOC's bill does not have an essential characteristic of the bill of lading, namely, a document conferring constructive possession.[97] In *Jones v European & General Express Co Ltd*,[98] Rowlatt J emphasised the functions of 'possession' and 'undertaking', when ruling that freight forwarders are not carriers, as follows:

> It must clearly be understood that a forwarding agent is not a carrier; he does not obtain the possession of the goods; he does not undertake the delivery of them at the other end.

---

[92] See Sections 20(2)(g) and 21(4) of the UK Senior Courts Act 1981.

[93] Comparatively, the court in *The Maheno* [1977] 1 Lloyd's Rep 81 (NZ SC) did not consider a through bill issued by a NVOC to be a document of title.

[94] Indeed, only the shipowner (disponent shipowner) can properly confirm or acknowledge 'shipped'.

[95] [1997] 1 Lloyd's Rep 153 (EW County Court).

[96] UCP 600, Article 20(c)(i).

[97] See *Barber v Meyerstein* (1870) LR 4 HL 317 (UK HL).

[98] (1920) 4 Ll L Rep 127 at 127 (EW HC).

The 'constructive possession' function is tied to the 'undertaking to deliver' characteristic. When a carrier having possession of the goods undertakes to deliver, the law considers that the person entitled under the undertaking, which is the holder of the bill of lading in the context here, has the constructive possession, i.e. the right to claim possession of the goods from the carrier. In the absence of such possession by the carrier, the undertaking to deliver does not have its value. It is this 'undertaking' that facilitates the merchants trading the goods in transit without sight based only on the carriage document issued by the carrier. 'Bill of lading' is not a mere label, it is a character. As an NVOC's bill cannot give constructive possession, it is not a bill of lading.

It follows that an NVOC's bill is not transferable as it does not represent possession of the goods. The bill cannot confer the constructive possession because the issuer of the bill does not have the actual possession. One himself not having an actual possession cannot give anyone by his document a right to claim against him the possession. A right to demand possession can only exist against one having actual possession.[99] To say otherwise will be illusory. The NVOC's bill has no more value than as a contract between the shipper and the NVOC, enforceable in an action directly between them only, by the doctrine of privity of contract. The proposition that only a bill of lading issued by a shipowner is a true bill of lading is supported authorities such as *The Julia*.[100] Robert Desty[101] emphasised the 'actual possession' by the carrier as an inevitable ingredient of the bill of lading in these words:

> There is a mixed possession: actual possession in the carrier, and an implied possession in the owner.

Under the UK Carriage of Goods by Sea Act 1992 Act, and its predecessor UK Bills of Lading 1885 Act, the contractual rights cannot be transferred unto another, in the case of an NVOC bill, as it is not in the first place a bill of lading. Both these Acts require it to be a 'bill of lading' in the first place for the rights under it to be transferred. No statute or convention has defined a bill of lading, hence one must go back to common law for the definition of the bill of lading. It cannot be escaped that it will be a bill of lading only if it embeds the three functions, namely: receipt, constructive possession and evidence of the contract of carriage.

There are more practical reasons for why NVOC's bills cannot give constructive possession. First, it will not be logical that there are two separate conferring constructive possession unto two separate persons for the same cargo, one issued by the NVOC to the end-shipper and another issued by the shipowner to the NVOC. Second, the duty of the shipowner will be to deliver the cargo only to the person

---

99 See *Primetrade AG v Ythan Ltd (The Ythan)* [2005] EWHC 2399 (Comm) at [68] [70], [2006] 1 All ER 367, [2006] 1 All ER (Comm) 157, [2006] 1 Lloyd's Rep 457, [2005] All ER (D) 05 (Nov) (EW HC).

100 *Comptoir d'Achat et de Vente du Boerenbond Belge S/A v Luis de Ridder Ltda (The Julia)* [1949] AC 293, (1948) 82 Ll L Rep 270 (UK HL).

101 Robert Desty, '*Manual of the Law relating to Shipping and Admiralty*', (San Francisco, S. Whitney, 1879), chap. X.

presenting the bill issued by it, and it will be inconsistent to say that any other person holding any other bill has the right of possession of the cargo. Hence, only a document issued by the shipowner can rightly give constructive possession and operate as a document of entitlement to possession of the goods and thus be transferable i.e. a bill of lading.

The Malaysian High Court in *Malayan Banking Bhd v Punjab National Bank*[102] accepted a bill, seemingly issued by a freight forwarder as a sufficient bill of lading. However, there is not sufficient reasoning in the judgment to support this conclusion, and the validity of the judgment on this point is highly dubious. In many cases, the question of whether an NVOC bill is a bill of lading within the common law has not been argued, even if that case concerned an NVOC bill.[103] The Court of Appeal[104] reversed the overall decision of the High Court, where it observed that the classical common law cases about bills of lading are largely about ocean bills, meaning shipowner's bills as opposed to NVOC's bills. The court also observed that the 'security' provided by an NVOC bill was inferior to the security provided by a shipped bill issued by the shipowner. However, to say it more accurately, there is no security in an NVOC bill save that an *in personam* claim against the NVOC can be taken.

The UCP 600 recognises a bill of lading to be issued by a carrier, owner (which means the shipowner), master or charterer (in the case of a charterparty bill, i.e. a bill subject to a charterparty).[105] The word 'carrier' is not defined in the UCP 600.[106] Again, when Article 22 permits a charterparty bill to be authenticated by a charterer, it does not limit it to a bill with a demise clause or an identity of carrier clause which will render it a shipowner's bill. If the 'carrier' is interpreted widely to refer to any contractual carrier, it will include NVOCs such as freight forwarders. However, if it is interpreted narrowly to refer only to the actual carrier who carries, then the reference will only be to the shipowner/disponent shipowner.[107] Whichever the approach is taken, it is sustainably arguable that only a shipowner's/disponent shipowner's bill is allowed by Article 20 of the UCP 600 because it is about issuance of a 'bill of lading', which by its very characteristics requires it to be issued by on or behalf of the shipowner/disponent shipowner. The same school of thought will afford a meritorious argument in case of Article 22 of the UCP 600 to restrict the authority given to the charterer to sign the bill of lading to signing a bill of lading with a demise clause/identity of carrier clause. Article 20(c) of the UCP 600 allows payment upon a bill of lading that envisages or allows transshipment. Again, for reasons said above, this can be narrowly interpreted to allow only a collective through bill as opposed

102 [2018] MLJU 1716 (MY HC).

103 E.g. *Minmetals South-East Asia Corp Pte Ltd v Nakhoda Logistics Sdn Bhd* [2019] 3 CLJ 19, [2018] 6 MLJ 152 (MY CA).

104 *Punjab National Bank v Malayan Banking Berhad* [2020] 1 LNS 232, [2020] 5 MLJ 732 (MY CA).

105 UCP 600, Articles 20 and 22.

106 See UCP 600, Articles 2 and 3.

107 Demise charterer.

to true or false through bills. It must be noted here that BIMCO forms of bills of lading, which do not have a demise clause or identity of carrier clause, recognises the possibility of an NVOC issuing the bill.[108] Even if an NVOC bill is recognised contractually by the form of the bill or for payment under a letter of credit,[109] that does not turn what is not a bill of lading, in law, into a bill of lading.

Comparatively, in the UCP 500,[110] Article 23 was the corresponding provision to the current Article 20 in the UCP 600. The Article 23 was entitled '*Marine/Ocean* Bill of Lading' and allowed the bill of lading to be signed by or on behalf of the *carrier or master*[111] only. The reference to 'ocean bill' in the heading arguably reinforced that the bill must be issued by the shipowner. The corresponding provision to the current Article 22 in the UCP 600 was Article 25 in the UCP 500, which permitted, in the case of a charterparty bill, only a bill of lading signed by or on behalf of *the master or the owner* but not the charterer.

Bills of lading issued by NVOCs on their own right are an anathema to the carriage of goods by sea and have caused numerous problems.[112] Such bills were not known a century ago but have come into the marketplace only recently. They are not bills of lading in the true sense[113] and are not transferable, but at best, they are merely contracts of carriage between the shipper and the freight forwarder, actionable only between them. Entitling them as a 'bill of lading' is deceptive.

Bills of lading issued by NVOCs on their own right are an anathema to the carriage of goods by sea and have caused severe commercial problems.[114] Such bills were not known a century ago but have come into the marketplace only recently over a century. They are not bills of lading in the true sense[115] and are not transferable, but at best, they are merely contracts of carriage between the shipper and the NVOC, actionable only between them. Entitling such bills as a 'bill of lading', with or without qualifications as 'house' bill of lading.[116]

---

[108] E.g. BIMCO CONGENBILL 2016, cl. 6(a); BIMCO CONLINEBILL 2016, cl. 15(a).

[109] Which is a matter between the seller and the buyer/buyer's bank.

[110] The predecessor to UCP 600.

[111] Who represents the shipowner or disponent shipowner.

[112] See *Minmetals South-East Asia Corp Pte Ltd v Nakhoda Logistics Sdn Bhd* [2019] 3 CLJ 19, [2018] 6 MLJ 152 (MY CA); *Malayan Banking Bhd v Punjab National Bank* [2018] MLJU 1716 (MY HC).

[113] John S Mo, 'Forwarder's Bill and Bill of Lading', *Asia Pacific Law Review*, vol. 5, no. 2 (Summer 1997): 96–110. This article was referred to in *Punjab National Bank v Malayan Banking Berhad* [2020] 1 LNS 232, [2020] 5 MLJ 732 (MY CA).

[114] See *Minmetals South-East Asia Corp Pte Ltd v Nakhoda Logistics Sdn Bhd* [2019] 3 CLJ 19, [2018] 6 MLJ 152 (MY CA); *Malayan Banking Bhd v Punjab National Bank* [2018] MLJU 1716 (MY HC).

[115] John S Mo, 'Forwarder's Bill and Bill of Lading', *Asia Pacific Law Review*, vol. 5, no. 2 (Summer 1997): 96–110. This article was referred to in *Punjab National Bank v Malayan Banking Berhad* [2020] 1 LNS 232, [2020] 5 MLJ 732 (MY CA).

[116] See Arun Kasi, "Freight Forwarders' Bill of Lading: Are they Bills of Lading?", THAC's Newsletter, No. 3, December 2020, p. 2, where the discussion herein also appears.

2.2.5.1 Combined Transport Bill of Lading and NVOC Bills

Combined transport is multimodal transport,[117] involving more than one mode of transport. It is common that a non-sea mode may be joined with a sea mode in a carriage contract. For example, a contract for carriage of containerised cargo by sea will commonly involve carriage from the door of the consignor to the door of the consignee (i.e. 'door to door' carriage contract), involving land-sea-land transport. In such cases, ordinarily, the bill will be a 'received for shipment' one. The bill will also have columns for 'place of receipt' and 'place of delivery' in addition to the port of loading and port of discharge.[118] Usage of a combined transport bill in containerised cargo is common.

The Hague and Hague-Visby Rules[119] may apply compulsorily to the sea voyage part only.[120] However, the 'period of responsibility' or 'before and after' clause may provide for the application of the Hague or Hague-Visby Rules to the road transport part with such modification as agreed between the parties.[121]

Before the Rules could apply, a difficult question arising is if it is a bill of lading in the first place, as the Rules will only apply if it is a 'bill of lading or any similar document of title'.[122] If the bill does not confer the constructive possession, then it cannot be a bill within the common law meaning of a bill of lading,[123] discussed above in detail. Such a bill will fail the test of a 'bill of lading' when different carriers are to perform different legs, as it will usually be. But it will pass the test if the issuer of the bill was to perform all the legs. The 'constructive possession' will mean the constructive possession from the moment of delivery to the carrier to the moment the carrier is obliged to deliver. If carrier A receives the goods and the delivery is intended to be made by carrier B, then the bill issued by the carrier A cannot give any assurance for delivery. But, there does not seem to be a compelling reason for why the bill should not be treated as such a document if the carrier has possession the goods throughout all the modes of transportation and some periods outside the carriage. The only limitation to this argument, namely the lack of 'security' feature, has been discussed above, when there is no *ship* to answer the claim when a loss or damage happens outside the carriage by the ship.

When the bill does not confer the 'constructive possession', it will not meet the standard of a bill of lading and hence will not be transferable within the *Barber v Meyerstein* principle or the 1992 Act as a bill of lading. However, there is nothing for it to be rendered transferable within the *Carlill v Carbolic* principle.

---

[117] The antonym to it is 'unimodal' bills, in which only one mode of transport is involve, e.g. sea voyage.

[118] See BIMCO MULTIDOC 2016 and BIMCO COMBICONBILL 1995 forms.

[119] In the case of Peninsular Malaysia, Sabah and Sarawak, the Hague Rules.

[120] Section 1(2) of the UK Carriage of Goods by Sea Act 1971; and Articles I(e) and II.

[121] Subject to any compulsory rules applicable for the land-transport legs.

[122] Article I(b), read together with Article II.

[123] *Barber v Meyerstein* (1870) LR 4 HL 317 (UK HL).

UCP 600[124] recognises combined transport bill for payment under a letter of credit. But this cannot affect the 'transferability' status of the bill as a matter of law. The popular standard forms used in connection with combined transport bills are:

(i) UNCTAD[125]/ICC[126] Rules for Multimodal Transport Documents 1992;
(ii) BIMCO COMBICONBILL (latest version 1995); and
(iii) BIMCO MULTIDOC (latest version 2016).

The last two documents above are full standard formats of combined transport bills of lading. They are not any conventions or laws but may be adopted by the parties purely voluntarily. These standard forms declare those bills to be 'negotiable'. But, despite the intention expressed therein to render them negotiable, that does not make it negotiable when it is not so as a matter of law.

All the above standard forms mix 'network solution' and 'uniform solution' to fill the convention gaps in combined transport bills. A network solution means that the mandatory regime applicable to different legs of the voyage will govern the respective legs. A uniform solution means that a uniform regime will apply throughout the voyage. Such a uniform regime has to be the most favourable one of all the available regimes to the lawful holder, as otherwise, the application of the regime will become invalid in respect of legs for which the regime is less favourable than the statutory minimum for that leg.

All the above said three popular standard forms, with a mixture of uniform and network solutions, generally render the contractual carrier responsible from the moment of receipt to the time of delivery, with some exceptions for the period of sea voyage consonant with the Hague and Hague-Visby Rules. They also provide for limitation and exceptions to limitation. They generally allow the carrier to restrict liability for delay and consequential loss to not more than the amount of freight or value of the cargo, whichever is less. In the event of any inconsistency between a mandatory regime and the standard form, of course, the mandatory regime will prevail. Both the BIMCO forms contain Himalaya and circular indemnity clauses.

2.2.6 *Bill of Lading Issued by Time-Charterers*

Bills of lading authenticated by time-charterers, who are NVOCs, will quite commonly have a demise clause or an identity of carrier clause, rendering it a bill issued the shipowner.[127] In such case, it will be a bill of lading in the legal sense and be transferable. In the absence of such a clause, the same consideration applicable to

---

[124] UCP 600, Article 19.

[125] 'United Nations Conference on Trade and Development'.

[126] 'International Chamber of Commerce'.

[127] Although they are not seen in the popular forms of charterparty bill of lading such as the BIMCO CONGENBILL 2016.

NVOC bills will apply to a pure charterer's bill and for the same reasons, it cannot be a document conferring constructive possession and thus cannot be transferable.

For completeness, there is no problem with a bill issued by a demise charterer, who will be the disponent owner of the ship. In the case of such a bill, an admiralty action *in rem* will be available against the ship.[128] The key difference between a time charterer's bill and a demise charterer's bill, for this purpose, is that in the case of the former the charterer is not in direct control of the master and over the carriage, whilst in the latter, the charterer is.

2.2.7 *Through Bill of Lading*

With a traditional ocean bill of lading, cargo is carried from the port of loading to the port of discharge by a single sea voyage. However, it is common nowadays that the carriage from the port of loading to the port of destination is performed by more than one sea voyage with transshipment at an intermediate port. A bill issued for a carriage performed by more than one leg of a sea voyage is called a 'through' bill. There are three types of through bills.

2.2.7.1 Pure and False Through Bills

First is a 'pure' through bill. In this, the principal carrier, who enters into a carriage contract with the shipper, will undertake responsibility for the entire voyage. The carrier will perform carriage by more than one leg of carriage. It will perform one or more of the legs on its own and may subcontract the carriage of some legs with on-carriers. For the sub-contracted parts, the principle carrier will be in the position of NVOC.

The second is a 'false' through bill. In this, the principal carrier effects one or more of the legs of the carriage. For the other legs, the principal carrier merely acts as a freight forwarder[129] (usually as agent for the shipper) and arranges carriage contracts with other on-carriers. The duty of the principal carrier is limited only to exercising reasonable care in appointing competent on-carriers for the other legs.

In the case of a pure through bill and false through bill, the on-carrier will issue a bill to the principal carrier, i.e. a transshipment bill. The transshipment bill may be made straight to the principal carrier or its order. If it is made straight to the principal carrier, then it will usually state that delivery will be made against presentation of the through bill. The transshipment bill may also be a sea waybill, in which event

---

[128] Section 20(2)(g) of the UK Superior Courts Act 1981.

[129] A freight forwarder will usually be an agent for the shipper when he merely arranges the carriage contract and earns a commission therefor. However, occasionally the forwarder will be the principle when he imposes on the shipper an all-in-all charge. It is unlikely that the forwarder will be the agent of any on-carrier. Generally, freight forwarders can be compared to travel agents.

the second carrier will not be entitled to rely on the Hague or Hague-Visby Rules protection except to the extent the same is contractually incorporated. Whichever type of bill is issued by the on-carrier to the principal carrier, the end consignee will, in practice, present the through bill, at the discharge port, to the principal carrier's agent, who will arrange the goods to be delivered by the last carrier to the end consignee.

Whether such a through bill is a bill of lading and is transferable is a difficult question. In the case of a pure through bill, first, it has to be determined, on the face of the bill, whether the carriage at different legs were all intended to be performed by the same shipowner who issued the bill. If so, the bill must be a bill of lading and transferable, as it will satisfy all the requirements of a bill of lading, namely: receipt, constructive possession and evidence of the contract of carriage.

However, if it was not intended that the shipowner will perform all the legs, then at some point, including possibly at the delivery point, the constructive possession will break. Similarly, there will be a break in the receipt function too. Under the Hague-Visby Rules say that the receipt acknowledged in the bill is conclusive evidence against the carriage at the suit of the transferee of the bill. This essentially assumes that the receipt, i.e. the bill of lading, was issued by the shipowner who performed the entire carriage. In such case, it cannot be a bill of lading and hence not be transferable.

In the case of a false bill, quite plainly, the carriage will be done by more than one shipowner, hence necessarily a break in the receipt and constructive possession functions. The obligation of the on-carrier will only be to deliver according to any bill that it has issued to the principal carrier. This will render the principal bill held by the holder valueless to claim delivery from the on-carrier at the destination port. Accordingly, if it appears on the face of the bill that it is intended to be a false bill, then it cannot be a bill of lading and hence cannot be a transferable document.

The Maheno[130] will to some extent support the above proposition, where the court was of the view that a through bill of lading issued by an NVOC, a freight forwarder, was not a bill of lading in the true sense. UCP 600[131] recognises a through bill of lading as a good tender in respect of the entire carriage. This practice cannot, as a matter of law, affect the status of the bill concerning possessory right and hence transferability.

Commonly, a pure through bill will often contractually incorporate the Hague or Hague-Visby Rules and contain 'Himalaya' and 'circular indemnity' clauses to extend the protection available to the principal carrier under the Rules to the on-carriers. A Himalaya clause will say that the on-carriers are entitled to the same protection and the circular indemnity clause will say that the lawful holder of the bill undertakes to the principal carrier that the lawful holder will not bring an action against the on-carriers on terms more favourable to the lawful holder than it would have been the case had the lawful holder taken the action against the principal carrier. However, if the Hague-Visby Rules apply, the on-carrier, as long as it issued a bill

---

130 *The Maheno* [1977] 1 Lloyd's Rep 81 (NZ SC).

131 UCP 600, Article 20(c)(i).

of lading to the principal carrier, will be protected by the Hague-Visby Rules despite that the action was in tort rather than under the bill of lading contract.[132]

A question that arises in conjunction with the above is about 'liberty to transship' clauses appearing in bills of lading, such as BIMCO CONLINEBILL 2016 form.[133] Such a clause does not by itself indicate that the goods will be transshipped. Nor does it indicate that in the event of a transshipment, a different carrier will perform the transshipped leg. Equally, it does not indicate that the transshipped leg will be performed by the principal shipowner. Arguably, as the document was issued as a 'bill of lading' by a shipowner, it should necessarily mean that any transshipped leg must be performed by the shipowner, as there is no authorisation for the principal shipowner to deliver the goods unto another shipowner to perform any transshipped leg. If this argument is accepted, then liberty clauses, or event clauses that says there will be a transshipment, will not disqualify the bill from being a bill of lading and hence transferable, unless there is something to indicate that a different shipowner will or may be engaged. This is a matter of construction of the bill of lading contract, and it does not appear that there is any reported case on this point.

UCP 600[134] allows a liberty clause or even a clause stating goods will be transshipped, even if the letter of credit prohibits transshipment, in the case of containerised cargo.

In *Mayhew Foods Ltd v Overseas Containers Ltd*,[135] a bill of lading was issued for loading in a UK port and discharge in a Saudi Arabian port. The bill of lading gave the carriers *liberty* to transship. The cargo was transshipped at a port in France. It was held by the English High Court that the Hague-Visby Rules applied throughout the carriage including the waiting period in the French port. In this case, it was treated that pure through bills with the liberty to transship was a document of title, hence the Hague-Visby Rules applied. Taking the facts of this case a step further, a through bill may state that the carriage will be by transshipment, as opposed to merely stating that the carrier has the *liberty* to transship.

2.2.7.2 Collective Through Bill

The third is a 'collective' through bill. In this, the principal carrier contracts on its own behalf for one or more of the legs of carriage. For other legs, it acts as an agent for the on-carriers. There will be no separate bills issued by the on-carriers, as the collective through bill incorporates the 'bill' of all the carriers in the same single document. By this structure, all the respective carriers become directly liable, as principals, under the bill to the shipper/any subsequent transferee of the bill. The

---

132 Articles I(b) and 4*bis*(1); *Pyrene Co Ltd v Scindia Navigation Co Ltd* [1954] 2 QB 402, [1954] 2 All ER 158, [1954] 2 WLR 1005, [1954] 1 Lloyd's Rep 321 (EW HC) (the common law position).

133 Cl. 7.

134 UCP 600, Article 20(c)(ii).

135 [1984] 1 Lloyd's Rep 317 (EW HC).

different legs can be subject to different rules or laws as the respective loading ports will be different.[136]

The bill can be treated as separate bills issued by the respective carriers. There is no difficulty in the bill giving constructive possession, as the bill is deemed issued by the respective carrier in possession of the goods for the respective legs. The last on-carrier will have the delivery obligation. However, the difficulty with such bills is with the 'receipt' function. The receipt was only issued by the principal carrier at the time of the first-point loading. Subsequently, there is no receipt issued by the on-carrier. One potential way to overcome this difficulty is to irrefutably assume that the on-carriers, by receiving the goods without any objection, have accepted the receipt as stated in the bill. If this argument is accepted, the cargo claimant will be able to take action, under the Hague-Visby Rules,[137] against the last on-carrier making the delivery in case of any damage or short delivery, as it is deemed he received the goods as stated in the receipt. In such a case, the on-carrier can hold any other carrier actually responsible for the loss or damage liable in indemnity. There is no compelling reason to dismiss this argument. On this basis, the collective bill will likely be a bill of lading and hence be transferable.

If the action is not under the Hague-Visby Rules but in negligence, then likely the action must lie against the carrier who damaged the goods. For the purpose of such an action, it cannot matter who the actual owner of the goods was at the time of the damage or loss, but the latest owner should be able to take the action, as there will be sufficient proximity between any on-carrier and the ultimate owner of the goods at the time of delivery within the *Donoghue v Stevenson*[138] neighbourhood principle.[139] In the case of an action in conversion[140] for misdelivery, that must lie against the last on-carrier who misdelivered, unless some other on-carrier or the principal carrier committed the misdelivery before the goods reached the final destination. An action may be taken in bailment by the owner of the goods at the destination port only if he was the holder of the bill at the time the defendant-carrier took charge of the goods.[141]

---

[136] A conflict of laws issue may arise because the single place of issuance of the bill may render a particular rule applicable for the entire carriage, while the different loading ports may call for different rules to apply based on the loading port for the voyage from that port to the next one.

[137] Article III(4).

[138] [1932] AC 562, [1932] All ER Rep 1.

[139] See *Homburg Houtimport BV v Agrosin Private Ltd (The Starsin)* [2003] UKHL 12, [2004] 1 AC 715, [2003] 2 All ER 785, [2003] 2 WLR 711, [2003] 1 All ER (Comm) 625, [2003] 1 Lloyd's Rep 571 [2003] All ER (D) 192 (Mar) (UK HL).

[140] A tort.

[141] Discussed in more detail in Chap. 4.

2.2.7.3 Convention Gap

When the cargo is in the intermediate port warehouse for transshipment, no mandatory rules may cover that period, unless contractually agreed. This is called a period of 'convention gap'.

Suppose that the port of loading is in Malaysia and the port of transshipment is in the UK and the port of discharge is in the USA, and the bill is issued in Malaysia which expressly spells out transshipment in the UK. Assuming it is a bill of lading to which the Hague/Hague-Visby Rules apply, the first leg will be subject to the Hague Rules, as the bill was issued in Malaysia, which still statutorily applies the Hague Rules. The second leg will be subject to the Hague-Visby Rules, as the transshipment is from a port in the UK, which statutorily applies the Hague-Visby Rules for shipments from any of its ports. The waiting period at a warehouse in the UK while awaiting transshipment will not be covered by any of the Rules (i.e. convention gap).

2.2.7.4 Meaning of 'Transshipment'

In *APV Hill & Mills (M) Sdn Bhd v AQ-Pacific Wide Sdn Bhd & Anor*,[142] a question arose as to the meaning of 'transshipment', however in the context of a dispute between a seller and purchaser in an international sale and purchase agreement. In this case, the seller agreed to ship equipment from Port Kelang[143] or Singapore to Benghazi,[144] and transshipment was prohibited. The seller arranged for the cargo to be first shipped from Port Kelang to Singapore and then from Singapore to Benghazi. The Malaysian Court of Appeal held that this would be a transshipment. However, if the shipper had got two separate bills of lading issued, one from Port Kelang to Singapore and another from Singapore to Benghazi, then it will be arguable whether it is a transshipment since the seller had the freedom to ship the cargo from Singapore and it might be up to him how he would get the cargo to Singapore, whether by road, plane or a feeder vessel.[145]

---

[142] [2006] 3 MLJ 235 (MY CA).

[143] In Malaysia.

[144] In Libya.

[145] However, the factual matrix of the case was highly different, as the seller procured a false bill stating that the cargo was shipped on board a vessel from Port Kelang when in fact the cargo was never shipped to Benghazi after arriving at Singapore. Accordingly, it was a straightforward case for the court to find for the buyer, as it did, even without deciding the question of meaning of 'transshipment'.

2.2.8 Document of Title v. Document of Possession

It is often said that a bill of lading is a 'document of title'. This description has its root in *Lickbarrow v Mason*, decided at the end of the 18th century.[146] In this case, in some way, the concept of property in the goods and the right to possession to the goods have been mixed up, at least seemingly. Clarity was added by the House of Lords by the third quarter of the 19th century in *Barber v Meyerstein*,[147] whereby it was made clear that a bill of lading, on its own right, is only a document conferring possession, but if parties intend to transfer the property in the goods together with the transfer of the bill, as it often happens, then the property will so be transferred.[148] Robert Desty[149] acknowledged this concept of the bill of lading as:

> The *prima facie* legal effect of a bill of lading is to vest the legal title to the property in the consignee, unless the contrary appears or is shown by extrinsic evidence.

Despite *Barber v Meyerstein*, the popular term to describe bills of lading has remained, and remains, 'document of title'. This term has been and is widely used in legal texts, judgements,[150] statutes[151] and international conventions.[152]

Plainly, a bill of lading is not a document of title, if the word 'title' is assigned the strict meaning of 'ownership'. A few things must be observed here. First, it is a document issued by the carrier. The carrier itself has not had, at any point in time, the title (in the sense of ownership). Hence, a document issued by the carrier cannot give the title. Second, the purpose for which a shipowner issues the document is not to represent the title to the goods but to identify who is entitled to claim delivery from the shipowner, i.e. a '*document of entitlement to delivery*'. Third, the dealing between the shipper/any subsequent transferee of the bill and the carrier is about the carriage only. It has nothing to do with the title. Hence, there is no reason to bind the concept of title with a carriage document. Fourth, delivery of the bill, as between the seller and the buyer, is tantamount to *delivery of the goods* rather than the *passing of the property in the goods*. The bill represents the *possession of the goods* that the carrier actually has (i.e. possessory right) rather than the *title to the goods* (i.e. proprietary right). Observing this, JK Roy[153] said:

---

146 (1794) 5 TR 683, 101 ER 380 (EW HC).

147 (1870) LR 4 HL 317 (UK HL).

148 Both *Lickbarrow* and *Barber* have been discussed in detail above in Chap. 2.2.2.

149 Robert Desty, '*Manual of the Law relating to Shipping and Admiralty*', (San Francisco, S. Whitney, 1879), chap. X.

150 E.g. *MacWilliam (JI) Co Inc v Mediterranean Shipping Co SA (The Rafaela S)* [2005] UKHL 11, [2005] 2 AC 423, [2005] 2 All ER 86, [2005] 2 WLR 554, [2005] 1 All ER (Comm) 393, [2005] 1 Lloyd's Rep 347 (UK HL); *Chan Cheng Kum v Wah Tat Bank* [1971] 1 Lloyd's Rep 439, [1971] 1 MLJ 177 (PC on appeal from Singapore); *Minmetals South-East Asia Corp Pte Ltd v Nakhoda Logistics Sdn Bhd* [2019] 3 CLJ 19, [2018] 6 MLJ 152 (MY CA).

151 E.g. UK Carriage of Goods by Sea Act 1971, Section 1(4).

152 Hague Rules/Hague-Visby Rules, Articles I(b) and III(7).

153 JK Roy, *Analysis of Carver's Carriage of Goods by Sea*, London, Stevens and Sons, 1913, p. 66.

> A *bill of lading is not a document of title in the sense of carrying title with it*, even to a buyer to takes it honestly and for full value. When goods have been shipped by one who has no property in them, and the shipper negotiates the bill of lading, his transferee does not get a title. [emphasis added].

Fifth, the property passes as *intended* by the parties.[154] Ordinarily, the intention may be that the property passes together with the bill, but not necessarily so. The now-repealed UK 1855 Act made it an additional requirement that the property must pass for the contractual rights to pass, making the distinction between the passing of the two quite clear. Similarly, when a bill is pledged to a bank, all that passes is the constructive possession without the title.

Accordingly, all that is meant by the 'document of title' in this context is merely a document of entitlement to claim delivery from the shipowner, i.e. a document conferring constructive possession. It has been said that the 'title' here refers to a special property, i.e. a right to possession. Labelling the bill of lading as a document of title has been sometimes a source of confusion where the courts have mixed up the possessory right (associated with the bill of lading) and the proprietary right (that would be associated with a document of title).[155] The better approach will be to avoid the term 'document of title', that can indeed be a misnomer, and to use the term 'document of constructive possession'.[156]

Any other document having the characteristics of the bill of lading will accordingly be treated and be transferable, even if it is not so labelled.[157] The vice versa is also true. A document does not become a bill of lading merely because it is so labelled. Accordingly, an analysis of the characteristics of the document has to be made to determine if it is a bill of lading.

In line with the above, the Privy Council in *Chan Cheng Kum v Wah Tat Bank*[158] recognised that a mate's receipt would be a document of title in place of the bill of lading when it is proved that by the custom of the trade in the relevant market it was so treated. In this case, in a case of shipment from Sarawak[159] to Singapore, the board found such a custom. However, the board held that the receipt was not a document of title in this case as it was marked 'Not negotiable'. Lord Devlin, delivering the judgment of the court, observed as follows:

> Their Lordships can see no reason in principle why a document of title should not be created by local custom. … It would be repugnant if it were inconsistent with any express term in

[154] Section 17 of the UK Sale of Goods Acts 1972.

[155] See Arun Kasi, 'A Critical Analysis of the Court of Appeal Decision on Misdelivery in Minmetals South-East Asia Corp Pte Ltd v Nakhoda Logistics Sdn Bhd', *The Law Review*, [2020] LR 105. This article was referred to in *Punjab National Bank v Malayan Banking Berhad* [2020] 1 LNS 232, [2020] 5 MLJ 732 (MY CA).

[156] See Arun Kasi, 'Bill of Lading: Document of Title or Possession?', *Journal of The Commonwealth Lawyers' Association*, vol. 30, no. 3, December 2020, p. 27.

[157] *Official Assignee of Madras v Mercantile Bank of India Ltd* [1935] AC 53 (PC on appeal from India).

[158] [1971] 1 Lloyd's Rep 439, [1971] 1 MLJ 177 (PC on appeal from Singapore).

[159] In Malaysia.

> any document it affects, whether that document be regarded as a contract or as a document of title. ... The form of mate's receipt used is similar to a bill of lading and there is no difficulty about treating it as an equivalent. ... Their Lordships can see nothing unreasonable in using the mate's receipt in this case as a document of title. ... The factor that in the end compels them to differ from his conclusion is the presence on the mate's receipt of the words 'Not negotiable'.

Similarly, in *Sarawak Electricity Supply Corp v MS Shipping Sdn Bhd*,[160] the Malaysian High Court recognised a 'shipping order' to be a document of title in the factual matrix of the case. There are statutes recognising other documents as documents of title, such as dock-warrant, warehouse keeper's certificate, wharfinger's certificate, warrant or order for delivery[161] such as railway receipt.[162]

2.2.9 *Negotiability v. Transferability*

The two words, 'negotiable' and 'transferable' has widely been used interchangeably in relation to bills of lading, the former word being more popular. The word 'negotiable' is a little vague one. For instance, UCP 600[163] defines 'negotiation' as 'purchase' in the context of letters of credit. Contrary to that, the Bills of Exchange Act, in the UK defines it as 'transfer'.[164] The Bills of Exchange Act covers bills of exchange, cheques on bankers and promissory notes.

In all these cases, of letter of credit and the bills of exchange, the document has a value on the face of it and it is a monetary value, unlike in the case of a bill of lading. In all these cases, the negotiation has to be for value in order to be effective, unlike in the case of a bill of lading. In all these cases, in effect, by the negotiation, the document will be discounted, unlike in the case of bills of lading. In all these cases, what is sold and purchased is in effect the document itself, whilst in the case of the bills of lading what is sold and purchased are the underlying goods and the bill of lading merely represents the constructive delivery of the goods.

The similarity between the bills of lading and the other documents is that all of them are transferable by the same methods, such as by indorsement and delivery in the case of a 'to order' document and by delivery in the case of a 'bearer' document. The UK Carriage of Goods by Sea Act 1992 uses the word 'transferable' rather than

---

[160] [2000] 5 MLJ 721 (MY HC in Sarawak).

[161] Malaysian Contracts Act 1950, Section 131: "A person who is in possession of any goods, or of any bill of lading, dock-warrant, warehouse-keeper's certificate, wharfinger's certificate, or warrant or order for delivery, or any other document of title to goods, may make a valid pledge of the goods or documents ..."

[162] *Official Assignee of Madras v Mercantile Bank of India Ltd* [1935] AC 53, 104 LJPC 1, 40 Com Cas 143, 4 LDAB 462, [1934] All ER Rep 237, 152 LT 170 (PC on appeal from India).

[163] UCP 600, Article 2.

[164] Section 31 of the UK Bills of Exchange Act 1882. Identical provision is found in the same numbered section in the Malaysian Bills of Exchange Act 1949 and the Singapore Bills of Exchange Act.

'negotiable'. Accordingly, the better and clearer concept to use in connection with the bills of lading is 'transferability' rather than 'negotiability'.

2.2.10 *Transferability of Bills of Lading*

There are two concepts of transferability in relation to bills of lading. One is the common law concept of transferability that has been recognised since *Lickbarrow v Mason*[165] decided in 1974, clarified in *Barber v Meyerstein*[166] decided in 1870. This is about transferability of the bill of lading at common law, with which passes the constructive possession of the goods, i.e. constructive delivery of the goods, enabling action conversion.[167]

The other is transferability of bills of lading for the purpose of transfer of contractual rights under the statute. The relevant statute in the UK is the Carriage of Goods by Sea Act 1992.

It must be observed that both the two regimes of transferability are independent of one another and both co-exist. One is for constructive possession and action in conversion. The other is for contractual action, that will bring in the Hague or Hague-Visby Rules. The parallel existence of two regimes will be clearer when the history of the bill of lading is looked at, dealt with earlier,[168] or the preamble to the UK Bills of Lading 1885 Act[169] that makes reference to the two parallel regimes. It reads as follows:

> WHEREAS by the Custom of Merchants a Bill of Lading of Goods being transferable by Endorsement the Property in the Goods may thereby pass, to the Endorsee, but nevertheless all Rights in respect of the Contract contained in the Bill of Lading continue in the original Shipper or Owner, and it is expedient that such Rights should pass with the Property ...

The statutory scheme has, in essence, adopted the common law scheme of transferability or negotiability as to indorsements, etc. However, the statutory scheme is more detailed than the common law scheme. A court will likely follow the same test of transfer both under the statutory regime and the common law regime.

2.2.10.1 Transfer of Rights (Section 2(1))

Unlike an ordinary contract, the bill of lading contract is transferable through indorsement by the lawful holder of the bill without the need for attornment by the carrier.[170]

---

[165] (1794) 5 TR 683, 101 ER 380 (EW HC).

[166] (1870) LR 4 HL 317 (UK HL).

[167] A tort.

[168] See Chap. 2.2.2.

[169] Now repealed and replaced with the UK Carriage of Goods by Sea Act 1992.

[170] It is taken that there is a *priori attornment*.

This is the same indorsement that transfers the constructive possession. The lawful holder may take action[171] against the carrier as if the lawful holder was a party to the bill. Any arbitration clause by which the original shipper would be bound will also bind any transferee of the bill by virtue of the Section 2(1) of the UK Carriage of Goods by Sea Act 1992, though Section 8(1) of the UK Contracts (Rights of Third Parties) Act 1999 (extending application of the arbitration clause to the third party covered by Section 1) does not apply to contracts for carriage of goods by sea by Section 6(5)(a) of the Act: *Sea Master Shipping Inc v Arab Bank (Switzerland) Ltd* [2018] EWHC 1902, [2018] Bus LR 1798 (EW HC). Originally, the UK Bills of Lading Act 1855,[172] in Section 1, provided for this. Now the UK Carriage of Goods by Sea Act 1992 provides for it in Section 2(1)[173] as follows:

> Subject to the following provisions of this section, a person who becomes—
>
> (a) the lawful holder of a bill of lading;
>
> (b) the person who (without being an original party to the contract of carriage) is the person to whom delivery of the goods to which a sea waybill relates is to be made by the carrier in accordance with that contract; or
>
> (c) the person to whom delivery of the goods to which a ship's delivery order relates is to be made in accordance with the undertaking contained in the order,
>
> shall (by virtue of becoming the holder of the bill or, as the case may be, the person to whom delivery is to be made) have transferred to and vested in him all rights of suit under the contract of carriage as if he had been a party to that contract.[174]

The repealed Section 1 of the UK Bills of Lading Act 1855,[175] provided:

> Every Consignee of Goods named in a Bill of Lading, and every Endorsee of a Bill of Lading to whom the Property in the Goods therein mentioned shall pass, upon or by reason of such Consignment or Endorsement, shall have transferred to and vested in him all Rights of Suit, and be subject to the same Liabilities in respect of such Goods ad if the Contract contained in the Bill of Lading had been made with himself.

Under the 1855 Act, the rights are transferred only upon the passing of property. This was a shortcoming as the banks holding the bill and financing the purchase could not have the contractual rights transferred to itself because there would be no intention

---

171 Contractual.

172 Now repealed and replaced by the Carriage of Goods by Sea Act 1992.

173 Read with Section 5(1).

174 Literally, the Section 2(1) transfers the contractual rights held by the contracting party. In a case where the shipper in the bill of lading is also the charterer of the vessel from the carrier, the bill has no contractual effect in the hands of the charterer. In such cases, a literal interpretation of the section will mean that there is no contractual right to transfer to the lawful holder. However, this section has been purposely interpreted so that the bill, insofar as it represents the contractual function, is treated as a as a contractual document meant to confer the rights thereunder on a holder other than the charterer.

175 Repealed and replaced by the UK Carriage of Goods by Sea Act 1992.

to pass the property to the pledgee. In *Sewell v Burdick*,[176] decided under the 1855 Act, the House of Lords found that by a mere pledge of the bill to the bank, the contractual rights were not transferred to the bank, nor the liability. In this case, the bank that had not taken delivery of the goods was not liable to the carrier under the terms of the bill.

For the purpose of transferability under the statues, it does not matter whether the bill is a 'shipped' one or 'received for shipment' one.[177] Accordingly, if a carrier issues a 'received for shipment' bill and subsequently does not ship as per the bill, it will be liable to the lawful holder of the bill for breach of the contract of carriage evidenced by the bill.[178]

Questions had arisen as to whether any terms agreed between the shipper and the carrier but not recorded in the bill of lading is transferred to a third-party consignee or indorsee. In *Leduc v Ward*,[179] decided under the Bills of Lading 1855 Act, the bill issued by the shipowner did not allow a deviation. However, according to the shipowner, the shipper knew that there would be a deviation by the ship first calling at an intermediate port. The English Court of Appeal held that it was immaterial whether the original shipper knew that there would be a deviation, as the indorsee is only bound by the terms of the bill of lading and not by any parol terms.

The same would be the position under Section 2(1) of the 1992 Act. In *The Michael S*,[180] decided under the 1992 Act, the English High Court held that a parol agreement between the carrier and the shipper to incorporate terms of charterparty into the bill of lading was not binding on the third party holder of the bill. Even in the absence of any construction of Section 1 of the 1855 Act or Section 2(1) of the 1992 Act to support this proposition, the carrier will still be estopped from relying on any parol terms with the original shipper, unless such terms were within the knowledge of the third-party consignee or indorsee at the time of the consignee or indorsee entering into the sale and purchase agreement or acquiring the bill.

When a lawful holder thus gets transferred the contractual rights under a bill of lading, he will be subject to any provision in the bill that binds the exercise of the rights. In *The Kribi*,[181] the court held that a jurisdiction clause in the bill was binding on the lawful holder.

Both 'holder' and 'lawful holder' are defined in Section 5(2) of the 1992 Act. Five points must be noted for a person to become the lawful holder. First, the person must

---

[176] (1884) 10 App Cas 74, [1881–5] All ER Rep 223 (UK HL).

[177] Indeed, Section 1(2)(b) of the UK Carriage of Goods by Sea Act 1992 expressly include 'received for shipment' bills into the definition of a bill of lading for the purpose of transferability. Even without such a provision, as in the case of Malaysia where the UK 1855 Act is largely applicable, a received for shipment bill of lading has been recognised as being transferable.

[178] *Playing Cards (Malaysia) Sdn Bhd v China Mutual Navigation Co Ltd* [1980] 2 MLJ 182 (MY FC).

[179] (1888) 20 QBD 475, [1886–90] All ER Rep 266, (1888) 20 EBD 475 (EW CA).

[180] *Evryalos Maritime Ltd v China Pacific Insurance Co Ltd (The Michael S)* [2001] All ER (D) 325 (Dec) (EW HC).

[181] *OT Africa Line Ltd v Hijazy and Others (The Kribi)* [2001] 1 Lloyd's Rep 76, [2000] All ER (D) 1571 (EW HC).

have physical possession of the bill. Second, he must have acquired such possession by delivery of the bill. Third, in the case of an order bill, it must be indorsed and transferred to him, and in the case of a bearer bill, it must be transferred to him. Fourth, if a person comes to possess the when the bill no longer represents the cargo, that does not stop him from becoming the lawful holder if (i) he so came to possess by virtue of a transaction made when the bill represented the cargo or (ii) the bill is returned to him upon rejection of the bill or goods by another.[182] Fifth and last, the person must have acquired the possession in good faith.[183] Section 5(2) of the UK Carriage of Goods by Sea Act 1992 reads as follows:

> References in this Act to the holder of a bill of lading are references to any of the following persons, that is to say—
>
> (a) a person with possession of the bill who, by virtue of being the person identified in the bill, is the consignee of the goods to which the bill relates;
>
> (b) a person with possession of the bill as a result of the completion, by delivery of the bill, of any indorsement of the bill or, in the case of a bearer bill, of any other transfer of the bill;
>
> (c) a person with possession of the bill as a result of any transaction by virtue of which he would have become a holder falling within paragraph (a) or (b) above had not the transaction been effected at a time when possession of the bill no longer gave a right (as against the carrier) to possession of the goods to which the bill relates;
>
> and a person shall be regarded for the purposes of this Act as having become the lawful holder of a bill of lading wherever he has become the holder of the bill in good faith.

Delivery of a bill has two components. One is tender by the transferor and another is acceptance by the transferee. Hence, if a bill is indorsed in favour of a person and passed to him, but he does not accept it, then he will not become the lawful holder. The following two cases will well demonstrate this. In *The Aegean Sea*,[184] the seller, by mistake, indorsed the bill to on-buyer instead of to the buyer. The seller delivered the bill to the buyer, who forwarded it to the on-buyer. The on-buyer returned it to the seller. The English High Court held that the on-buyer never became the lawful holder of the bill for two reasons. One, he did not accept the bill. Another, it was not indorsed and delivered by the seller to the on-buyer. In *The Erin Schulte*,[185] the seller tendered the bill of lading to the buyer's bank. However, the bank initially rejected the documents on non-compliance grounds but retained the document. Subsequently, the bank retracted and accepted the bill. The English Court of Appeal held that the bank did not become the lawful holder until the bank subsequently accepted the bill.

---

[182] E.g. buyer.

[183] 'Good faith' is what turns the holder into a 'lawful' holder: Section 5(2) of the UK Carriage of Goods by Sea Act 1992.

[184] *Aegean Sea Traders Corpn v Repsol Petroleo SA (The Aegean Sea)* [1998] 2 Lloyd's Rep 39, [1998] All ER (D) 135 (EW HC).

[185] *Standard Chartered Bank v Dorchester LNG (2) Ltd (The Erin Schulte)* [2014] EWCA Civ 1382, [2016] QB 1, [2015] 2 All ER 395, [2015] 3 WLR 261, [2015] 2 All ER (Comm) 362, [2015] 1 Lloyd's Rep 97, [2014] All ER (D) 273 (Oct) (EW CA).

In Singapore, questions as to the Sections 2(1)(a) and 5(2)(a) of the Singapore Bills of Lading Act, which are identical to the same numbered sections in the UK 1992 Act, came before the Court of Appeal in *UCO Bank v Golden Shore Transportation Pte Ltd.*[186] This case involved four shipments of logs from a Malaysian port to an Indian port, payment by way of letters of credit. The buyer arranged its bank to issue the letters of credit. The sellers shipped the cargoes. The shipowner issued bills of lading to the order of the buyer. Seemingly, the sellers were the shippers and accordingly named in the bills of lading. The sellers presented the bills to the sellers' bank together with the other required documents, which the bank forwarded to the buyer's bank for payment. There was no indorsement by the sellers to the seller's bank. There was also no indorsement by the seller's bank to the buyer's bank. The buyer's bank paid. Subsequently, the buyer defaulted in reimbursement to the buyer's bank and the bill was retained by the buyer's bank. The buyer's bank claimed delivery of the goods, as the holder of the bills, from the shipowner. The shipowner was not able to deliver, as there was a misdelivery. Thus, the buyer's bank sued the shipowner. The shipowner applied to strike out the claim, claiming that the buyer's bank was not a lawful holder because the bills were not indorsed by the shipper to the sellers' bank and were not on-indorsed by the sellers' bank to the buyer's bank, alternatively, the bills were not directly delivered by the shippers to the buyer's bank. The court dismissed the application, holding that there was no necessity to so indorse or to make a direct transfer from the shippers, as the named consignee (with 'to order' addition) was the buyer's bank. The court also acknowledged the commercial practice of such indorsement, that the court said was not necessary.

Such an indorsement would have no legal effect. If the buyer's bank transferred the bill to the buyer or any other, then such an indorsement by the buyer's bank and transfer of the bill by the buyer's bank would have been required. The court pointed out that the three conditions required to satisfy Section 5(2)(a) were that (a) the cargo claimant, that is the buyer's bank in this case, was in possession of the bill, (b) it was the named consignee on the bill, and (c) it was in possession of the bill in good faith, all of which were satisfied in this case. The court said that what the Section 2(1)(a) meant by 'lawful' holder is that the holder had come into possession of the bill 'in good faith' and satisfied the Section 5(2) requirements. The court also pointed out that any action available to the buyer's bank against any other party in this connection is not a bar to an action by the buyer's action against the shipowner under the bills of lading.

2.2.10.2 'Spent' Bills and Transfer of Rights (Section 2(2))

The general rule is that a bill must be 'transferred' at a time when the bill represents the cargo, i.e. the right to possession of the cargo.[187] If the ship sinks with a total loss of cargo, the bill cannot be transferred after that. The bill that no longer represents

[186] [2005] SGCA 42, [2006] 1 SLR 1 (SG CA).

[187] Section 2(2) of the UK Carriage of Goods by Sea Act 1992.

the cargo is called a 'spent' bill.[188] However, there are two exceptions to this general rule.[189] One is that the bill is transferred pursuant to a transaction made when the bill still represented the cargo.[190] Another is when the bill returns to the previous holder of the bill as a result of a rejection of the bill or cargo.[191] This is the effect of Section 2(2)[192] of the UK Carriage of Goods by Sea Act 1992, which reads as follows:

> Where, when a person becomes the lawful holder of a bill of lading, possession of the bill no longer gives a right (as against the carrier) to possession of the goods to which the bill relates, that person shall not have any rights transferred to him by virtue of subsection (1) above unless he becomes the holder of the bill—
>
> (a) by virtue of a transaction effected in pursuance of any contractual or other arrangements made before the time when such a right to possession ceased to attach to possession of the bill; or
>
> (b) as a result of the rejection to that person by another person of goods or documents delivered to the other person in pursuance of any such arrangements.

The question of whether the bill of lading represented the cargo at the time of indorsement and delivery to an innocent indorsee arose in a complex factual matrix before the Singapore High Court in *The Dolphina*.[193] In this case, the buyer received the cargo by giving a letter of indemnity to the carrier. Subsequently, he fraudulently indorsed and delivered the bill to his bank. Thereafter he did not settle the dues to the bank, and the latter claimed the cargo from the carrier, by virtue of the bill. The court held that the bank was not the lawful holder as the cargo was not in the hands of the carrier by the time of indorsement and delivery of the bill to the bank.

The rightness of the decision is dubious. When cargo is 'delivered', as opposed to being lost due to sinking etc., otherwise than in exchange for the bill, that will constitute a breach of contract and misdelivery.[194] This is so even if cargo is delivered to the consignee named in an order bill, in the absence of the original bill of lading

---

[188] A 'spent' bill can possibly be defined to mean an 'accomplished' bill, whereby the carrier has delivered cargo against presentation of the bill.

[189] Champerty or transfer of bare right of action is prohibited at common law.

[190] Section 2(2)(a) of the UK Carriage of Goods by Sea Act 1992.

[191] Provided that the principal transaction was made when the bill still represented the cargo: Section 2(2)(b) of the UK Carriage of Goods by Sea Act 1992.

[192] See Section 5(4) of the Act (which applies not only to bills of lading, but also to sea waybills and ship's delivery orders), which provides: "Without prejudice to Sections 2(2) …, nothing in this Act shall preclude its operation in relation to a case here the goods to which a document relates (a) cease to exist after the issue of the document; or (b) they cannot be identified (whether because they are mixed with other goods or for any other reason". Although the Section 5(4)(a) does not bar the operation of the Act in case of transfer of bills after the goods cease to exist, however it does not transfer the rights to the lawful holder of a bill of lading except otherwise than pursuant to Section 2(2) of the Act.

[193] *The Dolphina* [2012] 1 Lloyd's Rep 304, [2011] SGHC 273 (SG HC).

[194] *Chabbra Corporation Pte Ltd v Jag Shakti (Owners) (The Jag Shakti)* [1986] 1 MLJ 197, [1986] AC 337, [1986] 1 All ER 480, [1986] 2 WLR 87, [1987] LRC (Comm) 228, [1986] 1 Lloyd's Rep 1, 130 Sol Jo 51, [1986] LS Gaz R 45 (PC on appeal from Singapore); *Wolff v Trinity Logistics USA Inc*

being produced to the carrier.[195] Hence, arguably, as between the carrier and the innocent bill of lading holder, the bill still represents the cargo and *responsibility* on part of the carrier to deliver it to the lawful holder (i.e. the *right* of the holder of the bill to possession of the cargo). If a carrier were to be able to relinquish its responsibility by a misdelivery, then it would not even need to ask for a letter of indemnity from the person receiving the cargo.

In *The Yue You 902*,[196] also a Singapore case, a bank sued the carrier for misdelivery. The bill was pledged by the buyer to the bank after the misdelivery but under a loan agreement made before the misdelivery. The High Court held that the bill was not spent and that the bank was the lawful holder of the bill and transferee of rights thereunder.[197] Hence, the bank was entitled to take the action against the carrier.[198]

Another complex and interesting case in which the question as to transfer of a bill of lading, after the cargo was lost by an explosion and hence the bill did not represent the cargo, arose in *The Ythan*.[199] Some dangerous cargo was loaded into a ship. Order bill was issued, which the shipper indorsed in blank. The bill was then transferred to the buyer's bank under a letter of credit. While the bill was in the possession of the bank and payment not made yet, an explosion occurred causing total loss of the cargo and the ship. The buyer then instructed the bank to make payment under the letter of credit and to transfer the bill to the buyer's cargo insurers for payment-claim. The buyer's cargo insurers requested the P&I club for security for the claim.

With that set of facts, the shipowner instituted arbitration proceedings against the buyer under the bill of lading for about USD15 million for loss of the ship. It was the shipowner's claim that the buyer was the lawful holder of the bill, to whom the rights under the bill were transferred, under Sections 2(1)[200] and 5(2)(c) of the 1992 Act and that the buyer had taken the liability, under Section 3(1)(b) of the Act,[201] by virtue of the buyer's cargo insurers requesting the P&I club for security for the claim. The court had first to decide if the rights under the bill were transferred to the buyer, and if so, whether liability under the bill fell on the buyer.

[2018] EWCA Civ 2765, [2019] 1 WLR 3997, [2019] All ER (D) 37 (Jan) (EW CA)—Longmore LJ: "It has long been a cardinal principle of the English law of carriage by sea that the carrier should only deliver the goods to a person who presents an original bill of lading. If he delivers to anyone else he is liable for misdelivery."

[195] *The Stettin* (1889) 14 PD 142 (EW HC).

[196] *The Yue You 902* [2019] SGHC 106 (SG HC).

[197] Under Singapore Bills of Lading Act, which is for all practical purposes identical to the UK Carriage of Goods by Sea 1992 Act.

[198] *Standard Chartered Bank v Dorchester LNG (2) Ltd (The Erin Schulte)* [2014] EWCA Civ 1382, [2016] QB 1, [2015] 2 All ER 395, [2015] 3 WLR 261, [2015] 2 All ER (Comm) 362, [2015] 1 Lloyd's Rep 97, [2014] All ER (D) 273 (Oct) (EW CA) will support this position.

[199] *Primetrade AG v Ythan Ltd (The Ythan)* [2005] EWHC 2399 (Comm), [2006] 1 All ER 367, [2006] 1 All ER (Comm) 157, [2006] 1 Lloyd's Rep 457, [2005] All ER (D) 05 (Nov) (EW HC).

[200] Read with Section 2(2)(a).

[201] Transfer of liability under Section 3(1) is discussed in detail later in this chapter. In essence, a holder will only become liable under the bill if he makes a demand for delivery of goods, makes a claim or takes delivery under the bill.

The English High Court answered both questions in the negative. It was not in doubt that at the time the bill was transferred from the hands of the bank to the insurers, the bill no longer represented the cargo. The court held that the bill was not transferred pursuant to any prior trade arrangement but transferred only for purposes of claiming the insurance proceeds. Hence, the buyer did not become the lawful holder of the bill and was not entitled to the rights under the bill under Section 2(1) of the Act. The case did not fall within the Section 2(2)(a) exception to the general rule.

This rendered unnecessary to answer the second question. However, the court went on to answer the second question also in the negative. The court held that a mere request for security is not a claim that will suffice under Section 3(1)(b) of the Act to render any lawful holder liable under the bill. However, the court acknowledged that if the ship was arrested by the buyer, then that would have constituted a claim to burden the buyer with liability under Section 3(1)(b) of the Act. It followed that the buyer was accordingly not subject to the arbitration clause in the bill of lading. In the result, the arbitral award was overturned, and the buyer was relieved of the claim.

A case, in contrast, that fell within the exception to the general rule was *Motis Exports (No. 2)*.[202] In this case, a shipper-consignor transferred the bearer bill of lading to its bank by way of pledge. Subsequently, the sale to the buyer failed after the carrier misdelivered the cargo while the bill was still in the hands of the bank. The bank then transferred back the bill to the shipper. At this time, no doubt, the bill did not represent the cargo. However, under the Section 2(2)(b) exception, the shipper became the holder when the bank returned the bill to the shipper. The English High Court found that the transfer-back, though made after the goods were longer there, was made in good faith. Hence, Section 5(2) of the UK Carriage of Goods by Sea Act 1992 did not prevent the shipper from becoming the lawful holder. Accordingly, the rights under the bill were transferred back to the shipper.

The exceptions in Section 2(2)(a) of the Act applies only if the transfer of the bill, after the bill no longer represented the cargo, was made pursuant to an arrangement made at a time when the bill represented the cargo. Accordingly, in cases where the cargo is delivered to the consignee, before the surrender of the bill of lading, upon undertaking by the consignee to indemnify, the subsequent transfer of the bill will transfer the rights under the bill to the consignee. This is in a marked difference from the position under Section 1 of the UK Bills of Lading Act 1855, now repealed. Under the 1855 Act, the transfer of the bill after delivery of the goods would not transfer the rights under the bill. This was because the property in the goods would have been transferred to the consignee when the goods were delivered before the transfer of the bill to the consignee.[203] This was a troubling shortcoming of the 1855 Act as it was common for carriers to deliver the cargo to the consignee, before the surrender of the bill, upon the consignee's undertaking and agreement to indemnify.

---

[202] (2001) Admiralty Court, 2 Feb 2001 (EW HC).

[203] *Enichem Anic SpA and Others v Ampelos Shipping Co Ltd (The Delfini)* [1990] 1 Ll L Rep 252 (EW CA).

In *The David Agmashenebeli*,[204] the bill of lading was claused. This resulted in the bank refusing payment under the letter of credit and the bill returned to the seller. Then, the seller presented the set of all three original bills to the carrier for delivery and accordingly took delivery. The carrier kept one original bill and returned the balance two, marked "accomplished".[205] Subsequently, the seller successfully negotiated with the buyer a sale at a reduced price and the arrangement was that the buyer will settle the payment through the letter of credit against the accomplished bill. The accomplished bills were accordingly transferred to the bank, who paid under the letter of credit and passed on the bill to the buyer. Now the question was whether the transfer of the bill to the buyer conferred on the buyer the rights under the bill by virtue of Section 2 of the 1992 Act.[206] The English High Court held that the Section 2(2)(a) exception did not apply because the transfer of the bill was under the varied contract, which was made after delivery of the cargo by the carrier. Accordingly, at the time of the arrangement, the bill no longer represented the goods, hence the rights under the bill were not transferred to the buyer.

2.2.10.3 Transfer of Liability (Section 3(1))

Despite the transfer of rights by virtue of Section 2(1) of the UK Carriage of Goods by Sea Act 1992,[207] a carrier will not be able to take action on the bill against the lawful holder, for example, to claim freight,[208] except where the lawful holder (i) takes or demands delivery from the carrier, (ii) makes a claim under the bill of lading, took or (iii) took or demanded such delivery before he was entitled therefor.[209] Accordingly, a bill of lading is a partial[210] exception to the privity of contract rule.[211]

However, once the lawful holder does any of the three things said above, then he will become fully liable on the terms of the bill as if he was a party such as for freight, demurrage, general average, loss resulting from dangerous cargo, implied obligations arising from the terms of the bill, obligation to observe laytime (or implied obligation under the bill to discharge the cargo within a reasonable time where no laytime is stipulated)[212] and so forth. This is the effect of Section 3(1) of the 1992

[204] *The David Agmashenebeli (cargo owners) v The David Agmashenebeli (owners)* [2002] EWHC 104 (Admlty), [2002] 2 All ER (Comm) 806, [2003] 1 Lloyd's Rep 92, [2002] All ER (D) 535 (May) (EW HC).

[205] Meaning 'job completed'.

[206] Identically reproduced in the Singapore Bills of Lading Act with the same section numbering.

[207] Identically reproduced in the Singapore Bills of Lading Act with the same section numbering.

[208] Price payable to the carrier for the carriage.

[209] Section 3 of the UK Carriage of Goods by Sea Act 1992.

[210] One sided in the sense that the rights are *immediately* conferred on the holder but not on the carrier.

[211] A general rule whereby only parties to a contract may sue and be sued on the contract: *Provender v Wood* (1630) Hetley 30, (1627) 124 ER 318 (EW Court of Common Pleas).

[212] In *Tradigrain SA and Others v King Diamond Marine Ltd (The Spiros C)* [2000] All ER (D) 979, [2000] 2 Lloyd's Rep 319 (EW CA), the court observed that the end consignee will be under

Act. This section applies not only to bills of lading but equally to sea waybills and ship's delivery orders. The Section 3 reads as follows:

3. Liabilities Under Shipping Documents

(1) Where subsection (1) of section 2 of this Act operates in relation to any document to which this Act applies and the person in whom rights are vested by virtue of that subsection—

(a) takes or demands delivery from the carrier of any of the goods to which the document relates;

(b) makes a claim under the contract of carriage against the carrier in respect of any of those goods; or

(c) is a person who, at a time before those rights were vested in him, took or demanded delivery from the carrier of any of those goods,

that person shall (by virtue of taking or demanding delivery or making the claim or, in a case falling within paragraph (c) above, of having the rights vested in him) become subject to the same liabilities under that contract as if he had been a party to that contract.

(2) Where the goods to which a ship's delivery order relates form a part only of the goods to which the contract of carriage relates, the liabilities to which any person is subject by virtue of the operation of this section in relation to that order shall exclude liabilities in respect of any goods to which the order does not relate.

(3) This section, so far as it imposes liabilities under any contract on any person, shall be without prejudice to the liabilities under the contract of any person as an original party to the contract.

It must be noted from Section 3(3) that the liabilities of the shipper, the original party to the carriage contract, is not divested by transfer of the bill and thereby rendering the transferee liable under the bill. The purpose of this is that the carrier must have recourse to the original shipper for some reasons such as the freight is not paid or dangerous cargo had been loaded without proper notice to the carrier, particularly when the end consignee is not financially sound. Hence, the carrier has two potential parties to claim dues to it from.

A technical problem that may arise in imposing liabilities on the end consignee is that it may make a demand for delivery and take delivery from the shipowner when the bill of lading was issued by the charterer-carrier. In such cases, technically, the end consignee has neither made a demand against nor taken delivery from the carrier. However, the shipowner will in such cases act as the agent of the carrier in receiving the demand for delivery and in giving delivery. Hence, the end consignee will come within the scope of the Section 3 to take liability on terms of the bill of lading.

---

an obligation to discharge the cargo within a reasonable time when the original shipper was bound by such implied obligation.

2.2.10.4 Transferability: Analysis and Explanation

If not for such transferability, an assignment would be required. The difficulties with an assignment will be that a notice of the assignment must be given to the carrier.[213] Another requirement for a valid assignment is that the assignee must have a legitimate commercial interest in the cargo.[214] This will usually be satisfied if a consignor were to assign his rights under the bill to a consignee. However, if the ship sank and the parties with that knowledge contracts for the transfer of the bill to confer the '*bare* right of action' on the consignee, then the last requirement will not be satisfied, and the assignment will be bad.[215]

Transferability of bills of lading can also be explained differently, that is 'unilateral contract'.[216] The mechanism of bills of lading being transferred by the concept of a unilateral contract is as follows.[217] The carrier makes an offer to deliver the cargo to anyone lawfully acquiring and holding the bill of lading. The buyer accepts the offer by paying the seller for the cargo and acquiring the bill in reliance on the offer. Hence, a contract is concluded within the *Carlill v Carbolic Smoke Ball Company*[218] principle of unilateral contracts.

2.2.10.5 Return of Bill by Indorsee

When a bill reaches the hands of a bank or any other indorsee, whether the bank or the indorsee is named as the 'to order' consignee or is named in the indorsement, if the bank or the indorsee has for any reason to return the bill to the seller, then the bank or indorsee must indorse it back in favour of the seller. In *East West Corp v Dampskibsselskabet AF 1912*,[219] the bill was issued to order of the seller's bank. The bank returned the bill to the seller but did not indorse it to the seller. The seller claimed itself to be the lawful holder of the bill, but unsuccessfully, as the bill was not indorsed to it.

A similar decision was reached in Singapore in the case of *Bandung Shipping Pte Ltd v Keppel Tatlee Bank Ltd*.[220] In this case, bills of lading were issued by the shipowner to the order of the shipper. The shipper-seller indorsed them in blank and

---

[213] In the case of an assignment with notice, no attornment will be necessary. In Malaysia, the requirement for such notice in case of assignment is codified in Section 4(8) of the Singapore Civil law Act/Section 4(3) of the Malaysian Civil Law Act 1956.

[214] Common law prohibits champerty. Bare right of action cannot be assigned.

[215] Such an assignment of bare rights will be invalidated by the law of champerty.

[216] *Carlill v Carbolic Smoke Ball Company* [1892] EWCA Civ 1, [1893] 1 QB 256, [1891–94] All ER Rep 127 (EW CA).

[217] This explanation for transferability of bills of lading is novel and introduced in this work.

[218] [1892] EWCA Civ 1, [1893] 1 QB 256, [1891–94] All ER Rep 127 (EW CA).

[219] *East West Corp v Dampskibsselskabet AF, 1912, Aktieselskab; Utaniko Ltd v P&O Nedlloyd BV* [2003] EWCA Civ 174, [2003] 4 Costs LR 531, [2003] All ER (D) 249 (Feb), [2003] 1 Lloyd's Rep 265n (EW CA).

[220] [2003] 1 SLR 295 (SG CA).

delivered the same to the buyer. The buyer sold the cargo to a sub-buyer and delivered the bills to the buyer's bank, without any indorsement. The buyer's bank indorsed them to the sub-buyer's bank and forwarded the same to the latter. The sub-buyer did not pay and collect the bills. Hence, the sub-buyer's bank returned the bills to the buyer's bank, however without any indorsement. The buyer's bank then cancelled all the indorsements, namely the shipper's indorsement in blank and its own indorsement to the sub-buyer's bank, just by stamping "Cancelled" on the indorsements. In the meantime, the shipowner misdelivered the goods without presentation of the bills. The buyer's bank, holding the bills, sued the shipowner for the loss. The shipowner applied to strike out the claim. The Court of Appeal held that the bills, which were originally order bills became bear bills when they there indorsed in blank and delivered to the buyer. They then again became order bills when they were specifically indorsed by the buyer's bank to the sub-buyer's bank and delivered to the latter. Accordingly, when the sub-buyer's bank returned the bills, it should have indorsed them to the buyer's bank. As this was not done, the buyer's bank did not become the lawful holder of the bill. It was no open to any party to cancel an indorsement once made, hence the cancellation of the indorsements by the bank was of no effect. Accordingly, the court struck out the claim.

2.2.10.6 Extinction of Rights upon Transfer (Section 2(5))

Transfer of bill of lading, thus the rights thereunder on terms thereof, divests the original shipper, and all the previous lawful holders, of the rights under the bill. This is provided for by Section 2(5)[221] of the UK Carriage of Goods by Sea Act 1992, which reads as follows:

> Where rights are transferred by virtue of the operation of subsection (1) above in relation to any document, the transfer for which that subsection provides shall extinguish any entitlement to those rights which derives—
>
> (a) where that document is a bill of lading, from a person's having been an original party to the contract of carriage; or
>
> (b) in the case of any document to which this Act applies, from the previous operation of that subsection in relation to that document;
>
> but the operation of that subsection shall be without prejudice to any rights which derive from a person's having been an original party to the contract contained in, or evidenced by, a sea waybill and, in relation to a ship's delivery order, shall be without prejudice to any rights deriving otherwise than from the previous operation of that subsection in relation to that order.

What the original shipper is divested of, by virtue of the Section 2(5), are only the contractual rights under the bill. In *East West Corp v Dampskibsselskabet AF*

---

[221] In the case of ship's delivery orders, the rights of the last holder of the bill of lading, in exchange for which the ship's delivery orders were issued, are not divested. In the case of sea waybills, the rights of the original shipper are not divested.

1912,[222] the English Court of Appeal held that the original shipper, in the factual matrix of the case, retained the rights in bailment even after the transfer of the bill to the consignee and thereby the contractual rights. The case was decided in the context where the bill was indorsed to a bank and subsequently the bank returned the bill without indorsement back to the shipper. Hence, a cause of action in contract under the bill of lading was not available to the shipper, but it was able to take a bailment action on terms of the bill of lading.

It must be remembered that straight bills of lading are part of the definition of sea waybills[223] in the 1992 Act. Accordingly, the original shipper is not divested of his rights in the case of straight bills.[224] It was accordingly held in *East West Corp v Dampskibsselskabet AF 1912*.[225]

The importance of divesting the original shipper of his rights under the bill of lading is that, in the absence of such extinction, the carrier can be subjected to claims by multiple parties in respect of the same cause. However, not in all cases, the original shipper is divested of his right, for example, where he is also the charterer.

2.2.10.7 Extinction of Liability of Intermediate Holders

Although Section 3(1) of the 1992 Act is silent about the extinction of liabilities that fell on the intermediate holders of the bill of lading,[226] the intermediate holder will likely be divested of his liabilities under the bill upon transfer by him. First, it is unlikely that an issue as to this will arise since an intermediate holder will not ordinarily take or demand delivery or make a claim against the carrier. Second, if by any circumstances, he had taken the liability such as by demanding delivery and subsequently transfers the bill, then likely by a principle of mutuality he will be divested of the liabilities. In dealing with Section 1 of the UK Bills of Lading Act 1855 [transfer of rights],[227] the court in *Smurthwaite v Wilkins*[228] applied the principle of mutuality and held that a statutory burden and statutory right may only

---

[222] *East West Corp v Dampskibsselskabet AF, 1912, Aktieselskab; Utaniko Ltd v P&O Nedlloyd BV* [2003] EWCA Civ 174, [2003] 4 Costs LR 531, [2003] All ER (D) 249 (Feb), [2003] 1 Lloyd's Rep 265n (EW CA).

[223] Section 1(3) of the UK Carriage of Goods by Sea Act 1992.

[224] Original shipper in sea waybills and ship's delivery orders is not divested, by virtue of the Section 2(5), of his rights by statutory vesting of rights under the bill on a third party by operation of the Section 2(1).

[225] *East West Corp v Dampskibsselskabet AF, 1912, Aktieselskab; Utaniko Ltd v P&O Nedlloyd BV* [2003] EWCA Civ 174, [2003] 4 Costs LR 531, [2003] All ER (D) 249 (Feb), [2003] 1 Lloyd's Rep 265n (EW CA).

[226] Unlike what is provided in the Section 2(5) for extinction of rights of intermediate holders of bills of lading.

[227] That transferred rights in a bill of lading to the indorsee, prior to coming into force of the 1992 Act. The 1855 Act is now repealed by and replaced with the 1992 Act.

[228] 142 ER 1026, (1862) 11 CB NS 842, [1862] 2 WLUK 49 (EW Court of Common Pleas), approved by the House of Lords in *Borealis AB (formerly Borealis Petrokemi AB and Statoil Petrokemi AB) v Stargas Ltd (The Berge Sisar)* [2001] UKHL 17, [2002] 2 A.C. 205, [2001] 2 WLR 1118, [2001] 2

exit together. There is no reason to divert from such an approach in dealing with the transfer of rights under Section 2(1) of the 1992 Act.[229]

Support for the above proposition is found in *The Berge Sisar*.[230] In this case, a consignee awaiting bill of lading 'requested samples' before delivery at a time when he did not yet have the bill. After seeing the samples and receiving the bill, he did not take delivery but indorsed the bill to another buyer. An issue arose as to whether the intermediate holder, who requested the samples, had taken liability under Section 3(1) of the 1992 Act.[231] The House of Lords held that he was not liable. One of the reasons for the decision was that he could not have 'demanded' delivery at the time when he was not holding the bill. As a result of this decision, it seems that Section 3(1)(c) will be limited to cases where actual delivery was taken as opposed to a demand made, as a consignee not holding the bill at the time cannot 'demand' delivery. In any event, it must be noted that in this case the intermediate holder merely 'requested samples' and not 'demanded delivery'. Hence, it will not fall within Section 3(1). The fact that the bill had become 'spent' will not prevent the holder from taking liability as long as the spent bill was able to transfer rights under Section 2(1) of the 1992 Act.[232]

2.2.10.8 Bills of Lading Issued Under Charterparty

When the entire cargo-carrying capacity of a ship, or a substantial portion of it, is booked for a carriage, it is common for the shipper to take a voyage charter. The voyage charterparty[233] will be an agreement on its own, exhaustively setting out the terms of carriage.[234] Despite that, a bill of lading will be issued by the shipowner because the charterparty is only the carriage contract and does not evidence receipt of the cargo by the shipowner. Hence, only the bill of lading will evidence the receipt of cargo. In such cases, the bill of lading loses its function as the carriage contract as

All ER 193, [2001] 1 All ER (Comm) 673, [2001] 1 Lloyd's Rep 663, [2001] 3 WLUK 638, [2001] CLC 1084, (2001) 98(20) LSG 43, (2001) 145 SJLB 93 (UK HL).

229 Materially identical to Singapore Bills of Lading Act.

230 *Borealis AB (formerly Borealis Petrokemi AB and Statoil Petrokemi AB) v Stargas Ltd (The Berge Sisar)* [2001] UKHL 17, [2002] 2 AC 205, [2001] 2 WLR 1118, [2001] 2 All ER 193, [2001] 1 All ER (Comm) 673, [2001] 1 Lloyd's Rep 663, [2001] 3 WLUK 638, [2001] CLC 1084, (2001) 98(20) LSG 43, (2001) 145 SJLB 93 (UK HL).

231 The liability in question was as to liability for alleged damage to the ship resulting from corrosive state of the copper carried.

232 *Primetrade AG v Ythan Ltd (The Ythan)* [2005] EWHC 2399 (Comm), [2006] 1 All ER 367, [2006] 1 All ER (Comm) 157, [2006] 1 Lloyd's Rep 457, [2005] All ER (D) 05 (Nov) (EW HC) will support this proposition.

233 A popular standard form of such contract is BIMCO GENCON 1994.

234 Such terms will include details as to loading, carriage, discharge, freight, laytime, demurrage, etc.

between the carrier and the shipper.[235] However, when the bill is transferred to the hands of another lawful holder, it gains the status of carriage contract regulating the relationship between the carrier and the lawful holder.[236]

Article V of the Hague and Hague-Visby Rules expressly excludes the application of the Rules to charterparties, although parties are at liberty to voluntarily incorporate such terms into their charterparty.[237] In the same line, Article I(b), in the definition of "Contract of Carriage", includes a bill of lading issued under or pursuant to a charterparty but only from the moment the bill regulates the relationship between the carrier and the lawful holder of the bill. This refers back to common law on the question of when a bill regulates the relationship and when it does not. Under common law, a bill does not have the contractual effect when in the hands of a charterer, as said above.

2.2.11 *Period of Responsibility Under Bill of Lading*

The essential period of responsibility under a bill will, minimum, be the period between the loading of the goods onto the ship to the discharge of the goods from the ship. This is called 'tackle-to-tackle' or 'alongside' rule. This will be the only period of responsibility in the case of a 'free-in' and 'free-out' contract, whereby the consignor loads the goods and the consignee discharges the goods. Such a contract will be a pure carriage contract, the only thing that the carrier has undertaken is to 'carry', and the shipowner's obligations are that of a 'carrier'. In such cases, the delivery is not distinct from discharge and goes together with the discharge.

But, where the consignee has not undertaken to discharge, the obligation to deliver will be on the carrier, that will be a fundamental obligation under the bill of lading contract.[238] In such cases, the delivery will be after discharge, and the shipowner has necessarily undertaken not only to 'carry' but also to 'deliver', both arising from the carriage contract embodied in the bill of lading. Here, the obligation to deliver constitutes the second period of responsibility under the bill of lading contract. This second period is from the time of the completion of discharge to the time of delivery. The obligation of the carrier for the second period will be as that of a 'bailee' subject to any contractual terms in respect of the second period in the bill of lading.

---

[235] *Rodocanachi, Sons & Co v Milburn Bros* (1886) 18 QBD 67 (EW CA); *President of India v Metcalfe Shipping Co Ltd (The Dunelmia)* [1970] 1 QB 289, [1969] 3 All ER 1549, [1969] 3 WLR 1120 (EW CA).

[236] The bill will lose its contractual effect if it returns to the hands of the charterers after it was initially parted with by the charters: *President of India v Metcalfe Shipping Co Ltd (The Dunelmia)* [1970] 1 QB 289, [1969] 3 All ER 1549, [1969] 3 WLR 1120 (EW CA). However, the bill will not lose its contractual effect, if it returns to the charterer as pledgee: *Calcutta Steamship Co Ltd v Andrew Weir & Co* [1910] 1 KB 759 (EW HC).

[237] Such clauses are called 'clause paramount'.

[238] *Sze Hai Tong Bank Ltd v Rambler Cycle Co Ltd* [1959] AC 576, [1959] 3 All ER 182, [1959] 3 WLR 214, [1959] 2 Lloyd's Rep 114 (PC on appeal from Singapore).

There may also be another period of responsibility for the carrier, that is, the period before the shipment if the shipowner comes into possession of the goods before the shipment. This period will be from the moment of receipt of the goods to the moment of shipment. This period may or may not be subject to a bill of lading. When a 'received for shipment' is first issued and subsequently annotated as a 'shipped' bill or exchanged for a 'shipped' bill, then the period will be covered by the 'received for shipment' bill. Whether such a bill is issued or not, the duties of the shipowner for this period will be as a bailee. In the event of such a bill having been issued, the bailment will be subject to the terms of the bill. In this case, the undertaking of the carrier is to 'receive before shipment', to 'carry' and, if it is not a 'free-out' contract, to 'deliver'.

Typically, it was called an 'ocean bill of lading' when it was to carry goods by a *single* sea voyage so that it has the possession and control of the goods at all times during the sea voyage. However, the term nowadays is used more loosely to refer to a 'shipped' bill issued by a shipowner as opposed to any document issued by an NVOC.

The only period mandatorily covered by the Hague and Hague Visby Rules is the period of carriage, that is tackle-to-tackle, with a little extension to cover the entire loading operation and discharge operation.[239] Other than for this period, the contractual freedom is preserved, so that the parties can agree on terms in respect of the period before shipment and after discharge.[240]

It is common for bills of lading to have a 'period of responsibility' or 'before and after' clause to set out the carrier's responsibility for the outside period. Such a clause will often try to stipulate a uniform regime of liability in respect of the period outside carriage on the same terms as that applicable for the period of carriage. The freedom to enter into contractual relationships as regards the liability for the outside-period is expressly preserved in the Hague and Hague-Visby Rules,[241] while the contractual freedom in respect of the period from loading to discharge is restricted by the Rules.[242]

For example, in the case of a shipment from Malaysia, a bill may provide that 'the Hague-Visby Rules apply from the time the carrier received the cargo to the time the carrier delivers the cargo, except for any period to which the Hague Rules or any other rules apply statutorily.'[243] As Malaysia[244] statutorily applies the Hague Rules for shipments from Malaysia, in the case of this bill, the carriage will be subject to

---

[239] Article II; *Pyrene Co Ltd v Scindia Navigation Co Ltd* [1954] 2 QB 402, [1954] 2 All ER 158, [1954] 2 WLR 1005, [1954] 1 Lloyd's Rep 321 (EW HC). See also Article I(e), read together with Article II, for definition of 'carriage of goods' that means the 'tackle-to-tackle' period.

[240] Article VII of the Hague and Hague-Visby Rules.

[241] Article VII of the Hague/Hague-Visby Rules.

[242] Articles II and III(8).

[243] Contractual freedom is preserved by Article VII of the Hague/Hague-Visby Rules except for the period from loading to discharge regulated by the Rules.

[244] Largely.

the Hague-Visby Rules[245] for the warehouse period and subject to the Hague Rules for the sea voyage period. As to transshipments, it is common for bills of lading to contain a clause giving the liberty to the carrier to transship the goods or a statement that the carriage will be performed by transshipment (i.e. through bill).

2.2.12 Contract on Terms of the Would-Be Bill Even Before Issuance of Bill

The true carriage contract between the shipper and the carrier will likely be concluded before any bill of lading is issued. This may be done orally, by email or in the form of a 'booking note'. Subsequently, the bill of lading will be issued upon loading the cargo. It has been held that even before any bill of lading is issued, the terms of the contract between the parties will be governed by the bill of lading to be issued later. This point may be expressly mentioned[246] in the booking note, and if not, it will be implied.[247] Accordingly, as between the shipper and the carrier, irrespective of issuance of the bill of lading, the terms of the carriage contract at all material times will be on terms of the would-be bill of lading.

2.2.13 Application of International Conventions to Carriage Contracts

The terms of the bills of lading are largely controlled by the applicable international convention given effect to by the domestic legislation. At present, the international convention applicable to carriage of goods by sea for the UK is the Hague-Visby Rules of 1968 as amended by the SDR Protocol in 1979, by virtue of the UK Carriage of Goods by Sea Act 1971.

In Singapore, it is the Hague-Visby Rules of 1968 with its own scheme of liability-limitation and unit of currency.[248] In Malaysia,[249] it is the Hague Rules of 1924.[250]

---

[245] Which may be more favourable to the carrier, such as in case of liability-limitation—see Chap. 10.

[246] *Armour & Co Ltd v Leopold Walford (London) Ltd* [1921] 3 KB 473 (EW HC).

[247] *Pyrene Co Ltd v Scindia Navigation Co Ltd* [1954] 2 QB 402, [1954] 2 All ER 158, [1954] 2 WLR 1005, [1954] 1 Lloyd's Rep 321 (EW HC).

[248] By Section 3(1) of the Singapore Carriage of Goods by Sea Act, read together with para 2 of the Carriage of Goods by Sea (Singapore Currency Equivalents) Order.

[249] Largely.

[250] By Section 2 the Carriage of Goods by Sea Act 1950 for Peninsular Malaysia, by reg. 2 of the Merchant Shipping (Implementation of Conventions Relating to Carriage of Goods by Sea and to Liability of Shipowners and Others) Regulations 1960 for Sarawak and by reg. 3(1) of the Merchant Shipping (Applied Subsidiary Legislation) Regulations 1961 for Sabah, with Labuan left in lacuna since it was severed from Sabah in 1984.

Even if the Rules do not apply statutorily, bills of lading will commonly incorporate the Rules contractually, which clause is called 'clause paramount'.

2.2.14 Electronic Bills of Lading

There are two things to keep in mind when considering the idea of electronic bills of lading, as pointed out in a recent report called The Legal Status of Electronic Bills of Lading: A report for the ICC[251] Banking Commission (2018). First is the technical part, namely, the electronic system must be able to replicate the functions of the paper bill, namely, only one holder will exclusively have it any one time and thus only he will be able to present it. The carrier will have the comfort that it exchanges the goods for the bill (i.e. surrender of the bill), hence it cannot fall liable to another who may claim himself to be the lawful holder of the bill.

Second is the legal part. If the technical part can be accomplished with a system, then the law has to recognise it. This is also a difficult part as the law here means the law 'internationally'. Hence, if one or more countries amend their laws to facilitate electronic bills but not others, again, the electronic bill system cannot come into play, as the bill by its very nature will travel across the globe. It is unlikely that a country will want to legislate in favour of electronic bills unless there is a global motion for the major countries to so legislate. So far, no satisfactory solution has come up both in terms of technicality and legality.

Attempts have been made to introduce electronic bills of lading but without any good rate of success. One such attempt was by a scheme known as SEADOCS in the mid-1980s. Other attempts were by CMI[252] Rules for Electronic Bills of Lading Rules 1990, a project known as Bolero[253] launched in 1999, and a system called essDOCS established in 2005. Largely, these concepts were based on 'club' system, meaning that the system is available to the members of the club who contractually agree to abide by the system.

A few words about Bolero will help understand how the club system operates. Bolero members comprise carriers, shippers, consignees and banks. In Bolero, the holder is called 'holder to order'. The holder has the authority to designate, electronically, any other member as 'holder to order'. Then the designated person becomes the new holder to order, and so forth. This is equivalent to the transfer of the bill of lading. A holder may instead of designating a new holder to order pledge the bill. The pledgee is called pledgee to order. Now only the pledgee can designate any new holder to order or another pledgee to order. Any holder to order or pledgee to order may electronically surrender the bill so that he can take delivery. If the bill is to move to the hands of a non-member, then a paper bill will be issued. From this point onward, no more electronic transaction on the bill.

---

[251] 'International Chamber of Commerce'.

[252] 'Comité Maritime International'.

[253] 'Bills of Lading in Europe'.

Parallel to that, some attempts were made by United Nations Commission on International Trade Law (UNCITRAL), which came out with the UNCITRAL Model Law on Electronic Commerce of 1996 and subsequently UNCITRAL Model Law on Electronic Transferable Records of 2017. The former,[254] enacted in about 70 countries, allows transfer of a transport document to be effected by electronic data message. The latter,[255] enacted only in Baharain so far, allows replacement of a transferable document with an electronic transferable by a reliable method. None of the two model laws say how a bill of lading of which there may only be one exclusive holder at any time can be brought within an electronic transfer system. It must be noted that both these were model laws that a country may voluntarily adopt, as opposed to international convention. Both these attempts were not successful to bring into reality electronic bills.

It must be noted that the UK Carriage of Goods by Sea Act 1992,[256] in Section 1(5), empowers the Secretary of State to, 'by regulations, make provision for the application of this Act to cases where an electronic communication network or any other information technology is used for effecting transactions'. However, the Secretary of State has not made any such direction.[257] Given the challenges in implementing electronic bills of lading, as a matter of law, there does not seem any likelihood of the Secretary of State to make such regulations in any near future. However, Singapore, whose Bills of Lading Act is nearly identical to the UK Carriage of Goods by Sea Act 1992, has passed the Electronic Transactions (Amendment) Act on 1 February 2021 and brought it into force on 19 March 2021. This Act adopts the UNCITRAL Model Law on Electronic Transferable Records 2017 and makes necessary amendments to the Singapore Bills of Lading Act to legally recognise and facilitate e-bills of lading.

Glencore International v MSC Mediterranean Shipping Company,[258] decided by the English Court of Appeal, suggests that electronic bills will not be recognised as a matter of law, but they may be recognised in the event of contractual arrangements therefor. The 2018 report makes some comparison with the SWIFT[259] system successfully in operation to transact with electronic messages, but that does not answer the problem concerning electronic bills of lading. SWIFT is one-to-one electronic communication between the members.

A simple comparison, to understand the issue rightly, will be with cheques. Can a cash cheque function be replicated by an electronic cheque? Likely, the answer at this moment is 'no'. The same goes for bills of lading. But this does not mean a technological solution cannot be found in the future. An international convention, as opposed to mere model law, specifically to facilitate electronic bills of lading coupled with technological solution, might see the way forward.

---

[254] Article 17(1) and (3) read with Article 2(a) and (b).

[255] Article 10(1)(b) read with Article 17(1).

[256] Materially identical to the Singapore Bills of Lading Act, with the reference to 'Secretary of State' in Section 1(5) of the UK Act changed to 'Minister' in Section 1(5) of the Singapore Act.

[257] Similarly, in Singapore, the Minister has not made any such regulation.

[258] [2017] EWCA Civ 365 (EW CA).

[259] 'Society for Worldwide Interbank Financial Telecommunication'.

Electronic bills, if successfully introduced, will have two particular advantages or security features over the paper bills. One is that the indorsements cannot be easily forged or faked. Second is that there is no worry about loss of the physical bill which may end up in the hands of a fraudster.

2.3 Sea Waybill

Sea waybills are different from bills of lading in that the former does not confer constructive possession or title on the consignee. Sea waybills are not transferable. There is no 'to order' or 'bearer' consignee in sea waybills, but the consignee must always be straight named. The sea waybill need not be tendered or surrendered for the consignee to claim the cargo from the carrier. They can quite be compared with a courier consignment, where the carrier will drop it with the named consignee.

By virtue of Section 2(1), read with Section 5(1)(a), of the UK Carriage of Goods Act 1992, the person named as the consignee has a right of action against the carrier as if he was a party to the carriage contract on the terms of the bill.[260] However, the control remains with the shipper at all times until delivery. This is because the shipper may at any time, before delivery to the consignee, instruct the carrier to change the name of the consignee. For this reason, sea waybills cannot be used with letters of credit. However, this weakness can be overcome if the bank is named as the shipper. But a bank may not prefer this as it will render the bank directly liable, as the contracting party, to the carrier under the sea waybill. The Section 5(1)(a) reads as follows:

> (1) In this Act—
>
> "bill of lading", "sea waybill" and "ship's delivery order" shall be construed in accordance with section 1 above;
>
> "the contract of carriage"—
>
> (a) in relation to a bill of lading or sea waybill, means the contract contained in or evidenced by that bill or waybill; and
>
> (b) in relation to a ship's delivery order, means the contract under or for the purposes of which the undertaking contained in the order is given;

Accordingly, the payment mechanism becomes less secured with sea waybills. If the buyer makes an advance payment to the seller and subsequently the seller changes the consignee's name in the sea waybill, the buyer will be in difficulty. If the seller delivers before payment and the buyer subsequently defaults, the seller will be in difficulty.

However, the advantage of the sea waybills is that no original copy of the sea waybill is necessary for the consignee to claim cargo from the carrier. Comparatively,

[260] However, unlike in the case of bills of lading, this does not divest the shipper of his rights under the carriage of contract: Section 2(5) of the UK Carriage of Goods by Sea Act 1992.

with bills of lading, if the shipment arrives earlier than the document, the consignee will not be able to take the cargo until the document arrives.

In practice, in such a situation, the carrier under the bill of lading may release the cargo to the consignee either on the consignee's undertaking or the consignee's banker's undertaking.[261] If the carrier releases the cargo on the consignee's undertaking, the carrier takes the risk in the event the consignee subsequently defaults in tendering the bill of lading. If the carrier insists on a banker's guarantee for the release without surrender of the bill of lading, that will put the consignee to the cost and trouble of securing such a guarantee, if the consignee can.

With sea waybills, there is a risk to the carrier that it may deliver to a wrong person. However, such a risk is not present or is minimum with bills of lading as the delivery will be against the bill in the latter case. The bill of lading itself normally operates as a token or key and identifies the true consignee.

Sea waybills have some similarities with straight bills of lading. In both, the consignee is straight named. In the case of sea waybills, the shipper may have the consignee name changed at any time before delivery by the carrier of the cargo to the consignee. In the case of straight bills, the shipper may have the consignee name changed as long as the shipper has not parted with the straight bill. Both bills are not negotiable. Sea waybill is not necessary for consignee to claim cargo from the carrier, but a straight bill is necessary.[262] The Hague-Visby Rules apply compulsorily to straight bills[263] but not, unless expressly agreed between parties, to sea waybills.[264] The Singapore Court of Appeal took adopted the same position in *APL Co Pte Ltd v Voss Peer*[265] and explained that a straight bill of lading, although similar in some

---

[261] *Wolff v Trinity Logistics USA Inc* [2018] EWCA Civ 2765, [2019] 1 WLR 3997 (EW CA), speech of Longmore LJ: "It is by no means unknown for carriers … to succumb to pressure from the receivers/buyers of goods to release goods without production of an original bill. Any carrier who does so will be in breach of the contract of carriage. … He will therefore hardly ever release the goods without a guarantee or letter of indemnity from the receiver or whoever wants delivery of the goods."

[262] *MacWilliam (JI) Co Inc v Mediterranean Shipping Co SA (The Rafaela S)* [2005] UKHL 11, [2005] 2 AC 423, [2005] 2 All ER 86, [2005] 2 WLR 554, [2005] 1 All ER (Comm) 393, [2005] 1 Lloyd's Rep 347 (UK HL). Although a straight bill will usually, as in the case also of BIMCO standard forms, say that delivery is to be made against presentation of the bill, likely the obligation to deliver will be against presentation of the bill even if the absence of such statement in the bill: *Obiter* of Rix LJ at the Court of Appeal reported as [2003] EWCA Civ 556, [2004] QB 702 (EW CA).

[263] Section 1(4) of the UK Carriage of Goods by Sea Act 1971; Article I((b) read together with Article II; *MacWilliam (JI) Co Inc v Mediterranean Shipping Co SA (The Rafaela S)* [2005] UKHL 11, [2005] 2 AC 423, [2005] 2 All ER 86, [2005] 2 WLR 554, [2005] 1 All ER (Comm) 393, [2005] 1 Lloyd's Rep 347 (UK HL); *APL Co Pte Ltd v Voss Peer* [2002] 4 SLR 481 (SG CA), also reported as *Voss v APL Co Pte Ltd* [2003] 3 LRC 632, [2002] 2 Lloyd's Rep 707 (SG CA).

[264] Section 1(6)(b) of the UK Carriage of Goods by Sea Act 1971/Section 1(4)(b) of Singapore Carriage of Goods by Sea Act (however, there is a material difference between the two, namely "as if receipt were a bill of lading" in the closing is there in the UK provision, but not in the Singapore provision.

[265] [2002] 4 SLR 481 (SG CA), also reported as *Voss v APL Co Pte Ltd* [2003] 3 LRC 632, [2002] 2 Lloyd's Rep 707.

aspects to sea waybill, essentially retains other characteristics of a bill of lading except that it is not negotiable like order or bearer bills. The court further said that the fact that a bill of lading was issued must mean that the parties intended delivery against presentation of the bill unless otherwise said by clear words.

The consignee, in both sea waybills and straight bills, gets a right of action on terms of the bill against the carrier.[266] The rights of the shipper as the original contracting party with the carrier are not thereby extinguished.[267] Comparatively, in the case of negotiable bills, the lawful holder of the bill gets the right of action against the carrier on terms of the bill,[268] which extinguishes the right of action that the shipper possessed as the original contracting party under the bill.[269] The liabilities of the original shipper to the carrier under the sea waybills are never extinguished,[270] like bills of lading and ship's delivery orders.

That is because the 1992 Act groups, by Sections 1(2) and (3), bills into negotiable and not-negotiable categories. The former is called 'bill of lading' and the latter is called 'sea waybill'. Order and bear bills come under negotiable-category. Sea waybills and straight bills of lading come under the non-negotiable category. Comparatively, the distinction in the UK Carriage of Goods by Sea Act 1971, in applying the Hague-Visby rules to bills, is *between* bills of lading including straight bills *and* sea waybills. For the former, the Hague-Visby Rules statutorily apply, but not for the latter. The Section 1(3) of the 1992 Act reads as follows:

> References in this Act to a sea waybill are references to any document which is not a bill of lading but—
>
> (a) is such a receipt for goods as contains or evidences a contract for the carriage of goods by sea; and
>
> (b) identifies the person to whom delivery of the goods is to be made by the carrier in accordance with that contract.

Receipt in the straight bill, like order and bearer bills, constitutes *prima facie* evidence of the receipt of the cargo by the carrier and its condition as stated therein. It becomes conclusive evidence when transferred to the hands of a lawful holder in good faith.[271] However, it is not so in the case of sea waybills.[272] Hence, the evidentiary burden on the consignee to bring an action against the carrier under a sea waybill is higher than that under a bill of lading including a straight bill.

Comité Maritime International (CMI) has developed a set of rules for voluntary incorporation into sea waybills. This is known as Uniform Rules for Sea Waybill. The Rules attempt to match sea waybills with bills of lading in some aspects. The cl.

---

266 Section 2(1), read with Section 5(1), of the UK Carriage of Goods by Sea Act 1992.

267 Section 2(5) of the UK Carriage of Goods by Sea Act 1992.

268 Section 2(1), read with Section 5(1), of the UK Carriage of Goods by Sea Act 1992.

269 Section 2(5)(a) of the UK Carriage of Goods by Sea Act 1992.

270 Section 3(3) of the UK Carriage of Goods by Sea Act 1992.

271 Article III(4) of the Hague-Visby Rules.

272 The Hague-Visby Rules do not apply to sea waybills, unless contractually incorporated.

4 of the Rules provides for the application of international conventions or national laws that would apply if it was a bill of lading. Hence, this would incorporate the Hague-Visby Rules in the context of the UK. The cl. 5 renders the statements on the sea waybill *prima facie* evidence of the contents as between the carrier and the shipper.[273] It renders them conclusive evidence as between the carrier and consignee. The cl. 6 allows the carrier to charge the shipper for instruction to change the name of the consignee and require the shipper, if he so desires to change, to give reasonable notice. The cl. 7 relieves the carrier from liability for misdelivery if it has taken reasonable care to ascertain the identity of the consignee.

There has been a practice to include a 'No Disposal' (NODISP) clause into sea waybills. This clause will state that the shipper may not change the consignee. However, this clause is not effective because there is nothing to stop the shipper and the carrier from agreeing to vary this clause so that the shipper is permitted to change the consignee.

By virtue of Section 2(5) of the 1992 Act, the right of action held by the original shipper is not extinguished.[274] The liabilities of the original shipper are also not extinguished, by virtue of Section 3(1) of the 1992 Act. A commonly used form of sea waybill is BIMCO GENWAYBILL. The latest version of it is BIMCO GENWAYBILL 2016.

2.4 Ship's Delivery Order

A ship's delivery order is issued when it is necessary to split bulk cargo carried under one bill of lading to more than one consignee. In such cases, it will not be possible to issue more than one bill of lading as there is only one shipment of cargo. Accordingly, the lawful holder of the bill, whether consignor, shipper, 'to order' consignee or any other lawful holder, will issue merchant' delivery orders in favour of the respective consignees. The carrier will 'attorn' to the merchant's delivery orders. The 'attornment' is an undertaking by the carrier to the respective named consignees to deliver as per the terms of the ship's delivery order. An attorned delivery order is called a 'ship's delivery order', as it is now the ship's obligation to deliver accordingly. The carrier will only so attorn if the original bill of lading had been surrendered in return for the attornment.

Section 2(1)(c) of the UK Carriage of Goods by Sea Act 1992 now transfers to the person to whom the undertaking in the ship's delivery order is addressed the rights of action on the terms of the ship's delivery order. Such rights are, of course, limited to the part of the bulk cargo that the ship's delivery order relates to.[275] Similarly,

[273] The consignor.

[274] Unlike in the case of bills of lading.

[275] Section 2(3) of the UK Carriage of Goods by Sea Act 1992. This section reads "The rights vested in any person by virtue of the operation of subsection (1) above in relation to a ship's delivery order—(a) shall be so vested subject to the terms of the order; and (b) where the goods to

the liabilities of the consignee identified in the ship's delivery order is limited to his proportion.[276] This does not add much to the attornment, since the attornment would already give such right of action to the consignee, but perhaps the liability of the consignee now is clearer under the statutory scheme.

By Section 2(5) of the 1992 Act, the right of action held by the original shipper is not extinguished.[277] Similarly, the liabilities of the original shipper are not extinguished, by virtue of Section 3(1) of the 1992 Act.

Added to 1992 Act, now, Section 20A of the UK Sale of Goods Act 1979[278] allows passing of property in goods that are not yet to be ascertained.[279] This is a substantial improvement, as it will better facilitate sale of bulk goods in split quantity and payment transactions related to it since property can be passed in such split cargo. The Section 20A treats all the owners of the bulk cargo as owners in common. In the event, the total quantity. The Section 20A reads as follows:

20A. Undivided shares in goods forming part of a bulk

(1) This section applies to a contract for the sale of a specified quantity of unascertained goods if the following conditions are met—

(a) the goods or some of them form part of a bulk which is identified either in the contract or by subsequent agreement between the parties; and

(b) the buyer has paid the price for some or all of the goods which are the subject of the contract and which form part of the bulk.

(2) Where this section applies, then (unless the parties agree otherwise), as soon as the conditions specified in paragraphs (a) and (b) of subsection (1) above are met or at such later time as the parties may agree—

(a) property in an undivided share in the bulk is transferred to the buyer, and

(b) the buyer becomes an owner in common of the bulk.

(3) Subject to subsection (4) below, for the purposes of this section, the undivided share of a buyer in a bulk at any time shall be such share as the quantity of goods paid for and due to the buyer out of the bulk bears to the quantity of goods in the bulk at that time.

(4) Where the aggregate of the undivided shares of buyers in a bulk determined under subsection (3) above would at any time exceed the whole of the bulk at that time, the undivided share in the bulk of each buyer shall be reduced proportionately so that the aggregate of the undivided shares is equal to the whole bulk.

(5) Where a buyer has paid the price for only some of the goods due to him out of a bulk, any delivery to the buyer out of the bulk shall, for the purposes of this section, be ascribed in the first place to the goods in respect of which payment has been made.

---

which the order relates form a part only of the goods to which the contract of carriage relates, shall be confined to rights in respect of the goods to which the order relates."

[276] Section 3(2) of the UK Carriage of Goods by Sea Act 1992.

[277] Unlike in the case of bills of lading.

[278] Inserted into the Act in 1995.

[279] As an exception to the general rule in Section 16 of the UK Sale of Goods Act 1979 prohibiting the transfer of property in goods that are not ascertained. The Section 16, as amended, reads "Subject to section 20A below where there is a contract for the sale of unascertained goods no property in the goods is transferred to the buyer unless and until the goods are ascertained."

(6) For the purposes of this section payment of part of the price for any goods shall be treated as payment for a corresponding part of the goods.

The Section 20A is supplemented by Section 20B, which facilitates dealings by the owners in common in the bulk cargo.

Chapter 3
International Trade

This chapter introduces the law and practice of international trade. This includes a brief consideration of the various shipping terms, both classical and Incoterms. The classical terms considered are 'free on board' (fob), 'cost, insurance and freight' (cif), and 'cost and freight' (c&f). The three popular variants of the fob contract, namely, bare or straight fob, fob of classic type, fob with additional carriage services, are discussed. The shipping terms from Incoterms (including Incoterms 2020), a set of standard terms developed by International Chamber of Commerce (ICC), are briefly considered. They include 'Free on Board' (FOB), 'Cost and Freight' (CFR), and 'Cost, Insurance and Freight' (CIF). The E-Terms and D-Terms are noted, namely: Ex-Works (EXW), 'Delivered at Place Unloaded' (DPU) in the Incoterms 2020 replacing the 'Delivered at Terminal' (DAT) in the Incoterms 2010, 'Delivered at Place' (DAP), and 'Delivered Duty Paid' (DDP). Then is considered passing of risk and property under the Sale of Goods Act 1979, including Sections 20A and 20B allowing property in an unascertained portion of a bulk cargo to be passed and their relationship to sale of bulk goods in transit under ship's delivery orders. Finally, letter of credit and the fraud-exception to the autonomy of letters of credit are analysed.

3.1 Introduction

The laws concerning International trade, carriage of goods, and financing payment mechanism in international trade are all connected. For a good appreciation of the law of carriage of goods by sea, it is necessary to have a basic understanding of these laws, customs and practices, particularly, shipment terms in international trade contracts, passing of risk and property in international trade contracts, and payment mechanism through letter of credit. The same are the subject of this chapter.

A. Kasi, *The Law of Carriage of Goods by Sea*,
https://doi.org/10.1007/978-981-33-6793-7_3

3.2 Shipment Terms

Shipment terms are the terms of shipment agreed between a seller and a buyer, in an international trade contract, concerning the shipment, such as who arranges and pays for the freight and who arranges and pays for insurance, etc. There are many variants of shipment terms commonly used in international trade contracts. The classical ones are (i) 'free on board' [fob], (ii) cost and freight [c&f] and (iii) cost, insurance and freight [cif]. They have been conventionally called 'shipping terms'. International traders quote and offer prices commonly in one of these shipping terms, such as "US$1.25 per kg of salt *fob* Felixstowe" or "£2.50 per litre of sunflower oil *cif* Hamburg".

When parties conclude an international trade contract, it is common for them to record it down in a principle 'confirmation note' as opposed to a fully-fledged agreement of sale and purchase. This necessitates construing such contracts in light of trade custom, usage and practice including as to shipment terms. For instance, to determine what is meant by a reference to 'fob' or 'cif' in such a contract, one will have to look at the customary usage of these shipment terms. The English Court of Appeal held in *Euro-Asian Oil SA (formerly Euro-Asian Oil AG) v Credit Suisse AG and Another*[1] that the use of the terms such as CIF is not conclusive.[2] Accordingly, a court will have to consider the commercial intention of the parties as evidenced by the document.

There are also more formally documented shipment terms, such as those developed by the International Chamber of Commerce (ICC) called Official Rules for the Interpretation of Trade Terms (Incoterms®). Some of the common shipment terms of Incoterms[3] include FOB, CFR[4] and CIF. Incoterms have been published in numerous revised versions referenced by year of publication, such as Incoterms 2000, Incoterms 2010 and Incoterms 2020.[5] Many trade associations, such as the Grain and Feed Trade Association (GAFT) and the Federation of Oils, Seeds and Fact Association (FOSFA), also have their own documented contract forms which include their own shipment terms.

These standard terms are not conventions but are available for incorporation purely voluntarily. They will not be incorporated into an international trade contract except by clear and specific reference.[6] For instance, it will not suffice to merely generally refer to Incoterms, but the reference must specifically be to, for example, Incoterms

---

[1] [2018] EWCA Civ 1720, [2019] 1 All ER (Comm) 706, [2019] 1 Lloyd's Rep 444, [2018] All ER (D) 69 (Aug) (EW CA).

[2] *Comptoir d'Achat et de Vente du Boerenbond Belge S/A v Luis de Ridder Ltda (The Julia)* [1949] AC 293, [1949] 1 All ER 269 (UK HL).

[3] Discussed in more detail in later in Chap. 3.2.3.

[4] Cost and Freight (the Incoterms corresponding variant to classical shipping term 'c&f').

[5] The latest edition.

[6] *Stora Enso Oyj v Port of Dundee* [2006] CSOH 40, 2006 Scot (D) 18/3 (Scotland Court of Session, Outer House).

2020. Definitively, a mere reference to 'fob ' or 'cif ' will not be sufficient to trigger incorporation of Incoterms.

A problem caused by such incorporation is that it may be inconsistent with some other terms incorporated by reference into the contract or with express terms of the contract. These standard forms themselves may by reference incorporate the standard terms of another document. Hence, there could be multiple layers of sets of terms.

Which layer takes precedence over another in the event of conflict will be determined according to the intention of the parties as seen from the contract,[7] unless the contract itself expressly sets the order of precedence.[8] In practice, determining the intention of the parties may be an uphill task in many cases.

The general rule of construction of contractual terms in conflict is that a specifically negotiated term will prevail over a standard one. In the case of an unusual or unreasonable term incorporated by reference, a red hand notice may be required,[9] failing which courts or arbitrators may not admit that term as incorporated into the contract.[10] A visit to the popular shipment terms, namely, fob c&f and cif, the subvariants of fob-term and Incoterms are visited in this sub-chapter.

3.2.1 Classical Shipment Terms: fob, c&f, and cif

All fob, c&f and cif contracts are contracts to *ship* the cargo or to *procure the cargo already shipped* on board. When used in an international trade contract, these terms will be accompanied by a port name such as "fob Rotterdam" or "cif Singapore".

Contracts on fob, c&f or cif are all *shipment* contracts. This means that the obligation of the seller is only (i) to ship (i.e. load) the cargo on board a ship as per the contract and deliver the bill of lading to the buyer or (ii) to procure the cargo already shipped on board a ship as per the contract and deliver the bill of lading to

---

[7] *Charles Robert Leader and Henrietta Ada Leader v Duffey and Amyatt Edmond Ray* [1888] 13 App Cas 294 (UK HL).

[8] *Pagnan SpA v Tradax Ocean Transportation SA* [1987] 2 Lloyd's Rep 342, [1987] 3 All ER 565 (EW CA).

[9] In *Thornton v Shoe Lane Parking* [1971] 2 WLR 585 (EW CA), the Court of Appeal held that the more onerous the clause, the better notice of it needed to be given. In *Interfoto Picture Library Ltd v Stiletto Visual Programmes Ltd* [1989] QB 433, [1988] 1 All ER 348, [1988] 2 WLR 615 (EW CA), a contract for hire of photos at the rate of 50 pence per day for 14 days sought to incorporate a term that a holding charge of £5.00 would be charged if the photos were withheld beyond the 14 days. The Court of Appeal, in refusing to allow incorporation of the term, said that 'particularly onerous or unusual' terms require special notice and that when a term is particularly onerous the person seeking to rely on the term must take greater measures to bring it to the attention of the other party.

[10] *OK Petroleum AB v Vitol Energy SA* [1995] 2 Lloyd's Rep 160 (EW CA); *Ceval Alimentos SA v Agrimpex Trading Co Ltd (The Northern Progress) (No. 2)* [1996] 2 Lloyd's Rep 319 (EW HC).

the buyer.[11] The obligation is not to deliver the cargo in the port of discharge. This reinforces that the sale is *documentary* one.

For instance, in a 'fob Rotterdam' contract, the obligation of the seller terminates once he ships the cargo on board a ship arranged by the buyer. In a 'cif Singapore' contract, the obligation of the seller terminates when he ships the cargo on board a ship bound for Singapore. The obligation of the seller is not to deliver the cargo in Singapore or any other port of discharge.

In a fob contract, the seller invoices the buyer only for the price of the cargo. The costs of carriage and insurance are borne by the buyer. Usually, the buyer arranges the carriage and insurance. Generally, in bare fob contracts, the right to determine the exact time within the agreed shipment period at which the goods are to be shipped is with the buyer, subject to a requirement of reasonable notice to be given by the buyer to the seller.[12] However, in some variants of fob contract,[13] the seller may arrange the carriage and charge the buyer for that. Whichever variant of the fob contract, the buyer takes the risk of fluctuations in the cost of carriage and insurance.[14] The risk may be substantial as these markets highly fluctuate and the international trade contract may be concluded long before or after the shipment.

In a c&f contract, the seller invoices the buyer for the cost and freight. Usually, the cost of carriage (i.e. freight) is pre-bundled into the price offered to the buyer for the cargo, e.g. "€2.00 per 200 g bottle of soluble coffee *c&f* Le Havre". In a cif contract, the seller additionally invoices the buyer also for insurance, which is pre-bundled also into the price. This means the seller takes the risk of fluctuations in the carriage and insurance markets. In cif contracts, together with the transfer of the bill of lading, the seller also assigns and delivers the insurance policy to the consignee or next lawful holder of the bill.

3.2.2 Variants of Fob Term

The 'fob' referred to above is called 'bare' or 'straight' fob. A mere reference to 'fob' in an international trade contract will mean 'bare fob'. There are some other variants of 'fob'.

One such variant is 'fob of classic type'. In this variant, the seller will arrange the carriage contract as an agent for the buyer. The buyer will be the contracting party with the carrier and hence the buyer will be the shipper, just as in 'bare fob'. The

[11] *Manbre Saccharine Co v Corn Products Co* [1919] 1 KB 198, [1918-19] All ER Rep 980 (EW HC); *C Groom Ltd v Barbar* [1915] 1 KB 316, [1914-15] All ER Rep 194 (EW HC).

[12] *Dong Yuan Hang Trading Pte Ltd v Sunko (Singapore) Co Pte Ltd* [1994] 3 SLR 603 (SG CA): If the buyer fails to give reasonable notice, then the buyer may be taken to have repudiated the contract.

[13] Discussed later in Chap. 3.2.2.

[14] *Scottish & Newcastle Int Ltd v Othon Ghalanos Ltd* [2008] UKHL 11, [2008] 2 All ER 768, [2008] 2 All ER (Comm) 369, [2008] 1 Lloyd's Rep 462, [2008] All ER (D) 294 (Feb) (UK HL).

buyer will reimburse the seller for the freight paid to the carrier. Additionally, the seller will also charge the buyer a commission for making the carriage arrangement.

Another variant is 'fob with additional carriage services'. In this variant, the seller will enter into a carriage contract with the carrier in the seller's own name. Hence, the seller will be the shipper. Then, the seller will transfer to the bill of lading, hence the benefits of the carriage contract, to the buyer by indorsement in the bill of lading. The seller will charge the buyer the freight paid to the carrier plus a commission for making the carriage arrangement. In both the above-discussed variants of 'fob' contract, the buyer takes the risk of fluctuation in the freight market, unlike in c&f or cif contracts.

In fob, c&f and cif contracts, the risk passes to the buyer from the time of shipment, although the sale and purchase contract between the seller and the buyer may be made after shipment and the seller completes his obligation by procuring cargo already on board a ship according to the contract.[15]

3.2.3 *Incoterms: FOB, CFR, CIF, E Terms, D Terms*

The terms of Incoterms, corresponding to the fob, c&f and cif are FOB, CFR[16] and CIF. Unlike shipping terms (fob, c&f and cif), which are terms used customarily in international trade contracts and thus assigned meaning according to custom and usage, Incoterms FOB, CFR and CIF are documented standard form terms. They will only be incorporated into a contract if clear and specific clauses of incorporation are used.

In fob, c&f and cif contracts, the risk passes upon shipment (i.e. loading onto the ship). Thus, if the seller procures the cargo already on board the ship and indorses the bill of lading to the buyer, the risk retrospectively passes to the buyer from the moment of shipment and not from the time of procurement.[17] This is so even if the 'shipped' date is before the date of sale and purchase contract between the seller and the buyer.

However, in Incoterms[18] FOB, CFR and CIF contracts, the risk passes when the goods are delivered.[19] Delivery has been defined as (i) shipping the cargo on board a ship or (ii) procuring the cargo so shipped on board a ship, according to the contract. From this, it appears that the risk does not pass retrospectively in Incoterms contacts in the second scenario above where the seller procures the cargo already on board a ship to meet its contractual obligations to the buyer.

---

[15] *Manbre Saccharine Co v Corn Products Co* [1919] 1 KB 198, [1918-19] All ER Rep 980 (EW HC); *C Groom Ltd v Barbar* [1915] 1 KB 316, [1914-15] All ER Rep 194 (EWHC).

[16] Cost and freight.

[17] *Manbre Saccharine Co v Corn Products Co* [1919] 1 KB 198, [1918-19] All ER Rep 980 (EW HC); *C Groom Ltd v Barbar* [1915] 1 KB 316, [1914-15] All ER Rep 194 (EWHC).

[18] Incoterms 2020.

[19] Incoterms 2020, FOB/CFR/CIF, Cl. A3.

Under Incoterms, it appears that the risk will pass, where the seller procures cargo already on board a ship when the bill of lading is indorsed in favour of the buyer or buyer's bank. If the risk were to pass at the time of procurement of the cargo by the seller, then there is no assurance that that cargo will be assigned by the seller to the contract with the buyer. The seller may assign the procured cargo to contract with any other buyer. An assignment of the cargo to the buyer will only become crystallised when the bill of lading is indorsed in favour of the buyer or the buyer's bank.

The other Incoterms delivery terms are D terms and E terms. D terms comprise DPU (Delivered at Place Unloaded)[20] which was previously called DAT (Delivered at Terminal),[21] DAP (Delivered at Place) and DDP (Delivered Duty Paid). E terms, commercially called 'ex store' or 'ex warehouse' terms, comprise only EXW (Ex Works). The D terms and E terms are the two extreme opposites in delivery obligation and passing of risk.

Under EXW contracts, for example, 'EXW seller's warehouse in Cardiff', the delivery obligation of the seller completes when the seller places it at the disposal of the buyer in his warehouse in Cardiff. Risk passes to the buyer at the time the seller so places it at his warehouse, even before loading into any vehicle.

Under the D terms contracts at the other extreme, for example, 'DAP buyer's warehouse in Antwerp', the delivery obligation of the seller completes only upon delivery at the buyer's warehouse of cargo that answers the contractual description at the time of delivery. Hence, all risks, including any damage during transit, are with the seller until such delivery. If the cargo is found defective at delivery, the buyer may have the option of rejecting it.[22]

3.3 Passing of Risk

The general rule is that risk passes with property. This general rule has been codified in Section 20(1) of the UK Sale of Goods Act 1979, which reads as follows:

> Unless otherwise agreed, the goods remain at the seller's risk until the property in them is transferred to the buyer, but when the property in them is transferred to the buyer the goods are at the buyer's risk whether delivery has been made or not.

However, the general rule is often displaced in international trade contracts by an agreement to the contrary, expressly or by implication arising from trade usage, custom and practice.

In international trade, usually, the intention of the parties will be that the property would only pass upon payment by the buyer in exchange for the delivery of the bill of lading. As to risk, their intention, in fob, c&f and cif contracts, will be that the risk passes upon shipment (i.e. the moment when the cargo crosses the ship's rail).[23] In

---

[20] Incoterms 2020.

[21] Incoterms 2010.

[22] Provided that the defect is serious enough to trigger breach of a condition or a warranting breach of an innominate term in the contract.

[23] *Comptoir d'Achat et de Vente du Boerenbond Belge S/A v Luis de Ridder Ltda (The Julia)* [1949] AC 293, [1949] 1 All ER 269 (UK HL).

Incoterms[24] FOB, CFR and CIF contracts, by express terms of the Incoterms form, the risk passes upon shipment or procurement. Accordingly, the time risk passes will likely be in advance of the property passing.

The advance passing of the risk may be displaced by agreement of the parties, in particular, by 'out turn' clauses. An 'out turn' clause will say that if the cargo arrives short in quantity or *quality*, then a price adjustment will be made. This means that the intention of the parties is that the risk during transit will be with the seller.

Such clauses will be interpreted strictly against the party relying on it and will not cover a total loss of cargo. In *Soon Hua Seng Co Ltd v Glencore Grain Ltd*,[25] the English High Court said:

> If the goods covered by the shipping documents ... are lost in transit and do not arrive at all, the risk of loss remains on the buyers and no question of any adjustment to the payment ... can arise.

The above case seems to suggest that 'out turn' clauses do not alter the customary placement of risk on the buyer. There are four statutory exceptions to the advancepassing of the risk, provided by the UK Sale of Goods Act 1979,[26] which are:

(i) where delivery has been delayed through the fault of the seller, the loss which might not have occurred but for such fault[27];
(ii) where the seller acts as a bailee or custodian of the cargo, the loss arising from breach of duty to take reasonable care[28];
(iii) where the seller, in a fob of the classical type contract, fails to make a reasonable contract for carriage on behalf of the buyer, the loss or damage to cargo in transit[29];
(iv) where the seller fails to give such notice to the buyer as may enable the buyer to insure the cargo during sea transit, the loss or damage to cargo in transit.[30]

At common law, an exception to the passing of the risk to the buyer was when the condition of the cargo at the time of shipment was such that it could not likely withstand the sea transit.[31] In such cases, the risk of loss of or damage to the cargo would remain with the seller.

The passing of the risk is an important question when making a claim against the insurer. The loss is with the person who bears the risk. Hence, only he will be able to make a claim against the insurer for indemnity against the loss.

---

[24] Incoterms 2020.

[25] [1996] 1 Lloyd's Rep 398 at 405 (EW HC).

[26] In Singapore, the Sale of Goods Act. In Malaysia, the Sale of Goods Act 1957.

[27] Section 20(2) in the UK and Singapore. In Malaysia, Section 26.

[28] Section 20(3) in the UK and Singapore. In Malaysia, Section 26.

[29] Section 32(2) in the UK and Singapore. In Malaysia, Section 39(2).

[30] Section 32(3) in the UK and Singapore. In Malaysia, Section 39(2).

[31] *Mash & Murrell Ltd v Joseph I Emanuel Ltd* [1961] 2 Lloyd's Rep 326, [1962] 1 All ER 77, [1962] 1 WLR 16 (EW CA).

3.4 Passing of Property

For the passing of property, the general rule is that property passes when intended to pass.[32] This general rule has been codified in Section 17(1) of the UK Sale of Goods Act 1979. It reads as follows:

> Where there is a contract for the sale of specific or ascertained goods the property in them is transferred to the buyer at such time as the parties to the contract intend it to be transferred.

Section 18 of the UK Sale of Goods Act 1979 sets out some rules for ascertaining the intention.[33] Usually, the intention of the parties will be that the property passes upon payment by the buyer in exchange for the delivery of the bill of lading. Until then, the seller will retain the right of disposal, although the risk would have ordinarily passed to the buyer upon shipment or, in the case of Incoterms contract, upon shipment or procurement. The passing of property will be particularly important when a party becomes insolvent or a tort action needs to be taken in which case the ownership of the cargo will have to be established.[34]

3.5 Letter of Credit

In domestic trade, a seller could deliver the cargo at the door of the buyer and collect payment against delivery. However, this is not possible in international trade. A buyer will take the risk of losing his money if he pays in advance of shipment. A seller will take the risk of not being paid if he ships in advance of payment. A mechanism workable for both interests developed and that was 'letter of credit'.[35]

3.5.1 The Mechanism of Payment Through Letters of Credit

A letter of credit is an undertaking from the bank to the seller that the bank will pay the amount secured by the letter of credit or up to that amount against presentation of certain documents by the seller. This is directly between the bank and the seller and is independent of the underlying sale and purchase agreement between the seller and the buyer—this is also called the principle of autonomy of letters of credit.[36]

The mechanism of letters of credit is as this. The buyer will instruct his bank to open a letter of credit in favour of the seller. The buyer's bank is called the 'issuing bank'. The buyer's bank will either directly or through a correspondent bank communicate the letter of credit to the seller. The correspondent bank may either 'advise' the seller of the letter of credit and act merely as an agent of the

---

[32] It is conventionally thought that only an owner of cargo can suffer a loss of it, as denoted by the maxim *res perit domino*, meaning 'the thing is lost to the owner'.

[33] See Section 19(3).

[34] *Leigh and Sillavan Ltd v Aliakmon Shipping Co Ltd (The Aliakmon) (HL)* [1986] AC 785, [1986] 2 All ER 145, [1986] 2 WLR 902, [1986] 2 Lloyd's Rep 1 (UK HL).

[35] Also called 'documentary credit'.

[36] See *Malas (Hamzeh) & Sons v British Imex Industries Ltd* [1958] 2 QB 127, [1958] 1 All ER 262, [1958] 2 WLR 100, [1957] 2 Lloyd's Rep 549 (EW CA).

issuing bank or 'confirm' the credit and itself become liable to the seller on terms of the letter of credit. When it confirms, it is called a 'confirming bank' and when it merely advises, it is called an 'advising bank'. The use and role of the correspondent bank will follow the terms of the international trade contract between the buyer and seller. Usually, a seller will require, in the contract, a letter of credit 'confirmed' by a local bank in the country of the seller.

The letter of credit gives an additional layer of protection to the seller, as the bank is liable on it even if the buyer becomes insolvent. An added comfort to the seller with a local advising bank in the picture is that any legal or arbitral action arising in relation to the presentation of documents and payment will be within the local jurisdiction.[37] Another added comfort is that the obligation of the seller to present the documents will be to the local correspondent bank only.

The letter of credit will also usually be stated to be 'irrevocable', as ordinarily required in the contract between the seller and the buyer so that the bank cannot revoke it within the period allowed in the letter of credit for the seller to present the documents once the letter of credit reaches the hands of the seller.[38] This works as a unilateral contract,[39] binding the bank but not the seller, as between the bank and the seller.

The letter of credit will set out the documents to be 'presented' for payment within a certain time frame.[40] The list of documents will usually include the bill of lading, commercial invoice and in case of cif or CIF contract, insurance policy. The letter of credit will also normally require that the bill of lading must be 'shipped' and 'clean' one 'indorsed' to the order of the bank and that the insurance policy must be 'assigned' to the bank. The bill of lading must comply with all matters agreed between the parties, which will be repeated in the letter of credit, such as the time within which the cargo must be shipped, the port of loading and the port of discharge. The full set of original bill of lading must be tendered.[41]

The letter of credit, in standard form, may also require some documents which are not expressed in the contract between the seller and the buyer but implied. For example, a letter of credit may require presentation of a class certificate of the ship issued by a member of the International Association of Classification Societies

---

[37] However, subject to dispute resolution and jurisdiction clause applicable to the letter of credit.

[38] UCP 600, Article 2 renders (by definition) the letter of credit irrevocable. In *Standard Chartered Bank Malaysia Bhd v Duli Yang Maha Mulia Tuanku Ja'Afar Ibni Almarhum Tuanku Abdul Rahman, Yang Di Pertuan Besar Negeri Sembilan Darul Khusus* [2009] 4 MLJ 1 (MY CA), a bank issued, upon instruction of its customer, an irrevocable standby letter of credit (SBLC) subject to UCP 500, which is similar to a bank guarantee, to a beneficiary. Thereafter, the bank notified the beneficiary of the customer's intention to cancel the SBLC. The beneficiary did not respond, but subsequently a few months later made a call on the SBLC. The bank paid. In a suit between the bank and the customer, the Malaysian Court of Appeal held that the SBLC cannot be cancelled except by consent of the beneficiary and such a consent cannot be inferred from the failure of the beneficiary to respond to the cancellation notice. Accordingly, the bank rightly honoured the SBLC and the customer was liable to reimburse the bank.

[39] *Carlill v Carbolic Smoke Ball Company* [1892] EWCA Civ 1, [1893] 1 QB 256, [1891-94] All ER Rep 127 (EW CA).

[40] UCP 600, Article 6(e).

[41] UCP 600, Article 20(a)(iv).

(IACS), although not expressly required in the contract. Such a requirement may be implied in the contract between the seller and the buyer by virtue of trade usage, custom and practice.

In the case of fob of the classical type contracts, Section 32(2) of the UK Sale of Goods Act 1979[42] will apply. This imposes a duty on the seller to make reasonable carriage arrangements. This section reads as follows:

> Unless otherwise authorised by the buyer, the seller must make such contract with the carrier on behalf of the buyer as may be reasonable having regard to the nature of the goods and the other circumstances of the case; and if the seller omits to do so, and the goods are lost or damages in the course of transit, the buyer may decline to treat the delivery to the carrier as a delivery to himself or may hold the seller responsible in damages.

Courts have held that the 'reasonable' carriage contract stipulated in this section requires a carriage contract that (i) is on usual terms,[43] (ii) gives the buyer protective rights against the carrier[44] and (iii) is appropriate to sufficiently protect the cargo while in transit.[45] Incoterms[46] requires the seller, in a CIF contract, to make a carriage contract on usual terms for a carriage to the port of destination.[47]

However, a buyer when instructing the bank to issue the letter of credit must ensure that conditions not found, expressly or by implication, in the contract between the seller and the buyer are not imposed and must ensure that he does not tender a letter of credit that does not comply with the contract between the seller and buyer. If the buyer were to do so, the letter of credit will be a defective tender on behalf of the buyer, which the seller may accept by acting upon it or rejecting it.[48] Such a defective tender will put the seller in breach of the contract with the buyer.

In an international sale and purchase contract, usually, it will be a condition that the letter of credit is a 'confirmed' one. If the buyer breaches it, then the seller will be entitled to reject the letter of credit and withhold the shipment.[49] If a seller does not reject the letter of credit when it does not comply with the contract between the seller and the buyer, then the seller may be taken to have waived the right to reject, with the result that the seller will lose its right to subsequently insist on a compliant letter of credit and also lose the right to withhold shipment on this ground. Such acceptance has been held even to modify the contract between the seller and the buyer.[50]

Sometimes, the letter of credit may also require a certificate issued by an independent surveyor as to the quality, quantity and condition of the cargo. This is particularly

---

[42] Identically reproduced in Section 32(2) of the Singapore Sale of Goods Act, and in Section 39(2) of the Malaysian Sale of Goods Act 1975 with a coverage of 'wharfinger' in addition to 'carrier'.

[43] *Ceval Alimentos SA v Agrimpex Trading Co Ltd (The Northern Progress) (No. 2)* [1996] 2 Lloyd's Rep 319 (EW HC).

[44] *Elof Hansson v Hamel and Horley* [1922] 2 AC 36, [1922] All ER Rep 237 (UK HL).

[45] *Thomas Young and Sons Ltd v Hobson and Partners* [1949] 65 TLR 365 (EW CA).

[46] Incoterms 2020.

[47] Incoterms 2020, CFR/CIF, Cl. A4.

[48] If the breach is considered a breach of condition or of an innominate term ensuing in sufficiently serious consequences of the breach.

[49] *Soproma SpA v Marine and Animal By-Products Corp* [1966] 1 Lloyd's Rep 367 (EW HC).

[50] *Panoutsos v Raymond Hadley Corpn of New York* [1917] 2 KB 437, [1916-17] All ER Rep 448 (EW CA).

common in commodity trade, where price may grossly vary with specifications of the cargo. For instance, in sale and purchase of edible oil of certain specifications and chemical properties, a bill of lading could only confirm the fact that edible oil was shipped in a certain quantity in apparently good condition, but not the specifications of the oil. Hence, the only way to confirm it is by a lab test conducted by an independent surveyor on samples collected from the cargo to be shipped at the port of loading, so that buyer and buyer's bank can be satisfied that the cargo shipped answers the agreed specifications before payment is released. In such cases, it is also usual to find a term in the contract that the certificate is final and conclusive proof of what was shipped. If so agreed, the buyer or any lawful holder of the bill will be estopped from subsequently disputing the quality except in case of fraud.[51]

The letter of credit may be for payment against sight, meaning payment upon presentation of documents, or it can be for deferred payment, meaning payment in a certain number of days, e.g., 30 days or 60 days, after the presentation of documents or the date of the bill of lading. When it is a deferred payment letter of credit, it is common for the seller to arrange with a bank for discounting the letter and paying the discounted amount in advance to the seller. This is called 'negotiating' the letter of credit and, usually, such negotiation is permitted.

Almost always, letters of credit will be issued on terms of Uniform Customs and Practice for Documentary Credits (UCP) published by ICC, the current version of which is UCP 600, by express reproduction of the terms or more likely by incorporation by reference. This will be subject to any express modification or term to the contrary in the letter of credit.[52] However, it must be noted that UCP 600 is not a law or convention, and is incorporated purely on a voluntary basis, and accordingly, it will be subject to cannons of interpretation of contracts, including restrictive interpretation to avoid unjust results, where necessary.

Upon proper presentation of the documents by the seller, the correspondent bank[53] will pay the seller (or the obligation to pay will crystalize in) within five banking days, which is a requirement in UCP 600,[54] and will subsequently transfer the documents to the issuing bank and be reimbursed by the issuing bank, which in turn will deliver the documents to the buyer and be reimbursed by the buyer.[55] If the documents do not comply, then the bank must reject the documents.[56] If the bank fails to so reject within the five banking days, the bank will thereafter be estopped from denying compliance of the documents.[57]

If the bank rejects the documents, it must give notice to the seller within the five banking days, (i) stating it refuses to pay, (ii) listing the discrepancies and (iii)

---

[51] *Gill & Duffus SA v Berger & Co Inc* [1984] AC 382, [1984] 1 All ER 438, [1984] 2 WLR 95, [1984] 1 Lloyd's Rep 227 (UK HL).

[52] UCP 600, Article 1.

[53] Or the issuing bank where no correspondent bank is used.

[54] UCP 600, Articles 14(b) and 15.

[55] UCP 600, Articles 8 and 15.

[56] UCP 600, Article 16.

[57] UCP 600, Article 14(f)

indicating what it is doing with the documents. What the bank may do with the documents can be one of the following four actions: (i) holding the documents pending further instruction from the seller, (ii) holding the documents pending waiver from the seller, (iii) returning the document or (iv) acting in accordance with instruction already received from the seller.

There are many variants or classifications of the letters of credit. To comparatively outline some:

i) Revocable credit and irrevocable credit.
ii) Confirmed credit.
iii) Straight credit and negotiable credit.
A straight credit is payable to the seller (the beneficiary named in the credit) only. A negotiable credit is payable to any person in whose favour the credit has been validly negotiated. A negotiable credit may be open (that may be negotiated in favour of anyone) or restricted (that can be negotiated only to certain persons like the seller's bank).
iv) Sight credit and deferred payment/usance/acceptance credit.
A sight credit is payable upon presentation of compliant documents.
A deferred payment/usance/acceptance credit is payable in a certain number of days after presentation of the compliant documents.
v) Transferable credit.
This allows the seller to require the issuing bank to switch and split the credit to different persons. This happens where the seller is an intermediatory and a large portion of the credit needs to go to the manufacturer of the goods. The seller will return the credit to the issuing bank, which in turn will reissue two credits in the respective amounts for the intermediate seller and the manufacturer. Usually, the buyer will not know how the credit is switched and spilt, so that the manufacturer is kept behind the screen insofar as the buyer is concerned. A transferable credit is different from negotiable credit, where the entire credit is payable to the person in whose favour it has been negotiated. A transferable credit is also different from an assignment of the credit, in which case only the rights under the credit is assigned but not the obligations, whereas with a transferable credit both the rights and obligations are switched to the new beneficiaries under the credit, although the switching does not affect in any way the obligations of the seller to the buyer under the sale and purchase contract.
vi) Red clause/anticipatory/packing credit.
This allows the seller to drawdown the credit, usually a part of it, at certain stage before shipment, for example, upon presentation of warehouse receipt. The buyer (and not any bank) takes the risk of losing the money in case the seller subsequently does not ship the goods.
vii) Revolving credit.
By this, a single credit document is issued, under which multiple payments are to be respectively made upon multiple shipments over a period of time.

A letter of credit issues can be classified into all the above descriptions. For example, the letter of credit can be an irrevocable confirmed sight letter of credit.

Such a credit may either be straight or negotiable one. The terms of paymentmay be at sight or deferred. It may or may not be made transferable. Red clause can be added into it, and similarly revolving undertaking can also be added.

The UCP 600 rules as to the rejection of the documents also apply as between the confirming bank and the issuing bank.[58] In *Malayan Banking Bhd v Punjab National Bank,*[59] a letter of credit was issued by an issuing bank in India for USD1,962,500 plus/minus 2% in value in favour of a beneficiary (seller) in Malaysia. The letter of credit was payable in 60 days after the date of the bill of lading. It was confirmed to the beneficiary by a confirming bank in Malaysia. It was issued subject to UCP 600. The documents required under the letter of credit for payment included a bill of lading. It was one of the terms of the LC that "Short Form, Blank Back, Stale, Freight Forwarder, House Bill of Lading is not Acceptable." The bill of lading tendered was one issued by Diffreight Agencies (M) Sdn Bhd "on behalf of the carriers". It appears that the carriers were not named[60] and that the said Diffreight Agencies was a forwarding agent. Despite the differences, the confirming bank negotiated the letter of credit and paid the seller immediately upon presentation of the documents,[61] and forwarded the documents to the advising bank. The advising bank rejected the documents, however outside the five banking days' time-limit, and refused to pay. Sixty days after the date of the bill of lading, the confirming bank sued the issuing bank before the Malaysian High Court. The court held that the documents were compliant and that in any event as the advising bank missed the five banking days' time-limit, they had to pay. The decision is incorrect as far as the compliance issue was concerned. Insofar as the five banking days' time-limit was concerned, that is a more difficult issue. Although the issuing bank missed the time limit, the breach by the confirming bank to tender a bill of lading as expressly stipulated in the letter of credit is a fundamental one.[62] Even in the absence of any objection by the issuing bank, the burden on the confirming bank will be to establish before the court that it had complied with the terms of the letter of credit before it can found a valid cause of action. These points were not considered by the High Court, which resulted in its decision being overturned by the Court of Appeal.[63]

The Court of Appeal, in this case, held that Article 16[64] of UCP 600 will help a bank when the discrepancy is in the contents of the document as opposed to the document itself. In this case, the document tendered was a different one from that required, hence the question of discrepancy did not arise. The breach in this case is a fundamental one to which Article 16 is not a defence. The court further observed that Article1 of UCP 600 provides that the UCP standard terms are "binding … unless expressly modified or excluded by the credit." On this basis, the court added

---

[58] UCP 600, Article 16, read together with Article 2 definition of 'presenter'.

[59] [2018] MLJU 1716 (MY HC).

[60] Contrary to the UCP 600, Article 20 requirements as to form of bill of lading.

[61] The payment was made against a fax copy of the documents, against outside the scope of the letter of credit, whilst UCP 600, Article 17 requires original documents to be tendered for payment.

[62] See also UCP 600, Article 1.

[63] *Punjab National Bank v Malayan Banking Berhad* [2020] 1 LNS 232, [2020] 5 MLJ 732 (MY CA).

[64] About discrepancy in documents.

that the 'express exclusionary clause', in this case, prohibiting the house bills was a condition precedent that will render Article 16 inapplicable against a breach of this express clause. The school of thought adopted in the judgment of the Court of Appeal is a sound one.

In the event of a rejection by the bank, if the seller is within the time frame provided by the terms of the letter of credit, the seller may re-tender compliant documents within the time frame.[65] The bank has an onerous duty to check the documents presented and decide if they comply. If the bank wrongfully refuses to pay, then the bank will be liable both to the seller (by reason for issuing or confirming the credit)[66] and to the buyer (for failing to comply with the agreed instruction). If the bank wrongfully pays, then it will not be entitled to reimbursement by the buyer.[67]

The bank's duty to examine the documents is limited to documents alone[68] and to what they appear to be on their face.[69] Hence, the bank will not be liable in the event of forged documents.[70] There is some tolerance when the description of the goods in documents other than the invoice[71] is in general terms not inconsistent with the description of the goods in the letter of credit.[72]

At common law, the documents presented must strictly comply with the terms of the letter of credit.[73] There was no flexibility or application of the maxim *de minimis non curat lex.*[74] In *Moralice (London) Ltd v ED & F Man,*[75] the letter of credit was for 5,000 bags and the bill of lading stated 4,997. The buyer rejected the documents and the goods, which the court held the buyer was entitled to. One of the documents presented did not comply with this. The bank rejected the document for this. The House of Lords held that the bank was entitled to do so, despite that the non-compliance was so trivial. Rationale behind the strict-compliance duty is that it is the bank that determines the fitness of the document for payment and the bank, which is not an expert in the trade, cannot exceed the mandate of its customer and determine any issue of discrepancy whether it is trivial or not. Survey by ICC[76] and SITPRO[77] has shown the rejection rate at the first presentation as high as 50–60%.

UCP 600 requires the documents presented to be in accordance with the letter of credit, the terms of UCP 600 and *international standard banking practice.*[78] However,

---

[65] UCP 600, Article 16(c) and (e). See also *SIAT di Dal Ferro v Tradax Overseas SA* [1980] 1 Lloyd's Rep 53 (EW CA) for a similar position when the documents are tendered directly by the seller to the buyer. In the case of a direct tender, if the rejection by the buyer, in any particular case, is treated as a termination of the contract for breach by the seller in tendering defective documents, then the seller will not be able to re-tender any longer.

[66] But not by merely advising the credit.

[67] *Credit Agricole Indosuez v Generale bank and Seco Steel Trading Inc and Considar Inc (No. 2)* [2000] 1 Lloyd's Rep 123, [1999] 2 All ER (Comm) 1016 (EW HC).

[68] UCP 600, Articles 5 and 14(a).

[69] UCP 600, Article 14(a).

[70] *Gian Singh & Co Ltd v Banque De L'Indochine* [1972-1974] 1 SLR 28 (SG CA), speech of Tan Ah Tah J.

[71] Strict conformation in description of goods with that in the letters of credit is a must in invoice (UCP, Article 18(c)).

[72] UCP 600, Article 14(e), read together with Article 18(c).

[73] *Equitable Trust Co of New York v Dawson Partners Ltd* [1926] 27 Lll L Rep 49 (UK HL).

[74] 'The law does not concern itself with trifles'.

[75] [1954] 2 Lloyd's Rep 526 (EW HC).

[76] 'International Chamber of Commerce'.

[77] SITPRO Limited, formerly known as Simpler Trade Procedures Board.

[78] UCP 600, Article 6.

UCP 600 [79] exempts the bank from liability for "form, sufficiency, accuracy, genuineness, falsification or legal effect of any documents". This provision must not be misunderstood to dilute the strict compliance duty, called for in *Moralice*, in any way, which is always the standard.

UCP 600[80] requires the bill of lading to have the name of the carrier and to be signed by the carrier or its named agent or by the master or his named agent. It must be stated whether the signor is the carrier, master or agent. If agent, it must further state whether he is the agent for carrier or master. No notation of the bill being subject to charterparty, called 'charterparty bill of lading', is allowed unless the letter of credits permits the same.[81] In the case of a charterparty bill, an additional option is provided in that it may be signed by the charterer or its agent, with the same details as required in the case of a non-charterparty bill.[82]

In *HSBC Bank Malaysia Bhd v Dharani Sugars & Chemical Ltd and another appeal*,[83] the sugar was sold on FOB terms, buyer to arrange and nominate the ship and payment by letter of credit. The buyer chartered a ship and nominated her. The buyer got the letter of credit issued by its bank, which was silent about the charterparty . The letter of credit was subject to UCP 500,[84] which required the 'name of the carrier' to be stated in the bill [like UCP 600, Article 20(a)(i)] and prohibited charterparty bill [like Article 20(a)(vi)], unless permitted agreed between parties.[85] The carrier issued a bill subject to the charterparty.[86] The bill was signed "For UNICORN …" and "AS AGENTS". The seller presented the bill[87] to the buyer's bank for payment. The bank refused on grounds that the bill did not state whom 'Unicorn' was an agent for and that the bill was subject to charterparty. The seller sued the bank. The Malaysian Federal Court upheld both grounds advanced by the bank, resulting in the action being summarily struck out,[88] although it was the buyer's fault that it did not instruct its bank to permit charterparty bill in the letter of credit, knowing that it had contracted charterparty for the carriage. This was because the letter of credit transaction was an independent one between the bank and the seller and the terms between the buyer and the seller do not come into this. The bank's duty is only to act based on the documents on the face of them and to ensure that the documents tendered do comply with the terms of the letter of credit.

---

[79] UCP 600, Article 34.

[80] UCP 600, Article 20(a)(i).

[81] UCP 600, Article 20(a)(vi).

[82] UCP 600, Article 22(a)(ii).

[83] [2011] 1 MLJ 52 (MY FC).

[84] Predecessor to UCP 600.

[85] UCP 500, Article 25(a).

[86] In a BIMCO CONGENBILL form. 'BIMCO' is the abbreviation for Baltic and International Maritime Council.

[87] Along with other required documents.

[88] The court also made reference to UCP 500 , Article 25 that makes provision in relation to charterparty bills when such bills are permitted by the letter of credit. The quite similar provision to this in the UCP 600 is Article 22.

Additionally, in the event of non-complying documents, UCP 600 [89] makes provision for the bank to approach the buyer for a waiver in advance of payment.[90] If the waiver is granted, the bank will be relieved of any liability as a result of making the payment in respect of that waived non-compliance. Another avenue the banks have adopted to settle the remittance is by 'under reserve' payments. In such cases, the seller is liable to indemnify the bank in the event of any claim made by the buyer in respect of any defect in the documents.

At the tail end, the issuing bank will usually indorse the bill of lading in favour of the buyer (or to his order) and release the documents to the buyer upon payment or in exchange for 'trust receipt'. A trust receipt will make the buyer a trustee for the bank in respect of the cargo. The buyer may receive the cargo or sell the bill of lading. The buyer will hold the proceeds in trust for the bank. If the buyer defaults in payment, then the bank may equitably trace the proceeds. If the buyer defaults in making the payment or giving a trust receipt, as per agreement between the bank and the buyer, the bank as the pledgee may realise the security by collecting the cargo and selling it or by selling the bill of lading through indorsement.

In *Indian Overseas Bank v United Coconut Oil Mills Inc*,[91] a dispute arising from the tender of documents under letter of credit came before the Singapore Court of Appeal. In this case, a seller and buyer agreed on sale and purchase of two shipments[92] of cochin type or crude coconut oil, payment by letter of credit. The buyer arranged its bank to open a letter of credit.[93] The validity period of the letter of credit was until 15th October 1981. The documents required by the letter of credit included a 'certificate of analysis' issued by an independent laboratory, certifying free fatty acid (FFA) content in terms of 'lauric acid'.

The seller, through its bank, tendered the documents including a certificate issued by one company to the buyer's bank. The buyer's bank forwarded the same to the buyer on 1 October 1981.[94] The buyer rejected it on grounds that the certificate was not from an independent laboratory. The buyers' bank accordingly informed the seller's bank that the documents were rejected for the said reason. The seller then submitted another certificate, issued by Camino Chemicals Inc on, which again the buyer's bank forwarded to the buyer. The buyer once again rejected, on 7th October 1981, claiming that a defective tender cannot be subsequently made good. The buyer's bank conveyed it to the seller's bank on 10th October 1981. The seller's bank protested, saying the re-tender was good as it was made within the validity period of the letter of credit. Then, on 16th October 1981, the buyer came out with new and switched reasons for rejecting, namely[95] that the Camino report was not a

[89] UCP 600, Article 16(b).

[90] In the case of a correspondent bank, it will approach the buyer through the issuing bank.

[91] [1993] 1 SLR 141 (SG CA).

[92] Among others.

[93] Subject to Uniform Customs and Practice for Documentary Credits (1974 Revision) Rules (UCP Rules).

[94] The procedure for the bank to check with the buyer on any discrepancy is in Article 16(b) of the current UCP 600. This does not, however, extend the five banking days' time-limit, in Article 14(b), to determine documents' compliance in sub-article 14(b).

[95] Among others.

certificate of analysis and that the FFA was described in terms of 'lauric and oleic acid'. This was again conveyed to the seller's bank on 20th October 1981.

The seller sued the buyer's bank. On the question of the Camino report, the court held that the Camino report was a certificate of analysis. The court said that the requirement of strict compliance with the terms of the letter of credit did not mean literal compliance and inconsequential discrepancies can be disregarded. The test was whether the documents, properly read and understood, do not contain any discrepancy that called for an inquiry or investigation or invited litigation. On the question of the description of the FFA content, the court agreed that it was not conforming. There was evidence before the court to say that by trade usage 'lauric' and 'oleic' measurements were interchangeable. But the court pointed out that a bank's acceptance or rejection of the documents are based on what was on the face of the documents, by a standard of an ordinary and competent banker, and a banker would not be expected to undertake an examination of the trade usage. However, the court held that the buyer's bank was estopped by conduct from raising this as it did not raise this objection until the expiry period of the letter of credit although it had the option of doing so. Accordingly, the seller was entitled to assume that there was no objection on this count. Hence, judgement for the seller.

In another case in Singapore, *Bhojwani & Anor v Chung Khiaw Bank Ltd*,[96] the Court of Appeal there again had an opportunity to deal with the practical scope of the strict conformity requirement, construction of the documents tendered and the procedure for resolving discrepancies. In this case, Buyer's bank opened 2 letters of credit for shipments of motor vehicles in identical terms. Each was for four units of new motor cars of specific make and model, shipment from Hamburg to Singapore. Pursuant to the terms of the letter of credit, the seller was to furnish among others insurance policy covering the transit-risks from seller's warehouse to buyer's warehouse and a certificate of shipment issued by the shipowner, and the full set of bills of lading. The seller tendered the documents. There was one certificate of shipment only covering both bills of lading and issued by the shipowner's agent. The certificate described the car as in the letters of credit save that the word 'new' was not included. The bank notified the buyer only of the discrepancy that the certificate was issued by the shipowner's agent. The buyer replied, accepting the discrepancy. The insurance policy coverage was from 'warehouse West Germany to warehouse Singapore'. The bill of lading showed that the goods were received in Stuttgart and the loading port was Hamburg, both in West Germany, and the port of discharge was Singapore. The bank made the payment.

The buyer failed to reimburse the bank. The bank sued the buyer and obtained summary judgment. In an attempt to set aside the summary judgment, the buyer argued that the bank should not have paid because there was no strict compliance. This allegation was premised upon four grounds. One, there should have been two separate certificates of shipment, one for each bill of lading, and the certificate should have been issued by the shipowner. Second, the bills were not originals. Third, the insurance policy coverage differed from that required in the letters of credit. Fourth, the certificate of shipment missed the word 'new'.

---

[96] [1990] 1 SLR 128 (SG CA).

As to the first ground, the court held whilst there must be strict conformation, that was not all and that could not be rigidly applied to all situations. Conformation was a matter of construction and each case must be decided on its own merits. As it was not expressly said in the letters of credit that there must be a separate certificate, the single certificate tendered satisfied the purchase, hence no non-conformity on this count. On the objection of the buyer that the certificate was issued by the shipowner's agent, the court held that the discrepancy was waived by the buyer by accepting it, although the buyer did not sign the acceptance on the certificate itself. When the bank considers there is a discrepancy, this is what the bank must do, that is, ask the buyer for its instructions and follow the same, which the bank did.[97] As to the second ground, the court found that the bills appeared to have been properly signed, and dismissed this ground. As to the third ground, the court held that the insurance policy was merely more specific and not discrepant. As to the fourth ground, the court held that it was permissible to describe the goods in general terms not inconsistent with the description in the letter of credit, other than in invoice. This was allowed by Article 32(c) of the UCP for Documentary Credits (1974 Revision).[98] In this case, the missing 'new' was not inconsistent with the letter of credit but was merely more general and less specific than the letters of credit description. Accordingly, the court dismissed this ground too. Accordingly, the court found for the bank, by way of summary judgment.

A similar decision was reached in *JH Rayner & Co Ltd v Hambro's Bank Ltd,*[99] where the letter of credit was for 'coromandel groundnuts', but the bill of lading tendered described it as 'machine shelled groundnuts kernels'. They meant the same thing in the trade. However, a bank is not expected to know customary trade terms and hence the English Court of Appeal held that it was rightly entitled to reject the documents.

3.5.2 Fraud Exception to Autonomy of Letters of Credit

Whilst it is the absolute and strict obligation of the issuing or confirming bank to pay upon presentation by the seller the documents complying with the terms of the letter of credit, there is one exception to it, namely the 'fraud exception '. Even if the documents on the face of them strictly comply with the terms of the letter of credit, the bank should not pay if it is aware of the fraud, such as the bill of lading stating the goods are shipped when they were not. Although contractual terms like UCP 600 Article 34 will relieve the bank if it pays upon documents that are false, that protection will only be available when the bank pays *without knowledge* of the

---

[97] Now the procedure for the bank to check with the buyer on any discrepancy is in Article 16(b) of the current UCP 600. This does not, however, extend the five banking days' time-limit, in Article 14(b), to determine documents' compliance in sub-article 14(b).

[98] Article 32(c) of the UCP 1974 version. This is now provided in the current UCP 600, Articles 18(c) and 14(e).

[99] [1943] KB 37, [1942] 2 All ER 694 (EW CA).

falsification but not if the bank pays with a clear knowledge of the falsification or fraud. The burden on the bank in this respect is onerous in that if it refuses to pay and later it transpires there was no fraud and the bank's perception of the fraud was wrong, then the bank will be liable to the seller for failing to honour the letter of credit.

It must be noted that although it is said that the fraud is tested only in relation to the documents, the fact that the documents falsely describe the goods or their order and condition within the knowledge of the seller, will relate the goods-fraud to the documents. There can be some frauds that are document-centric such as false shipment date in the bill.

There is no doubt that the general rule is that the bank's obligation is independent of the underlying sale and purchase transaction and that the bank cannot put its head into any dispute between the seller and the buyer. In *Deutsche Ruckversicherung AG v Walbrook Insurance Co Ltd & Ors,*[100] the English High Court said this general principle[101] as follows:

> It is the policy of the law, save in cases of fraud or illegality, not to interfere by injunction with the operations of banks under letters of credit and similar instruments, but to leave the plaintiff [buyer] to his remedy against the beneficiary [seller] for breach of the underlying contract. Where an injunction is sought against a bank, the plaintiff must make out a clear case of fraud to the knowledge of the bank.

The only exception to it is fraud in relation to the documents, such as tendering a false 'shipped' bill, tendering a 'clean' bill when the seller knows that the goods shipped are defective or tendering the bill with false quantity when the seller knows the quantity loaded is short of that stated in the bill. In *Edward Owen Edward Owen Engineering Ltd v Barclays Bank International Ltd,*[102] Lord Denning MR said the exception to the autonomy of letters of credit as "[t]he only exception is when there is a clear fraud of which the bank has had notice." The English Court of Appeal in *RD Harbottle (Mercantile) Ltd v National Westminster Bank*[103] emphasised that the letters of credit are the "the life blood of international trade" and it must be "a clear case of established fraud to prevent payment under a credit" to invoke the fraud exception.

English courts seem to have kept the fraud exception within narrow confines. In *Montrod v Frandkotter Fleischvertriebs GmbH,*[104] Potter LJ did not favour an

---

[100] [1995] 1 Lloyd's Rep 153, [1994] 4 All ER 181, [1995] 1 WLR 1017 at 1027 (EW HC), affirmed on appeal by CA [1996] 1 All ER 791, [1996] 1 WLR 1152, [1996] 1 Lloyd's Rep 345, [1996] 5 Re LR 91.

[101] The general rule is the same in Malaysia. See *Kiramas Sdn Bhd v Federal Land Development Authority* [1991] 2 MLJ 1998 (MY HC). It is also same in Singapore. See *Beam Technology (MFG) Pte Ltd v Standard Chartered Bank* [2003] 1 SLR 597 (SG CA).

[102] [1978] 1 All ER 976, [1977] 3 WLR 764, [1978] 1 Lloyd's Rep 166, [1978] QB 159 at 171 (EW CA).

[103] [1977] 2 All ER 862, [1977] 3 WLR 752, [1978] QB 146 (EW CA).

[104] [2002] CLC 446, [2001] EWCA Civ 1954, [2002] 3 All ER 697, [2002] 1 WLR 1975, [2002] 1 All ER (Comm) 257, [2001] All ER (D) 335 (Dec) (EW CA).

extension of the fraud exception to a 'general nullity exception' as 'it would place banks in a further dilemma as to the necessity to investigate facts which they are not competent to do'. However, fraud and other elements like forgery or nullity can be interconnected. If the document forged and hence a nullity, and the bank comes to know that, then there will also be fraud within the knowledge of the bank in relation to the document. Sir John Donaldson MR in *Bolivinter Oil v Manhattan Bank*[105] explained the rationale behind the narrow approach as that it was to protect the "bank's greatest asset ... namely its reputation for financial and contractual probity".

Singapore courts seem to take a wider approach to the fraud exception. In *Beam Technology (MFG) Pte Ltd v Standard Chartered Bank,*[106] the Singapore Court of Appeal[107] said *obiter* that the "bank is not obliged to pay if it has established within the seven-day period that a material document required under the credit is forged and null and void and notice of it is given within that period."

In *The American Accord,*[108] a loading broker, acting as agents for the carrier, issued the bill of lading with a false shipment date stated as 15 December 1976 when the actual shipment date was 16 December 1976. The loading brokers did this in order to match the deadline for shipment allowed in the letter of credit. The seller had no knowledge of this falsification and presented the documents to the bank for payment under the letter of credit. The bank rejected the documents saying it "had information in their possession which suggested that shipment was not effected as it appears in the bill of lading" and refused to pay. The seller sued the bank and the banked relied on the fraud exception. The House of Lords held that the case did not fall within the fraud exception as the seller did not commit any fraud, but it was committed by the carrier's agent.

The American Accord took too narrow an approach which will mean that the bank should pay even if the bank knew that the material information in the documents had been falsified. What about then if the bank knew that the goods were not even loaded by the carrier's agents onto the ship? Will the bank still have to pay? Here, not only the buyer's interest is affected but also the bank's interest in the sense that the bank might have financed the purchase. Irrespective of who committed the fraud, the commercial interest in the documents is with the seller who relies on the false documents to claim its payment, even if the seller did not know it is false. The *ratio* in *The American Accord* might be revisited by a court in the future.

[105] [1984] 1 All ER 351, [1984] 1 WLR 392, [1984] 1 Lloyd's Rep. 251 (EW CA).

[106] [2003] 1 SLR 597 (SG CA).

[107] When deciding an interlocutory application.

[108] *United City Merchants (Investments) Ltd and Others v Royal Bank of Canada and Others (The American Accord)* [1983] 1 AC 168, [1982] 2 All ER 720, [1982] 2 WLR 1039, [1982] 2 Lloyd's Rep 1 (UK HL).

Part II
Bills of Lading

Chapter 4
Cargo Claims: Legal Bases

This chapter considers the possible branches of law under which cargo claims may be mounted. They are: contract, bailment, tort of negligence and tort of conversion. This chapter considers cargo claims brought by the bill of lading holder, seller, owner of cargo, etc. against the contractual carriers, shipowners, independent contractors like strovedores, etc. The utility of each type of action and a comparison between them, when more than one is available, are set out. The question of existence of contract in carriage transactions is examined. This covers direct contract (including one by demise clause), statutory contact by Bills of Lading Act 1855/Carriage of Goods by Sea Act 1992, contract by agency on loading and implied contracts before loading/on loading or discharge. The distinction between misdelivery (for which an action lies in conversion) and a mere non-delivery (for which an action lies only in contract) are clearly set out. The difference between proprietary interest and possessory interest are observed in the study of conversion. The application of contractual limitations in negligence actions are observed. Burden of proof in bailment actions, head bailments, sub-bailments, terms of bailment and incorporation of jurisdiction and choice of law clauses into bailment terms are dealt with.

4.1 Introduction

The branches of law relevant to cargo claims are laws of contract, tort (negligence or conversion) and bailment. It is common for a cargo claim to be pleaded under multiple branches of the law, concurrently or in the alternative.

Cargo claims will commonly be bought by the holder of the bill of lading against the carrier when the goods are not delivered, short delivered, delivered in damaged condition or late delivered. The holder of the bill taking the action, quite commonly, will be the end-consignee but it can be others such as the consignor, shipper, seller or the banker to whom the bill has been pledged. It will be the seller, for instance, where the buyer has defaulted in payment and the bill of lading has not been parted with. It

A. Kasi, *The Law of Carriage of Goods by Sea*,
https://doi.org/10.1007/978-981-33-6793-7_4

can also be because seller has retained the risk of damage to the goods until delivery, though this is not the popular norm in international trade. It will be a banker when the banker is the lawful holder of the bill as pledgee and the buyer has defaulted in payment to the bank.

There are also other instances of cargo claims such as those by the holder of the bill of lading against the shipowner[1] who is not the contractual carrier, against an on-carrier who performed a transshipment leg, a warehouse operator, a stevedore and so forth. An action may also lie against a non-vehicle owning carrier (NVOC) such as a freight forwarder when the NVOC is the contractual carrier.[2]

An incentive for a cargo claimant in taking the action, under whatever branch of the law, against the shipowner is that the ship (or sister ship) can be arrested, which will normally result in the Protection and Indemnity (P&I) Club giving security, by way of undertaking to pay any award, for release of the ship. Other than that, an action may lie at the instance of a cargo owner who is not the holder of the bill of lading in negligence for damage caused to his goods.

This chapter is to consider the actions in contract, bailment, negligence and actions for misdelivery (conversion) and non-delivery (contract). The next chapter is, among others, for the third-party protection mechanisms, namely, the UK Contracts (Rights of Third Parties) Act 1999, Himalaya clause and circular indemnity clause.

4.2 Contract-Action

The terms of the contract of carriage will be contained in the applicable shipping document, which can be a bill of lading, sea waybill, ship's delivery order. The terms may be in the time or voyage charterparty, if there is one. In such case, the charterparty terms will supersede, as between the carrier and the charterer, any terms in any bill of lading issued in respect of the carriage.

It has not been a straightforward question, in the carriage of goods by sea, whether there is a contract between certain parties. A contractual link can be there in many scenarios, some of which are these. A direct contract between the parties, e.g. between a shipper and carrier on terms of the bill of lading or sea waybill, or between a shipowner and time or voyage charterer on terms of the charterparty. A contract by agency, e.g. where the shipper contracts with the charterer for the carriage and subsequently the charterer issues the bill on behalf of the shipowner—here the contract, from the time of issuance of the bill, is between the shipowner and the shipper. A statutory contract by operation of the relevant statute that transfers the contractual rights under a bill of lading or other shipping documents to the transferee of the bill or the consignee—the statutory contract is between the transferee of the bill/consignee

[1] References to 'shipowner' includes disponent shipowner (i.e. demise charterer). See *The Pacific Wisdom* [1998] 3 SLR 705 (SG CA): "In admiralty proceedings, the phrase 'owners of a ship or vessel' was capable of encompassing the bareboat or demise charterers of the ship or vessel."

[2] See Chapter 2.2.5 for a discussion of the status and transferability of bills issued by NVOCs.

and the carrier. An implied contract between the *consignor* (who may be a different person from the shipper such as in a pure fob contract) and the shipowner on loading or delivery of goods by the consignor to the shipowner. An implied contract between the holder of the bill/consignee and the shipowner upon discharge by the said holder or consignee, where the shipowner is not the contractual carrier. This sub-chapter is for the study of the direct contract, statutory contract, contract by agency principle and implied contract.

4.2.1 Direct Contract

There will be a direct contract between a shipper and a carrier or between a shipowner and a charterer—the most obvious cases. The shipowner may act directly or through the master in signing the shipowner's bills—when a master signs, it is usually deemed that the master signed it for the shipowner. Parol terms agreed between the carrier and the shipper, outside or contrary to the terms of the bill of lading contract, are admissible as between the carrier and the shipper to supersede the terms of the bill of lading.

4.2.1.1 Between Shipper and Carrier

A shipper may deal directly with the shipowner. This is a straightforward case, where the contract is directly between the shipper and the shipowner. Alternatively, the shipper may deal with a time-charterer. In this case, the contract will initially be between the shipper and the charterer. Subsequently, the charter may issue the bill of lading with a demise or identity of carrier clause that will declare the charterer to be an agent of the shipowner.[3] This will render it a shipowner's bill of lading. Thus, bill of lading contract will be between the shipowner and the shipper.

A demise clause will declare that at all times, even before the bill was issued, the charterer was acting as an agent for the shipowner—thus, retrospective effect.[4] This will mean that the shipowner was an *undisclosed* principal from the beginning to the time the bill was issued. The concept of undisclosed principal is well recognised in law. While it is so recognised in England and Wales[5] at common law, this has been codified in many Commonwealth countries, including Malaysia,[6] that has a Contract Act modelled on the Indian Contract Act 1872. The result of the principal

---

[3] In *MB Pyramid Sound NV v Briese Schiffahrts GmbH and Co KG MS Sina and Latvian Shipping Assoc Ltd (The Ines)* [1995] 2 Lloyd's Rep 144 (EW HC), it was accepted without challenge that when a time-charterer issues a bill to the shipper with a demise clause, the relationship (and prior contract) between the time-charterer and the shipper disappears upon the bill being issued.

[4] Discussed in detail later in this chapter.

[5] And Singapore.

[6] Malaysian Contracts Act 1950.

being undisclosed is that the other contracting party has the option of taking action against the principal or agent for events until disclosure.[7] As far as an action against the shipper[8] is concerned, it may only be taken by the shipowner as the principal but not the agent even for the events until disclosure.[9] A typical demise clause would read as follows:

> If the ship is not owned by (or chartered by demise) to the company or line by whom the bill of lading is issued (as may be the case notwithstanding anything that appears to the contrary) this bill of lading shall take effect only as a contract with the owner (or demise charterer) as the case may be as principal made through the agency of the said company or line who acts as agents only, and who shall be under no personal liability whatsoever in respect thereof.

A similar effect will be achieved by an identity of the carrier clause, which will be simpler and clearer than a demise clause. An identity of carrier clause will typically read as follows:

> The contract evidenced by this bill of lading is between the Merchant and the Owner of the vessel named herein and it is, therefore, agreed that the said shipowner alone shall be liable for any damage or loss due to any breach or non-performance of any obligation arising out of the contract of carriage.

A direct contract is actionable two-way. The shipper may take action against the shipowner (or charterer, in the case of a pure charter's bill) under the bill such as for damages to the goods.[10] Similarly, the shipowner (or charterer, in the case of a pure charter's bill) may take action against the shipper under the bill such as for freight.[11]

In *The Berkshire*,[12] a bill issued by the charterer with a demise clause was accepted as the contract between the shipowner and the shipper without challenge.[13] In *The Jalamohan*,[14] the charterer issued a bill with a demise clause. The freight was collected by the charterer and the bill was marked "Freight Prepaid". However, the shipowner was not paid by the charterer and the shipowner made a claim for *quantum meruit* freight against the shipper. The claim failed because the bill constituted the

[7] In the UK and Singapore, the position of an agent where the principal is not disclosed will be regulated by the common law. In India, it is codified in Section 231 (para 1) of the Indian Contract 1872 Act. In Malaysia, the Indian provision is reproduced in Section 184(a) of the Contracts Act 1950.

[8] Or transferee of the bill if the liabilities under the bill has been transferred subject to the relevant statutory scheme. See Chapter 2.2.10.3.

[9] In the UK and Singapore, this is regulated by the common law. In India, this has been codified in Sections 226, 230 and 232 of the Indian Contract Act 1872. In Malaysia, this has been codified in Sections 179, 183 and 185 of the Contracts Acts 1950.

[10] E.g. for damage to or loss of cargo, short delivery, non-delivery, delayed delivery, etc.

[11] E.g. for freight, shipping dangerous cargo without sufficient notice, etc.

[12] *The Berkshire* [1974] 1 Lloyd's Rep 185 (EW HC).

[13] Similarly, it was accepted without challenge in *Ngo Chew Hong Edible Oil Pte Ltd v Scindia Steam Navigation Co Ltd (The Jalamohan)* [1988] 1 Lloyd's Rep 443 (EW HC).

[14] *Ngo Chew Hong Edible Oil Pte Ltd v Scindia Steam Navigation Co Ltd (The Jalamohan)* [1988] 1 Lloyd's Rep 443 (EW HC).

contract between the shipowner and the shipowner by virtue of the demise clause. Hence, the shipowner was bound by the "Freight Prepaid" annotation.

Similarly, in *Cho Yang Shipping Co Ltd v Coral (UK) Ltd*,[15] the English Court of Appeal refused to allow the shipowner to claim freight from the shipper, however, for a different reason. In this case, the freight rate between the shipowner and the charterer was different from the freight rate between the charterer and the shipper. This led the court to find that the charterer contracted with the shipper as principal rather than as an agent of the shipowner. The result was that the shipowner could not make a claim against the shipper under the bill of lading contract. In any event, in this case, the bill of lading issued to the shipper was marked "Freight Prepaid". Hence, even if the shipowner was a party to the bill of lading contract, the shipowner would have been bound by the "Freight Prepaid" annotation and would not have been able to recover any freight from the shipper. In *The Ines*,[16] it was accepted without challenge that when a time-charterer issues a bill to the shipper with a demise clause, the relationship (and prior contract) between the time-charterer and the shipper disappears upon the bill being issued.

If the shipowner wished to intercept and collect the freight directly from the shipper, the shipowner must give notice directly to the shipper of the termination of the agency of the charterer and claim any freight unpaid under the bill.[17] Usually, as between the shipowner and the charterer, the charterparty will give a lien on sub-freight to the shipowner, which it may exercise when the charterer is in default. The lien may be exercised only by giving the notice directly to the shippers.[18]

This was well demonstrated by *Cascade Shipping Inc v Eka Jaya Agencies (Pte) Ltd*,[19] decided by the Singapore Court of Appeal. In this case, a ship was on time charter. The charterparty authorised the charterer to issue bills of lading, as agents for the shipowner, with a demise clause. It also included a lien clause which gave the shipowner a lien on sub-freight. The charterer had an agent who issued bills and collected freight. The charterer defaulted in payment of hire. The shipowner gave notice to the charterer's agents that the shipowner had exercised the lien and accordingly asked the agent to pay, to the shipowner, any freight they have collected and were holding as well as the freight that they will collect in the future. Then the shipowner quickly switched its position by saying it was claiming freight as the principal in the bills of lading issued.

The agent refused to pay, and the shipowner sued the agent. The court summarily dismissed[20] the claim of the shipowner holding that the shipowner did not have a

---

[15] [1997] 2 Lloyd's Rep 641 (EW CA).

[16] *MB Pyramid Sound NV v Briese Schiffahrts GmbH and Co KG MS Sina and Latvian Shipping Assoc Ltd (The Ines)* [1995] 2 Lloyd's Rep 144 (EW HC).

[17] If a shipowner were to do so otherwise than pursuant to the terms of the charterparty, the shipowner will be liable in breach of contract to the charterer.

[18] Even if the notice is given otherwise than pursuant to the charterparty, the notice will bind the shipper from the moment of the notice.

[19] [1993] 1 SLR 980 (SG CA).

[20] At the instance of an application by the shipowner for summary judgment.

right to intercept otherwise than by the exercise of the lien. The exercise must be by giving notice to the shippers asking them to pay any freight, not paid yet, to the shipowners. It could not be exercised by giving notice to the charterer or its agent to on-pay any freight collected or to be collected.

However, if no bill of lading is subsequently issued or a pure charterer's bill is issued, then the contract will be between the shipper and the charterer. A bill signed by a charterer will be a pure charterer's bill when there is no demise or identity of carrier clause to render it a shipowner's bill. It may sometimes happen that no bill is subsequently issued such as where the goods are damaged before loaded onto the ship.[21]

The effect of the direct contract will partly be lost when the bill is transferred into the hands of a consignee or a third party who has acquired the rights under the bill by the statutory operation. The statutory transfer is effected by Section 2(1) of the UK Carriage of Goods by Sea Act 1992. Section 2(5) divests the shipper of his rights under the bill of lading upon such statutory transfer. However, the liabilities of the original shipper are preserved by Section 3(3). Prior to the 1992 Act, a similar result was achieved by virtue of Sections 1 and 2 of the UK Bills of Lading Act 1855.

In *Evergreen Marine Corp v Aldgate Warehouse (Wholesale) Ltd*,[22] a buyer regularly engaged a carrier to transport goods by sea. The carrier and the buyer had a standard freight rate agreement. The system in practice was that buyers would buy goods from various suppliers on fob terms and instruct the suppliers to ship on board the carrier's ships. The carrier will then issue bills of lading naming the supplier as the shipper, a bank as the 'to order' consignee, and the buyer merely as the 'notify party'. The bills will be marked 'Freight Collect', as the buyer would pay the freight as per the freight rate agreement. In the case of some of the bills, a problem arose as the buyer rejected the bills tendered by the suppliers because of late shipment. This put the carrier in difficulty as the freight was not paid and, added to that, demurrage was running. Hence, the carrier took action against the buyer for freight and demurrage. The English High Court held that the buyer was not liable for freight, because it was not named as the shipper and did not accept the bills. This was so despite the standard freight rate agreement between the carrier and the buyer. This case reinforces the principle that the direct contract is between the shipper and the carrier, and the one liable for freight and demurrage is the shipper unless the transferee of the bill makes a demand under the bill and hence takes liability under Section 3(1) of the UK Carriage of Goods by Sea Act 1992.

However, if a party is named as a shipper on behalf of another, then the principal will be the shipper. In *The Xingcheng and The Andros*,[23] the goods were carried under a through bill. The principal carrier issued a bill of lading, naming China

---

[21] As it happened in *Pyrene Co Ltd v Scindia Navigation Co Ltd* [1954] 2 QB 402, [1954] 2 All ER 158, [1954] 2 WLR 1005, [1954] 1 Lloyd's Rep 321 (EW HC). However, sometime a 'received for shipment' bill would be issued even before the goods are loaded onto the ship.

[22] [2003] EWHC 667 (Comm), [2003] 2 Lloyd's Rep 597, [2003] All ER (D) 430 (Mar) (EW HC).

[23] *China Ocean Shipping Co (Owners of Xingcheng) v Andros (Owners of The Andros)* [1987] 1 WLR 1213, [1987] 2 Lloyd's Rep 210 (PC on appeal from Hong Kong).

National Textiles Import and Export Corporation (CNTIE) as the shipper, and it was consigned to order of the shipper. On transshipment, the on-carrier issued a bill of lading, naming the original carrier's representatives as the shipper on behalf of CNTIE. The Privy Council found that the shipper, for the purposes of both the bills, was CNTIE.

Right of Shipowner for Freight/Sub-Freight from Shipper

A question arises in cases where a time-charterer issues a bill of lading with a demise/identity of carrier clause or the shipowner directly issues to the bill to the shipper when the booking was made to the time or voyage charterer. The question is whether the shipowner may directly claim the freight from the shipper[24]/any subsequent holder of the bill.[25]

This question arose in a complex factual matrix in *Wehner v Dene Steam Shipping Co.*[26] In this case, a ship was let on a time-charter by the shipowner to a head charterer. The head charterer let the ship on a sub-chartered, which was a voyage charter, to a sub-charterer. The sub-charterer contracted to carry some goods for a shipper and freight was not paid in advance. A shipowner's bill was issued to the shipper. In the meantime, the head charterer defaulted in payment of hire to the shipowner. Upon completion of the carriage of goods of the shipper, the shipowner successfully claimed the bill of lading freight from the shipper. This was because the bill of lading created a direct contract between the shipowner and the shipper. The result would be a loss to the sub-charterer, who did not default in the hire-payment to the head charterer but lost the freight.

In *Samuel,Samuel & Co v West Hartlepool Steam Navigation Co*,[27] the English High Court found the bill to be a pure charterer's bill, so that the shipowner could not claim the freight from the shipper through the bill of lading contract. However, the court held that the shipowner had a lien over the freight because the charterparty expressly provided for the lien and the charterparty was incorporated by reference into the bill of lading, which was not annotated as 'freight prepaid'. The decision in this case does not disturb the position taken in the *Wehner* case.

In *Molthes Rederi Aktieselskabet v Ellerman's Wilson Line Ltd*,[28] the English High Court allowed the shipowner to collect the sub-freight from the end sub-charterer, a voyage charterer, when the head-charterer defaulted in the hire-payment to the shipowner. However, the court criticised the 'bill of lading contract' approach taken by *Wehner* case to arrive at this conclusion. Rather, the court based its decision on the right of lien on sub-freight that the shipowner was entitled to pursuant to the charterparty, which was in turn incorporated by reference into the bill of lading issued to the end sub-charterer.

---

[24] Between the shipowner and the shipper, there is a direct contract.

[25] Between the shipowner and any subsequent holder of the bill, there is a statutory contract.

[26] [1905] 2 KB 92 (EW HC).

[27] (1907) 12 Com Cas 203 (EW HC).

[28] [1927] 1 KB 710, [1926] All ER Rep 417 (EW HC).

Conflicting Clauses

Complexity has arisen in identifying the carrier as a result of the pathological placement of conflicting clauses in bills of lading. A good example of such a case is *The Starsin*,[29] in which the House of Lords adopted the commercial-sense approach to determine the question of who the carrier was. The House gave importance to what appeared prominently on the face of the bill in deciding this question.

In this case, the ship was chartered by Continental Pacific Shipping. The charterer was a shipowner in its own right. The charterer issued the bill in its standard format that it would issue when carrying goods by its own ships. The bill prominently displayed the name of the charterer on the top right-hand corner of the front page. At the bottom right-hand corner was a printed attestation clause, which stated that the bill was signed by the master. Below that, there was the signature box, into which was typed "As Agent for Continental Pacific Shipping (the Carrier)". While a master's signature, without more, will suggest that this was a shipowner's bill, the typed clause will suggest that the carrier was the charterer and hence charterer's bill. Added to this, at the rear page of the bill, the small-size printed clauses included a demise clause and an identity of carrier clause. To further complicate, another clause at the rear—cl. 1c—stated that the carrier was "the party on whose behalf this Bill of Lading has been signed". While the demise and identity clauses will suggest a shipowner's bill, the cl. 1c read together with the attestation at the front will suggest a charterer's bill. The House of Lords held this to be a charterer's bill, giving importance to what was visible at a reading of the front page of the bill and to commercial certainty to the bill. The House decision has been welcomed for construing the bill in line with commercial reality.

In *The Flecha*,[30] another bill, issued by the same charterer in *The Starsin* in a similar format and under similar circumstances, came before the English High Court before the House of Lords Decision in *The Starsin*. The court held that it was a shipowner's bill. This decision no longer represents the good law by virtue of the subsequent House of Lords decision in *The Starsin*.

In *The Hector*,[31] a bill of lading was issued in the format of a time-charterer. The bill in the front page prominently displayed the name of the charterer as the carrier. However, it was signed on behalf of the master. At the rear page was a demise clause, printed in the usual small size. The signature on behalf of the master and the demise clause would suggest a shipowner's bill. However, the prominently displayed carrier identification clause would suggest a charterer's bill. The English High Court gave importance to what appeared prominently at the face of the bill and held it to be a charterer's bill. This decision will be in line with the commercial reality and with the House of Lords decision in *The Starsin*.

---

[29] *Homburg Houtimport BV v Agrosin Private Ltd (The Starsin)* [2003] UKHL 12, [2004] 1 AC 715, [2003] 2 All ER 785, [2003] 2 WLR 711, [2003] 1 All ER (Comm) 625, [2003] 1 Lloyd's Rep 571, [2003] All ER (D) 192 (Mar) (UK HL).

[30] *Fetim BV v Oceanspeed Shipping Ltd (The Flecha)* [1999] 1 Lloyd's Rep 612 (EW HC).

[31] *Sunrise Maritime Inc v Uvisco Ltd (The Hector)* [1998] 2 Lloyd's Rep 287 (EW HC).

Identifying Carrier

Identifying who the carrier has proved to be a challenging task in many cases.[32] The difficulty may be aggravated when the ship was under a charterparty or a chain of charterparties. A plain reading of the bill may only result in a confusion as to who the carrier is or may be misleading as to it. Even a demise or identity of the carrier clause will not tell the name of the carrier, but merely will declare that the shipowner or the demise shipowner is the carrier. One may have to do searches like Sea-web (of IHS Markit) or Seasearcher (of Lloyd's List Intelligence) or a search at the ship's registry if it is known to find out who the shipowner/demise charterer is.

All these difficulties can be prejudicial to the cargo interest given the one-year time limit for cargo claims.[33] If a wrong person is sued and subsequently it is found out the suit should have been against another, then it may not be possible to so bring the action against the other if by then the one-year time limit was over.

The problem of the identification was glaring in many cases such as *Colgate-Palmolive (Asia) Ltd v Swedish East Asia Co Ltd*,[34] where the bill prominently displayed 'Malaya Indonesia Line', which was only a call-name shared by three cargo lines and the cargo claimant sued the carrier in this name. Subsequently, after the one-year time-limit had set in, the Malaysian Federal Court allowed the cargo claimant to correct the misnomer.

Freight Forwarder's Bill

When a shipper deals with a freight forwarder, there are three possible legal scenarios. One is that the freight forwarder may be the agent of the shipper. Another, it is the agent of the carrier. The last, it is the principal and hence the contractual carrier as far as the shipper is concerned and it is the shipper as far as the shipowner is concerned. In this last scenario, the bill issued by the shipowner will be to the freight forwarder and the bill will not be transferred to the end-shipper but the freight forwarder will issue its own bill to the end-shipper.[35] In such a case, the shipowner will not be able to rely on the terms of its bill against the end-shipper.

---

[32] As it was, for example, in *Colgate-Palmolive (Asia) Ltd v Swedish East Asia Co Ltd* [1967] 1 MLJ 115 (MY FC). See Chapter 10.2.1 for facts of this case.

[33] Article III(6) of the Hague/Hague-Visby Rules: the time-limit to take action in respect of loss or damage caused during the carriage is one year from the date of delivery or the date when the goods should have been delivered.

[34] [1967] 1 MLJ 115 (MY FC). For more detailed facts, see Chapter 10.2.1.

[35] Such bills are quite commonly called 'house' bill of lading: *Minmetals South-East Asia Corp Pte Ltd v Nakhoda Logistics Sdn Bhd* [2019] 3 CLJ 19, [2018] 6 MLJ 152 (MY CA). In this case, it seems that the shipowner issued an ocean bill naming the shipper in the house bill as the shipper for the ocean bill. This appears not to be right practice. This will not be the right practice, as the freight forwarder will be principal *vis-a-vis* both the end-shipper and the shipowner. It will be hard to say that the freight forwarder contracted with the shipowner as an agent of the end-shipper, particularly when the freight rates are different, as it will likely be so. In the case of house bills, ordinarily, when they are presented to the freight forwarder, it will exchange them for the ocean bills so that the presenter can present the ocean bills to the shipowner in order to collect the cargo from the shipowner. See Arun Kasi, 'A Critical Analysis of the Court of Appeal Decision on Misdelivery in Minmetals South-East Asia Corp Pte Ltd v Nakhoda Logistics Sdn Bhd', *The Law Review*, [2020]

This scenario was well demonstrated by *Ocean Projects Inc v Ultratech Pte Ltd*,[36] where the Singapore Court of Appeal there dealt with a situation where competing bills were issued by the freight forwarder and the disponent shipowner for the same shipment to the same shipper. In this case, the buyers contracted with a freight forwarder to ship the buyer's cargo from Houston[37] to Damai.[38] In turn, the freight forwarders contracted with a disponent shipowner for the carriage. The buyers paid the freight to the freight forwarder. The freight forwarder returned a clean bill of lading issued to the buyer's bank, noting 'freight prepaid', issued by someone other than the disponent shipowner. Subsequently, the disponent shipowner issued another bill also to the buyer's bank. This bill was claused and noted freight was not paid. This bill, as usual, also conferred on it the right of lien on cargo for the freight. The buyer did not come forward to pay the freight once again. The disponent shipowner discharged the cargo in Singapore without completing the voyage and claimed its right of lien under its bill of lading. In turn, the respondent claimed damages for breach of contract based on the bill given by the freight forwarder. The freight forwarder has gone into liquidation.

The court found the freight forwarder was the principal contracting party *vis-a-vis* the buyer and the disponent owner.[39] One contract of carriage between the buyer and the freight forwarder, and another between the freight forwarder and the disponent shipowner. Thus, the court held that the disponent shipowner would not be able to rely on the lien clause in its bill of lading[40] against the buyer. Although a private carrier who carries a cargo of a cargo-owner to the destination intended by him will be entitled to a lien even without any direct contract between them, that did not help the disponent shipowner here because it did not complete the voyage to Damai. The disponent shipowner was also not entitled to any *quantum meruit* claim as there was no contract of carriage, express or implied, between the buyer and the disponent shipowner.

It has earlier been considered whether the bills issued by freight forwarders on their own right, as an NVOC, can be a bill of lading in the true sense and a transferable document.[41] Such bills, which have come into the industry over the last century only, are an anathema to the carriage of goods by sea and have caused numerous problems, discussed earlier.[42] Such bills cannot be bills of lading in the true sense and cannot thus be not transferable. At best, they can merely be contracts of carriage between

---

LR 105. This article was referred to in *Punjab National Bank v Malayan Banking Berhad* [2020] 1 LNS 232, [2020] 5 MLJ 732 (MY CA).

[36] [1994] 2 SLR 369 (SG CA).

[37] In the USA.

[38] In Malaysia.

[39] Prior to making the final decision, the court made an interim order for release of the cargo to the respondents subject to the respondent furnishing a banker's guarantee for any lien claim.

[40] I.e. Contract between the disponent shipowner and the freight forwarder.

[41] See Chapter 2.2.5.

[42] See *Minmetals South-East Asia Corp Pte Ltd v Nakhoda Logistics Sdn Bhd* [2019] 3 CLJ 19, [2018] 6 MLJ 152 (MY CA); *Punjab National Bank v Malayan Banking Berhad* [2020] 1 LNS 232, [2020] 5 MLJ 732 (MY CA).

the shipper and the freight forwarder, actionable only between them. Entitling them as a 'bill of lading' is deceptive.

Bills Signed on Behalf of Master

A shipowner may act through the master. Thus, if the bill is signed by or on behalf of the master,[43] then, generally, it will be a shipowner's bill.[44] In *Baumwoll Manufactur von Carl Scheibler v Furness*,[45] the master signed the bill. The House of Lords found this to be a shipowner's bill.

The courts have held this to be so even where the charterparty designates the master as the servant of the charterer and the terms of the charterparty are incorporated by reference into the bill of lading. When the charterer signs on behalf of the master, the charterer is considered to have at least the implied or ostensible authority to so sign irrespective of whether the charterer had the express or actual authority.

In *Manchester Trust Ltd v Furness Withy & Co Ltd*,[46] the ship was under a time charter. The charterparty included an employment and agency clause that provided that the master and the crew were at the disposal of the charterer, which is a usual clause in time-charterparties. The clause also expressly provided that the master was to be regarded as the servant of the charterer when signing the bills of lading. The master signed a bill. The bill incorporated by reference the terms of the charterparty, which is quite usual when the ship is under a time-charterparty. Such bills are called 'charterparty bill of lading'. This does not denote it is a charterer's bill but merely that the bill (usually a ship owner's bill by virtue of a demise or identity of carrier clause) is subject to the terms of the charterparty. In contrast, it will be a pure 'charterer's bill' when the charterer issues a bill as the *principal* without any demise or identity of carrier clause. The bill, in this case, was indorsed to a third party. The third-party, as the lawful holder of the bill, sued the shipowner under the bill of lading contract for an alleged fraud. An issue that arose was whether the contract created by the bill of lading was between the shipowner and the holder of the bill *or* between the charterer and the holder of bill. The English Court of Appeal held the bill to be a shipowner's bill, despite the employment and agency clause in the charterparty and despite the incorporation of the terms of charterparty into the bill of lading.

In *The Vikfrost*,[47] a charterer signed the bill on behalf of the master. The English High Court held this to be a shipowner's bill, because the charter had the implied authority to sign on behalf of the master even if not expressly stated in the charterparty.

---

[43] Usually, the shipowner will appoint and have control over the master, even if the ship is time chartered or voyage chartered.

[44] Or demise charter's bill, where the ship has been demise chartered. This is because in such cases, the master will be appointed by and under the control of the demise charterer.

[45] [1893] AC 868, [1891–4] All ER Rep Ext 1710 (UK HL).

[46] [1895] 2 QB 539 (EW CA).

[47] *Fletcher (W & R) (New Zealand) v Sigurd Haavik A/S (The Vikfrost)* [1980] 1 Lloyd's Rep 560 (EW CA).

In *The Nea Tyhi*,[48] the English Court of Appeal held that the charter has the ostensible authority to sign on behalf of the master, even if the charterer did not actually have such authority. However, the English High Court in *The Hector*[49] seemed to have the contrary view, by way of an *obiter* statement. It appears that the view taken in *The Nea Tyhi* is the better one because the shipowner, who allows the charterer to trade with the shippers, should be taken to have authorised the charterer to so sign on behalf of the master and should be held take the responsibility for the charterer's actions.

Parol Terms

The shipper and carrier may agree to certain terms, which are not stated in the bill of lading or even contrary to the terms of the bill of lading.[50] In such cases, as between the shipper and the carrier, the parol terms will be binding and will take precedence over the bill terms.

In *The Ardennes*,[51] a load of oranges was shipped. The shipowner, through an agent, verbally agreed that the cargo would be carried from Cartagene[52] directly to London. Upon shipment, the shipowner issued the bill of lading, which allowed deviation. In carrying the cargo, the shipowner deviated to Antwerp and finally reached London later than it should have reached if no deviation. By the time of late arrival, the price of oranges in London had dropped and the import duty had risen. The shipper took action against the shipowner to claim these economic losses. The shipowner's defence was that deviation was justified by the terms of the bill. The English High Court rejected this argument and held the shipowner liable. The court pointed out that the actual contract between the parties is not in the bill of lading and that the bill is merely the excellent evidence of the terms of the actual contract. However, if the bill is transferred to the hands of another, then as between the transferee and the carrier, the parol terms are of no effect.[53]

[48] *The Nea Tyhi* [1982] 1 Lloyd's Rep 606, [1982] Com LR 9 (EW HC).

[49] *Sunrise Maritime Inc v Uvisco Ltd (The Hector)* [1998] 2 Lloyd's Rep 287 (EW HC).

[50] Which may be in a standard form.

[51] *SS Ardennes (Cargo Owners) v SS Ardennes (Owners)* [1951] 1 KB 55, [1950] 2 All ER 517 (EW HC).

[52] In Spain.

[53] *Leduc v Ward* (1888) 20 QBD 475, [1886–90] All ER Rep 266 (EW CA).

Incorporation Clauses

It is common that bills of lading, sea waybills, ship's delivery orders or sub-charters issued by a charterer will incorporate the terms of a charterparty[54] between the charterer and the shipowner.[55] A bill of lading so incorporating the terms of the charterparty is called a '*charterparty* bill of lading'.[56] This does not denote it is a *charterer's* bill but merely that the bill is subject to the terms of the charterparty. Most of the times, such a bill will be a *shipowner's* bill by virtue of a demise or identity of carrier clause there.

The practice of incorporating charterparty terms into the bill of lading has given rise to difficulties. Such incorporation clauses may import jurisdiction, choice of law and arbitration clauses into the bill of lading. They may even import liability of the charterer to pay demurrage and deadfreights, which will on the face of it be unfair. Accordingly, the courts have to be, and have been, vigilant about such incorporation clauses. This was well pointed out in *The Federal Bulker*[57] by Bingham LJ as follows:

> Generally speaking, the English law of contract has taken a benevolent view of the use of general words to incorporate by reference standard terms to be found elsewhere. But in the present field a different, and stricter, rule has developed, especially where the incorporation of arbitration clauses is concerned. The reason no doubt is that a bill of lading is a negotiable commercial instrument and may come into the hands of a foreign party with no knowledge and no ready means of knowledge of the terms of the charterparty. The cases show that a strict test of incorporation having, for better or worse, been laid down, the Courts have in general defended this rule with some tenacity in the interests of commercial certainty. If commercial parties do not like the English rule, they can meet the difficulty by spelling out the arbitration provision in the bill of lading and not relying on general words to achieve incorporation.

A few types of control-mechanisms have been deployed by the courts to curtail the effect of the clause. The common ones of them follow. First, limiting the incorporation, when it is a general incorporation clause, to those provisions of the charterparty that will logically fit into the bill, i.e. the provisions that are germane to the bill.[58]

Second, limiting the manipulation of the charterparty provisions that will determine whether the provision can have any meaning in the context of the bill of lading or other shipping document. Quite normally, many provisions in the charterparty will require some manipulation to apply between the shipper and the carrier. For instance, an arbitration clause cause will refer to all the disputes between the parties.

---

[54] Such incorporation, literally, may even have a chain effect, when there are multiple layers of charterparty. For instance, a shipowner may give the ship on a demise charter, who may in turn give her on a time charter. At the end of the chain, the time charterer may issue the bill of lading, incorporating the terms of the time charterparty. The time charterparty itself may incorporate the terms of the demise charterparty. Hence, if literally read, both the terms of the demise charterparty and the time charterparty will be incorporated into the bill of lading.

[55] Or disponent shipowner or head charterer.

[56] For example, see UCP 600, Article 22.

[57] *Federal Bulker Federal Bulker Carriers Inc v C Itoh & Co Ltd (The Federal Bulker)* [1989] 1 Lloyd's Rep 103 (EW CA).

[58] *Hogarth Shipping Co Ltd v Blyth, Greene, Jourdain & Co Ltd* [1917] 2 KB 534 (EW CA).

Strictly speaking, the reference to parties here will only mean the shipowner and the charterer. Accordingly, a judicial manipulation will be required if the meaning is to be extended to the context of a bill of lading or other shipping documents. Here is where the courts will exercise the control mechanism, for example, by holding that the courts will so manipulate only if the bill expressly and specifically refers to the arbitration clause. An example of a judicial manipulation can be seen in *Adamastos Shipping Co Ltd v Anglo-Saxon Petroleum Co Ltd*.[59] In this case, a charterparty incorporated the US Carriage of Goods by Sea Act of 1936. The House of Lords allowed manipulation of references in the Act to 'charterparty' to 'bill of lading' in order to give effect to the incorporation.

Third, requiring an express, specific and unequivocal reference for certain types of provisions in the charterparty to be incorporated into a bill of lading or other shipping documents. Such a requirement has been called for in the case of dispute resolution, law and jurisdiction clauses.[60]

Fourth, requiring a certain degree of notice in case of very onerous clauses. This can be relevant when an attempt is made to import into the bill of lading orother shipping documents the liability of the charterer to pay the freight and demurrage to the shipowner.[61] The more onerous the provision sought to be incorporated is, the higher the degree of notice or specific reference that is called for. The term 'red hand clause' has been used to refer to very onerous provisions sought to be incorporated to symbolically say that they require a red hand notice for the incorporation. In *Thornton v Shoe Lane Parking*,[62] the English Court of Appeal held that the more onerous the clause, the better notice of it needed to be given. In *Interfoto Picture Library Ltd v Stiletto Visual Programmes Ltd*,[63] the respondent hired 47 photos from the appellant at a rate of 50 pence[64] per photo per day. The delivery note *inter alia* included a term that if the photos were held for more than 14 days, a holding charge of £5.00[65] per photo per day would be charged, which was 10 times the original rate. The respondent held the photos for 14 days beyond the initial 14 days. The appellant billed the respondent a sum of £3,290.00[66] for the additional period. The English Court of Appeal said, as a guideline, that in deciding whether a clause was incorporated into the contract between the parties, regard should be had to the nature of the transaction, the character of the parties, the sufficiency and proportionality of the notice, and whether it would be fair to hold the parties to the condition in question. Having taken these factors into consideration, the court held that the onerous term in

[59] [1959] AC 133, [1958] 1 All ER 725, [1958] 2 WLR 688, [1958] 1 Lloyd's Rep 73 (UK HL).

[60] See *TW Thomas & Co Ltd v Portsea Steamship Co Ltd* [1912] AC 1 (UK HL); *Skips A/S Nordheim v Syrian Petroleum Co Ltd (The Varenna)* [1984] QB 599, [1983] 3 All ER 645, [1984] 2 WLR 156, [1983] 2 Lloyd's Rep 592 (EW CA).

[61] See *Gray v Carr* (1871) LR 6 QB 522, 25 LT 215 (EW Court of Exchequer Chamber).

[62] [1971] 2 WLR 585, [1971] 1 All ER 686, [1971] 2 QB 163 (EW CA).

[63] [1989] QB 433, [1988] 1 All ER 348, [1988] 2 WLR 615 (EW CA).

[64] Plus VAT at 15%.

[65] Plus VAT at 15%.

[66] Plus VAT at 15%.

that case was not incorporated into the contract. The court also said that 'particularly onerous or unusual' terms require special notice and that when a term is particularly onerous the person seeking to rely on the term must take greater measures to bring it to the attention of the other party. Although the last two cases were not shipping law cases, there is nothing to prevent the general principle enunciated in those case to be applied in the context of the charterparty bills of lading or other shipping documents.

Fifth, other fetters like, for terms of a charterparty to be incorporated into a bill of lading or other shipping documents, the charterparty must be in writing.[67] In *The Epsilon Rosa*,[68] the charterparty was not signed, but there was a recap telex confirming the terms, and this was held sufficient to satisfy the requirement that the charterparty was in writing for its terms to be incorporated into a bill.

Arbitration, Jurisdiction and Choice of Law Clauses

Arbitration and exclusive jurisdiction clauses have been held not to be incorporated in the absence of a specific reference to them.[69] But that is a matter of construction in each case. In *The Merak*,[70] there was a general incorporation clause in the bill of lading, which did not make specific reference to the arbitration clause in the charterparty. However, the arbitration clause in the charterparty was drafted so as to apply in the bill of lading context. It read "any dispute arising out of the charter or any bill of lading issued hereunder was to be referred to arbitration". The English Court of Appeal held that the arbitration clause was incorporated into the bill of lading.

In *The Channel Ranger*,[71] a clause in a bill of lading incorporated "law and arbitration clause" in a charterparty. However, in the charterparty there was only an English law and court clause, but not an arbitration clause. The English Court of Appeal held that the English law and court clause was incorporated and hence granted an anti-suit injunction to restrain Moroccan proceedings. The court noted that the question, in this case, was not one of incorporation but of construction of the clause.

An arbitration clause in a charterparty, incorporated into the bill by specific reference, may refer to disputes between the shipowner and the charterer. Hence, it will have to be manipulated to refer to the charterer and the holder of the bill, in order to make any sense in the context of the bill.

[67] *Partenreederei M/S Heidberg v Grosvenor Grain and Feed Co Ltd (The Heidberg)* [1994] 2 Lloyd's Rep 287 (EW HC).

[68] *Welex AG v Rosa Maritime Ltd (The Epsilon Rosa)* [2002] EWHC 762 (Comm), [2002] 1 All ER (Comm) 939, [2002] 2 Lloyd's Rep 81, [2002] All ER (D) 236 (Apr) (EW HC).

[69] *TW Thomas & Co Ltd v Portsea Steamship Co Ltd* [1912] AC 1 (UK HL); *Skips A/S Nordheim v Syrian Petroleum Co Ltd (The Varenna)* [1984] QB 599, [1983] 3 All ER 645, [1984] 2 WLR 156, [1983] 2 Lloyd's Rep 592 (EW CA). See also *Federal Bulker Federal Bulker Carriers Inc v C Itoh & Co Ltd (The Federal Bulker)* [1989] 1 Lloyd's Rep 103 (EW CA).

[70] *Owners of Cargo on Board The Merak v The Merak (Owners) (The Merak)* [1965] P 223, [1964] 3 All ER 638, [1965] 2 WLR 250, [1964] 2 Lloyd's Rep 283 (EW CA).

[71] *Caresse Navigation Ltd v Zurich Assurances MAROC (The Channel Ranger)* [2014] EWCA Civ 1366, [2015] QB 366, [2015] 2 WLR 43, [2015] 1 Lloyd's Rep 256, [2014] All ER (D) 248 (Oct) (EW CA).

Courts have been more willing to manipulate when the clause has been specifically incorporated. In *The Nerano*,[72] an arbitration clause in a charterparty was specifically incorporated into the bill of lading and the English Court of Appeal manipulated the arbitration clause to apply as between the charterer and the holder of the bill. Similarly, in *The Channel Ranger*,[73] an English law and arbitration clause in a charterparty was specifically incorporated into the bill of lading. The English Court of Appeal manipulated the clause to apply as between the charterer and the holder of the bill.

Demurrage and Dead freight Clauses

Coming to the question of incorporation demurrage and dead freight from the charterparty into a bill of lading or other shipping document, the courts have construed such incorporation clauses narrowly against the shipowner. The court have been reluctant in manipulating the clause to render the holder of the bill liable to pay the demurrage or deadfreight, in the absence of an express reference in the bill or other shipping documents specifically to those clauses.

A classical case on this point is *Gray v Carr*,[74] a charterparty obliged the charterer to load "full cargo" and conferred a lien on the cargo in favour of the shipowners "for all freight, deadfreight, demurrage, and average". It also provided for "the charterer's responsibility to cease on shipment of the cargo."[75] The demurrage was specified at a certain rate up to 10 days beyond the laytime.[76] However, the charterparty was silent about any detention charges should the 10-day demurrage period be exceeded. The charters took, for loading, 18 days in addition to the laytime and the demurrage period. The charterer did also not load 'full cargo'. The shipowner issued a bill of lading, stating:

> [the cargo] to be delivered at the port of discharge, *as per the aforesaid charterparty*… unto order, or to his or their assigns, *he or they paying freight and all other conditions or demurrage.* [emphasis added]

Notably, deadfreight, unlike demurrage, was not expressly mentioned in the bill of lading, although mentioned in the charterparty, whilst detention charges were not even mentioned in the charterparty. The bill was transferred to a subsequent purchaser. Upon arrival at the discharge port, the shipowner sought to recover from the subsequent purchaser, by exercising a lien on the cargo, the payment for the 10-day demurrage, 18-day detention charges and dead freight of an amount unascertained. The English Court of Exchequer allowed the claim for demurrage by a majority, dismissed the claim for detention charges unanimously and dismissed the claim for

---

[72] *Daval Aciers d'Usinor et de Sacilor v Armare Srl (The Nerano)* [1994] 2 Lloyd's Rep 50 (EW CA).

[73] *Caresse Navigation Ltd v Zurich Assurances MAROC (The Channel Ranger)* [2014] EWCA Civ 1366, [2015] QB 366 (EW CA).

[74] (1871) LR 6 QB 522, 25 LT 215 (EW Court of Exchequer Chamber).

[75] Provided it be of sufficient value to cover the freight and charges on arrival at port of discharge.

[76] 50 days.

deadfreight by a majority. In a nutshell, the court allowed only what was expressly stated in the bill of lading, i.e. demurrage.

More recently, in *The Miramar*,[77] a charterparty[78] provided that "*[c]harterer* shall pay demurrage". The bill of lading incorporated the charterparty with a general incorporation clause stating "[t]his shipment is carried under and pursuant to the terms of the charter ... and all the terms whatsoever of the said charter except the rate and payment of freight specified therein apply ..." The House of Lords refused to manipulate the word 'charterer' in the demurrage clause in the charterparty to refer to the 'holder of the bill' in the context of the bill of lading, hence refused to hold the holder of the bill liable for the demurrage. A reason for the reluctance of the House to hold the transferee of the bill liable on the demurrage clause was that it would impose a 'liability of an unknown extent', as it would be contrary to good commercial sense for a transferee to take such liability in the absence of clear words to that effect in the bill of lading.

A similar conclusion was arrived at by the Court of Appeal in *Spiros C*,[79] where the demurrage clause in the charterparty, incorporated into a bill of lading, specifically obliged the charterer to pay the demurrage, hence no liability on the transferee of the bill to pay. Comparatively, when a charterparty says in a neutral tone that 'freight to be paid', courts have held that a general incorporation clause would bind the transferee of the bill.[80]

In Singapore, the issue came up before the Court of Appeal in *The Daphne L*,[81] but in a different and peculiar context, namely in a dispute between the shipowner and the owner of the cargo who was not the holder of the bill. In this case, a cargo of crude oil was carried under a charterparty and bill of lading. The charterparty had a lien clause that said:

> The Owner shall have an absolute *lien on the cargo* for all freight, deadfreight, demurrage ...". It also had a demurrage clause stating "*[c]harterer* shall pay demurrage per running hour ..." [emphasis added]

The bill of lading incorporated the charterparty in these words:

> [F]reight payable as per charter party ... all terms and conditions, liberties and exceptions of the charter party are herewith incorporated.

At the discharge point, the owner of the cargo was not able to produce the original bill of lading and the shipowner refused to deliver the cargo. The shipowner obtained an order for sale of the cargo and the cargo was sold by the Sheriff. There was a

---

77 *Miramar Maritime Corpn v Holborn Oil Trading Ltd (The Miramar)* [1984] AC 676, [1984] 2 All ER 326, [1984] 3 WLR 1, [1984] 2 Lloyd's Rep 129 (UK HL).

78 In EXXONVOY 1969 form.

79 *Tradigrain SA and Others v King Diamond Marine Ltd (The Spiros C)* [2000] All ER (D) 979, [2000] 2 Lloyd's Rep 319 (EW CA).

80 *Compania Comercial y Naviera San Martin SA v China National Foreign Trade Transportation Corporation (The Constanza M) (CA)* [1981] 2 Lloyd's Rep 147 (EW CA).

81 *Feoso (Singapore) Pte Ltd v Faith Maritime Co Ltd (The Daphne L)* [2003] SGCA 34 (SG CA).

delay of 130 days before discharge and the shipowner claimed demurrage for this and sought to recover the same from the proceeds of the sale. The owner of the cargo, who was not holding the bill, objected to this and claimed that the shipowner was liable for conversion in selling off the cargo.

The High Court allowed the shipowner's claim for demurrage and dismissed the cargo owner's conversion claim. In the High Court, the owner of the cargo conceded that if the shipowner could exercise a lien, then the same can be satisfied on the proceeds of the sale but argued that the shipowner was not entitled to demurrage and was not entitled to exercise the lien. The High Court held that the shipowner was entitled to demurrage and to exercise the lien, hence allowed the demurrage claim and recovery of the same from the proceeds of the sale. On appeal, the owner of the cargo attempted to introduce a new argument namely under the charterparty the liability to pay demurrage was only on the charterer and hence same cannot be claimed against the proceeds of the sale of the cargo belonging to the owner of the cargo. The Court of Appeal refused to allow this argument to be introduced and upheld the decision of the High Court.

Even if the new argument was allowed to be introduced, the decision might not have been different, as this was not a regular case where the litigation was between the shipowner and the bill of lading holder, where the bill of lading holder would try to push the liability onto the charterer. In this case, irrespective of whether it was the charterer or the bill of lading holder (who did not come into the picture) was liable, the shipowner would have had a lien on the cargo when demurrage was not paid, if the bill of lading was not annotated with 'freight prepaid' statement. When the shipowner rightly exercises the lien, any right of the cargo owner to the proceeds of the sale will be for the proceeds less the sum of the demurrage payable to the shipowner. In order for the shipowner to rightly exercise the lien, the lien clause must be properly incorporated into the bill of lading and take effect between the shipowner and the holder of the bill. This will more likely be so in a lien clause as it will be stated in neutral terms binding the cargo rather than any party.

Although a contractual lien, unlike a common law lien, will only bind the parties to the contract rather than the cargo itself,[82] this analysis will not help the subsequent purchaser like the one in the Singapore case. This is because the contractual lien,[83] in that case, was rightly given by the lawful owner of the cargo at the time when it was given through the charterparty, the terms whereof was incorporated into the bill of lading, hence binding the holder of the bill as long as the bill is not marked 'freight prepaid'.

The question of whether the demurrage or other payment obligation in the charterparty will bind the transferee of the bill is a question of construction of the bill and the charterparty in every case, with some scope for judicial flexibility and ingenuity depending on the specific circumstances of each case. What can be broadly and generally deduced from the cases are as these. If a bill specifically refers to

[82] See *Welsh Development Agency(Holdings) Ltd v Modern Injection Mouldings Ltd* [1986] Lexis Citation 1535 (EW HC).

[83] See Chapter 13.7 for a more detailed discussion of 'lien'.

demurrage, then the transferee of the bill will likely be liable. If the charterparty specifically imposes the obligation on the charterer, then it might not bind the transferee of the bill. If the obligation in the charterparty is neutrally worded, then there is some possibility that it may bind the transferee.

4.2.1.2 Between Charterer and Shipowner

In the case where the shipper charters the ship, by time or voyage charter, there will be two documents in relation to the carriage. One is the charterparty and the other is the bill of lading. A bill of lading is still necessary as the charterparty is not the evidence of receipt of the goods.[84]

The charterparty will exhaustively set out the terms of the carriage contract between the parties. In such a case, the bill of lading issued to the charterer-shipper is not intended to be, and it is not, a document of contract as between the charterer-shipper and the shipowner. However, if the bill is subsequently transferred to a third party, the bill will gain its contractual effect in the hands of the third party.

In *Rodocanachi, Sons & Co v Milburn Bros*,[85] the English Court of Appeal found that, in the case of a bill of lading issued to a charterer, it was not the intention of the parties that the bill had any contractual effect as between them and accordingly held that it was not a document of contract as between the parties.

In *The Dunelmia*,[86] the bill of lading issued under a charterparty was found not to have the contractual effect between the parties because the charterparty provided that the bill would be issued "without prejudice to the terms of this charter". However, even in the absence of such a provision, it would not have been the intention of the parties that the bill of lading had any effect as the contract between them.

However, exceptionally, a bill of lading may have the contractual effect when in the hands of a charterer. This happened in *Calcutta Steamship Co Ltd v Andrew Weir & Co*.[87] In this case, the bill issued to the charterer was transferred to a third party, hence it gained the contractual effect. Subsequently, it was indorsed back to the charterer as a pledgee. The English High Court held that the bill had the contractual effect between the charterer holding it as a pledgee and the shipowner. This was because the bill came back to the charterer as the pledgee and not as the charterer. However, if the bill was returned to the charterer because the buyer did not pay and accept the bill, then the bill would have lost the contractual effect once returned to the charterer.

---

[84] The other functions served by a bill of lading, that cannot be accomplished with a charterparty, are document of title, document giving constructive possession to its holder, a transferability of contract of carriage.

[85] (1886) 18 QBD 67 (EW CA).

[86] *President of India v Metcalfe Shipping Co Ltd (The Dunelmia)* [1970] 1 QB 289, [1969] 3 All ER 1549, [1969] 3 WLR 1120 (EW CA).

[87] [1910] 1 KB 759 (EW HC).

4.2.2 *Statutory Contract*

The statutory contract comes into play by statutory transfer of rights of the shipper under a shipping document to the consignee or transferee. This is effected by Sections 2 and 5 of the UK Carriage of Goods by Sea Act 1992.

The 1992 Act provides for the transfer of rights under bills of lading, sea waybills and ship's delivery orders. For the purpose of this Act, a straight bill of lading is treated as a sea waybill, and thus the rights are transferred to the consignee. Under the 1855 Act, only the rights under a bill of lading are transferred, but the reference to the 'bill of lading' must include a straight bill of lading.

Under the scheme of the 1992 Act, an order bill of lading is transferable by indorsement and delivery. A bearer bill is transferable by delivery. A straight bill of lading, treated as a sea waybill,[88] has been held to be transferable once only to the consignee by delivery.[89]

Section 2(1) of the 1992 Act[90] transfers the rights of action under the contract embodied in order and bearer bills to the transferee as if he was a party to the contract from the beginning. In the case of a straight bill, sea waybill and ship's delivery order the transfer is to the consignee in the same way. Thereby it is said that a statutory contract is created between the carrier and the lawful holder of the bill of lading, when it is an order or bearer bill,[91] on terms of the bill. The statutory contract will be with the consignee if it is a straight bill, sea waybill[92] or ship's delivery order.[93]

However, this does not create a full contract between the carrier and the transferee of the bill, in the strict sense, because the imposition of liability on the transferee is deferred until one of the three conditions in Section 3(1) of the Act is satisfied.[94] Likely, a similar effect was achieved by Section 1 of the Bills of Lading Act 1855.

4.2.2.1 Parol Terms

The shipper and carrier may agree to certain terms, which are not stated in the bill of lading or even contrary to the terms of the bill of lading.[95] In such cases, as between the shipper and the carrier, the parol terms will be binding and will take precedence

---

[88] Section 1(2) read together with (3).

[89] *MacWilliam (JI) Co Inc v Mediterranean Shipping Co SA (The Rafaela S)* [2005] UKHL 11, [2005] 2 AC 423, [2005] 2 All ER 86, [2005] 2 WLR 554, [2005] 1 All ER (Comm) 393, [2005] 1 Lloyd's Rep 347 (UK HL).

[90] This must be read with Section 2(2) and Section 5.

[91] Section 2(1)(a).

[92] Section 2(1)(b).

[93] Section 2(1)(c).

[94] See Chapter 2.2.10.4.

[95] Which may be in a standard form.

over the bill terms.[96] However, if the bill is transferred to the hands of another, then as between the transferee and the carrier, the parol terms are of no effect as between the innocent transferee and the carrier.

In *Leduc v Ward*,[97] the shipowner committed a deviation. The deviation was not justified by the terms of the bill of lading. The bill of lading was indorsed by the shipper to a third party. Finally, the indorsee took action against the shipowner for the unauthorised deviation. It was the defence of the shipowner that the original shipper knew that the carriage would be performed subject to the deviation and hence the indorsee was bound by that. The English Court of Appeal rejected this argument and held the shipowner liable to the indorsee. However, if the action was between the original shipper and the shipowner, then the parol terms would have been effective.

4.2.3 *Contract by Agency Principle*

There may exist a contract by agency principle in a few circumstances. One of that is by the demise or identity of carrier clause in the bill of lading, already visited above. A contract by agency principle may be inferred between a *consignor* and a *shipowner* on loading or delivery of the goods by the consignor to the shipowner, where the contract of carriage is made by a fob buyer.

4.2.3.1 Between Consignor and Shipowner on Loading

The classical case on this point is *Pyrene Co Ltd v Scindia Navigation Co Ltd*,[98] the English High Court found that there was a contract between the consignor-seller and the shipowner on loading on the terms of the bill of lading to be issued, where the carriage contract was made by the fob buyer. Although one of the reasons given for this conclusion was that it was an implied contract, the other reason given was that the buyer was an agent of the seller when making the contract of carriage insofar the loading-part was concerned. Hence, the seller was bound by the carriage-contract for the loading-part. Accordingly, the shipowner was protected by the liability-limitation in the Hague Rules that was an implied term of the pre-bill contract of carriage.[99]

---

[96] *SS Ardennes (Cargo Owners) v SS Ardennes (Owners)* [1951] 1 KB 55, [1950] 2 All ER 517 (EW HC).

[97] (1888) 20 QBD 475, [1886–90] All ER Rep 266 (EW CA).

[98] [1954] 2 QB 402, [1954] 2 All ER 158, [1954] 2 WLR 1005, [1954] 1 Lloyd's Rep 321 (EW HC).

[99] This concept has some similarity in effect to the 'vicarious immunity' concept recognised in the bailment-case of *Elder, Dempster & Co Ltd v Paterson, Zochonis & Co, Griffiths Lewis Steam Navigation Co v Paterson, Zochonis & Co Ltd* [1923] 1 KB 420, [1924] AC 522, [1924] All ER Rep 135 (UK HL).

4.2.4 *Implied Contract*

Courts have, by judicial ingenuity, inferred implied contracts particularly in three situations in the context of carriage of goods by sea. First, between the shipper and the carrier before issuance of the bill of lading on terms of the bill of lading intended to be issued. Second, between the consignor and the carrier at the time of delivery of the goods to the carrier or loading them onto the ship. Third, between the receiver[100] of the goods at the destination port and the carrier at the time of delivery or when a demand is made for delivery or between the receiver and the shipowner on delivery of the goods. Each of these implied contract concepts is, in turn, looked at below.

4.2.4.1 Implied Contract Between Shipper and Carrier

In *Armour & Co Ltd v Leopold Walford (London) Ltd*,[101] the English High Court held that the terms of the bill of lading to be issued governed the relationship between shipper and the carrier, as an implied contract, even before issuance of the bill of lading. In that case, the booking note issued by the carrier at the outset referred to the bill of lading to be issued. However, it appears that even in the absence of such a reference in the booking note, the court would have found an implied contract on standard terms in which a bill of lading would ordinarily be issued in the market.

4.2.4.2 Implied Contract Between Consignor and Shipowner on Loading

In *Pyrene Co Ltd v Scindia Navigation Co Ltd*,[102] a seller and buyer contracted a sale and purchase of a fire tanker on fob terms. The buyer made the carriage contract with the carrier. While the fire tanker was being loaded, before crossing the ship's rail, it was dropped and damaged. At this point, the risk was still with the seller, as the loading was not completed. No bill of lading was then issued and none would be issued, as the cargo was not loaded. The seller sued the shipowner for the full quantum of loss. The shipowner admitted liability but sought to protect itself under the liability-limitation in the Hague Rules. Two pertinent questions arose. First, whether the Hague Rules applied when the bill of lading was not issued. Second, even if the Hague Rules applied, whether it may be invoked against the seller, who was not the shipper. The English High Court held that even before issuance of any bill of lading, the contract between the shipper and the carrier was on the terms of the bill that would be issued upon goods being loaded. In this case, if the bill was issued it

[100] Who will be the lawful holder of the bill or the consignee.

[101] [1921] 3 KB 473 (EW HC).

[102] [1954] 2 QB 402, [1954] 2 All ER 158, [1954] 2 WLR 1005, [1954] 1 Lloyd's Rep 321 (EW HC).

would have extended the Hague Visby Rules liability-limitation to also loading.[103] Accordingly, the Hague Rules applied to the incident in question as between the buyer and the shipowner. The court also held that the seller was bound by the terms of the intended bill of lading so that the seller could claim no more than the limited amount allowed by the Hague Rules. One of the reasons offered by the court for coming to this conclusion was that there was an implied contract between the seller and the shipowner created by the seller tendering the cargo for loading on terms of the bill that would be issued upon loading. However, the other preferred reason offered for the conclusion was that the buyer was an agent of the seller in making the carriage contract with the shipowner insofar as the part of loading was concerned. In the absence of the court, by judicial ingenuity, binding the seller to the terms of the intended bill of lading, the shipowner would have been liable for full loss without the benefit of the Hague Rules liability-limitation.

Similarly, in *The Dunelmia*,[104] the English Court of Appeal favoured the implication of a contract on loading between the consignor and the shipowner because the consignor would be able to instruct the shipowner and the Hague or Hague-Visby Rules should apply. Such implication is important in cases, particularly when the sale and purchase contract is on fob terms, where there is no direct contract between the consignor and shipowner.

Although an implied contract is found on loading, that will be only in respect of goods accepted by the shipowner for loading. Accordingly, if a shipowner refuses to load a part of the goods tendered, the consignor has no claim against the shipowner for the refusal to load part of the goods. This scenario happened in *The Barranduna and Tarago*.[105] The Privy Council refused to find any implied contract between the consignor and the shipowner that a certain quantity of the goods would be loaded. However, this does not affect any right of the shipper against the carrier where the carrier has undertaken to carry a certain quantity under the carriage contract between them. The law concerning such implied contracts will be equally applicable where the goods are not loaded unto the ship but delivered to the carrier and damaged before shipment.

4.2.4.3 Implied Contract Receiver and Shipowner on Discharge

In *Brandt v Liverpool, Brazil and River Plate Steam Navigation Co Ltd*,[106] a bank advanced finance to a buyer of goods and held the bill of lading as security. The buyer defaulted in the payment to the bank. Hence, the bank discharged the goods from the ship and thereby took delivery fo the goods. Upon the discharge and receipt of the

---

[103] This was a common practice in the industry.

[104] *President of India v Metcalfe Shipping Co Ltd (The Dunelmia)* [1970] 1 QB 289, [1969] 3 All ER 1549, [1969] 3 WLR 1120 (EW CA).

[105] *Scancarriers A/S v Aotearoa International Ltd (The Barranduna and Tarago)* [1985] 2 Lloyd's Rep 419 (PC).

[106] [1924] 1 KB 575, [1923] All ER Rep 656 (EW CA).

goods, the bank found them to be damaged and sued the shipowner. The bank did not have the rights under the bill of lading transferred and pledged to it, as this was an early 20th century case to which the UK 1855 Act applied. Under the Section 1 of this Act, rights under the bill of lading would pass to the transferee only if the property in the goods also passed to the transferee, which requirement was later removed in the UK 1992 Act. As there will be no intention to pass the property to a pledgee, unlike in the case of a transfer of the bill to the buyer, banks at that time could not have the contractual rights passed to them. Accordingly, the English Court of Appeal, by judicial ingenuity, had to find an implied contract between the bank as the receiver and the shipowner to limit the liability of the shipowner to that it would be liable if the action was by the buyer.[107] Without such a finding, the shipowner would be liable for more if a bank to which the buyer pledged the bill sues, but it will be for less if the buyer sues. However, the need to find such a contract is no longer there under the UK 1992 Act,[108] whereby the rights are transferred to the lawful holder of the bill, irrespective of whether the property in the goods is transferred to the holder of the bill.

Even before the 1992 Act, the *Brandt* case was not favoured by subsequent case law and its effect was limited. *The Aramis*[109] and *The Gudermes*,[110] both decided just before the 1992 Act came into existence, found that a mere discharge would not be sufficient to create a contractual relationship between the receiver and the shipowner. The courts, in these two cases, were of the view that there must be some unusual degree of cooperation to find an implied contract. The effect of *The Aramis* and *The Gudermes* is that, ordinarily, a *Brandt* implied contract on discharge or delivery cannot be found. The principle in these two cases can easily be extended to limit the *Pyrene v Scindia Navigation* implied contract on loading or delivery to the carrier, although in the *Pyrene v Scindia Navigation* scenario there may be no bill of lading, whilst in the *Brandt* scenario there will be a bill of lading. The law concerning such implied contracts will be equally applicable where the receiver does not discharge the goods from the ship but takes delivery of them from the carrier or probably even makes a demand for such delivery.

---

[107] *Leigh and Sillivan Ltd v Aliakmon Shipping Co Ltd (The Aliakmon) (HC)* [1983] 1 Lloyd's Rep 203 at 207 (EW HC), speech of Staughton J, who commented on this as: "The doctrine of *Brandt v Liverpool Steam Navigation Co Ltd* is far more often pleaded than established by judicial decision." The decision in this case was reversed by the House of Lords in [1986] AC 785, [1986] 2 All ER 145, [1986] 2 WLR 902, [1986] 2 Lloyd's Rep 1 (UK HL), which however did not have an effect on the comment made by Staughton J.

[108] Section 2(1) and (2) read together with Section 5.

[109] *The Aramis (CA)* [1989] 1 Lloyd's Rep 213 (EW CA).

[110] *Mitsui & Co Ltd v Novorossiysk Shipping Co (The Gudermes) (CA)* [1993] 1 Lloyd's Rep 311 (EW CA).

4.3 Bailment-Action

A bailment is created when one person delivers goods to another for safekeeping, carriage or a purpose, on certain terms, pursuant to which the goods must be returned or otherwise disposed of. The obligations under bailment continues even after the contractual period of responsibility has come to an end, for example, where the goods are discharged but the bailor has failed to take delivery, thus the bailor involuntarily holding on to the goods.[111] The person delivering the goods is called the bailor. The person taking delivery is called the bailee. If the goods are damaged or lost while in the custody of the bailee, the bailor has a cause of action against the bailee in bailment. Bailment is a *suis generis*.[112] This is not part of the law of tort or contract and is distinct from any action in tort that the bailor may have against the bailee i.e. in negligence or conversion.

In *Spectra International plc v Hayesoak Ltd*,[113] the English County Court seemed to suggest that to constitute bailment, the delivery and receipt of goods need not be physical but can be legal. It was held that a freight forwarder who issued a combined transport bill of lading was a bailee, although it did not take physical possession of the goods. This meant that it was sufficient that the goods were at its disposal as freight forwarders to arrange warehousing, transportation and delivery. The validity of this view and decision is highly questionable.

The bailee may pass on the goods to another for the safekeeping, carriage or the purpose. In such a case, the bailee is called head bailee, the other is called sub-bailee and the transaction is called sub-bailment. The sub-bailee will owe a duty directly to the bailor. Accordingly, the bailor has a cause of action both against the bailee and the sub-bailee. Similarly, a sub-bailee is liable both to the head-bailor and to the bailor.

When a head-bailor appoints a sub-bailee, the head bailor owes, in particular, two duties to the bailor. One is to ensure that the fundamental obligations of the head-bailee are maintained in the terms of the sub-bailment, such as the obligation to deliver the goods against presentation of the bill of lading. The other is to ensure that the sub-bailee is reasonably competent.

---

[111] *Owners of the ship or vessel 'Kota Bakti' v Douglas Fraser & Sons (London) Ltd (The Kota Bakti)* [1993] 1 SLR 849 (SG CA).

[112] 'Of its own kind'.

[113] [1997] 1 Lloyd's Rep 153 (EW County Court).

4.3.1 Bailment-Action Only for Bailor Against Head or Sub-Bailee

A bailment-action is available only to a bailor.[114] The bailee in such an action can be the head bailee with whom the bailor entrusted the goods or it can be a sub-bailee to whom the head-bailor passed the goods on behalf of the principal bailor.[115] In *The Pioneer Container*[116] the Privy Council held that a sub-bailee was liable to the owner of the goods, this was because the sub-bailee for all legal purposes is a bailee to the bailor. This is analogous to treating sub-agent as the agent to the principal. To be a bailor, it is not necessary to be the owner of the goods.[117] They are two different concepts.

This tells that a transferee of a bill of lading will not be able to take action in bailment unless there is an attornment by the bailee in favour of the transferee of the bill. There is one exception to this, that is, where the goods are transshipped and at the time of the transshipment the transferee was already holding the bill. In such a case, the principal carrier will be deemed to effect the transshipment on behalf of whoever the holder of the principal carrier's bill at that time. Accordingly, the transferee will become the bailor in the transshipment and the bailee will be the on-carrier. Notably, the on-carrier will not be a sub-bailee in such case, but rather straight the bailee, because the principal carrier was never a bailee to the transferee of the bill.

In this context, it must be noted that the UK Carriage of Goods by Sea Act 1992 does not transfer the rights in bailment but transfers the rights in contracts only. The same was true of the now-repealed UK Bills of Lading Act 1855. The rights under the relevant Hague or Hague-Visby Rules are transferred with the contract because the Rules render the contract of carriage subject to the liabilitiess and immunities provided in the Rules.[118]

In *Sonicare International Ltd v East Anglia Freight Terminal Ltd*,[119] the English County Court held that the bailee could be liable to a named 'consignee' in bailment

---

[114] *Leigh and Sillavan Ltd v Aliakmon Shipping Co Ltd (The Aliakmon) (HL)* [1986] AC 785 at 815, [1986] 2 All ER 145, [1986] 2 WLR 902, [1986] 2 Lloyd's Rep 1 (UK HL), dictum of Lord Brandon. In Singapore, the position will be same as that in England, as bailment is regulated by the common law in both these jurisdictions. In India, Section 148 (and Part IX) of the Indian Contract Act 1872 is consonant with this. The Malaysia, the Indian provision is reproduced in Section 101 (and Part IX) of the Contracts Act 1950.

[115] If one bails the goods on behalf of another, then the principal will be the bailor. But, if a pledgee bails the goods, he does so on his own behalf rather than on behalf of the owner and accordingly will be himself the bailor.

[116] *KH Enterprise v Pioneer Container (The Pioneer Container)* [1994] 2 AC 324, [1994] 2 All ER 250, [1994] 3 WLR 1, [1994] 1 LRC 465, [1994] 1 Lloyd's Rep 593 (PC on appeal from Hong Kong).

[117] Part X of the Indian Contract Act 1872/Malaysian Contracts Acts 1950 is consonant with this proposition; *Scipion Active Trading Fund v Vallis Group Ltd (formerly Vallis Commodities Ltd)* [2020] EWHC 795 (Comm) (EW HC).

[118] Article II.

[119] [1997] 2 Lloyd's Rep 48 (EW County Court).

without the need for any attornment. This is not correct as the consignor cannot be treated as bailing the goods to the carrier on behalf of the consignee even if named in a straight bill. This is because, until the bill is delivered to the consignee, the consignee does not get the rights under the bill.[120] In *The Future Express*,[121] the English Court of Appeal found that merely naming a bank as the consignee was not sufficient to dispense with the need for attornment.

If the shipper and the consignor are different persons, as it would be in a pure fob contract, the question of who the bailor is may prove to be a difficult one. Arguably, the consignor delivers (i.e. bails) the goods to the carrier on behalf of the shipper. If so, the shipper is the bailor. This is consonant with the Hague and Hague-Visby Rules that render the bill of lading deliverable to the shipper rather than to the consignor.[122] These rules do not recognise the concept of 'consignor'. However, there are limitations to this argument. Cases have recognised the relationship between the consignor and the carrier independently of the relationship between the shipper and the carrier. a limitation to this argument is that. They have even treated the shipper as the agent for the consignor.[123] Treating the consignor as the agent of the shipper is also contrary to reality. The consignor will normally retain the property and not pass the bill until paid. The risk will be with the consignor, even after delivery of the goods to the carrier, until they are shipped. In the event the buyer does not pay for the goods and take the bill, the right must be with the consignor to return the bill to the carrier to take delivery or to switch the bill. There is nothing to prevent an implied contract between the carrier and the consignor being inferred to this effect. All the references in this sub-chapter to 'shipper' as the one entitled in bailment could alternatively mean the 'consignor' if the second line of argument is right.

4.3.2 Burden of Proof in England and Wales

In England and Wales, both the laws of bailment and evidence are largely regulated by the common law. All that the bailor has to establish in an action in bailment, unless the terms of the bailment provide otherwise, is that the goods were entrusted with the bailee in a certain condition and that they were lost or damaged at the time of return by the bailee to the bailor. Then, the burden shifts to the bailee to prove that the bailee took reasonable care of the goods.[124]

---

[120] *MacWilliam (JI) Co Inc v Mediterranean Shipping Co SA (The Rafaela S)* [2005] UKHL 11, [2005] 2 AC 423, [2005] 2 All ER 86, [2005] 2 WLR 554, [2005] 1 All ER (Comm) 393, [2005] 1 Lloyd's Rep 347 (UK HL).

[121] *The Future Express* [1993] 2 Lloyd's Rep 542, [1993] 7 WLUK 364, [1994] CLY 4046 (EW CA).

[122] Article III(3).

[123] *Pyrene Co Ltd v Scindia Navigation Co Ltd* [1954] 2 QB 402, [1954] 2 All ER 158, [1954] 2 WLR 1005, [1954] 1 Lloyd's Rep 321 (EW HC).

[124] *Port Swettenham Authority v The Borneo Co (Malaysia) Sdn Bhd* [1975] 2 MLJ 80 (MY FC): Cargo owner proved 173 cartons delivered into custody of the port godown and only 70 cartons

When the bailment is on the terms of the bill of lading and the action is against the contractual carrier, the bill of lading will serve as either *prima facie* or conclusive evidence of the condition of the goods at the time of delivery to the bailee.[125] In *Tithes Dental & Photo Supply Sdn Bhd v Empresa Lineas Maritimes Argentinas & Ors*,[126] an action in bailment was taken against the port authority as the warehouse operator. In this case, the goods were discharged from the ship into a lighter and taken to the warehouse. The claimant was not able to prove the condition of the goods at the time of receipt by the warehouse, after changing of hands from the ship to the lighter and then from the lighter to the warehouse. In this context, mere proof of damage and loss at the time of receipt by the cargo claimant compared against the description of the goods in the bill of lading did not shift the burden onto the port authority. Accordingly, the Malaysian Federal Court found against the claimant. The same will be the position if the case had appeared before an English court.

A bailment action is different from an action in negligence, where the burden of proof will be on the cargo claimant to prove that the defendant was negligent which resulted in the damage to or loss of the goods. However, in practice, the difficulty in the negligence-action will usually be mitigated by the doctrine of *res ipsa loquitur*,[127] that will place the burden on the carrier.[128] Conversely, the burden in a bailment-action can be contractually placed on the cargo claimant, except in respect of the mandatory period covered by the Hague or Hague-Visby Rules.

4.3.3 Burden of Proof in Commonwealth Countries with Evidence Act and Contract Act

In many Commonwealth countries, including Malaysia, both the laws of bailment (when contractual, as it will be in most of the cases of head bailment in the context of contracts for carriage of goods by sea) and evidence are statutorily regulated. The statutes, in many cases, are largely based on the models of Indian Contract Act 1872 and Indian Evidence Act 1872. The Indian Acts, in turn, are quite substantially codification of the English common laws on these subjects.

---

were delivered by the port authority to the cargo claimant. Burden then shifted to the port authority to prove it had taken all reasonable care of the goods in its custody. Thus, the court held the port authority liable. Another very similar case and decision in *Port Swettenham Authority v Tw Wu and Company (M) Sdn Bhd* [1978] 2 MLJ 137 (PC on appeal from Malaysia).

[125] Under Article III(4) of the Hague-Visby Rules, in the case of an action by the shipper against the carrier, the descriptions stated in the bill are prima facie evidence. In the case of a suit by a third-party holder of the bill in good faith, the descriptions are conclusive evidence. Under Article III(4) of the Hague Rules, the descriptions are only prima facie evidence, irrespective of whether the suit is by the shipper or a third party holder of the bill.

[126] [1977] 2 MLJ 13 (MY FC).

[127] 'The thing speaks for itself'.

[128] By an inference that the loss or damage could not have happened in the absence of negligence of the carrier, unless the carrier can show otherwise.

The relevant provisions in the Indian Contracts Act are Sections 148, 151, 152 and 161, materially identically reproduced in Sections 101, 104, 105 and 114 of the Malaysian Contracts Acts 1950. They provide as follows:

> **148. "Bailment", "bailor" and "bailee"**
>
> A "bailment" is the delivery of goods by one person to another for some purpose, upon a contract that they shall, when the purpose is accomplished, be returned or otherwise disposed of according to the directions of the person delivering them. The person delivering the goods is called the "bailor". The person to whom they are delivered is called, the "bailee". ...
>
> **151. Care to be taken by bailee**
>
> In all cases of bailment the bailee is bound to take as much care of the goods bailed to him as a man of ordinary prudence would, under similar circumstances, take of his own goods of the same bulk, quality and value as the goods bailed.
>
> **152. Bailee when not liable for loss, etc., of thing bailed**
>
> The bailee, in the absence of any special contract, is not responsible for the loss, destruction or deterioration of the thing bailed, if he has taken the amount of care of it described in section 151.[129]
>
> **161. Bailee's responsibility when goods are not duly returned**
>
> If, by the fault of the bailee, the goods are not returned, delivered, or tendered at the proper time, he is responsible to the bailor for any loss, destruction, or deterioration of the goods from that time.

It was observed by the Privy Council in *Irrawaddy Flotilla Co v Bugwandas*[130] on an appeal from India that the provisions in the Indian Contract Act 1872 as to bailment are not exhaustive, as follows:

> The Act ... does not profess to be a complete code dealing with the law relating to contracts. It purports to do no more than to define and amend certain parts of that law. No doubt it treats of bailments in a separate chapter. But there is nothing to show that the Legislature intended to deal exhaustively with any particular chapter or subdivision of the law relating to contracts.

However, the applicability of this observation to Malaysia is quite arguable, but not with any great force, on the basis that the view was to some extent based on the preamble to the Indian Contracts Act stating "To define and amend certain parts of the law relating to contracts". In Malaysia, the preamble states only "An Act relating to contracts". But likely, even without reference to the preamble, the fact remains that those provisions are not intended to be exhaustive.

None of those sections says anything about on whom the burden of proof lies. In the absence of such a statement, the burden will be regulated by the relevant Evidence Act. The relevant sections in the Indian Evidence Act 1872 are Sections 101, 102, 103, 106 and 114, materially identically reproduced in the Malaysian Evidence Act 1950 with the same section numbering and in the Singapore Evidence Act by Sections 103, 104, 105, 108 and 116. They read as follows[131]:

---

[129] Section 104 in the Malaysian Contracts Act 1950.

[130] (1891) 18 IA 121 (PC on appeal from India).

[131] In the Indian Act.

101. Burden of proof

Whoever desires any court to give judgment as to any legal right or liability, dependent on the existence of facts which he asserts, must prove that those facts exist.

When a person is bound to prove the existence of any fact, it is said that the burden of proof lies on that person.

102. On whom burden of proof lies

The burden of proof in a suit or proceeding lies on that person who would fail if no evidence at all were given on either side.

103. Burden of proof as to particular fact

The burden of proof as to any particular fact lies on that person who wishes the court to believe in its existence, unless it is provided by any law that the proof of that fact shall lie on any particular person.

106. Burden of proving fact especially within knowledge

When any fact is especially within the knowledge of any person, the burden of proving that fact is upon him.

114. Court may presume existence of certain fact

The court may presume the existence of any fact which it thinks likely to have happened, regard being had to the common course of natural events, human conduct, and public and private business, in their relation to the facts of the particular case.

Illustration

The court may presume—

...

(g) that evidence which could be and is not produced would if produced be unfavourable to the person who withholds it;

...

Sections 101–103 will place the burden on the claimant to prove that the loss or damage occurred by the bailee's failure to exercise reasonable care. In such a case, Section 114 *illustration (g)* will enable the court to infer the contrary when the bailee fails to put before the court material relevant to the question of his care, such as by calling the relevant witnesses—but this will still not place the legal burden on the bailee.

However, Section 106 will place the legal burden on the bailee once the bailor has proved that the goods were delivered to the bailee in a certain condition and order. Sections 101–103 are general in nature and Section 106 is specific when the facts are especially within the knowledge of a party. Hence, Section 106 will prevail over Sections 101–103 in the context of the burden of proof in bailment cases.[132] Hence, the legal burden is on the bailee, and there is no need to invoke Section 114 *illustration (g)*.

In *Port Swettenham Authority v Tw Wu and Company (M) Sdn Bhd*,[133] 173 cartons of pharmaceutical products were delivered into the custody of port godown. The port

---

[132] By rule of interpretation known as *lex specialis derogat legi generali* ('specific prevails over the general').

[133] [1978] 2 MLJ 137 (PC on appeal from Malaysia).

returned only 70 cartons to the cargo owner. The cargo owner proved the quantity delivered to the godown and the quantity returned by the godown. The Privy Council held that once the cargo owner had proved them, the burden shifted to the port authority to prove it had taken all reasonable care of the goods in its custody. The port authority failed to call any of the clerks in charge of the operation of the godown as witnesses. The board found that the port authority failed to discharge the burden on it to prove it had taken reasonable care and hence held it liable.[134]

In coming to this decision, the board made it clear that effect of the Section 106 was not merely to put the duty on the port authority to make available relevant witnesses but to prove that it had taken reasonable care. On this point, the Privy Council expressed its disagreement with a speech in *Dwarkanath Raimohan Chaudhuri and Another v The Rivers Steam Navigation Company Limited*,[135] where it was said when dealing with the same Section 106 of the Indian Evidence Act 1872 as follows:

> … Evidence Act of 1872, section 106 … it was therefore right that the defendant Company should call the material witnesses who were on the spot … But this provision of the law of evidence does not discharge the plaintiffs from proving the want of due diligence, or … the negligence, of the servants of the defendant Company. It may be for the Company to lay the materials before the court; but it remains for the plaintiffs to satisfy the court that the true inference from these materials is that the servants of the defendant Company have not shown due care, skill and nerve.

The Privy Council's decision in the Malaysian case is sound as both Sections 102–104 and Section 106 all talk about 'burden'. Hence, when the burden referred to in Sections 102–104 is legal burden, then the burden referred to in Section 106 is also the legal burden and there is no reason to reduce it to evidentiary burden. This decision will render *Volcafe* applicable and effective in jurisdictions with a similar Evidence Act.[136]

It must be observed that even without relying on Section 106, a claimant may base its case on breach of contract, independent of any special laws concerning bailment, when goods are *lost* in the sense they are not returned or returned in short quantity as opposed to being merely *damaged*. This is clear, by the definition of bailment in the Indian Contract Act 1872[137] whereby a bailment is a *contract* whereby the bailee has agreed to return the goods or otherwise dispose of them as per the directions of the bailor. When he does not thus return, he will be liable for breach of contract. A statutory defence available to the bailee, in Section 150 of the Indian Contract Act,[138] is that the loss was not due to his fault. For this defence, the burden to prove no-fault

---

[134] Another very similar case and decision in *Port Swettenham Authority v The Borneo Co (Malaysia) Sdn Bhd* [1975] 2 MLJ 80 (MY FC).

[135] [1917] UKPC 108 (PC on appeal from India), speech of Sir Walter Phillimore.

[136] Including India, Singapore and Malaysia. See Arun Kasi, "Burden of Proof in Cargo Claims: Volcafe v CSAV in Commonwealth", *Current Law Journal*, [2020] 1 LNS(A) v, where a discussion of this subject appears.

[137] Section 148 in the Indian Ac; Section 101 in the Malaysian Contracts Act 1950.

[138] Section 105 in the Malaysian Contract Act 1950.

will be on the bailee by Sections 101–103 of the Indian Evidence Act 1950,[139] and there is no need for the cargo claimant to rely on Section 106 of the Indian Evidence Act.[140]

In *Vitachem (M) Sdn Bhd v Ing Hua Fu Marine Line Sdn Bhd*,[141] a cargo of agrochemicals was shipped from Penang[142] to Miri[143] under a clean bill of lading and carried on deck. The bill of lading stated that the cargo was shipped on deck at shipper's risk. The shipper had declared them to be dangerous cargo within the knowledge of the shipowner.[144] During the voyage, the cargo caught fire and an explosion happened, resulting in the ship sinking with a total loss of the cargo. The shipper sued the shipowner for the loss in negligence and bailment. At the trial, neither the master nor the chief officer gave evidence. The Malaysian Court of Appeal found for the shipper and held the shipowner liable. Although the court did not say that the basis of the decision was the breach of bailee's duty by the shipowner, it appears to be so as a bailee has to deliver the cargo in the like condition as received, and the bailee will not be held responsible for any loss or damage only if the bailee proves that such loss or damage happened without its fault. In this case, the shipowner did not call the master or chief officer as a witness to explain how the carriage was performed. If they were called, it might or might not have turned fatal to the shipowner. The failure to call may attract an adverse inference by the court. The duties of the bailee can include an obligation to properly carry by a system suitable to carry the particular cargo based on the information it has about the cargo[145] and even to make inquiries if reasonably needed in the circumstances.

However, the analysis adopted in the judgement had numerous shortfalls. First, the court relied on the Hague Rules Article IV(6) obligations of the shipper when shipping dangerous cargo. This is more commonly invoked as a defence for the shipowner when the shipowner has landed, destroyed or rendered innocuous the dangerous cargo before discharge by reason of the danger exposed by the cargo.[146]

---

[139] Sections 101–103 in the Malaysian Evidence Act 1950; Sections 103–105 in the Singapore Evidence Act.

[140] Section 106 in the Malaysian Evidence Act 1950; Section 108 in the Singapore Evidence Act.

[141] [2014] 6 MLJ 566 (MY CA).

[142] In Peninsular Malaysia.

[143] In Sarawak, Malaysia.

[144] The shipowner charged an extra fee for carrying the 'dangerous' cargo.

[145] For the duty of the carrier to adopt a suitable system and method of carriage for the particular cargo, see *Volcafe Ltd and others v Compania Sud Americana De Vapores SA* (t/a CSAV) [2018] UKSC 61, [2019] AC 358, [2019] 2 All ER 81, [2018] 3 WLR 2087, [2019] 1 All ER (Comm) 397, [2019] 1 Lloyd's Rep 21, [2018] All ER (D) 16 (Dec) (UK SC); *Albacora SRL v Westcott & Laurance Line Ltd (The Maltasian)* [1966] 2 Lloyd's Rep 53 (UK HL). As to dangerous cargo and the information to be furnished by the shipper, see *Atlantic Oil Carriers Ltd v British Petroleum Co Ltd (The Atlantic Duchess)* [1957] 2 Lloyd's Rep 55, [1957] 7 WLUK 46, [1957] CLY 3303 (EW HC); *General Feeds Inc v Burnham Shipping Corpn (The Amphion)* [1991] 2 Lloyd's Rep 101 (EW HC); *Mediterranean FreightServices Ltd v BP Oil International Ltd (The Fiona)* [1994] 2 Lloyd's Rep 506 (EW CA); *The Athanasia Comninos and Georges Chr Lemos* [1990] 1 Lloyd's Rep 277 (EW HC).

[146] The subject of liability for shipping dangerous cargo is covered in Chapter 11.

Second, the Hague Rules did not apply because the cargo was stated in the bill to be carried on deck and was accordingly carried (Article 1(c)).[147] Third, the court commented that the bill issued was a 'clean' one in suggesting that the shipowner must be liable. Clean bill or claused bill is not about dangerous cargo, but about defects in condition or order of cargo.[148] Fourth, the court's focus was centred around the question of whether the cargo shipped was 'fundamentally different' from that contracted for. This type of question is not supported by precedents.[149] Fifth, the court did not take the right direction by asking the question whether the shipowner had breached its duties as a bailee that can include the duty to carry properly adopting a system appropriate to carry the cargo in question based on the information available to the shipowner. The only basis that the decision can be sustained is perhaps by an adverse inference that can be drawn against the shipowner for failing to call the relevant witnesses to establish how the carriage was performed.

The other matters discussed in relation to the burden of proof in connection with England and Wales will be relevant also to these Commonwealth countries. The effect of Evidence Act in arbitral proceedings is discussed later.[150]

4.3.4 Burden of Proof in Commonwealth Countries with Evidence Act but not Contract Act

An example of a jurisdiction that has an Evidence Act based on the Indian Evidence Act 1872 model but no Contract Act, where the contract law is regulated by the common law is Singapore. The provisions corresponding to Sections 101–103, 106 and 114 of the Indian Evidence Act 1872 are respectively Sections 103–105, 108 and 116 in the Singapore Evidence Act. They are identical, and the discussion made in respect of the burden of proof in Commonwealth countries with both Evidence Act and Contract Act[151] will apply also to Singapore. Accordingly, in Singapore, the burden will be on the bailee once the claimant has proved that the cargo of a certain quantity in a certain condition was delivered to the bailee and that it was returned in a different quantity or condition or that it was not returned.[152]

The other matters discussed in relation to the burden of proof in connection with England and Wales will be relevant also to Singapore. The effect of the Evidence Act in arbitral proceedings is discussed later.[153]

---

[147] The subject of application of the Rules is covered in Chap. 8.

[148] The subject of clausing bills of lading is covered in Chapter 6.5.

[149] The subject of fundamental breach is covered in Chapter 7.

[150] See Chapter 9.

[151] See Chapter 4.3.3.

[152] Section 108 of the Singapore Evidence Act, identical to Section 106 of the Indian Evidence Act 1872.

[153] See Chapter 9.

4.3.5 Utility of Bailment-Action in Carriage of Goods by Sea

In the context of carriage of goods by sea, it is unlikely that a shipper/any subsequent holder of the bill of lading[154] will want to sue the contractual carrier in bailment. This is because the bailment in such cases will be on terms of the bills of lading including exclusions, limitation, and law, jurisdiction clauses and dispute resolution clauses. Hence, the shipper would rather sue the carrier contractually under the bill of lading. However, there may be rare instances where a shipper may want to sue the carrier in bailment. Such an instance happened in *East West Corp v Dampskibsselskabet AF 1912*.[155] In this case, the shipper indorsed the bill to a bank. The bank did not pay but returned the bill. However, the bank did not indorse the bill back to the shipper when returning. Accordingly, the original shipper was unable to take action against the carrier under the bill of lading but had to take action in bailment on terms of the bill of lading. The English Court of Appeal held that the shipper may do so.

Another such instance happened in the Singapore Court of Appeal case of *The Kota Bakti*,[156] where the cargo was carried from Bangkok[157] to Khorramshahr in Iran on board the vessel Kota Sejarah. She could not discharge in Khorramshahr due to labourers' strike there. She proceeded to Porbander in India as the final destination and discharged the cargo there into the port godown. The shipowner was authorised to do so by a contingencies-clause in the bill of lading in the event of contingencies like strike, etc. It was not disputed that the shipowner was so authorised. Thereafter, on 1st March 1979, the shipowner and the cargo owners discussed further arrangements, but no agreement was reached. Then, around early May 1979, the shipowner loaded the cargo on board vessel Kota Agung bound for Khorramshahr, without any notice to the cargo owners. Just after that, on 10th May 1979, when the vessel had not set on the voyage yet, the cargo owners instructed the shipowners to hold on to the cargo, as the Iranian buyers had defaulted in payment and the cargo owners further undertook to pay the storage charges. However, the shipowner refused to off-load the cargo, but parties came to an agreement for reshipment of the cargo from Khorramshahr to Bangkok at a certain rate. Upon arrival at Khorramshahr, the vessel caught fire and the cargo was destroyed totally. The cargo owner sued the shipowner in trespass to goods and bailment.[158]

The court found that the contingencies-clause did not authorise transshipment after the cargo was discharged at the Indian port as the final destination, at which

---

[154] If he was holding the bill at the time when the goods were passed to the carrier, such as at the time of transshipment, and the goods were so passed to the carrier on his behalf, e.g. when a principal carrier passes the goods to an on-carrier, he may do not on behalf of the current holder of the bill of lading at that time.

[155] *East West Corp v Dampskibsselskabet AF, 1912, Aktieselskab; Utaniko Ltd v P&O Nedlloyd BV* [2003] EWCA Civ 174, [2003] 4 Costs LR 531, [2003] All ER (D) 249 (Feb), [2003] 1 Lloyd's Rep 265n (EW CA).

[156] *Owners of the ship or vessel 'Kota Bakti' v Douglas Fraser & Sons (London) Ltd (The Kota Bakti)* [1993] 1 SLR 849 (SG CA).

[157] In Thailand.

[158] Among others.

point the voyage was abandoned and the contract for carriage terminated. Upon discharge at the Indian port, the shipowners became bailee involuntarily. The court held that transshipping without, or contrary to, the cargo owner's instruction was a trespass to the goods.[159] As a trespasser, the shipowner stood in the place of an insurer and had to pay for the loss, irrespective of any negligence. On another count, as a bailee too, the shipowner is liable for the loss, as the shipowner was not able to prove that the fire happened without its fault.

The court also held that the shipowner had committed a 'conversion' by transshipping the cargo. The validity of this point is arguable, as the shipowner did not pass on the goods to any other by the transshipment but was still holding it for the cargo owner. However, any finding on this will not affect the judgement as the shipowner was already found liable on trespass and bailment.[160]

The practical utility of the bailment action in the context of carriage of goods by sea is where the bill is issued by a non-vehicle-owning carrier (NVOC) such as a time-charterer or freight forwarder and the shipper wants to sue the shipowner rather than the NVOC. This is because, by suing the shipowner, the cargo claimant will be able to arrest the ship (or sister ship) and procure security from the P&I Club. The shipper cannot sue the shipowner contractually as the bill of lading contract is between the NVOC and the shipper. Hence, the only avenue to sue the shipowner is in bailment or tort (negligence or conversion).

Particularly in two scenarios, a cargo interest may want to sue the shipowner where there is no contractual relationship between them. One is where the bill was issued by a time-charterer on its own account[161] or a combined transport bill was issued by a freight forwarder. Another is where a pure through bill was issued by the principal carrier. In the first case, the shipper may want to sue the shipowner if the damage or loss occurred while the goods were in the latter's custody. In the second case, the cargo claimant may want to sue the on-carrier if the damage or loss occurred while the goods were in the latter's custody.

In the case of a false through bill, the shipper can likely sue the on-carrier contractually. In the case of a false through bill, the shipper will be regarded as the party to the bill issued by the on-carrier to the principal carrier, because the principal carrier would have acted as an agent (like a freight forwarder) for the shipper in contracting for the on-carriage. (i.e. agent).[162] At the time when the goods are passed by the principal carrier to the on-carrier, if the principal bill of lading was held by a transferee of the bill, then the party to the on-carriage bill will be the holder of the bill at this time. This is because the principal carrier's intention will be to act as an agent for whoever may be the holder of the bill at that time. In the case of a collective bill, the shipper/any holder of the bill of lading may directly sue the on-carrier in contract

---

[159] Removing one's goods against his wishes or wrongful interference with another's goods is a trespass to goods. A bailee may move the goods to a safer or suitable place, but not return to perform the terminated contract for carriage.

[160] The subject of conversion is covered later in this chapter.

[161] Without a demise or identity of carrier clause.

[162] The shipper may even be an undisclosed principal in this case.

because the principal carrier would have issued the bill on behalf of itself and the on-carrier.

4.3.6 Terms of Bailment in Carriage of Goods by Sea

In a bailment-action,[163] the terms of the bailment will first have to be ascertained. When a pure time-charterer's bill is issued, there are two schools of thought in answering the question as to the terms of the bailment. One is that the shipowner is the bailee on terms of the charter's bill of lading issued to the shipper. Another is that the shipowner is a sub-bailee on terms of the shipowner's charterparty with the charterer. The first school of thought is footed on the basis that the shipper directly delivers the goods to the shipowner. The second school of thought is footed on the basis that the charterer took legal possession of the goods and delivered the same to the shipowner.

In *Elder, Dempster v Paterson Zochonis*,[164] the House of Lords adopted the first school of thought. It found that, when the bill was issued by a time-charterer, the shipowner was a bailee on terms of the bill of lading issued by the charterer to the shipper. Accordingly, the shipowner was able successfully to rely on the terms of the bill to limit its liability.

However, in *The Starsin*,[165] Lord Hobhouse favoured the second school of thought and was of the view that the shipowner was a sub-bailee on terms of the charterparty. The school of thought adopted in *Elder Dempster* case appears to be a better one than the view of Lord Hobhouse because the shipper will have no access to the charterparty,[166] whereas the shipowner may have access to the bill of lading issued by the charterer. A time-charterer will issue the bill pursuant to the terms of the charterparty and as allowed by the shipowner. Hence, it will be fairer to bind the shipowner to the terms of the bill of lading issued by the charterer rather than to bind the shipper to the terms of the charterparty.

In *The Pioneer Container*,[167] a transshipment case, the Privy Council held that the on-carrier was a sub-bailee to the shipper on terms of the on-carrier's bill issued to the principal carrier. It was well decided so in the context of a transshipment case where the on-carrier will have no control over the terms of the bill of lading between the principal carrier and the shipper, unlike in the case of a charterer's bill where the

---

[163] If it is a case of bailment on terms, as it will almost always be in shipping cases.

[164] *Elder, Dempster & Co Ltd v Paterson, Zochonis & Co, Griffiths Lewis Steam Navigation Co v Paterson, Zochonis & Co Ltd* [1923] 1 KB 420, [1924] AC 522, [1924] All ER Rep 135 (UK HL).

[165] *Homburg Houtimport BV v Agrosin Private Ltd (The Starsin)* [2003] UKHL 12, [2004] 1 AC 715, [2003] 2 All ER 785, [2003] 2 WLR 711, [2003] 1 All ER (Comm) 625, [2003] 1 Lloyd's Rep 571 [2003] All ER (D) 192 (Mar) (UK HL).

[166] This is practically so even if the bill of lading incorporates by reference the charterparty.

[167] *KH Enterprise v Pioneer Container (The Pioneer Container)* [1994] 2 AC 324, [1994] 2 All ER 250, [1994] 3 WLR 1, [1994] 1 LRC 465, [1994] 1 Lloyd's Rep 593 (PC on appeal from Hong Kong).

shipowner will have some control over the terms of the bills issued by the charterer to the shippers.

In this case, the board placed reliance on a clause in the bill of lading issued by the principal carrier to the shipper, by which the principal carrier was allowed to transship the goods on 'any terms whatsoever'. However, even in the absence of such a liberty-clause, the board should have reached the same conclusion. Donaldson J in the earlier case of *Johnson Matthey & Co Ltd v Constantine Terminals Ltd*[168] was of the view that such consent of the bailor was not necessary to constitute a sub-bailment on terms of the sub-bailee's document. Although the Privy Council in *The Pioneer Container* case did not prefer the view of Donaldson J, it appears that the view of Donaldson J should be the preferred one as a sub-bailee should not be liable more than by the terms on which it has accepted, or fairly said to have accepted, the sub-bailment. *Sonicare International Ltd v East Anglia Freight Terminal Ltd*[169] supports a proposition that such consent of the bailor may be implied. This can harmonise the difference on this point between *The Pioneer Container* and *Johnson Matthey v Constantine Terminals.*

It must be noted that any exclusion or limitation clause that a shipowner or a subcontractor may rely on, in a bailment action where there is no contractual[170] relationship between the parties, will be subject to a test of reasonableness[171] by virtue of Section 2(2) of the UK Unfair Contract Terms Act 1977[172] insofar as the clause attempts to exclude or limit liability for *negligence.*

In visiting the 1977 Act in the context of carriage of goods by sea, two matters must be borne in mind. One is that that para 2 of the Schedule 1 to the Act excludes the operation of Section 2(2) to contracts for carriage of goods by ship. However, this does not prevent the operation of the Section 2(2) when there is no such contract for carriage of goods between the parties as in a *pure* bailment action. The other is that Section 27 of the Act excludes the application of Section 2 when the Act applies only because of choice of law by the parties. The Sections 2(1) and (2) of the Act reads as follows:

> (1) A person cannot by reference to any contract term or to a notice given to persons generally or to particular persons exclude or restrict his liability for death or personal injury resulting from negligence.
>
> (2) In the case of other loss or damage, a person cannot so exclude or restrict his liability for negligence except in so far as the term or notice satisfies the requirement of reasonableness.

The Section 27(1) of the Act reads as follows:

> Where the law applicable to a contract is the law of any part of the United Kingdom only by choice of the parties (and apart from that choice would be the law of some country outside

---

[168] [1976] 2 Lloyd's Rep 215 (EW HC).

[169] [1997] 2 Lloyd's Rep 48 (EW County Court).

[170] Including a statutory contractual relationship created by the UK Carriage of Goods by Sea Act 1992.

[171] Set out in Section 11 of the Act (for England and Wales and N. Ireland). Section 24 for Scotland.

[172] Applies to the whole of the UK.

the United Kingdom) Sections 2 to 7 and 16 to 21 of this Act do not operate as part of the law applicable to the contract.

The para 2 of the Schedule 1 to the Act reads as follows:

Section 2(1) extends to—

(a) any contract of marine salvage or towage;

(b) any charterparty of a ship or hovercraft; and

(c) any contract for the carriage of goods by ship or hovercraft;

but subject to this Sections 2, 3 and 7 do not extend to any such contract …

4.3.6.1 Jurisdiction and Choice of Law Clauses

In the case of a pure time-charterer's bill, although the shipowner may be a bailee on terms of the charterer's bill, the shipowner has not been allowed to rely on the jurisdiction and choice of law clauses in the charterer's bill of lading. In *The Forum Craftsman*,[173] the English Court of Appeal refused to allow the shipowner to rely on the jurisdiction and choice of law clause in the bill issued by the charterer. Similarly, in *The Mahkutai*,[174] the court refused such reliance, however, on grounds that the Himalaya clause did not make provision for this. These clauses are considered to be not about bailment per se but about dispute resolution between the direct parties only, namely, the charterer and the shipper. They are said to be intended for their mutual benefit only. It appears to be sustainable that the shipowner should not be allowed to rely on such a dispute resolution mechanism in a third-party document.

However, at present, the Himayala clause appearing in Baltic and International Maritime Council (BIMCO) forms of bill of lading and sea waybill[175] expressly extend the jurisdiction clause in the bill to the subcontractors, servants and agents of the carrier. In such a case, the shipowners will be able to rely also on the jurisdiction clause in the charterer's bill of lading. The clause in the BIMCO forms of bill of lading and sea waybill[176] reads as follows:

(c) Without prejudice to the generality of the foregoing provisions in this clause, every exemption, limitation, condition and liberty contained herein (other than Art III Rule 8 of the Hague/Hague-Visby Rules if incorporated herein) and every right, exemption from liability, defence and immunity of whatsoever nature applicable to the carrier or to which the carrier is entitled hereunder including the right to enforce any jurisdiction or arbitration provision contained herein shall also be available and shall extend to every such Servant of the carrier, who shall be entitled to enforce the same against the Merchant.

---

173 *The Forum Craftsman* [1985] 1 Lloyd's Rep 291 (EW CA).

174 *The Mahkutai* [1996] AC 650, [1996] 3 All ER 502, [1996] 3 WLR 1, [1996] 2 LRC 599, [1996] 2 Lloyd's Rep 1 (PC on appeal from Hong Kong).

175 BIMCO CONLINEBILL 2016 (Liner Bill of Lading). BIMCO CONGENBILL 2016 (Bill of Lading). BIMCO GENWAYBILL 2016 (Non-Negotiable General Sea Waybill). BIMCO MULTIDOC 2016 (Negotiable Multimodal Transport Bill of Lading).

176 BIMCO CONLINEBILL 2016 (Liner Bill of Lading). BIMCO CONGENBILL 2016 (Bill of Lading). BIMCO GENWAYBILL 2016 (Non-Negotiable General Sea Waybill). BIMCO MULTIDOC 2016 (Negotiable Multimodal Transport Bill of Lading).

Contrary to the position of a shipowner in the case of a pure time-charterer's bill, an on-carrier who issued its bill to the principal carrier in a transshipment has been allowed to rely on the jurisdiction and choice of law clauses in the on-carrier's bill. In *The Pioneer Container*,[177] the on-carrier, who was a sub-bailee to the shipper on terms of the sub-bailee's bill issued to the principal carrier, was allowed to rely on the jurisdiction and choice of law clauses in the bill. This was well so because the on-carrying was relying on its own document to which it was a party. It must be noted that when a shipper seeks to rely on a third-party document, i.e. the bill issued by the on-carrier to the principal carrier, to found a case in bailment, the shipper should also be subject to the jurisdiction and choice of law clauses therein. This is different from the case of a pure time-charterer's bill, where the shipowners had unsuccessfully attempted to rely on the jurisdiction and choice of law clauses in a third-party document, i.e. the charterer's bill.

4.4 Tort-Action: Negligence

In the UK, the law of tort, that covers negligence, is largely regulated by the common law. The position in many Commonwealth countries, including Singapore and Malaysia, is largely the same.

4.4.1 Negligence Action in General

Carriers and contractors in the carriage of goods by sea will come within the *Donoghue v Stevenson*[178] neighbourhood principle to owe a duty of care to the cargo interest, who may be a different person from the shipper, consignor and holder of the bill of lading. It will be recalled that in this landmark case, the House of Lords held that a manufacturer of a bottled drink, putting the same for sale through retailers, owed a duty of care to the consumers of the drink, although there was no contractual link between the manufacturer and the consumers.

---

[177] *KH Enterprise v Pioneer Container (The Pioneer Container)* [1994] 2 AC 324, [1994] 2 All ER 250, [1994] 3 WLR 1, [1994] 1 LRC 465, [1994] 1 Lloyd's Rep 593 (PC on appeal from Hong Kong).

[178] [1932] AC 562, [1932] All ER Rep 1 (UK HL).

4.4.2 Limitations to Negligence Action in Carriage of Goods by Sea

The negligence-action was originally available to the cargo owners and those entitled to immediate possession of the goods. However, subsequently, it was restricted to cases where the claimant had such interest at the time of the first significant damage to the goods. The reason for this restrictive approach seems to be for curbing the attempts of the cargo claimants to circumvent the application of the Hague or Hague-Visby Rules, under which the carriers would be entitled to liability-limitation,[179] by bringing an action in negligence. Courts have also been restrictive in finding a duty of care against independent contractors. This again seems to be to rule out attempts of cargo claimant to recover in total more than that limited by the Rules.

In *The Aliakmon*,[180] the House of Lords held that negligence-action was available to both the cargo owners and those entitled to immediate possession of the goods. If the owner of the goods is not holding the bill, perhaps because it is stuck somewhere in the passage through banks, he may still take action in negligence as the owner of the goods. Alternatively, if the holder of the bill is not the owner, such as a pledgee-bank, then it too may take the action.

Subsequently, the House of Lords in *The Starsin*[181] restricted its availability by holding that the cargo claimant must establish ownership or right to possession *at the time of first significant damage to the goods*. This is a major limitation. In this case, the bill of lading was issued by the charterer. The cargo claimants sued the shipowner for negligent stowage, namely condensation damage, resulting progressively. The requirement of establishing ownership or right to possession at the time of first significant damage shut off the claimants, except in the case of one of them. The first significant damage did not occur in this case at the outset as the damage by condensation was progressive.

In *The Nicholas H*,[182] the cargo owners sued the classification society for loss to the cargo owners resulting from negligent classification. The suit came after the cargo owners had already successfully recovered the maximum amount recoverable from the shipowners subject to the applicable limitations. The House of Lords turned down the action holding[183] that the classification society did not owe a duty of care to the cargo owners.

---

[179] Article IV(5).

[180] *Leigh and Sillavan Ltd v Aliakmon Shipping Co Ltd (The Aliakmon) (HL)* [1986] AC 785, [1986] 2 All ER 145, [1986] 2 WLR 902, [1986] 2 Lloyd's Rep 1 (UK HL).

[181] *Homburg Houtimport BV v Agrosin Private Ltd (The Starsin)* [2003] UKHL 12, [2004] 1 AC 715, [2003] 2 All ER 785, [2003] 2 WLR 711, [2003] 1 All ER (Comm) 625, [2003] 1 Lloyd's Rep 571 [2003] All ER (D) 192 (Mar) (UK HL).

[182] *Marc Rich & Co AG v Bishop Rock Marine Co Ltd (The Nicholas H)* [1996] AC 211, [1995] 3 All ER 307, [1995] 3 WLR 227, [1995] 3 LRC 120, [1995] 2 Lloyd's Rep 299 (UK HL).

[183] Possibly by judicial ingenuity.

4.4.3 Rule Against Recovery of Economic Loss in Negligence-Action

Pure economic loss is not recoverable in a negligence-action. The advantage of action in contract is that such economic loss may be recovered. The 'pure economic' loss has been widely defined.

In *Murphy v Brentwood District Council*,[184] the local authority negligently approved the plans for a house footing. The plaintiff purchased the house, which subsequently started to subside as a result of the defective footing. Hence, the plaintiff had to sell the house at a loss. The plaintiff then sued the local authority for the loss. The House of Lords refused remedy to the plaintiff as the loss claimed was purely economic as opposed to material or physical damage.

The same approach has been followed in shipping cases. In *The Gudermes*,[185] a cargo of oil was shipped. The shipowner failed to heat the oil, resulting in unsuitability of the oil to be discharged through the receiver's pipeline. Hence, the receiver incurred an additional cost of transshipment to enable the oil to be discharged through the pipeline. At the High Court, Hirst J was of the view, *obiter*, that this loss was pure economic loss and could not be recovered in a negligence-action.

In *The Orjula*,[186] the shipowners suffered loss as a result of defective drums containing chemicals loaded onto the ship, which drums leaked the chemicals on the deck. This resulted in the shipowner having to remove the drums, clean the deck and re-stow the drums. The shipowner sued the supplier of the drums in negligence. The English Court of Appeal refused remedy to the shipowner, holding the loss complained of to be purely economic.

4.4.4 Negligence Action Subject to Contractual Limitations

A negligence-action will normally be taken by a cargo claimant against the party with whom the cargo claimant has no contractual nexus. If a cargo claimant were to take a negligence-action against a respondent in contractual nexus, then the negligence-action will be subject to exclusions and limitations in contract, hence no utility in such an action. This has been the position both at common law[187] and under the Hague-Visby Rules. Article IV*bis*(1) of the Hague-Visby Rules provides as follows:

---

184 [1990] 2 All ER 908, [1990] 3 WLR 414, [1990] 2 Lloyd's Rep 467 (UK HL).

185 *Mitsui & Co Ltd v Novorossiysk Shipping Co (The Gudermes) (HC)* [1991] 1 Lloyd's Rep 456 (EW HC). The decision made by the High Court was reversed by the Court of Appeal in [1993] 1 Lloyd's Rep 311 (EW CA).

186 *Losinjska Plovidba v Transco Overseas Ltd (The Orjula)* [1995] 2 Lloyd's Rep 395 (EW HC).

187 See *Henderson v Merrett* [1995] 2 AC 145 (EW HL); *BSkyB Ltd v HP Enterprise Services UK Ltd* [2010] EWHC 86 (TCC), 129 ConLR 147, [2010] IP & T 597, [2010] IP & T 811, [2010] All ER (D) 192 (Jan) (UK HL); *Pyrene Co Ltd v Scindia Navigation Co Ltd* [1954] 2 QB 402, [1954] 2 All ER 158, [1954] 2 WLR 1005, [1954] 1 Lloyd's Rep 321 (EW HC).

> The defences and limits of liability provided for in these Rules shall apply in any action against the carrier in respect of loss or damage to goods covered by a contract of carriage whether the action be founded in contract or tort.

Similarly, the law, jurisdiction and dispute resolution clauses in the contract will bind the action in tort between the same contractual parties. It must be noted that the subjection operates only when there is a contractual nexus between the parties.

Hence, it does not apply where the charterer issued the bill on its own right[188] and the holder of the bill directly sues the shipowner. Hence, when a holder of a pure charterer's bill,[189] sues a stevedore or the shipowner, the liability of the stevedore or the shipowner in negligence is not limited by the Hague or Hague-Visby Rules. Thence came the practice of including a Himalaya and circular indemnity clauses in bills of lading. These clauses will extend the protection accorded to the carrier to all servants, agents and subcontractors of the carrier, including the shipowner.[190] Such clauses have limited the utility of action in negligence against any such contractors, etc. However, a benefit of taking action against the *shipowner* in negligence, when it is not the contractual carrier, is that the ship (or sister ship) can be arrested to procure security from the P&I Club.[191] In such an action against the shipowner, all the limitations in the bill issued by the charterer will apply when there is a Himalaya clause.

4.4.5 Action in Negligence Versus Action in Bailment

In the case of an action in bailment, the liability of the bailee will be limited per the terms of bailment. The terms of bailment may be those found in a bill of lading issued to the shipper. In the case of a sub-bailment by transshipment, the terms of the sub-bailment will be found in the bill issued by the on-carrier to the principal carrier.

To the contrary, in the case of an action in negligence against anyone other than the carrier, in theory, the terms of the bill have no role to play. However, in practice, by the widespread use of Himalaya clauses, the terms of the bill will be relevant, as the clauses will extend the protection accorded to the carrier to the non-carrier respondent.[192]

---

[188] Without a demise or identity of carrier clause.

[189] Without a demise or identity of carrier clause.

[190] In the case of a pure charterer's bill.

[191] Security for payment of any award sum as a condition for release of the ship from arrest.

[192] Such as the agents, servants and subcontractors of the carrier, including the shipowner.

4.5 Conversion (Tort)/Non-delivery (Contract)

The obligation of the carrier to deliver the goods at the destination port against the presentation of the bill of lading is a fundamental one. If the carrier fails to do so, it will be liable in *contract* for *non-delivery* and, if that is because of *misdelivery* to a wrong person, also in *conversion*.[193] The obligation for delivery is *on* the person obliged to deliver, that is the carrier. The obligation is *to* the person entitled to possession or immediate possession of the goods, that is the lawful holder[194] of the bill of lading, or in the case of a straight bill, to the named consignee in possession of the bill. Accordingly, ordinarily, an action in conversion between the cargo claimant and the carrier will be available only when there is a contractual nexus between them. It is not doubted that a conversion-action against the carrier, being an action in tort, is subject to the contractual limitations and exceptions found in the bill of lading.[195] Hence, the utility of a conversion-action is limited[196] since it is in parallel to a cause of action in contract. Two things must be noted. First, a conversion-action is based on the *right to possession*[197] and it is irrelevant whether the claimant is the owner of the goods. Second, not only the carrier but also others[198] such as the person wrongfully receiving the goods[199] can be liable in conversion.

4.5.1 *Non-delivery v. Misdelivery*

The two, mere non-delivery and misdelivery, seem to have been confused at times. In *Minmetals South-East Asia Corp Pte Ltd v Nakhoda Logistics Sdn Bhd*,[200] the Malaysian Court of Appeal seemed to have treated indifferently misdelivery and a mere non-delivery not amounting to misdelivery. In this case, there were cargoes of timber carried on board a few vessels from Port Klang[201] to Shanghai.[202] The cargoes

---

[193] A tort.

[194] More accurately, the transferee of the bill within the *Barber v Meyerstein* (supra) principle.

[195] *Pyrene Co Ltd v Scindia Navigation Co Ltd* [1954] 2 QB 402, [1954] 2 All ER 158, [1954] 2 WLR 1005, [1954] 1 Lloyd's Rep 321; Article IV*bis*(1) of the Hague-Visby Rules.

[196] As between cargo owner and carrier.

[197] As far as cargo claims are concerned.

[198] Joint tortfeasors.

[199] *Mewah-Oils Sdn Bhd v Lushing Traders Pte Ltd* [2018] 5 CLJ 185, [2017] 2 MLJ 592 (MY CA).

[200] [2019] 3 CLJ 19, [2018] 6 MLJ 152 (MY CA). See also Arun Kasi, 'A Critical Analysis of the Court of Appeal Decision on Misdelivery in Minmetals South-East Asia Corp Pte Ltd v Nakhoda Logistics Sdn Bhd', *The Law Review*, [2020] LR 105. This article was referred to in *Punjab National Bank v Malayan Banking Berhad* [2020] 1 LNS 232, [2020] 5 MLJ 732 (MY CA).

[201] In Malaysia.

[202] In China.

were covered by 25 house bills of lading issued by a Malaysian freight forwarder—a NVOC. A Singapore trader purchased the cargoes for about USD13 million and fully paid for them and obtained the 25 house bills. Thereafter, the freight forwarder refused to furnish,[203] to the Singapore trader, the agent's details to arrange collection. Thereafter, the Singapore trader, as the holder of the bills, demanded delivery but again, no avail. Hence, the Singapore trader sued the freight forwarder, in effect for non-delivery. The court found the freight forwarder liable and ordered it to pay damages to the Singapore trader.[204] However, in coming to the conclusion, the court treated non-delivery and misdelivery indifferently. This will not be correct.

A carrier will be liable[205] when it fails to deliver against the presentation of the bill issued by it. The liability will be in contract when it is mere non-delivery (such as where the goods are lost). In addition to that, it will be in conversion for misdelivery (where the goods are delivered to a wrong person i.e. a person not holding the bill).[206]

It must be observed that, at common law, the tort of conversion[207] is committed only in the case of the latter (misdelivery), but not in the case of the former (mere non-delivery not amounting to misdelivery). 'Conversion' has not been an easy thing to define or understand. In *Hiort v London and North Western Railway Co*,[208] Bramwell LJ said that he had frequently stated that he never understood with precision what a conversion was. The English Court of Appeal in *Kuwait Airways Corpn v Iraqi Airways Co (Nos4 and 5) (CA)* [209] was guided by the following definition of conversion by Salmond on Torts[210]:

> [T]he wrong of conversion consists in any act of willful interference with a chattel, done without lawful justification, whereby any person entitled thereto is deprived of the use and possession of it.

The court similarly was guided also by the following definition of conversion by Clerk & Lindsell[211]:

---

[203] Other than perhaps asking the Singapore trader to contact the 'notify party' named in the bills.

[204] The decision would have been correct if the claimant was the shipper or the bill was issued by the shipowner so that it would be transferable within the *Barbar v Meyerstein* principle. This was a point not considered by the court.

[205] In the case of an NVOC, the liability is to the shipper. See Chapter 2.2.5 for a detailed consideration of the question of 'transferability' of bills issued by NVOCs.

[206] *Chabbra Corporation Pte Ltd v Jag Shakti (Owners) (The Jag Shakti)* [1986] 1 MLJ 197, [1986] AC 337, [1986] 1 All ER 480, [1986] 2 WLR 87, [1987] LRC (Comm) 228, [1986] 1 Lloyd's Rep 1, 130 Sol Jo 51, [1986] LS Gaz R 45 (PC on appeal from Singapore).

[207] Also called 'trover'.

[208] (1870) 4 Ex D 188 at 194 (EW CA).

[209] [2001] 3 WLR 1117 (EW CA), affirmed by the House of Lords in [2002] UKHL 19 at [129], [2002] 2 AC 883, [2002] 3 All ER 209, [2002] 2 WLR 1353, [2002] 1 All ER (Comm) 843, [2003] 1 LRC 430, [2002] All ER (D) 252 (May) (UK HL).

[210] John W. Salmond, *Salmond on Torts*, UK, Stevens and Haynes, 1907, p 284.

[211] Latest edition: Michael A Jones, *Clerk & Lindsell on Torts*, 23nd edn., UK, Sweet & Maxwell, 2020, at para 16–07.

> [A]n act of deliberate dealing with a chattel in a manner inconsistent with another's right whereby that other is deprived of the use and possession of it.

Conversion is a tort of strict liability,[212] 'in which the moral concept of fault in the sense of either knowledge by the doer of an act that it is likely to cause injury, loss or damage to another, or lack of reasonable care to avoid causing the injury, loss or damage to another, plays no part'.[213] At the same time, conversion is a 'voluntary' or 'deliberate' act. Hence there will be no conversion if the bailee merely lost the goods or the goods were destroyed by negligence of the bailee but without his voluntary act. There will be a conversion where one voluntarily gives away or takes the goods belonging to another without authority. such a voluntary act when one wrongfully gives away or takes. Similarly, there will be a conversion where on voluntarily retains, uses or destroys the goods belonging to another without authority. For a conversion, i.e. interference with another's right to possession, to be committed it is not necessary that the tortfeasor gains possession of the converted goods.[214] A wrongful refusal of access to one entitled to the possession will also be a conversion. While all these are conversion at common law, a statutory conversion was created by Section 2(2) of the Torts (Interference with Goods) Act 1977,[215] namely, loss of goods by breach of bailee's duties. This will cover loss by negligence.

In jurisdictions where the common law applies and there is no statutory extension to it,[216] a mere non-delivery, not amounting to misdelivery, will not be a conversion. Hence, for such an instance, a suit for non-delivery has to be taken in contract based on the bill of lading, or in bailment or negligence.[217] As far as England, Wales and N. Ireland is concerned, an action in conversion will be additionally available by virtue of Section 2(2) of the Torts (Interference with Goods) Act 1977, provided that the defendant is a bailee, e.g. shipowner.[218]

---

[212] *Kuwait Airways Corpn v Iraqi Airways Co (Nos 4 and 5) (HL)* [2002] UKHL 19 at [129], [2002] 2 AC 883, [2002] 3 All ER 209, [2002] 2 WLR 1353, [2002] 1 All ER (Comm) 843, [2003] 1 LRC 430, [2002] All ER (D) 252 (May) (UK HL), speech of Lord Hoffman.

[213] *Marfani & Co Ltd v Midland Bank Ltd* [1968] 1 WLR 956 at 970–971 (EW CA), speech of Diplock LJ.

[214] *Amixco Asia Pte Ltd v Bank Negara Indonesia* [1992] 1 SLR 703 (SG CA).

[215] There is no equivalent statutory provision in many commonwealth countries including Singapore and Malaysia, where conversion can only be found by common law principles.

[216] E.g. Singapore/Malaysia.

[217] Depending on availability of actions in the factual matrix of the case.

[218] Whether an NVOC, like a freight forwarder who does not take physical possession of the goods, is a bailee is arguable. In *Spectra International plc v Hayesoak Ltd* [1997] 1 Lloyd's Rep 153, an English County Court held that a freight forwarder who issued a combined transport bill of lading was a bailee, although it did not take physical possession of the goods, and it was sufficient that goods were at its disposal as freight forwarder to arrange warehousing, transportation and delivery. Despite that, the point can be open to argument.

4.5.2 Misdelivery

It will be a misdelivery when goods are delivered otherwise than against presentation of the bill of lading. Lord Longmore well reminded this point of law in *Wolff v Trinity Logistics USA Inc*[219] as follows:

> It has long been a cardinal principle of the English law of carriage by sea that the carrier should only deliver the goods to a person who presents an original bill of lading. If he delivers to anyone else he is liable for misdelivery.[220]

At the same time his Lordship also referred to the practice as this:

> It is by no means unknown for carriers … to succumb to pressure from the receivers/buyers of goods to release goods without production of an original bill. Any carrier who does so will be in breach of the contract of carriage.[221] He will therefore hardly ever release the goods without a guarantee or letter of indemnity from the receiver or whoever wants delivery of the goods.[222]

The duty to delivery only against the presentation of the bill is a strict one. It is not delegable, so it is not a defence for the carrier to say that the goods were misdelivered by a competent subcontractor appointed by it such as a warehouse operator. It is a misdelivery even if the delivery was made to the owner of the goods[223] or a consignee named in an order bill[224] without presentation of the bill of lading but against indemnity-undertaking, which is quite common in the industry. This will be crucial when the bill of lading had been pledged to a bank, which is still holding it, but delivery made to the buyer against indemnity-undertaking.

At most of the times, the delivery obligation will crystallise after the discharge of the goods from the ship. However, it may sometimes crystallise simultaneously at the time of discharge. In cases where the goods were carried on 'free-out' terms, the consignee will arrange the discharge of the goods from the ship. In such cases, the carrier must ensure that the bill has been surrendered to it before the discharge operation starts. Otherwise, the carrier can become liable for misdelivery.

---

[219] [2018] EWCA Civ 2765, [2019] 1 WLR 3997, [2019] All ER (D) 37 (Jan) (EW CA).

[220] For application of this principle in Singapore, see *The Cherry and Others* [2003] 1 SLR 471 (SG CA).

[221] See *Sze Hai Tong Bank Ltd v Rambler Cycle Co Ltd* [1959] AC 576, [1959] 2 Lloyd's Rep 114 at 120, [1959] 3 All ER 182, [1959] 3 WLR 214 (PC on appeal from Singapore), speech of Lord Denning: "It is perfectly clear law that a shipowner who delivers without production of the bill of lading does so at his peril. The contract is to deliver, on production of the bill of lading, to the person entitled under the bill of lading."

[222] Similarly, in *Kuwait Petroleum Corpn v I & D Oil Carriers Ltd (The Houda)* [1994] 2 Lloyd's Rep 541 (EW CA), the court refused to recognise the trade practice to deliver cargo without presentation of the bill as a defence to misdelivery claim.

[223] *Chabbra Corporation Pte Ltd v Jag Shakti (Owners) (The Jag Shakti)* [1986] 1 MLJ 197, [1986] AC 337, [1986] 1 All ER 480, [1986] 2 WLR 87, [1987] LRC (Comm) 228, [1986] 1 Lloyd's Rep 1, 130 Sol Jo 51, [1986] LS Gaz R 45 (PC on appeal from Singapore).

[224] *The Stettin* (1889) 14 PD 142 (EW HC).

4.5.2.1 Charterparty Allowing or Requiring Delivery Against Indemnity

It is common that charterparties will permit or even require the shipowner, in cases where the bills of lading are issued by the shipowner, to deliver against indemnity-undertaking. Courts have held that despite such a provision in the charterparty, the shipowner will be liable for misdelivery if it delivers without the surrender of the bill.[225] In *The Sormovskiy 3068*,[226] the charterparty *authorised* the shipowner to deliver against an indemnity-undertaking. The terms of the charterparty were incorporated into the bill of lading issued by the shipowner. The court held that despite this arrangement, the shipowner will be liable for misdelivery if it delivers goods otherwise than against the bill. Courts have found that a carrier will be liable for misdelivery even if the charterparty *required* the shipowner to deliver against indemnity-undertaking.[227]

In *The Epic*,[228] decided by the Singapore Court of Appeal, the owner of the cargo requested the shipowner to deliver without production of the bill of lading upon a letter of indemnity and payment of the sub-freight. The shipowner first agreed and then changed its mind and refused. Accordingly, the shipowners did not deliver the goods and detained them. The owner of the cargo sued the shipowner for wrongful detention. The court found that the parties had entered into a collateral contract for delivery against the letter of indemnity and that the shipowner breached it. Hence, the court held the shipowner liable and awarded damages against it.

However, the court did not consider the legality, existence of consideration and binding force of agreement in light of the settled law that it would be a misdelivery to deliver the cargo without presentation of the bill. The purpose of the rule against delivery otherwise than by the production of the bill is for the protection of third parties who may come to hold the bill, i.e. to safeguard them from being defrauded, and is a cardinal principle concerning the transferability of the bill of lading,[229] that is central to international trade.

Although a shipowner is not bound to deliver against an indemnity-undertaking, if it delivers, then it would be able to enforce the indemnity-undertaking. An indemnity-undertaking is not illegal or unenforceable although delivery otherwise against the bill is contrary to the law. It must be noted that P&I insurance does not cover liability for misdelivery.

---

[225] In *Olivine Electronics Pte Ltd v Seabridge Transport Pte Ltd* [1995] 3 SLR 143 (SG HC), the Singapore High Court held that a clause in the bill of lading saying "if required by the carrier one (1) original bill of lading must be surrendered" did not actually give any option to the carrier to deliver otherwise than against presentation of the bill.

[226] *Sucre Export SA v Northern Shipping Ltd (The Sormovskiy 3068)* [1994] 2 Lloyd's Rep 266 (EW HC).

[227] *The Aegean Sea* [1998] 2 Lloyd's Rep 39, [1998] All ER (D) 135 (EW HC); *The Dolphina* [2012] 1 Lloyd's Rep 304, [2011] SGHC 273 (SG HC).

[228] *The Epic* [2000] 3 SLR 735 (SG CA).

[229] See *Barber v Meyerstein* (1870) LR 4 HL 317, [1861–73] All ER Rep Ext 1810 (UK HL).

4.5.2.2 'Possessory Right' as the Key to Conversion-Action

The requirement that the claimant in a conversion-action held the 'possessory right' is a one, and 'proprietary right' is irrelevant. This can be seen from the case of *The Cherry and Others*,[230] decided by the Singapore Court of Appeal. In this case, fuel oil belonging to the claimant, carried on board the vessel The Hyperion from Iran to Fujairah, was misdelivered into another tanker, namely The Cherry, owned by another carrier. The owners of The Cherry then wrongfully on-carried the cargo to Singapore and misdelivered the same to a wrong person. The claimant, however, did not hold the bill of lading. The claimant brought an action in conversion[231] against the owners of The Cherry. The court disallowed the claim, as a claim in conversion was only available to a person who held the immediate right to possession, i.e. holder of the bill. The result would have been the same even if the action was brought against the former carrier who misdelivered to the latter carrier.

This was a consolidated appeal case, in which the court also decided a claim brought by the claimant against the owners of The Cherry, but in respect of a different shipment of fuel oil from Kuwait to Fujairah and two other claims brought by the same claimant against the owners of two other tankers, The Epic and The Addax. In the case of these three shipments, carried by The Cherry, The Epic and The Addax, the bills of lading were endorsed to and held by a sister company of the Swiss-based claimant[232] in the UK.[233] The sister company was holding these three bills as agents for the claimant, hence the claimant was considered the holder of these bills. All the cargo of the three shipments were misdelivered by the respective owners of the three tankers without presentation of the bill.[234] The claims in respect of these three shipments, based on the bills of lading contract,[235] were allowed.

However, the procedural correctness of the decision in relation to the three shipments is questionable, as the bills were not merely held by the UK company, but were indorsed to the UK company. Hence, the UK company was the holder of the bill in the eyes of the law, even if they held it for the benefit of the Swiss company. Section 2(1) of the Singapore Bills of Lading Act, which is identical to Section 2(1) of the UK Carriage of Goods by Sea Act 1992, makes provision for this scenario by allowing the holder of the bill to take action for the benefit of the owner of the cargo. Hence, as a matter of procedure, the better and safer approach, particularly taking into account the short time limit,[236] would have been at least to join the UK company as a claimant.

---

[230] *The Cherry and Others* [2003] 1 SLR 471 (SG CA).

[231] Among others.

[232] Glencore International AG, Switzerland.

[233] Glencore UK Ltd, UK.

[234] Upon instruction of the seller, who also happened to be the time-charterer of the three carrying ships.

[235] Among others.

[236] Article III(6) of the Hague Rules/Hague-Visby Rules: time limit of one year to bring suit from the date of delivery or from the date when the cargo should have been delivered.

The possessory right as the basis of the conversion action was emphasised by the Privy Council in an appeal from Singapore in *Chan Cheng Kum v Wah Tat Bank*.[237] In this case, the Privy Council held that a bank that was holding a non-negotiable mate's receipts,[238] issued in place of the bill of lading by the custom of the trade in that marketplace at that time, had the possessory rights over the goods. Hence, the bank was able to bring an action in conversion against the shipowner when the latter delivered the goods to the shipper without any indorsement by the bank on the receipt. For the bank to the acquire possessory title, there must be delivery of the cargo and a pledge of the same to the bank. In this case, the shipment of the cargo was considered delivery of it to the bank.[239] Delivery of the mate's receipts to the bank completed the pledge of the cargo. Thus, the bank acquired the possessory right, that in turn gave it the right to sue for conversion. As the shipowner delivered the cargo to the shipper, knowing of the bank's interest but without indorsement from the bank, the shipowner was held liable in conversion to the bank.

4.5.2.3 Time at Which Possessory Right Must Have Been Held

The time at which the claimant in a conversion-action must have had the possessory right is a highly controversial subject. It has attracted conflicting authorities and different schools of thought. It is not doubted that, in the general context, the liability in conversion is to the person who had the possessory right at the time of the conversion. But in the context of transfer of bills, the question is whether the transfer passes the possessory right attached to the bill and all the privileges bound with it from the moment of the transfer or from the moment the bill was originally issued.

In *The Future Express*,[240] a bank received the bill of lading after the cargo had been misdelivered by the carrier. The bank sued the carrier for conversion. The English Court of Appeal disallowed the claim on the ground that the bank did not have the possessory right at the time of conversion. In *The Cherry and Others*,[241] decided by the Singapore Court of Appeal, the owners of the vessel The Cherry misdelivered the goods. The cargo owner, who did not hold the bill at the time of the misdelivery but received it after that. The cargo owner sued the shipowner for conversion. The Singapore Court of Appeal disallowed the claim, holding that a claim in conversion was only available to a person who held the immediate right to possession, i.e. holder of the bill, at the time of the conversion. In this case, as the carrier no longer had the actual possession at the time the buyer received the bill, the buyer could not, and did

237 [1971] 1 Lloyd's Rep 439, [1971] 1 MLJ 177 (PC on appeal from Singapore).

238 Because the mate's receipts were not negotiable and the bank was not a party to it, it had no rights of suit under it although named as the consignee. In fact, the shipper can at any time change the consignee.

239 It was the intention of the shipper and the bank that the bank would finance the transaction (which the bank did) and the shipper would pledge the cargo to the bank.

240 *The Future Express* [1993] 2 Lloyd's Rep 542, [1993] 7 WLUK 364, [1994] CLY 4046 (EW CA).

241 *The Cherry and Others* [2003] 1 SLR 471 (SG CA).

never, acquire any immediate right to possession against the carrier. In both these cases, the court assumed that a transfer of bill passed the possessory right from the moment of the transfer.

A contrary decision was arrived at in late 19th century by the English Court of Appeal in *Bristol and West of England Bank v Midland Railway Company*.[242] In this case, an action was taken by a holder of a bill of lading, namely, the bank to which the bill was pledged, against the carrier for conversion committed before the bank came to hold the bill. The English Court of Appeal allowed the claim. It appears that the court was of the view that the rights of suit for the conversion, from the issuance of the bill, had been transferred to the subsequent holder of the bill.

In attempting to understand the conflict between the two approaches, it will be helpful to compare the interference with possessory rights in the case of bills of lading with that in the case of physical chattels. Suppose there is an interference with the possession of physical chattels and subsequently the possession is transferred to a transferee. Any suffering as a result of the interference was borne by the transferor and he only has the right to sue for the interference. The transferee is not affected by the past interference in any way. There can be no doubt that the transferee does not inherit the cause of action associated with the interference.

Now, a look at the bill of lading scenario. Suppose there is an interference with the possessory rights, namely, misdelivery by the carrier, and subsequently the bill (and therefor the possessory right) is transferred to a transferee. Here, neither the transferor nor the transferee sees the goods by their eyes. It is only a presumed possession by the carrier. This presumption necessarily arises from the undertaking, embedded in the bill of lading, by the carrier to deliver, that necessarily constitutes a warranty by the carrier that he has the actual possession. The warranty is a unilateral one given by the carrier to anyone trading on the strength of the bill in good faith. The misdelivery by the carrier does not interfere in any way with the said presumption or the warranty. The innocent transferee here traded and paid on the strength of the said warranty in the bill of lading and the strength of the carrier, and not on the strength of the transferor. Although a conversion might have happened before the transferee came to hold the bill, the crystallisation, maturity and true value of the bill is only at time it is due for delivery. Here, the loss resulting from the conversion falls only on the transferee and not he transferor. This is a unique thing for goods at sea represented by a bill of lading. Accordingly, the carrier must be liable to the holder of the bill, at the minimum, for breach of the warranty.

As far as the contractual rights are concerned, when the bill is transferred, the contractual rights passes from the time when the bill was issued rather than from the time of the transfer, as if the transferee was a party to the bill of lading contract. This was so both under the 1855 Act regime and the 1992 Act regime, although there is a fetter in the 1855 Act regime, namely, the property must pass for the contractual rights to pass. In a contractual action, there is no need for any concept of unilateral warranty to overcome the prior misdelivery, as the carrier will be liable for non-delivery without any valid excuse.

---

[242] [1891] 2 QB 653, 61 LJQB 115, 7 Asp MLC 69, 40 WR 148, 65 LT 234, 7 TLR 627 (EW CA).

It is arguable that *Bristol v Midland* conclusion is to be preferred to that of *The Future Express* and *The Cherry*, taking into account the peculiar aspects of bill of lading as opposed to physical chattels. It is also counter-arguable that there is no utility in or reason for extending the availability of a conversion-action as held in *Bristol v Midland* because an action in contract for non-delivery is statutorily available to the lawful holder of the bill of lading. Such a counterargument would be supported by *The Ythan*,[243] where the English High Court observed the following:

> [T]here cannot be a right (against the carrier) to possession of the goods if the goods no longer exist … If the reason for the loss is a breach of contract by the carrier, there may at that stage spring up a contractual right to damages.

Although the question of validity of *Bristol v Midland* may appear to be a merely academic one in the UK in view of the 1992 Act, it is not so in those jurisdictions like certain parts of Malaysia where the UK 1855 Act applies.[244] This is because a transferee of the bill will not acquire the contractual rights under the 1855 Act unless the property in the goods also passes.

4.5.2.4 Conversion-Action Against Persons Other Than Carrier

An action may lie in conversion in respect of misdelivery against persons other than the carrier. Such an action lay against the person who received the cargo in *Mewah-Oils Sdn Bhd v Lushing Traders Pte Ltd*,[245] decided by the Malaysian Court of Appeal. This was in a complex factual scenario where the owner of the cargo did not have the bill of lading at the time of misdelivery but had it after that, although the owner had paid in full for the cargo in advance of the shipment. In this case, a buyer purchased about half a million tons of crude palm oil from a seller, shipment from Belawan[246] to Chittagong.[247] The buyer paid the full contract price to the seller in advance of the shipment. The shipment was made on board the carrying vessel[248] on 8 November 2003. Bills of ladings were issued on the same date. In the meantime, the buyer had made an arrangement to on-sell the cargo to a sub-buyer, which did not go through. On 9 November 2003, seemingly at the instance of the sub-buyer, the shipowner deviated and delivered the cargo at Port Kelang[249] to the sub-buyer's

---

[243] *Primetrade AG v Ythan Ltd (The Ythan)* [2005] EWHC 2399 (Comm) at [68] [70], [2006] 1 All ER 367, [2006] 1 All ER (Comm) 157, [2006] 1 Lloyd's Rep 457, [2005] All ER (D) 05 (Nov) (EW HC).

[244] See Chapter 1.3.6.2.

[245] [2018] 5 CLJ 185, [2017] 2 MLJ 592 (MY CA). See Arun Kasi, 'A Critical Analysis of the Court of Appeal Decision on Misdelivery in Minmetals South-East Asia Corp Pte Ltd v Nakhoda Logistics Sdn Bhd', *The Law Review*, [2020] LR 105. This article was referred to in *Punjab National Bank v Malayan Banking Berhad* [2020] 1 LNS 232, [2020] 5 MLJ 732 (MY CA).

[246] In Indonesia.

[247] In Bangladesh.

[248] The Suppavan 1.

[249] In Malaysia.

nominee without presentation of the bills. The delivery was made by discharge of the oil into the nominee's shore tanks on 9 and 10 November 2003. On 10 November 2003, the buyer received the bills. After 10 November, the nominee processed the cargo and produced resultant products.

The buyer sued the nominee for 'conversion'. The nominee challenged the action with the following contentions.[250] First, the buyer obtained the bills only on 10 November 2003 and hence did not at the time of the alleged conversion have the possessory right (immediate right to possession) to maintain an action in conversion. Second, the nominee was a purchaser of the cargo in good faith by a chain of further sub-sale transactions flowing from the sub-buyer. Third, the buyer had sued the sub-buyer for the sub-sale price as well as conversion in two other actions and had obtained a judgment in one of them and lost the other. However, no payment was received from the sub-buyer who had by then been wound up.

The court there held, on the first contention, that the proprietary and possessory rights were interconnected and that the buyer as the owner of the cargo at the time of misdelivery may bring an action in conversion although it was not holding the bills at that time. On the second contention, the court held that *bona fide* of the nominee was irrelevant in a conversion-action and also that the nominee did not acquire any good title to the goods by the principle *nemo dat quod non habet*. On the third contention, the court held that a claimant may maintain actions against multiple tortfeasors in connection with the same loss[251] and one does not bar the other.[252] The court held that it was an act of conversion for the nominee to receive the cargo on 9 and 10 November, hence the conversion claim must be allowed. The court further held that, in any event, it was an act of conversion for the nominee to retain the cargo and process it after 10 November, by when the buyer had the bills. Accordingly, the court allowed the claim.

The decision of the court that the proprietary right and possessory rights are interconnected and that the buyer may bring an action in the conversion when it did not have the bill is contrary to the established principles of conversion-action and does not represent the good law to be followed. However, the overall result arrived at by the court may be sustainable on the grounds that the nominee retaining and processing the cargo after 10 November, by when the buyer had the bill, rendered the nominee liable to the buyer for conversion.

The facts of this case present an opportunity for analysis of the law concerning conversion and related subjects such as the passing of property, the distinction between passing of property and passing of possessory right, the time at which the

---

250 Among others.

251 However, this must be subject to the rule against double recovery.

252 This principle is in essence codified in Malaysia by Section 10 of the Civil Law Act 1956. Similarly, in Singapore, by Section 10 of the Civil Law Act. In *Wah Tat Bank Ltd & Ors v Chan Cheng Kum* [1975] 1 MLJ 97 (PC on appeal from Singapore), the Privy Council upheld this principle by holding that a judgement secured by the claimant against a tortfeasor for conversion by misdelivery is not a bar to the claimant proceeding with any other joint tortfeasor, under Section 10 of the Singapore Civil Law Act, commenting that the same would be the position under common law.

possessory right is switched to a conversion-claim, *nemo dat quod non habet*, conversion as recurring tort, detachment and attachment-back of possessory right from and to the proprietary right, detinue-action as an alternative to conversion-action, and remedies for interference with *proprietary* right. The same will be analysed below.[253]

Passing of Property in Goods

The *property in goods* passes when it is intended to pass as between the seller and the buyer.[254] Generally, the goods must be ascertained and unconditionally appropriated to the contract.[255] By way of exception to the general rule, the property in a portion of a bulk cargo may pass though not ascertained and unconditionally appropriated.[256] When goods are delivered to the carrier to transmit them to the buyer, without reservation of the right of disposal, unconditional appropriation is deemed to happen, so the property will pass.[257] Where a bill of lading is to the order of the seller, the right of disposal is *prima facie* reserved, so the property will not pass.[258] When goods are shipped and payment is made, generally, the property will pass. In this case, the *property* (also called '*title*' and '*proprietary right*') would have passed when the cargo was shipped on 8 November, since full payment was already made by then.

In *The Ciudad de Pasto and The Ciudad de Neiva*[259] the English Court of Appeal held that when 80% of the contract price was paid in advance of shipment the property in the goods still did not pass to the buyer. In this case, Staughton LJ observed the relationship between payment and passing of property as follows:

> [I]n the ordinary way a seller will not wish to part with the property in his goods if they are shipped overseas until he has been paid in full.

Passing of Property v. Passing of Possessory Right

The two are different. As early as 1839 it was held in *Dunlop v Lambert*[260] that the holder of the bill who has suffered no substantial damages may, at common law, obtain substantial damages for the benefit of a third party who has those losses. Lord

---

[253] See Arun Kasi, 'Mewah-Oils Sdn Bhd v. Lushing Traders Pte Ltd—Court of Appeal Decision on Conversion: A Critical Analysis', *The Law Review*, [2020] LR 209. This article was referred to in *Punjab National Bank v Malayan Banking Berhad* [2020] 1 LNS 232, [2020] 5 MLJ 732 (MY CA).

[254] Section 17 of the UK Sale of Goods Act 1979.

[255] Sections 16 and 18 r. 5(1) of the UK Sale of Goods Act 1979.

[256] Section 20A and 20B of the UK Sale of Goods Act 1979. The same is the position in Singapore. But there is no such exception in the Malaysian Sale of Goods Act 1957. See Chapter 2.4.

[257] Section 18 r. 5(2) of the UK Sale of Goods Act 1979.

[258] Section 19(2) of the UK Sale of Goods Act 1979.

[259] *Mitsui & Co Ltd v Flota Mercante Grancolombiana SA (The Ciudad de Pasto and The Ciudad de Neiva)* [1989] 1 All ER 951 at 957, [1988] 2 Lloyd's Rep 208, [1988] 4 WLUK 98, [1989] CLY 3330 (EW CA).

[260] (1839) 6 Cl & F 600 (EW HC).

Mustill in *The Delfini*[261] described the relationship between the passing of proprietary right and the passing of possessory right as follows:

> [T]he bill of lading fulfills two distinct functions. 1. It is a symbol of constructive possession of the goods which … can transfer constructive possession by endorsement and transfer; it is a transferable 'key to the warehouse'. 2. It is a document which, although not itself capable of directly transferring the property in the goods which it represents, merely by endorsement and delivery, nevertheless is capable of being part of the mechanism by which property is passed.

The buyer would acquire the possessory right when it received the bill, in the *Mewah-Oils* case on 10 November.[262] However, on 10 November, the shipowner did not have the actual possession any longer for the buyer to have a possessory right against the shipowner.[263] Accordingly, if the school of thought in *The Future Express* and *The Cherry* is adopted, the buyer would not acquire any possessory right, but the seller will have it until 10 November. If the school of thought in *Bristol v Midland* is adopted, the buyer will have sufficient standing to sustain an action for the conversion that happened after the bill was issued on 8 November.

It must be noted that if a bill has not gone out of the hands of a shipper-consignor, *irrespective of 'to order' of whom it is issued*, he must have the right to *return* the bill to the carrier for any correction, changing the consignee column information, switching, etc. In this line of thought, the possessory right must also be with him, hence the right to claim delivery of the cargo if the bill is never passed to any others.[264]

Switching of Possessory Right to Conversion-Claim

Conversion is a single wrongful act, unlike detinue that is a continuing cause of action until the tortfeasor delivers up the goods.[265] It is a fact that once the conversion has happened the holder of the bill no longer has any right to possession against the carrier, as the carrier himself does not have the possession.[266] Hence, what happens is that at the time of conversion, the right to possession against the carrier that existed

[261] *Enichem Anic SpA and Others v Ampelos Shipping Co Ltd (The Delfini)* [1990] 1 Ll L Rep 252 at 268 (EW CA).

[262] *Barber v Meyerstein* (1870) LR 4 HL 317, [1861–73] All ER Rep Ext 1810 (UK HL).

[263] *Primetrade AG v Ythan Ltd (The Ythan)* [2005] EWHC 2399 (Comm) at [68] [70], [2006] 1 All ER 367, [2006] 1 All ER (Comm) 157, [2006] 1 Lloyd's Rep 457, [2005] All ER (D) 05 (Nov) (EW HC).

[264] This is so even if the bill was issued to the order of a person to whom the shipper-consignor never passed the bill.

[265] *General and Finance Facilities Ltd v Cooks Cars (Romford) Ltd* [1963] 2 All ER 314 at 317, [1963] 1 WLR 644 (EW CA), speech of Diplock LJ: "There are important distinctions between a cause of action in conversion and a cause of action in detinue. The former is a single wrongful act and the cause of action accrues at the date of the conversion; the latter is a continuing cause of action which accrues at the date of the wrongful refusal to deliver up the goods and continues until delivery up of the goods or judgment in the action for detinue."

[266] *Primetrade AG v Ythan Ltd (The Ythan)* [2005] EWHC 2399 (Comm) at [68] [70], [2006] 1 All ER 367, [2006] 1 All ER (Comm) 157, [2006] 1 Lloyd's Rep 457, [2005] All ER (D) 05 (Nov) (EW HC).

up to and at the time conversion is turned into a right for damages for the conversion against the carrier as the tortfeasor.

Acquisition of Title by Nominee

The general rule is that *nemo dat quod non habet*, that is, 'no one gives what he does not have.' This in effect means that only an owner of the goods can pass title, hence if a purchaser purchases or gets them from someone who is not the owner, the purchaser will not acquire the title. This rule has been statutorily codified in Malaysia, Singapore and the UK. In Malaysia, the general rule is in Section 27 of the Sale of Goods Act 1957, and the exceptions in Sections 27–30. In Singapore, the general rule is in Section 21 of the Sale of Goods Act, and the exceptions in Sections 21, 23–26. In the UK, materially identical provisions are in the same numbered sections of the Sale of Goods Act 1979, except that there is an additional exception in Section 22. Generally, the exceptions are when a buyer purchases the goods in good faith for value where (i) the goods had been sold with the authority of the owner; (ii) the owner is estopped from denying the seller's authority by conduct; (iii) sale is by a person holding a voidable title that has not been avoided at the time of the sale; (iv) sale is by the seller or purchaser in possession after the sale or sub-sale of the goods or document of title to the goods; or (v) sale is by a mercantile agent, having customary authority, of the said seller or purchaser. If a purchaser purchases the goods in transit, in an ordinary way, by transfer of the bill of lading, then he will fall within the exception nos. (i), (ii) or (iv).[267] It must be observed that the 'good faith' of the purchaser is irrelevant unless the purchase falls within one of the excepted categories.

In this case, the nominee purchased it without the bill of lading. Hence, no exception to the general rule will apply and the nominee could not get the title. This will mean the title at all material times from 8 November has been with the buyer.

Conversion by Nominee in Receiving Cargo.

Wrongfully receiving a cargo will amount to conversion as much as wrongfully giving the cargo. As the nominee received the cargo, without the bill of lading and without the authority of the person having the possessory rights at that time, namely, the seller, the nominee had committed a conversion. The *bona fide* argument, which it will be hard to advance when a purchaser purchased goods in transit without the bill of lading, is nevertheless irrelevant to a case in conversion—a strict liability tort. A purchaser who purchases goods in transit without the bill of lading should know the risk that he takes in doing so and that any of his remedies will be against the seller if subsequently there is a claim by any other person entitled to the cargo.

Conversion by Nominee in Retaining and Processing Cargo

One of the categories of conversion is the wrongful retention of the goods against the one having the possessory rights—this recognises that a conversion can be a recurring tort. Another is wrongfully denying access to the person having the possessory

---

[267] His good faith will usually not be an issue, as he has purchased by transfer of bill of lading—an instrument recognised as a document of title.

rights. *General and Finance Facilities Ltd v Cooks Cars (Romford) Ltd*[268] says that conversion is a single wrongful act as opposed to a *continuing cause*, but that does not mean that conversion cannot be committed by a *recurring cause* such as the continued retention. In this case, likely, the nominee would have committed a recurring conversion by retaining the cargo until they were processed and transformed into some other products.

Detachment and Attachment-Back of Possessory Right from and to Proprietary Right

Most of the times, the person having the proprietary right will also have the possessory right, in the context of international trade contracts done with bills of lading. However, by action subsequent to his becoming the owner or by circumstances subject to which he became the owner, his possessory rights might be or become detached and pass on to another. For example, one buys a car. Upon becoming the owner, he must also have the possessory right. But if he lets the car on hire, then he has parted with his possessory rights for the period of the let. The same thing may be true if he buys a car that is already subject to a lease held by a hirer. During the period of the let or lease, if the owner interferes with the possession of the hirer, the hirer will have an action in conversion against the owner.[269]

A bill of lading is a document that will so detach the possessory rights from the owner to the holder, where the two are different persons. When the bill of lading is spent, by delivery of the goods by the carrier whether rightly or wrongly, the bill no longer represents the goods and the detachment by the bill comes to an end. After this, if there is no person other than the owner acquiring the possessory rights as allowed by the law, then they must come back to or vest in the owner.

Accordingly, in this case, the possessory rights after 10 November must have been held by the buyer. This proposition is supported by the fact that after 10 November, the buyer could have gone to the court for an order of specific relief[270] to compel the nominee to deliver the cargo to the buyer. Hence, the buyer would have the right of action in respect of any conversion that has happened after 10 November. When the nominee retained the cargo after 10 November, that was contrary to the possessory rights of the buyer. Hence, the nominee committed conversion. Similarly, the nominee acted contrary to the possessory rights of the buyer by processing the cargo to produce other products and hence committed the conversion. However, once the cargo has been processed, there will no longer be any immediate right to possession of the cargo that no longer exists. Accordingly, the buyer would have a right of action in conversion against the nominee for the conversion that took place from the starting time of retention after 10 November to the time of processing.

Detinue v. Conversion

[268] [1963] 2 All ER 314 at 317, [1963] 1 WLR 644 (EW CA).

[269] See *Brierly v Kendall* (1852) 17 QB 937, 21 LJQB 161, 16 Jur 449, 117 ER 1540, 18 LTOS 254 (EW HC).

[270] Perpetual mandatory injunction.

Detinue is another possible action in tort. Detinue is similar to conversion but is more centred on the refusal by a person to deliver up the goods when demanded by a person having the immediate right to possession. If the buyer, in this case, had demanded such delivery before the goods were processed, then it will also have an action in detinue. A claim in detinue will be for the return of the goods coupled with a claim for the value of the goods as damages in the alternative.[271]

The time for assessment of damages will be at the time of judgment rather than at the time when the wrong was committed, demand was made or when they should have been returned.[272] This is because detinue, unlike conversion, is considered to be a continuing wrong and the action will in principle be for delivery of the goods, with only an alternative claim for the value of the goods. Only when the court turns down the claim for delivery of the goods, the alternative claim triggers, i.e. at the time of judgement.[273]

Whilst 'detinue' as a cause of action survives in Malaysia[274] and Singapore,[275] it was abolished in England, Wales and N. Ireland by Section 2(1) of the Torts (Interference with Goods) Act 1977 and was replaced with a scheme of tort called 'interference with goods'. If an action in detinue was to be taken, that must have been by the buyer, as the person who has the immediate right to possession and upon whose demand the nominee refused to deliver up the cargo.

Remedies for Interference with Proprietary Right as Opposed to Possessory Right

This is an area of a gap at the common law. That was well said by Lady Hale in *OBG Ltd and another v Allan and others Douglas and others v Hello! Ltd and others (No.3) Mainstream Properties Ltd v Young*[276] as follows:

> The common law, as is well known, lacked any general proprietary remedy equivalent to the Roman law *vindicatio*. It provided three separate remedies for wrongfully taking away, keeping, or disposing of another's goods: trespass, detinue and trover or conversion.

Trespass to goods will be where, for example, one interferes with the goods in possession of another with the result that the latter suffers a loss. For example, in *Transco plc v United Utilities Water plc*,[277] the court held that it was a trespass to goods where workmen performing repairs underground mistakenly closed a gas

---

[271] See *Rosenthal v Alderton & Sons Ltd* [1946] KB 374, [1946] 1 All ER 583, 174 LT 214 (EW CA).

[272] See *Rosenthal v Alderton & Sons Ltd* [1946] KB 374, [1946] 1 All ER 583, 174 LT 214 (EW CA).

[273] *General and Finance Facilities Ltd v Cooks Cars (Romford) Ltd* [1963] 2 All ER 314 at 317, [1963] 1 WLR 644 (EW CA).

[274] See Rules of Court 2012—Order 13 rule 3 and Order 19 rule 4.

[275] See *Antariksa Logistics Pte Ltd and others v McTrans Cargo (S) Pte Ltd* [2012] SGHC 154 at [158], [2012] 4 SLR 250 (SG HC).

[276] *OBG Ltd and another v Allan and others Douglas and others v Hello! Ltd and others (No. 3) Mainstream Properties Ltd v Young* [2008] 1 AC 1 at [308], [2007] UKLH 21 (UK HL), speech of Lady Hale.

[277] [2005] EWHC 2784, [2005] All ER (D) 281 (Oct) (EW HC).

stopcock servicing the claimant, and hence liable for the interrupted gas supply to the claimant. It must be observed that all the three causes of action in relation to interference with goods—(i) conversion (also called trover); (ii) detinue and (iii) trespass to goods—are all based on possession or possessory right of the claimant, and not the proprietary right.

Comparatively, under the Roman law, there is a direct relief when a person's ownership in goods has been infringed by another interfering with the goods. There is no equivalent to this at the common law.

But what is available in England and Wales,[278] is largely what is there at the common law and equity, subject to some statutory additions. In England, Wales and N. Ireland, there is the Torts (Interference with Goods) Act 1977. In many Commonwealth jurisdictions,[279] including Malaysia,[280] there is a statute modelled on the Indian Specific Relief Act 1872. This Act deals with reliefs of equitable nature and injunctions and will be of relevance in restoring when one's proprietary rights have been wrongfully interfered with or infringed. Sometimes, the courts have used the words 'proprietary right' and 'possessory right' interchangeably when dealing with conversion. That does not seem to be in line with the established principles. In any event, that does not seem to be intended to extend the law of conversion, by *ratio*, to proprietary rights. The statement by Lady Hale in *OGB Ltd*[281] appears to accurately state the position of the common law in this area.

4.5.3 Assessment of Damages for Misdelivery/Non-delivery

In a conversion-action, both the value of the goods and consequential loss will be recoverable.[282] Any recovery on account of the conversion will be subject to the normal tort principles including the remoteness of damages and foreseeability.

The general rule is that the damages will be assessed by the market value of the goods at the time and place they should have been delivered. In *The Jag Shakti*,[283] the Privy Council took the position that the value of the goods will be that at the supposed time and place of delivery. In this case, salt was shipped from Tuticorin in India to Chittagong in Bangladesh on board the vessel The Jag Dhir under a bill of lading. The bills were indorsed to a pledgee who financed the transaction. The cargo was misdelivered by the shipowner. The pledgee brought an action for

---

[278] And Singapore and Malaysia.

[279] But not Singapore.

[280] Specific Relief Act 1950.

[281] [2008] 1 AC 1 at [308], [2007] UKHL 21 (UK HL), speech of Lady Hale.

[282] *Kuwait Airways Corpn v Iraqi Airways Co (Nos 4 and 5) (HL))* [2002] UKHL 19, [2002] 2 AC 883, [2002] 3 All ER 209, [2002] 2 WLR 1353, [2002] 1 All ER (Comm) 843, [2003] 1 LRC 430, [2002] All ER (D) 252 (May) (UK HL).

[283] *Chabbra Corporation Pte Ltd v Jag Shakti (Owners) (The Jag Shakti)* [1986] 1 MLJ 197, [1986] AC 337, [1986] 1 All ER 480, [1986] 2 WLR 87, [1987] LRC (Comm) 228, [1986] 1 Lloyd's Rep 1, 130 Sol Jo 51, [1986] LS Gaz R 45 (PC on an appeal from Singapore).

damages. The right of the pledgee to possession of the cargo was not disputed. The pledgee commenced an *in rem* action against a sister ship of The Jag Dhir, namely, The Jag Shakti. The Singapore Court of Appeal gave an award of damages on the basis of the sums expended by the pledgee in financing the transaction and refused to award damages on the basis of the market value of the cargo at the time and place of delivery. The pledgee claimed a higher sum based on an alleged sub-sale of the cargo and appealed. The Privy Council held that the correct measure of damages was the market value of the cargo at the supposed time and place of delivery,[284] and not the cost of financing. However, the burden is on the claimant to prove the market value, which the claimant failed, as there was no reliable evidence of the alleged sub-sale. Although the Court of Appeal based its decision on a wrong basis of measure, that is the only award that can be justifiably made as the pledgee failed to discharge its burden of proving the market value. In this case, the shipowner did not take a challenge to say that the amount of finance was higher than the market value of the goods at the relevant place and time, which it would have been open for the shipowner to do so if it wanted to.

Similarly, in Malaysia, the Court of Appeal in *Minmetals South-East Asia Corp Pte Ltd v Nakhoda Logistics Sdn Bhd*[285] has held that damages for conversion and non-delivery would generally be assessed by fair market value at the destination port at the time of the breach.[286] However, in this case, the court allowed an alternative basis of assessment based on the cost of the goods to the holder of the bill, i.e. the price which the holder of the bill bought them for, which is the actual loss to it. The better approach would have been to call the cost of the goods to the holder of the bill as 'evidence' of the value of the goods at the relevant place and time rather than as an 'alternative' method of assessment.[287] It will be open to the carrier to challenge any such alternative evidence such as by tendering better evidence of the more precise value of the goods at the relevant place and time if it wishes to do so.

However, in *The MSC Amsterdam*,[288] the English Court of Appeal assessed the value of the goods at the time of the judgement, by when the value had appreciated. The position taken by *The Jag Shakti* and *Minmetals v Nakhota*[289] seems to represent the right law as the loss would crystallise at the time of conversion and the time of judgment may have no relevance in such a pure damages-claim. The same rules should apply in the case of a non-delivery or short delivery, not amounting to misdelivery.

---

[284] *The Arpad* [1934] All ER Rep 326, [1934] P 189, 152 LT 521 (EW CA).

[285] [2019] 3 CLJ 19, [2018] 6 MLJ 152 (MY CA). See also Arun Kasi, 'A Critical Analysis of the Court of Appeal Decision on Misdelivery in Minmetals South-East Asia Corp Pte Ltd v Nakhoda Logistics Sdn Bhd', *The Law Review*, [2020] LR 105. This article was referred to in *Punjab National Bank v Malayan Banking Berhad* [2020] 1 LNS 232, [2020] 5 MLJ 732 (MY CA).

[286] The date of delivery or the date when the goods should have been delivered.

[287] Although the two practically mean the same thing.

[288] *Mediterranean Shipping Co SA v Trafigura Beheer BV and Another (The MSC Amsterdam)* [2007] EWCA Civ 794, [2008] 1 All ER (Comm) 385, [2007] 2 Lloyd's Rep 622, [2007] All ER (D) 444 (Jul) (EW CA).

[289] Save for the 'alternative' measure part.

4.5.4 Excluding or Limiting Liability for Misdelivery/Non-delivery

Finally, an interesting question that arises in relation to liability for misdelivery is whether it can be excluded or limited. It must be noted that delivery will usually be after discharge,[290] hence not covered within the mandatory period of the Hague or Hague-Visby Rules.[291] The Rules themselves allow liability outside the loading-to-discharge period to be contractually excepted or limited. Despite that, the courts have regarded the obligation to deliver to be a fundamental one, so that it cannot ordinarily be excluded. There have been different approaches to how the courts reached this conclusion. In *Sze Hai Tong Bank Ltd v Rambler Cycle Co Ltd*,[292] the Privy Council held that ordinarily, *as a matter of construction*, an exclusion clause will not be found to cover liability for misdelivery, however, if it covered such liability in most obvious terms, then *as a matter of law* the clause will be ineffective insofar as misdelivery was concerned as the obligation to delivery was a fundamental one—the concept of fundamental breach. In this case, the relevant clause read "the responsibility of the carrier … shall be deemed … to cease absolutely after [the goods] are discharged". Lord Denning, delivering the judgement of the board, said:

> If the exemption clause, on its true *construction*, absolved the shipping company from an act such as that … they would have been absolved if they had given the goods away to some passer-by or had burnt them or thrown them into the sea. If it had been suggested to the parties that the condition exempted the shipping company in such a case, they would both have said: "Of course not". There is, therefore, an *implied limitation on the clause, which cuts down the extreme width of it*; and, as a matter of *construction*, their Lordships *decline to attribute to it the unreasonable effect* contended for. *But their Lordships go further*. If such an extreme width were given to the exemption clause, it would run counter to the main object and intent of the contract. For the contract … has, as one of its main objects, the proper delivery of the goods by the shipping company, "unto order or his or their assigns", against production of the bill of lading. It would defeat this object *entirely* if the shipping company was at liberty, at its own will and pleasure, to deliver the goods to somebody else, to someone not entitled at all, without being liable for the consequences. The *clause must, therefore, be limited and modified to the extent necessary to enable effect to be given to the main object and intent of the contract* … It must, at least, be modified so as not to permit the shipping company deliberately to disregard its obligations as to delivery … No court can allow so *fundamental a breach* to pass unnoticed under the cloak of a general exemption clause. [emphasis added]

However, subsequently, in *Photo Production Ltd v Securicor Transport Ltd*,[293] not a shipping case, the House of Lords ruled out the concept of fundamental breach, so that

---

[290] Outside the tackle to tackle period, that will include the whole of loading and discharge operations for purposes of the Rules: *Pyrene Co Ltd v Scindia Navigation Co Ltd* [1954] 2 QB 402, [1954] 2 All ER 158, [1954] 2 WLR 1005, [1954] 1 Lloyd's Rep 321 (EW HC).

[291] Articles I(e) and II.

[292] [1959] AC 576, [1959] 3 All ER 182, [1959] 3 WLR 214, [1959] 2 Lloyd's Rep 114 (PC on appeal from Singapore).

[293] [1980] AC 827, [1980] 1 All ER 556, [1980] 2 WLR 283, [1980] 1 Lloyd's Rep 545 (UK HL).

a clause suitably drafted can even exclude or limit liability for a fundamental breach. However, this did not affect what Lord Denning said about restrictive construction of exclusion and limitation clauses when they are relied on to exclude or limit liability for fundamental breach. This point was made clear in *Motis Exports Ltd v Dampskibsselskabet AF 1912, A/S and another*.[294] In this case, the responsibility-clause stated:

> Where the carriage called for commences at the port of loading and/or finishes at the port of discharge, the Carrier shall have no liability whatsoever for any loss or damage to the goods while in its actual or constructive possession before loading or after discharge over ship's rail, or if applicable, on the ship's ramp, however caused.

The Court of Appeal agreed that 'Article VII permits the carrier to exclude or limit liability for loss of damage to goods in his custody prior to loading and after discharge from the ship'. However, the court narrowly construed the clause as being 'concerned with responsibility for physical peril to the goods and was not apt to cover misdelivery by the carriers' and hence held that it did not cover liability for misdelivery. The court referred, with approval, to the following speech of Lord Herschell LC in *Glynn v Margetson & Co*[295]:

> [T]he main object and intent … is the carriage of oranges from Malaga to Liverpool. That is the matter with which the shipper is concerned; and it seems to me that *it would be to defeat what is the manifest object and intention of such a contract* to hold that it was entered into with a power to the shipowner to proceed anywhere that he pleased, to trade in any manner that he pleased, and to arrive at the port at which the oranges were to be delivered when he pleased. … Where *general words are used in a printed form* which are obviously intended to apply, so far as they are applicable, to the circumstances of a particular contract, which particular contract is to be embodied in or introduced into that printed form, *I think you are justified in looking at the main object and intent of the contract and in limiting the general words used, having in view that object and intent.* Therefore, it seems to me that the construction contended for would be an unreasonable one, and there is no difficulty in construing this clause to apply to a liberty in the performance of the stipulated voyage to call at a particular port or ports in the course of the voyage. [emphasis added]

In line with the above passage, the court went on to say that if the clause could have sufficient meaning without covering liability in respect of a fundamental obligation, then the clause will be construed not to cover the liability. This means that if liability for breach of a fundamental obligation is to be covered, almost specific and express words referring to such liability will have to be in the clause and any general clause will be insufficient to cover such liability. The court said this as follows:

> [E]ven if the language was apt to cover such a case, it is not a construction which should be adopted, involving as it does excuse from performing an obligation of such *fundamental importance*. As a matter of construction the courts lean against such a result if *adequate content* can be given to the clause. In my view it can …; it is wide enough also to cover loss caused by negligence, provided the loss is of the appropriate kind. [emphasis added]

---

[294] *Motis Exports Ltd v Dampskibsselskabet AF 1912 Aktieselskab and Aktieselskabet Dampskibsselskabet Svendborg* [2000] 1 All ER (Comm) 91, [2000] 1 Lloyd's Rep 211, [1999] All ER (D) 1490 (EW CA).

[295] [1893] AC 351 at 355, [1891–4] All ER Rep 693 (UK HL).

Mance LJ in the case stressed the importance of the carrier's obligation to delivery only against presentation of a genuine bill of lading[296] as follows:

> The shipowners' construction of [the clause] would appear to go to the extreme of protecting against any misdelivery, however negligent, and to undervalue the importance which both parties must be taken to have attached to the ship's obligation to deliver against presentation of original bills of lading.

Having said that, the court made a distinction when it is a case of non-delivery as opposed to misdelivery such as where the goods are stolen from the custody of the carrier. The court said *obiter:*

> [T]hat theft by taking without the bailee's consent would be covered by the clause, as would loss or damage by fire, flood or other perils.

The court positively referred to the dictum of Clarke J in *The Ines,*[297] who said when dealing with a similar clause that:

> [T]he clause seems to me to be concerned with the case where the goods are lost or damaged, and may include the case where they are stolen, but does not include delivery without production of an original bill of lading.

In *The Arktis Sky,*[298] the Singapore High Court arrived at a similar decision in construing a clause relieving the carrier from liability "after … proper discharge". In line with *Motis Exports*, the later case of *The Sormovskiy 3068*[299] holds that very clear or express wording if liability for misdelivery is to be excluded. In this case, the English High Court held that a general clause excluding or limiting liability for loss or damage to goods after discharge was insufficient to cover liability for misdelivery.

Adding to the above, it will be possible to argue if a clause in most clear terms excepted liability for misdelivery, then it is invalid on *public policy* grounds, as it will render the bill of lading lose its core effect whilst the bill is the key document in the international cargo trade and render illusory the consideration given by the carrier when the exclusion clause is triggered.[300] Public policy is a wide avenue available to the court to strike down an agreement when the agreement may not be struck down by any other means. Burrough J in *Richardson v Mellish,*[301] in his oft-quoted speech

---

[296] In this case, the cargo was misdelivered against presentation of forged bill of lading.

[297] *MB Pyramid Sound NV v Briese Schiffahrts GmbH and Co KG MS Sina and Latvian Shipping Assoc Ltd (The Ines)* [1995] 2 Lloyd's Rep 144 (EW HC).

[298] *The Arktis Sky* [2000] 1 SLR 57 (SG HC).

[299] *Sucre Export SA v Northern Shipping Ltd (The Sormovskiy 3068)* [1994] 2 Lloyd's Rep 266 (EW HC).

[300] See *Empire Meat Co Ltd v Patrick Empire Meat Co Ltd* [1939] 2 All ER 85, [1939] 2 All ER 85: a clause in restraint of trade was void for offending public policy, but the rest of the agreement was not affected by the illegality. Severability of an illegal clause from the main agreement was recognised in Malaysia in *Murugesan v Krishnasamy & Anor* [1958] MLJ 92 (MY HC) under Section 25 of the Malaysian Contracts Act 1950.

[301] (1824) 2 Bing 252, (1824) 130 ER 294, [1824–34] All ER Rep 258 (EW Court of Common Pleas).

two centuries ago, said this as: "Public policy is a very unruly horse, and when you get astride, you never know where it will carry you".

To the contrary, the Malaysian Court of Appeal in *Sebor (Sarawak) Trading Sdn Bhd & Anor v Syarikat Cheap Hin Toy Manufacture Sdn Bhd*,[302] held a general post-discharge exclusion to be effective to cover liability for misdelivery. In this case, three containers of firecrackers were shipped from Port Klang[303] to Sibu[304] under a bill of lading. The bill provided:

> [T]he responsibility of the carrier whether as carrier or as custodian or bailee of the goods shall be deemed to commence only when the goods are loaded on the ship and to cease absolutely on discharge when they are free of the ship's tackle.

The vessel reached Sibu and discharged the cargo. Thereafter, the cargo was misdelivered. The cargo interest sued the carrier for the value of the cargo. The court held that the responsibility clause exempted the carriers from liability for the misdelivery.[305] This decision is against sound established authorities, which were not sufficiently considered by the court in arriving at the decision, and hence does not represent the good approach to be followed.

It must be noted that the doctrine of fundamental breach, now ruled out in the English law, could not be imported into the Malaysian jurisprudence by Sections 3(1) and 5 of the Civil Law Act 1956, as the validity of agreements in Malaysia is regulated by the Contracts Act 1950. See Sections 10(1), 24 and 25.[306] The Act determines when an agreement is a contract and when it is not, hence the question of validity of an agreement must be decided within the four corners of the Act.[307] The illegality argument, based on public policy ground said earlier, will be a potential argument in Malaysia that will yield an analogous result to that of the doctrine of fundamental breach. The same 'public policy' tool will also be available in England and Wales and Singapore under the common law in addition to the judicial tools of restrictive interpretation of such exclusion or limitation clauses.

---

[302] [2003] 2 MLJ 486, [2003] 3 AMR 354, [2003] 2 CLJ 381 (MY CA). See Arun Kasi, 'A Critical Analysis of the Court of Appeal Decision on Misdelivery in Minmetals South-East Asia Corp Pte Ltd v Nakhoda Logistics Sdn Bhd', *The Law Review*, [2020] LR 105. This article was referred to in *Punjab National Bank v Malayan Banking Berhad* [2020] 1 LNS 232, [2020] 5 MLJ 732 (MY CA).

[303] In Malaysia.

[304] In Sarawak, Malaysia.

[305] A similar result was achieved by an Australian Court of Appeal in *Glebe Island Terminals Pty Ltd v Continental Seagram Pty Ltd (The Antwerpen)* [1994] 1 Lloyd's Rep 213, (1993) 40 NSWLR 206(1993), Aust Contract R 90-032 (NSW CA), where the court held that a clause exempting the carrier from liability in respect of loss or damage occurring after discharge even in the event of a fundamental breach was sufficient to exempt the carrier from liability for misdelivery.

[306] See Sections 10(1), 24 and 25.

[307] Unlike the Indian Contract Act 1872, the preamble to the Malaysian Act reads only "An Act relating to contracts", whilst the preamble to the Indian Act reads "To define and amend certain parts of the law relating to contracts".

4.5.5 *Spent Bills*

A bill is normally issued in a set of three originals. All that is required for the carrier to deliver the goods is the surrender of one of them.[308] Upon such delivery, the bill becomes 'spent' and no longer good to claim delivery. The carrier is not liable to any other person subsequently presenting any other originals of the bill as long as the carrier had no notice of any want of title in the party who first presented the bill.[309]

However, a carrier will be strictly liable in conversion if he delivers against a forged bill,[310] even if there was no means of the carrier knowing it was a forged bill.[311] The same is true when a carrier delivers against a stolen pin code, as happened in *MSC Mediterranean Shipping Company SA v Glencore International AG*.[312] In this case, the carrier regularly carried cargo for Glencore under bills of lading. The bills were standard ones that required the surrender of the bill to obtain delivery or delivery order. The practice was for the carrier to issue an electronic delivery order in the form of a release note with a pin code. The release note will instruct the terminal operator to deliver the cargo against the pin code. In one instance, the pin code electronically given to Glencore's agents without presentation of the bill was accessed by a wrong person, who collected the cargo with the pin code. Glencore sued the carrier for misdelivery. The carrier argued that delivery of the pin code was as good as the issuance of the delivery order stated in the bill, hence the obligations of the carrier was discharged. The English Court of Appeal rejected this argument and held that the delivery order referred to in the bill was the 'ship's delivery order' and not the delivery order or release note that merely instructs the terminal operator to deliver the cargo. The court held the carrier liable for misdelivery, also rejecting the carrier's argument that in the past Glencore had accepted the pin codes to collect cargoes from the terminal operator. In arriving at the decision, the court noted that there was no term in the bill of lading authorising delivery against any such pin code.

In the case of a misdelivery, the question of whether the genuine bill has become 'spent' is academic, as there is no doubt about the carrier's liability. For academic argument, in such a case the bill may better not be called 'spent' as the bill was not used to claim delivery and is still good for a conversion-action.

---

[308] *Motis Exports Ltd v Dampskibsselskabet AF 1912 Aktieselskab and Aktieselskabet Dampskibsselskabet Svendborg* [2000] 1 All ER (Comm) 91, [2000] 1 Lloyd's Rep 211, [1999] All ER (D) 1490 (EW CA).

[309] *Glyn Mills Currie & Co v The East and West India Dock Co* (1882) 7 App Cas 591 (UK HL).

[310] *The Jian He* [2000] 1 SLR 8 (SG CA).

[311] *Motis Exports Ltd v Dampskibsselskabet AF 1912 Aktieselskab and Aktieselskabet Dampskibsselskabet Svendborg* [2000] 1 All ER (Comm) 91, [2000] 1 Lloyd's Rep 211, [1999] All ER (D) 1490 (EW CA).

[312] [2017] EWCA Civ 365, [2017] 2 All ER (Comm) 881, [2017] 2 Lloyd's Rep 186, [2017] All ER (D) 02 (Jun) (EW CA).

Chapter 5
Protection and Action for Third Parties

This chapter considers the mechanisms by which the protection afforded to the carrier may be extended to others such as stevedores, etc. This includes a study of the Contracts (Rights of Third Parties) 1999 Act, Himalaya clause and circular indemnity clause. This chapter also considers the action that a bill of lading holder may take against the carrier, under the common law and under the Carriage of Goods by Sea Act 1992, for the benefit of a third party such as the owner of the goods. Then, a brief visit to representative actions by a cargo claimant representing its own interest and that of the others, such as where a ship sinks with a total loss of cargo belonging to many owners insured by a few insurers.

5.1 Introduction

In certain circumstances, cargo claims may be brought by a cargo claimant against a person with whom the claimant does not have a contractual nexus, such as an independent contractor (e.g. stevedore) or servant of the carrier.[1] By bringing such an action, the claimant may attempt to be relieved from the exclusion and limitation clauses in the contract. Such a measure has been countered by the carriers by extending the contractual protection to the third parties by clauses known as Himalaya clauses and circular indemnity clauses. Other than this, a statutory extension is also available to such third parties, subject to certain conditions, under the UK Contracts (Rights of Third Parties) Act 1999. In order to make the protection to the carrier under the Hague or Hague-Visby Rules, usually, the Rules will be *contractually incorporated* into the bill of lading and then extended to the third party by a Himalaya or circular indemnity clause or with both these clauses. It is not necessary to contractually incorporate the Rules where they already statutorily attach to the bill of lading. In such a case, a Himalaya or circular indemnity clause will automatically include the benefits

[1] Dealt with in the last chapter.

A. Kasi, *The Law of Carriage of Goods by Sea*,
https://doi.org/10.1007/978-981-33-6793-7_5

of the protection to the carrier under Rules statutorily attached to the contract of carriage evidenced by the bill of lading.

The said three avenues of extending the contractual protection to the third parties, namely, the UK Contracts (Third Parties) Protection Act 1999, Himalaya clause and circular indemnity clause are the subject of this chapter. Added to that, a visit is last made in this chapter to the ability of a holder of a bill to bring an action for the benefit of another such as the owner of the cargo who is unable to bring such an action because the latter is not holding the bill.

5.2 Contracts (Rights of Third Parties) Act 1999

It is a trite principle of common law that only parties to a contract may sue and be sued on it—the doctrine of privity of contract.[2] However, the UK Contracts (Rights of Third Parties) Act 1999 provide some exceptions to it, discussed here.

Section 1(1)(a) of the Act allows a party to enforce a contract where the contract expressly allows the same. Section 1(2)(b) allows a third party to enforce where the contract purports to confer a benefit on the third party, except where the parties did not intend the contract to be enforced by the third party.[3]

Section 1(3) provides that the third party may be identified by description and need not be in existence at the time of the contract. Section 1(4) subjects enforcement of the contract by the third party to the terms of the contract. Hence, a third party cannot merely take the benefits of the contract without taking the burdens of the contract. The Section 1(1)–(4) read as follows:

> (1) Subject to the provisions of this Act, a person who is not a party to a contract (a "third party") may in his own right enforce a term of the contract if—
>
> (a) the contract expressly provides that he may, or
>
> (b) subject to subsection (2), the term purports to confer a benefit on him.
>
> (2) Subsection (1)(b) does not apply if on a proper construction of the contract it appears that the parties did not intend the term to be enforceable by the third party.
>
> (3) The third party must be expressly identified in the contract by name, as a member of a class or as answering a particular description but need not be in existence when the contract is entered into.
>
> (4) This section does not confer a right on a third party to enforce a term of a contract otherwise than subject to and in accordance with any other relevant terms of the contract.

Section 1(6) allows a third party to take the benefit of exclusion or limitation of liability provided in his favour in the contract. The Section 1(6) reads as follows:

---

[2] *Provender v Wood* (1630) Hetley 30, (1627) 124 ER 318 (EW Court of Common Pleas).

[3] Section 1(2).

> Where a term of a contract excludes or limits liability in relation to any matter references in this Act to the third party enforcing the term shall be construed as references to his availing himself of the exclusion or limitation.

By virtue of Section 6(5), read together with Section 6(6) and (7), all contracts covered by UK Carriage of Goods by Sea Act 1992—order and bearer bills of lading, straight bills of lading, sea waybills and ship's delivery order—are exempted, except that a third party may take advantage of Section 1(6) of the UK 1999 Act, i.e. taking benefit of an exclusion or limitation clause in the bill or ship's delivery order in his favour. The exemption is provided because the third party, usually the lawful holder of the bill, is accorded his remedies under the UK Carriage of Goods by Sea Act 1992. The Section 6(5)–(7) of the UK 1999 Act reads as follows:

> (5) Section 1 confers no rights on a third party in the case of—
>
> (a) a contract for the carriage of goods by sea, or
>
> (b) a contract for the carriage of goods by rail or road, or for the carriage of cargo by air, which is subject to the rules of the appropriate international transport convention,
>
> except that a third party may in reliance on that section avail himself of an exclusion or limitation of liability in such a contract.
>
> (6) In subsection (5) "contract for the carriage of goods by sea" means a contract of carriage—
>
> (a) contained in or evidenced by a bill of lading, sea waybill or a corresponding electronic transaction, or
>
> (b) under or for the purposes of which there is given an undertaking which is contained in a ship's delivery order or a corresponding electronic transaction.
>
> (7) For the purposes of subsection (6)—
>
> (a) "bill of lading", "sea waybill" and "ship's delivery order" have the same meaning as in the Carriage of Goods by Sea Act 1992, and
>
> (b) a corresponding electronic transaction is a transaction within section 1(5) of that Act which corresponds to the issue, indorsement, delivery or transfer of a bill of lading, sea waybill or ship's delivery order.

It must be noted that the Section 6(5) exemption does not apply charterparties. It is common that a brokerage commission will be specified in the charterparty, although the broker is not a party to the charterparty.[4] The Section 6(5) is no barrier to the claim of the broker for the commission under Section 1(2)(b). In *Nisshin Shipping Co Ltd v Cleaves & Co Ltd,*[5] a broker was able to claim the commission reserved for him in the charterparty, subject to arbitration clause therein.

---

[4]E.g. NYPE 2015, cl. 53. 'NYPE' is the abbreviation for New York Produce Exchange' form.

[5][2003] EWHC 2602 (Comm), [2004] 1 All ER (Comm) 481, [2004] 1 Lloyd's Rep 38, [2003] All ER (D) 106 (Nov) (EW HC).

5.3 Himalaya Clause

Claims by cargo claimants against non-contractual parties like stevedores,[6] to circumvent the Hague or Hague Visby Rules and avoid liability-limitation applicable to bills of lading, became rampant.

5.3.1 Himalaya Clauses Recognised

In *Alder v Dickson*,[7] a passenger on board SS Himalaya sued the master and another member of the crew in negligence for injuries sustained by her when boarding the ship. She did not sue the shipowner due to a liability exclusion clause in the ticket. The Court of Appeal held that a carrier may limit liability not only for its own benefit but also for the benefit of others engaged by the carrier in performing the voyage. However, the court found that the exclusion clause, in this case, was not for the benefit of any party than the shipowner. Hence, the court decided that the master and the other members of the crew were not entitled to be protected under the exclusion clause.[8]

In *Midland Silicones Ltd v Scruttons Ltd*,[9] a cargo owner sued stevedores in negligence. Stevedores attempted to rely on package limitation under the Hague Rules applicable to the bill of ladings. The House of Lords refused this because the stevedore, to whom goods are delivered merely for loading but not for safekeeping or carrying, was not a bailee. This decision seems to contradict the decision of the House of Lords in *Elder, Dempster v Paterson Zochonis*,[10] where the shipowner, as a bailee, was able to rely on the liability-limitation clause in the bill of lading issued by the charterer. The House of Lords in *Midland Silicones* limited *Elder, Dempster v Paterson Zochonis* to bailment cases. The House set out four conditions to be satisfied for a third party to be protected by terms of the bill through agency principle. The four conditions are:

(i) The parties must intend to protect the third party.
(ii) The carrier must contract also as an agent of the third party.
(iii) The third-party must have authorised[11] the carrier to contract on its behalf.
(iv) The third-party must have given consideration.

---

[6] Also called 'dockers'.

[7] [1955] 1 QB 158, [1954] 3 All ER 397 (EW CA).

[8] It must be noted that if the same facts were to happen today, the exclusion clause would be invalid as Section 2(1) of the UK Unfair Contract Terms Act 1977 do not allow liability in negligence for personal injury and death to be excluded or limited.

[9] [1962] AC 446, [1962] 1 All ER 1, [1962] 2 WLR 186, [1961] 2 Lloyd's Rep 365 (UK HL).

[10] *Elder, Dempster & Co Ltd v Paterson, Zochonis & Co, Griffiths Lewis Steam Navigation Co v Paterson, Zochonis & Co Ltd* [1923] 1 KB 420, [1924] AC 522, [1924] All ER Rep 135 (UK HL).

[11] Or subsequently ratified.

In this case, the protection in the bill was for 'carrier'. Hence, the required intention of the parties to protect the stevedores was missing and thus the House held that the stevedores were not entitled to the protection.

Following this case, the carriers started to include a clause in the bills that will satisfy the four conditions to extend the protections in the bill to others engaged in the voyage, in particular, stevedores. Such a clause came to be popularly known as the Himalaya clause following the name of the ship in *Alder v Dickson.*[12] A Himalaya clause appearing in BIMCO[13] forms of bill of lading and sea waybill[14] is as follows:

> (a) …
>
> (b) It is hereby expressly agreed that no Servant shall in any circumstances whatsoever be under any liability whatsoever to the shipper, consignee, receiver, holder, or other party to this contract (hereinafter termed "Merchant") for any loss, damage or delay of whatsoever kind arising or resulting directly or indirectly from any act, neglect or default on the Servant's part while acting in the course of or in connection with the performance of this contract.
>
> (c) Without prejudice to the generality of the foregoing provisions in this clause, every exemption, limitation, condition and liberty contained herein (other than Art III Rule 8 of the Hague/Hague-Visby Rules if incorporated herein) and every right, exemption from liability, defence and immunity of whatsoever nature applicable to the carrier or to which the carrier is entitled hereunder including the right to enforce any jurisdiction or arbitration provision contained herein shall also be available and shall extend to every such Servant of the carrier, who shall be entitled to enforce the same against the Merchant.
>
> (d) …
>
> (e) For the purpose of sub-paragraphs (a)-(d) of this clause the Carrier is or shall be deemed to be acting as agent or trustee on behalf of and for the benefit of all persons mentioned in sub-clause (a) above who are its Servant and all such persons shall to this extent be or be deemed to be parties to this contract.

In *The Eurymedon,*[15] the Privy Council found that all the four *Midland* conditions were satisfied and accordingly the stevedoring company was protected by the liability-limitation regime applicable to the bill of lading. In this case, a clause in the bill provided that the protection accorded to carriers extended to stevedores. It was not doubted that the carrier acted as the agent for the stevedores in contracting this clause and that the stevedoring company had authorised the carrier contract the same because the stevedoring company was an associated company of the carrier.

---

[12] [1955] 1 QB 158, [1954] 3 All ER 397 (EW CA).

[13] 'Baltic and International Maritime Council'.

[14] BIMCO CONLINEBILL 2016 (Liner Bill of Lading). BIMCO CONGENBILL 2016 (Bill of Lading). BIMCO GENWAYBILL 2016 (Non-Negotiable General Sea Waybill). BIMCO MULTIDOC 2016 (Negotiable Multimodal Transport Bill of Lading) .

[15] *New Zealand Shipping Co Ltd v AM Satterthwaite (The Eurymedon)* [1975] AC 154, [1974] 1 All ER 1015, [1974] 2 WLR 865, [1974] 1 Lloyd's Rep 534 (PC on appeal from New Zealand).

The board found that consideration was given by the stevedoring company by performance. This was because of the doctrine that the performance of a pre-existing duty owed to a third party[16] constitutes good consideration.[17]

5.3.2 Event within Responsibility Period of Carrier

For a third party to seek protection through the Himalaya clause, it is important to determine whether the event in question fell within the *responsibility period* of the carrier under the bill. Only if it falls within such period, the third party will be able to rely on the protection accorded to the carrier under the bill. If it so falls, it does not matter that it falls outside the *'tackle to tackle' period.*

In *The New York Star,*[18] the Privy Council upheld the Himalaya clause. In this case, a clause in the bill of lading acknowledged liability of the carrier as a bailee when it held the goods after discharge from the ship.[19] Another clause in the bill of lading set a time limit for any action at one year after delivery or the date when the goods should have been delivered.[20] A Himalaya clause in the bill extended all protection afforded to the carrier to stevedores.[21] After discharge from the ship, the goods came into the possession of stevedores, who misdelivered them. The holder of the bill of lading sued stevedores a year after the date when the goods should have been delivered. The issue was whether the stevedores may rely on the terms on the bill of lading, namely the one-year time limit to defeat the claim. The board held that the stevedores may, hence the stevedores were not liable. The board observed that it did not matter that misdelivery happened outside the tackle to tackle period, as the carrier was responsible for delivery even after the discharge.[22] It must be noted that in the absence of a clause in the bill stating the one-year time limit, the one-year time limit in the Hague Rules Article III(6)[23] will not apply to cases of non-delivery and misdelivery as these happen outside the 'tackle to tackle' scope of the *Rules.*[24] When the time limit is stated in the bill, it will also cover non-delivery and misdelivery that

[16]The duty owed by the stevedoring company to the shipowner.

[17]*Scotson v Pegg* (1861) 6 H & N 295, 30 LJ Ex 225, 9 WR 280, 158 ER 121, 3 LT 753 (EW Court of Exchequer Chamber).

[18]*Port Jackson Stevedoring Pty Ltd v Salmond & Spraggon (Australia) Pty Ltd (The New York Star)* [1981] 1 WLR 138, [1980–84] LRC (Comm) 105, [1980] 3 All ER 257, [1980] 2 Lloyd's Rep 317 (PC on appeal from NSW).

[19]Cl. 5.

[20]Cl. 17.

[21]Cl. 2.

[22]A similar point was made out by the Singapore Court of Appeal in *The Jian He* [2000] 1 SLR 8.

[23]Similar to that in the Hague-Visby Rules.

[24]Article II of the Hague/Hague-Visby Rules; *Peninsular & Oriental Steam Navigation Co Ltd & Ors v Rambler Cycle Co Ltd* [1964] 30 MLJ 443 (MY FC); *The Lung Yung & Thai Yung, Owners & Ors v Sadit Timber Sdn Bhd & Ors* [1984] 1 MLJ 29 (MY FC); *Deep Sea Maritime Ltd v Monjasa A/S (The Alhani)* [2018] EWHC 1495 (Comm), [2018] 2 Lloyd's Rep 563 (EW HC).

happen outside the 'tackle the tackle' period because the responsibility scope under the *bill* is beyond the 'tackle to tackle' period and until delivery to the right person.

In *Raymond Burke v Mersey Docks and Harbour Board*,[25] the cargo was carried under a 'port to port' bill with a Himalaya clause. The cargo was damaged while in the hands of the terminal operator before loading operation commenced, hence outside the 'tackle to tackle' period i.e. 'port to port' period. The English High Court held that the Himalaya clause did not protect the terminal operators as the damage occurred outside the responsibility period of carriers under the 'port to port' bill.

5.3.3 Third-Party Dealing with Shipper on Third Party's Own Terms

However, if the third party has dealt directly with the shipper on its own terms, then the third party will lose the benefit of any Himalaya clause in the bill. This happened in *The Rigoletto*.[26] A terminal operator directly issued its receipt to the shipper. The receipt contained its own terms and conditions. This constituted a bailment on terms of the receipt. Accordingly, when sued by the shipper in bailment, the terminal operator was able to rely on the terms of the receipt, however not on the Himalaya clause in the bill of lading. If the terminal operator did not issue its own receipt directly to the shipper but issued it to the carrier, then the options available to the terminal operator would have been to rely on the terms in the receipt issued to the carrier as sub-bailee on those terms or to rely on the Himalaya clause in the bill of lading. If the receipt had referred to and incorporated the bill of lading, then the terminal owner would have been able to rely on the Himalaya clause in the bill.

5.3.4 Himalaya Protection to Shipowner Limited to Rules Threshold

When a shipowner, as opposed to other contractors like stevedores, seeks to rely on a Himalaya clause in the charterer's bill, courts[27] have imposed a limitation. It is that if the Himalaya clause seeks to exclude liability in total or below the threshold of the applicable Hague or Hague-Visby Rules, then clause will be invalid as far as the shipowner is concerned. The courts have relied on Article III(8) of the Hague and Hague-Visby Rules to justify the limitation. Article III(8) reads as follows:

---

[25][1986] 1 Lloyd's Rep 155 (EW HC).

[26]*Lotus Cars Ltd v Southampton Cargo Handling plc and Others (The Rigoletto)* [2000] 2 All ER (Comm) 705, [2000] 2 Lloyd's Rep 532, [2000] All ER (D) 1125 (EW CA).

[27]*Homburg Houtimport BV v Agrosin Private Ltd (The Starsin)* [2003] UKHL 12, [2004] 1 AC 715, [2003] 2 All ER 785, [2003] 2 WLR 711, [2003] 1 All ER (Comm) 625, [2003] 1 Lloyd's Rep 571, [2003] All ER (D) 192 (Mar) (UK HL).

> Any clause, covenant, or agreement in a contract of carriage relieving the carrier or the ship from liability for loss or damage to, or in connexion with, goods arising from negligence, fault, or failure in the duties and obligations provided in this Article or lessening such liability otherwise than as provided in this Convention, shall be null and void and of no effect. A benefit of insurance in favour of the carrier or similar clause shall be deemed to be a clause relieving the carrier from liability.

In the strictest sense, Article III(8) applies only to contractual carriers, which will be the charterer in the case of goods carried under charterer's bill, and not to the shipowner. However, because the charterer contracts as an agent of the shipowner for purposes of the Himalaya clause, the shipowner becomes a party to the bill for this purpose. Accordingly, the courts have justified, by judicial ingenuity, binding the shipowner to Article III(8) although it is the carrier in the bill in the strictest sense. In a nutshell, the courts do not allow the shipowners, who are the true carriers although may not be the contractual carriers, to escape liability under the Hague or Hague-Visby Rules by such loophole. This approach of the courts makes commercial sense and will be welcome.

In *The Starsin,*[28] the cargo was carried under a charterer's bill. The shipowner was sued in negligence in respect of stowage. The bill contained a wide Himalaya clause exempting the charter's subcontractors, which would include the shipowner, from liability. The bill provided that the subcontractors were deemed to be parties to the bill. The House of Lords held that the exemption clause was void under Article III(8) of the Hague-Visby Rules for attempting to exempt a carrier, in the true sense, from the liabilities imposed by the Rules.

The exemption clause would not have gone void if a stevedore, instead of the shipowner, attempted to rely on it. The result is that a shipowner will be protected as much as the charterer-carrier but not more than that.

5.3.5 Jurisdiction and Choice of Law Clauses

A defendant relying on a Himalaya clause in the bill, to which the defendant is not directly a party, has not been allowed to rely on jurisdiction and choice of law clauses. This is because jurisdiction and choice of law clauses are considered to be meant for the mutual benefit of direct parties only. In *The Mahkutai,*[29] the Privy Council held accordingly. However, *The Mahkutai* effect has been limited by the current BIMCO

[28] *Homburg Houtimport BV v Agrosin Private Ltd (The Starsin)* [2003] UKHL 12, [2004] 1 AC 715, [2003] 2 All ER 785, [2003] 2 WLR 711, [2003] 1 All ER (Comm) 625, [2003] 1 Lloyd's Rep 571, [2003] All ER (D) 192 (Mar) (UK HL).

[29] *The Mahkutai* [1996] AC 650, [1996] 3 All ER 502, [1996] 3 WLR 1, [1996] 2 LRC 599, [1996] 2 Lloyd's Rep 1 (PC on appeal from Hong Kong).

forms of bill of lading[30] and sea waybill[31] that expressly allow the third party to rely on the jurisdiction clause in the bill.[32]

5.4 Circular Indemnity Clause

A circular indemnity clause in a bill of lading or sea waybill is another way of protecting the subcontractors, agents and servants. The clause will usually provide that no action will be taken by the person entitled under the bill, such as the lawful holder of a bill of lading, against such subcontractors, agents and servants, meaning a blanket exemption. Alternatively, it may provide that the person entitled will not take any action against them on terms more favourable than an action available against the carrier, thereby entitling them to the protection available to the carrier. In either case, it will also say that if the person entitled were to take action in breach of the clause, it will 'indemnify' the carrier. It is common that both Himalaya and circular indemnity clauses are included in bills of lading and sea waybills.

BIMCO forms of bill of lading and sea waybill,[33] contain a circular indemnity clause together with a Himalaya clause. The circular indemnity clause reads as follows:

(d)

(i) The Merchant undertakes that no claim or allegation whether arising in contract, bailment, tort or otherwise shall be made against any Servant of the carrier which imposes or attempts to impose upon any of them or any vessel owned or chartered by any of them any liability whatsoever in connection with this contract whether or not arising out of negligence on the part of such Servant. The Servant shall also be entitled to enforce the foregoing covenant against the Merchant; and

(ii) The Merchant undertakes that if any such claim or allegation should nevertheless be made, it will indemnify the carrier against all consequences thereof.

(e) For the purpose of sub-paragraphs (a)-(d) of this clause the Carrier is or shall be deemed to be acting as agent or trustee on behalf of and for the benefit of all persons mentioned in sub-clause (a) above who are its Servant and all such persons shall to this extent be or be deemed to be parties to this contract.

---

[30] E.g. BIMCO CONGENBILL 2016, cl. 6(c); BIMCO CONLINEBILL 2016, cl. 15(c).

[31] BIMCO GENWAYBILL 2016, cl. 3(c).

[32] Discussed earlier at Chap. 4.3.6.1.

[33] BIMCO CONLINEBILL 2016 (Liner Bill of Lading). BIMCO CONGENBILL 2016 (Bill of Lading). BIMCO GENWAYBILL 2016 (Non-Negotiable General Sea Waybill). BIMCO MULTIDOC 2016 (Negotiable Multimodal Transport Bill of Lading).

In cases where, by law, third parties cannot get rights under a contract, as in Malaysia[34] and unlike in England or Singapore,[35] the clause (e) above in BIMCO forms seems to have the effect of making the subcontractors a party to the bill for purposes of the circular indemnity clause, so that the subcontractor may directly seek the stay or anti-suit injunction. However, this concept will not enable the subcontractor to claim indemnity since the indemnity is in favour of the carrier and the carrier may only claim it if the three conditions, set out earlier, are satisfied.

5.4.1 Utilities of Circular Indemnity Clause

The circular indemnity clause has two utilities. One is that the carrier may invoke it against the cargo claimant[36] to obtain a stay or anti-suit injunction of any action that the cargo claimant may take against the subcontractors, agents or servants. Another is that the carrier may invoke it, as indemnity in the strict sense, to make a monetary claim against the cargo claimant to recover any damages paid by the subcontractors, agents or servants to the cargo claimant. The former is more popular than the latter.

In *The Elbe Maru*,[37] the cargo was carried under a combined transport bill of lading. The bill contained a circular indemnity clause. A part of the carriage was done by a road carrier, who was a subcontractor to the contractual carrier. Upon damage to the cargo whilst in the road carriage, the bill of lading holder directly sued the road carrier in tort. The carrier applied to the English High Court for a perpetual stay of the suit, which the court granted.

Similarly, in *The Marielle Bolten*,[38] the cargo was carried under a bill of lading, that contained Himalaya and circular indemnity clauses. The bill also contained a choice of English law clause and an exclusive English jurisdiction clause. Despite these clauses, the cargo insurers sought to sue the subcontractors outside of English courts. The carrier applied to the English court for an interim anti-suit injunction to restrain such suits out of the jurisdiction. The English High Court granted the same.

---

[34] For all the states and territories other than Penang, Malacca, Sabah, Sarawak and Labuan.

[35] Section 1(1) and (6), read together with Section 6(5) of the Contracts (Rights of Third Parties) Act 1999.

[36] Such as the lawful holder of a bill of lading.

[37] *Nippon Yusen Kaisha v International Import and Export Co Ltd (The Elbe Maru)* [1978] 1 Lloyd's Rep 206 (EW HC).

[38] *Whitsea Shipping and Trading Corp v El Paso Rio Clara Ltda (The Marielle Bolten)* [2009] EWHC 2552 (Comm), [2010] 1 Lloyd's Rep 648, [2009] All ER (D) 300 (Oct) (EW HC).

5.4.2 *Limitations to Effectiveness of Circular Indemnity Clause*

There are various limitations to the effectiveness of a circular indemnity clause. They are only actionable by the carrier by not the subcontractor. However, this limitation will be overcome,[39] with Sections 1(1) and 1(6) read together with Section 6(5) of the UK Contracts (Rights of Third Parties) Act 1999, which will allow the subcontractor to directly rely on the circular indemnity clause, as a clause excluding or limiting the liability of the third party, in an action by a cargo claimant against the subcontractor.

A stay or an anti-suit injunction here is a relief in the nature of the specific performance of circular indemnity clause and is granted at the discretion of the court. The court may not grant it in favour of a carrier unless the carrier had a real financial interest in the suit of the cargo claimant against the subcontractor.[40] A cargo claimant may successfully resist the stay or anti-suit injunction application if there is a serious triable issue as to whether the suit against the subcontractor is in respect of an event covered within the responsibility period of the carrier under the bill.[41]

5.4.3 *Pure Indemnity Claim*

Where a stay or an anti-suit injunction is not obtained by the carrier, it will be able to obtain 'indemnity' in monetary terms, from a successful cargo claimant, if a few conditions are satisfied. First, there must be a contract between the carrier and subcontractor whereby the carrier has agreed to protect the subcontractor or to indemnify the subcontractor in the event of a successful claim by the cargo interest against the subcontractor. Second, the subcontractor must have been found liable to the cargo claimant. Third, the subcontractor must have held the carrier liable for the damages the subcontractor has paid or has to pay the bill of lading holder. It must be noted that in a suit by the subcontractor against the carrier, the carrier may bring the successful cargo claimant as a third party liable to indemnify the carrier.

5.5 Suit for Benefit of Another

It is not uncommon for bills of lading to get stuck on its passage from the consignor to the end consignee through banks and other intermediate buyers. Any delay in getting hold of the bill of lading is a sensitive issue in the law of carriage of goods

---

[39] Where English law applies.

[40] *Nippon Yusen Kaisha v International Import and Export Co Ltd (The Elbe Maru)* [1978] 1 Lloyd's Rep 206 (EW HC).

[41] *Neptune Orient Lines Ltd v JVC (UK) Ltd (The Chevalier Roze)* [1983] 2 Lloyd's Rep 438 (EW HC).

by sea because of the narrow one-year time limit to bring any cargo claim against the carrier, by virtue of Article VI of the Hague and Hague-Visby Rules.

To partly redress the predicament, Section 2(4) of the UK Carriage of Goods by Sea Act 1992 allows an action by a lawful holder of the bill of lading[42] to take action against the carrier for the benefit of a person interested in the goods. The Section 2(4) reads as follows:

> (4) Where, in the case of any document to which this Act applies—
>
> (a) a person with any interest or right in or in relation to goods to which the document relates sustains loss or damage in consequence of a breach of the contract of carriage; but
>
> (c) subsection (1) above operates in relation to that document so that rights of suit in respect of that breach are vested in another person,
>
> The other person shall be entitled to exercise those rights for the benefit of the person who sustained the loss or damage to the same extent as they could have been exercised if they had been vested in the person for whose benefit they are exercised.

This is not a new principle enacted in the 1992 Act. This principle was a long-established one since the 1839 case of *Dunlop v Lambert.*[43] In this case, it was held that a shipper, who has suffered no substantial damages, may obtain substantial damages from a carrier to hold the proceeds in trust for the third party who has actually suffered those losses.[44]

However, the shortfall here is that the discretion to exercise the relief available in the Section 2(4) is with the lawful holder of the bill.[45] He is not under any legal obligation to exercise it.

5.6 Representative Action

It is unlikely that a cargo claimant will bring a representative action against the carrier, i.e. for loss sustained by the claimant and other cargo interests.[46] Even if such a representative action is brought, it is doubtful whether it will be allowed to continue as such, as a matter of civil procedure.

In *Markt & Co Ltd v Knight Steamship Co Ltd*,[47] a representative action for the cargo interest was not allowed to be continued as such. In contrast to that, in *The*

---

[42] Or transferees of the rights in a sea waybill or ship's delivery order, by virtue of Section 2(1) of the Act.

[43] (1839) 6 Cl & F 600.

[44] Accordingly, the position in Malaysia where the 1855 Act applies will be the same, despite lack of any statutory provision like the Section 2(4) of the UK 1992 Act.

[45] Or such other persons entitled to the rights in a sea waybill or ship's delivery order, by virtue of Section 2(1) of the Act.

[46] E.g. Where the ship sank with total loss of all the cargo on board the ship.

[47] [1910] 2 KB 1021, [1908–10] All ER Rep Ext 1031 (EW CA, by majority).

Irish Rowan,[48] a shipowner brought an indemnity claim against the single largest insurer cum leading underwriter in respect of damages that the shipowner had paid to the cargo owners. The insurer was named on its own behalf and as representative of the other insurers. The insurer applied to strike out the 'representative' part. The English Court of Appeal refused, holding that all the insurers had the 'same interest'.

[48] *Irish Shipping Ltd v Commercial Union Assurance Co plc (The Irish Rowan)* [1991] 2 QB 206, [1989] 3 All ER 853, [1990] 2 WLR 117, [1989] 2 Lloyd's Rep 144, [1990] 5 LS Gaz R 39 (EW CA).

Chapter 6
Proof of Damages: Presumptions and Estoppels

This chapter analyses presumptions and estoppels in proof of cargo damage during transit. First, 'clausing' of bills and evidentiary value of the statements in the bill are introduced. The evidentiary value may be that the statements are conclusive evidence, *prima facie* evidence or no evidence. Second, the sources of the presumptions and estoppels are analysed. They are at common law, the Hague Rules, the Hague-Visby Rules, the Carriage of Goods by Sea Act 1992. Standing of the charterer to rely on Hague-Visby Rules Article III(4) (conclusive evidence) is also considered. Third, the role and significance of presumptions and estoppels in this area of law are examined. Fourth, the various popular clauses such as 'quantity or weight not known', 'contents not known', 'said to contain', 'condition not known', 'Relta' clausing are dealt with. Fifth, the standard statement that goods are received in 'apparent good order and condition' is considered. Sixth, the shipper's liability to indemnify to the carrier for statements made by the shipper to the carrier, reflected in the bill of lading. is briefly looked at. Last, the actions available to cargo interest, when a statement in a bill goes wrong, in tort of deceit, tort of negligent misrepresentation and the Misrepresentation Act 1967 are visited.

6.1 Introduction

In proving loss or damages in a cargo claim, there are various presumptions or estoppels that will come into play. These presumptions or estoppels arise from the representations appearing in the bill of lading or other shipping documents like the sea waybill or ship's delivery order. Indeed, in the absence of such presumptions or estoppels, a claimant may not be able to establish a cargo claim since the claimant, who may be a transferee of the bill, may not have the direct knowledge of or access to various facts including the condition of the cargo at the time of loading. It would have purchased the cargo relying on the bill. Hence, the necessity for the various presumptions or estoppels.

A. Kasi, *The Law of Carriage of Goods by Sea*,
https://doi.org/10.1007/978-981-33-6793-7_6

Presumptions as to order and condition of the goods at the time of the shipment as stated in the bill of lading is an important aspect of the law of cargo-shipping. These presumptions are what give the bill its full value as a receipt. Carriers have attempted to circumvent this by clausing the bill with clauses such as 'quantity and weight not known'. Such clauses, if upheld, will render the bill of lesser value. The Rules have some provisions that can arguably control such clausing. Other than this, the courts have employed restrictive interpretation as a tool for controlling the effect of such clauses. It appears what the courts have not yet considered is using public policy grounds to strike down such clauses.

The complexity associated with claused bills has been compounded by the growing use of containerised shipments. In such shipments, the carriers will annotate the bill with a 'said to contain' clausing. This may render the receipt function of the bill of little value.

In this chapter, first an introduction is made to claused and clean bills and to the three levels of evidentiary value of representations in the bill, namely conclusive proof, *prima facie* evidence and no evidentiary value. That is followed by an analysis of the sources of the presumptions and estoppels, and the role they play in proof of damages by a cargo claimant. Then, a some of the popular clausings are considered, namely, 'Quantity or Weight Not Known', 'Contents Not Known', 'Said to Contain', 'Condition Not Known' and 'Relta' clause. Then an analysis is made of the popular statement 'Apparent Good Order and Condition' commonly found in shipping documents and the statutory indemnity by the shipper for the information as to the quantity of the goods shipped furnished by it to the carrier. Thereafter, alternative actions available to the cargo claimant are visited, such as an action in deceit , negligence and misrepresentation for misstatements in the bill, e.g. wrong date. A wrong date will be an crucial, for example, when the shipment is made outside the period allowed by the letter of credit but the bill is mis-dated it as if the shipment was made within the allowed period in order to facilitate the seller presenting the bill for payment under the letter of credit.

6.2 Preliminaries

Here will be visited claused and clean bills of lading, and the three levels of evidentiary value of representations in the bill.

6.2.1 Claused and Clean Bill

The representations made on a bill by the carrier will usually be as to the description of the cargo, packing of the cargo, its condition, quality, quantity and date of shipment.[1] Such representations may be qualified, which is called 'clausing'. The qualification may take one of two forms. One is that the bill notes a *defect*, for example, the steel bars loaded were rusty. This is an *affirmation* of the carrier's knowledge of the condition of the cargo. Another is that the shipowner will *disclaim* knowledge of it, such as when a container stuffed by the consignor is shipped, in which case the bill will note the above description of cargo "said to contain". This is a *negation* of any knowledge of the cargo. A bill that is qualified whether by affirmation or negation is said to be 'claused'. When a bill is not claused in either way, it is called a 'clean' bill. An interesting case concerning the dividing line between a claused bill and a clean bill is *The Galatia. M Golodetz & Co Inc v Czarnikow-Rionda Co Inc (The Galatia)* [1980] 1 All ER 501, [1980] 1 WLR 495, [1980] 1 Lloyd's Rep 453 (EW CA). This case concerned a C&F contract for 12,000 – 13,000 tons of sugar. The buyer was to pay against a clean shipped on board bill of lading. While the cargo was being loaded into the ship, after a part of it was loaded, a fire broke out damaging 200 tons of sugar. The damaged sugar was unloaded, and the remainder of the cargo was loaded. The shipowner issued two bills, one for the 200 tons that noted shipment in apparent good order and condition with an additional typewritten annotation that the sugar was discharged because it was damaged by fire. Another for the remainder of the cargo. The buyer paid for the bill in respect of the remainder of the cargo but not the one in respect of the 200 tons. The dispute reached the English Court of Appeal, that held that the bill was a 'clean' shipped bill, as the goods were in apparent good order and condition at the time of loading. What happened after that did not render the bill a claused one. This case also demonstrates the passing of risk upon loading, even if it is a part of the cargo only.

6.2.2 Three Levels of Evidentiary Value of Representations

The evidentiary value of such representations subject to any clausing may be at one of three levels. One is that it is presumed to be conclusive evidence so that the carrier is estopped from adducing evidence to the contrary. Another is that it is a *prima facie* evidence so that the burden of disproving it is on the carrier. The last is that it has no evidentiary value, with the result that the burden is on the claimant to prove it.

[1] They are considered to be representations rather than terms of the bill. However, details of the carrying vessel, port of loading and port of discharge are considered to be terms of the bill.

6.3 Sources of Presumptions and Estoppels

There are presumptions provided for by the Hague and Hague-Visby Rules and statutes, and estoppels by the common law. Article III(4)[2] of the Hague Rules of 1924 gives a rebuttable presumption arising from the receipt of goods acknowledged in the bill of lading, i.e. leading marks, quantity and condition. This was amended in the Hague-Visby Rules of 1968,[3] that turned the presumption into conclusive evidence when relied on by a transferee of the bill in good faith against the carrier. An addition was made to this by the UK Carriage of Goods Act 1992, and similarly the Singapore Bills of Lading Act, in Section 4, whereby similarly statement of 'shipment' or 'received for shipment' in a bill of lading was made conclusive evidence against the carrier at the suit of a transferee of the bill in good faith.

It must be observed that none of these presumptions or estoppel has any place in a dispute between the buyer and the seller or in any dispute other than one between the carrier and the shipper/the transferee of the bill. In *China Steel Corporation v Pan Asia Shipyard & Engineering Co (Pte) Ltd,*[4] the Singapore Court of Appeal rightly disallowed a seller from relying on the 'apparent good order and condition' statement in the bill of lading to claim that the goods were shipped in such order and condition. However, the reasoning of the court seemed quite insufficient. In this case, a seller sold and shipped steel plates to the buyer. The shipowner issued a clean bill of lading. Upon delivery of the goods, the buyer complained they were damaged. The buyer made a claim against the seller for the resultant loss. The court found that the cause of damage was threefold. First, defects in the plates present at the time of shipment. Second, spillage of salt onto the plates during discharge. Third, exposure to weather in the buyer's open yard after delivery. The seller relied on the clean bill of lading to argue that it had shipped the goods in good order and condition. The court rejected this argument on grounds that it may not show qualitative defects and it only shows the 'apparent' order and condition. The court also doubted if the statements made in the bill of lading could serve as evidence of the quality of the goods in a suit between the seller and the buyer.[5] The court held the seller was only liable in respect of the first cause, but not the second and the third ones. In the circumstances, the court apportioned liability 50:50 between the seller and the buyer, and it ordered the seller to pay 50% of the total loss.

It is settled that, in the absence of a contrary intention, the seller's responsibility is only until the goods pass the rail of the ship at the time of loading, thereafter the risk (though not necessarily the property) passes to the buyer.[6] Hence, in this case, for

[2] Read together with Article III(3).

[3] In the same Article.

[4] [1988] 1 SLR 458 (SG CA).

[5] The court also refused to disturb the apportionment decided by the trial court, as it was based on findings of fact and there was no error of law. Accordingly, the court affirmed the trial court's decision.

[6] *Manbre Saccharine Co v Corn Products Co* [1919] 1 KB 198, [1918-19] All ER Rep 980 (EW HC); *C Groom Ltd v Barbar* [1915] 1 KB 316 (EW HC).

the damage that occurred during discharge, the risk was with the buyer, for which the buyer may have a claim against the shipowner if the spillage was the latter's fault.[7]

A bill of lading will merely be a hearsay evidence when it is relied on to prove the statements therein, and it may either be inadmissible or of limited value if admitted. In those Commonwealth countries, including Singapore and Malaysia, with an Evidence Act modelled on the Indian Evidence Act 1872 hearsay evidence is generally inadmissible. Sections 32(1) and 60 of the Indian Evidence Act 1872, which is materially identically reproduced, with the same section numbering in the Singapore Evidence Act and the Malaysian Evidence Act 1950, prohibits such hearsay evidence. However, an exception in Section 32(1)(b) of the Act may apply in case of bills of lading. The Section 32(1)(b) reads as follows:

> 32. (1) Statements, written or verbal, of relevant facts made by a person ... whose attendance cannot be procured without an amount of delay or expense which under the circumstances of the case appears to the court unreasonable, are themselves relevant facts in the following cases:
>
> (a) ...
>
> (b) when the statement was made by any such person in the ordinary course of business ... or of a document used in commerce, written or signed by him.

Comparatively, in England and Wales, hearsay evidence is admissible by virtue of Section 1 of the UK Civil Evidence Act 1995 and CPR[8] Rules 33.1–33.6, subject to procedural safeguards in Sections 2 and 3 of the Act and in the said Rules. However, the weight to be attributed to the evidence is a matter for the court to determine, depending on the circumstances, as provided in Section 4 of the Act.

In Malaysia, a question as to the evidentiary value of the bill of lading in a dispute between the consignee and a warehouse operator came before the Federal Court in *Borneo Co (M) Sdn Bhd v Penang Port Commission.*[9] In this case, two boxes alleged to contain pharmaceutical were discharged at the Penang[10] port and stored in the port's godown. Subsequently, the two boxes went missing and the port authority was not able to deliver them to the consignee. The consignee sued the port authority for the value of the goods. It was the case of the consignee that the boxes contained the goods as described in the bill of lading. The port authority challenged this. The court held that the bill of lading was *prima facie* evidence . Accordingly, the court decided that, since the port authority was not able to disprove it, the port authority was liable for the loss.[11] This authority does not represent the right law. A bill of lading is *prima facie* evidence of the contents of the boxes. Rather, it was hearsay evidence, of which admissibility should have been considered under Section 32(1)(b) of the Malaysian

---

[7] See the Hague and Hague-Visby Rules—Articles II(1), II(2), III(6) and IV(2).

[8] Civil Procedure Rules (of England and Wales).

[9] [1975] 2 MLJ 204 (MY FC).

[10] In Malaysia.

[11] The court considered neither Section 32 of the Malaysian Evidence Act 1950 nor Article III(4) of the Hague Rules (largely applicable in Malaysia) in deciding the case.

Evidence Act 1950 as well as under Section 114 of the Act[12] (read together with *illustration (f)* thereto). The Section 114 and the *illustration (f)* read as follows:

> The court may presume the existence of any fact which it thinks likely to have happened, regard being had to the common course of natural events, human conduct, and public and private business, in their relation to the facts of the particular case.
>
> *Illustration*
>
> ...
>
> (f) that the common course of business has been followed in particular cases; ...

6.3.1 Estoppels at Common Law

At the common law , originally estoppel against carriers based on representations was not recognised. Later development of the common law resulted in the estoppel being recognised, as it is today. In the mid- 19th century, in *Grant v Norway*,[13] a bill of lading was signed by the master when no cargo was received. The English Court of Common Pleas held the bill to be a nullity, with the result that the shipowner was not estopped by the quantity-representation made in the bill. There are two limitations to the application of the case in the current time. First, at that time, the ostensible authority of agents was not recognised, which is not so today. Second, at that time, 'received for shipment' bills were not recognised and it was a bill of lading only when the goods were laden on board the ship, i.e. 'shipped' bill. Contrary to this, today, 'received for shipment' bills are recognised.[14]

Then, in the late 19th century, in *Thorman v Burt*,[15] the court recognised the quantity-representation in the bill as *prima facie* evidence and allowed the carrier to adduce evidence to prove that only a lesser quantity was actually loaded. In the early 20th century, in *The Skarp*,[16] a clean bill of lading was issued by the shipowner despite a defect in the apparent condition of the cargo. The bill was then transferred to the buyer. Upon receipt of the cargo, the buyer sued the shipowner. The issue of estoppel arose, that is, whether the shipowner was estopped from adducing evidence to the effect that the goods were, in fact, defective at the time of loading and hence there was no breach of contract of carriage. The English High Court held that the shipowner was not estopped because, under the sale and purchase contract between the seller and the buyer, the latter was obliged, quite unusually, to accept the bill and pay upon it even if it was claused. The court assumed that this meant that the buyer did not rely on the representation to its detriment i.e. paying upon the bill.

---

[12] Equivalent to Section 114 of the Indian Evidence Act 1872 and Section 116 of the Singapore Evidence Act.

[13] (1851) 10 CB 665 (EW Court of Common Pleas).

[14] With some limitations, discussed in Chap. 2.

[15] *Thorman v Burt, Boulton & Co* (1886) 54 LT 349, [1886-90] All ER Rep 787 (EW CA).

[16] *The Skarp* [1935] P 134, [1935] All ER Rep 560 (EW HC).

The limitation to the concept of estoppel seen in *The Skarp* was diluted in the late 20th century case of *The Dona Mari.*[17] In this case, the English High Court held that if a buyer would not have paid had the bill been claused, irrespective of any terms of the contract between the buyer and the seller, then the buyer may raise on estoppel, as there is a detriment. Hence, the question is whether the buyer *in fact* relied on the bill to make payment to the seller rather than whether he was *obliged* to make the payment. *The Dona Mari*, rather than *The Skarp*, rightly represents the common law i.e. the concept of 'detriment' to raise estoppel.

At common law, in its present state, it is not doubted that the representations made in a bill will estop the carrier from disputing the truth of the representations when the cargo claimant had relied on the representations to its detriment. This is not something unique to shipping law, but a basic principle of any estoppel at common law.[18]

The estoppel will be available only when such representations are relied on by a transferee of the bill in good faith but not when relied on by a consignor as he will not rely on the representations to his detriment.[19] The estoppel will be applicable to a shipper when the shipper is not the consignor, as in a pure fob contract, since he will rely on it to pay the consignor and receive the bill. When the claim is by the *consignor*, the representations are relevant evidence as admission[20] and its weight is for the court to determine.

The estoppel concept will, of course, not help a cargo claimant when the discrepancy between the representation and the goods shipped is immaterial. In *Parsons v New Zealand Shipping*,[21] carcasses of frozen lamb were shipped. The bill described the leading marks as "Sun Brand 622x". However, some of the carcasses were actually marked "Sun Brand 522x". The character and value of the carcasses, whether marked with 622x or 522x, were the same. Accordingly, the cargo claimant had no valid claim against the shipowner for this as any difference in the markings on the cargo did not cause any prejudice to the cargo claimant.

6.3.2 Presumptions Under Hague Rules (Prima Facie Evidence)

Under the Hague Rules, the representations in the bill of lading as to leading marks, quantity and apparent condition is a *prima facie* evidence of those facts under Article

[17] *Cremer v General Carriers SA (The Dona Mari)* [1973] 2 Lloyd's Rep 366, [1974] 1 All ER 1, [1974] 1 WLR 341 (EW HC).

[18] See *Redgrave v Hurd* (1881) 20 Ch D 1 (EW CA); *Peekay Intermark Ltd v ANZ Banking Group Ltd* [2006] EWCA Civ 386, [2006] 2 Lloyd's Rep 511 (EW CA); *Colchester BC v Smith* [1991] Ch 448 (EW HC, affirmed by the Court of Appeal in [1992] Ch 421 (EW CA).

[19] The transferee may even be the named consignee or shipper-buyer in a fob contract.

[20] Codified in Malaysia and Singapore in Section 23 of the respective Evidence Acts.

[21] [1901] 1 QB 548 (EW CA).

III(4), read together with Article III(3). Hence, the burden of proving otherwise is on the carrier. For this, it does not matter whether such representations are relied on by the shipper, consignor or a transferee of the bill. However, practically, a transferee will rely on the common law estoppel based on detrimental reliance on the bill, that will completely bar the carrier from adducing evidence to prove the representations to be wrong. Article III(3) and (4) of the Hague Rules read as follows:

> 3. After receiving the goods into his charge the carrier or the master or agent of the carrier shall, on demand of the shipper, issue to the shipper a bill of lading showing among other things:
>
> (a) The *leading marks* necessary for identification of the goods as the same are furnished in writing by the shipper before the loading of such goods starts, provided such marks are stamped or otherwise shown clearly upon the goods if uncovered, or on the cases or coverings in which such goods are contained, in such a manner as should ordinarily remain legible until the end of the voyage.
>
> (b) Either the *number of packages or pieces, or the quantity, or weight*, as the case may be, as furnished in writing by the shipper.
>
> (c) The *apparent order and condition of the goods.*
>
> Provided that no carrier, master or agent of the carrier shall be bound to state or show in the bill of lading any marks, number, quantity or weight which he has reasonable ground for suspecting not accurately to represent the goods actually received, or which he has had no reasonable means of checking.
>
> 4. Such a bill of lading shall be *prima facie evidence* of the receipt by the carrier of the goods as therein described in accordance with paragraph 3 (a), (b) and (c). [emphasis added]

6.3.3 Presumptions Under Hague-Visby Rules (Conclusive Evidence)

The *prima facie* evidence provided for by the Hague Rules is also available under the Hague-Visby Rules. The latter Rules added that when the representations are relied on by a transferee of the bill of lading in good faith, the representations are conclusive evidence against the carrier so that the carrier cannot adduce evidence to the contrary. This is to a large extent a codification of the common law estoppel principle, with one modification, namely, reliance to the detriment is not necessary but the transferee must have acted in good faith in receiving the bill. This was made by an addition to Article III(4), which with the addition reads as follows in the Hague-Visby Rules:

> 4. Such a bill of lading shall be *prima facie evidence* of the receipt by the carrier of the goods as therein described in accordance with paragraph 3 (a), (b) and (c). <u>However, proof to the contrary shall not be admissible when the bill of lading has been transferred to a third party acting in good faith.</u> [emphasis added]

The underlined portion was the one added in the Hague-Visby Rules over the Hague Rules.

6.3.3.1 Non-availability of Article III(4) to Charterer

The presumption/conclusive evidence rule in Article III(4), read together with Article III(3), is not available to a charterer-buyer to whom the bill is transferred by a consignor-seller. This happens when the buyer charters the ship and the shipowner issues the bill to the seller, who transfers the bill to the buyer.[22] This is because a bill of lading does not regulate the relationship between the parties when the bill is in the hands of a charterer. This is the result of the definition of 'carriage of contract' in Article I(b) of the Hague and Hague-Visby Rules. Article I(b) reads as follows:

> 'Contract of carriage' applies only to contracts of carriage covered by a bill of lading or any similar document of title, in so far as such document relates to the carriage of goods by sea, including any bill of lading or any similar document as aforesaid issued under or pursuant to a charter party *from the moment at which such bill of lading or similar document of title regulates the relations between a carrier and a holder of the same.* [emphasis added]

Practically, this does not affect a charterer for two reasons. First, the charterer will still be able to rely on the common law estoppel, as the charterer would pay the seller-consignor relying on the representations made in the bill. Second, the charterparty will usually contractually incorporate the Rules.[23] Such a clause is called 'clause paramount' and is commonly found in the standard forms of charterparties.[24]

6.3.4 *Presumptions Under COGSA 1992 Section 4 (Conclusive Evidence)*

An addition was made by Section 4 of the UK Carriage of Goods by Sea Act 1992, whereby the representation in the bill of lading of the fact of 'shipment' or 'received for shipment' is conclusive evidence of the fact against the carrier at the suit of a transferee of the bill in good faith. The Section 4 of the UK Carriage of Goods by Sea Act 1992 reads as follows:

> **4. Representations in Bills of Lading**
>
> A bill of lading which—
>
> (i) represents goods to have been *shipped on board* a vessel or to have been *received for shipment* on board a vessel; and
>
> (ii) has been signed by the master of the vessel or by a person who was not the master but had the express, implied or apparent authority of the carrier to sign bills of lading,
>
> shall, in favour of a person who has become the *lawful holder* of the bill, be *conclusive evidence* against the carrier *of the shipment of the goods* or, as the case may be, of their *receipt for shipment.* [emphasis added]

---

[22] E.g. *President of India v Metcalfe Shipping Co Ltd (The Dunelmia)* [1970] 1 QB 289, [1969] 3 All ER 1549, [1969] 3 WLR 1120 (EW CA).

[23] Called 'clause paramount'.

[24] E.g. BIMCO forms of charterparty.

This is largely a codification of the common law estoppel with a modification that the requirement of detrimental reliance is not there but the transferee must have received the bill in good faith. Interestingly, it expressly provides for this effect of the bill of lading when it is signed by the master or by anyone with the express, implied or apparent authority of the carrier. This section was aimed at expressly reversing the effect of *Grant v Norway*. Even in the absence of such statutory provision, the position must almost be the same at the common law concerning estoppels, as it is now. There is no limitation to the application of this section when the bill is in the hands of the charterer as long as the charterer is a transferee of the bill in good faith.

6.4 Role of Presumptions in Proof of Transit-Damage

Presumptions and estoppels are very important for a cargo claimant in proving damages during transit. Without them, the cargo claimant may have no access to what transpired during transit. The important of establishing that the damage occurred during the carriage is dealt with first below, followed by the role of the presumptions and estoppel in proving such damage. Then, a note of what the period of carriage in this context means.

6.4.1 Why is Time of Damage Crucial?

What the claimant will seek to prove will be that the goods were damaged or lost by fault attributable to the carrier. The time when the damage or loss occurred is crucial. This is because the carrier's liability will be statutorily regulated, through the Hague or Hague-Visby Rules,[25] *during* the period of carriage, which the carrier cannot exclude or limit.[26] For the period *before and after* the carriage, if the carrier has control of the cargo, the liability will only be regulated by the terms of the contract between the parties, the laws of bailment, negligence and conversion. Such a clause is called 'before and after' clause Typically a carrier will place, into the bill of lading, exclusion and limitation clauses in respect of the liability for the 'before and after' periods. The obligation to 'deliver' is one of the important obligations in the 'after' period, not mandatorily covered by the Rules.[27] When a cargo claimant desires to hold the carrier responsible for loss or damage, usually, it will endeavour to establish that the loss or damage happened during the period of 'carriage', so that no exclusion or limitation clause will be effective in respect of the liability for the loss or damage.

---

[25] Whichever is applicable depending on the facts of the case.

[26] Article III(8) of the Hague and Hague-Visby Rules.

[27] Unless it is a 'free-out' contract, where the consignee performs the discharge and takes delivery together with that.

6.4.2 Role of Presumptions in Proof of Damages During Carriage

That is where the presumptions or estoppels play an important role. Damage might actually have happened before the carriage commenced or even before the goods were received by the carrier. But the bill may mistakenly acknowledge receipt in 'apparent good order and condition', hence a 'clean bill'. This will bind the carrier, who will be estopped from adducing evidence to the contrary against an innocent transferee of the bill. This will enable the cargo claimant to obtain compensation as if the goods were damaged during the carriage and hence within the scope of the Hague/Hague-Visby Rules.

Interestingly, in such a case, there is actually no breach of the carriage-contract on the part of the carrier. The actual fault of the carrier is that it mistakenly issued a clean bill. This has occasioned to the transferee the loss of the opportunity to reject the documents, which it might have done had the bill been properly claused. However, the award of damages will be for breach of the carriage contract.

6.4.3 Period of Carriage Under Hague or Hague-Visby Rules

The period covered by the Hague/Hague-Visby Rules is colloquially said to the 'tackle-to-tackle', also called the 'alongside' rule, that is, from the time the goods cross the rail of the ship inward on loading and to the time the goods pass the rail of the ship outward on discharge. However, this is not accurate, as the Rules cover from the loading to the discharge, meaning the entire loading and operations included. Article I(e) of the Rules[28] defines carriage of goods as follows:

> Carriage of goods" covers the period from the time when the goods are *loaded on to* the time they are *discharged from* the ship. [emphasis added]

The period referred to by Article I(e) seems, by a literal reading, to mean the 'tackle to tackle' period because loading on *to the ship* and discharge *from the ship* happens when the goods cross the ship's rail inward or outward respectively. However, Article II of the Rules[29] renders the Rules applicable to loading and discharge and all that falls in between them. It reads as follows:

> Subject to the provisions of Article VI, under every contract of carriage of goods by sea the carrier, in relation to the *loading*, handling, stowage, carriage, custody, care and *discharge* of such goods, shall be subject to the responsibilities and liabilities and entitled to the rights and immunities hereinafter set forth. [emphasis added]

Article II refers to loading and discharge, without the addition of '*on to the ship*' or '*from the ship*'. Loading and discharge, literally read, seems to mean the entire

[28] The Hague and Hague-Visby Rules.

[29] The Hague and Hague-Visby Rules.

operation of loading and discharge. Support for this proposition is added by Article III(2) that similarly imposes the duty for loading and discharge on the carrier, without the additions. Article III(2) reads as follows:

> Subject to the provisions of Article IV, the carrier shall properly and carefully load, handle, stow, carry, keep, care for, and discharge the goods carried.

Accordingly, the responsibility period under the Rules is from the start of the loading to the end of discharge, meaning the entire period of the loading and discharge covered. In *Pyrene Co Ltd v Scindia Navigation Co Ltd,*[30] the English High Court held accordingly.[31]

6.5 Popular Clausings

Some clausing are commonly found in bills of lading, including in BIMCO[32] standard forms of bills. A discussion of such clauses follows.

6.5.1 'Quantity or Weight Not Known' Clausing

At common law, when a bill has been claused with a disclaimer stating that the quantity or weight is unknown, that rendered the representation as to quantity or weight of no evidentiary value.[33] However, courts have construed such disclaimers narrowly against the carrier. In *Attorney General of Ceylon v Scindia Steam Navigation Co Ltd,*[34] a cargo of rice was shipped. The bill was claused with a disclaimer "*weight* unknown". The Privy Council held that this clausing did not qualify the representation as to the *number of bags* loaded. The same approach, under the Hague Rules, in *Oricon Waren-Handels GmbH v Intergraan NV,*[35] required the consignee to prove the weight of the cargo against the carrier when the number of packages shipped, and only that, was evidenced by the bill.

Article III(3)(b) of the Hague and Hague-Visby Rules requires the carrier to issue a bill stating "the number of packages or pieces, or the quantity or weight", with only two exceptions. First, where the carrier has 'reasonable grounds' to suspect the accuracy of those matters. Second, where the carrier has 'no reasonable means' of verifying them. However, the Rules require the carrier to issue such a bill only

---

[30] [1954] 2 QB 402, [1954] 2 All ER 158 (EW HC).

[31] With a set of complex reasons. See Chap. 4.2.3 for a summary of the case.

[32] 'Baltic and International Maritime Council'.

[33] *New Chinese Antimony Co Ltd v Ocean Steamship Co Ltd* [1917] 2 KB 664 (EW CA).

[34] [1962] AC 60, [1961] 3 All ER 684, [1961] 3 WLR 936, [1961] 2 Lloyd's Rep 173 (PC on appeal from Ceylon).

[35] [1967] 2 Lloyd's Rep 82 (EW HC).

when requested by the shipper. This may look a little odd because the carrier will have to issue a bill of lading upon receipt of the cargo, even in the absence of any such provision in the Rules, as this will be an implied and customary term of the space booking contract. A harmonious construction of the Article will be that, while it is not doubted that the carrier will have to issue a bill in any event, the carrier will have to compulsorily state those details if required by the carrier when the bill issued does not have any of those details.

As per this suggested construction, if a carrier qualifies the quantity or weight with a clausing like 'quantity or weight not known', then the shipper or any subsequent holder of the bill can go back to the carrier to remove the clausing and to state the quantity or weight unless of course one of the two exceptions apply. However, if the shipper or subsequent holder of the bill does not exercise this right, then it cannot rely on the bill as evidence of the quantity or weight against the carrier. This proposition will be supported by *The Atlas.*[36] In this case, steel billets were shipped from Russia to Taiwan. The bill of lading[37] was issued in Hong Kong, hence subject to the Hague-Visby Rules. The bill that stated the weight of the steel billets to be about 12,000 metric tons was claused with a quantity and weight unknown statement. The bill was transferred to the cargo claimant. Upon delivery, it transpired that the steel billets weighed only about 10,800 metric tons. The cargo claimant sued the carrier for short delivery and relied on the quantity-statement in the bill as evidence of the goods shipped. The court refused this as the bill was claused with quantity and weight unknown statement.[38] A similar approach was taken in Singapore by the Court of Appeal in *Kwantung Provincial Bank v Osaka Shoshen Kaisha.*[39] It must be noted that various BIMCO standard forms of bill of lading have such clausing.[40]

However, a natural limitation to *The Atlas* approach will be where a carrier issues a bill of lading stating quantity, qualified by the clausing when the carrier knew that its statement of quantity was inaccurate, or was at least negligent about that. In such cases, there does not seem to be anything to stop the innocent transferee of the bill of lading from suing the carrier in deceit or negligence.

Another difficulty that may arise is when the carrier first issues a bill with a quantity or weight statement but qualified with a 'quantity and weight unknown' clause although the carrier had every means of verifying the quantity or weight. The shipper subsequently requests for a bill with the clause removed but the carrier refuses. Two questions arise from this scenario. First, does the quantity or weight stated in the claused bill is *prima facie* evidence between the shipper and the carrier? Second, does the quantity or weight stated is *prima facie* or conclusive evidence between a subsequent holder of the bill and the carrier? For the first question, although

---

[36] *Noble Resources Ltd v Cavalier Shipping Corpn (The Atlas)* [1996] 1 Lloyd's Rep 642, [1996] CLC 1148 (EW HC).

[37] A 'switch bill'.

[38] For a similar decision, see *Agrosin Pte Ltd v Highway Shipping Co Ltd (The Mata K)* [1998] 2 Lloyd's Rep 614 (EW HC).

[39] [1967] 2 Lloyd's Rep 82 (SG CA).

[40] *Henry Smith & Co v Bedouin Steam Navigation Co Ltd* [1896] AC 70 (UK HL).

the carrier is in breach of the statutory obligation, that does not trigger the operation of Article III(4) when the bill is claused. No doubt, the shipper will in such case be entitled to claim damages for the breach, which will be the loss that the shipper suffered by holding a bill that is not so tradable with a non-binding representation as to the quantity. For the second question, as the subsequent buyer accepted the bill with the clausing, arguably, he should be bound by it, so that the quantity or weight statement should not have any evidentiary value. *The Atlas* will support this proposition.

6.5.2 'Contents not Known' Clausing

It is common for bills of lading to contain a representation that goods have been loaded in 'apparent good order and condition' and a clause to say 'contents unknown'. Most of the BIMCO forms of bills of lading and sea waybills have both these statements.[41] Although there appears to be a contradiction between the two statements, courts have harmonised them by holding that the cargo loaded, as far as apparently appearing, were in good order and condition, but the master has no knowledge of the contents.

In *The Peter der Grosse*,[42] the English High Court held that 'contents … unknown' clause did not dilute the 'apparent good order and condition' representation, and that it rather meant the outside packages loaded were in apparent good condition, but the master had no knowledge of the contents inside.

6.5.3 'Said to Contain' Clausing

In *The Esmeralda 1*,[43] containerised cargo, stuffed by the consignor, was shipped. The bill contained the statement "said to contain" above the details of the cargo carried. The Australian court upheld this statement. This is not in conflict with Article III(3) of the Hague Rules, because, by virtue of the proviso to Article III(3), a carrier is not obliged to state any quantity that it has no reasonable means of checking.

The Singapore Court of Appeal in *The American Astronaut*[44] reinforced the principle that as long as the carrier had no means of checking the contents of the cargo and the fact is clear on the bill, by whatever notation or statement in the bill, Article

---

[41] See BIMCO CONGENBILL 2016 (charterparty bill of lading) and BIMCO CONLINEBILL 2016 (liner bill of lading), BIMCO GENWAYBILL 2016 (sea waybill). However, BIMCO MULTIDOC 2016 (Negotiable Multimodal Transport Bill of Lading) does not have the 'unknown' clause.

[42] *The Peter der Grosse* (1875) 1 PD 414 (EW HC).

[43] *Ace Imports Pty Ltd v Companhia de Navegacao Lloyd Brasileiro (The Esmeralda 1)* [1988] 1 Lloyd's Rep 206 (NSW SC).

[44] *The American Astronaut* [1978-1979] 1 SLR 187 (SG CA).

III(4) presumption does not arise. In this case, a container was shipped from New York to Singapore. The contents of the containers apparently included 580 cartons of soaps shipped by the shipper to the consignee.[45] The container was stuffed and sealed by shipper's agent and delivered to the carrier for carriage. The carrier issued a bill of lading stating the number of packages to be 580, description of package and goods to be cartons of toilet soap. The bill was subject to the US Carriage of Goods by Sea Act 1936, which has largely adopted the Hague Rules.[46] The notations in the bill included:

(i) 'House to Pier Container';
(ii) 'Shipper's load, stowage and count';
(iii) 'the goods or the containers ... other packages said to contain goods herein mentioned were received in apparent good order and condition, except as otherwise indicated herein to be transported to the port of discharge named.'; and
(iv) 'Received the container ... said to contain goods herein mentioned in apparent good order and condition ...'

Upon discharge at the Singapore port, the shipowner's agent unpacked the container and stacked the soap cartons in the designated area of the port's godown. When the goods were delivered to the consignee, there were only 375 cartons, short of 205 cartons. Unpacking and stacking were done by contractors of the carrier, without the presence of any representative of the carrier, consignee or port authority. There was no explanation for the shortage.

The consignee sued the carrier. The consignee argued that the bill was *prima facie* evidence of shipment of 580 cartons, relying on Section 3(4) of the Act,[47] which is materially identical to Article III(4) of the Hague Rules. The carrier argued that the bill was only evidence of receipt of the container and not the contents inside the container which the carrier had no opportunity of checking. It was established by evidence that 'House to Pier Container' meant that the packaging was done in the supplier's warehouse or factory and the container will be towed to the pier intact". 'Shipper's load, stowage and count' meant that the shipper stuffs the container, stow them and count them without any representative from the carrier and seals the container and ships it on board. Accordingly, the court held that the bill did not raise any presumption as to the cargo inside the container shipped and that the burden of proving it rested with the consignee, which it failed to discharge.

The consignee further argued that any notation to the effect that the acknowledgement was limited to receipt of a container rather than the contents of the container

---

45 Transferee of the bill.

46 The USA is not a signatory to The Hague or Hague-Visby Rules, but has enacted in line with the Hague Rules in its Carriage of Goods by Sea Act 1936.

47 Section 3(4): "Such a bill of lading shall be prima facie evidence of the receipt by the carrier of the goods as therein described in accordance with paragraphs (3)(a), (b), and (c), of this section ...".

was contrary to Section 3(8) of the Act,[48] which is materially identical to Article III(8) of the Hague Rules. The court rejected this argument, holding such notations are not a non-responsibility clause and hence do not contravene the Section 3(8). Accordingly, the court disallowed the claim and found for the carrier.

BIMCO CONLINEBILL 2016 (Liner Bill of Lading) states, in pre-printed form, below description of goods "particulars declared by the shipper but not acknowledged by the carrier". This will have the same effect as "said to contain" and will be upheld when used in conjunction with a container stuffed by the consignor.[49]

6.5.4 'Condition not Known' Clausing

BIMCO CONGENBILL 2016 form (Bill of Lading to be used with charterparties) has a statement that declares the condition unknown. It also has the usual statement that goods were loaded in 'apparent good order and condition'. The two statements are in direct contradiction to one another. It is unlikely that a court will uphold the 'condition unknown' clause, taking into account the contradicting 'apparent good order and condition' clause and Article III(3) of the Hague and Hague-Visby Rules. It will be expected that BIMCO will visit the conflict and resolve the same.

6.5.5 'Retla' Clausing

In *Tokio Marine & Fire Insurance Co Ltd v Relta Steamship Co*,[50] a cargo of metal pipes was shipped. The bill contained an 'apparent good order and condition' statement and a statement qualifying that, also at the front of the bill, as follows:

> The term 'apparent good order and condition ' when used in this bill of lading with reference to iron, steel or metal products does not mean that the goods, when received, were free of visible rust or moisture.

The American court, in this case, held that it excluded the liability of the carrier for any rust of whatever degree on the surface of the pipe. This approach negated the 'apparent good order and condition' clause as far as surface rust was concerned.

In *The Saga Explorer*,[51] the English High Court recognised the Relta clause but limited it to "minor or superficial rust that would be present on any steel cargo." By

---

[48] Section 3(8): "Any clause, covenant, or agreement in a contract of carriage relieving the carrier or the ship from liability for loss or damage to or in connection with the goods, arising from negligence, fault, or failure in the duties and obligations provided in this section, or lessening such liability otherwise than as provided in this Act, shall be null and void and of no effect. ...".

[49] Or where for other reasons the carrier cannot check the contents.

[50] [1970] 2 Lloyd's Rep 91 (US CA 9th Circuit).

[51] *Brefka & Hehnke GmbH & Co KG v Navire Shipping Co Ltd (The Saga Explorer)* [2012] EWHC 3124 (Comm), [2013] 1 Lloyd's Rep 401, [2012] All ER (D) 81 (Nov) (EW HC).

such limitation, the court harmonised the 'apparent good order and condition' statement and the Relta clause, without negating the 'apparent good order and condition' statement. The court held that the Relta clause, in this case, did not protect the carrier as the visible rust was of a severe degree.

6.6 'Apparent Good Order and Condition' Statement

A common and a very important statement found in the bills is that the goods were received in apparent good order and condition. All BIMCO forms of bills of lading and sea waybills have this statement printed on the front of the bill, inside a box at the right-side bottom.[52] Most of them limit it with a provision like "unless otherwise stated".[53] Most of them are also qualified by a clause like "weight, measure, marks, numbers, quality, quantity, contents and value unknown".[54]

6.6.1 Condition Different from Quality

'Condition' is different from 'quality'. The 'condition' refers to external aspects of the cargo loaded, whereas 'quality' will mean the internal aspects of the cargo. The dividing line between the two may be a narrow one. For instance, salt may be described as "free-flowing iodised salt". If a consignor loads the salt in bulk with this description, but it is not iodised, that will not make the carrier liable, because 'iodisation' goes to quality and not apparent condition. Both the salts will apparently look alike and only a chemical examination will tell if it is iodised. However, if the salt is highly moisturised and is not free-flowing, then the carrier will be liable as the 'free flow' refers to the apparent condition of the salt.

In *The Peter der Grosse*,[55] the English High Court well said that the 'apparent good order and condition' means "apparently, and so far as meets the eye, and externally, they were placed in good order on board this ship". A good example of the application of the test was in *Silver and Layton v Ocean Steamship Co Ltd*.[56] In this case, a cargo of cans of frozen eggs was shipped. The usual bill with 'apparent good order and condition' was issued, without any clausing. A dispute arose between a third-party

---

[52] See the sample BIMCO bills of lading forms: CONGENBILL 2016, CONLINEBILL 2016 and MULTIDOC 2016. For sea waybill, see BIMCO GENWAYBILL 2016 form.

[53] Except BIMCO CONGENBILL 2016 (Bill of Lading to be used with charterparties). However, this form, in contradiction to the "apparent good order and condition" provision, declares condition unknown.

[54] Except BIMCO MULTIDOC 2016 (Negotiable Multimodal Transport Bill of Lading). BIMCO CONLINEBILL 2016 (Liner Bill of Lading) states, in pre-printed form, below description of goods "particulars declared by the shipper but not acknowledged by the carrier".

[55] *The Peter der Grosse* (1875) 1 PD 414 at 420 (EW HC).

[56] [1930] 1 KB 416, [1929] All ER Rep 611 (EW CA).

holder of the bill and the shipowner. The English Court of Appeal decided that the shipowner was estopped from adducing evidence of any insufficient packing by the nature and shape of the cans. Similarly, the shipowner was not estopped from proving the cans were seriously gashed, as such a serious gash would be apparent. However, the shipowner was allowed to establish that the cans were pinhole-punctures, which would not have been apparent. It is important to note that 'packing' goes to apparent condition.

In *The Athelviscount*,[57] a cargo of kerosene was loaded by being pumped through pipe-lines. The kerosene was discoloured, which rendered it defective. The English High Court held that discolouration went to 'quality' and not to 'condition'. In the case of containerised cargoes, stuffed into the container by the consignor, the carrier will have no idea of the contents inside the container. In such cases, the 'apparent good order and condition' statement will only mean the apparent condition of the container.[58] Similarly, in *Cox, Patterson & Co v Bruce & Co*,[59] the English Court of Appealheld that markings indicating the quality of jute loaded in bales did not estop the shipowner from proving otherwise, because it was not within the scope of the master to verify this representation and any buyer should know that it is a mere repetition by the shipowner of information furnished by the consignor. In *The Skarp*,[60] the English High Court delved into the difference between the apparent condition and real condition and said as follows:

> There is no question that there are many classes of goods as to which there may be a distinction when one is speaking of their *apparent* condition and of their *real* condition. [emphasis added]

6.6.2 Specific Clausing to Limit 'Apparent Good Order and Condition'

Any notation by the carrier as to an adverse condition of the cargo must be prominent in order to rebut the 'apparent good order and condition' statement. In *The Skarp*,[61] timber was shipped. The master noted some adverse remarks as to the condition of the cargo loaded at the reverse of the bill. The English High Court held this to be insufficient to rebut the 'apparent good order and condition' statement at the front of the bill. In *Canadian and Dominion Sugar Co Ltd v Canadian National (West Indies) Steamship Ltd*,[62] the bill was stamped with a statement "signed under guarantee to

---

[57] *National Petroleum Co v Athelviscount (Owners) (The Athelviscount)* (1934) 48 Ll L Repl 164 (EW HC).

[58] *Marbig Rexel Pty Ltd and Another v ABC Container Line NV (The TNT Express)* [1912] 2 Lloyd's Rep 636 (NSW SC).

[59] (1886) 18 QBD 147 (EW CA).

[60] *The Skarp* [1935] P 134, [1935] All ER Rep 560 (EW HC).

[61] *The Skarp* [1935] P 134, [1935] All ER Rep 560 (EW HC).

[62] [1947] AC 46, [1947] LJR 385 (PC on appeal from Canada).

produce ship's clean receipt". The Privy Council held that this statement overruled and rendered ineffective the 'apparent good order and condition statement'.

6.7 Shipper's Indemnity

Article III(5) of the Hague and Hague-Visby Rules renders the shipper liable to the carrier for certain details furnished by the consignor, namely: marks, number, quantity and weight. Usually, the details furnished by the consignor will form the basis of the representations made by the carrier in the bill of lading. Article III(5) reads as follows:

> The shipper shall be deemed to have guaranteed to the carrier the accuracy at the time of shipment of the marks, number, quantity and weight, as furnished by him, and the shipper shall indemnify the carrier against all loss, damages and expenses arising or resulting from inaccuracies in such particulars. The right of the carrier to such indemnity shall in no way limit his responsibility and liability under the contract of carriage to any person other than the shipper.

However, Article III(5) is between the shipper and the carrier. It appears that it has no role in the case of a claim by a transferee of the bill against the carrier. It must be observed that the convention-indemnity is placed on the shipper and not the consigner who may be a different person from the shipper, e.g. in a pure fob contract.

Apart from the convention-indemnity, there is also a practice whereby a consignor will give an indemnity-undertaking to the carrier in order to induce the carrier to issue a clean bill. Such an indemnity will be invalid if that means a fraud on any transferee of the bill since a clean bill will be issued when the carrier knows that is not true. In *Brown Jenkinson & Co Ltd v Percy-Dalton (London) Ltd*,[63] the shipowner issued a clean bill upon the indemnity of the consignor, when the shipowner knew that it should have issued a claused bill. In an action by the shipowner against the consignor under the indemnity, the English Court of Appeal held the indemnity to be illegal for defrauding the transferees of the bill and hence void. Accordingly, the shipowner was not able to rely on the indemnity to claim against the consignor.

6.8 Other Actions for Misstatements in Bill of Lading

There are some representations in bills that do not fall within the scope of Article III(3) of the Hague and Hague-Visby Rules, Section 4 of the UK Carriage of Goods by Sea Act 1992 and the common law estoppel. For instance, the statement of the date of shipment in the bill will be such a representation that does not fall within any of those laws. If the carrier states the date wrongly, that will not be a breach of contract of carriage. In such cases, a cargo claimant may have an alternative action

[63] [1957] 2 QB 621, [1957] 2 All ER 844, [1957] 3 WLR 403, [1957] 2 Lloyd's Rep 1 (EW CA).

against the carrier in tort of deceit, tort of negligent misstatement or under the UK Misrepresentation Act 1967.[64] These alternative bases of actions are discussed in turn below.

6.8.1 Action for Tort of Deceit

If the carrier makes a statement incorrectly in the bill knowingly or recklessly, then the carrier may be liable in tort of deceit for any loss that occurs to the cargo interest as a result of the inaccurate statement. That happened in *The Saudi Crown.*[65] In this case, the cargo was shipped after the agreed date between the seller and the buyer. However, the master ante-dated the bill, so that it would appear that the shipment was made within the contractual period as between the seller and the buyer. The buyer paid for the bill not knowing the ante-dating. Had the bill been correctly dated, the buyer would have rejected the tender of the bill, by when the market value of the cargo had fallen. Hence, the buyer sued the shipowner in deceit for economic loss,[66] which the English High Court allowed.

In *Standard Chartered Bank v Pakistan National Shipping Corp (No 2),*[67] the letter of credit was issued by a Vietnamese bank upon the instruction of the buyer, requiring shipment by 25 October 1993. The letter of credit was confirmed by the Standard Chartered Bank (SCB) to the seller. The seller on 7 November 1993 tendered documents to SCB together with a bill of lading stating the goods were shipped by the stipulated date. There were some discrepancies in the documents, which the SCB overlooked. SCB paid. Thereafter, the Vietnamese bank rejected the documents and did not reimburse SCB on grounds of those discrepancies. Subsequently, it transpired that the goods were shipped only on 5 December 1993, meaning if the shipowner and the seller had acted honestly, there would have been no shipped bill of lading for tender on 7 November 1993 and there would have been no payment by SCB, irrespective of the discrepancies in the other documents. Then SCB sued the shipowner and the seller[68] in deceit. The English Court of Appeal allowed the claim.[69]

---

[64] Applicable to England and Wales.

[65] [1986] 1 Lloyd's Rep 261 (EW HC).

[66] Vicarious liability for the tortious action committed by the master.

[67] [2000] 1 All ER (Comm) 1, [2000] 1 Lloyd's Rep 218 (EW CA).

[68] And the seller's managing director who tendered the documents on behalf of the seller with knowledge of falsity.

[69] But the Court of Appeal disallowed the claim against the seller's managing director, as he tendered the documents merely on behalf of the seller. On further appeal by SCB to the House of Lords, the House reversed this and held the managing director too liable. The House of Lords also rejected a contention by the managing director that the bank was liable for contributory negligence in respect of the other discrepancies. The decision of the House of Lords is reported in [2002] UKHL 43, [2003] 1 AC 959, [2003] 1 All ER 173, [2002] 3 WLR 1547, [2002] 2 All ER (Comm) 931, [2003] 1 BCLC 244, [2003] 1 Lloyd's Rep 227, [2002] All ER (D) 67 (Nov) (UK HL).

Ante-dating of the shipment date in the bill posed a peculiar issue in *Procter & Gamble Philippine Manufacturing Corpn v Kurt A Becher GmbH & Co KG.*[70] In this case, the bill was ante-dated, but the shipment was actually made within the time frame allowed by the letter of credit. The buyer, upon subsequently discovering the misdating, sued the buyer. The English Court of Appeal found for the seller, granting no more than nominal damages to the buyer.

6.8.2 Action for Tort of Negligent Misstatement

Another potential alternative will be an action in tort of negligent misstatement. Negligent misstatement was recognised as a cause of action in *Hedley Byrne & Co Ltd v Heller & Partners Ltd.*[71] In this case, an advertising agency received a large order from a client on credit terms. Before providing the services, the agency sought to check the credit standing of the client. The agency requested its bankers to check with the client's bank. The client's bank wrote about the client like this: "considered good for its ordinary business engagements". However, the client's bank disclaimed all liability. The House of Lords found there was sufficient proximity between the client's bank and the agency so that the client's bank owed a duty of care to the agency. The House held that a person making a statement voluntarily assumes liability to the person to whom the statement is made when the maker knows or ought to know the statement will be relied on by the other to his detriment. Accordingly, the House recognised negligent misstatement as a cause of action in tort. However, it turned down the action on account of the disclaimer provision in the advice.

The same principle can be applied to the relationship between the carrier and the holder of the bill. However, this tort was limited subsequently by *Caparo Industries plc v Dickman.*[72] In this case, a shareholder relied on the audited accounts prepared by the company's auditors to buy more shares in the company. Subsequently, the shareholder found that the accounts were incorrect and were negligently prepared by the auditors. The shareholder sued the auditors under the *Hedley Byrne v Heller* principle. However, the House of Lords turned down this action, holding that the auditors did not owe a duty of care to the shareholder for purposes of investment. This was because the House found that the purpose of the report was merely to enable the shareholders to exercise their rights in a general meeting. Here, the shareholder acted as an investor rather than as a shareholder.

In the context of an action by a buyer against the carrier for a negligent statement of the shipment date, it appears that the stringent threshold laid down in *Caparo Industries* will be satisfied. This is because one of the purposes of the shipment date is to enable the buyer to accept or reject the bill according to the contract between the buyer and the seller.

---

70 [1988] 2 Lloyd's Rep 21 (EW CA).

71 [1964] AC 465, [1963] 2 All ER 575, [1963] 3 WLR 101, [1963] 1 Lloyd's Rep 485 (UK HL).

72 [1990] 2 AC 605, [1990] 1 All ER 568, [1990] 2 WLR 358, [1990] BCLC 273 (UK HL).

6.8.3 Action Under Section 2(1) of UK Misrepresentation Act 1967

This is another potential alternative cause of action. This section renders a person making a misrepresentation liable if the other party enters into a contract as a result of the misrepresentation and suffers a loss. Interestingly, under this section, once the plaintiff proves that the statement is a misrepresentation, the burden shifts to the person who made the statement to prove that he was not negligent. Once the threshold is met, the section also renders the person who made the statement liable as if it was made fraudulently. The Section 2(1) of the UK Misrepresentation Act 1967 reads as follows:

> Where a person has *entered into a contract after a misrepresentation* has been made to him by another party thereto and as a result thereof he has suffered loss, then, if the person making the misrepresentation would be liable to damages in respect thereof had the misrepresentation been made fraudulently, *that person shall be so liable notwithstanding that the misrepresentation* was not made fraudulently, *unless he proves that he had reasonable ground to believe and did believe up to the time* the contract was made the facts represented were true. [emphasis added]

The action under this section will be more straightforward for a cargo claimant than the common law action for negligent misstatement, which will be subject to the stringent proximity test laid down in *Caparo Industries*.

6.8.4 Tort or Misrepresentation Act Action Subject to Hague or Hague-Visby Limitations?

This is an interesting question. The actions in tort of deceit, tort of negligent misstatement or under the UK Misrepresentation Act 1967 are not contractual actions. The Hague Rules do not have any provision to extend the limitations therein to tort or other actions. However, there is a general common law principle that when there is a contract between the parties, a tort action[73] will be subject to the same limitations as in the contract between the parties.[74] It is likely that the actions in tort of negligent misstatement, though not one for tort of deceit, will be caught by this general common law principle.

The Hague-Visby Rules have a specific provision[75] to deal with the applicability of limitations under the Rules when a non-contractual action is brought. Article IV*bis*(1) reads as follows:

---

[73] Other than tort of deceit.

[74] See *Henderson v Merrett* [1995] 2 AC 145 (EW HL); *BSkyB Ltd v HP Enterprise Services UK Ltd* [2010] EWHC 86 (TCC), 129 ConLR 147, [2010] IP & T 597, [2010] IP & T 811, [2010] All ER (D) 192 (Jan) (UK HL); *Pyrene Co Ltd v Scindia Navigation Co Ltd* [1954] 2 QB 402, [1954] 2 All ER 158, [1954] 2 WLR 1005, [1954] 1 Lloyd's Rep 321 (EW HC).

[75] Article IV*bis*(1).

> The defences and limits of liability provided for in these Rules shall apply in any action against the carrier in respect of *loss or damage to goods* covered by a contract of carriage whether the action be founded in contract or in tort. [emphasis added]

Notably, the extension of limitation in the Article is in respect of loss or damage to goods. Literally, this will not cover when a misstatement is made as to the date of shipment resulting in an economic loss. Hence, the Article will not be of assistance in the case of legal bases of actions for misstatement discussed in this sub-chapter. However, even in the absence of application of this Article, the general common law principle that extends contractual limitation in tortious actions will apply and import the Hague-Visby limitations into the tortious action.

As far as an action under the UK Misrepresentation Act 1967 is concerned, any limitation in the Hague or Hague-Visby Rules will be extended to the action only if the limitation passes a test of reasonableness, by virtue of Section 3(1) of the Act. The burden to satisfy the test of reasonableness is on the carrier. The Section 3(1) reads as follows:

> If a contract contains a term which would exclude or restrict—
>
> (a) any liability to which a party to a contract may be subject by reason of any misrepresentation made by him before the contract was made; or
>
> (b) any remedy available to another party to the contract by reason of such a misrepresentation,
>
> that term shall be of no effect except in so far as it satisfies the requirement of reasonableness as stated in section 11(1) of the Unfair Contract Terms Act … and it is for those claiming that the term satisfies that requirement to show that it does.

6.8.5 Action Under Contract Act 1950 in Malaysia

There is no statute in Malaysia similar to the UK Misrepresentation Act. In Malaysia, relief for misrepresentation is provided for in the Contracts Act 1950 by Section 19, namely the aggrieved party is entitled to rescind or claim damages to be put in a position as if the misrepresentation was true, where he was influenced by the misrepresentation to enter into the contract. Section 18 defines 'misrepresentation'. The Sections 18 and 19, which are materially identical to the same numbered sections in the Indian Contract in the Indian Act 1872,[76] read as follows:

18. "Misrepresentation"

"Misrepresentation " includes—

(a) the positive assertion, in a manner not warranted by the information of the person making it, of that which is not true, though he believes it to be true;

(b) any breach of duty which, without an intent to deceive, gives an advantage to the person committing it, or anyone claiming under him, by misleading another to his prejudice, or to the prejudice of anyone claiming under him; and

---

[76] Without *Illustrations*.

(c) causing, however innocently, a party to an agreement to make a mistake as to the substance of the thing which is the subject of the agreement.

19. Voidability of Agreements Without Free Consent

(1) When consent to an agreement is caused by coercion, fraud, or misrepresentation, the agreement is a contract voidable at the option of the party whose consent was so caused.

(2) A party to a contract, whose consent was caused by fraud or misrepresentation, may, if he thinks fit, insist that the contract shall be performed, and that he shall be put in the position in which he would have been if the representations made had been true.

Exception—If such consent was caused by misrepresentation or by silence, fraudulent within the meaning of section 17, the contract, nevertheless, is not voidable, if the party whose consent was so caused had the means of discovering the truth with ordinary diligence.

Chapter 7
Implied Terms and Exclusion Clauses

This chapter deals with obligations imposed on the carrier by implied terms at common law and clauses in contracts of carriage intending to exclude them. The implied terms considered are: the obligation of the shipowner to provide a seaworthy and cargoworthy ship, the duty not to deviate, the duty not to carry the cargo on deck, and the duty to take reasonable care of the cargo. The relationship between seaworthiness and cargoworthiness is considered. The scope and standard of seaworthiness and the absoluteness of the seaworthiness-duty at common law are explained. The relationship between the Rules-obligations and the common law obligations, and their co-existence, are analysed. The doctrine of stages and its co-existence with the Rules-obligations is examined. The burden of proof and causation in relation to unseaworthiness are considered.

7.1 Introduction

At common law, certain obligations of the carrier have been implied in contracts of carriage of goods by sea, which includes bills of lading, sea waybills, ship's delivery orders and charterparties. The popular implied terms are as to seaworthiness and cargoworthiness of the ship, duty not to deviate, prohibition against carriage on deck, and obligation to take reasonable care of the cargo.

Some of them have been modified by the Hague or Hague-Rules. This does not undermine the significance of the common law implied terms for a few reasons. First, the Rules do not apply, unless contractually made to apply, in many cases such as in the case of a sea waybill, ship's delivery order, bill of lading in the hands of a charterer, carriage on deck[1] or of live animal.[2] In such cases, the modifications are not relevant. Second, in cases where the Rules apply, the common law is intact save

[1] Agreed to be carried on deck and is so carried; Article I(c).

[2] Article I(c).

A. Kasi, *The Law of Carriage of Goods by Sea*,
https://doi.org/10.1007/978-981-33-6793-7_7

for the modifications made by the Rules.[3] Third, the Rules, where they apply, are not exhaustive, hence the necessity for the common law implied terms.[4] Forth, where the Rules apply, they statutorily cover only from the beginning of the loading to the end of discharge.[5] Hence, the common law implied terms will be the relevant for events that take place outside the coverage-period of the Rules. Fifth, irrespective of whether the Rules apply to a given case, the common law implied terms are relevant to and have influenced the interpretation of the Rules.[6] For example, the Rules impose an obligation on the carrier as to seaworthiness of the ship but they do not define 'seaworthiness', hence the relevance of the wealth of common law jurisprudence on this point.

Unlike the obligations imposed by the Rules and statutorily implemented, the common law obligations are in the form of 'implied terms', hence may be avoided by well-drafted exclusion clauses. However, the court have countered such clauses with a restrictive interpretation.

This chapter analyses the common law implied terms and how the courts deal with the contractual measures attempting to exclude or limit liability for the implied terms, named above.

7.2 Common Law Implied Terms

At common law, the most important implied terms are the following:

(i) The ship will be seaworthy at the beginning of sailing—absolute warranty of seaworthiness.
(ii) The ship is cargoworthy during loading—absolute warranty of cargoworthiness.
(iii) The shipowner will not voluntarily deviate from the contracted voyage without lawful justification—the term with the most drastic consequences of breach.
(iv) The shipowner will not carry the cargo on deck—quasi-deviation.
(v) The shipowner will take reasonable care of the cargo.

The first one has been quite substantially modified by the Hague/Hague-Visby Rules[7] and statute.[8] The second one has been modified by the Rules. The third and fourth ones are not stated in the Rules. The fifth one is substantially repeated in the Rules.[9]

---

[3] Including in cases to which the Rules apply.

[4] Whether applicable statutorily or contractual incorporation.

[5] The period statutorily covered by the Rules is from the start of loading to end of discharge. However, contractually, usually, the period will be extended beyond the statutory period.

[6] *Maxine Footwear Co Ltd v Canadian Government Merchant Marine Ltd* [1959] AC 589, [1959] 2 Lloyd's Rep 105 (PC on appeal from Canada).

[7] Article III(1).

[8] UK Carriage of Goods by Sea Act 1972, Section 3.

[9] Article III(2).

The above list is not exhaustive. There are other implied terms such as about the duty not to voluntarily reduce speed,[10] the duty to prosecute the voyage with reasonable dispatch[11] which is largely relevant to charterparties rather than to bills of lading. There is no corresponding duty to this in the Rules. Arguably, Article III(2) duty to 'properly carry' may encompass a duty to proceed with reasonable dispatch one the voyage has commenced. However, this argument will not in practice be important as the duty is anyway imposed by the common law implied terms. In this sub-chapter, the implied terms listed above will be the subject of discussion, and before that, the relationship between the common law implied terms and the Rules and the relationship between the concepts of seaworthiness and cargoworthiness will be visited first.

7.2.1 *Relationship Between Common Law and the Rules*

The relationship between the common law and the Hague/Hague-Visby Rules must be rightly understood. First, the Rules, and the statutes giving effect to them, do not overrule the common law, save for declaring that there is no absolute warranty of seaworthiness of the ship in cases to which the Rules apply.

Second, the common law does not impose those duties as a matter of law but do find implied terms to those effects as a matter of fact. Thus, by very nature, the implied terms are subject to any clear modification or exclusion by unequivocal contractual provisions. The courts have been very restrictive about such contractual provisions because those implied terms are about core[12] duties of the shipowner in a contract for carriage of goods by sea.

Accordingly, the common law implied terms will be applicable in cases to which the Rules applies, except where (i) the implied term has been *directly modified* by the Rules or (ii) having the implied term will be *inconsistent* with the provisions made in the Rules. Subject to this, when the common law implied terms apply in cases to which the Rules apply, it must be borne in mind that the application will be subject to an overriding limitation, namely the statutory abolition of the warranty of an 'absolute warranty of seaworthiness'.

---

[10] Treated as deviation or quasi-deviation.

[11] See *Freeman v Taylor* (1831) 8 Bing 124, 131 ER 348, [1831] 11 WLUK 107 (EW Court of Common Pleas).

[12] Fundamental.

7.2.2 *Relationship Between Seaworthiness and Cargoworthiness*

'Seaworthiness' refers to the fitness of the ship to perform and complete the contracted voyage. 'Cargoworthiness' refers to the fitness of the ship to safely receive, carry and discharge the particular cargo contracted to be carried. At common law, the implied term is that the ship must be seaworthy at the time the ship starts sailing. For cargoworthiness, the relevant time is when the cargo is loaded. These two obligations have been treated in a similar way in many aspects, e.g. both are absolute duties at common law.

Legal texts have sometimes treated the word 'seaworthiness' as encompassing cargoworthiness. Classical definitions of 'seaworthiness' do not include cargoworthiness,[13] and the same is true in the case of the Hague and Hague-Visby Rules.[14] Arguably, by natural meaning, 'seaworthiness' is connected with the ship and the voyage and 'cargoworthiness' is connected with the ship and the cargo. Anyway, this is not a matter of substance but the choice of words only. In this work, the two words will be assigned their respective meanings and treated distinctly as much as practicable.

7.2.3 *Seaworthiness*

Seaworthiness will be analysed below in this sub-chapter by a visit to the basis of the implied term, the various definitions of 'seaworthiness', the 'standard' of seaworthiness required, what is meant by 'absolute warranty' of seaworthiness, the time during which the duty attaches, burden of proof associated with the concept of seaworthiness, the degree of causal link required between the unseaworthiness and the damage or loss in a sea carriage environment where always there will be some other causes joining hands with the unseaworthiness and the type of the implied term.[15]

7.2.3.1 Basis of the Implied Terms

The basis of implying the term as to seaworthiness was well said by Lord Ellenborough CJ in *Lyon v Mells*,[16] in the course of restrictively interpreting a general exclusion clause and holding that it did not cover the loss caused by unseaworthiness, as follows:

---

[13] Discussed in Sects. 7.2.2 and 7.2.4.

[14] See Article III(1)(a) and (c).

[15] Condition, warranty or innominate.

[16] (1804) 5 East 428 (EW HC).

> In every contract for carriage of goods between a person holding himself forth as the owner of a … vessel ready to carry goods for hire, and the person putting goods on board … his vessel … for that purpose, it is a term of the contract on the part of the carrier …, implied by law, that his vessel is right and fit for the purpose … for which he offers and holds it forth to the public; it is the very foundation and immediate substratum of the contract that it is so: the law presumes a promise to that effect on the part of the carrier without any actual proof; and every reason of sound policy and public convenience requires it should be so.

7.2.3.2 Definition

In the third quarter of the 19th century, Field J delivering the judgment of the three-member panel court in *Kopitoff v Wilson*[17] did *define* 'seaworthiness' of a ship as being:

> [F]it to meet and undergo the perils of sea and other incidental risks to which of necessity she must be exposed in the course of a voyage.

But that did not cover all aspects of seaworthiness but covered only the 'physical' aspect. By end of the 19th century, AL Smith LJ in *The Vortigern*[18] said this in wide terms of 'seaworthiness':

> [T]he ship shall be seaworthy for the voyage at the time of sailing, by which is meant that the vessel shall be in a fit state as to repairs, equipment, and crew, and in all other respects, sufficient to take her in ordinary circumstances to her port of destination, though there is no warranty that the ship shall continue seaworthy during the voyage.

It is not doubted that 'seaworthiness' covers physical fitness, legal fitness and crew-competency. Cresswell J in *The Eurasian Dream*[19] summarised the scope of matters covered by the 'seaworthiness' and 'cargoworthiness' obligations as follows:

The components of the duty (as illustrated by the case law) are as follows:

(1) The vessel must be in a suitable condition and suitably manned and equipped to meet the ordinary perils likely to be encountered while performing the services required of it. This aspect of the duty relates to the following matters.

  (a) The physical condition of the vessel and its equipment.
  (b) The competence/efficiency of the master and crew.
  (c) The adequacy of stores and documentation.

(2) The vessel must be cargoworthy in the sense that it is in a fit state to receive the specified cargo.

The Hague/Hague-Visby Rules do not provide any definition of seaworthiness and cargoworthiness. Thus, the common law definition will be relevant to cases under the Rules.

---

[17] [1874–80] All ER Rep 609, (1876) 1 QBD 377, 45 LJQB 436 (EW HC).

[18] *The Vortigern* [1899] P 140 (EW CA).

[19] *Papera Traders Co Ltd v Hyundai Merchant Marine Co Ltd (The Eurasian Dream) (No. 1)* [2002] EWHC 118 at [128], [2002] 1 Lloyd's Rep 719, QBD (Comm) (EW HC).

Legal Fitness

In *Ciampa and Others v British India Steam Navigation Co Ltd,*[20] the ship did not have a 'clean bill of health' certificate. This was legally required because she had called at Mombasa during the outbreak of plague. This was a reason, among others, for the English High Court to find that the ship was unseaworthy. In *The Derby,*[21] the English Court of Appeal held that not having the blue card required by the International Transport Workers' Federation (ITF) did not render the ship unseaworthy, as this was not a legal requirement. In The *CMA CGM Libra, Alize 1954 and another v Allianz Elementar Versicherungs AG and others (The GMA CGM Libra)* [2020] EWCA Civ 293, [2020] Bus LR 1590 (EW CA) [appeal to Supreme Court outstanding]. the passage plan was defective in that did not sufficient note that the approaches to the port had depths less than those in the chart. As a result, the vessel grounded on an uncharted shoal as she was leaving the port. The Court of Appeal held that the defective passage plans rendered the ship unseaworthy. This was as a case under the Hague Rules, where the court held that there was a breach of the Article III(1) obligation by reason of the defective plan and that *Northern Shipping Co v Deutsche Seereederei GmbH and Others (The Kapitan Sakharov)* [2000] 2 Lloyd's Rep 255 (EW CA) did not support, when there was a breach of Article III(1), the proposition that loss caused by navigational faults was outside the responsibility of the shipowners.

Crew-Competency

If the crew is *negligent*, then that is not related to the question of seaworthiness of the ship. If the crew is *incompetent*, then that may amount to unseaworthiness.

The significance of the difference is that the liability for negligence is quite largely excluded by the Hague or Hague-Visby Rules. Where the Rules do not apply, the liability for negligence can ordinarily be excluded by contractual provisions. However, when it is about *seaworthiness*, the liability cannot be so easily excluded. Under the Rules, the liability in respect of unseaworthiness can be excluded only if it was not caused by want of due diligence on the part of the carrier.[22] Under the common law, the 'seaworthiness' obligation is a fundamental one the liability for which can only be excluded by specific exclusion clauses.[23]

The difference between negligence and incompetence can be a fine one. Some cases are visited below that will offer some light in understanding the difference. A comparison will be made between the positions under the common law and the Rules, where appropriate.

---

[20] [1915] 2 KB 774 (EW HC).

[21] *Alfred C Toepfer Schiffahrtsgesellschaft Gmbh v Tossa Marine Co Ltd; Tossa Marine Co Ltd v Alfred C Toepfer Schiffahrtsgesellschaft Gmbh (The Derby)* [1985] 2 Lloyd's Rep 325 (EW CA).

[22] Article IV(1).

[23] *Phillips Petroleum Co v Cabaneli Naviera SA (The Theodegmon)* [1990] 1 Lloyd's Rep 52 (EW HC).

In *Hong Kong Fir Shipping Co Ltd v Kawasaki Kisen Kaisha Ltd*,[24] the ship's engines and machinery were old and required experienced engine room staff to maintain. This did not, by itself, render the ship unseaworthy. However, the engine room staff was incompetent to manage the old engines and machinery.[25] The English Court of Appeal held that the incompetence of the engine room staff rendered the ship unseaworthy.

In *Standard Oil Co of New York v Clan Line Steamers Ltd*,[26] the lack of knowledge of the master in handling the ballast, resulting from the failure of the shipowner to forward the shipbuilder's manual on ballast to the master, was held to constitute unseaworthiness. Quite similarly, in *The Star Sea*,[27] the master was not familiar with the fire-fighting system in the ship, which the English High Court held to amount to unseaworthiness, in the context of liability of the insurer to the shipowner.[28]

In *International Packers London Ltd v Ocean Steam Ship Co Ltd*,[29] a ship commenced voyage with tarpaulins over hatch covers but without the tarpaulin locking bars being fastened. The tarpaulins were there to prevent water from entering the hatch covers. After the ship started sailing, a storm threw away the tarpaulins, as the locking bars were not fastened. The reason the crew did not fasten the locking bars was that it was not expected, at the start of sailing, any such storm would come. Though the crew might have been negligent in not fastening the locking bars, the English High Court held that this did not go to the incompetence of the crew. However, had the crew not known that locking bars were there or how to fasten them, then that would have gone to the incompetence of the crew, hence unseaworthiness, if that was the reason for not fastening them.

The dividing line between crew negligence and incompetence will become thinner when the crew negligence was the result of the failure of the shipowner to train the crew and put a proper operating *system* in place. This can be something relative to the state of law and technology at the relevant time. What would be considered to be 'negligence' at one time may later be considered as 'incompetence'. For instance, the ISM[30] Code was introduced into SOLAS[31] in 1993 and came into force as law

---

[24] [1962] 2 QB 26, [1962] 1 All ER 474, [1962] 2 WLR 474, [1961] 2 Lloyd's Rep 478 (EW CA).

[25] Added to this, the chief engineer was addicted to drink.

[26] [1924] AC 100, [1923] All ER Rep 73 (UK HL).

[27] *Manifest Shipping & Co Ltd v Uni-Polaris Insurance Co Ltd and La Reunion Europeene (The Star Sea)* [1995] 1 Lloyd's Rep 651 (EW HC).

[28] Under Section 39(5) of the UK Marine Insurance Act 1906, which relieves the insurer of liability 'where, with the privity of the assured, the ship is sent to sea in an unseaworthy state'. The Singapore Marine Insurance Act is materially identical to the UK 1906 Act with the same section numbering. There is no such Act in Malaysia, but there is a general Insurance Act 1996.

[29] [1955] 2 Lloyd's Rep 218 (EW HC).

[30] 'International Safety Management' Code.

[31] The International Convention on Safety of Life at Sea of 1974.

in the UK in 2002 insofar as cargo ships were concerned.[32] The code is also in force in Singapore[33] and Malaysia[34] This code, in essence:

(i) sets a standard of safety management objective;
(ii) requires shipowners to have in place a safety management system (SMS) and policy to achieve the said safety management objective;
(iii) requires shipowners to have a safety management manual on board, comprising the SMS.

If the shipowner fails to comply with the ISM Code, hence the crew is not familiar with the safety management objectives, that will render the crew incompetent, hence ship unseaworthy. The ISM Code is likely to dilute and make less available the defence in Article IV(2)(a) of the Hague/Hague-Visby Rules by rendering the ship unseaworthy[35] for what would otherwise be negligence excepted under Article IV(2)(a). Article IV(2)(a) reads as follows:

2. Neither the carrier nor the ship shall be responsible for loss or damage arising or resulting from:

> (a) Act, *neglect, or default* of the master, mariner, pilot, or the servants of the carrier in the *navigation or in the management* of the ship. [emphasis added]

Similarly, the ISM Code may have an impact on a few other exceptions in Article IV(2), namely, (b), (p) and (q), all of which are defences available to the carrier if the carrier is not, in effect, negligent. The said Article IV(2)(b), (p) and (q) respectively provide as follows:

> (b) Fire, unless caused by the actual fault or privity of the carrier.
> (p) Latent defects not discoverable by due diligence.
> (q) Any other cause arising *without the actual fault or privity of the carrier, or without the fault or neglect of the agents or servants of the carrier*, but the burden of proof shall be on the person claiming the benefit of this exception to show that neither the actual fault or privity of the carrier nor the fault or neglect of the agents or servants of the carrier contributed to the loss or damage. [emphasis added]

In *The Eurasian Dream*,[36] cars were loaded into a car-carrying vessel by stevedores. The stevedores were simultaneously refuelling and jump-starting the cars. This resulted in a fire and consequent damage to the cars. the English High Court

---

[32] On 1st July 2002 insofar as cargo ships were concerned. Insofar as passenger ships were concerned, it was brought into force on 1st July 1998. This was done by the UK Merchant Shipping (International Safety Management Code) Regulations 1998, supplemented by 2014 Regulations.

[33] By Merchant Shipping (Safety Convention) Regulations.

[34] By Merchant Shipping Ordinance 1952 through an amendment made by the Merchant Shipping (Amendment) Act 1991, that renders the Convention applicable with any amendments made thereto.

[35] Falling foul of Article III(1).

[36] *Papera Traders Co Ltd v Hyundai Merchant Marine Co Ltd (The Eurasian Dream) (No.1)* [2002] EWHC 118, [2002] 1 Lloyd's Rep 719, QBD (Comm) (EW HC).

found this to be a dangerous practice. The officers of the carrier should have supervised and avoided such practice, which they failed. The court found this to be the incompetence of the crew, hence the ship held unseaworthy.

In this case, the dangerous practice was supplemented by lack of *training* for the crew to fight a fire and lack of *equipment* like walkie-talkies for effective communication during times of emergency and lack of *system or procedure* in place to deal with emergencies. All these factors will point to the unseaworthiness of the ship.

7.2.3.3 Standard

Channel J in *McFadden & Co v Blue Star Line*[37] endorsed the *standard* of seaworthiness as stated in Carver on Carriage by Sea,[38] which was as follows:

> [T]hat degree of fitness which an ordinary careful and prudent owner would require his vessel to have at the commencement of her voyage having regard to all the probable circumstances of it.

The above statement has been repeated with approval numerous times over a century by the courts, including the House of Lords.[39] The above definition goes to the *standard* of seaworthiness, which is a *relative* one, i.e. relative to the industry standard at the relevant time. This was expressed in the same case as follows:

> Seaworthiness develops over time to reflect evolving knowledge and standards of ship construction… [and]… varies according to the voyage to be undertaken.

The Hague/Hague-Visby Rules do not provide any standard to test seaworthiness and cargoworthiness. Thus, the common law standard will be applicable to cases under the Rules.

A few cases decided under the common law will not be visited and a comparison will be made with the position under the Rules, where appropriate. In *Kopitoff v Wilson*,[40] the shipowner received three armour plates for shipment, each weighing about 18 tonnes. The shipowner stowed them on top of a cargo of railway iron and secured them with wooden shores. The wooden shores could not hold them in the heavy weather encountered during the voyage. One of the plates moved from its place and pierced the cargo holds, resulting in loss of the cargo and the ship. Although the ship by itself was seaworthy, the English High Court held that the bad stowage of cargo rendered the ship unseaworthy. Even if the shipper had undertaken stowage, such as under a 'free-in' contract, the decision would likely have been the same. This is because, under such a contract, the responsibility of the shipper would merely be

[37] [1905] 1 KB 697 (EW HC).

[38] The last edition of which is Carver, '*Carriage by Sea*', 13th edn., UK, Stevens & Sons, 1982.

[39] *FC Bradley & Sons Ltd v Federal Steam Navigation Co Ltd* (1927) 27 Ll L Rep 395 (UK HL); *Papera Traders Co Ltd v Hyundai Merchant Marine Co Ltd (The Eurasian Dream) (No. 1)* [2002] EWHC 118, [2002] 1 Lloyd's Rep 719, QBD (Comm) (EW HC).

[40] [1874–80] All ER Rep 609, (1876) 1 QBD 377, 45 LJQB 436 (EW HC).

to stow the cargo and hence the duty to ensure seaworthiness of the ship would still be on the carrier.

The above case was one of pre-Hague Rules era. Under the Hague/Hague-Visby Rules, the obligation for stowage is on the carrier[41] and liability in respect of that cannot be *excluded*.[42] However, this does not prevent the parties from allocating responsibilities concerning loading or stowage. The House of Lords in *The Jordan II*[43] held the rule does not prevent 'free-in' contracts where the shipper had undertaken the responsibility for stowage and confirmed that such contracts do not fall foul of Article III(8)[44] that renders any contractual exclusion or limitation of the carrier's liability under the Rules to be null and void. The decision of the House is in line with commercial reality. It must be observed that such a contractual allocation of responsibility is not an exclusion or limitation of liability. However, the question of whether a particular clause is an exclusion or responsibility-allocation clause must be answered in the factual matrix of the case. If a liner bill of lading, of which an essential characteristic is that the carrier must arrange and pay for the stevedoring, attempts to pass the responsibility for loading or unloading onto the cargo interest, that must fall foul of Article III(8).[45] This is because the intention of the clause in such a bill is rather for the shipowner to wash its hands of the liability for any damage caused by stevedores during the loading or unloading rather than to allocate the responsibility for it.

If *Kopitoff v Wilson* were to be decided under the Rules,[46] the result would likely be the same. Under the Rules, the carrier will be relieved of liability for failing to provide a seaworthy ship only if the carrier can prove that it had exercised all due diligence to provide a ship that is seaworthy before and at the start of the voyage.[47] Due diligence would include the responsibility on the shipowner to monitor the stowage and to check that it has been done satisfactorily and that it is safe for the ship to sail with that.

---

[41] Article III(2).

[42] Article III(8).

[43] *Jindal Iron and Steel Co Ltd v Islamic Solidarity Shipping Co Jordan Inc (The Jordan II)* [2004] UKHL 49, [2005] 1 All ER 175, [2005] 1 WLR 1363, [2005] 1 All ER (Comm) 1, [2005] 1 Lloyd's Rep 57, [2004] All ER (D) 388 (Nov) (UK HL).

[44] Article III(8): "Any clause, covenant, or agreement in a contract of carriage relieving the carrier or the ship from liability for loss or damage to, or in connection with, goods arising from negligence, fault, or failure in the duties and obligations provided in this article or lessening such liability otherwise than as provided in these Rules, shall be null and void and of no effect. A benefit of insurance in favour of the carrier or similar clause shall be deemed to be a clause relieving the carrier from liability."

[45] In practice, usually, a stevedoring company will do the loading and unloading. The servants of stevedoring companies are treated as the servants of the carrier, so that the carrier will be vicariously liable for their negligence in the loading and unloading operation: *RF Brown & Co Ltd v T & J Harrison* (1927) 43 TLR 633.

[46] Article III(1).

[47] Article IV(1).

In *Sunlight Mercantile Pte Ltd and Another v Ever Lucky Shipping Co Ltd*,[48] decided by the Singapore Court of Appeal, cargoes of logs were carried by a shipowner on deck, under a few bills of lading. The agreement was to carry them on deck. Hence, the Hague-Visby Rules did not apply, and the carriage was subject to common law. The bills of lading provided that the cargoes were carried on deck 'at [s]hipper's risk; the [c]arrier not being responsible for loss or damage howsoever arising [or howsoever caused]'.

The ship was unseaworthy at the outset of the voyage and broke-down during the voyage. She was towed to the discharge port. The shipowner claimed general average contribution from the cargo owners, in respect of the towage costs, and sued the cargo owners for this. Under the York Antwerp Rules,[49] if the general average arose due to an 'actionable fault' of the shipowner, then the shipowner will not be entitled to general average contribution. In this case, whether the shipowner committed an actionable fault was dependent on two things. One, the seaworthiness of the ship. Another, the exclusion clause.

At common law, the shipowner's obligation to provide a seaworthy ship at the beginning of the sailing is an absolute one, that can only be excluded by specific reference and not by any general exclusion clause.[50] It was the finding of the trial court that the ship was unseaworthy at the outset of the voyage. As the exclusion clause here was not one specifically referring to the seaworthiness-obligation, the court held that it did not relieve the owner from the liability. Hence, there was an actionable fault on the part of the shipowner and the court disallowed the general average claim of the shipowner. In arriving at this conclusion, the court criticised *The Imvros*,[51] which held that a general exclusion clause exempted the shipowner from liability for seaworthiness, as being out of line with the precedents and refused to follow it.

In the case of piracy, it may attract the liability for unseaworthiness, if it happened because the ship did not have suitable security features such as ShipLoc,[52] when many thousand ships, relatively, had already installed this. The same can be true when the crew is not reasonably trained in anti-piracy measures.

---

[48] [2003] SGCA 47, [2004] 1 SLR 171 (SG CA).

[49] Rule D of the York Antwerp Rules, as interpreted by *Goulandris Brothers Ltd v B Goldman & Sons Ltd* [1957] 3 WLR 596, [1957] 3 All ER 100, [1957] 2 Lloyd's Rep 207, [1958] 1 QB 74 (EW HC). These rules are normally voluntarily incorporated into bills of lading, as seemingly was so in this case. The Rule D, in the latest 2016 version of the Rules was materially the same in its predecessors 2004 and 1994 versions.

[50] The subject of exclusion clauses in respect of the common law implied terms, including seaworthiness objection, is dealt with in more detail later in this chapter.

[51] *Transocean Liners Reederei GmbH v Euxine Shipping Co Ltd (The Imvros)* [1999] 1 All ER (Comm) 724, [1999] 1 Lloyd's Rep 848, [1999] All ER (D) 237 (EW HC).

[52] Produced by the International Maritime Bureau in collaboration with Collecte Localisation Satellites ('CLS'). ShipLoc is designed to locate vessels at sea or in port.

7.2.3.4 Absoluteness of Duty

The duty, at common law, is an *absolute* one, as said in *Steel v State Line Steamship Co.*[53] It is said to be a 'warranty' of seaworthiness. This means it is no *defence* for the shipowner to say that he did not know of the defect or that even due diligence would not have revealed the defect or that a prudent owner would not have discovered it i.e. latent defect or that he was not negligent about it.[54]

Common examples of unseaworthiness per se include leaky hull,[55] leaking hatch covers,[56] leaking sea valve,[57] porthole not fit to be closed during the voyage,[58] defectively weld crankshaft,[59] faulty propellers,[60] carrying insufficient or unsuitable spare parts,[61] slug in lubrication oil,[62] insufficient or contaminated fuel,[63] contaminated cargo holds or tanks,[64] insufficient chats and navigation aids.[65]

Section 2 of the UK Carriage of Goods by Sea Act 1924 abolished the absolute warranty of seaworthiness, insofar as bills of lading are concerned. There are two things that must be observed here. First, it abolished the 'absoluteness' of the duty but did not provide the definition and standard of 'seaworthiness'. Second, it does not seem to encompass cargoworthiness. The Section 2 read as follows:

> There shall not be implied in any contract for the carriage of goods by sea to which the Rules apply by virtue of this Act any absolute undertaking by the carrier of the goods to provide a seaworthy ship.

The same provision has been repeated in the Section 3 of the UK Carriage of Goods by Sea Act 1971 that repealed and replaced the 1924 Act. Whilst the absolute warranty in the case of bills of lading has been abolished in cases to which the Hague/Hague-Visby Rules statutorily apply, the Rules provide the corresponding

---

53 (1877) 3 App Cas 72.

54 See *McFadden & Co v Blue Star Line* [1905] 1 KB 697 (EW HC).

55 *Lyon v Mells* (1804) 5 East 428 (EW HC).

56 *Itoh & Co Ltd v Atlantska Plovidba (The Gundulic)* [1981] 2 Lloyd's Rep 418 (EW HC).

57 *McFadden & Co v Blue Star Line* [1905] 1 KB 697 (EW HC).

58 *Steel v State Line Steamship Co* (1877) 3 App Cas 72, 3 Asp MLC 516 (UK HL).

59 *The Glenfruin* (1885) 10 PD 103 (EW HC).

60 *Snia Societa di Navigazione Industria e Commercio v Suzuki & Co* (1924) 29 Com Cas 284, (1924) 18 Ll L Rep 333 (EW CA).

61 *The Pride of Donegal* [2002] EWHC 24, [2002] 1 Lloyd's Rep 659 (EW HC); *Guinomar of Conakry and Another v Samsung Fire & Marine Insurance Co Ltd (The Kamsar Voyager)* [2002] 2 Lloyd's Rep 57 (EW HC).

62 *Fyffes Group Ltd. And Caribbean Gold Ltd v Reefer Express Lines Pty Ltd and Reefkrit Shipping Inc (The Kriti Rex)* [1996] 2 Lloyd's Rep 171 (EW HC).

63 *The Vortigern* [1899] P 140 (EW CA); *Owners of cargo lately laden on board ship or vessel Makedonia v Makedonia (Owners) (The Makedonia)* [1962] P 190, [1962] 2 All ER 614, [1962] 3 WLR 343, [1962] 1 Lloyd's Rep 316 (EW HC).

64 *Vinmar International Ltd v Theresa Navigation SA (The Atrice)* [2001] 2 All ER (Comm) 243, [2001] 2 Lloyd's Rep 1, [2001] All ER (D) 107 (Mar) (EW HC).

65 *Rey Banano Del Pacifico CA and Others v Transportes Navieros Ecuatorianos and Another (The Isla Fernandina)* [2000] 2 Lloyd's Rep 15 (EW HC).

obligation, with significant modification by replacing the *absolute* duty at the start of every *sailing* with a duty to exercise *due diligence* at the start of *the voyage*, in Article III(1), which reads as follows:

1. The carrier shall be bound before and at the beginning of the voyage to exercise due diligence to:

(a) Make the ship seaworthy;
(b) Properly man, equip and supply the ship;
(c) Make the holds, refrigerating and cool chambers, and all other parts of the ship in which goods are carried, fit and safe for their reception, carriage and preservation.

Article IV(1) qualifies Article III(1) as follows:

> 1. Neither the carrier nor the ship shall be liable for loss or damage arising or resulting from unseaworthiness unless caused by want of due diligence on the part of the carrier to make the ship seaworthy, and to secure that the ship is properly manned, equipped and supplied, and to make the holds, refrigerating and cool chambers and all other parts of the ship in which goods are carried fit and safe for their reception, carriage and preservation in accordance with the provisions of paragraph 1 of Article III. Whenever loss or damage has resulted from unseaworthiness the burden of proving the exercise of due diligence shall be on the carrier or other person claiming exemption under this article.

Although Article IV(1) seems to qualify Article III(1), in fact, the former merely adds that the burden of proving the due diligence mentioned in Article III(1) is on the carrier.

7.2.3.5 Time at Which Duty Attaches: Doctrine of Stages

At common law, the seaworthiness/cargoworthiness obligations recur in stages.[66] The first stage is during loading, as regards cargoworthiness.[67] Next, when the ship starts sailing from the port of loading, as regards seaworthiness.[68] After this, the seaworthiness-obligation recurs every time the ship starts sailing again from any intermediate port, for example, after re-bunkering en route. This is called the 'doctrine of stages'. There is a gap period between the completion of loading and start of sailing, for which period the duty does not attach, at common law. The gap period is called the 'lying stage'.

At the loading stage, the ship need not be seaworthy to sail, but she must be fit to safely receive the cargo. This is because there may be something that needs to be done before the ship sets sail. At the first sailing stage, she must be fit to sail to the destination port or the next scheduled port such as an intermediate port en route for bunkering. At the stage of re-sailing from the intermediate port, she must similarly

66 *The Vortigern* [1899] P 140 (EW CA).

67 *McFadden & Co v Blue Star Line* [1905] 1 KB 697 (EW HC).

68 *Cohn v Davidson* (1877) 2 QBD 455, 46 LJQB 305 (EW HC)—a voyage charterparty case.

be fit to reach the destination or next scheduled port. It can be seen that the essence of the obligation, insofar as it relates to sailings, is that a shipowner must not set sail unless the ship is fit to complete the part of the voyage for which she is scheduled at that stage.

Lord Wensleydale in *Biccard v Shepherd*,[69] delivering the judgment of the Privy Council, noted the different standards the obligation at different stages as follows:

> [If] the voyage, be such as to require a different complement of men, or state of equipment, in different parts of it, as, if it were a voyage down a canal or river, and thence across to the open sea, it would be enough if the vessel were at the commencement of each stage of the navigation properly manned and equipped for it.

The above passage was referred to with approval by Wiles J in *Bouillon v Lupton*,[70] where his Lordship well noted the different 'degrees' of seaworthiness at different stages and said:

> [The] warranty of seaworthiness must have a different meaning as applied to the two different portions of the voyage.

In *The Vortigen*,[71] the ship was on a voyage from Cebu to Liverpool. En route, she was to call at Colombo port and then at Suez port for coaling. At Colombo, she did not take sufficient coal to reach Suez. The Court of Appeal held that the ship was not seaworthy at the stage of the commencement of sailing from Colombo due to insufficient coal. The same was the case in *Northumbrian Shipping Company Limited v Timm And Son Limited*,[72] where the ship left the loading port without sufficient bunkers to reach her next port to call.

The same principle as to the stages was repeated by Channel J in *McFadden & Co v Blue Star Line*[73] in the following words:

> There is, of course, no warranty at the time the goods are put on board that the ship is then ready to start on her voyage; for while she is still loading there may be many things requiring to be done before she is ready to sail. … When a voyage is in stages the warranty is that the ship on starting on each particular stage is fit for that stage. Thus, if she is going to stop at an intermediate port, she must have sufficient coals to take her to that port, but she is not bound to have sufficient coals to take her the whole voyage.

In this case, the ship arrived at the loading place on 11 November. The loading was commenced on 12 November and completed in the morning of 24 November. The cargo claim arose in respect of a cargo of cotton that were loaded on 12 and 13 November and subsequently damaged by sea water ingress into the cargo holds in

---

[69] (1861) 14 Moo PCC 471, 1 Mar LC 165, 10 WR 136, 15 ER 383, 5 LT 504 (PC).

[70] (1863) 15 CBNS 113, 33 LJPC 37, 10 Jur NS 422, 1 Mar LC 347, 2 New Rep 393, 11 WR 966, 143 ER 726, 8 LT 575 (EW HC).

[71] [1895–99] All ER Rep 387, 68 LJP 49, [1899] P 14080 LT 382, 47 WR 437, 15 TLR 259, 43 Sol Jo 330, 8 Asp MLC 523, 4 Com Cas 152 (EW CA).

[72] [1939] AC 397, [1939] 2 All ER 648, 108 LJKB 503, 19 Asp MLC 290, 44 Com Cas 278, 83 Sol Jo 563, 160 LT 573, 55 TLR 770 (UK HL).

[73] [1905] 1 KB 697, 74 LJKB 423, 10 Asp MLC 55, 10 Com Cas 123, 53 WR 576, 93 LT 52, 21 TLR 345 (EW HC).

the night of 23 November. The reasons for the water ingress were that an insufficient joint of a valve-chest which was remade shortly before the cargo in question was loaded, insufficient closure of seacock 23 November after it was opened on the same day, insufficient closure of sluice-door on 23 November. The court held that the relevant period for which the obligation seaworthiness in respect of the loading stage attaches is between 12 and 13 November when the cargo in question was loaded. Hence, the failure to properly close the seacock and the sluice-door would not be taken into account. But the ship was unseaworthy during the relevant period because of the insufficiency of the valve-chest joint.

Under the Hague/Hague-Visby Rules, the duty to exercise due diligence for both seaworthiness and cargoworthiness is before and at the start of the voyage. This in effect covers the period from the start of the loading to the start of the voyage in common to both seaworthiness and cargoworthiness obligations. Hence, no gap period during the lying stage, under the Rules.

Coming to seaworthiness, the obligation at common law is at the time the ship starts sailing, meaning every sailing. Under the Rules, it is at the time of the start of the voyage, meaning the first sailing. The Rules do not interfere with or modify the common law obligation insofar as *subsequent* sailing are concerned and they go only up to the commencement of the voyage. There is nothing in the Rules to displace the implied term (reflecting the commercial intention of the parties) that the ship will be seaworthy at any subsequent sailing such as where the ship starts sailing again from any intermediate port. Of course, there can be no absolute warranty as to seaworthiness at the time of the start of the subsequent sailing, as the same has been completely statutorily removed in cases to which the Rules apply. Some legal texts have expressed the contrary view on the question of applicability of doctrine of stages under Hague/Hagu-Visby Rules. Such a view would be supported by *The Makedonia.*[74] This subject is considered in detail later.[75]

7.2.3.6 Burden of Proof

The burden of proving the unseaworthiness is on the cargo claimant as the person alleging it. However, unseaworthiness may readily be inferred by the court. In such cases, the evidentiary burden will be on the carrier to prove otherwise.

For instance, if a ship sinks on her voyage in normal or expected weather, a court may infer that the ship was unseaworthy at the start of the voyage. This happened in *The Torenia*[76] and the inference was that the ship was unseaworthy at the start of the

---

[74] *Owners of cargo lately laden on board ship or vessel Makedonia v Makedonia (Owners) (The Makedonia)* [1962] P 190, [1962] 2 All ER 614, [1962] 3 WLR 343, [1962] 1 Lloyd's Rep 316 (EW HC).

[75] See Chap. 9.2.1.

[76] *Aktieselskabet de Danske Sukkerfabrikker v Bajamar Compania Naviera SA (The Torenia)* [1983] 2 Lloyd's Rep 210 (EW HC).

voyage. In this case, Hobhouse J well observed the following as to the evidentiary burden and inferences that a court will nowadays make concerning seaworthiness:

> Whereas in the days of wooden ships or in the days when the design of steel ships and their construction was less well advanced or the forces they were liable to encounter were less well known and understood there may have been many instances where unexplained losses at sea gave rise to no inference of unseaworthiness, it will not be rare for such an inference not to arise in the absence of some overwhelming force of the sea or some occurrence affecting the vessel from outside. In the present case the shipowners, whilst proving the loss of the cargo, have proved also the loss of the vessel in conditions which ought not to have led to the loss of a seaworthy ship. Similarly in proving that the incursion of seawater was fortuitous they have proved that the structure of the vessel was defective …

Similarly, in *The Theodegmon*[77] it was inferred that the ship was unseaworthy at the start of the voyage when the ship's steering gearbox failed soon after she started to sail. In *Fiumana Società di Navigazione v Bunge & Co Ltd,*[78] the English High Court inferred unseaworthiness when four different bunker spaces caught fire. This would not ordinarily happen unless there was something wrong in the bunker that the ship took before the start of the voyage. However, such an inference might not have been drawn if the fire caught was only in one of such spaces.

7.2.3.7 Causation

It is a basic principle of the laws of contract and tort that a claimant will be entitled to damages only if the impugned event caused the loss. The same principle applies in the case of a claim against a carrier for breach of the implied term as to seaworthiness of the ship.[79] However, this is a complex question in shipping cases because unseaworthiness would likely have joined with other causes in causing the loss or damage.[80] It has been held that it is sufficient if the unseaworthiness is 'a' cause of the loss or damage, hence there may be other causes. In *Smith, Hogg v Black Sea and Baltic General Insurance,*[81] Lord Wright[82] explained this as follows:

> In truth, unseaworthiness … can never be the sole cause … At least I have not thought of a case where it can be the sole cause. It must, I think, always be one of several co-operating causes. In this connection, I can draw no distinction between cases where the negligence

---

[77] *Phillips Petroleum Co v Cabaneli Naviera SA (The Theodegmon)* [1990] 1 Lloyd's Rep 52 (EW HC).

[78] [1930] 2 KB 47 (EW HC).

[79] *Kish v Taylor* [1912] AC 604, [1911] 1 KB 625 (EW CA).

[80] *Smith, Hogg v Black Sea and Baltic General Insurance* [1940] AC 997 (UK HL).

[81] [1940] AC 997 (UK HL).

[82] With whom Lord Atkin was in agreement. However, Lord Porter and Lord Romer did not suggest that it was sufficient for unseaworthiness to be 'a' cause. They agreed with the conclusion that the shipowner was liable but that seems to be because they considered the unseaworthiness was the cause of the loss or damage. In a later case, *Papera Traders Co Ltd v Hyundai Merchant Marine Co Ltd (The Eurasian Dream) (No. 1)* [2002] EWHC 118, [2002] 1 Lloyd's Rep 719, QBD (Comm) (EW HC), the court followed the position taken by Lord Wright and Atkin.

> conduct of the master is a cause and cases in which any other cause, such as perils of the seas, or fire, is a co-operating cause. A negligent act is as much a co-operating cause, if it is a cause at all, as an act which is not negligence. *The question is the same in either case, it is, would the disaster not have happened in the ship had fulfilled the obligation of seaworthiness.*
>
> The sole question ... '*Was that breach of contract "a" cause of the damage.*' It may be preferred to describe it as an effective or real or actual cause though the adjectives in my opinion in fact add nothing. If the question is answered in the affirmative, the shipowner is liable though there were other co-operating causes ... as perils of the seas, fire, ... human action ... whether negligent or a combination of both kind ...
>
> In cases of the type ... the negligence, if any, must almost inevitably occur in the course of the voyage ... I doubt whether there could be any event which could supersede or override the effectiveness of the unseaworthiness if it was 'a' cause. [emphasis added]

The approach of Lord Wright has gained recognition as shown by the cases visited below. In *McFadden & Co v Blue Star Line,*[83] there were three factors that rendered the ship unseaworthy and caused the damage. First, the failure of the crew to close the seacock properly. Secondly, the defect in the valve chest. Thirdly, open sluice door. When the first and the third causes took place and rendered the ship uncargoworthy, the ship was in lying stage, hence no obligation for cargoworthiness was attached. However, the second cause was present during the loading of the cargo. This was sufficient for the English High Court to hold the shipowner liable for breach of seaworthiness obligation and to compensate the cargo interest for the damage the cargo, although this was only one of the three causes of the loss.

In *The Christel Vinnen,*[84] the ship carried a cargo of maize. It was damaged by seawater ingress through a rivet hole which was not closed with a rivet. This rendered the ship unseaworthy. However, had the crew observed soundings, which ordinarily they should have done but failed, they would have closed the rivet and any damage to the cargo would have been minimal. Here, there were two causes of the resultant damage. One was the unseaworthiness of the ship at the start of the voyage. Another was the negligence of the crew that aggravated the damage. The English Court of Appeal held the shipowner liable for all the loss on account that the unseaworthiness was one of the causes.

In *The Europa,*[85] a ship collided with the dock. As a result, a pipe in the ship broke that allowed water ingress into an upper deck, damaging the cargo on the upper deck. The water further flowed into the lower deck and damaged the cargo there because some scupper holes in the upper deck were not properly closed. An exclusion clause excluding collision liability protected the shipowner from the damage to the cargo at the upper deck. However, the shipowner was liable for the damage to the cargo at the lower deck. It must be noted that the unseaworthiness, in this case, was not one of the causes of damage to the cargo at the upper deck, which damage was solely attributable to the collision. In the case of damage to the cargo at the lower deck, the unseaworthiness was one of the causes, the other being the collision.

---

[83] [1905] 1 KB 697 (EW HC).

[84] *The Christel Vinnen* [1924] P 208, [1924] All ER Rep 197 (EW CA).

[85] *The Europa* [1908] P 84, [1904–7] All ER Rep 394, (1863) 167 ER 313 (EW HC).

In *The Atrice*,[86] the English High Court refused the argument of the carrier that the decision of the cargo interest to continue loading ethylene even after coming to know that the cargo was getting contaminated broke the chain of causation. The court accordingly held the carrier liable for unseaworthiness caused by unclean tanks, which was a cause of the damage, although supplemented by the decision of the cargo interest to load despite knowledge of the unseaworthiness.

In *Monarch Steamship Co Ltd v A/B Karlshamns Oljefabriker*,[87] a shipper contracted with a carrier to transport a cargo of beans by sea. The voyage was delayed due to unseaworthiness of the ship. Before the ship can reach the discharge port, the Second World War set in. As a result, the ship was prevented by the British Government from continuing on the voyage. If not for the unseaworthiness, the ship would have arrived at the discharge port before the war outbreak. Now there are two causes for the failure of the carrier to complete the carriage contract. One is the unseaworthiness of the ship. The other is the order of the British Government upon the outbreak of the war. The carrier argued that the chain of causation was broken insofar as the unseaworthiness was concerned so that the carrier would be covered by a war-exception clause. The House of Lords refused this argument and held the carrier liable for the unseaworthiness of the ship.

7.2.3.8 Type of the Implied Term

The implied term as to seaworthiness[88] is treated as an innominate term.[89] Only if the consequences are so serious that it will frustrate the commercial objective of the carriage contract, then the cargo interest may elect to terminate the contract.[90]

In *Hong Kong Fir Shipping Co Ltd v Kawasaki Kisen Kaisha Ltd*,[91] a ship was not seaworthy at the appointed date for delivery in a two-year time charterparty. It would take a delay of more than four months[92] to put the ship to a seaworthy condition. The English Court of Appeal held that the delay—the consequence of the breach of the innominate term—was sufficiently serious to warrant termination by the charterer of the charterparty.

The implied term as to seaworthiness is conventionally labelled as “warranty of seaworthiness”. This is mere labelling and does not affect the legal effect of it as an innominate term. Unlike in the case of deviation, a breach of the innominate term

---

[86] *Vinmar International Ltd v Theresa Navigation SA (The Atrice)* [2001] 2 All ER (Comm) 243, [2001] 2 Lloyd's Rep 1, [2001] All ER (D) 107 (Mar) (EW HC).

[87] [1949] AC 196, [1949] 1 All ER 1 (UK HL).

[88] Including cargoworthiness.

[89] *Hong Kong Fir Shipping Co Ltd v Kawasaki Kisen Kaisha Ltd* [1962] 2 QB 26, [1962] 1 All ER 474, [1962] 2 WLR 474, [1961] 2 Lloyd's Rep 478 (EW CA).

[90] Unlike an innominate term, a breach of a ‘condition’ will entitle the innocent party to terminate the contract, whereas there will be no right to terminate for a breach of a ‘warranty’.

[91] [1962] 2 QB 26, [1962] 1 All ER 474, [1962] 2 WLR 474, [1961] 2 Lloyd's Rep 478 (EW CA).

[92] About 20 weeks.

as to seaworthiness does not disentitle the carrier to rely on the terms of the bill to exclude or limit liability[93] or to claim any freight[94] due under the bill.

7.2.4 Cargoworthiness

Cargoworthiness will be analysed below in this sub-chapter by a visit to its scope, its relationship to contractual description of cargo holds, issues of cargoworthiness arising from the growing practice of containerisation, the time at which the duty attaches, and the applicability of some of the seaworthiness-principles to cargoworthiness.

7.2.4.1 Scope

Cargoworthiness is both generic and specific. A ship will be uncargoworthy in a *generic* way when, for example, the cargo gears are faulty[95] or the hatch covers are leaky[96] so that the ship is not fit to carry *any* cargo.[97] The uncargoworthiness will be *specific* when the ship is not fit to carry the particular cargo loaded onto her, though she may be fit to carry other cargo. Both types of uncargoworthiness will render the ship unseaworthy. Hence, a ship that is seaworthy to carry one cargo may not be so to carry another cargo.

In *Tattersall v National Steamship Co*,[98] it was held that a ship offered to carry livestock was uncargoworthy when her holds were not disinfected after carrying cattle infected with foot and mouth disease. In *The Maori King*,[99] a cargo of frozen mutton was shipped. The ship's refrigeration system failed, resulting in damage to the cargo. The English Court of Appeal held the ship was uncargoworthy. In *Stanton v Richardson*,[100] the ship's pumps were inadequate to deal with the moisture from the cargo of wet sugar, that rendered the ship uncargoworthy, although the pumps would have been able to deal with dry sugar.[101] If billion room is not reasonably fit

---

[93] Subject to any applicable rules like the Hague or Hague-Visby Rules.

[94] And lien on freight.

[95] *Hang Fung Shipping and Trading Co Ltd v Mullion & Co Ltd* [1966] 1 Lloyd's Rep 511 (EW HC).

[96] *Itoh & Co Ltd v Atlantska Plovidba (The Gundulic)* [1981] 2 Lloyd's Rep 418 (EW HC).

[97] Though she may be fit to sail.

[98] (1884) 12 QBD 297 (EW HC).

[99] *Owners of Cargo on The Maori King v Hughes (The Maori King)* [1895] 2 QB 550, [1895] 7 WLUK 104 (EW CA).

[100] (1875) 45 LJCP 78 (UK HL).

[101] The shipowner's argument that the charterer had the option of loading wet or dry sugar did not hold good.

to resist bullion thieves, that will render the ship uncargoworthy.[102] A ship with no dunnage mats when carrying dry cargo may be uncargoworthy.[103]

The common law scope of cargoworthiness is not modified by the Hague/Hague-Visby Rules in any way. Hence the same will be relevant to cases under the Rules.

7.2.4.2 Cargoworthiness and Contractual Description of Cargo Holds

In *The Asia Star*,[104] a charterparty case, the Singapore Court of Appeal held that a ship was not cargoworthy when 40% of epoxy coating of her tanks were gone, in a context where the ship was offered to carry palm and it was part of the description of the ship in the contract[105] that the ship was epoxy coated. However, the shipowner was not held liable on account of uncargoworthiness as a result of a clause in the charterparty that allowed the shipowner to cancel the charter if the ship's tank were found defective upon arrival at the port of loading and the same could not be repaired within 24 h.[106] In this case, upon being reported of the epoxy coating failure at the port of loading, the shipowner invoked the cancellation clause and cancelled the charter.

But the shipowner was found liable[107] on another account, namely for failure to provide a ship that answered the contractual description because the magnitude of the failure of the epoxy coating was so large that the ship was considered not epoxy coated. The court held that the contractual description of the ship, such as 'epoxy-coated', constituted a separate and independent obligation from any other obligation to exercise due diligence to provide a seaworthy and cargoworthy ship.[108] Accordingly, even if the ship was cargoworthy, the shipowner can still be found liable for consequences of the breach of the independent obligation to make available a ship answering the contractual description, as it happened in this case. The court also held that the exemption clause did not protect the shipowner from liability for breach of the contract description. Under the Hague/Hague-Visby Rules, the cargoworthiness-obligation is stated in Article III(1)(c).[109]

---

[102] *Queensland National Bank v Peninsular and Oriental Steam Navigation Co* [1898] 1 QB 567, 67 LJQB 402 (EW CA).

[103] *Hogarth v Walker* [1899] 2 QB 401 (EW HC).

[104] *The Asia Star* [2007] SGCA 17, [2007] 3 SLR 1 (SG CA).

[105] In the charterparty fixture.

[106] VEGOILVOY Tanker Voyage Charterparty 1950 form, cl. 1(b).

[107] For damages suffered by the charterer as a result of consequent inability of the charterer to perform its contracts with its suppliers and customers.

[108] VEGOILVOY Tanker Voyage Charterparty 1950 form, cl. 1(a).

[109] Article III(1)(c): "Make the holds, refrigerating and cool chambers, and all other parts of the ship in which goods are carried, fit and safe for their reception, carriage and preservation."

7.2.4.3 Containerised Cargo

In the case of containerised cargo, it is possible that the container is treated as part of the ship's stowage compartment. In that case, if the container is supplied by the carrier and is defective, that may render the ship uncargoworthy. The following speech of Beeks DJ in the US case of *The Aegis Spirit*,[110] when dealing with the package limitation under the Hague Rules, will support this proposition:

> I would liken these containers to detachable stowage compartments of the ship. They simply serve to divide the ship's overall cargo space into smaller, more serviceable *loci*. Shipper's packages are quite literally 'stowed' in the containers utilising stevedoring practices and materials analogous to those employed in traditional on board stowage. The logic of this view is made plainer yet upon noting ... that Tokai's bill of lading covers every piece of cargo packaged by Matshushita/Japan but in no way affects title to the containers which remains in Tokai [the time charterer who issued the 'charterer's bills']. This fact underscores the fundamental distinction between shipper-packaged goods and the carrier-owned containers.

In *The Red Jacket*,[111] a defective container supplied by the carrier broke during the voyage, resulting in many other containers washed overboard. The US court held the ship was uncargoworthy for purposes of the US Carriage of Goods by Sea Act of 1936. This will support the proposition that a container, supplied by the carrier, may be treated as a goods-carrying compartment of the ship.

In one case, where the defective container was supplied by the shipper, the court has refused to hold the carrier liable.[112] However, the result will be dependent on the factual matrix of each case, as the carrier will have an obligation to clause the bill if the damage to the container is apparent at least for the benefit of subsequent buyers who may come to hold the bill or to refuse to carry the container if it will endanger the other cargo or the ship, rendering the ship uncargoworthy or unseaworthy.

7.2.4.4 Time at Which Duty Attaches: Doctrine of Stages

Under the common law that the ship must be cargoworthy during loading. Under the Hague/Hague-Visby Rules, due diligence must be exercised to ensure that the ship is cargoworthy before and at the time of the beginning of the voyage, as Article III(1) provides a uniform period for both seaworthiness and cargoworthiness. This will cover from the beginning of the loading to the start of the voyage including the lying stage. Hence, the obligations under the Rules include the common law implied term for cargoworthiness during loading, by a standard of due diligence as opposed to absolute warranty. The common law 'absolute warranty' concept in relation to cargoworthiness cannot apply under the Rules, as that is in direct contradiction to

---

[110] *The Aegis Spirit* [1977] 1 Lloyd's Rep 93 (US District Court in Washington).

[111] *Houlden & Co Ltd and Others v SS Red Jacket and American Export Lines Ltd; Metal Traders Inc, Third Party; United States Fourth Party (The Red Jacket)* [1978] 1 Lloyd's Rep 300 (US District Court in New York).

[112] *Empire Distributors v United States Lines* [1987] AMC 455, SD Ga 1986 (US District Court in Georgia).

the standard imposed by the Rules. The cargoworthiness-obligation, under the Rules unlike common law, is present continuously from the start of the loading to the start of the voyage.

The ship may be uncargoworthy even if the uncargoworthiness was latent, under the common law, during loading. This happened in *Ciampa and Others v British India Steam Navigation Co Ltd*[113] decided under the common law. In this case, the ship called at Mombasa during the outbreak of plague. Subsequently, at Naples, a cargo of lemons was loaded onto the ship for discharge in Marseilles. At the time of discharge, the port authorities required the ship to be fumigated before discharge, because she had previously called at Mombasa. During the fumigation, the lemons were damaged. on to the ship was loaded a cargo of lemons at Naples. The English High Court held the ship to be uncargoworthy because the need for fumigation at discharge port was latent at the time of loading.

The factual matrix was different in *Elder, Dempster v Paterson Zochonis.*[114] In this case, barrels of palm oil were first loaded. Subsequently, heavy palm kernels were loaded on top of the barrels, that affected the palm oil. The House of Lords, under the common law, did not find the ship to be uncargoworthy insofar as the cargo of palm oil was concerned because, at the time of loading the palm oil, the ship was cargoworthy as the palm kernels came in only later. However, had this case come under the Rules, the House would likely have decided otherwise, as the uncargoworthiness is tested also at the time of the start of the voyage.

A similar case decided under the common law was *The Thorsa.*[115] This was a case of bad stowage, resulting in damage to the cargo. In this case, a cargo of chocolate was loaded and stowed. Then, adjacent to it, a cargo of cheese was loaded and stowed. The cheese tainted the cargo of chocolate. In the action by cargo interests of the chocolate consignment, the English Court of Appeal held that the ship was not uncargoworthy, because at the time the chocolate was loaded, the cheese was not there. As the court did not find this to be a case of uncargoworthiness the carrier escaped liability with a clause excepting liability for bad stowage. It seems that the court would have found the ship to be uncargoworthy, had the cheese been first loaded and then the chocolate. In such a case, the exception for bad stowage would not have saved the carrier. If the case was decided under the Rules, the result would likely have been different as the uncargoworthiness would be tested also at the later time of the start of the voyage, hence it would not matter which cargo was loaded first.

7.2.4.5 Absoluteness of Duty

The absoluteness of the obligation at the common law was demonstrated by the case of *Petrofina SA of Brussels v Compagnia Italiana Trasporto Olii Minerali of*

[113] [1915] 2 KB 774 (EW HC). Decided under the common law in the pre-Hague Rules era.

[114] *Elder, Dempster & Co Ltd v Paterson, Zochonis & Co, Griffiths Lewis Steam Navigation Co v Paterson, Zochonis & Co Ltd* [1923] 1 KB 420, [1924] AC 522, [1924] All ER Rep 135 (UK HL).

[115] *The Thorsa* [1916] P 257, 116 LT 300 (EW CA).

Genoa.[116] In this case, a load of benzine was shipped. It was discoloured because of the lack of cleanliness of the ship's tanks. Cargo interest claimed against the shipowner for breach of the implied term to provide seaworthy ship (in the sense of being cargoworthy). It was the defence of the shipowner that the charterer had inspected the tanks prior to shipment by its surveyors as required by the charterparty and was satisfied. The English Court of Appeal found for the cargo interest, as the obligation to provide a seaworthy and cargoworthy ship was an absolute one.

Similarly, in *The Atrice*,[117] a gas-carrier vessel was engaged to carry a cargo of ethylene. Prior to this shipment, the vessel carried butadiene and the carrier[118] did not clean the tanks of butadiene. This resulted in the ethylene being contaminated and suit by cargo interest against the carrier. It was the defence of the cargo interest that the cargo interest was aware of the contamination at the early stage of loading as reported by the cargo interest's surveyor. However, the cargo interest proceeded to load and took a substantial risk. Accordingly, the carrier argued that the conduct of the cargo interest had broken the chain of causation. The English High Court disagreed with this argument and held the carrier liable. The court noted that the cargo interest was put to this condition, whereby it had to take such risk, by the fault of the carrier.

In cases to which the Rules applies, the cargoworthiness-obligation at the time of loading by virtue of the common law implied term is likely one to exercise due diligence rather than of absolute duty, for reasons earlier said.

7.2.4.6 Applicability of Seaworthiness Principles

Various aspects discussed earlier in respect of seaworthiness-obligation will also be largely relevant to cargoworthiness-obligation, such as the standard and causation.

7.2.5 Deviation

Deviation will be analysed below in this sub-chapter by a visit to its origin and scope, the defence of 'justification' at common law compared with that under Article IV(4) of the Hague/Hague-Visby Rules, the extent to which liberty clauses could negate any 'deviation', and the consequences of deviation under the common law with a consideration of the position under the Rules coupled with a discussion of the doctrine of fundamental breach.

---

[116] (1937) 53 TLR 650, (1937) 57 Ll L Rep 247 (EW CA).

[117] *Vinmar International Ltd v Theresa Navigation SA (The Atrice)* [2001] 2 All ER (Comm) 243, [2001] 2 Lloyd's Rep 1, [2001] All ER (D) 107 (Mar) (EW HC).

[118] Demise charterer.

7.2.5.1 Origin and Scope

At common law, it is a duty, by implied term, not to voluntarily deviate from the proper route without lawful justification. The term is implied into every contract for carriage of goods by sea, including time and voyage charterparties. There is no corresponding obligation imposed by the Hague/Hague-Visby Rules, and the common law implied terms are applicable also in cases to which the Rules apply. The consequences of the breach of this implied term are the most serious of all the implied terms. Having said that, this being an implied term, it is subject to any express term in the contract of carriage to the contrary. Hence, if the contract expressly provides a route or allows cargo to be carried on deck, it will be no deviation for the shipowner to carry by that route (even if that is not the usual or reasonable route) or to carry the cargo on deck, respectively. However, the courts have restrictively interpreted any clause in the contract to dilute the obligation not to deviate. The origin of this implied term can be traced to the early 19th century case, *Davis v Garrett*,[119] where Tindal CJ held that:

> [T]he law does imply a duty in the owner of a vessel, whether a general ship or hired for the special purpose of the voyage, to proceed without unnecessary deviation in the usual and customary course.

It appears that the reason for the implication of such a term or imposition of the duty was that the only risk that a shipper had agreed to take was that in the course of the proper route and any other route would void the cargo insurance.[120] But the reason is not expressed anywhere in the judgment, although arguments by the counsel for the cargo claimant may suggest it. This case was about a deviation by the shipowner to facilitate smuggling. However, the judgment did not confine the result reached to illegal activities. Tindal CJ seemed to acknowledge that it would have been a defence to the shipowner if the loss would have necessarily happened even if the ship had taken the proper route. Some support for the proposition that the insurance-point is a factor that influenced the rigours of the law of deviation[121] can be seen in the judgement of Cockburn CJ in *Scaramanga & Co v Stamp and Another*,[122] where his Lordship said, in the context of holding that it was a deviation to take another ship on tow to save property although it would not be a deviation to do so to save life at sea:

> [D]eviation for the purpose of saving life is protected, and involves neither forfeiture of insurance or liability to the goods' owner which would otherwise be within the exception of 'perils of the seas'

---

[119] (1830) 6 Bing 716 (EW Court of Common Pleas).

[120] The validity of this rationale at the current time is questionable, as insurance coverage can be made to extend to loss or damage caused during a deviated route.

[121] *Glynn v Margetson & Co* [1893] AC 351, [1891–4] All ER Rep 693 (UK HL).

[122] (1880) 5 CPD 295 (EW CA).

In the second quarter of the 20th century, Lord Porter in *The Indian City*[123] said this of the duty not to deviate:

> It is the duty of a ship, at any rate when sailing upon an ocean voyage from one port to another, to take the usual route between those two ports. If no evidence be given, that route is presumed to be the direct geographical route, but it may be modified in many cases for navigational or other reasons, and evidence may always be given to show what the usual route is, unless a specific route be prescribed by the charter party or bill of lading. ... In some cases there may be more than one usual route. ... difficult to say a ship sailing from New Zealand to this country deviated ... whether she sailed by the Suez Canal, the Panama Canal, round the Cape of Good Hope or through the Straits of Magellan. Similarly the exigencies of bunkering may require the vessel to depart from the direct route ...
>
> It is not the geographical route but the usual route which has to be followed, though in many cases the one may be the same as the other. ... a route may become ta usual route in the case of a particular line though that line is accustomed to follow a course which is not that adopted by the vessels belonging to other lines ... It is sufficient if there is a well known practice of that line ...

In this case, the ship carrying ore from Poti[124] to Sparrow's Point[125] departed from her route to take bunkers at Constantza. The departure would lengthen the voyage by about 200 miles. Constantza was not a popular port at which ships on this route take bunkers but about one-quarter of the ships on this route called at Constantza. The House of Lords held that this was not a deviation, taking into account that the departure was for bunkering.

Carrying the cargo beyond the contracted port of discharge can be a deviation.[126] Only a departure that is *voluntary* will be a deviation. In *Rio Tinto v Seed Shipping*,[127] the ship departed from the proper route because the master made a mistake as to the compass course, whilst the master had no intention to leave the route of the voyage. Roche J held that this was not a deviation. His Lordship emphasised:

> It is a change of voyage, a radical breach of the contract, that is required to, and essentially does, constitute a deviation ...

Other than deviation per se in this sense, some other matters have also been classified as deviation or quasi-deviation, such as a voluntary reduction of speed or carrying cargo on deck. The purpose of such a classification seems to emphasise the seriousness of the consequences of breach. In *Scaramanga & Co v Stamp and Another*,[128] a ship carrying a cargo of wheat from Cronstadt to Gibraltar took another on tow to Texel and hence had to prosecute at reduced speed. The English Court of Appeal considered both, the departure and the reduction of speed, to be respectively breaches of the duty, by implied term, not to deviate. Cockburn CJ said:

---

[123] *Reardon Smith Lines Ltd v Black Sea and Baltic General Insurance Co Ltd (The Indian City)* [1939] AC 562, [1939] 3 All ER 444 (UK HL).

[124] In Black Sea.

[125] In Baltimore, USA.

[126] *Cunard Steamship Co Ltd v Buerger* [1927] AC 1, [1926] All ER Rep 103 (UK HL).

[127] (1926) 23 LI L Rep 316 (EW HC).

[128] (1880) 5 CPD 295 (EW CA).

> [T]here was here a twofold deviation … in the first place … departure … from her proper course in going to the Texel … secondly, in her taking the Arion in tow (since) the effect of taking another vessel in tow is necessarily to retard the progress of the towing vessel and thereby to prolong the risk of the voyage.

Such implied terms as to the other deviations or quasi-deviations are relevant also in cases to which the Rules apply, as the Rules do not provide for the same. Hence, the common law implied terms will be imposed, although the consequences may be modified by virtue of various exclusions and limitations in the Rules applicable to contracts of carriages covered by the Rules.

The two defences or rebuttals to a deviation-claim, at common law, are liberty clauses and justification i.e. to save life or avoid imminent peril. The liberty-clause, to say it strictly, is not a defence to deviation because it negates any deviation in the first place.

7.2.5.2 Justification

Justification may be available at common law or under the Hague/Hague-Visby Rules. Both co-exist. Justification under each head is, respectively, be visited below.

Under Common Law

At common law, only two classes of justification have been recognised. One is the justification of saving life at sea. In fact, the obligation for saving life at sea is even made obligatory by various conventions and statutes.[129] Another is the justification of avoiding imminent peril. 'Saving property at sea' has not been recognised at common law. Three cases will demonstrate the classes of justification and their availability at common law.

In *Scaramanga & Co v Stamp and Another*,[130] a ship, The Olympias, carrying wheat from Cronstadt to Gibraltar sighted another ship, The Arion, stranded at sea due to engine failure. The weather and the sea were good. The Olympias agreed to take The Arion on tow to Texel for £1,000. In the deviated course, The Olympias with the cargo was lost. The English Court of Appeal found this to be a twofold deviation. One was towing another ship and thereby having to reduce speed. Another was to depart off the course to Texel. The court held that it was not justified as it was for saving property rather than life at sea. In consequence, the shipowner was not able to rely on the 'perils of the seas' exception. Cockburn CJ said:

> [D]eviation for the purpose of communicating with a ship in distress is allowable, inasmuch as the state of the vessel in distress may involve danger to life. On the other hand, deviation

---

[129] Section 93(1) of UK Merchant Shipping Act 1995: "… master of a ship …on receiving a signal of distress … shall proceed with all speed to assistance of the persons in distress". Similarly, International Convention for the Safety of Life at Sea 1974 (SOLAS) and International Convention on Maritime Search and Rescue 1979 (SAR) have provisions mandating the same. The Malaysian Merchant Shipping Ordinance 1952 imposes an identical burden on the master of a ship, by Section 280(1), however limited only to master of a 'British or Malaysian' ship.

[130] (1880) 5 CPD 295 (EW CA).

> for the sole purpose of saving property is not thus privileged, but entails all the usual consequences of deviation. ... If, therefore, the lives of the persons on board a disabled ship can be saved without saving the ship, as by taking them off, deviation for the purpose of saving the ship will carry with it all the consequences of an unauthorized deviation.

In *Phelps, James & Co v Hill*,[131] the ship was carrying tin plates from Swansea to New York under a bill of lading. About five days out, the ship suffered damage requiring repair before she could proceed on her voyage. The shipowner ordered the master to bring her to its shipyard in Bristol for the repairs although Swansea would have been a little nearer than Bristol to reach. In Bristol, the spare parts were readily available, and the repairs could be done more quickly and cheaply. A transshipment would also be possible in Bristol. In the course to Bristol, a collision happened, and the ship sank with the cargo. The cargo interest sued the shipowner for non-delivery. The bill contained a usual exclusion clause in respect of loss resulting from collision. However, if there was an unjustified deviation, the shipowner would not be able to rely on the exclusion clause. The jury found that there was no deviation, and the English Court of Appeal held accordingly. In this case, the shipowner was not at fault in respect of the damage first suffered by the ship as a result of the storm and there was no complaint that the ship was unseaworthy at the beginning of the voyage.

In contrast to that, in *Kish v Taylor*,[132] a pre-Hague Rules charterparty case, the ship was unseaworthy at the beginning of the voyage by the fault of the master in accepting overload of cargo on board. During the voyage, the unseaworthiness posed a danger to the ship and the crew. Accordingly, the master had to deviate to take refuge in order to save the ship and the crew. The English Court of Appeal held that the deviation was reasonable and in determining this question it did not matter whether the deviation became necessary because of an initial unseaworthiness. Hence, the shipowner would not lose the benefits of exception clauses but will still have to answer for the unseaworthiness at the outset. Subsequently, the House of Lords in *Monarch Steamship Co Ltd v A/B Karlshamns Oljefabriker*,[133] a charterparty case decided under the common law, followed *Kish v Taylor* and held "deviation necessarily made to remedy unseaworthiness does not amount to unjustifiable deviation". Again, this would relieve the shipowner from the drastic consequences of deviation, but not from the liability for the unseaworthiness at the outset.

Under Hague and Hague Visby Rules

The Hague/Hague-Visby Rules, in Article IV(6), made an express extension to cover 'saving property at sea' as a defence to deviation-claim. Other than this, the rule also provides a defence when it is the deviation is reasonable—this is open and wider than the common law 'justification' limited to two classes of justification. Lord Warrington in *Stag Line Ltd v Foscolo, Mango & Co Ltd*[134] observed when dealing with Article IV(6), that what is reasonable is 'a question of fact and has to be answered

[131] [1891] 1 QB 604 (EW CA).

[132] [1912] AC 604, [1911] 1 KB 625 (EW CA).

[133] [1949] AC 196, [1949] 1 All ER 1 (UK HL).

[134] [1932] AC 328, [1931] All ER Rep 666 (UK HL).

after giving due consideration to all the relevant circumstances' of the case. Article IV(6)[135] reads as follows:

> 4. Any deviation in saving or attempting to save life or property at sea or any reasonable deviation shall not be deemed to be an infringement or breach of this Convention or of the contract of carriage, and the carrier shall not be liable for any loss or damage resulting therefrom.

The Rules do not expressly impose any obligation not to deviate. Hence, the defence in the Rules is meant purely to answer a claim in the common law for deviation. Although the Rules do not expressly state the justification of avoiding imminent peril, that is readily available in the common law, applicable also to cases to which the Rules apply. However, what is arguable is whether the principle enunciated in *Kish v Taylor* and *Monarch Steamship* will help the shipowner in a case to which the Rules apply. This is because it is likely that it is sufficient if the unseaworthiness is 'a' cause of the loss or damage.[136]

In *Stag Line Ltd v Foscolo, Mango & Co Ltd,*[137] the ship deviated to take replacement crew. After that, the ship took a time-saving route that was unsafe. The House of Lords held the first deviation to take replacement crew to be reasonable under the Rules, but not the subsequent unsafe route.

In *The Al Taha,*[138] the ship and its boom were damaged, due to heavy weather, on her approach voyage to the loading port. Repairs to the ship were carried out at the loading port. For the damage to the boom, it was sent to another port for repair. Subsequently, to avoid delay in getting back the boom by road due to bad weather, the ship sailed to the other port where the repaired boom was lying. The English High Court held this deviation to be reasonable under the Rules.

7.2.5.3 Liberty Clauses

Effective liberty clauses will negate any deviation in the first place so that the question of justification or any other defence such as it was not done voluntarily does not arise. However, the courts usually restrictively interpret them with the result that they may not have the intended effect.

In *Leduc v Ward,*[139] the bill of lading gave open liberty to the shipowner as "liberty to call at any ports in any order". The English Court of Appeal narrowly interpreted this clause so that it did not allow a deviation off the track to Glasgow whilst on a voyage from Fiume to Dunkirk. Lord Esher MR said:

---

[135] Hague/Hague-Visby Rules.

[136] *Smith, Hogg v Black Sea and Baltic General Insurance* [1940] AC 997 (UK HL); *Papera Traders Co Ltd v Hyundai Merchant Marine Co Ltd (The Eurasian Dream) (No. 1)* [2002] EWHC 118, [2002] 1 Lloyd's Rep 719, QBD (Comm) (EW HC).

[137] [1932] AC 328, [1931] All ER Rep 666 (UK HL).

[138] *Lyric Shipping Inc v Intermetals Ltd (The Al Taha)* [1990] 2 Lloyd's Rep 117 (EW HC).

[139] (1888) 20 QBD 475, [1886–90] All ER Rep 266, (1888) 20 EBD 475 (EW CA).

> In the present case liberty is given to call any ports in any order. It was argued that that clause gives liberty to call at any port in the world. Here, again, it is a question of the construction of a mercantile expression used in a mercantile document, and I think that as such the term can have but one meaning, namely, that the ports, liberty to call at which is intended to be given, must be ports which are substantially ports which will be passed on the named voyage. … the invariable construction has been that she old only be entitled to call at such ports in their geographical order … when … ship went off the ordinary track of a voyage from Fiume to Dunkirk to a port not on the course of that voyage, such as Glasgow, there was a deviation, and she was then on a voyage different from that contracted for to which the excepted perils clause did not apply; and therefore the shipowners are responsible for the loss of the goods …

In *Glynn v Margetson & Co*,[140] the ship was on a voyage from Malaga[141] to Liverpool.[142] She deviated off the route to Burriana, a port in the east coast of Spain. The bill of lading contained a liberty clause as follows:

> [L]iberty to proceed to and stay at any port or ports in any station in the Mediterranean Levant, Black Sea or Adriatic or on the coast of Africa, Spain, Portugal, France, Great Britain and Ireland, for the purpose of delivery coals, cargo or passengers or for any other purpose whatsoever.

The House of Lords held that 'these words are printed words in a document evidently intended to be used in relation to a variety of contracts of affreightment' and construed it narrowly to mean only 'ports which are in the course of the voyage'. Lord Halsbury went further than merely dealing with the clause as a matter of construction and said that "one must reject words … if they are inconsistent with what one assumes to be the 'main purpose' of the contract". His Lordship pointed out that it was impossible to insure the cargo if a wide construction was given to the clause.[143] Hence, the carrier was liable for the deviation.

In *Connolly Shaw Ltd v Nordenfjeldske Steamship Co*,[144] the ship carried a cargo of lemon from Palermo to London. However, she deviated to Valencia to load potatoes and then to Hull to discharge the potatoes, before proceeding to London. This resulted in a delay of three days. The bill of lading contained a wide liberty clause as follows:

> The ship is to be at liberty either before or after proceeding towards the port of delivery of the said goods, to proceed to or return to and stay at any ports or places whatsoever (although in a contrary direction to or out of or beyond the route of the said port of delivery) once or oftener in any order, backwards or forwards, for loading or discharging cargo … or for any purpose whatsoever, whether in relation to her homeward voyage, or to her outward voyage, or to an intermediate voyage, and all such ports, places and sailings shall be deemed included within the intended voyage of the said goods

The English High Court so construed the liberty clause as to cover the deviation complained of, as the deviation complained of did not frustrate contract, unlike in the

[140] [1893] AC 351, [1891–4] All ER Rep 693 (UK HL).

[141] In Spain.

[142] In the UK.

[143] Relying on *Robertson v French* [1803–13] All ER Rep 350, (1803) 4 East 130, 102 ER 779 (EW HC).

[144] (1934) 49 Ll L Rep 183 (EW HC).

case of non-delivery after discharge or misdelivery. In this case, the delay of merely three days was not something that was out of contemplation in a sea voyage such as this. Accordingly, the carrier was not liable.

Under the Rules, there is nothing to invalidate liberty clauses. Such clauses will not fall foul of Article III(8) of the Rules for restricting any liability imposed by the Rules since the Rules did not impose any duty not to deviate.

The difference between a clause negating an obligation and one excepting liability for breach of the obligation will best be demonstrated by *Renton (GH) & Co Ltd v Palmyra Trading Corpn of Panama*,[145] in which the Rules were applicable. In this case, the cargo was carried under bills of lading for delivery in London and Hull. The bills of lading contained a 'strike' clause that allowed the shipowner to deliver at an alternative port in the event of a strike at the named port of discharge. At the material time, both the named ports were strike-bound. Hence, the shipowner discharged the cargo in Hamburg. The cargo owner sued the shipowner for deviation and argued that it was an unreasonable deviation not allowed by Article IV(4) and that the 'strike' clause was invalid falling foul of Article III(8). The House of Lords[146] rejected the argument and held that there was no obligation on the carrier under the bills to delivery in London or Hull when these ports are strike-bound. The obligation was only to delivery at an alternative port, in the event of such strike, as did by the shipowner. As there was no breach of the obligation (not to deviate), the question of whether it was a reasonable deviation under Article IV(4) did not arise. As the 'strike' clause defined or modified the obligation rather excepting liability for deviation, that did not fall foul of Article III(8). However, the dividing line between a clause rightfully defining an obligation and one excepting liability for breach of an obligation can be thin in many cases. This can be a matter of construction by the court in any case before it, taking into account the commercial intention of the parties.

7.2.5.4 Consequences of Deviation

The consequences of deviation under the common law and the Hague Rules and Hague-Visby Rules considered below, after a visit to the doctrine of fundamental breach that will help a better understanding of the consequences of deviation.

Doctrine of Fundamental Breach

It will be helpful to visit the doctrine of fundamental breach before visiting the consequences of deviation. There is some relationship or similarity between the two. Possibly, one may have an influence over the other. An understanding of the one may also help understand the other. However, the two concepts are different. It is important to take note that they are different, because the doctrine of fundamental breach has now become extinct in England and Wales and in effect replaced with a

---

[145] [1957] AC 149, [1956] 3 All ER 957[1957] 2 WLR 45[1956] 2 Lloyd's Rep 379 (UK HL).

[146] By majority.

judicial control mechanism of contractual clauses excluding or limiting liability for fundamental breach by a narrow interpretation of them against the carrier.

In those Commonwealth countries[147] with a Contract Act modelled on the Indian Contract Act 1872, a court may find any exclusion of liability for a fundamental breach to be contrary to *public policy* and hence invalid.[148] The illegality argument, based on the said public policy ground, can potentially yield an analogous result to that of the doctrine of fundamental breach. An argument against exclusion or limitation of fundamental breach on public policy grounds will also be available under the English law, in addition to the other judicial tools of restrictive interpretation.

The law on this subject can be traced to, at least, as early as *Glynn v Margetson & Co*,[149] decided by the House of Lords in 1893. In this case, the contract was for carriage of oranges from Malaga to Liverpool. The bill of lading contained a printed clause that allowed wide liberty to the carrier, which read

> [L]iberty to proceed to and stay at any port or ports in any station in the Mediterranean, Levant, Black Sea, or Adriatic, or on the coasts of Africa, Spain, Portugal, France, Great Britain, and Ireland, for the purpose of delivering coals, cargo or passengers, or for any other purpose whatsoever.

The House of Lords said that 'these words are printed words in a document evidently intended to be used in relation to a variety of contracts of affreightment' and construed it narrowly to mean only 'ports which are in the course of the voyage'. Lord Halsbury went further than merely dealing with the clause as a matter of construction and said that "one must reject words ... if they are inconsistent with what one assumes to be the 'main purpose' of the contract".

Subsequently, by the mid-20th century, the 'main purpose' concept was extended into general contract law and developed more than as a means of construction, and called the doctrine of 'fundamental breach' and 'hard core of the contract'.[150] A fundamental breach was one that would go to the 'root of the contract', a good example of which is the case of *Karsales v Wallis*,[151] decided by the Court of Appeal in 1956. In this case, a buyer inspected a used car for purchase from a dealer. Later the car was towed and delivered in non-working condition. It was substantially modified before delivery including replaced older tyres, burnt valves, missing parts, etc. Upon action by the buyer, the dealer attempted to rely on a clause in the contract that disclaimed any warranty of roadworthiness and fitness for any purpose. The Court of Appeal held that the dealer had committed a 'fundamental breach' that barred it from relying on the exception clause.

However, the doctrine of fundamental breach in the context of general contract law did not long live. It was not favoured by the House of Lords in *Suisse Atlantique*

---

[147] Including Malaysia.

[148] Section 23 (sub-para 5) of the Indian Contract Act 1872/s. 24(e) of the Malaysian Contracts Act 1950.

[149] [1893] AC 351, [1891–4] All ER Rep 693 (UK HL).

[150] *Karsales v Wallis* [1956] EWCA Civ 4, [1956] 2 All ER 866, [1956] 1 WLR 936 (EW CA). Lord Denning contributed to the development of this doctrine in many of His Lordship's judgments.

[151] [1956] EWCA Civ 4, [1956] 2 All ER 866, [1956] 1 WLR 936 (EW CA).

Société d'Armement Maritime SA v Rotterdamsche Kolen Centrale NV.[152] Subsequently by 1980, the doctrine was ruled out, in the context of general contract law, by the House of Lords in *Photo Production Ltd v Securicor Transport Ltd.*[153] But, this did not affect how the courts would deal with deviation cases.

Consequences of Deviation under Common Law

At common law, the consequences of deviation are drastic for the carrier. The deviation is considered to be a change of the voyage and so radical a breach of the contract[154] that the carrier is no longer treated as being in the course of performing the contracted voyage.[155] The result of such a treatment is that the carrier can no longer rely on any term of the contract, including exclusion and limitation clauses[156] and possibly those provisions giving it a right such as to claim freight[157] or demurrage. As the carrier cannot rely on the contract, it cannot also bind the shipper to any agreed laytime.[158] However, the carrier can claim *quantum meruit* freight[159] and demurrage for the loading and unloading time beyond reasonable laytime.[160]

It appears that at common law, in effect, a deviation will reduce the status of the carrier from a contractual carrier to a common carrier. A common carrier is one who will carry the goods of anyone paying its charges for the carriage. A good example will be the post office. This can be compared with that of bus service in the carriage of passengers. This is different from a mere carrier for reward, under which the duties of the carrier are those as a bailee for reward. Examples of this will be a hired truck, house mover and voyage charterparty. It was once not clear whether a carrier in a bill of lading or other types of bills were considered a common carrier or carrier for rewards. If a carrier is a common carrier, it has an absolute obligation to deliver

---

152 [1967] 1 AC 361, [1966] 2 All ER 61, [1966] 2 WLR 944, [1966] 1 Lloyd's Rep 529 (UK HL).

153 [1980] AC 827, [1980] 1 All ER 556, [1980] 2 WLR 283, [1980] 1 Lloyd's Rep 545 (UK HL).

154 *Rio Tinto v Seed Shipping* (1926) 23 LI L Rep 316 (EW HC).

155 *Leduc v Ward* (1888) 20 QBD 475, [1886–90] All ER Rep 266, (1888) 20 EBD 475 (EW CA).

156 *Glynn v Margetson & Co* [1893] AC 351, [1891–4] All ER Rep 693 (UK HL); *Joseph Thorley Ltd v Orchis Steamship Co Ltd* [1907] 1 KB 660, 96 LT 488 (EW CA); *James Morrison & Co Ltd v Shah, Savill and Albion Co Ltd* [1916] 2 KB 783, [1916–17] All ER Rep 1068 (EW CA); *Internationale Guano en Superphosphaat-Werken v Robert Macandrew & Co* [1909] 2 KB 360, 100 LT 850 (EW HC); *Hain Steamship Co Ltd v Tate & Lyle Ltd* (1936) 41 Com Cas 350, [1936] 2 All ER 597, (1936) 55 Ll L Rep 159 (UK HL).

157 A contrary view was held by the courts in *Cole v Shallet* (1682) 3 Lev 41, 83 ER 567 (EW Court of King's Bench) and *Davidson v Gwynne* (1810) 1 Camp 376, 12 East 381, 104 ER 149 (EW Court of King's Bench).

158 *United States Shipping Board v Bunge y Born Ltda Sociedad (The Alamosa)* (1925) 42 TLR 174, [1925] All ER Rep 173 (UK HL).

159 In *Tate & Lyle Ltd v Hain Steamship Co Ltd; sub nom. Hain Steamship Co Ltd v Tate & Lyle Ltd* (1936) 41 Com Cas 350, [1936] 2 All ER 597, (1936) 55 Ll L Rep 159 (UK HL), it was said that a reasonable freight was payable despite that the carrier was not able to claim freight as a matter of contract.

160 A right for the carrier to claim damages for delay in unloading, despite that the carrier did not have a right to claim contractual demurrage, was assumed in *United States Shipping Board v Bunge y Born Ltda Sociedad (The Alamosa)* (1925) 42 TLR 174, [1925] All ER Rep 173 (UK HL).

the goods in the like condition that it received, subject only to four defences. They are: act of God, act of Queen's enemies, inherent vice of the goods and fault of the consignor. Otherwise than in the context of deviation, the category of common carriers is no longer existent.[161]

Liver Alkali Co v Johnson[162] treated the sea carriers of cargo as common carriers or as taking liability as a common carrier. *Nugent v Smith*[163] seemed to suggest that a sea carrier of cargo need not necessarily be a common carrier. In *Paterson Steamship Ltd v Canadian Co-operative Wheat Producers,*[164] Lord Wright equated the sea carrier of cargo with an insurer, that will come near to a common carrier. Finally, the question of whether a shipowner or a carrier in a bill of lading is a common carrier or a mere carrier for reward was authoritatively answered by the UK Supreme Court in the recent case of *Volcafe v CSAV.*[165] The court held that they are merely carriers for reward and the category known as the 'common carrier' had almost become extinct for a long time. The court well defined a common carrier, now almost extinct, and its duties as follows:

> The characteristic feature of a common carrier was that he held himself out as accepting for carriage the goods of all comers on a given route, subject to capacity limits. As such, he was strictly liable at common law for loss of or damage to the cargo subject only to exceptions for acts of God and the Queen's enemies. The absence of negligence was irrelevant.

Quite plainly, carriers that are referred to in bills of ladings or other shipping documents will not fit the above definition of common carriers. Some cases decided under the common are visited below.

In *Rio Tinto v Seed Shipping,*[166] Roche J described deviation as a 'change of voyage, a radical breach of the contract'. In *Leduc v Ward,*[167] the Court of Appeal found that by deviating, a ship sets 'on a voyage different from that contracted for to which the excepted perils clause did not apply; and therefore the shipowners are responsible for the loss of the goods …'[168]

In *Joseph Thorley Ltd v Orchis Steamship Co Ltd,*[169] a shipowner deviated. Subsequently, during discharge, stevedores negligently damaged the cargo. There was a clause in the bill of lading excepting liability for damage to cargo by stevedores'

---

[161] *Volcafe Ltd Ltd and others v Compania Sud Americana De Vapores SA (t/a CSAV)* [2018] UKSC 61, [2019] AC 358, [2019] 2 All ER 81, [2018] 3 WLR 2087, [2019] 1 All ER (Comm) 397, [2019] 1 Lloyd's Rep 21, [2018] All ER (D) 16 (Dec) (UK SC).

[162] (1874) LR 9 Ex 338, 43 LJ Ex 216, 2 Asp MLC 332, 31 LT 95 (EW Court of Exchequer Chamber).

[163] (1876) 1 CPD 423, 34 LT 827, 41 JP 4, 45 LJQB 697, 3 Asp MLC 198, 25 WR 117 (EW CA).

[164] [1934] AC 538, [1934] All ER Rep 480 (PC on appeal from Quebec).

[165] *Volcafe Ltd and others v Compania Sud Americana De Vapores SA (t/a CSAV)* [2018] UKSC 61, [2019] AC 358, [2019] 2 All ER 81, [2018] 3 WLR 2087, [2019] 1 All ER (Comm) 397, [2019] 1 Lloyd's Rep 21, [2018] All ER (D) 16 (Dec) (UK SC).

[166] (1926) 23 LI L Rep 316 (EW HC).

[167] (1888) 20 QBD 475, [1886–90] All ER Rep 266, (1888) 20 EBD 475 (EW CA).

[168] Speech of Lord Esher MR.

[169] [1907] 1 KB 660, 96 LT 488 (EW CA).

negligence. The Court of Appeal treated the implied term not to deviate as a condition precedent,[170] the breach of which will disentitle the shipowner from relying on any term of the contract. Accordingly, the court held that the shipowner cannot rely on that clause as a result of the deviation. This was so despite that the damage had nothing to do with the deviation. The justification for such a strict approach in case of deviation was that the cargo owner would lose the benefit of cargo insurance by the deviation.[171]

In *James Morrison & Co Ltd v Shah, Savill and Albion Co Ltd*,[172] the ship sank as a result of a collision with a submarine while deviating during the First World War. The Court of Appeal refused to allow the shipowner to even raise the defence of the act of enemies, which would be available to a common carrier. This was because the loss happened when deviating, and hence even the defences available to a common carrier were lost.

Internationale Guano en Superphosphaat-Werken v Robert Macandrew & Co[173] took the rigours of deviation further by holding that the shipowner may not rely on any exclusion clause in the bill of lading even in respect of any loss that happened before the deviation. The extremity of the decision may be hard to be justified. [174] In *Hain Steamship Co Ltd v Tate & Lyle Ltd*[175] , the House of Lords held, prior to *Photo Production v Securicor*, Photo Production Ltd v Securicor Transport Ltd [1980] AC 827, [1980] 1 All ER 556, [1980] 2 WLR 283, [1980] 1 Lloyd's Rep 545 (UK HL). settled that a deviation is such a fundamental breach, even if it is one of a slightest degree only, in the context of carriage of goods by sea, that it gave the option to the cargo interest to affirm the contract or to treat itself as not bound by any term of the contract. This means, if the cargo interest takes the second option, the contract will be nullified in entirety from the inception, and not merely the selected clauses or exception clauses. In such a case, the cargo interest does not have to pay the contractual freight as it is not bound by any terms of the carriage contract. However, the House left open the question whether the shipowner may in certain circumstances claims reasonable remuneration for the carriage performed, although the House seemed to favour an answer to this question in the affirmative. Upon notifying its election to treat the contract as nullified, the cargo interest may claim back the goods. If the cargo interest does not so notify, the cargo interest will not be lightly taken to have affirmed the contract and waived the deviationunless there are 'acts which plainly show that the [cargo interest] intends to treat the contract as still binding'. This is because, with a bill of lading, the cargo interest may not have an

---

[170] A similar point was made in *Balian & Sons v Joly, Victoria & Co* (1890) 6 TLR 345 (EW CA).

[171] It must be noted that the cover can be extended to include a deviation, that will cost an additional premium.

[172] [1916] 2 KB 783, [1916–17] All ER Rep 1068 (EW CA).

[173] [1909] 2 KB 360, 100 LT 850 (EW HC).

[174] Notably, the cargo insurance will remain effective in respect of any damage that happened before the deviation.

[175] *Tate & Lyle Ltd v Hain Steamship Co Ltd; sub nom. Hain Steamship Co Ltd v Tate & Lyle Ltd* (1936) 41 Com Cas 350, [1936] 2 All ER 597, (1936) 55 Ll L Rep 159 (UK HL).

option practically to call back the goods while they are at sea even if it comes to know of the deviation while the voyage is still being prosecuted. Hence, a mere failure to call back will not be taken as an affirmation of the contract. An election made by a charterer will not bind the transferee of the bill who had no knowledge of the deviation and thus who may make such election when he comes to know of the deviation. Any proposition that a deviation will put an automatic end to the contract of carriage was ruled out. The House noted that the reason for the drastic consequences of deviation may have its root in voyage insurance policies that was avoided the moment the ship deviated, and that policies were now available to cover even in the case of deviation. But this did not bar the House from taking the position that it did. In saying so, the House observed that the rigours of the legal consequences of deviation is 'balanced by the fact that the ship can, and often does, have liberties [contractually] to deviate'. In *Photo Production v Securicor*, Photo Production Ltd v Securicor Transport Ltd [1980] AC 827, [1980] 1 All ER 556, [1980] 2 WLR 283, [1980] 1 Lloyd's Rep 545 (UK HL). the House of Lords abolished the doctrine of fundamental breach. A factor that influenced the House to do so was the enactment of the Unfair Contract Terms Act 1977 to regulate and control, in certain circumstances, unfair contractual terms. The clauses that this Act may catch includes ones that exempt liability for fundamental breach. In abolishing the doctrine, the House, through the speech of Lord Wilberfore, treated deviation cases as a sui generis to which special rules were applicable derived from historical and commercial reasons and did not wish to disturb them. It followed, in The Sur, Dera Commercial Estate v Derya Inc (The Sur) [2019] 1 All ER 1147 (UK HC). that the English High Court recently held that the law concerning effect of deviation, as enunciated in Hain Steamship case survives Photo Production case. It was noted that the concept of fundamental breach applicable in the context of contracts of carriage, enunciated in Hain Steamship case, was somewhat different from the doctrine of fundamental breach that of general application to contracts prior to Photo Production case in two aspects. First, 'even a trivial deviation which does not cause any loss of or damage to the cargo will be sufficient' to entitle the cargo interest to exercise its rights of termination for deviation. Second, the 'effect of termination is that the entire contract is displaced'. Thus, the undertaking not to deviate was treated as a 'condition precedent to the right of the shipowner to put the contract in suit'.

In *Hain Steamship*, it was held that deviation in the context of a charterparty was a breach of condition, entitling the innocent party to elect to keep the contract alive or to terminate it. In this case, the charterers were held to have elected to keep it alive by ordering the ship to load at the next port after becoming aware of the deviation. However, it also held that, in the context of a bill of lading, the deviation automatically terminated the contract, as there was not a way that the bill of lading holder can elect to keep the contract alive or to terminate. Even if the bill of lading holder presents the bill to receive the goods, that will not amount to an election to keep the contract alive. Accordingly, the carrier in the bill of lading contract was not able to claim the contractual freight. The decision, insofar as the bill of lading scenario is concerned, makes a departure from the established principles of contract law by providing an automatic termination for breach of a condition. This departure may be re-visited by the court in the future.

Consequences of Deviation under Hague and Hague-Visby Rules

At common law, a deviation will deprive the carrier of the benefit of the contract, particularly exclusion and limitation clauses. The question here is whether it will similarly deprive the carrier of the benefits of defences and limitation in the Hague and Hague-Visby Rules. This has been a difficult question.

If it can be said that the carrier is no longer in the course of performance of the contract of carriage because of deviation, then arguably, the limitations and defences available to the carrier under the Rules are no longer applicable. Thus, the liability of the carrier will be as a common carrier. This would mean the position under the common law and the Rules are at par. This is the position taken by the House of Lords in *Stag Line Ltd v Foscolo, Mango & Co Ltd,*[176] where Lord Atkinson said:

> [T]he general principles of English law are still applicable to the carriage of goods by sea except as modified by the Act; and I can find in the Act nothing which makes its statutory exceptions apply to a voyage which is not the voyage the subject of "the contract of carriage of goods by sea" to which the Act applies.

In this case, the ship left Swansea for Constantinople, carrying coal under a bill of lading subject to Hague Rules. At Swansea, engineers got on board to test the heating system of the ship. However, they could not complete the job and get off because some of the firemen were drunk. Hence, the ship carried the engineers and had to make a deviation to St Ives. On leaving St Ives, the ship met an accident, seemingly due to a navigational decision or error, with a total loss of the ship and the cargo. Hence, the cargo interest sued the shipowner. The shipowner attempted to rely on Article IV(2)(a)[177] and (c)[178] of the Hague Rules. The House of Lords held that the shipowner may not rely on them because the ship had deviated.

As per this case, the carrier will lose all the benefits of the entire Hague Rules contract. This will include loss of the time-limitation,[179] liability-limitation,[180] exceptions[181] and reduced obligation for seaworthiness and cargoworthiness.[182]

However, under the Hague-Visby Rules, there are authorities to say that the carrier does not lose the benefits. In *The Antares,*[183] the English Court of Appeal held that deviation did not deprive the carrier of the one-year time limit in Article III(6) of the Hague-Visby Rules. This seems to be because there is an additional word, 'whatsoever', in Article III(6) of the Hague-Visby Rules, which word is not there

[176] [1932] AC 328, [1931] All ER Rep 666 (UK HL).

[177] Navigational error of the master, mariner or pilot.

[178] Perils, dangers and accidents of the sea.

[179] Article III(6).

[180] Article IV(5).

[181] Article IV(2).

[182] Article III(1).

[183] *Kenya Railways v Antares Co Pte Ltd (The Antares)* [1987] 1 Lloyd's Rep 424 (EW CA).

in the same Article in the Hague Rules. Article III(6) of the Hague Rules reads as follows:

> In any event the carrier and the ship shall be discharged from all liability in respect of loss or damage unless suit is brought within one year after delivery of the goods or the date when the goods should have been delivered.

The same Article in the Hague-Visby Rules reads as follows:

> [T]he ship shall in any event be discharged from all liability *whatsoever* in respect of the goods, unless suit is brought within one year of their delivery or of the date when they should have been delivered. [emphasis added].

The Antares school of thought may suggest that all protection given by the Hague-Visby Rules to the carrier, namely the liability-limitation,[184] exceptions[185] and reduced obligation for seaworthiness and cargoworthiness[186] will be available despite a deviation, as a result of Article IV(5)(e) of the Hague-Visby Rules, which is not there in the Hague Rules. Article IV(5) of the Hague-Visby Rules reads as follows:

> (e) Neither the carrier nor the ship shall be entitled to the benefit of the *limitation* of liability *provided for in this paragraph* if it is proved that the damage resulted from an act or omission of the carrier *done with intent to cause damage*, or *recklessly and with knowledge that damage would probably result*. [emphasis added]

Arguments have been advanced that *The Antares* school of thought is supported also by Article IV(5), that includes the words 'in any event' when providing the liability-limitation. Article IV(5) in the Hague Rules reads as follows:

> 5. Neither the carrier nor the ship shall *in any event* be or become liable for any loss or damage to or in connexion with goods in an amount exceeding 100 lb sterling per package or unit, or the equivalent of that sum in other currency unless the nature and value of such goods have been declared by the shipper before shipment and inserted in the bill of lading. [italic added]

The corresponding Article IV(5)(a) in the Hague-Visby Rules (without SDR Protocol) reads as follows:

> 5. (a) Unless the nature and value of such goods have been declared by the shipper before shipment and inserted in the Bill of Lading, neither the carrier nor the ship shall *in any event* be or become liable for any loss or damage to or in connection with the goods in an amount exceeding the equivalent of 10,000 francs per package or unit or 30 francs per kilo of gross weight of the goods lost or damaged, whichever is the higher. [emphasis added]

The same Article in the Hague-Visby Rules (as amended by SDR Protocol) reads as follows:

---

[184] Article IV(5).

[185] Article IV(2).

[186] Article III(1).

> 5. (a) Unless the nature and value of such goods have been declared by the shipper before shipment and inserted in the bill of lading, neither the carrier nor the ship shall *in any event* be or become liable for any loss or damage to or in connection with the goods in an amount exceeding 666.67 units of account per package or unit or 2 units of account per kilogramme of gross weight of the goods lost or damaged, whichever is the higher. [emphasis added]

The shortcoming of *The Antares* school of thought is that it bypasses the fact that all those provisions—Article III(6), Article IV(5)(a) and Article IV(5)(e)—are relevant only for a contract for carriage of goods under a bill of lading, as per the approach of the House of Lords in *Stag Line*. But by voluntarily deviating without justification, the carrier had stepped out of the performance of the carriage contract, hence disentitled to rely on any provision of the Hague-Visby Rules.

This argument is not without limitations, as Article IV(4) provides a defence for deviation. Such a defence will arguably be meaningless if the carrier cannot rely on the Hague/Hague-Visby Rules because of a deviation. If this line of argument has any merit, then it will equally apply to the Hague Rules, since Article IV(4) is the same in both the Rules, hence run contrary to the position taken by the House of Lords *Stag Line*. Harmony may be found here if the carrier is barred only from relying on defences and limitations in the Rules but not from relying on other parts of the Rules. The discussion in the following sub-chapter of *The Chanda*[187] and *The Kapitan Petko Voivoda*[188] are also relevant here.

7.2.6 Quasi-deviation (Carriage on Deck)

It is an implied term at the common law that the carrier will not carry the cargo on deck. Of course, this will be subject to any express contract to the contrary, which can be in the form of an agreement that the goods *will be* carried on deck or that the carrier has the *liberty* to carry on deck. If the carrier carries the cargo on deck without authority to carry on deck, that is called 'quasi-deviation'. It appears the words 'quasi-deviation' is used to denote a breach that is as serious as deviation and attracting similar consequences as a deviation.

In *Royal Exchange Shipping Co Ltd v Dixon,*[189] bales of cotton were carried on deck, without authority to so carry on deck. During the voyage, the ship was grounded and the master had to jettison some of the bales. The bill of lading contained a 'jettison' exception. The House of Lords held that the carrier lost the benefit of the exception as a result of the unauthorised carriage of cargo on deck. By carrying on deck, it was treated that the carrier was no longer in the performance of the contracted carriage, like how it will be treated in the case of a deviation.

---

[187] *Wibau Maschinenfabric Hartman SA and Another v Mackinnon Mackenzie & Co (The Chanda)* [1989] 2 Lloyd's Rep 494 (EW HC).

[188] *Daewoo Heavy Industries Ltd v Klipriver Shipping Ltd (The Kapitan Petko Voivoda)* [2003] EWCA Civ 451, [2003] 1 All ER (Comm) 801, [2003] 2 Lloyd's Rep 1, [2003] All ER (D) 46 (Apr) (EW CA).

[189] (1886) 12 App Cas 11.

The Rules do not expressly provide any corresponding duty. In fact, the Hague/Hague-Visby Rules render themselves inapplicable where the cargo is agreed to be carried on deck and is so carried.[190] There is nothing in the Rules to displace the common law implied term against carriage on deck.

Coming to the question of whether a quasi-deviation will deprive the carrier of the protection under the Hague or Hague-Visby Rules, the same considerations discussed in respect of the deviation will be relevant. In *The Chanda*,[191] the court refused to allow a carrier to rely on the Hague Rules package limitation by applying the 'four corners' rule[192] when there was a quasi-deviation by the unauthorised carrying of the cargo on deck. The Court of Appeal in *The Kapitan Petko Voivoda*,[193] overruled *The Chanda* and allowed the carrier to rely on the Hague Rules package limitation.

7.2.7 Obligation to Take Reasonable Care of Cargo

In *Notara v Henderson*,[194] Willes J recognised the wide scope of the duty of the shipowner to take reasonable care of the cargo. In this case, some beans were carried. The bill of lading excepted liability for "loss or damage arising from … accidents of the seas". During the voyage, a collision happened that resulted in the beans getting wet by seawater. The master stopped at a nearby port for repairs, and after repairs, proceeded to the discharge port. On discharge, it was found that the beans had been damaged by seawater. The cargo interest sued the carrier for the damage. The English Court of Exchequer found that it would have been reasonable for the master to temporarily discharge the beans and to allow them to be dried in a warehouse there. This was not done. The court held that the carrier was not entitled to rely on the exception which did not exclude liability for negligence. The corresponding obligation in the Hague/Hague-Visby Rules is in Article III(2), which provides as follows:

> 2. Subject to the provisions of Article IV, the carrier shall properly and carefully load, handle, stow, carry, keep, care for, and discharge the goods carried.

Article III(2) nearly includes the common law implied term in entirety with the words "care for". Hence, the utility of the common law implied term here is minimal in cases to which the Rules apply, save for any period that the common law may

---

190 Article I(c) of the Hague/Hague-Visby Rules.

191 *Wibau Maschinenfabric Hartman SA and Another v Mackinnon Mackenzie & Co (The Chanda)* [1989] 2 Lloyd's Rep 494 (EW HC).

192 When the performance is *radically* different from that agreed, the party is no longer performing that contract and is not entitled to rely on the terms of the contract.

193 *Daewoo Heavy Industries Ltd v Klipriver Shipping Ltd (The Kapitan Petko Voivoda)* [2003] EWCA Civ 451, [2003] 1 All ER (Comm) 801, [2003] 2 Lloyd's Rep 1, [2003] All ER (D) 46 (Apr) (EW CA).

194 (1872) LR 7 QB 225 (EW Court of Exchequer Chamber).

cover outside the coverage of the Rules.[195] Article III(2) is expressly made subject to Article IV defences. Article IV(2) of the Hague/Hague-Visby Rules accords to the carrier wide range of exclusions, which are as follows:

2. Neither the carrier nor the ship shall be responsible for loss or damage arising or resulting from:

> (a) Act, neglect, or default of the master, mariner, pilot, or the servants of the carrier in the navigation or in the management of the ship.
> (b) Fire, unless caused by the actual fault or privity of the carrier.
> (c) Perils, dangers and accidents of the sea or other navigable waters.
> (d) Act of God.
> (e) Act of war.
> (f) Act of public enemies.
> (g) Arrest or restraint or princes, rulers or people, or seizure under legal process.
> (h) Quarantine restrictions.
> (i) Act or omission of the shipper or owner of the goods, his agent or representative.
> (j) Strikes or lockouts or stoppage or restraint of labour from whatever cause, whether partial or general.
> (k) Riots and civil commotions.
> (l) Saving or attempting to save life or property at sea.
> (m) Wastage in bulk or weight or any other loss or damage arising from inherent defect, quality or vice of the goods.
> (n) Insufficiency of packing.
> (o) Insufficiency or inadequacy of marks.
> (p) Latent defects not discoverable by due diligence.
> (q) Any other cause arising without the actual fault or privity of the carrier, or without the actual fault or neglect of the agents or servants of the carrier, but the burden of proof shall be on the person claiming the benefit of this exception to show that neither the actual fault or privity of the carrier nor the fault or neglect of the agents or servants of the carrier contributed to the loss or damage.

7.3 Exclusion Clauses

Exclusion and limitation clauses have been interpreted restrictively not to cover a breach of an implied term unless the clause specifically covers such breach.[196] In *The Theodegmon*,[197] the English High Court refused to allow a carrier to rely on a general exclusion clause in respect of damage by grounding when the grounding was

---

[195] From the beginning of loading to the end of loading: Article II of the Hague/Hague-Visby Rules; *Pyrene Co Ltd v Scindia Navigation Co Ltd* [1954] 2 QB 402, [1954] 2 All ER 158, [1954] 2 WLR 1005, [1954] 1 Lloyd's Rep 321 (EW HC).

[196] *Lyon v Mells* (1804) 5 East 428 (EW HC).

[197] *Phillips Petroleum Co v Cabaneli Naviera SA (The Theodegmon)* [1990] 1 Lloyd's Rep 52 (EW HC).

caused by the unseaworthiness of the ship at the start of the voyage. In *The Maori King*,[198] similarly a clause excluding the liability of the shipowners for "failure or breakdown of machinery, insulation and other appliances" was held not to apply when the refrigeration system of the ship carrying a cargo of frozen mutton did not work properly at the start of the voyage. This rendered the ship uncargoworthy to carry a cargo of frozen mutton.

A similar restrictive approach was taken by the Singapore Court of Appeal when dealing with a question of seaworthiness-obligation.[199] In another Singapore case, *The Asia Star*,[200] a case decided by the Singapore Court of Appeal, a charterparty[201] for carrying palm provided in cl. 1(a) that the shipowner would exercise due diligence to make the ship seaworthy and the tanks cargoworthy before and at the commencement of the voyage. In cl. 1(b) it provided that if the tanks were found defective upon arrival at the loading port and could not be repaired within 24 h, the shipowner had the option of cancelling the charterparty. In this case, upon arrival of the ship at the loading port, the tanks were found defective which could not be repaired within 24 h and the shipowner invoked cl. 1(b). The court acknowledged that seaworthiness-obligation was a fundamental one and can only be excepted by 'express, pertinent and apposite' words. However, in this case, the court opined that cl. 1(b) and its invocation were sufficient to exempt the shipowners from seaworthiness-obligation.[202]

In a Malaysian case, *Playing Cards (Malaysia) Sdn Bhd v China Mutual Navigation Co Ltd*,[203] a carrier issued a 'received for shipment' bill naming the vessel The SS Priam. However, the carrier missed shipping on board that vessel, and subsequently shipped on board another vessel, resulting in a delay in the arrival of about six months. The holder of the bill sued the carrier. The carrier relied on an exclusion clause that exempted the carrier from any liability for delay. The Malaysian Federal court allowed the carrier to successfully rely on the clause. This decision is against the line of authorities and does not seem to represent the good law to be followed. It would have been more in line with authorities to refuse to allow the carrier to rely on the exclusion clause for two reasons. First, the exclusion clause did not relate to any breach of the obligation to ship on board the particular vessel The SS Priam. If the goods were shipped on board this vessel and there was a delay in the arrival of the ship for whatever reason, only then the exclusion clause could cover. Second, the breach here is, at least arguably, about the failure of the carrier to proceed with reasonable dispatch, a common law implied term, which can only be excepted by direct reference and not by a clause merely excepting liability for delay.

---

[198] *Owners of Cargo on The Maori King v Hughes (The Maori King)* [1895] 2 QB 550, [1895] 7 WLUK 104 (EW CA).

[199] *Sunlight Mercantile Pte Ltd and Another v Ever Lucky Shipping Co Ltd* [2003] SGCA 47, [2004] 1 SLR 171 (SG CA). See Chap. 7.2.3.3.

[200] *The Asia Star* [2007] SGCA 17, [2007] 3 SLR 1 (SG CA).

[201] In VEGOILVOY 1950 form (tanker voyage-charterparty) .

[202] However, the court held the shipowner liable, as it breached the contractual description of the ship as epoxy quoted, which was not excepted by the cl. 1(b), and hence it was not so necessary to decide the seaworthiness and cargoworthiness obligations.

[203] [1980] 2 MLJ 182 (MY FC).

7.3.1 'Perils of the Sea' Exception

One of the popular exclusion clauses found in contracts for carriage of goods by sea, particularly those contracts to which the Hague or Hague-Visby Rules do not apply, is the 'perils of the sea' exception. For an event to be classified as a peril of the sea, it must be a fortuitous one and must be peculiar to carriage by sea, as opposed to carriage by any other modes of transport. The damage caused by it must be a 'sea damage, occurring at sea and nobody's fault'.[204] In *The Stranna*,[205] the carrier successfully relied on a 'peril of the sea' exception clause to protect itself when the cargo fell overboard while loading when the ship listed. Other common examples of the perils of the sea include collision,[206] grounding[207] and ingress of water.[208]

However, the 'peril of the sea' exception will not protect the carrier when the event was the result of a breach of one of the implied terms. For instance, ingress of water will be a peril of the sea. However, the clause will not cover the loss when the ingress was the result of the unseaworthiness of the ship. The burden of proving that the event falls within the exception clause will be on the party relying on the clause, that is, the carrier. In *The Torenia*,[209] the ship sank. The carrier was not able to rely on a 'peril of the sea' cause as the most likely cause of the sinking was a defect in the structure of the ship that would amount to the unseaworthiness of the ship at the start of the voyage. The burden of proving otherwise was on the carrier which it failed to discharge. Courts will restrictively construe any exclusion clause relied on to exclude or limit liability for breach of an implied term.[210]

7.3.2 Excluding Liability for 'Negligence'

Similarly, a clause excepting liability for 'errors of navigation' has been held not to cover *negligent* errors of navigation.[211] Ordinarily, liability for negligence can only be excepted by a clause specifically or necessarily covering negligence.

---

[204] Per Lopes LJ in *Hamilton, Fraser & Co v Pandorf & Co* (1885) 16 QBD 629 (EW HC). Although the decision in this case was reversed by the House of Lords in (1887) 12 App Cas 518, [1886–90] All ER Rep 220 (UK HL), that did not disturb quotation of Lopes LJ referred to above.

[205] *The Stranna* [1938] P 69, [1938] 1 All ER 458 (EW CA).

[206] *Thomas Wilson, Sons & Co v Owners of the Cargo per The Xantho (The Xantho)* (1887) 12 App Cas 503, [1886–90] All ER Rep 212 (UK HL).

[207] *Phillips Petroleum Co v Cabaneli Naviera SA (The Theodegmon)* [1990] 1 Lloyd's Rep 52 (EW HC).

[208] *Hamilton, Fraser & Co v Pandorf & Co* (1887) 12 App Cas 518, [1886–90] All ER Rep 220 (UK HL).

[209] *Aktieselskabet de Danske Sukkerfabrikker v Bajamar Compania Naviera SA (The Torenia)* [1983] 2 Lloyd's Rep 210 (EW HC).

[210] Discussed at length earlier.

[211] *Industrie Chimiche Italia Centrale SpA v Nea Ninemia Shipping Co SA (The Emmanuel C)* [1983] 1 Lloyd's Rep 310, [1983] 1 All ER 686 (EW HC).

It must be noted that Section 2(2) of the UK Unfair Contract Terms Act 1977 does not come into play in the context of the Hague/Hague-Visby Rules. This is because paragraph 2 of Schedule 2 to the Act excludes the operation of the Section 2(2) in the case of a contract for carriage of goods by ship. However, other than for the period of carriage, there is nothing to prevent the Section 2(2) coming into operation, with the result that any exception will be subject to a test of reasonableness. By virtue of Section 27(1), the Section 2 will apply only if the UK law is applicable not by choice of parties only.

7.3.3 Burden of Proof

In *The Glendarroch,*[212] the Court of Appeal held that once the shipowner had brought itself within the scope of the exceptions clause, then it will be protected unless the claimant can prove negligence on part of the shipowner or breach of an implied term that is not excepted. However, *The Glendarroch* was overruled by the House of Lords in *Volcafe v CSAV,*[213] whereby the carrier will only be able to rely on the exceptions clause if it can prove lack of negligence on its part. This is in somewhat endorsement of the view of Lord Sumner in *FC Bradley & Sons Ltd v Federal Steam Navigation Co Ltd*[214] that it is a condition precedent for the carrier to rely on an exceptions clause that it first proves it was not negligent and was not in breach of the implied terms.

Accordingly, now the burden of proof is on the carrier to establish not only that the event falls within the exceptions clause but also that the carrier was not in breach of one of the three implied terms and that, unless the exceptions clause necessarily covers negligence, it was not negligent. This is tantamount to putting the carrier nearly in the position of a bailee.[215]

---

212 *The Glendarroch* [1894] P 226, [1891–4] All ER Rep 484 (EW CA)

213 *Volcafe Ltd and others v Compania Sud Americana De Vapores SA (t/a CSAV)* [2018] UKSC 61, [2019] AC 358, [2019] 2 All ER 81, [2018] 3 WLR 2087, [2019] 1 All ER (Comm) 397, [2019] 1 Lloyd's Rep 21, [2018] All ER (D) 16 (Dec) (UK SC).

214 (1927) 27 Ll L Rep 395 at 396 (UK HL).

215 Called the 'bailment reasoning'.

Chapter 8
Hague/Hague-Visby Rules: Application

This chapter analyses the statutory and voluntary application of the Hague/Hague-Visby Rules. The significance of the difference between the two types of application are set out clearly and it is considered how conflicts between the provisions of the Rules and the terms of the bill of lading are resolved by the courts. The criteria for statutory application of the Rules based on the Hague Rules and the Hague-Visby Rules and the Carriage of Goods by Sea Act 1971 are critically examined. The various measures employed by parties to circumvent the Rules, including jurisdiction and choice of law clauses, and how courts control such measures are considered in case of the Hague Rules and Hague-Visby Rules are visited. The Article IV*bis* introduced in the Hague-Visby Rules to extend the protection under the Rules to servants and agents of the carrier is considered. Finally, the principles applicable in interpreting the Rules are looked at.

8.1 Introduction

The Hague/Hague-Visby Rules[1] may apply statutorily or contractually in any given case.[2] When the Rules apply statutorily, they may not be contractually ousted. But the provisions in the Rules may be ousted or modified, when the Rules are voluntarily incorporated. A clause incorporating the Rules, called 'clause paramount', is common in charterparties and sea waybills. It may not always be straightforward question whether the Rules apply in a given case by operation of statute or by voluntary incorporation. The complexity surrounding this question will be dealt with in this chapter.

---

[1] For the relevant rules applicable in the case of the UK, Malaysia and Singapore, see Chap. 1.3.1.

[2] They can also apply to charterparties, but only by voluntary incorporation—without statutory force. In the circumstances mentioned in Section 1(6)(c) of the UK Carriage of Goods by Sea Act 1971/Section 3(4) of the Singapore Carriage of Goods by Sea Act, the Hague-Visby Rules will apply statutorily to sea waybills.

A. Kasi, *The Law of Carriage of Goods by Sea*,
https://doi.org/10.1007/978-981-33-6793-7_8

When the Rules would apply statutorily, carriers have attempted to employ certain mechanisms to be out of the Rules or a particular set of Rules. For example, a carrier may place into the bill of lading jurisdiction and choice of law clauses pointing to a jurisdiction and law which either has not subscribed to any Rules or has subscribed to a set of Rules that is more favourable to the carrier.[3] The courts have been vigilant about such mechanisms and construed such clauses narrowly[4] or even have held them to be invalid.[5]

The significance of the distinction between statutory application of the Rules and the contractual application will first be briefly looked at, followed by a consideration of conflicts between the terms of the Rules and the terms of the bill. Then, the criteria for the statutory application of the Rules will be analysed and it will be seen how the courts deal with parties' measures to circumvent the statutory application of the Rules such as by jurisdiction clauses. That is followed by a visit to Article IV*bis* of the Hague-Visby Rules that was introduced into the Rules to extend the protection accorded to the carriers under the Rules to actions in tort and to third parties such as the servants and agents. Finally, a note about rules applicable in interpreting the Rules.

8.2 Significance of Distinction Between Statutory and Contractual Application

The significance of the distinction between the statutory application and contractual application of the Rules is that in the case of the former the Rules may not be ousted by any term of the bill of lading so as to render it more unfavourable to the shipper than that under the Rules, by virtue of Article III(8) of the Hague/Hague-Visby Rules.[6] When they apply by voluntary incorporation only, then any part of the Rules may be modified or ousted by the terms of the bill of lading or the shipping document. Article III(8) reads as follows:

> 8. Any clause, covenant, or *agreement in a contract of carriage relieving the carrier* or the ship from liability for loss or damage to, or in connection with, goods arising from negligence, fault, or failure in the duties and obligations provided in this article *or lessening such liability* otherwise than as provided in these Rules, shall be null and void and of no effect. A benefit of insurance in favour of the carrier or similar clause shall be deemed to be a clause relieving the carrier from liability. [emphasis added]

---

[3] *Vita Foods Products Inc v Unus Shipping Co Ltd* [1939] AC 277, [1939] 1 All ER 513 (PC on appeal from Nova Scotia).

[4] *The Fehmarn* [1958] 1 All ER 333, [1958] 1 WLR 159, [1957] 2 Lloyd's Rep 551 (EW CA).

[5] *The Hollandia* [1983] 1 AC 565, [1982] 3 All ER 1141, [1982] 3 WLR 1111, [1983] 1 Lloyd's Rep 1 (UK HL); *The Epar* [1985] 2 MLJ 3 (SG HC).

[6] In *Shun Cheong Steam Navigation Co Ltd v Wo Fong Trading Co* [1979] 2 MLJ 254 (MY FC), the Malaysian Federal Court held a clause in the bill of lading, to which the Hague Rules was applicable, limiting liability to HKD300 to be invalid by virtue of Article III(8).

8.3 Conflict Between Terms of Bill and the Rules

When the Rules apply by voluntary incorporation, if there is an inconsistency between the Rules and an express term of the bill of lading or other shipping document, usually the express term will prevail over an incorporated term, in the event of inconsistency.[7] However, if the Rules apply statutorily, then, of course, the Rules will prevail over any term of the contract.

In *The Strathnewton*,[8] a time charterparty voluntarily incorporated both Inter-Club Agreement and the Hague-Visby Rules. The Hague-Visby Rules has a one-year time limit for cargo claims,[9] while the Inter-Club Agreement has a three-year time limit. The English Court of Appeal held that the Hague-Visby Rules time limit did not apply for an indemnity claim by the charterer against the shipowner, hence the Inter-Club Agreement time limit applied.

In *Finagra (UK) Ltd v OT Africa Line Ltd*,[10] the Hague Rules were voluntarily incorporated into a bill of lading. The Hague Rules provides a time limit of one year to bring cargo claims.[11] However, an express term of the bill limited the time to bring a cargo claim to nine months. The English High Court gave effect to the one-year time limit in the Hague Rules against the express nine-month period time limit. To the contrary, in a New Zealand case, *The Tasman Discoverer*,[12] the Court of Appeal gave effect to an express specific package limitation in the bill against the package limitation in the Hague Rules, when the Hague Rules applied by voluntary incorporation.

8.4 Statutory Application of the Rules

The Rules have certain criteria for their application. The criteria in the Hague Rules and the Hague-Visby Rules differ. As far as these criteria are concerned, there is no difference between the Hague-Visby Rules without SDR Protocol and the Hague-Visby Rules as amended by SDR Protocol. The applicable statute giving effect to the Rules will have some criteria for the application of the Rules. Accordingly, the

---

[7] *Homburg Houtimport BV v Agrosin Private Ltd (The Starsin)* [2003] UKHL 12, [2004] 1 AC 715, [2003] 2 All ER 785, [2003] 2 WLR 711, [2003] 1 All ER (Comm) 625, [2003] 1 Lloyd's Rep 571 [2003] All ER (D) 192 (Mar) (UK HL).

[8] *D/S A/S Idaho v Peninsular and Oriental Steam Navigation Co (The Strathnewton)* [1983] 1 Lloyd's Rep 219 (EW CA).

[9] Article III(6).

[10] [1998] 2 Lloyd's Rep 622, [1998] All ER (D) 296 (EW HC).

[11] Article III(6).

[12] *Dairy Containers Ltd v Tasman Orient Line CV (The Tasman Discoverer)* [2002] 1 Lloyd's Rep 528, [2002] 3 NZLR 353 (NZ CA), affirmed by the Privy Council in [2004] UKPC 22, [2005] 1 WLR 215, [2004] 2 All ER (Comm) 667, [2004] 5 LRC 511, [2004] 2 Lloyd's Rep 647.

criteria in both the applicable Rules and the applicable Act must be read together to determine when statutory force will be given to the Rules.

In the UK, the applicable Rules are the Hague-Visby Rules and the applicable statute is the 1971 Act. Accordingly, the criteria applicable in the UK and Singapore are largely similar. This will differ from country to country. In the case of Singapore, they are the Hague-Visby Rules and the Singapore Carriage of Goods by Sea Act.[13] In Malaysia, the applicable Rules are the Hague Rules and the applicable statute is the Carriage of Goods by Sea Act 1950.[14]

It must be noted that Section 4 of the Malaysian 1950 Act, which is materially identical to Section 3 of the repealed UK 1924 Act, requires the fact of application of the rules to be declared in the bill of lading. Many jurisdictions that remain with the Hague Rules have an Act modelled on the UK 1924 Act with a similar requirement. The Section 4 of the Malaysian 1950 Act reads as follows:

> Every bill of lading, or similar document of title, issued in Malaysia which contains or is evidence of any contract to which the Rules apply shall contain an express statement that it is to have effect subject to the said Rules as applied by this Act.

However, if the clause paramount is missed, it has no impact on the statutory application of the Rules. This point was emphasised by the Privy Council in *Vita Foods Products Inc v Unus Shipping Co Ltd*[15] as follows:

> [T]he omission of what is called the clause paramount does not make the bills of lading illegal documents, in whole or in part, either within Newfoundland or outside it. Section 3 is in their Lordships' judgment directory. It is not obligatory, nor does failure to comply with its terms nullify the contract contained in the bill of lading. This, in their Lordships' judgment, is the true construction of the statute, having regard to its scope and its purpose and to the inconvenience which would follow from any other conclusion.

It was similarly said by the Malaysian High Court, when dealing with Malaysian Carriage of Goods by Sea Act 1950, which is materially identical to the UK 1924 Act, in the case of *Sarawak Electricity Supply Corp v MS Shipping Sdn Bhd*,[16] where the High Court expressed:

> [T]he shipping order is as good as a document of tile … This is notwithstanding the absence of an endorsement on the shipping order that it is subject to the Hague Rules because the failure to comply with reg [or s] 4[17] did not render the shipping order an illegal document or render the contract of carriage illegal.

---

[13] Which is largely similar to the UK 1971 Act.

[14] Which is materially identical to the now repealed UK Carriage of Goods by Sea Act 1924.

[15] [1939] AC 277 at 295, [1939] UKPC 7 (PC on appeal from Nova Scotia).

[16] [2000] 5 MLJ 721 (MY HC in Sarawak).

[17] Section 4 of the Malaysian 1950 Act is equivalent to Section 3 of the UK 1924 Act.

8.4.1 Criteria for Application of the Rules

The criteria in the Hague and Hague-Visby Rules are contained in Articles I(b), I(c), I(e), II and X. Except for Article X, these Articles mentioned are the same in the Hague Rules and the Hague-Visby Rules. Criteria in the UK Carriage of Goods by Sea Act 1971 are contained in Sections 1(3), 1(4), 1(6) and 1(7). In the case of Singapore, the corresponding statutory provisions are Sections 3(2), 3(3), 3(4), 3(5), 3(6) and 3(7) of the Carriage of Goods by Sea Act, which are materially identical to the UK provisions.[18] Each of these provisions, based on the UK 1971 Act is considered below.[19]

8.4.1.1 Article II

Article II renders the Rules applicable to contracts of carriage of goods by sea. Article II reads as follows:

> Subject to the provisions of Article VI, under every *contract of carriage* of *goods* by sea the carrier, in relation to the loading, handling, stowage, carriage, custody, care and discharge of such goods, shall be subject to the responsibilities and liabilities and entitled to the rights and immunities hereinafter set forth. [emphasis added]

In turn, Article I(b) defines 'contract of carriage', Article I(c) defines 'goods' and Article I(e) defines 'carriage of goods'.

8.4.1.2 Article I(b)

Article I(b) of the Rules defines 'contract of carriage' as follows:

> (b) 'Contract of carriage' applies *only* to *contracts of carriage covered by a bill of lading* or any similar document of title, in so far as such document relates to the carriage of goods by sea, including any bill of lading or any similar document as aforesaid issued under or pursuant to a charter party from the moment at which such bill of lading or similar document of title regulates the relations between a carrier and a holder of the same.

The conditions in Article I(b) are that the contract of carriage is covered by a bill of lading. Literally, this will cover both 'shipped' bills and 'received for shipment' bills.[20] The words 'or any similar document of title' may cover when a document

---

[18] In Malaysia, the relevant statutory provisions are in Sections 2 and 4 of the Carriage of Goods by Sea Act 1950, which is materially similar to the repealed UK 1924 Act.

[19] But not necessarily in the order stated above.

[20] There can be instances where a 'received for shipment' bill may be issued and subsequently the goods will be carried but no shipped bill delivered to the consignor.

such as a mate's receipt[21] is treated as a document of title by trade custom.[22] In *Chan Cheng Kum v Wah Tat Bank*,[23] the Privy Council, when recognising, by relevant trade custom at that time in relation to shipments from Sarawak[24] to Singapore, a mate's receipt as a negotiable document of title in place of a bill of lading, said this:

> A good and established custom 'obtains the force of a law, and is, in effect, the common law within that place to which it extends'. Thus the custom in this case, if proved, takes effect as part of the common law of Singapore. As such it will be applied by any court dealing with any matter which that court treats as governed by the law of Singapore. In this sense it is binding not only in Singapore but on anyone anywhere in the world." This was said by the court when dealing with negotiability of mate's receipt that was issued in place of bill of lading by trade custom in relation to shipments from Sarawak (Malaysia) to Singapore at that time.

In *Official Assignee of Madras v Mercantile Bank of India Ltd*,[25] the Privy Council held[26] that railway receipts were documents of title.[27] Similarly, the Rules recognises and covers carriages under 'received for shipment' bills of lading. This will be made clearer by a reading of Articles III(3) and III(7) of the Rules.[28] The Articles III(3) reads as follows:

> 3. After *receiving* the goods *into his charge* the carrier or the master or agent of the carrier shall, on demand of the shipper, issue to the shipper a *bill of lading* showing among other things:
>
> (a) The leading marks necessary for identification of the goods as the same are furnished in writing by the shipper before the loading of such goods starts, provided such marks are stamped or otherwise shown clearly upon the goods if uncovered, or on the cases or coverings in which such goods are contained, in such a manner as should ordinarily remain legible until the end of the voyage.
>
> (b) Either the number of packages or pieces, or the quantity, or weight, as the case may be, as furnished in writing by the shipper.
>
> (c) The apparent order and condition of the goods.
>
> Provided that no carrier, master or agent of the carrier shall be bound to state or show in the bill of lading any marks, number, quantity or weight which he has reasonable ground for suspecting not accurately to represent the goods actually received, or which he has had no reasonable means of checking. [emphasis added]

---

21 *Chan Cheng Kum v Wah Tat Bank* [1971] 1 Lloyd's Rep 439, [1971] 1 MLJ 177 (PC on appeal from Singapore).

22 In effect, the reference to document of title here is one to a document conferring entitlement to claim the goods from the carrier and that is transferable—see Chap. 2.2 for a detailed discussion.

23 [1971] 1 Lloyd's Rep 439, [1971] 1 MLJ 177 (PC on appeal from Singapore).

24 Malaysia.

25 [1935] AC 53, 104 LJPC 1, [1934] All ER Rep 237, 4 LDAB 462 (PC on appeal from India).

26 By specific reference to the *then* Section 178 of the Indian Contract Act 1872, which provided "A person who is in possession of any goods, or of any bill of lading, order for delivery, or any other document of title to goods, may make a valid pledge of such goods, or documents ..."

27 In the sense that it conferred the possessory right on the holder of the receipts.

28 Same both in the Hague and Hague-Visby Rules.

Article III(7) reads as follows:

> 7. After the goods are *loaded* the bill of lading to be issued by the carrier, master, or agent of the carrier, to the shipper shall, if the shipper so demands be a *'shipped' bill of lading*, provided that if the shipper shall have previously taken up any document of title to such goods, he shall surrender the same as against the issue of the 'shipped' bill of lading, but at the option of the carrier such document of title may be noted at the port of shipment by the carrier, master, or agent with the name or names of the ship or ships upon which the goods have been shipped and the date or dates of shipment, and when so noted, if it shows the particulars mentioned in paragraph 3 of Article III, shall for the purpose of this article be deemed to constitute a 'shipped' bill of lading. [emphasis added]

Article III(3) confers a right on the shipper to demand a *bill of lading* after the goods are *received* by the carrier into its charge. Article III(7) confers a right on the shipper to demand a *shipped* bill of lading after the goods have been *loaded*. When cargo has been delivered to the carrier prior to loading, Article III(3) will mean a right to demand 'received for shipment' bill. Article III(7) expressly means the right to demand 'shipped' bill after loading, subject to the surrender of any prior document, which must necessarily include 'received for shipment' bill.

It has been held that the reference in the Article to the bill of lading encompasses also 'straight' bills.[29] In the case of a bill of lading in the hands of a charterer, the Rules do not apply as long as the bill is in the hands of the charterer, as the relationship between the carrier and the charterer will be regulated by the charterparty.[30]

A literal reading of the Article will suggest that it does not cover when no bill has been issued. The Privy Council in *Vita Foods Products Inc v Unus Shipping Company Ltd*[31] expressed this to be the position. In this case, the Hague Rules was applicable under the regime of an Act similar to the UK 1924 Act.

However, courts have held that this shortfall has been redressed by the UK 1971 Act, by interpreting Section 1(4) as extending the application of the Rules to cases where no bill of lading is issued but one was contemplated. The Section 1(4) provides:

> Subject to subsection (6) below, nothing in this section shall be taken as applying anything in the Rules to any contract for the carriage of goods by sea, unless *the contract expressly or by implication provides for the issue of a bill of lading* or any similar document of title. [emphasis added]

In cases where the goods have been damaged while loading, there may be no bill issued. In such cases, the question of whether the Rules apply becomes a crucial one as the liability of the carrier[32] will vastly vary depending on whether the Rules apply.

---

[29] *MacWilliam (JI) Co Inc v Mediterranean Shipping Co SA (The Rafaela S)* [2005] UKHL 11, [2005] 2 AC 423, [2005] 2 All ER 86, [2005] 2 WLR 554, [2005] 1 All ER (Comm) 393, [2005] 1 Lloyd's Rep 347 (UK HL); *APL Co Pte Ltd v Voss Peer* [2002] 4 SLR 481 (SG CA), also reported as *Voss v APL Co Pte Ltd* [2003] 3 LRC 632, [2002] 2 Lloyd's Rep 707 (SG CA).

[30] See Chap. 2.2.10.8 for a more detailed discussion of this subject.

[31] [1939] AC 277 at 287–288, [1939] 1 All ER 513 (PC on appeal from Nova Scotia), speech of Lord Wright delivering the judgment of the board.

[32] And its entitlement to limit any liability.

This happened in *The Happy Ranger*,[33] where the English Court of Appeal held the Rules to be applicable by virtue of the Section 1(4). In this case, a large heavy reactor was to be carried from Italy, which at that time had not legislated the Hague-Visby Rules. During loading, the reactor fell and was damaged before crossing the ship's rail, for which the carrier was responsible. No bill of lading was issued. The cargo owner brought a claim against the carrier for damage to the reactor in the sum of about USD2.4 million. As per the terms of the contract between the carrier and the shipper, where the Hague-Visby Rules did not apply statutorily (as in this case), the contract was subject to the Hague-Rules and a liability-limitation of £100 per package. If the Hague-Visby Rules applied, then the liability-limitation, in this case, will be on the weight, which will come to about USD2 million. Accordingly, it was crucial to decide whether the Hague-Visby Rules applied statutorily despite that no bill of lading was issued. The court found that the contract between the parties contemplated issuance of a bill of lading, which if issued would undoubtedly have been subject to the Hague-Visby Rules. The court held that the Hague-Visby Rules statutorily applied. Thus, the carrier was liable on a weight basis as opposed to a package basis.

Similarly, in *The Maersk Tangier*,[34] more than a thousand pieces of frozen tuna were carried from Spain, which applied the Hague-Visby Rules. The 1971 Act was applicable in this case. The cargo was stuffed as unpackaged pieces into three freezer containers. The contract between the carrier and the shipper contemplated issuance of a bill of lading. However, due to some issues in transshipment, to avoid delay, parties agreed that a sea waybill would be issued respectively for each container, which was accordingly issued. They described the goods carried like "1 Container Said to Contain *xxx* pcs—Frozen Bluefin Tuna Loins *xxx* kgs'. The cargo arrived in damaged condition due to failure of the reefer. The English Court of Appeal followed *The Happy Ranger* and held that the Hague-Visby Rules applied by virtue of Section 1(4) of the 1971 Act, despite that a sea waybill was issued because the contract originally contemplated issuance of bills of lading. The court also held that for purposes of package limitation in the Hague-Visby Rules, each piece of unpackaged tuna constituted a unit of package.

For jurisdictions that remain with the UK 1924 Act model adopting the Hague Rules, like Malaysia,[35] *The Happy Ranger* and *The Maersk Tangier* position will not be applicable. Rather, the position expressed in *Vita Foods* will be applicable—if no bill of lading is issued, no application of the Rules.

An issue with Article III(3) is that it requires the bill to be given to the shipper on demand by the shipper. However, in practice, a bill should be given to the consignor,

---

[33] *Parsons Corp v CV Scheepvaartonderneming (The Happy Ranger)* [2002] EWHC Civ 649, [2002] 2 All ER (Comm) 24, [2002] 2 Lloyd's Rep 357, [2002] All ER (D) 278 (May) (EW CA).

[34] *Kyokuyo Co Ltd v AP Møller-Maersk A/S (trading as 'Maersk Line') (The Maersk Tangier)* [2018] EWCA Civ 778, [2018] 3 All ER 1009, [2018] 2 All ER (Comm) 503, [2018] 2 Lloyd's Rep 59, [2018] All ER (D) 90 (Apr) (EW CA).

[35] Except for the federal territory of Labuan. See Chap. 1.3.6.2 for a detailed discussion of this point.

who may be a different person from the shipper, such as in the case of a pure fob[36] contract. This, by custom, must be done even without any requirement of demand by any person. The significance of the bill being given to the consignor is that the consignor may have to tender the bill to the buyer or the buyer's bankers for payment under letter of credit. As the bill is a document of receipt of cargo, it should only be given to the consignor as the person who delivers the goods. Giving a receipt to any other will be inconsistent with reality. Despite the defective drafting of the Article III(3), there does not seem to be any case where it was argued that the bill must be given to the shipper as opposed to the consignor.

8.4.1.3 Article I(c)

Article I(c) of the Rules defines 'goods' as follows:

> (c) 'Goods' includes goods, wares, merchandise, and articles of every kind whatsoever except live animals and cargo which by the contract of carriage is stated as being carried on deck and is so carried.

Deck cargo will go out of coverage of the Rules only if both conditions are satisfied, namely, it is agreed to be so carried and is so carried. This is called 'deck cargo', which falls outside the mandatory coverage of the Rules.

In *Svenska Traktor Aktiebolget v Maritime Agencies (Southampton) Ltd*,[37] a clause in the bill of lading gave the 'liberty' to the carrier to carry on deck. The English High Court held this not to attract Article I(c) exception, with the result the Hague-Rules applied.

8.4.1.4 Article I(d)

Article I(d) of the Rules defines 'ship' as follows:

> (d) 'Ship' means any vessel used for the carriage of goods by sea.

In *National Jaya (Pte) Ltd v Hong Tat Marine Shipping Pte Ltd*,[38] the Singapore High Court held that rudderless barge, having the cargo claimant's cargo, on tow by another vessel was a ship within the definition in Article I(d).

8.4.1.5 Article I(e)

Article I(e) of the Rules defines 'goods' as follows:

---

[36] 'Free on board'.

[37] [1953] 2 QB 295, [1953] 3 WLR 426, [1953] 2 All ER 570, [1953] 2 Lloyd's Rep 124, (1953) 97 SJ 525 ABD (EW HC).

[38] [1979] 2 MLJ 6 (SG HC).

(e) 'Carriage of goods' covers the period from the time when the goods are loaded on to the time they are discharged from the ship.

It is trite that the period of carriage of goods referred to by the Rules includes the entire loading and discharge operations, which will be more than the strict 'tackle to tackle' period.[39] Article II will support this position as it applies the rights and immunities under the Rules to 'loading, handling, storage, carriage, custody, care and discharge'. The loading and discharge referred to in Article II will, by a literal reading, refer to the entire operation of loading and discharge.

When the carriage involves transshipment, questions have arisen as to whether the Rules apply when the goods are in the intermediate port while waiting for transshipment. This is called a period of 'convention gap'. It is settled that if the contract was for carriage with transshipment, then the Rules cease to statutorily apply when they have been discharged at the transshipment port and will apply again when reloaded.[40] Upon reloading, the Rules that apply may be a different one from that which applied from the original port. For instance, if the carriage is from London to Sydney, with transshipment in Kuala Lumpur,[41] then statutorily, the Hague-Visby Rules will apply for the leg from London to Kuala Lumpur, and the Hague Rules from the leg from Kuala Lumpur to Sydney—because Malaysia[42] statutorily applies the Hague Rules.

In *The Rafaela S*,[43] some printing equipment was carried from Durban to Boston. The bill of lading provided for carriage from Durban to Felixstowe, and onward to Boston. The House of Lords held that the contract contemplated two voyages, one from Durban to Felixstowe and another from Felixstowe to Boston. In other words, the contracted carriage was by transshipment. At that time, Durban applied the Hague Rules and Felixstowe applied the Hague-Visby Rules. Accordingly, the House held that the Hague Rules applied for the first leg and the Hague-Visby Rules of the second leg.

It is quite accepted that if the transshipment is effected by a 'liberty' clause, in the bill of lading, to transship, then the operation of the Rules will not break while the goods are transshipped. In the above example, if the bill of lading does not say that the goods *will be* transshipped at Kuala Lumpur but merely states that the carrier has the *liberty* to transship, then the Hague-Visby Rules for the entire period from London to Sydney including the holding period in Kuala Lumpur.

---

[39] *Pyrene Co Ltd v Scindia Navigation Co Ltd* [1954] 2 QB 402, [1954] 2 All ER 158, [1954] 2 WLR 1005, [1954] 1 Lloyd's Rep 321 (EW HC). It has been held in the same way in Malaysia: *KMA Abdul Rahim & Anor v Owners of Lexa Maersk & Ors* [1954] 2 QB 402 (MY HC).

[40] *Captain v Far Eastern Shipping Co* [1979] 1 Lloyd's Rep 595 (Canada SC).

[41] Port Kelang, Malaysia.

[42] Except for the federal territory of Labuan. See Chap. 1.3.6.2 for a detailed discussion of this point.

[43] *MacWilliam (JI) Co Inc v Mediterranean Shipping Co SA (The Rafaela S)* [2005] UKHL 11, [2005] 2 AC 423, [2005] 2 All ER 86, [2005] 2 WLR 554, [2005] 1 All ER (Comm) 393, [2005] 1 Lloyd's Rep 347 (UK HL).

In *Mayhew Foods Ltd v Overseas Containers Ltd*,[44] the cargo was carried from Sussex to Jeddah. The cargo was transshipped at Le Havre.[45] The bill of lading was issued at Le Havre and it contained a 'liberty to transship' clause. The English High Court held that the Hague-Visby Rules applied from the point of loading in Sussex to the point of discharge in Jeddah, including the holding period at Le Havre.

Although in strict transshipment cases, the Rules will not apply during the period of storage in the transshipment port, commonly, the bill of lading will provide for the application of one of the Rules. In such cases, the Rules will apply by voluntary incorporation subject to other terms of the bill of lading, rather than with statutory force. Even if the bill of lading does not so provide, by implication, one of the Rules may apply.[46]

8.4.1.6 Article X

Article X set out the applicability of the Rules per se. Article X in the Hague Rules and Hague Visby Rules differ. In the Hague Rules, Article X reads as follows:

> The provisions of this Convention shall apply to all *bills of lading issued in any of the Contracting States*. [emphasis added]

The criteria for application of the rules, in the Hague Rules, are only that (i) the shipping document is a bill of lading and (ii) it is issued in a Contracting State. In *Mayhew Foods Ltd v Overseas Containers Ltd*,[47] the cargo was shipped from Sussex to Jeddah. The bill of Lading was only issued at Le Havre at the point of transshipment. The English High Court held that the Rules applied to the entire carriage from Sussex to Jeddah. This case was decided in a different context where both the shipment was from the UK, that applied the Hague-Visby Rules and the bill was issued in France, which too applied the Hague-Visby Rules. The point that is relevant from this case to the Hague Rules is that if a shipment is from a non-contracting State and the bill is subsequently issued in a contracting State, then the Hague Rules will apply for the entire carriage. In the Hague-Visby Rules, Article X reads as follows:

> The provisions of these Rules shall apply to every *bill of lading* relating to the carriage of goods *between ports in two different States* if
>
> (a) the bill of lading is *issued in a contracting State*, or
>
> (b) the carriage is from a port in a contracting State, or

---

[44] [1984] 1 Lloyd's Rep 317 (EW HC).

[45] France.

[46] *Mediterranean Shipping Co SA v Trafigura Beheer BV and Another (The MSC Amsterdam)* [2007] EWCA Civ 794, [2008] 1 All ER (Comm) 385, [2007] 2 Lloyd's Rep 622, [2007] All ER (D) 444 (Jul) (EW CA).

[47] [1984] 1 Lloyd's Rep 317 (EW HC).

(c) the contract contained in or evidenced by the *bill of lading provides* that these Rules or legislation of any State giving effect to them are to *govern* the contract;

whatever may be the nationality of the ship, the carrier, the shipper, the consignee, or any other interested person.

Each Contracting State shall apply the provisions of this Convention to the bills of lading mentioned above.

This Article shall not prevent a Contracting State from applying the Rules of this Convention to bills of lading not included in the preceding paragraphs. [emphasis added]

Thus, as per the Rules, it applies in case of international carriages where (i) the bill of lading is issued in a contracting state, (ii) the shipment is from a contracting state, or (iii) the bill of lading provides for the application of the Rules or the legislation giving effect to the Rules.[48]

Bill of Lading—Extended to Sea Waybills

Although the opening words of Article X renders the Hague-Visby Rules applicable only to a bill of lading, Section 1(6)(b) of the UK 1971 Act provides for the application of the Rules to be extended to sea waybills if it expressly provides that the Rules are to govern the contract as if the receipt were a bill of lading. The Section 1(6) reads as follows:

Without prejudice to Article X(c) of the Rules, the Rules shall have the force of law in relation to—

(a) any bill of lading if the contract contained in or evidenced by it expressly provides that the Rules shall govern the contract, and

(b) any receipt which is a *non-negotiable document* marked as such if the contract contained in or evidenced by it is a contract for the carriage of goods by sea which *expressly provides that the Rules are to govern the contract as if the receipt were a bill of lading*, [emphasis added]

In *The Vechscroon*,[49] the English High Court held that the general incorporation clause was sufficient to attract the operation of Section 1(6)(b) of the UK 1971 Act. This will dilute the difference between statutory application of the Rules and voluntary incorporation of the Rules, as voluntary incorporation will trigger the statutory application of the Rules so that no part of the Rules can be ousted by any term of the sea waybill.

To the contrary, subsequently, in *The European Enterprise*,[50] the English High Court held that a general incorporation clause will not be sufficient, and it must be specified that the Rules are to govern the contract 'as if it were a bill of lading'. This sets a high threshold to trigger the statutory application of the Rules which will oust

---

[48] Article X of the Hague-Visby Rules.

[49] *McCarren & Co Ltd v Humber International Transport Ltd and Truckline Ferries (Poole) Ltd (The Vechscroon)* [1982] 1 Lloyd's Rep 301 (EW HC).

[50] *Browner International Ltd v Monarch Shipping Co Ltd (The European Enterprise)* [1989] 2 Lloyd's Rep 185 (EW HC).

contractual freedom of parties contract any term out of the Rules. This approach is to be welcomed as being in line with commercial reality as well as the intention of the legislature by specifically providing those words in the Section 1(6)(b).

In Singapore, the corresponding provision to Section 1(6) of the 1971 Act are Sections 3(4) and (5) of the Singapore Carriage of Goods by Sea Act. They read as follows:

> (4) Without prejudice to paragraph (c) of Article X of the Rules, the Rules shall have the force of law in relation to—
>
> (a) any bill of lading if the contract contained in or evidenced by it expressly provides that the Rules shall govern the contract; and
>
> (b) any receipt which is a non-negotiable document marked as such if the contract contained in or evidenced by it is a contract for the carriage of goods by sea which expressly provides that the Rules are to govern the contract.
>
> (5) Where subsection (4)(b) applies, the Rules shall apply—
>
> (a) as if the receipt referred to therein were a bill of lading; and
>
> (b) subject to any necessary modifications and in particular with the omission of the second sentence of paragraph 4 and of paragraph 7 in Article III of the Rules.

Interestingly, in Singapore, the words 'as if the receipt were a bill of lading' is not there in Section 5(b). Hence, it is not necessary for the sea waybill to state that the Rules are to apply 'as if it was a bill of lading', unlike in the case of the UK. Accordingly, *The Vechscroon*, but not *The European Enterprise*, will apply in Singapore. Further, in Singapore, unlike the UK, in the case of sea waybills (as opposed to bills of lading), the statements therein are not conclusive evidence thereof and there is no right to demand a shipped bill.[51] In Malaysia, like those countries that remain with the relevant Act modelled on the UK 1924 Act adopting the Hague Rules, the question of the Hague Rules applying statutorily to sea waybills is not there, as the Malaysian Carriage of Goods by Sea Act 1950 renders the Rules applicable only to bills of lading.[52]

International Ports—Extended to Domestic Ports

The Rules, again in the opening words of Article X, provides for its application only when the shipment is from a port in a contracting State to a port in a different State, that is, international shipments. However, Section 1(3) of the UK 1971 Act extends the application of the Rules to domestic shipments, that is to shipments from a port in the UK to another within the UK. The Section 1(3) reads as follows:

> Without prejudice to subsection (2) above, the said provisions shall have effect (and have the force of law) in relation to and in connection with the carriage of goods by sea in ships

---

[51] Second sentence of Article III(4) and (7) excluded by Section 3(5)(b).

[52] In Malaysia, the Carriage of Goods by Sea (Amendment) Act 2020 has now been passed to amend the 1950 Act, which, when it comes into force in July 2021, will extend the application of the Act to sea waybills and is expected to bring home the Hague-Visby Rules (as amended by SDR Protocol).

> where the port of shipment is a port in the United Kingdom, whether or not the carriage is between ports in two different States within the meaning of Article X of the Rules.

In Malaysia, like those countries that remain with the relevant Act modelled on the UK 1924 Act adopting the Hague Rules, similarly, Section 4 of the Malaysian Carriage of Goods by Sea Act 1950 extends the application of the Hague Rules to shipments "from any port in Malaysia to any other port whether in or outside Malaysia".[53]

Bill Issued in Contracting State or Carriage from Contracting State

In *Mayhew Foods Ltd v Overseas Containers Ltd*,[54] the shipment was from the UK to Saudi Arabia. The bill was only issued, subsequent to the shipment, in France, at the time of transshipment. The English High Court held that the Hague-Visby Rules applied to the entire carriage from the UK to Saudi Arabia. In this case, both Articles X(a) and X(b) were satisfied, although any one of them will suffice to trigger the statutory application of the Hague-Visby Rules.

If the Hague-Visby Rules applies in the country of shipment and the Hague Rules in the country of issuance of the bill, or vice versa, then it will be a matter of which country's law applies to the case and in which country the case is tried that will determine which Rules apply. If a shipment is from the UK and the bill is issued in a non-contracting State to the Hague-Visby Rules such as Malaysia, then, if the case is tried before the UK court, the Hague-Visby Rules will apply by virtue of Article X(a). The same will likely be the result where the shipment is from a non-contracting State and the bill is issued in the UK. This is because the statutory application of the Hague-Visby Rules will be triggered when any one of the three sub-articles of Article X is satisfied.

Bill of Lading Providing for Hague-Visby Rules to Govern Contract

By virtue of Article X(c), a bill of lading may provide for the application, with statutory force, of the Hague-Visby Rules, when otherwise it will not statutorily apply, in two ways. One is by declaring that the Hague-Visby Rules shall *govern* the contract. Another is by declaring that legislation, such as the UK 1971 Act, giving effect to it shall *govern* the contract. Section 1(6)(a)[55] of the UK 1971 Act in effect repeats the first way. A general clause paramount, that does not provide that the Rules shall *govern* the contract, will not be sufficient to meet the Article X(c) or Section 1(6)(a) threshold, though such a clause will be sufficient to incorporate the Rules contractually. When the Rules are incorporated merely contractually, any provision of the Rules may be ousted or modified contractually. The observation made by the English High Court in *The European Enterprise* will be relevant to strict construction of the requirement in Article X(c)/Section 1(6)(b) that the bill of lading provides that the Rules shall *govern* the contract, although in that case the

---

53 Materially corresponding provision is in the Sarawak Regulations (applicable also to Sabah).

54 [1984] 1 Lloyd's Rep 317 (EW HC).

55 This section is identical to Section 3(4)(a) of the Singapore Carriage of Goods by Sea Act.

question was about interpretation of the words ‘expressly provides that the Rules are to *govern* the contract as if the receipt were a bill of lading’ in Section 1(6)(b) in relation to a sea waybill.

A clause saying that the Rules will apply ‘if they apply compulsorily’ is of no effect, because if the Rules apply compulsorily then there is no need for the contract to say that it will apply. If the Rules do not apply compulsorily (i.e. statutorily), then these causes do not provide for its application. Such clauses do not attract the operation of Article X(c).[56] In *The BBC Greenland*,[57] the bill of lading stated the cargo was to be carried on deck and it was carried on deck. Accordingly, the bill of lading attracted the exception in Article 1(c). However, the bill also stated that the Hague-Visby Rules would be incorporated if they applied compulsorily. The English High Court found that the Hague-Visby Rules were not imported by this clause.

However, if the bill, in that case, had provided that the contract would be governed by the Hague-Visby Rules despite cargo being carried on deck, then the Hague-Visby Rules would have applied with the force of law, by virtue of Section 1(7). The Section 1(7) of the 1971 Act provides as follows:

> If and so far as the contract contained in or evidenced by a bill of lading or receipt within paragraph (a) or (b) of subsection (6) above applies to deck cargo or live animals, the Rules as given the force of law by that subsection shall have effect as if Article I(c) did not exclude deck cargo and live animals.
>
> In this subsection “deck cargo” means cargo which by the contract of carriage is stated as being carried on deck and is so carried.

In the case of a ‘deck cargo’, where the bill of lading provides that the Hague-Visby Rules are to govern the contract, still Section 1(7) is necessary to give the statutory effect to it. This is because, in the absence of Section 1(7), even if the Hague-Visby Rules are made applicable by virtue of Article X(c), the application of Rules will be excluded by Article I(c).[58]

A *choice of law* of the UK law, by itself, is not sufficient to attract the operation of Article X(c). This is because when the UK law applies, statutory force is given to the Rules. However, under the Rules, the Rules apply only if the conditions in Article X are satisfied, along with other requirements in Article. Accordingly, when none of the three conditions in Article X are satisfied, under the UK law, the Hague-Visby Rules do not apply. Similarly, where the *choice of jurisdiction* is the UK, that does not trigger the application of the Rules, as what is required is a provision in the bill of lading that the Rules or a statute giving effect to it like UK 1971 Act governs the contract of carriage.

---

[56] *Mediterranean Shipping Co SA v Trafigura Beheer BV and Another (The MSC Amsterdam)* [2007] EWCA Civ 794, [2008] 1 All ER (Comm) 385, [2007] 2 Lloyd’s Rep 622, [2007] All ER (D) 444 (Jul) (EW CA).

[57] *Sideridraulic Systems SpA v BBC Chartering & Logistic GmbH & Co KG (The BBC Greenland)* [2011] EWHC 3106 (Comm), [2012] 1 Lloyd’s Rep 230 (EW HC).

[58] This excludes application of the Rules to ‘deck cargo’.

In *The Komninos S*,[59] the English Court of Appeal agreed that an agreement to submit to the *jurisdiction* of the English court[60] would by implication render the English *law applicable*. However, the court refused the argument that it necessarily meant that the Hague-Visby was to *govern* the contract. The court found that none of the conditions of Article X was satisfied because the shipment was from Greece and the bill was issued in Greece, which at that time applied the Hague Rules, and the bill did not provide that the Hague-Visby Rules or a statute giving effect to it like UK 1971 Act would 'govern the contract'.

Section 1(6)(a) of the UK 1971 Act provides that the Hague-Visby Rules shall statutorily apply when a bill of lading expressly provides that the Rules shall govern the contract.[61] This materially repeats Article X(c), however with an addition that the bill *expressly* states the Rules to be applicable. Article X(c) does not require the bill to state that expressly. Accordingly, reading both Section 1(6)(a) and Article X(c), it may be safely said that it is not a requirement that the bill *expressly* makes such provision. However, in practice, it is unlikely that a court will hold that a bill impliedly provided that the Hague-Visby Rules or legislation giving effect to it should govern the contract.

8.4.2 Circumventing Rules by Choice of Law and Jurisdiction Clauses

There is some difference in the legal position concerning the parties' measures to circumvent the application of the Rules between the Hague Rules regime and the Hague-Visby Rules regime. Accordingly, the two regimes is considered separately below.

8.4.2.1 Hague Rules Regime

Under the Hague Rules regime, the statutes usually require that every bill of lading contains a statement that the bill was to take effect subject to the Hague Rules. When the statement is included in the bill, that will operate as a clause paramount so that the Hague Rules will be contractually applicable even if the case is heard before a court that does not statutorily enforce the Hague Rules. However, a shortfall in those Acts is that they do not provide any sanction against the carrier if it misses out the statement in the bill. Hence, it is possible for a carrier to miss out the statement and to include a jurisdiction and choice of law clause pointing to a jurisdiction and law in which the Rules do not statutorily apply to the carriage. Even if the clause pointed to

---

59 *Hellenic Steel Co v Svolamar Shipping Co Ltd (The Komninos S)* [1991] 1 Lloyd's Rep 370 (EW CA).

60 The reference was to the 'British court', which the court agreed meant English court, in this case.

61 This sub-section is expressly declared to be 'Without prejudice to Article X(c)'.

a jurisdiction and law where the Rules are ratified, still the Rules may not apply for the carriage when, for example, the carriage is not from a port in that jurisdiction as required by the law of that jurisdiction for the Rules to apply. For instance, if a bill of lading for a shipment from a port in Thailand[62] and makes applicable the law of Malaysia, a contracting State to the Hague Rules at that time, then the Hague Rules will not apply. This is because, under the Malaysian Carriage of Goods by Sea Act 1950,[63] the Rules apply only to shipments from a Malaysian port to any port in or outside Malaysia.

The tactical scenario happened in *Vita Foods Products Inc v Unus Shipping Company Ltd.*[64] In this case, a bill of lading was issued in Canada for a shipment from a Canadian port to a port in the USA. The Canadian law,[65] at that time, required the bill to contain a statement that it was subject to the Hague Rules. However, the bill did not contain such a statement. Instead, the bill had contained a choice of law clause that made the English law applicable. Under the English law, application of the Hague Rules, by the statement, was only compulsory for shipments out of the UK. Accordingly, the Privy Council held that the Hague Rules did not apply in this case.

8.4.2.2 Hague-Visby Rules Regime

Under the Hague-Visby Rules, there is no requirement to include the clause paramount statement. However, the application of the Rules, by Article X, has been widened from that in the Hague Rules and the Acts implementing the 1924 regime.

It is not unknown for carriers to attempt to circumvent the Hague-Visby Rules by providing for a choice of law and jurisdiction clause that refers to a non-contracting State. However, the courts have limited the effectiveness of such measures. In *The Hollandia*,[66] a road-finishing machine was shipped from a port in Scotland. The bill of lading provided for disputes to be submitted to the exclusive jurisdiction of Netherlands, which at that time applied the Hague Rules. Under the Hague Rules, package limitation, that will be more favourable to the carrier than the weight limitation in the Hague-Visby Rules was applicable. At this time, the UK 1971 Act was effective, that applied to all shipments from the UK[67] and rendered the Hague-Visby Rules applicable to all such shipments. The machine was damaged and the cargo owners brought an action before the English court. The carrier applied for a stay

---

[62] Where no convention relating to bills of lading applies.

[63] Section 2: "Subject to this Act, the Rules set out in the First Schedule (hereinafter referred to as "the Rules") shall have effect in relation to and in connection with the carriage of goods by sea in ships carrying goods from any port in Malaysia to any other port whether in or outside Malaysia."

[64] [1939] AC 277, [1939] 1 All ER 513 (PC on appeal from Nova Scotia).

[65] Canadian Carriage of Goods by Water Act 1936.

[66] *The Hollandia* [1983] 1 AC 565, [1982] 3 All ER 1141, [1982] 3 WLR 1111, [1983] 1 Lloyd's Rep 1 (UK HL).

[67] Section 1(3).

of the action on grounds that the action may only be commenced before a court in the Netherlands, in order that the carrier will enjoy the package limitation under the Hague Rules. The House of Lords refused the stay, as granting a stay will in effect be to contradict the 1971 Act. Lord Diplock pointed out that:

> [I]n so far as [jurisdiction clause] purports to lessen the liability of the carrier as it expressly does … it unquestionably contravenes art 3.8".

This decision was adopted and followed in Singapore in a similar case, *The Epar*,[68] where the Singapore High Court refused to uphold an Indonesian jurisdiction clause in a bill of lading for a carriage of goods from Singapore to Indonesia. While Indonesia had not subscribed to any of the Rules, the Hague-Visby Rules were applicable in Singapore.

Another avenue by which courts have limited the effect of such jurisdiction clauses is by narrowly construing them or rejecting them when they lack certainty. In *The Fehmarn*,[69] the cargo was shipped from Russia to England. The English buyer claimed that the cargo arrived damaged. The bill of lading provided for a jurisdiction and choice of law clause pointing to Russia but did not express it to be exclusive. Despite that, the buyer sued the carrier, a German company, before an English court. The carrier applied for a stay of the action on grounds of lack of jurisdiction in the English court, whilst at that time the applicable rules in England were the Hague Rules, and no international rules were applicable in Russia. The English Court of Appeal held, as a matter of construction, a clause does not oust the jurisdiction of a court merely by providing that another court has jurisdiction.

Even if the jurisdiction clause is an exclusive one, that does not assure that a court of another jurisdiction will stay the action to refer to the court of contracted jurisdiction, as the stay is discretionary and will be considered by application of principles applicable to such a stay as a matter of civil procedure. In *The Armar*,[70] the English Court of Appeal rejected a 'floating' choice of law clause that provided like this:

> [G]eneral average shall be adjusted stated and settled according to York-Antwerp Rules 1950 … at such port or place *as maybe selected by the carrier*. Matters not provided for by these rules to be adjusted stated and settled according to the laws and usage at such port or place *as maybe selected by the carrier*. [emphasis added]

The court held a contract must have a proper law at the time it was made, it could not be left to be fixed retrospectively and the proper law cannot change from one jurisdiction to another upon the happening of subsequent events. In *The Benarty*,[71] the shipments were from European ports, most of which subscribed to the Hague-Visby

[68] *The Epar* [1985] 2 MLJ 3 (SG HC).

[69] *The Fehmarn* [1958] 1 All ER 333, [1958] 1 WLR 159, [1957] 2 Lloyd's Rep 551 (EW CA).

[70] *Armar Shipping Co Ltd v Caisse Algérienne d'Assurance et de Réassurance (The Armar)* [1981] 1 All ER 498, [1981] 1 WLR 207, [1980] 2 Lloyd''s Rep 450 (EW CA).

[71] *RA Lister & Co Ltd v EG Thomsom (Shipping) Ltd (The Benarty)* (No. 2) [1985] QB 325, [1984] 3 All ER 961, [1984] 3 WLR 1082, [1984] 2 Lloyd's Rep 244 (EW CA).

Rules, to Indonesia. The bills of lading incorporated the Hague Rules. They also contained a choice of law clause and jurisdiction clause, both referring to Indonesia, that has not subscribed to the Hague or Hague-Visby Rules. Cargo claims arose out of the carriages and the cargo owners took action before the English courts. The carrier applied for a stay of the action on grounds that the action should be taken before an Indonesian court. Two advantages would be earned by the carrier if the action was before an Indonesian court. First, only the Hague Rules will apply as incorporated by the bill. Second, the domestic laws of Indonesia on liability-limitation (i.e. tonnage limitation) will be available to the carrier, which would be more favourable to it than that in Article IV(5) of the Hague-Visby Rules. The English Court of Appeal allowed the stay upon the carrier's undertaking that it will not take any benefit of the first advantage said above, that is, the application of the Hague-Rules as opposed to the Hague-Visby Rules. However, the carrier was entitled to take the benefit of the second advantage said above because that was permitted by the Hague-Visby Rules, in Article VIII. Article VIII is materially the same in both the Rules. The said Article reads as follows, with those in brackets only in the Hague Rules and those in the square bracket only in the Hague-Visby Rules:

> The provisions of (this Convention) [these Rules] shall not affect the rights and obligations of the carrier under any statute for the time being in force relating to the limitation of the liability of owners of (sea-going) vessels.

What must be observed from the above decision is that the liability-limitation regime in the Hague or Hague-Visby Rules[72] is, within its own scope, subject to any applicable domestic laws on liability-limitation, although not subject to any contrary terms of the bill of lading.[73] Article VI, which is present and the same in both the Hague and Hague-Visby Rules, seems to have some provision to prevent the carriers from avoiding the Rules by issuing shipping documents other than bills of lading. Article VI reads as follows:

> Notwithstanding the provisions of the preceding articles, a carrier, master or agent of the carrier and a shipper shall in regard to any particular goods be at *liberty to enter into any agreement in any terms as to the responsibility and liability of the carrier for such goods, and as to the rights and immunities of the carrier in respect of such goods, or his obligation as to seaworthiness*, so far as this stipulation is not contrary to public policy, or the care or diligence of his servants or agents in regard to the loading, handling, stowage, carriage, custody, care and discharge of the goods carried by sea, *provided that in this case no bill of lading has been or shall be issued* and that the terms agreed shall be embodied in a receipt which shall be a non-negotiable document and shall be marked as such.
>
> An agreement so entered into shall have full legal effect.
>
> *Provided that this article shall not apply to ordinary commercial shipments* made in the ordinary course of trade, *but only to other shipments* where the character or condition of the property to be carried or the circumstances, terms and conditions under which the carriage is to be performed are such as *reasonably to justify a special agreement*. [emphasis added]

[72] Article IV(5).

[73] Article III(8).

It is hard to make any meaning of the Article. It gives the freedom to the parties to enter into any agreement where no bill of lading is issued. However, where no bill is issued, the Rules has no application, by virtue of Article I(b) read together with Article II. Article VI additionally has a proviso that the Article shall not apply to ordinary commercial shipments but only where it is reasonable to justify a special agreement. In other words, it says that only in special cases, parties may enter into any agreement as to rights and immunities where no bill of lading is issued. Again, the proviso does not seem to be of any substance as the Rules has no application where no bill is issued. To say it simply, Article VI attempts to deal with matters where no bill is issued, in which case the Rules has no application, unless Article VI is argued to take precedence over Article II. In the context of the UK law, Article VI will also not align with Section 1(4) of the UK 1971 Act that excludes the application of the Rules where no bill of lading has been issued or contemplated.[74] For Malaysia, like those countries that remain with the relevant Act modelled on the UK 1924 Act adopting the Hague Rules, Article VI will apply, as modified by Section 5 of the 1950 Act. The Section 5 reads as follows:

> **5. Modification of Article VI of Rules in relation to *local trade***
>
> Article VI of the Rules shall, in relation to—
>
> (a) the carriage of goods by sea in sailing ships carrying goods from any port in Malaysia to any other port whether in or outside Malaysia; and
>
> (b) the carriage of goods by sea in ships carrying goods from any port in Malaysia to any other port in Malaysia, have effect as though the said Article referred to goods of any class instead of to particular goods and as though the *proviso to the second paragraph of the said Article were omitted*. [emphasis added]

Exclusion of the proviso seems only to more suggest that parties have the freedom of contract as to terms of the responsibility of the carrier when no bill of lading has been issued. However, the provision is unlikely to be of any relevance now as it refers to 'sailing' ships which are practically obsolete in commercial carriage market now. Although this section largely corresponds with Section 4 of the repealed UK 1924 Act, the words 'sailing' is not there in the Section 4 of the UK 1924 Act.

8.5 Article IV*bis* of Hague-Visby Rules

This entire Article was newly added by the Hague-Visby Rules.

[74] The Section 1(4) has been reproduced earlier in this chapter. The same is true of Singapore by Section 3(3) of the Singapore Carriage of Goods by Sea Act.

8.5.1 *Article IV*bis*(1)*

Article IV*bis*(1) expressly states that the defences and limitations in the Hague-Visby Rules apply whether the case has been framed in contract or tort. Article IV*bis*(1) reads as follows:

> 1. The *defences and limits* of liability provided for in these Rules shall apply in any action against the carrier in respect of *loss or damage to goods* covered by a contract of carriage whether the action be founded in *contract or in tort*. [emphasis added]

A literal interpretation of this Article may suggest that the defences and the liability-limitation are available to the carrier whether there is a contractual nexus between the cargo claimant and the carrier or not. However, the English Court of Appeal in *The Captain Gregos*[75] held that this Article applies only where there is a contractual nexus between the parties. A suit by a cargo owner against a carrier, where there is no contractual nexus is possible. For instance, where a buyer does not get the bill that has been stuck in the course of transfer through banks. In such a case, if the cargo has been damaged, the buyer may opt to sue the shipowner in negligence and there will be no contractual nexus between them since the bill has not been transferred to the buyer. In such cases, as per *The Captain Gregos*, the Hague-Visby Rules do not apply.

Even in the absence of this Article, where there is a contractual nexus between the parties, an action in tort is always subject to exceptions and limitations in the contract.[76] Accordingly, the position under the Hague Rules is no different from that under the Hague-Visby Rules in this respect.

8.5.2 *Article IV*bis*(2)*

This Article IV*bis*(2) extends the protection given to the carrier under the Hague-Visby Rules to its agents and servants but not to independent contractors. Action against such agents and servants will necessarily be in tort. Article IV*bis*(2) reads as follows:

> 2. If such an action is brought against a servant or agent of the carrier (such servant or agent not being an independent contractor), such servant or agent shall be entitled to avail himself of the defences and limits of liability which the carrier is entitled to invoke under these Rules.

Even before the introduction of this Article, Himalaya and 'circular indemnity' clauses were widely found in bills of lading that extended the protection under

[75] *Cia Portorafti Commerciale SA v Ultramar Panama Inc (The Captain Gregos)* [1990] 1 Lloyd's Rep 310, [1990] 3 All ER 967 (EW CA).

[76] *Pyrene Co Ltd v Scindia Navigation Co Ltd* [1954] 2 QB 402, [1954] 2 All ER 158, [1954] 2 WLR 1005, [1954] 1 Lloyd's Rep 321 (EW HC).

the terms of the bill of lading to agents, servants and independent contractors.[77] In addition to them, since the coming into force of the UK Contracts (Rights of Third Parties) Act 1999,[78] these third parties, including independent contractors, are entitled to rely on exclusion and limitation clauses in the bills of lading where it is expressly provided that those third parties may rely on the clauses or the clause was intended to confer a benefit on them.[79]

*8.5.3 Article IV*bis*(3)*

Article IV*bis*(3) caps the aggregate amount recoverable by a cargo claimant from all defendants—the carrier, agents and servants—to the amount of limited liability pursuant to the Hague-Visby Rules. Article IV*bis*(3) reads as follows:

> 3. The aggregate of the amounts recoverable from the carrier, and such servants and agents, shall in no case exceed the limit provided for in these Rules.

This Article means actions both in contract and tort and whether there is a contractual nexus between the parties or not, as necessarily any action against the agents and servants will be in tort. Before this, the English courts had employed judicial ingenuity to prevent recovery beyond the limitation amount in the Rules, as the court did in *The Nicholas H*.[80] In this case, the cargo owners sued the classification society for loss to the cargo owners resulting from negligent classification. The suit came after the cargo owners had already successfully recovered the maximum amount recoverable from the shipowners subject to applicable limitations. The House of Lords turned down the action holding[81] that the classification society did not owe a duty of care to the cargo owners. Although such judicial ingenuity may no longer be needed in jurisdictions like the UK that have subscribed to the Hague-Visby Rules, it will be relevant in jurisdictions like Malaysia that have still subscribed only to the Hague Rules.[82]

---

[77] For a detailed discussion of Himalaya clauses, see Chap. 5.3, and for 'circular indemnity' clauses, see Chap. 5.4.

[78] Section 1(6). For a detailed discussion of the application of the UK 1999 Act to protect third parties in the context of carriage of goods by sea, see Chap. 5.2.

[79] Section 1(1)–(4).

[80] *Marc Rich & Co AG v Bishop Rock Marine Co Ltd (The Nicholas H)* [1996] AC 211, [1995] 3 All ER 307, [1995] 3 WLR 227, [1995] 3 LRC 120, [1995] 2 Lloyd's Rep 299 (UK HL).

[81] Possibly by judicial ingenuity.

[82] In Malaysia, the Carriage of Goods by Sea (Amendment) Act 2020 has now been passed to amend the 1950 Act, which, when it comes into force in July 2021, is expected to bring home the Hague-Visby Rules (as amended by SDR Protocol).

*8.5.4 Article IV*bis*(4)*

Article IV*bis*(4) provides as follows:

> 4. Nevertheless, a servant or agent of the carrier shall not be entitled to avail himself of the *provisions of this article*, if it is proved that the damage resulted from an act or omission of the servant or agent done with *intent to cause damage* or *recklessly and with knowledge* that damage would *probably* result. [emphasis added]

This is quite similar to Article IV(5)(e) that makes unavailable the liability-limitation in the Hague-Visby Rules unavailable to the carrier when damages were caused by similar intent or recklessness of the carrier. To fall within Articles IV(5)(e) and IV*bis*(4), there must be either intent to cause damage or there must be recklessness *coupled with knowledge* that damage *will probably* result. The mere knowledge that damage *may* result is insufficient. This is a formidable threshold and will not be met in any ordinary case.

There is no equivalent provision in the Hague Rules. However, it is unlikely that a court will allow the carrier or its agents or servants to rely on the protection in the Rules when the damage was intended or so recklessly caused. In fact, in such a case, a court may utilise canons of interpretation like 'four corners' rule to hold what the carrier was doing was so radically different from that contracted for that it stepped out of the contractual performance. The result will be that the culpable carrier, agent or servant cannot rely on the defences and limitations in the contract of carriage.[83] Then, last, a note about considerations relevant to interpretation of the rules.

8.6 Interpretation

The objective of the Hague/Hague-Visby Rules is to provide an internationally uniform regime of laws on this subject applicable in all the member states. The objective of the Rules requires two things to be kept in mind when interpreting the Rules. First, the interpretation must not be over-influenced by pre-Rules domestic precedents. Second, foreign authorities may be considered. Added to them, in interpreting the Rules, regard must be had to the Vienna Convention on the Law of Treaties,[84] particularly Article 31, and domestic Interpretation Acts. A detailed consideration of the principles applicable in interpreting the Rules is covered in the next chapter,[85] as part of the discussion of Article IV(2) Defences.

---

[83] See *Royal Exchange Shipping Co Ltd v Dixon* (1886) 12 App Cas 11 (UK HL), in the context of quasi-deviation cases (carriage on deck without authorisation).

[84] Ratified by the UK in 1971 and came into force in 1980. Singapore has not ratified this treaty, but has its own statutory provision facilitating purposive construction of treaties. Malaysia ratified (by accession) this treaty in 1994.

[85] See Chap. 9.4.

Chapter 9
Hague/Hague-Visby Rules: Carriers' Obligation and Defences

This chapter discusses the carrier's obligations and defences under the Hague and Hague-Visby Rules. The obligations are those in Article III(1) (obligation to provide a seaworthy and cargoworthy ship) and Article III(2) (duty to properly and carefully load, stow, carry and discharge). The defences are those in Article IV(1) that relates to Article III(1) obligation and Article IV(2) that relates to Article III(2) obligation. It is noted that the Article IV(2) puts the burden of proofing due diligence on the carrier rather than providing any substantive defence to Article III(1). The Article IV(2)(a)–(q) defences are separated into two groups broadly and analysed. One is Article IV(2)(a)–(b) and another is Article IV(2)(c)–(q). It is noted that the latter is not a defence in the true sense, as there is no corresponding obligation in respect of them in the first place. That is followed by a consideration of burden of proof associated with the Article IV(2) defences and a detailed study of the UK Supreme Court's *Volcafe* decision in 2018 is undertaken. The application of the *Volcafe* position in Commonwealth countries with a statute regulating the law of evidence/contracts (including bailments) is also considered.

9.1 Introduction

The substantive obligations of the carrier are set out in Article III(1) and (2) of the Hague/Hague-Visby Rules. They are in essence obligations as to seaworthiness and cargoworthiness of the ship (Article III(1)) and as to proper and careful loading, carriage and discharge of the goods (Article III(2)). Article IV(1) makes provision as to the burden of proof related to the obligation set out in Article III(1). Article IV(2) provides some substantive defences available to the carrier in respect of the obligations set out in Article III(2). In both the Hague and Hague-Visby Rules, these provisions are the same.

A. Kasi, *The Law of Carriage of Goods by Sea*,
https://doi.org/10.1007/978-981-33-6793-7_9

The obligations set out by the Rules are not exhaustive. The obligations imposed by the implied terms at common law are not excluded by the Rules and they co-exist with the Rules, but some of them are modified to some extent.[1]

In this chapter, the Article III(1) and (2) obligations and the Article IV(2) Defences are analysed at depth. This includes a consideration of each of the 17 sub-limbs [(a)–(q)] of defences under Article III(2). That is followed by a consideration of the burden of proof associated with these Article III(2) and IV(2). This includes a detailed study includes the UK Supreme Court decision in *Volcafe v CSAV* in 2018. The next chapter will cover Article III(6) (time limit in respect of cargo claims brought against the carrier) and Article IV(5) (liability (quantum) limitation of the carrier's liability for cargo claims).[2]

9.2 Articles III(1) and IV(1)

These Articles are the same in both the Hague and Hague-Visby Rules. Article III(1) reads as follows:

1. The carrier shall be bound *before and at* the beginning of the *voyage* to exercise *due diligence*:
   (a) Make the ship seaworthy;
   (b) Properly man, equip and supply the ship;
   (c) Make the holds, refrigerating and cool chambers, and all other parts of the ship in which goods are carried, fit and safe for their reception, carriage and preservation.

Article III(1) provides for seaworthiness obligation. This largely resembles the implied term at common law as to seaworthiness. Articles III(1)(a) and (b) are for seaworthiness whilst Article III(1)(c) is about cargoworthiness.

However, there are some differences. First, the obligation is only to exercise *due diligence* to render the ship seaworthy and cargoworthy, as opposed to an *absolute obligation* to provide a seaworthy and cargoworthy ship implied by the common law. The common law absolute obligation of seaworthiness of the ship expressly abolished originally by Section 2 of the UK Carriage of Goods Act 1924 (now repealed),[3] and the abolition is identically repeated in the UK Carriage of Goods Act 1971 (in force now), by Section 3, which reads as follows:

---

[1] Discussed at length earlier.

[2] The liability-limitation in the Hague and Hague-Visby Rules are in addition to the tonnage limitation available to shipowners, discussed later in Chap. 10.2.

[3] Section 2: "There shall not be implied in any contract for the carriage of goods by sea to which this Act applies any absolute undertaking by the carrier of the goods to provide a seaworthy ship." An identical provision is also found in the Malaysian Carriage of Goods by Sea Act 1950 in Section 3.

> There shall not be implied in any contract for the carriage of goods by sea to which the Rules apply by virtue of this Act any absolute undertaking by the carrier of the goods to provide a seaworthy ship.

The abolition of the absolute warranty is almost universal in jurisdictions that has adopted the Hague or Hague-Visby Rules. The same is true of those jurisdictions, like Malaysia, that has an Act modelled on the UK 1924 Act adopting the Hague Rules, where the absolute warranty is similarly abolished by identical provision.[4] The same is also true of those jurisdictions, like Singapore, that has an Act modelled on the UK 1971 Act adopting the Hague-Visby Rules, where the absolute warranty is similarly abolished by identical provision.

The abolition seems only to refer to the 'seaworthiness of the ship' but not the common law absolute warranty of cargoworthiness. However, as the absolute warranty of cargoworthiness is an implied term, by the necessary intention of the legislation abolishing, in essence, the concept of *absolute* warranty, there will likely be no longer any *absolute* warranty of cargoworthiness implied by the common law in cases to which the Rules apply.

Second, the obligation starts from the beginning of the loading and continues up to the start of the voyage. This is the effect of the words 'before and at' in the Article. The period denoted by the word 'before' here starts at the time of loading, as the coverage of the Rules, in general, is from the beginning of loading to the end of discharge.[5] The word 'at' extends the obligation up to and terminates it at the point of the start of the voyage. This is common for both the seaworthiness and cargoworthiness obligations. Hence, the carrier must exercise due diligence to ensure seaworthiness and cargoworthiness *up to* the time of the start of the voyage. Comparatively, the implied term at the common law is to provide a cargoworthy ship *during loading* and a seaworthy ship *at the start of sailing*. At common law, there is a gap period after the completion of loading and before the start of sailing. During the gap period, the seaworthiness and cargoworthiness obligations do not attach. However, there is no such gap period in Article III(1) as the obligation is to exercise due diligence to provide a seaworthy and cargoworthy ship from the start of the loading to the start of the voyage.

In *Maxine Footwear Co Ltd v Canadian Government Merchant Marine Ltd*,[6] the ship caught fire, by negligence of the crew, near to the end of loading operation at Halifax.[7] As a result, the master had to order scuttling[8] of the ship, that resulted in the loss of the claimant's cargo of three crates and one drum of shoe leather and findings. The cargo interest instituted an action against the carrier for the loss and argued that the ship was unseaworthy within the scope of Article III(1). The carrier argued that

---

[4] In Malaysia, by Section 4 of the Carriage of Goods by Sea Act 1950.

[5] Article II; *Pyrene Co Ltd v Scindia Navigation Co Ltd* [1954] 2 QB 402, [1954] 2 All ER 158, [1954] 2 WLR 1005, [1954] 1 Lloyd's Rep 321 (EW HC).

[6] [1959] AC 589, [1959] 2 Lloyd's Rep 105 (PC on appeal from Canada).

[7] In Canada.

[8] Deliberately sinking the ship.

Article III(1) was not applicable as the fire took place during the gap period. The Privy Council[9] held that the seaworthiness obligation under Article III(1) attached from the start of loading to the start of the voyage—in this case until the ship sank—unlike the position at common law. In this connection, the board said:

> "before and at the beginning of the voyage" means the period from at least the beginning of the loading until the vessel starts on her voyage. The word "before" cannot in their opinion be read as meaning "at the commencement of the loading."

The board also held that the carrier had failed to exercise due diligence in ensuring seaworthiness of the ship during the relevant period as the fire broke out as a result of the negligence of the crew, and accordingly held the carrier liable for the loss. But if the fire had happened by negligence of the crew after the ship had started her voyage, then the carrier might have been able to rely on Article IV(2)(a)[10] or (b) exceptions.[11]

Third, the obligation ceases once the *voyage* has started. 'Voyage' is a journey that starts at the port of loading and ordinarily ends at the port of discharge.[12] Accordingly, for different cargo loaded at different ports on the same ship over a particular route, the starting point of the voyage will be different for the respective cargoes. Hewson J in *The Makedonia*[13] well defined 'voyage' as "the *contractual voyage* from the port of loading to the port of discharge as declared in the appropriate bill of lading." If a ship loads a cargo at Felixstowe for Southampton and en-route stops at London to load another cargo for Southampton, then as far as the first cargo is concerned the voyage started at Felixstowe, and for the second cargo, the voyage starts at London. Similarly, if a ship stops, during the voyage, at an intermediate port for bunkering and sails again from the intermediate port, no voyage starts at the intermediate port.[14] Thus, the 'beginning of the voyage' in Article III(1) refers to the port of loading,[15] where the seaworthiness obligation in the Article attaches. Comparatively, at common law, the obligation will attach every time the ship starts *sailing*. This will include the intermediate ports that the ship stops at. In the first example above, under common

[9] Overturning the decision of the Canadian Supreme Court.

[10] "(a) Act, neglect, or default of the master, mariner, pilot, or the servants of the carrier in the navigation or in the management of the ship."

[11] "(b) Fire, unless caused by the actual fault or privity of the carrier."

[12] *Owners of cargo lately laden on board ship or vessel Makedonia v Makedonia (Owners) (The Makedonia)* [1962] P 190, [1962] 2 All ER 614, [1962] 3 WLR 343, [1962] 1 Lloyd's Rep 316 (EW HC).

[13] *Owners of cargo lately laden on board ship or vessel Makedonia v Makedonia (Owners) (The Makedonia)* [1962] P 190, [1962] 2 All ER 614, [1962] 3 WLR 343, [1962] 1 Lloyd's Rep 316 (EW HC).

[14] *Owners of cargo lately laden on board ship or vessel Makedonia v Makedonia (Owners) (The Makedonia)* [1962] P 190, [1962] 2 All ER 614, [1962] 3 WLR 343, [1962] 1 Lloyd's Rep 316 (EW HC).

[15] *Owners of cargo lately laden on board ship or vessel Makedonia v Makedonia (Owners) (The Makedonia)* [1962] P 190, [1962] 2 All ER 614, [1962] 3 WLR 343, [1962] 1 Lloyd's Rep 316 (EW HC).

law, the seaworthiness obligation will attach again at the time the ship starts re-sailing from London and in the second example, it will attach again when the ship starts re-sailing from the intermediate port. This is called 'doctrine of stages' at common law, meaning the seaworthiness obligation recurs in stages—at the time of loading and at the beginning of every sailing. It has been noted earlier that there is nothing in the Rules to displace the doctrine of stages being effective for sailings starting from intermediate ports, subject only to the abolition of the absoluteness of the obligation and modification of the same to a duty to exercise due diligence. This is considered in detail below.

9.2.1 Operation of Doctrine of Stages Under the Rules Regime

The conventional view is that the seaworthiness obligation has been modified by the Rules and that the common law doctrine of stages has been abolished in cases to which the Rules apply. Of course, the Rules do not apply to certain instances of carriages such as those under a sea waybill,[16] ships' delivery order,[17] and bill of lading in the case of deck cargo or carriage of live animals.[18]

The conventional view was upheld in *The Makedonia.*[19] In this case, the ship carried timber from west Canadian ports to the UK ports under various bills of lading subject to the Canadian Water Carriage of Goods Act 1936 which gives effect to the Hague Rules.[20] En route, she was to take, and took, fuel at San Pedro and then at Balboa ports. The fuel taken at Balboa was contaminated with sea water. As a result, the ship was completely immobilised in the sea and had to be towed to the port of Ponta Delgada, as the port of refugee, with salvage assistance. As part of this exercise, some of the forward deck cargo had to be jettisoned to trim the ship by stern, some timber had to be burned as fuel, and expenses at the port of refuse were incurred. This gave rise to claims concerning salvage costs, general average claims and claims for loss of the jettisoned cargo. The cargo interests argued that the duty on the shipowner to exercise due diligence to provide a seaworthy ship under Article III(1) recurred at every intermediate port.[21] Hewson J rejected this argument and held that the duty on the shipowner was only, at the outset of the voyage, to:

---

[16] Hague/Hague-Visby Rules, Article I(b).

[17] Hague/Hague-Visby Rules, Article I(b).

[18] Hague/Hague-Visby Rules, Article I(c).

[19] *Owners of cargo lately laden on board ship or vessel Makedonia v Makedonia (Owners) (The Makedonia)* [1962] P 190, [1962] 2 All ER 614, [1962] 3 WLR 343, [1962] 1 Lloyd's Rep 316 (EW HC).

[20] Applicable through the Canadian Water Carriage of Goods Act 1936.

[21] 'Doctrine of stages' argument.

> [Have] the vessel adequately bunkered for the first stage to San Pedro, and to arrange for adequate bunkers of a proper kind at the San Pedro and other selected intermediate ports on the voyage so that the contractual voyage might be performed.

Thus, his Lordship rejected the operation of common law doctrine of stages in cases to which the Rules apply. In so rejecting, his Lordship was influenced by Article IV(2)(a) of the Rules, which is identical in both the Hague and the Hague-Visby Rules and reads as follows:

2. Neither the carrier nor the ship shall be responsible for loss or damage arising or resulting from:

   (a) *Act, neglect, or default* of the master, mariner, pilot, or the servants of the carrier in the navigation or *in the management of the ship.* [emphasis added]

His Lordship was of the view that the natural construction of Article IV(2)(a) precluded liability for any default, including one rendering the ship unseaworthy, unless the unseaworthiness fell within Article III(1), hence negating the doctrine of stages in relation to the subsequent sailings. Although his Lordship found that the fuel-contamination incidence at Balboa, by itself, did not constitute a breach of Article III(1) duty, the shipowner had breached Article III(1) duty because the engineers, at the outset of the voyage from the loading ports, 'were not properly instructed or experienced in the use of the oil' and the shipowners had 'failed to exercise due diligence to see that the engineers were so properly instructed or experienced'.

There are some limitations to the view of Hewson J and his Lordship's reliance on Article IV(2)(a) to reject the doctrine of stages. First, as per the view, Article IV(2)(a) will negate the doctrine of stages and save the shipowner only if the unseaworthiness at the subsequent sailing was caused by an 'act, neglect or default' of 'the master, mariner, pilot or the servants of the carrier'. Notably, this excludes two things. One, a situation where the subsequent unseaworthiness is the result of a fortuity, an unknown cause or was not otherwise caused by such an 'act, neglect or default'. Another, a situation where the subsequent unseaworthiness is caused by an act, neglect or default, but not of the master/mariner/pilot/servants of the carrier, e.g. unseaworthiness caused by an independent contractor or an accident that happened by fault of another ship or the port authority.

Second, Article IV(2)(a) in effect provides an exception to liability. It is well settled that in the case of the implied terms at common law, including the seaworthiness obligation, the liability may only be excluded by a specific exception clause that is intended to exclude liability for the implied terms, e.g. seaworthiness, but not by a general exception clause which is capable of having effect without necessarily covering the liability for breach of the implied terms. In *Lyon v Mells*,[22] the bill of lading contained a general exception clause that read:

---

[22] (1804) 5 East 428, 1 Smith KB 478, 102 ER 1134 (EW Court of King's Bench).

> We will not be answerable for any loss or damage which shall happen to any cargo which shall be put on board any of our vessels, unless such loss or damage shall happen or be occasioned by want of ordinary care and diligence in the master or crew of the vessel, in which case we will pay [£10] per cent, upon such loss or damage, so as the whole amount of such payment shall not exceed the value of the vessel and the freight.

The Court of King's Bench held that the exception clause did not cover liability for breach of implied obligation for seaworthiness. Similarly, in *The Theodegmon*,[23] Phillips J refused to allow a carrier to rely on a general exclusion clause in respect of damage by grounding when the grounding was caused by the unseaworthiness of the ship at the start of the voyage. In the same vein, in *The Maori King*,[24] a clause excluding the liability of the shipowners for "failure or breakdown of machinery, insulation and other appliances" was held by the Court of Appeal not to apply when the refrigeration system of the ship carrying a cargo of frozen mutton did not work properly at the start of the voyage. This rendered the ship unseaworthy in the sense of being uncargoworthy to carry the cargo of frozen mutton.

If this principle of construction is adopted in interpreting Article IV(2)(a), then the Article will not interfere with the common doctrine of stages insofar as it relates to the subsequent sailings. If the principle is not followed, that would only produce an anomalous result in that if the ship is unseaworthy by fault of the shipowner at the subsequent sailing, then the shipowner will have a defence, but if she is unseaworthy not by fault of the shipowner, then the shipowner will not have the defence. It unlikely that the Rules, by Arts. III(1) and IV(2)(a), intended to modify the common law position so as to allow the shipowner to set sail from an intermediate port despite knowledge that she is unseaworthy (an obligation fundamental in nature).

A few other factors will support the proposition that the doctrine of stages, insofar as subsequent sailings are concerned, co-exists with Article III(1), in cases to which the Rules apply. In general, the Rules are not intended to displace or replace the common law position, save in the areas dealt with by the Rules. Rather, the Rules co-exist with the common law and in the event of a conflict, of course, the Rules will prevail.

Lord Sumption JSC, delivering the judgment of the Supreme Court, in *Volcafe v CSAV*,[25] noted that Rules "are not exhaustive of all matters relating to the legal responsibility of carriers for the cargo". In this case, a cargo of coffee beans was damaged in transit. The cargo interest made a claim for breach of the bailee-duties and of Article III(2) duty to properly and carefully handle and carry.[26] The carrier

---

[23] *Phillips Petroleum Co v Cabaneli Naviera SA (The Theodegmon)* [1990] 1 Lloyd's Rep 52, (1989) Times 15 June (EW HC).

[24] *Owners of Cargo on The Maori King v Hughes (The Maori King)* [1895] 2 QB 550, 65 LJQB 168, 8 Asp MLC 65, 14 R 646, 44 WR 2, 39 Sol Jo 688, 73 LT 141, 11 TLR 550 (EW CA).d

[25] *Volcafe Ltd and others v Compania Sud Americana De Vapores SA (t/a CSAV)* [2018] UKSC 61, [2019] AC 358, [2019] 2 All ER 81, [2018] 3 WLR 2087, [2019] 1 All ER (Comm) 397, [2019] 1 Lloyd's Rep 21, [2018] All ER (D) 16 (Dec) (UK SC).

[26] Hague/Hague-Visby Rules, Article III(2): "Subject to the provisions of Article IV, the carrier shall properly and carefully load, handle, stow, carry, keep, care for, and discharge the goods carried."

relied on Article IV(2)(m) exception (damage due to inherent vice of the goods).[27] A question arose as to who bears the legal burden of proof. At common law, the burden of proving that a bailee was not negligence for damage that happened to the bailed goods was on the bailee. Lord Sumption JSC observed that "[nothing] in the Hague Rules alters the status of a contract of carriage by sea as a species of bailment for reward on terms". With that observation, the court held that the burden of proving discharge of Article III(2) duty, i.e. that the carrier was not negligent, was on the carrier, before the carrier could rely on Article IV(2)(m) exception.

Another example of the Rules and the common law working together is in relation to deviation. At common law, it is an implied term that the shipowner will not voluntarily deviate from the proper route without lawful justification.[28] There is no corresponding obligation in the Rules. But the Rules provide a defence to deviation in Article IV(4).[29] The defence will only be relevant if the common law implied obligation not to deviate is applicable under the Rules regime.

Accordingly, the preferred position is that the doctrine of stages, insofar as it relates to subsequent sailings, is not displaced by the Rules. If this proposition is accepted, the next question is about the absoluteness of the obligation in relation to the subsequent sailing. At common law, the obligation is an absolute one. However, Section 2 of the Carriage of Goods by Sea Act 1924 Act (now repealed) and Section 3 of the Carriage of Goods by Sea Act 1971 Act (now in force) has abolished the 'absoluteness' of the obligation in cases to which the Rules apply. Accordingly, the Acts modify the common law obligation, in relation to the subsequent sailings, to one that is not absolute. This will practically align the common law obligation, as modified by the Acts, with that under the Rules, i.e. to a duty to exercise due diligence only to ensure seaworthiness at the subsequent sailings.

The common law jurisprudence is relevant to cases to which the Rules apply also in interpreting various terms in the Rules. For instance, the Rules do not define what 'seaworthiness' or 'cargoworthiness' is. For that, one will still resort to common law. Now some cases in Singapore and Malaysia on the seaworthiness-obligation under the Rules will be visited below.

In *Guan Bee & Co v Palembang Shipping Co Ltd*,[30] the Singapore High Court dealt with Article III(1) seaworthiness-obligation. In this case, goods were damaged by the entry of water into the cargo hold. It was not known when the water entered. After the water was finally pumped out, it transpired that there the scupper pipes were very rusty resulting from poor maintenance and had holes. The court found that a careful and proper examination by a reasonably skilled and careful man would have revealed the weakened condition of the pipes requiring repair before the ship

[27] Hague/Hague-Visby Rules, Article IV(2)(m): "Wastage in bulk or weight or any other loss or damage arising from inherent defect, quality or vice of the goods."

[28] *Davis v Garrett* (1830) 6 Bing 716 (EW Court of Common Pleas).

[29] Hague/Hague-Visby Rules, Article IV(4): "Any deviation in saving or attempting to save life or property at sea or any reasonable deviation shall not be deemed to be an infringement or breach of this Convention or of the contract of carriage, and the carrier shall not be liable for any loss or damage resulting therefrom."

[30] [1969] 1 MLJ 90 (SG HC).

was sent to sea. Accordingly, the court held the sea to be unseaworthy at the outset of the voyage contrary to Article 3 and held the shipowner liable.

In *Sarawak Electricity Supply Corp v MS Shipping Sdn Bhd*,[31] the Malaysian High Court said that a ship seaworthy in herself may be rendered unseaworthy by reason of her cargo and that it was essential that she should be fit to encounter the perils of the voyage as a laden ship. The court said that a ship otherwise seaworthy may become unseaworthy by being overloaded or by reason of inappropriate stowage.

9.2.2 Due Diligence and Burden of Proof

The burden of proving unseaworthiness is on the cargo claimant. Once this is done, the burden of proving due diligence, which will negate the obligation in Article III(1), is on the carrier. Article IV(1) reads as follows:

> 1. Neither the carrier nor the ship shall be liable for loss or damage arising or resulting from unseaworthiness unless caused by want of due diligence on the part of the carrier to make the ship seaworthy and to secure that the ship is properly manned, equipped and supplied, and to make the holds, refrigerating and cool chambers and all other parts of the ship in which goods are carried fit and safe for their reception, carriage and preservation in accordance with the provisions of § 1 of Article 3. *Whenever loss or damage has resulted from unseaworthiness the burden of proving the exercise of due diligenceshall be on the carrier or other person claiming exemption under this Article.* [emphasis added]

This Article, save for its last sentence, substantially repeats the opening part of Article III(1). The last sentence maintains the duty to prove unseaworthiness on the cargo claimant, and once this is done, it shifts the burden to prove due diligence onto the carrier.[32] In *The Hellenic Dolphin*,[33] Lloyd J well said this[34] as follows:

> The cargo owner can ... proving that the vessel was unseaworthy at the commencement of the voyage and that the unseaworthiness was the cause of the loss. Then burden in relation to seaworthiness does not shift. Naturally the court can draw inferences ... But if at the end of the day ... the court is left on the razor's edge, the cargo owner fails on unseaworthiness ... If, on the other hand, the court comes down in favour of the cargo owners on unseaworthiness, the shipowners can still escape by proving that the relevant unseaworthiness was not due to any want of diligence on their part or on the part of their servants or agents.[35]

---

[31] [2000] 5 MLJ 721 (MY HC).

[32] Or any other person claiming the benefit of 'due diligence' requirement in Article III(1), such as a servant or agent, under Article IV*bis*(1) of the Hague-Visby Rules.

[33] *The Hellenic Dolphin* [1978] 2 Lloyd's Rep 336 (EW HC).

[34] Following *Ministry of Food v Reardon Smith Line Ltd* [1951] 2 Lloyd's Rep 265 (EW HC).

[35] This has been followed by many cases such as *Phillips Petroleum Co v Cabaneli Naviera SA (The Theodegmon)* [1990] 1 Lloyd's Rep 52 (EW HC), *The Toledo* [1995] 1 Lloyd's Rep 40 (EW HC), and *Papera Traders Co Ltd v Hyundai Merchant Marine Co Ltd (The Eurasian Dream) (No.1)* [2002] EWHC 118, [2002] 1 Lloyd's Rep 719, QBD (Comm) (EW HC).

It is a settled law that the duty to exercise due diligence is a non-delegable one.[36] Lord Steyn in *The Jordan II*[37] made this point as follows:

> [I]t is obvious that the obligation to make the ship seaworthy under article III, r. 1, is a fundamental obligation which the owner cannot transfer to another. The Rules impose an inescapable personal obligation …"

In *The Muncaster Castle*,[38] to facilitate a special survey, immediately prior to the onward voyage to the load port, the shipowner engaged a reputable ship repairer to open up all inspection covers. When closing back after inspection, a fitter of the repairer was negligent and did not secure the nuts sufficiently. Thereafter, the ship arrived at the load port and the cargo was loaded. Subsequently, as a result of the loosened nuts, seawater entered and damaged the goods. As the inspection covers were insufficiently secured at the time of loading, the ship was unseaworthy. The House of Lords held that the shipowner was liable under Article III(3) as it was no excuse for the shipowner to say that it was caused by the negligence of the repairs. This case was referred to with approval in Singapore by *Guan Bee & Co v Palembang Shipping Co Ltd*.[39]

In *The Happy Ranger*,[40] a newly built heavy-lift ship was employed to carry three heavy reactors each weighing about 800 tonnes. The ship was delivered by the shipbuilder to the shipowner with defective crane hooks. During loading of the reactors, a hook broke, resulting in a reactor falling and suffering substantial damage. The shipowner did not proof-test the cranes after taking delivery of the ship from the shipowner. Had the shipowner done so, it would have discovered the defect. The cargo interests instituted an action against the shipowner. The shipowner argued that it had engaged a reputable shipbuilder to build the ship and there was no lack of due diligence to ensure seaworthiness on the shipowner's part. It was also the shipowner's argument that the defect, caused by the negligence of the shipbuilder, was there prior to the ship coming into the shipowner's orbit for which the shipowner should not be held liable. The English Court of Appeal rejected the first argument above and held that the shipowner had failed in its duty to exercise due diligence to ensure that the ship was seaworthy at the time of loading. As to the second argument, the court agreed that there was no obligation on the shipowner to ensure seaworthiness before the ship came into the shipowner's orbit, however, held that it did not save the shipowner as the shipowner's duty was to ensure that it was seaworthy once it came into the shipowner's orbit, which the shipowner failed. Accordingly, the shipowner

---

[36] *The Toledo* [1995] 1 Lloyd's Rep 40 (EW HC).

[37] *Jindal Iron and Steel Co Ltd v Islamic Solidarity Shipping Co Jordan Inc (The Jordan II)* [2004] UKHL 49, [2005] 1 All ER 175, [2005] 1 WLR 1363, [2005] 1 All ER (Comm) 1, [2005] 1 Lloyd's Rep 57, [2004] All ER (D) 388 (Nov) (UK HL).

[38] *Riverstone Meat Co Pty Ltd v Lancashire Shipping Co Ltd (The Muncaster Castle)* [1961] AC 807, [1961] 1 All ER 495, [1961] 2 WLR 269, [1961] 1 Lloyd's Rep 57 (UK HL).

[39] [1969] 1 MLJ 90 (SG HC).

[40] *Parsons Corp v CV Scheepvaartonderneming (Happy Ranger)* [2002] EWHC Civ 649, [2002] 2 All ER (Comm) 24, [2002] 2 Lloyd's Rep 357, [2002] All ER (D) 278 (May) (EW CA).

was held liable. Had the shipowner proof-tested the cranes after delivery of the ship by the shipbuilder and before loading, the shipowner would have discharged its duty to exercise due diligence to ensure seaworthiness.

In *The Theodegmon,*[41] the ship's steering gear failed shortly after she left the port of loading. Although the duty to prove unseaworthiness before or at the beginning of the voyage was on the claimant, the English High Court made an inference that if the gear can fail so shortly after leaving the port, it must have been defective by the time of the beginning of the voyage. Accordingly, in the absence of an explanation from the shipowner as to how the gear failed, the court found the ship unseaworthy.

In contrast to The *Theodegmon*, the facts of *The Hellenic Dolphin*[42] did not warrant making of any inference as to seaworthiness. In *The Hellenic Dolphin*, a cargo of asbestos was found damaged by seawater on arrival. It was found that seawater entered into the cargo hold through an indented ship's shell plating. The question was whether the indent was there by the time of the beginning of the voyage or had happened after that. There was no evidence to establish when the indent happened. Accordingly, the court was left on razor's edge and had to rule against the cargo interest on the question of seaworthiness, as the fact did not warrant making any inference as to the time when the indent was present. However, if there was evidence that the seawater entered into the cargo hold shortly after the ship started to sail from the port of loading, the court might have been warranted to make an inference of unseaworthiness by the time of the beginning of the voyage. As the court did not decide the point of seaworthiness in favour of the claimant, the question of whether the shipowner exercised due diligence to ensure seaworthiness did not arise. However, the court went on to consider and answer this question. The ship had undergone her annual dry-docking recently and was fully classed at the material time. A superintending engineer had performed an inspection before the commencement of the round voyage from Europe to Africa. The master and chief engineer had performed routine inspections during the voyage. With these factors, the court answered the question of due diligence in favour of the shipowner. The court rejected the argument of the cargo interests that a superintending engineer should have performed another inspection in the midst of the voyage. The court pointed out that what was expected from the shipowner is only a reasonable action and not perfection.

In *The Amstelslot,*[43] the ship broke down because the reduction gear failed as a result of fatigue cracks in the gearbox. As a result, cargo interests suffered general average loss and they instituted action against the shipowner to recover the loss. The shipowner had a careful survey conducted prior to the loading, which did not reveal the problem. The cargo interests argued that the shipowner should have conducted further tests that would have revealed the problem. The House of Lords held that the shipowner had acted with due diligence to ensure seaworthiness and had no

---

[41] *Phillips Petroleum Co v Cabaneli Naviera SA (The Theodegmon)* [1990] 1 Lloyd's Rep 52 (EW HC).

[42] *The Hellenic Dolphin* [1978] 2 Lloyd's Rep 336 (EW HC).

[43] *Union of India v NV Reederij Amsterdam (The Amstelslot)* [1963] 2 Lloyd's Rep 223 at 235 (UK HL).

obligation to take additional steps to ensure seaworthiness more than exercising due diligence. Lord Devlin explained the dividing line between due diligence and what will be beyond that as "[what] has to be balanced is in the one scale the extreme unlikelihood of there being any crack to be found and in the other scale the serious damage and loss that would occur if there was a crack." In this case, it was a common ground that if the survey had indicated something abnormal such as corrosion or pitting more than usual, then more tests would have been warranted to discharge the due diligence duty. In this case, Lord Devlin equated lack of due diligence with negligence by saying "lack of due diligence is negligence". More recently, Staughton LJ in *The Antigoni*[44] similarly equated lack of due diligence with negligence.

Similarly, in *The Yamatogowa*,[45] the ship broke down due to failure of the reduction gear, resulting in loss to the cargo interests by general average and salvage. The first question was whether the ship was unseaworthy by the time of the beginning of the voyage. The answer to this question was in the affirmative as the defect was there by the time of the beginning of the voyage. The second question was whether the shipowner had failed in its due diligence duty. In this case, the shipowner had not properly inspected the gear and thus the English High Court found that it had breached the due diligence duty. Now the third question was whether the failure to exercise due diligence was the cause of the loss. In answer to this question, the court found that even if the shipowner had properly inspected the gear, the defect was so latent and would not have been discovered through any diligent inspection. Accordingly, the court answered this question in the negative, with the result the claim of the cargo interests failed.

In *The Kapitan Sakharov*,[46] one of the containers loaded on deck contained some dangerous cargo unknown to the shipowner and exploded with the result of a fire outbreak. That was followed by a second explosion of containers containing isopentane, a highly volatile and flammable liquid even at room temperature, stowed under deck, resulting from the heat transfer from the first explosion. As a result of the second explosion, water entered into the ship and the ship sank with a total loss of cargo. Isopentane was carried with knowledge of the shipowner. The ship was not fit to carry isopentane as there was no mechanical ventilation under deck.[47] Accordingly, the ship was unseaworthy by reason of carrying isopentane. The shipowner made a claim against the cargo interests of the on-deck cargo for loss of the ship, etc. The cargo interests of the on-deck cargo counterclaimed against the shipowner for loss of the on-deck cargo, etc. The English Court of Appeal held that, although the ship was unseaworthy, that did not cause any loss of cargo to the on-deck cargo interests, but rather their loss was caused by their own cargo that exploded. In coming to this

---

[44] *The Antigoni* [1991] 1 Lloyd's Rep 209 (EW CA).

[45] *Kuo International Oil Co Ltd v Daisy Shipping Co Ltd (The Yamatogawa)* [1990] 2 Lloyd's Rep 39 (EW HC).

[46] *Northern Shipping Co v Deutsche Seereederei GmbH and Others (The Kapitan Sakharov)* [2000] 2 Lloyd's Rep 255 (EW CA).

[47] Carrying this substance without mechanical ventilation was also against the International Maritime Dangerous Goods Code (IMDG Code), which was applicable in this case as the ship was flying under the flag of Russia that implemented the code.

conclusion, the court also found that there was no want of due diligence on part of the shipowner in respect of the on-deck cargo, as they could not have known what cargo was stuffed into the container by any exercise of due diligence. Accordingly, the shipowner was not liable to the cargo interests for the loss of the on-deck cargo. Coming to the shipowner's claim, the court held that the loss of the ship was caused by want of due diligence on part of the shipowner, as the shipowner carried highly volatile and flammable material when the ship was not fit to carry such material. Accordingly, the English Court of Appeal refused the shipowner's claim save to the extent of damage to the ship caused by the first explosion. Hobhouse J in *The Torenia*[48] well said of the inferences to be made as to seaworthiness that will shift the evidentiary burden in these modern days as follows:

> Whereas in the days of wooden ships or in the days when the design of steel ships and their construction was less well advanced or the forces they were liable to encounter were less well known and understood there may have been many instances where unexplained losses at sea gave rise to no inference of unseaworthiness, it will not be rare for such an inference not to arise in the absence of some overwhelming force of the sea or some occurrence affecting the vessel from outside. In the present case the shipowners, whilst proving the loss of the cargo, have proved also the loss of the vessel in conditions which ought not to have led to the loss of a seaworthy ship. Similarly in proving that the incursion of seawater was fortuitous they have proved that the structure of the vessel was defective …

In *The MV Kantang*,[49] the Singapore High Court said that due-diligence duty limited to what a prudent and careful carrier would do whether personally or through his servants and agents reasonably skilled and competent, and that the shipowner will be liable if the servants or agents are found to be negligent. In this case, the court held that the shipowner had discharged the duty by the master performing a visual inspection with reasonable skill and competition and without any negligence. The court said that it was not 'obligatory upon a ship's officer on the commencement of a voyage to go and tap every plank in the hull to find if it has a defect or not'.

In *Sarawak Electricity Supply Corp v MS Shipping Sdn Bhd*,[50] limited that areas in respect of which a shipowner will have to prove exercise of due diligence. The Malaysian High Court held that the shipowner is only required to show the exercise of due diligence in respect of areas where a plaintiff has alleged it was lacking. The court also said that it would be an impossibility for the shipowner to prove exercise of due diligence in all respects which have not been put into a challenge by the cargo claimant. The process of establishing an Article III(1) claim can be summarised as follows:

(i) The cargo interest must show that the ship was unseaworthy by the time of the beginning of the voyage through direct evidence or by inference that the court may draw [unseaworthiness].

---

[48] *Aktieselskabet de Danske Sukkerfabrikker v Bajamar Compania Naviera SA (The Torenia)* [1983] 2 Lloyd's Rep 210 (EW HC).

[49] *Zuellig (Gold Coin Mills) v MV Antoly (Owners) (The MV Kantang)* [1971] 1 MLJ 183 (SG HC).

[50] [2000] 5 MLJ 721 (MY HC in Sarawak).

(ii) Then the cargo interest must show that the damage or loss was caused by the unseaworthiness [causation].

(iii) If the cargo interest fails in the above, then Article III(1) claim ends there. However, if the cargo interest succeeds in the above, then the burden shifts to the carrier to show that it had exercised due diligence [due diligence] - or that no exercise of due diligence would have uncovered the unseaworthiness [causation].

9.2.3 Article IV(2) Defences not Apply to Article III(1) Obligations

There are a few defences in Article IV(2) including those in respect of negligence in navigation and management of the ship and in respect of fire caused without actual fault or privity of the carrier. The Privy Council in *Maxine Footwear Co Ltd v Canadian Government Merchant Marine Ltd*[51] held that Article IV(2) defences do not apply in respect of the obligations in Article III(1).[52] In Malaysia, it was similarly held in *Sarawak Electricity Supply Corp v MS Shipping Sdn Bhd*.[53] In Singapore, by *National Jaya (Pte) Ltd v Hong Tat Marine Shipping Pte Ltd*.[54] In *Maxine Footwear*, in so holding, the Privy Council emphasised:

> Article III(1) is an overriding obligation. If it is not fulfilled and the nonfulfilment causes the damage the immunities of article IV cannot be relied on. This is the natural construction apart from the opening words of article III(2). The fact that that rule is made subject to the provisions of article IV and article III(1) is not so conditioned makes the point clear beyond argument.

One may argue that, in such cases, Article III(1) is not expressly made subject to Article IV(1). However, Article IV(1) does not really provide any defence to Article III(1) obligation, but merely provides for burden of proof in relation to unseaworthiness and exercise of due diligence. More, Article IV(1) expressly refers to unseaworthiness and the exercise of due diligence, which can be related only to Article III(1)(a) and (b) obligation. Notably, the shifted burden of proof does not refer to cargoworthiness but only seaworthiness.

However, the difficulty with *Maxine Footwear* emphasis is that, if it was literally taken, then it would mean that the entire Article IV including Article IV(5) providing for liability-limitation[55] will not be applicable when Article III(1) is invoked. But, it has always been accepted that Article IV(5) limitation is available also in cases of Article III(1) breach. In any event, a proper reading of the Privy Council judgment in

---

[51] [1959] AC 589, [1959] 2 Lloyd's Rep 105 (PC on appeal from Canada).

[52] *Glencore Energy UK Ltd & Anor v Freeport Holdings Ltd (The Lady M)* [2019] EWCA Civ 388, [2019] 2 All ER (Comm) 731, [2019] All ER (D) 25 (Apr) (EW CA).

[53] [2000] 5 MLJ 721 (MY HC in Sarawak).

[54] [1979] 2 MLJ 6 (SG HC).

[55] Article IV(5) is dealt with in detail in the next chapter.

full would reveal that the passage was said merely to add support to the proposition and it was not intended to have an effect such as rendering the limitations in the Rules unavailable when there is a breach of Article III(1).

A more persuasive reason for rejecting Article IV(2) defences in cases of breach of Article III(1) obligation is that when a loss or damage results from an excepted event in Article IV(2), which itself is caused by unseaworthiness/cargoworthiness, then the true cause of the loss or damage is the unseaworthiness/cargoworthiness through the excepted event. Adding to this, it has been held that it is sufficient if the unseaworthiness (that must encompass uncargoworthiness in this context) is 'a' cause of the loss or damage.[56] For instance, if the carrier mans the ship with an incompetent master, who subsequently commits a navigational error that no competent master would have committed, then at least one of the effective causes of the loss or damage is the unseaworthiness at the outset. Unless such a construction is adopted, the carrier will escape liability for breach of Article III(1) obligation by relying on Article IV(2)(b). Hence, the only defence available to the carrier in such a case should be the one in Article IV(1) and not Article IV(2). An added reason for rejecting Article IV(2) defences to Article III(1) breach is that the seaworthiness/cargoworthiness obligation is a very fundamental one,[57] which constituted at common law an absolute warranty.[58]

9.3 Articles III(2)

Article III(2) provides for an obligation on the carrier, independent of Articles III(1) obligation, to exercise due care in performing the carriage operations from loading to discharge. Article III(2), which is the same in both the Rules, reads as follows:

> 2. Subject to the provisions of *Article 4*, the carrier shall *properly and carefully load*, handle, *stow, carry*, keep, care for, and *discharge* the goods carried. [emphasis added]

The duty imposed by this Article is similar to that imposed by the common law on a bailee for reward. There is also an implied term at the common law to similar effect,[59] which will now have no significant utility in cases to which the Rules apply, as the duty has essentially been restated in this Article.

---

[56] *Smith, Hogg v Black Sea and Baltic General Insurance* [1940] AC 997 (UK HL).

[57] *Jindal Iron and Steel Co Ltd v Islamic Solidarity Shipping Co Jordan Inc (The Jordan II)* [2004] UKHL 49, [2005] 1 All ER 175, [2005] 1 WLR 1363, [2005] 1 All ER (Comm) 1, [2005] 1 Lloyd's Rep 57, [2004] All ER (D) 388 (Nov) (UK HL), speech of Lord Steyn: "...article III, r. 1, is a fundamental obligation ... article III, r. 2, provides for functions some of which [although very important] are of a less fundamental order ...".

[58] By implied term. The 'absoluteness warranty' has now been statutorily abolished in cases to which the Rules apply.

[59] *Notara v Henderson* (1872) LR 7 QB 225 (EW Court of Exchequer Chamber).

9.3.1 Free-In and Free-Out

Before delving into the obligation imposed by this Article and the defences to it provided in Article IV(2), a closer look at the obligation to 'load' and to 'discharge' must be taken to appreciate the extent of coverage of the obligation. Literally reading, the obligation to 'load' and 'discharge' in Article III(2) could mean that the obligation is always on the carrier to load and to discharge. However, the intended meaning cannot be that, given the trade practice whereby the carrier and the shipper may agree on 'free-in' and/or 'free-out', meaning the shipper or consignee is to perform some or all part of, respectively, loading and/or discharge. The carriage contract may allocate the responsibility for loading, stowing and trimming on the cargo interest with clauses known as 'free-in, out, stowed and trimmed' clause, abbreviated as 'fiost'. Courts have upheld such clauses. In *Pyrene Co Ltd v Scindia Navigation Co Ltd*,[60] Devlin J well said the intention of Article III(2) and its proper interpretation[61] as follows:

> The phrase 'shall properly and carefully load' may mean that the carrier shall load and that he shall do it properly and carefully; or that he shall do whatever loading he does properly and carefully. The former interpretation perhaps fits the language more closely, but the latter may be more consistent with the object of the Rules ... It is difficult to believe that the Rules were intended to impose a universal rigidity in this respect, or to deny freedom of contract to the carrier. The carrier is practically bound to play some part in the loading and discharging, so that both operations are naturally included in those covered by the contract of carriage. But I see no reason why the Rules should not leave the parties free to determine by their own contract the part which each has to play. On this view the whole contract of carriage is subject to the Rules, but the extent to which loading and discharging are brought within the carrier's obligations is left to the parties themselves to decide.

Challenges have been taken to 'free-in' and 'free-out' clauses on the basis that they contravene Article III(2) obligations to 'load' and 'discharge' and hence invalid pursuant to Article III(8). Courts have turned down such challenges and held the clauses not to infringe Article III(2) and hence valid.[62]

---

[60] [1954] 2 QB 402, [1954] 2 All ER 158, [1954] 2 WLR 1005, [1954] 1 Lloyd's Rep 321 (EW HC).

[61] Purposive interpretation. In jurisdictions with an Interpretation Act like Malaysia, purposive interpretation is statutorily supported. In Malaysia, Section 17A of the Interpretation Acts 1948 and 1967 provides for purposive interpretation of statutes. In Singapore, Section 9A of the Interpretation Act.

[62] *Jindal Iron and Steel Co Ltd v Islamic Solidarity Shipping Co Jordan Inc (The Jordan II)* [2004] UKHL 49, [2005] 1 All ER 175, [2005] 1 WLR 1363, [2005] 1 All ER (Comm) 1, [2005] 1 Lloyd's Rep 57, [2004] All ER (D) 388 (Nov) (UK HL); *Societe De Distribution De Toutes Merchandises En Cote D'Ivoire (t/a "SDTM-CI") v Continental Lines NV (The Sea Mirror)* [2015] EWHC 1747 (Comm), [2016] 1 All ER (Comm) 1016, [2015] 2 Lloyd's Rep 395[2015] All ER (D) 206 (Jun) (EW HC).

9.3.2 *Properly and Carefully*

The obligation is both to carry out those functions 'properly' and 'carefully'. At a reading of the Article, one might think that the words 'properly and carefully' mean the same thing or that the word 'properly' does not really add anything to the word 'carefully'. However, a close reading will reveal that they could mean different things and that the word 'properly' may add something to the word 'carefully'. 'Properly' refers to a system or standard. For instance, it is not proper to smoke in public places. This is a certain standard in society. A smoker so smoking is not careless but is committing an improper act. If a repairer leaves an inspection cover open, having forgotten that to close it, then he was careless. However, if he left it open mistakenly thinking that it must be left open for emergency checking when it is not so, then he was not in any way careless in doing his job. But he did not know what the right thing was to do, and what he did can only be said to be an improper thing, but not a careless thing.

In *The Maltasian*,[63] the House of Lords said that the word 'properly' added a duty to have in place a sound system to perform the carriage. In this case, a cargo of fish was damaged because it was not carried in a temperature below 5 °C. The carrier had no knowledge of, or reason to suppose, such requirement and the shipper did not require a refrigerated container but merely asked not to stow near the ship's boilers. Accordingly, the House of Lords held that Article III(2) duty was not breached. Supposing the shipowner knew that this cargo can only be carried safely in refrigeration despite want of instruction by the shipper and carried it without refrigeration, then the shipowner would have committed improper carriage.

9.3.3 *Non-Delegable Nature of Duty*

The obligation imposed by Article III(2) has been recognised to be a non-delegable one.[64]

9.4 Article IV(2) Defences

Article IV(2) provides for a number of exceptions to the liability of carriers in cargo claims, popularly called 'defences' available to the carrier under the Rules. The Article, which is the same in both the Rules, reads as follows:

---

[63] *Albacora SRL v Westcott & Laurance Line Ltd (The Maltasian)* [1966] 2 Lloyd's Rep 53 (UK HL).

[64] *Brown & Co Ltd v Harrison, Hourani v Harrison* (1927) 96 LJKB 1025, [1927] All ER Rep 195, 137 LT 549, 17 Asp MLC 294, 32 Com Cas 305 (EW CA).

2. Neither the carrier nor the ship shall be responsible for loss or damage arising or resulting from:

(a) Act, neglect, or default of the master, mariner, pilot, or the servants of the carrier in the navigation or in the management of the ship;
(b) Fire, unless caused by the actual fault or privity of the carrier;
(c) Perils, dangers and accidents of the sea or other navigable waters;
(d) Act of God;
(e) Act of war;
(f) Act of public enemies;
(g) Arrest or restraint of princes, rulers or people, or seizure under legal process;
(h) Quarantine restrictions;
(i) Act or omission of the shipper or owner of the goods, his agent or representative;
(j) Strikes or lockouts or stoppage or restraint of labour from whatever cause, whether partial or general;
(k) Riots and civil commotions;
(l) Saving or attempting to safe life or property at sea;
(m) Wastage in bulk or weight or any other loss or damage arising from inherent defect, quality or vice of the goods;
(n) Insufficiency of packing;
(o) Insufficiency or inadequacy of marks;
(p) Latent defects not discoverable by due diligence;
(q) Any other cause arising without the actual fault or privity of the carrier, or without the actual fault or neglect of the agents or servants of the carrier, but the burden of proof shall be on the person claiming the benefit of this exception to show that neither the actual fault or privity of the carrier nor the fault or neglect of the agents or servants of the carrier contributed to the loss or damage.

9.4.1 Initial Observation

Before delving into each of the exceptions in detail, it will be worth making some initial observations on Article IV(2).

9.4.1.1 'Neither the Carrier nor the Ship'

The Article's opening words 'Neither the carrier nor the ship' confer the protection on both the carrier and the ship, although the obligations under Article III is only imposed on the carrier. The word 'ship' here can only refer to *in rem* action.[65] An *in rem* action is in effect an action against the owner or disponent owner[66] of the ship.

[65] For cargo claims, *in rem* action is provided for by Section 20(2)(g) of the UK Senior Courts Act 1981.

[66] Demise charterer.

Hence, when a carrier, who is the owner or disponent owner of the ship, is sued, it makes no difference whether it is sued *in personam* or *in rem*, as in both it is an action against the carrier, to which the Rules will apply.

The reason a cargo claimant will prefer an *in rem* action when the carrier is also the owner or disponent owner of the ship is that the cargo claimant can effect service of cause papers on the ship, the ship will be arrested to obtain security and a direct order for sale may be obtained at the end of a successful action without having to go through separate execution proceedings where no security was given and the ship was not released. All these benefits to the cargo claimant do not affect the true status of the action as an action against the owner or disponent of the ship and the action has the same effect as an action *in personam* except for those benefits to the cargo claimant. Accordingly, those additional words 'nor the ship' do not, in fact, add anything to the protection given to the 'carrier'.

9.4.1.2 'Loss or Damage'

There is no doubt that the 'loss or damage' referred to in the Rules will cover physical loss or damage. However, questions had arisen whether that includes economic loss. This question perhaps is not just about Article IV(2) but also about Article III(2), as Article IV(2) provides defences to Article III(2) claim. The courts have held that the loss or damage referred to under the Rules include economic loss.[67] In *Adamastos Shipping Co Ltd v Anglo-Saxon Petroleum Co Ltd*,[68] the House of Lords considered the meaning of 'loss or damage' appearing in Section 4 of the US Carriage of Goods by Sea Act 1936, which is materially identical to Article IV of the Hague/Hague-Visby Rules, and held that it included economic loss suffered by a charterer as a result of the ship breaking down during the first ballast voyage to the loading port. This interpretation protected the shipowner also from economic-loss claims where one of the defences in Article IV(2) was relevant.

9.4.1.3 Exception to Article III(2) Obligation Only

In *Maxine Footwear Co Ltd v Canadian Government Merchant Marine Ltd*,[69] the Privy Council held that Article IV(2) exceptions are limited to Article III(2) obligation and do not extend to Article III(1) obligation. The Privy Council supported this proposition with that Article IIII(2), but not Article III(1), is expressly made subject

---

[67] *Renton (GH) & Co Ltd v Palmyra Trading Corpn of Panama* [1957] AC 149, [1956] 3 All ER 957, [1957] 2 WLR 45, [1956] 2 Lloyd's Rep 379 (UK HL); *Adamastos Shipping Co Ltd v Anglo-Saxon Petroleum Co Ltd* [1959] AC 133, [1958] 1 All ER 725, [1958] 2 WLR 688, [1958] 1 Lloyd's Rep 73 (UK HL).

[68] [1959] AC 133, [1958] 1 All ER 725, [1958] 2 WLR 688, [1958] 1 Lloyd's Rep 73 (UK HL).

[69] [1959] AC 589, [1959] 2 Lloyd's Rep 105 (PC on appeal from Canada).

to Article IV. The limitations to literally following this rationale has been discussed earlier in this chapter.

9.4.1.4 Real Exceptions Only in (a) and (b)

Although there are 17 limbs of exceptions from (a) to (q) in Article IV(2), the real exceptions are only (a) and (b). Article IV(2)(a) is an exception relieving liability of the carrier for *act, neglect and default* of *Master, mariner, pilot and servants of the carrier* in *navigation or management of the ship*. In the absence of this exception, if loss ensues, for example, from the negligence of the master in navigation or management of the ship, the carrier would be liable under Article III(2) for failing to carefully carry the goods.

Article IV(2)(b) is to except liability for fire unless the same was caused by *actual fault or privity of the carrier*, meaning involvement of the carrier at management level in the cause of the fire. In the absence of this exception, if loss ensues from fire caused by, for example, negligence of a crew member throwing a lighted cigarette, the carrier would be liable under Article III(2) for failing to properly and carefully carry, keep and care for the goods.

Basically, Article III(2) obligation is to exercise due diligence and *care* for safe carriage of the goods. Article IV(2)(a) and (b) directly except liability for *negligence* in certain cases. Hence, Article IV(2)(a) and (b) are defences to liability arising from a breach of Article III(2).

Article IV(2)(c)–(q) declares that the carrier is not liable for loss or damage caused in effect by perils of the sea, act of God, act of war, act of public enemies, arrest pursuant to law, quarantine restrictions, act or omission of the shipper, strikes, riots and civil commotions, saving life or property at sea, inherent vice of the goods, insufficiency of packing, insufficiency of marks, latent defects not discoverable by due diligence, and any other cause without fault of the carrier or its agents and servants.

In fact, none of the events mentioned in Article IV(c)–(q), are per se within the scope of the obligation imposed by Article III(2) or the common law. For instance, Article III(2) does not impose any responsibility on the carrier for damage caused by an act of God or war. Accordingly, Article IV(2)(c)–(q) do not in fact provide a defence to Article III(2).[70]

However, interestingly, when a carrier proves any of the events mentioned in Article IV(c)–(q), that will negate any breach in the first place of Article III(2). In *The Maltasian*,[71] the carrier established, under Article IV(2)(m), that the damage to the cargo of fish was caused by the inherent vice of the goods. The same fact also

---

[70] This proposition will be supported by the judgment of the UK Supreme Court in *Volcafe Ltd and others v Compania Sud Americana De Vapores SA (t/a CSAV)* [2018] UKSC 61 at [28], [2019] AC 358, [2019] 2 All ER 81, [2018] 3 WLR 2087, [2019] 1 All ER (Comm) 397, [2019] 1 Lloyd's Rep 21, [2018] All ER (D) 16 (Dec) (UK SC).

[71] *Albacora SRL v Westcott & Laurance Line Ltd (The Maltasian)* [1966] 2 Lloyd's Rep 53 (UK HL).

showed that, in fact, the carrier did not commit any breach of Article III(2). Thus, the true value of Article IV(2)(c)–(q) is mere guidance to rebut an allegation of want of due diligence and care under Article III(2).

9.4.1.5 Interpretation of the Rules

The objective of the Rules is to provide an internationally uniform regime of laws on this subject applicable in all the member states. The objective was said by Lord Steyn in *The Giannis NK*[72] as follows:

> This much we know about the broad objective of the Hague Rules: it was intended to reign in the unbridled freedom of contract of owners to impose terms which were 'so unreasonable and unjust in their terms as to exempt from almost every conceivable risk and responsibility' ...; it aimed to achieve this by a pragmatic compromise between interests of owners and shippers; and the Hague Rules were designed to achieve a part harmonization of the diverse laws of trading nations at least in the area which the convention covered.

The objective of the Rules requires two things to be kept in mind when interpreting the Rules. First, the interpretation must not be over-influenced by pre-Rules domestic precedents. Second, foreign authorities may be considered. The first point was said by Lord Macmillan in *Stag Line Ltd v Foscolo, Mango & Co Ltd*[73] as follows:

> It is important to remember that the [Carriage of Goods by Sea Act 1924] was the outcome of an International Conference, and that the rules in the Schedule have an international currency. As these rules must come under the consideration of foreign courts it is desirable in the interests of uniformity that their interpretation should not be rigidly controlled by domestic precedents of antecedent date, but rather that the language of the rules should be construed on broad principles of general acceptance.

The same point was emphasised by the UK Supreme Court recently in *Volcafe v CSAV*[74] in the following words:

> It is well established that even in a contract governed by English law, provisions derived from an international convention are intended to have an internationally uniform effect and should not be construed by national courts by reference to principles of purely domestic application: *Stag Line Ltd v Foscolo, Mango & Co Ltd*[75]; *James Buchanan & Co Ltd v Babco Forwarding and Shipping (UK) Ltd.*[76] [emphasis added]

---

[72] *Effort Shipping Co Ltd v Linden Management SA (The Giannis NK)* [1998] AC 605, [1998] 1 All ER 495, [1998] 2 WLR 206, [1998] 4 LRC 97, [1998] 1 Lloyd's Rep 337, [1998] All ER (D) 10 (UK HL).

[73] [1932] AC 328, [1931] All ER Rep 666 (UK HL).

[74] *Volcafe Ltd and others v Compania Sud Americana De Vapores SA (t/a CSAV)* [2018] UKSC 61, [2019] AC 358, [2019] 2 All ER 81, [2018] 3 WLR 2087, [2019] 1 All ER (Comm) 397, [2019] 1 Lloyd's Rep 21, [2018] All ER (D) 16 (Dec) (UK SC).

[75] [1932] AC 328 at 350, [1931] All ER Rep 666 (UK HL), speech of Lord MacMillan.

[76] [1978] AC 141 at 152, [1977] 3 All ER 1048, [1977] 3 WLR 907, [1978] 1 Lloyd's Rep 119 (UK HL), speech of Lord Wilberforce.

The second point was said by Lord Phillips in *The River Gurarra*[77] as follows:

> The Hague Rules were the product of international Convention. They were incorporated into the domestic legislation of a large number of seagoing nations and became widely used as the terms governed the international carriage of goods by sea. … [P]articular respect should be paid to the decisions of other jurisdictions in respect of the meaning of the rules, for the stated object of the Convention was the unification of domestic laws of the Contracting States relating to bills of lading.

The point was taken further by the English Court of Appeal in *The Lady M.*[78] The court made reference to the Vienna Convention on the Law of Treaties,[79] particularly Article 31 thereof, which reads as follows:

> 1. A treaty shall be interpreted in good faith in accordance with the ordinary meaning to be given to the terms of the treaty in their context and in the light of its object and purpose.
>
> …
>
> Recourse may be had to supplementary means of interpretation including the preparatory work of the treaty and the circumstances of its conclusion, in order to confirm the meaning resulting from the application of article 31, or to determine the meaning when the interpretation according to article 31: (a) leaves the meaning ambiguous or obscure, or (b) leads to a result which is manifestly absurd or unreasonable.

The court observed that even before the Vienna Convention came into force in the UK in 1980, the rules for the interpretation of international conventions were in effect the same. The court made the following important observations on Article 31 of the Vienna Convention:

(1) An international convention should be interpreted in accordance with the ordinary meaning to be given to its terms.
(2) In interpreting the convention, its objective and purpose must be kept in mind.
(3) Recourse should be had to *travaux préparatoires* only when the object and purpose of the international convention cannot be ascertained without recourse to it.
(4) Substantively,[80] an international convention should not be interpreted in light of domestic legal background, to allow international uniformity in interpretation and application of the convention.

---

[77] *Owners of Cargo lately on board River Gurara v Nigerian National Shipping Line Ltd (The River Gurara)* [1998] 1 Lloyd's Rep 225 at 228, [1998] QB 610, [1997] 4 All ER 498, [1997] 3 WLR 1128 (EW CA).

[78] *Glencore Energy UK Ltd & Anor v Freeport Holdings Ltd (The Lady M)* [2019] EWCA Civ 388, [2019] 2 All ER (Comm) 731, [2019] All ER (D) 25 (Apr) (EW CA).

[79] Ratified by the UK in 1971 and came into force in 1980. Singapore has not ratified this treaty, but has its own statutory provision facilitating purposive construction of treaties. Malaysia ratified (by accession) this treaty in 1994.

[80] This does not cover procedural and evidentiary aspects: *Volcafe Ltd and others v Compania Sud Americana De Vapores SA (t/a CSAV)* [2018] UKSC 61, [2019] AC 358, [2019] 2 All ER 81, [2018] 3 WLR 2087, [2019] 1 All ER (Comm) 397, [2019] 1 Lloyd's Rep 21, [2018] All ER (D) 16 (Dec) (UK SC).

More than 110 countries have ratified the Vienna Convention, including the UK.[81] Apart from the Vienna Convention, interpretation statutes of some of the States may also mandate interpretation of any statute in accordance with the purpose of the statute. For example, the Interpretation Acts 1948 and 1967 of Malaysia provides in Section 17A as follows:

17A. Regard to be had to the purpose of Act

In the interpretation of a provision of an Act, a construction that would promote the purpose or object underlying the Act (whether that purpose or object is expressly stated in the Act or not) shall be preferred to a construction that would not promote that purpose or object.

Interestingly, Singapore has a more complex and detailed provision for interpreting a statute in accordance with the purpose of the Act and as to making reference to *travaux préparatoires*.[82] It is in Section 9A of the Singapore Interpretation Act, which reads as follows:

9A. Purposive interpretation of written law and use of extrinsic materials

(1) In the interpretation of a provision of a written law, an interpretation that would promote the purpose or object underlying the written law (whether that purpose or object is expressly stated in the written law or not) shall be preferred to an interpretation that would not promote that purpose or object.

(2) Subject to subsection (4), in the interpretation of a provision of a written law, if any material not forming part of the written law is capable of assisting in the ascertainment of the meaning of the provision, consideration may be given to that material —

(a) to confirm that the meaning of the provision is the ordinary meaning conveyed by the text of the provision taking into account its context in the written law and the purpose or object underlying the written law; or

(b) to ascertain the meaning of the provision when —

(i) the provision is ambiguous or obscure; or

(ii) the ordinary meaning conveyed by the text of the provision taking into account its context in the written law and the purpose or object underlying the written law leads to a result that is manifestly absurd or unreasonable.

(3) Without limiting the generality of subsection (2), the material that may be considered in accordance with that subsection in the interpretation of a provision of a written law shall include —

(a) all matters not forming part of the written law that are set out in the document containing the text of the written law as printed by the Government Printer;

[81] And Malaysia, but not Singapore, which has its own statutory provisions enabling purposive construction of treaties, discussed below.

[82] This is not substantially difference from the position in Article 31 of the Vienna Convention as to interpretation of international conventions.

(b) any explanatory statement relating to the Bill containing the provision;
(c) the speech made in Parliament by a Minister on the occasion of the moving by that Minister of a motion that the Bill containing the provision be read a second time in Parliament;
(d) any relevant material in any official record of debates in Parliament;
(e) any treaty or other international agreement that is referred to in the written law; and
(f) any document that is declared by the written law to be a relevant document for the purposes of this section.

(4) In determining whether consideration should be given to any material in accordance with subsection (2), or in determining the weight to be given to any such material, regard shall be had, in addition to any other relevant matters, to —

(a) the desirability of persons being able to rely on the ordinary meaning conveyed by the text of the provision taking into account its context in the written law and the purpose or object underlying the written law; and
(b) the need to avoid prolonging legal or other proceedings without compensating advantage.

However, that does not mean that the courts do nor or will not refer to common law for guidance on many questions which have not been altered by the Rules. For example, the Rules do not define what is seaworthiness. Best guidance can only be obtained from English common law cases, which have been widely adopted in many jurisdictions. This wealth of precedents cannot be set aside. In fact, if a court were to ignore the wealth of precedents, that would only result in largely inconsistent decisions.

9.4.2 Article IV(2)(a) and (b)

These two defences, the most material ones, are considered in turn below.

9.4.2.1 Article IV(2)(a): Fault in Navigation and Management of Ship

The exception is for acts, neglect or default—of the master, mariner, pilot or servant of the carrier—in the navigation or management of the ship. Although liability for negligence is excluded by the Article, it is limited to matters only of (i) navigation and (ii) management of the ship. This is where the courts can control the scope of this exception as a matter of construction of these two words—navigation and management of the ship.

Navigation

In *The Hill Harmony*,[83] a dispute arose out of a time charterparty that incorporated the Hague Rules. Pursuant to the terms of the charterparty, the master was to take orders and directions of the charterers as regards the *employment* of the vessel.[84] The charterers instructed the master to follow a particular route[85] to the discharge port. However, the master opted to follow a different route[86] to the discharge port, which will be longer than the one opted by the charterer. The charterer instituted arbitration claiming that the shipowner had breached the provision as to the employment of the vessel. The shipowner defended itself with Article IV(2)(a) of the Hague Rules, whereby a carrier is not liable for any act of the master as to navigation. The arbitral tribunal[87] decided that the choice of the master was not a navigational one but rather one as to the employment of the vessel. Accordingly, they decided that the shipowner breached its obligation and was not protected by Article IV(2)(a). On appeal against the award, the English High Court and, on further appeal, the Court of Appeal found in favour of the shipowner. The charterer appealed to the House of Lords. The House held that whether the decision of the master to take a particular route is one as to navigation is a question of degree. The House pointed out that a navigation decision may be taken while sailing or even before the ship sets sail. If the decision of the master to refuse the route proposed by the charterer and to take another route is based on safety or other navigational reasons, then it is a navigational decision protected under Article IV(2)(a). If the decision is not made for *safety*[88] *or other navigational reasons*, then it is not a decision as to navigation and not protected under Article IV(2)(a). The burden is on the carrier to satisfy that the decision was a navigational one. In this case, evidence showed that more than 300 vessels had used the route proposed by the charterers over the last three months, it was the usual route recommended by Ocean Routes and there was no valid reason for the master to opt for the other route.[89] Accordingly, the House held that the decision of the master was

---

[83] *Whistler International Ltd v Kawasaki Kisen Kaisha Ltd (The Hill Harmony)* [2001] 1 Lloyd's Rep 147, [2001] 1 AC 638, [2001] 1 All ER 403, [2000] 3 WLR 1954, [2001] 1 All ER (Comm) 76, [2001] 4 LRC 142, [2000] All ER (D) 2178 (UK HL).

[84] The time charterparty was in the form of New York Produce Exchange (NYPE) 1946 form, wherein cl. 8 provided as follows: "Captain (although appointed by the Owners), shall be under the orders and directions of the Charterers as regards employment and agency; and Charterers are to load, stow, and trim the cargo at their expense under the supervision of the Captain, who is to sign Bills of Lading for cargo as presented, in conformity with Mate's or Tally Clerk's receipts."

[85] Northerly 'Great Circle Route'.

[86] Southerly 'Rhumb Line Route'.

[87] By majority.

[88] Of the ship, crew and cargo.

[89] Although the actual reason was that the vessel had suffered typhoon damage on a previous voyage when using that route—an explanation found to be unreasonable.

not a navigational one, but rather one as to the employment of the vessel, and thus was not protected by Article IV(2)(a).[90]

In the New Zealand Supreme Court case of *The Tasman Pioneer,*[91] the master took a risky shortcut to save time, which resulted in the ship grounding. Thereafter, the master, instead of reporting to the coastguard and owner immediately and seeking assistance, told the crew to cover up for saving the master from blame. Subsequently, the master sought assistance, by when the cargo was also substantially damaged as a result of the delay in seeking assistance. The cargo interest, to whom the bill of lading subject to the Hague-Visby Rules had been issued, sued the carrier. The carrier defended itself with Article IV(2)(a) exception. The High Court, although agreed that post-grounding operations can be a matter of navigation or management of the ship, held that the event was not covered by Article IV(2)(a) because the act of the master here was not done in good faith to save the ship, cargo or crew, but rather to save himself from blame. This analysis will align with *The Hill Harmony,* as a navigational decision is one made in the interests of safety or for navigational reasons. The Court of Appeal[92] upheld the decision. The carrier appealed to the New Zealand Supreme Court, which found there was no barratry and reversed the decision. The court held that Article IV(2) covered the event and hence protected the carrier because the exception was designed to protect carriers from the acts of their employees, provided the conduct did not amount to barratry. In coming to the conclusion, the Supreme Court made reference to the *travaux préparatoires* and resorted to the pre-Hague Rules common law authorities to interpret the rules. The English Court of Appeal, in a subsequent case about Article IV(2)(b), *The Lady M,*[93] disagreed with the position of the New Zealand Supreme Court that Article IV(2)(a) would not cover if there was barratry. It also disagreed with the approach of the New Zealand Supreme Court in making reference to the *travaux préparatoires.* If a case such as *The Tasman Pioneer* comes up before an English court, it is likely the that it court will rule that barratry is irrelevant, and hold in favour of the cargo interest, because the decision of the master not to report to coastguard was not one made for navigational reason but made rather for another reason, namely to protect the master from blame.[94]

The words 'in the navigation' and 'in the management of the ship' themselves has an element of intention with which, or the purpose for which, the act in question must be done or default or neglect in question must be committed. If the intention or purpose, associated navigation or ship management, is missing, as in *The Hill*

[90] The House found that the charterer had also breached the duty to proceed with utmost dispatch by failing to take the usual shorter and quicker route and opting a longer route without valid reason.

[91] *Tasman Orient Line CV v New Zealand China Clays (The Tasman Pioneer)* [2010] NZSC 37 (NZ SC).

[92] New Zealand.

[93] *Glencore Energy UK Ltd & Anor v Freeport Holdings Ltd (The Lady M)* [2019] EWCA Civ 388, [2019] 2 All ER (Comm) 731, [2019] All ER (D) 25 (Apr) (EW CA).

[94] Following *Whistler International Ltd v Kawasaki Kisen Kaisha Ltd (The Hill Harmony)* [2001] 1 Lloyd's Rep 147, [2001] 1 AC 638, [2001] 1 All ER 403, [2000] 3 WLR 1954, [2001] 1 All ER (Comm) 76, [2001] 4 LRC 142, [2000] All ER (D) 2178 (UK HL).

Harmony and *The Tasman Pioneer*, then it will not qualify for the exception in Article IV(2)(a) as it will not be an act 'in the navigation or in the management of the ship'.

Management of Ship

In *The Canadian Highlander*,[95] a cargo of tinplate was carried. During the voyage, the ship suffered a casualty. To repair, the cargo holds had to be assessed and for this purpose, the hatch covers were opened. It was raining at that time and tarpaulins were not placed to cover the open hatch covers. As a result, rain entered the cargo holds and damaged the cargo of tinplate. The cargo interest sued the carrier. The carrier defended itself with Article IV(2)(a) by claiming that the error in not covering the hatch covers with tarpaulins was one as to the management of the ship. The House of Lords rejected this argument and held the carrier liable, as tarpaulins are purely used to protect the cargo only and has nothing to do with 'management of the ship'. Lord Hailsham differentiated 'want of care of the cargo' from 'want of care of the vessel indirectly affecting the cargo'. The former will not be excepted under Article IV(2) but the latter will be because that is a shortfall in relation to 'management of the ship'. The House of Lords was in favour of the three-point test, formulated by Greer LJ in his Lordship's dissenting judgment at the Court of Appeal,[96] to determine if a case falls within this exception. It will be so when the damage to the cargo was an indirect result of an act, or neglect, which can be described as either:

(i) negligence in caring for the safety of the ship;
(ii) failure to take care to prevent damage to the ship or some part of the ship; or
(iii) failure in the management of some operations connected with the movement or stability of the ship or otherwise for ship's purposes.

Difficulties have arisen when a system that was mismanaged was in relation both to cargo safety and ship safety. In *International Packers London Ltd v Ocean Steam Ship Co Ltd*,[97] the English High Court held that a failure of the crew to properly secure locking bars on the hatch covers, resulting in seawater entering the cargo holds and damaging the cargo, was covered by Article IV(2)(a). This was because ensuring the locking bars were properly secured was also for the safety of the ship and was part of the management of the ship. Even if there was no cargo in the holds, the locking bars must be securely locked for the safety of the ship. In fact, this is also mandated by the Load Line Rules, which was one of the factors that influenced the court to arrive at the decision that it did.

---

[95] *Gosse Millerd Ltd v Canadian Government Merchant Marine Ltd (The Canadian Highlander)* [1929] AC 223, [1928] All ER Rep 97 (UK HL).

[96] *Gosse Millerd Ltd v Canadian Government Merchant Marine Ltd* [1928] 1 KB 717 (EW CA). Although this decision was reversed by the House of Lords in [1929] AC 223, [1928] All ER Rep 97, the three-point test referred to here found favour in the House of Lords.

[97] [1955] 2 Lloyd's Rep 218 (EW HC).

Questions had arisen as to the application of Article IV(2)(a) when the damage occurred due to a fault in management of the inert gas system in ships. The inert gas system is installed in oil tankers that carry flammable material. The purpose is to render the atmosphere of the cargo tanks non-flammable and to prevent any explosion. Hence, the system has two functions: one to protect the cargo and another to safeguard the ship from the danger that the cargo poses to the ship.

When the cargo was damaged due to the carrier's fault in management of the system, the question that arises is whether it is in relation to the management of the ship or management of the cargo. In the former case, the carrier will be protected by Article III(2)(a) exception, but not in the latter. In two cases,[98] one in England and another in New South Wales, the courts held that the management of the inert gas system was in relation to the management of cargo rather than of the ship. Hence, the courts refused to allow the carrier to rely on Article IV(2)(a) exception. These are razor-edge cases and the correctness of the decisions is dubious. Although the inert gas also protects the cargo, without a proper administration of it, the ship will be in danger. Hence, it will be hard to say that an inert gas system, or anything that is in relation to the *safety* of the ship, is not about the management of the ship. The right question to ask will likely be whether the system is one in relation to the management of the ship rather than whether it is concerning the management of cargo. Once the answer to the former question is that it is about the management of the ship, then arguably it does not matter that it is *also* about the management of cargo.

Performing work concerning the cargo-carrying facilities, when cargo was not carried in those facilities, have been held to fall within this exception. In the Singapore Court of Appeal case of *The Dagny Skou,*[99] a cargo of paper was carried from Buenos Aires[100] to Singapore under a bill of lading subject to US Carriage of Goods by Sea Act 1936, which has largely adopted the Hague Rules.[101] The cargo was damaged by water. The facts leading up to the damage were as follows. The paper was stowed in a hold at the stern.[102] Below the hold, there were two deep tanks with manhole access from the main deck. The purpose of the tanks was twofold. One, to carry a cargo of vegetable oil[103] and another to store fuel oil for the ship's propulsion. At the time of the incident, both tanks were originally empty having discharged the last cargo of vegetable oil. The crew went into the tanks to clean them. The master ordered filling the tanks with about 350 tons of water, which will be done with one hour of pump operation. The total capacity of the two tanks was 780 tons. The engineer turned the pump on at 6 pm and was supposed to turn it off at 7.00 pm. He forgot to turn it off

[98] *The Petroleum Oil and Gas Corporation of South Africa (Pty) Ltd v Fr8 Singapore Pte Ltd (The Eternity)* [2009] 1 Lloyd's Rep 107, [2008] EWHC 2480 (Comm), [2009] 1 All ER (Comm) 556, [2008] All ER (D) 236 (Oct) (EW HC); *Caltex Refining Co Pty Ltd v BHP Transport Ltd (The Iron Gippsland)* [1994]1 Lloyd's Rep 335 (NSW SC).

[99] *The Dagny Skou* [1980-1981] 1 SLR 200 (SG CA).

[100] In Argentina.

[101] The USA is not a signatory to the Hague or Hague-Visby Rules.

[102] Rear side of the ship.

[103] Or dry cargo.

until 8.30 pm, with the result the pump filled up the tanks to the full capacity and further exceeded the capacity. The water entered the main deck and the cargo hold where the paper was stored since manholes were left open at that time to facilitate inspection of the water levels. Thus, the paper was damaged.

The consignee[104] sued the carrier. The carrier claimed that the damage was caused by an 'act, or neglect or default in the management of the ship', so that liability for that would be excluded by Section 4(2)(a) of the Act. The said section is identical to Article IV(2)(a) of the Hague/Hague-Visby Rules. The court agreed with this contention and held that the carrier was not liable because the negligence was not concerning any particular cargo but was about the management of the ship.

It must be observed that in this case, although the holds had a dual purpose—carriage of cargo and storing of fuel oil for the ship—at the time of the negligent act or omission, it was not carrying any cargo and the actions performed were concerned with the management of the ship or ship's cargo carrying facilitates but not any cargo itself. The reason for performing the work in relation to the cargo carrying facilities might have been to prepare the ship to carry next cargo or fuel oil, but that did not affect the ability of the carrier to rely on the exception and the decision.

The effect of Article IV(2) exception insofar as it is for 'management of the ship' is quite limited, as this will easily overlap in many cases[105] with a failure to have in place a proper management system at the outset of the voyage and hence will become a breach of Article III(1). This is more so with safety systems required to be in place by the International Safety Management Code (ISM Code). See *Papera Traders Co Ltd v Hyundai Merchant Marine Co Ltd (The Eurasian Dream) (No. 1)* [2002] EWHC 118, [2002] 1 Lloyd's Rep 719, QBD (Comm) (EW HC).

9.4.2.2 Article IV(2)(b): Fire Without Actual Fault or Privity of Carrier

This exception is for fire caused otherwise than by actual fault or privity of the carrier.

Actual Fault or Privity of Carrier

The two exclusions in Article IV(2) to the application of fire-exception are where the fire happened by 'actual fault of the carrier' and when it happened by 'privity of the carrier'. Each of them is disjunctive, as they are separated by 'or'. The 'privity' on its own right seems to suggest that the carrier can be liable even if there was no fault of the carrier but there was privity in the sense of 'personal involvement' in the events that caused the fire. In *The Apostolis,*[106] the English High Court interpreted the two exclusions cumulatively to mean fault of a servant of the carrier of a certain

[104] Indorsee of the bill.

[105] Though not necessarily always, e.g. management of the inert gas system during the voyage.

[106] *Meredith Jones (A) & Co Ltd v Vangemar Shipping Co Ltd (The Apostolis)* [1996] 1 Lloyd's Rep 475 (EW HC).

seniority, such as the general manager, who can be said to be the alter ego of the carrier-company. The English Court of Appeal in *The Lady M,*[107] when dealing with a case of loss resulting from a fire caused by barratry, seemed to have assumed that actual fault or privity of the carrier referred to a fault at the management level of the carrier-company and no argument otherwise was advanced.

This seems to suggest 'personal fault' as opposed to 'imputed fault'. That does not answer the question of what is meant by 'actual fault of the carrier' and what is meant by 'privity of the carrier'. It seems that an attempt has not been made to authoritatively answer this point. Perhaps the current interpretation will better fit 'privity of carrier' than 'actual fault of carrier'. On a plain reading of the Article, it is hard to interpret '*actual* fault of the carrier' to mean the *personal* fault of the carrier.

If the Article had merely said 'fault of the carrier', then it should possibly include servants and agents of the carrier. But it adds the word 'actual'. Literally, the addition of the word 'actual' cannot add anything as there is no such thing as a non-actual fault unless one is dealing with a presumption of fault. One could argue that this was intended to mean 'personal' fault of the carrier, i.e. the fault of the alter ego of the carrier-company, as seems to be thought by the court in *The Apostolis* and *The Lady M*. This complexity owes to the insufficient drafting of the Rules.[108]

Some support for *The Apostolis* and *The Lady M* position can be derived from the fact that the Rules in certain parts refer to 'carrier' and in some other part[109] to 'agents or servants of the carrier'. Arguably, this divorces the carrier from its agents and servants for purposes of interpreting the Rules, with the result that the fault of the carrier will mean fault of the alter ego of the carrier-company rather than a fault of other agents or servants of the carrier. In line with this school of thought, *The European Enterprise,*[110] the English High Court was of the view that 'carrier' in Article IV(5)(e) meant a person of sufficient seniority in the management of the carrier-company, which did not include the master in this case.[111] This line of thought seems to have been adopted generally in cases.

In *The Garden City,*[112] the senior officers operating a fleet of vessels were not considered to be the alter ego of the carrier-company. Rather, the director of technical services was thought to be the one who may be considered to be such an alter ego.

---

[107] *Glencore Energy UK Ltd & Anor v Freeport Holdings Ltd (The Lady M)* [2019] EWCA Civ 388, [2019] 2 All ER (Comm) 731, [2019] All ER (D) 25 (Apr) (EW CA).

[108] That the UK Supreme Court in *Volcafe Ltd and others v Compania Sud Americana De Vapores SA (t/a CSAV)* [2018] UKSC 61, [2019] AC 358, [2019] 2 All ER 81, [2018] 3 WLR 2087, [2019] 1 All ER (Comm) 397, [2019] 1 Lloyd's Rep 21, [2018] All ER (D) 16 (Dec) (UK SC) described as 'notoriously unsatisfactory'.

[109] Article IV(2)(q).

[110] *Browner International Ltd v Monarch Shipping Co Ltd (The European Enterprise)* [1989] 2 Lloyd's Rep 185 (EW HC).

[111] Carrier' was similarly treated in *Tasman Orient Line CV v New Zealand China Clays (The Tasman Pioneer)* [2010] NZSC 37 (NZ SC), which did not agree with a contradicting view stated in a previous New Zealand case *Nelson Pine Industries Ltd v Seatrans New Zealand Ltd (The Pembroke)* [1995] 2 Lloyd's Rep 290 (NZ HC)

[112] *The Garden City* [1982] 2 Lloyd's Rep 382 (EW HC).

However, there have been avenues of mitigating the effect of that line of thought. In *The Lady Gwendolen,*[113] the English Court of Appeal interpreted 'actual fault or privity of owner' appearing in Section 503 of the UK Merchant Shipping Act 1894 which provision limited the liability of the shipowner in certain cases where there was no 'actual fault or privity' of the shipowner. The court refused defence to the shipowner when the master was negligent. In this case, the managing director, the alter ego of the carrier-company, had appointed the master and left matters relating to safe navigation, the procuring of navigational information and publications to the matter. Similarly, in *The Marion,*[114] the House of Lords refused the Section 503 limitation to the shipowner when the ship did not have up-to-date charts and sailing schedules. In this case, the House said that it was the director's duty to ensure that the master had the latest charts and to supervise the master and pointed out that "it is no longer sufficient that having appointed a competent master". The House held that the carrier liable for failing in these duties.

Fire, Perils of Sea and Barratry

This exception, interestingly, is not limited to the fire happening as a peril of the sea—a fortuitous event peculiar to carriage by sea. A good case that will demonstrate this is *The Lady M,*[115] In this case, during the voyage, the chief engineer deliberately started a fire, the reason for which was not known precisely, but possibly that he was suffering from depression. As a result, salvage cost and the cost of defending the salvage action were incurred by the cargo interest. The cargo interest brought an action against the carrier-shipowner to recover the loss under Article III(1) and (2). The shipowner agreed that the fire was so started by the chief engineer but argued that it was not liable for it by virtue of Article IV(2)(b) because the fire took place without actual fault or privity of the carrier. The response of the cargo interest to this was that the act of the chief engineer constituted barratry and that Article IV(2)(b) did not protect the carrier when there was barratry.

The English Court of Appeal disagreed with the cargo interest's argument and held that even fire caused by barratry is covered within Article IV(2)(b) exception so that the carrier will not be liable for it. The court observed that there was nothing in the wording of Article IV(2)(b) to say that a shipowner will lose the protection if there was barratry. In fact, the court observed that barratry is a very thing covered in Article IV(2)(b) as "in cases of barratry the carrier's agents are acting contrary to the carrier's interests and in breach of the trust reposed in them." The court rejected the argument of the cargo interest to refer to the domestic law prior to the Rules as

113 *Arthur Guinness, Son & Co (Dublin) Ltd v The Freshfield (Owners) (The Lady Gwendolen)* [1965] P 294, [1965] 2 All ER 283, [1965] 3 WLR 91, [1965] 1 Lloyd's Rep 335 (EW CA).

114 *Grand Champion Tankers Ltd v Norpipe A/S (The Marion)* [1984] AC 563, [1984] 2 All ER 343, [1984] 2 WLR 942, [1984] 2 Lloyd's Rep 1 (UK HL).

115 *Glencore Energy UK Ltd & Anor v Freeport Holdings Ltd (The Lady M)* [2019] EWCA Civ 388, [2019] 2 All ER (Comm) 731, [2019] All ER (D) 25 (Apr) (EW CA).

to fire exception and barratry and to interpret the Article in light of the pre-Hague Rules[116] common law cases.[117] The court also disagreed with the cargo interest's argument that there was any need to refer to *travaux préparatoires* in interpreting the Article, although the court did not rule out the possibility of making such reference when the meaning of the Rules cannot be ascertained from the Rules themselves. The court did not regard as right the position taken by the New Zealand Supreme Court in case of *The Tasman Pioneer*[118] that if there was barratry then the exception in Article IV(2)(a) would not apply. The court emphasised the need to interpret the Rules, being an international convention, in accordance with its ordinary meaning in their context and in the light of its object and purpose pursuant to the Vienna Convention.[119]

Non-Vehicle Owning Carriers

It has been observed earlier, following a detailed discussion, that 'carrier' in the Hague/Hague-Visby Rules can only mean a shipowner because a document will qualify to be a bill of lading only if it is issued by the shipowner.[120] This is a highly controversial point.

However, if the Rules could apply where the carrier is a non-vehicle owning carrier (NVOC) such as freight forwarders, then the NVOC will almost always be entitled to the protection in Article IV(2)(b) as any fault will be that of the shipowner rather than the NVOC. This will be an anomalous position crated, at least literally, if the Rules were to apply to bills issued by NVOCs.

---

[116] 1924.

[117] *Gard Marine and Energy Ltd v China National Chartering Co Ltd; China National Chartering Co Ltd v Gard Marine and Energy Ltd; Daiichi Chuo Kisen Kaisha v Gard Marine and Energy Ltd (The Ocean Victory)* [2017] 1 WLR 1793 at [70], [2017] UKSC 35, [2018] 1 All ER 832, [2017] 1 WLR 1793, [2018] 1 All ER (Comm) 1, [2017] 1 Lloyd's Rep 521, [2017] All ER (D) 54 (May) (UK SC); *Stag Line Ltd v Foscolo, Mango & Co Ltd* [1932] AC 328, [1931] All ER Rep 666 (UK HL).

[118] *Tasman Orient Line CV v New Zealand China Clays (The Tasman Pioneer)* [2010] NZSC 37 (NZ SC).

[119] Article 31 of the Vienna Convention.

[120] See Chap. 2.2 .

Fire-Exception and Unseaworthiness

If a fire happens before the voyage starts, that will render the ship unseaworthy within the province of Article III(1), hence Article IV(2) will be of no application.[121] The only defence will be that the carrier exercised due diligence to ensure seaworthiness.[122]

Section 186 of the UK Merchant Shipping Act 1995 Exception for Domestic Ships

Independently of the Rules, Section 186 of the UK Merchant Shipping Act 1995 The Section 186 is expressly preserved by Section 6(4) of the Carriage of Goods by Sea Act 1971 read together with Article VIII of the Hague/Hague-Visby Rules. also provides a fire-exception, in wider terms than in Article IV(2)(b), in the case of ships registered in the UK. The Section 186, in relevant part and together with relevant schedule, reads as follows:

> **186. Exclusion of liability**
>
> (1) Subject to subsection (3) below, the owner of a United Kingdom ship shall not be liable for any loss or damage in the following cases, namely—
>
> (a) where any property on board the ship is lost or damaged by reason of fire on board the ship;
>
> …
>
> (2) This section does not exclude the liability of any person for any loss or damage resulting from any such personal act or omission of his as is mentioned in Article 4 of the Convention set out in Part I of Schedule 7.
>
> **SCHEDULE 7**
>
> **Convention on Limitation of Liability for Maritime Claims 1976**
>
> …
>
> **Article 4: Conduct barring limitation**
>
> A person liable shall not be entitled to limit his liability if it is proved that the loss resulted from his personal act or omission, committed with the intent to cause such loss, or recklessly and with knowledge that such loss would probably result.

In Singapore, Section 135 of the Merchant Shipping Act makes a materially identical provision to that in the Section 186 of the 1995 Act. [123]

---

[121] *Maxine Footwear Co Ltd v Canadian Government Merchant Marine Ltd* [1959] AC 589, [1959] 2 Lloyd's Rep 105 (PC on appeal from Canada); *Glencore Energy UK Ltd & Anor v Freeport Holdings Ltd (The Lady M)* [2019] EWCA Civ 388, [2019] 2 All ER (Comm) 731, [2019] All ER (D) 25 (Apr) (EW CA).

[122] Article IV(1).

[123] any loss or damage happening without his actual fault or privity in the following cases: (a) where any goods, merchandise or other thing whatsoever taken in or put on board his ship are lost or damaged by reason of fire on board the ship; or …".

A question arising from the Section 186 of the UK 1995 Act is whether it covers fire caused by unseaworthiness at the outset of the voyage that will fall foul of Article III(1). Where the cause of the fire is attributable to unseaworthiness, then, in fact, the effective cause of the loss *vis-a-vis* the fire is the unseaworthiness. If this analysis is correct, then the Section 186 does not protect the UK shipowner from unseaworthiness-claim. The shipowner will be left with his only defence of due diligence in Article IV(2). This analysis will find support from the accepted interpretation of the Rules, whereby Article IV(2) exceptions do not except Article III(1) seaworthiness-obligation. Accordingly, the Section 186[124] does not really add to Article IV(2)(b). Section 6(4) of the Carriage of Goods by Sea Act 1971 expressly declares the Section 186 of the UK 1995 Act to be a provision relating to limitation of liability for purposes of Article VIII. The Article VIII declares that any statute relating to limitation of liability is not affected by the Rules. Hence, operation of the Section 186 is not subject to the Rules, and it will, likely, be available even if the fire itself was caused by unseaworthiness of the ship at the outset of the voyage.

9.4.3 *Article IV(2)(c)-(q)*

Each of the defences in Article IV(2)(c) through (q), which are not in fact defences as there is no corresponding liability but perhaps have value as guidance only, are briefly visited in turn below.

9.4.3.1 Article IV(2)(c): Perils, Dangers and Accidents of Sea

This exception is for perils, dangers and accidents of the sea or other navigable waters. This covers three matters. One is perils of the sea, second is dangers in the sea and the last is accidents at the sea.

'Peril' is not defined in the Hague/Hague-Visby Rules. 'Peril' in relation to sea adventure has always meant a fortuitous event peculiar to carriage by sea such as stranding, sinking, a collision of the vessel, striking a submerged object, or encountering heavy weather or other unusual forces of nature. As such it will cover dangers at sea. However, whether it covers all incidents of accidents is questionable, because an accident may happen with or without the master's negligence. If it happens without the master's negligence, then 'peril' will cover it. However, if it happens by master's or crew's negligence, then the cause of the loss will be negligence rather than the peril of the sea.

Prior to the Rules, 'perils of the sea' was a popular exception found in bills of lading and other shipping documents. The need for this exception was there because it was not clear if a shipowner was a common carrier or merely bailee for reward. If it was merely a bailee for reward, then all its duty to take proper and due care of

---

[124] And similar provisions in other countries.

the goods entrusted with it, and it is not an insurer. In such a case, the 'perils of the sea' exception would not be necessary as the bailee is not liable for damage or loss caused by perils of the sea. However, if it was a common carrier,[125] then the only defences it had were the act of God, act of Queen's enemies, inherent vice of the goods and fault of the consignor. In such a case, the carrier would be liable for perils of the sea, unless contractually excepted. Hence, the need for this popular contractual exception. Common law cases[126] on the meaning of 'perils of the sea' will still be relevant under the Rules, but not the substantive common law.

'Danger' and 'accident' are not defined in the Rules. 'Danger' seems to cover matters over which the master will have no control, such as a sudden heavy wave overturning the ship. 'Accident' seems to cover matters such as collision over which master will have some control or at least there will be an element of some human-control. What 'danger' and 'accident' cover may, in fact, be more than this and it is not attempted here to exhaustively define them. An accident may be committed by negligence of the master[127] or without such negligence.

If a loss or damage is caused by a peril of the sea, including danger and accident, that does not automatically bring the incident within the exception in this Article. If the peril is attributable to the negligence on part of the carrier, then the effective cause is negligence rather than the peril. Hence, liability will not be excepted.[128] In fact, even under the common law, this was the position.[129]

Foreseeable Bad Weather and Perils of the Sea

While it is not doubted that bad weather encountered during the voyage is a peril of the sea, it is questionable whether the exception will protect the carrier if the bad weather was foreseeable before starting to sail. If it was so foreseeable that no reasonable shipowner would proceed to set sail, then it would amount to negligence on part of the carrier, with the result perils of the sea exception is no longer available to the carrier. To decide if there was negligence on part of the shipowner, a court will have to balance the foreseen danger against the commercial commitment and need to

[125] A category of sea carriers of cargo, now almost extinct: Supreme Court in *Volcafe Ltd and others v Compania Sud Americana De Vapores SA (t/a CSAV)* [2018] UKSC 61, [2019] AC 358, [2019] 2 All ER 81, [2018] 3 WLR 2087, [2019] 1 All ER (Comm) 397, [2019] 1 Lloyd's Rep 21, [2018] All ER (D) 16 (Dec) (UK SC).

[126] Discussed earlier in this sub-chapter.

[127] Or crew.

[128] *Maxine Footwear Co Ltd v Canadian Government Merchant Marine Ltd* [1959] AC 589, [1959] 2 Lloyd's Rep 105 (PC on appeal from Canada).

[129] *Industrie Chimiche Italia Centrale SpA v Nea Ninemia Shipping Co SA (The Emmanuel C)* [1983] 1 Lloyd's Rep 310, [1983] 1 All ER 686 (EW HC): in this case, 'errors of navigation' were contractually excepted, however, the court held that it did not cover when the error was committed by negligence.

set sail.[130] However, an Australian court has said *obiter* that advance foreseeability of bad weather does not affect the ability of the carrier to rely on the perils of the sea exception.[131] These authorities have not considered that setting sail when bad weather was foreseeable could constitute negligence as the cause of loss rather than the peril. In Canada, it has been held that the carrier cannot rely on the peril of the sea exception where the peril was foreseeable and could have been guarded against.[132] The Australian authorities are unlikely to be followed in the UK.

In *The MV Kantang*,[133] the Singapore High Court held that this exception was not available when the ship sank in heavy weather, which was not of such a catastrophic nature or so overwhelming as to constitute perils of the sea. In this case, the court held that the ship sank because she was unseaworthy in that the fastenings of the bow planking of the vessel were unsound whereby the bow planking worked loose in the heavy seas allowing water to enter the vessel causing her to sink. However, the analysis that a weather of catastrophic or overwhelming nature was required to constitute this exception is not so correct approach. Rather the better approach is to ask if such weather was such weather was something beyond the reasonable foreseeability of an ordinarily competent shipowner at the outset of the voyage, and if so whether sufficient precaution was taken to sail during that weather or to other appropriate measures such as changing the route or postponing the voyage. The discussion made below in respect of *The MV Thonfullin*[134] under Article IV(2)(d) is also applicable to Article IV(2)(c) exception, as the two can be intertwined.

Exception Unnecessary for Bailee for Reward

As it is now settled that a sea carrier now is merely a bailee for reward and not a common carrier, hence the exception is unnecessary.

9.4.3.2 Article IV(2)(d): Act of God

This exception is for act of God. In means incidents beyond human control, e.g. tsunami. In fact, it will also encompass some of the perils of the sea such as an

---

[130] *The Tilia Gorthon* [1985] 1 Ll Rep 552 (EW HC) has some passages that will lend support to the proposition that when so bad weather is foreseeable that it cannot be ignored, proceeding to sail can constitute negligence on part of the shipowner.

[131] *Great China Metal Industries Co Ltd v Malaysian International Shipping Corporation Berhad (The Bunga Seroja)* [1999] 1 Lloyd's Rep 512 (Australian HC); *Shipping Corp of India Ltd v Gamlen Chemical Co (A/Asia) Pty Ltd* 147 CLR 142, 32 ALR 609, 55 ALJR 88 (Australian HC).

[132] *Charles Goodfellow Lumber Sales Ltd v Verreault, Hovington and Verreault Navigation Inc* [1971] 1 Lloyd's Rep 185 (Canada SC).

[133] *Zuellig (Gold Coin Mills) v MV Antoly (Owners) (The MV Kantang)* [1971] 1 MLJ 183 (SG HC).

[134] *Kuok Ling Timber Industries Sdn Bhd v The Owners of and Other Persons Interested in the Vessel MV Thonfullin (The MV Thonfullin)* [2000] 2 MLJ 615 (MY HC).

unexpected bad weather setting during the voyage. This exception is unnecessary, as a carrier, whether a common carrier[135] or merely a bailee for reward, is not liable for acts of God. The Malaysian Federal Court in *Kwan Sun Ming v Chak Chee Hing*[136] referred with approval to the definition of 'act of God' given in Halsbury's Laws of England,[137] which was as follows:

> [A]n extraordinary occurrence or circumstance which could not have been foreseen and which could not have been guarded against; or, more accurately, as an accident due to natural causes, directly and exclusively without human intervention, and which could not have been avoided by any amount of foresight and pains and care reasonably expected of the person sought to be made liable for it, or who seeks to excuse himself on the ground of it ...

Following that, the Malaysian High Court in *The MV Thonfullin*,[138] held that the storm relied on by the shipowner to constitute the act of God did not entitle the shipowner to this exception because it was not shown to be a sudden violent storm or an extraordinary high tide. Again, the better and right approach would have been to test it with 'reasonable foreseeability' test as said in Halsbury rather than 'extraordinary event' test. However, the extraordinariness can be an aspect to be considered as part of the reasonable foreseeability test. When something is so extraordinary, that may be the reason that it was not reasonably foreseen. But sometimes, even extraordinary events might be within reasonable foresight, such as when out-of-ordinary weather was already forecast before the voyage commenced. If this point is argued under the perils of the sea exception in Article IV(2)(c), the same would be the position.

9.4.3.3 Article IV(2)(e): Act of War

This exception is for act of war. The discussion made in respect of the act of God above is relevant here. However, if a carrier sails into a war zone taking an unproportionate risk, then the effective cause of any loss or damage may be the negligence, for which liability is not excepted.

9.4.3.4 Article IV(2)(f): Act of Public Enemies

This exception is for act of public enemies, which will include pirates. It will be arguable that piracy[139] was a result of unseaworthiness at the outset of the voyage

---

[135] Now almost extinct: *Volcafe Ltd and others v Compania Sud Americana De Vapores SA (t/a CSAV)* [2018] UKSC 61, [2019] AC 358, [2019] 2 All ER 81, [2018] 3 WLR 2087, [2019] 1 All ER (Comm) 397, [2019] 1 Lloyd's Rep 21, [2018] All ER (D) 16 (Dec) (UK SC).

[136] [1965] 1 MLJ 236 (MY FC).

[137] (3rd edn.), at p. 183.

[138] *Kuok Ling Timber Industries Sdn Bhd v The Owners of and other persons interested in the vessel (The MV Thonfullin)* [2000] 2 MLJ 615 (MY HC).

[139] For case on consequences of piracy in relation to cargo claim, see *Petroships Pte Ltd of Singapore v Petec Trading and Investment Co of Vietnam and Ors (The Petro Ranger)* [2001] EWHC 418 (Comm) (EW HC).

if the piracy was a result of the ship not having suitable security features or crew trained in anti-piracy. The discussions made in respect of the act of God and act of war above are relevant here.

9.4.3.5 Article IV(2)(g): Arrest, Seizure Under Legal Process, etc

This exception is for arrest of the ship, seizure under legal process, restraint by princes and rulers, and restraint by people. Arrest[140] and seizure under legal process are beyond the control of the shipowner. Restraint by princes and rulers will include requisition to the government. Even if the cause of the arrest or legal process is the negligence of the carrier, such as a previous collision, still a carrier still likely to be entitled to the exception under this Article, because negligence, in this case, will be too remote a cause for the subsequent loss occasioned to the cargo interest as a result of the arrest or legal process.

9.4.3.6 Article IV(2)(h): Quarantine Restrictions

This exception is for quarantine restrictions. The discussions made in respect of act of God and act of war above are relevant here.

9.4.3.7 Article IV(2)(i): Act or Omission of Shipper or Owner of Goods

This exception is for acts or omission—of the shipper or owner of the goods—his agents or representative. Notably, this exception does not cover acts or omission of the consignor who may be different from the shipper and the owner of the goods and whose acts or omission may be the person culpable for anything wrong with the goods.

If the loss or damage to cargo is the result of an act or omission of the shipper or owner of the goods, then the carrier is not liable for it. This is a simple logical position as one cannot claim against another for consequences of his own act or omission. There are three limitations to this exception. First is that it does not relieve the carrier of its obligation to perform the carriage function properly and carefully. Second is that it does not relieve the carrier from seaworthiness-obligation. The third is that it does not protect the carrier where the carrier is estopped from setting up the defence in a suit by a third-party holder of a clean bill of lading.

Some examples will help understand the three limitations. Suppose that cargo is so badly stowed by a shipper in a 'free-in' carriage contract that the carrier knows or ought to know that it cannot be safely carried but the carrier does not intervene. This will constitute a breach of Article III(2) and Article IV(2). If the non-intervention is construed to be the negligence of the carrier, then the effective cause of the loss will be the negligence of the carrier rather than bad stowage by the shipper. In such a case, the carrier will not be able to rely on the exception.

If the bad stowage by the shipper renders the ship unseaworthy at the outset of the voyage, then this exception will not protect the carrier against breach of the

[140] Sections 20 and 21 of UK Senior Courts Act 1981.

seaworthiness-obligation, as it is a settled position that Article IV(2) exceptions do not apply when there is a breach of Article III(1) obligation.[141]

If the suit against the carrier is by a third party holder of a clean bill of lading in good faith, then the carrier will be estopped from setting up Article IV(2)(i) defence.[142] In *Silver and Layton v Ocean Steamship Co Ltd*,[143] the English Court of Appeal estopped the carrier from setting up Article IV(2)(n) defence of insufficient packaging against the holder of a clean bill of lading in good faith.

9.4.3.8 Article IV(2)(j): Strikes or Lockouts or Stoppage or Restraint of Labour

This exception is for strikes, lockouts and restraints of labour—from whatever cause—whether partial or general. The 'whatever cause' seems to make a wide coverage including a scenario where the cause of the strike is attributable to a fault on the carrier's part.

9.4.3.9 Article IV(2)(k): Riots and Civil Commotions

This exception is for riots and civil commotions. The discussions made in respect of the act of God, act of war and act of public enemies above are relevant here.

9.4.3.10 Article IV(2)(l): Saving or Attempting to Save Life or Property at Sea

This exception is for saving or attempting to save—life or property—at sea. This exception is wider than the defence in Article IV(4) of the Rules, which provides this defence in respect of a claim for deviation only.

9.4.3.11 Article IV(2)(m): Inherent Defect, Quality or Vice of Goods

This exception is for inherent defect, quality or vice of the goods. Naturally, a carrier cannot take responsibility for the inherent vice of the gods. However, this point is not as simple as that. This exception has been a subject of controversy in a number of cases.

In *Volcafe v CSAV*,[144] a cargo of coffee beans was damaged by water condensed on the container walls. The condensation was caused by the inherent vice of the coffee beans themselves which will emit moisture when carried from a colder climate to a

[141] *Maxine Footwear Co Ltd v Canadian Government Merchant Marine Ltd* [1959] AC 589, [1959] 2 Lloyd's Rep 105 (PC on appeal from Canada).

[142] *Ismail v Polish Ocean Lines (The Ciechocinek)* [1976] QB 893, [1976] 1 All ER 902, [1976] 2 WLR 477, [1976] 1 Lloyd's Rep 489 (EW CA).

[143] [1930] 1 KB 416, [1929] All ER Rep 611 (EW CA).

[144] *Volcafe Ltd and others v Compania Sud Americana De Vapores SA (t/a CSAV)* [2018] UKSC 61, [2019] AC 358, [2019] 2 All ER 81, [2018] 3 WLR 2087, [2019] 1 All ER (Comm) 397, [2019] 1 Lloyd's Rep 21, [2018] All ER (D) 16 (Dec) (UK SC).

warmer climate, as happened in this case. However, the carrier could have avoided it by lining the container walls and roof with paper or card, which was the practice. The carrier was unable to prove that it had sufficiently done so, although it had lined the walls with some paper. Accordingly, the UK Supreme Court held that the cause of the damage was the failure of the carrier to properly and carefully carry and to care for the goods rather than the inherent vice. All Article IV(2)(c)–(q) exceptions do not save a carrier when there was a fault on its part constituting a breach of Article III(2) obligation.

In *The Maltasian*,[145] a cargo of fish was damaged because they were not carried in a refrigerated container. Neither the carrier nor the shipper was aware of this requirement. The shipper did not book a refrigerated container. The House of Lords held that the cargo was damaged by inherent vice and the carrier was able to rely on Article IV(2)(m) exception as the carrier was not at fault in connection with it. In deciding the question of the fault of the carrier, Lord Reid connected it to the terms of the contract of carriage and said as follows:

> [W]hether there is inherent defect or vice must depend on the kind of transit required by the contract. If this contract had required refrigeration there would have been no inherent vice. But as it did not, there was inherent vice because the goods could not stand the treatment which the contract authorised or required."

Even before the Hague Rules, this was the position and the defence was only available when the loss by inherent vice was not associated with any fault on the carrier's part. In *Nugent v Smith*,[146] a pre-Hague Rules case, a mare was carried in the hold and died. The cause of her death was both bad weather and her own fright as a result of which she struggled and injured herself. The Cockburn CJ described the law in relation to inherent vice as this:

> [T]he carrier is not liable where the thing carried perishes or sustains damage, *without any fault of his*, by reason of some quality inherent in its nature.

The same principle was said in the case by Mellish LJ as this:

> [I]f the jury had found that the injury was caused solely by the conduct of the mare herself by reason of fright and consequent struggling, *without any negligence on the part of the defendant's servants*, ... a plea that the injury to the mare was caused by the vice of the mare herself would have been proved.

In *The Cendor Mopu*,[147] the UK Supreme Court considered the inherent vice defence in the context of an insurance policy that excluded liability for inherent vice. In this

---

[145] *Albacora SRL v Westcott & Laurance Line Ltd (The Maltasian)* [1966] 2 Lloyd's Rep 53 (UK HL).

[146] (1876) 1 CPD 423 at 438 -439, 41 JP 4, 45 LJQB 697, 3 Asp MLC 198, 25 WR 117, 34 LT 827 (EW CA).

[147] *Global Process Systems Inc v Syarikat Takaful Malaysia Bhd (The Cendor Mopu)* [2011] UKSC 5, [2011] 1 All ER 869, [2012] 1 All ER (Comm) 111, [2011] 1 Lloyd's Rep 560, [2011] All ER (D) 10 (Feb) (UK SC).

case, an oil rig was carried on a barge. The rig comprised a platform and three legs. The three steel legs, each of longer than 300 feet weighing more than 400 tonnes, were into the air during the carriage on the barge. As a result of strong waves, metal fatigue developed, resulting in all the three legs falling off one by one. The cargo interest sued the insurer under the policy. The insured claimed that the loss was due to the inherent vice of the goods. The court narrowly defined 'inherent vice' and refused the insurer's argument. The court held that the loss was not by inherent vice but by 'leg-breaking wave' which was a covered peril. The court held that the inherent vice defence is not available when some external fortuity had interfered to cause the loss. But it will be available only when the fortuity came from the goods themselves.

9.4.3.12 Article IV(2)(n): Insufficiency of Packing

This exception is for insufficiency of packing. Naturally, this is an act of the shipper. However, that does not mean that the carrier cannot be held liable for a loss arising from it, for example, if it had issued a clean bill of lading and a third-party bill holder in good faith sues the carrier. There cannot be doubt in that this exception will be a defence if the claimant is the shipper itself. However, estoppel will bar the carrier from setting up this defence when sued by the third-party bill holder in good faith.

In *Silver and Layton v Ocean Steamship Co Ltd,*[148] a cargo of frozen eggs was shipped. The packages had sharp edges. Because of the sharp edges, one package will damage another. The cargo arrived thus damaged. A clean bill of lading was issued by the carrier, which bill was subsequently transferred to a holder in good faith. The English Court of Appeal held that the insufficient packing referred to in Article IV(2)(n) also covers the case where the package is good in itself but will damage other packages carried together with it, as it happened in this case. However, the court held that the carrier was estopped from establishing this defence against the third party bill of lading holder in good faith.

In *Goodwin, Ferreira & Co Ltd v Lamport & Holt Lines Ltd,*[149] Roche J was of the view that 'insufficiency of packaging' will include cases where the insufficient packaging of one consignor's goods damages the goods of another consignor. However, in that case, Roche J decided the case on Article IV(2)(q) exception rather than on Article IV(2)(n) exception. The view of Roche J does not seem to accord with the purpose of the exception in Article IV(2)(n) which appears to exonerate the carrier when the blame is attributable to the shipper, as with Article IV(2)(i). As a convention must be interpreted in accordance with its purpose,[150] the view of Roche J is unlikely to be sustainable. Suppose that the packing is insufficient, resulting in damage to cargo, and the claim is made by the consignor itself, only then this exception will protect the carrier, however likely subject to the three limitations discussed above in relation to Article IV(2)(i).

---

[148] [1930] 1 KB 416, [1929] All ER Rep 611 (EW CA).

[149] (1929) 34 Ll L Rep 192, [1929] All ER Rep 623 (EW HC).

[150] *Glencore Energy UK Ltd & Anor v Freeport Holdings Ltd (The Lady M)* [2019] EWCA Civ 388, [2019] 2 All ER (Comm) 731, [2019] All ER (D) 25 (Apr) (EW CA); Vienna Convention, Article 31.

9.4.3.13 Article IV(2)(o): Insufficiency or Inadequacy of Marks

This exception is for insufficiency or inadequacy of marks. In practice, this is unlikely to be an issue, unless the insufficiency led to the carrier mistaking the goods of one owner for another and thereby making a mistaken delivery, provided that the carrier was not negligent in making those mistakes.

9.4.3.14 Article IV(2)(p): Latent Defect Not Discoverable by Due Diligence

This exception is for latent defects—that cannot be discovered by due diligence. At the outset, it must be noticed that the question is not whether due diligence was exercised, but whether objectively the defect was discoverable by due diligence.

In a nutshell, this provides that if a loss or damage occurs by a cause that the carrier could not have found out by due diligence then the carrier is not liable. In fact, if the loss or damage is caused by a latent defect not discoverable by due diligence, then there would in the first place be no breach of Article III(2) obligation, essentially, to exercise due care and diligence in performing the functions related to the carriage.

The Antigoni[151] demonstrates the close relationship between this exception and Article III(1) duty to exercise due diligence to ensure the ship is seaworthy at the outset of the voyage. In this case, the shipowner argued that the casualty was caused by a latent defect that could not be discovered by due diligence, hence sought to rely on Article IV(2)(p) exception. At the same time, the shipowner also argued that there was no breach of Article III(1) as the casualty was not due to any want of due diligence on its part. In either case, Staughton LJ pointed out that the burden to prove exercise of due diligence was on the shipowner.

9.4.3.15 Article IV(2)(q): Any Other Cause not Attributable to Fault of Carrier

This exception is for any other cause not attributable to fault or neglect of the carrier, including its servants and agents. Like some other provisions of the Rules, this Article is also drafted in a difficult style.

This Article opens by excepting any cause 'without actual fault or privity of the carrier *or* without the fault or neglect of the servants or agents of the carrier'. This will suggest that there are two different causes excepted by this Article, one is where the cause arose without the actual fault or privity of the carrier and another is where it arose without the fault or neglect of the carrier's servants and agents. However, at the closing, the Article requires the carrier to prove, in order to rely on this exception, that there was 'neither the actual fault nor privity of the carrier *nor* the fault or neglect of the agents or servants of the carrier'. This will mean that the excepted cause is only one, that is one that arose without actual fault or privity of the carrier *and* without fault or neglect of the servants or agents of the carrier.

---

[151] *The Antigoni* [1991] 1 Lloyd's Rep 209 (EW CA).

Sellers LJ in *The Chyebassa*[152] said that theft would fall within this exception only if it was without carrier's "actual fault or privity" and "also … it was without the fault or neglect of their agents or servants."

In fact, if there was no fault, neglect attributable to the carrier, including its servants and agents, then in the first place there is no liability on the carrier. Hence, this exception is unlikely to be of any utility, other than as serving as guidance to, and reiteration of, Article III(2) obligation, as like the other exceptions in Article IV(2)(c)–(p).

9.5 Article III(2) and IV(2): Burden of Proof

Prior to the recent Supreme Court decision in *Volcafe v CSAV*,[153] the position in the English law was that the legal burden to prove breach of Article III(2) obligation was on the cargo interest and the legal burden to prove Article IV(2) exception was on the carrier. If a carrier proves an Article IV(2) defence, then the burden shifts onto the cargo interest to prove negligence on part of the carrier to debar the carrier from taking the benefit of Article IV(2) exception. Despite this being the position in law, in practice, when a cargo loaded in good state arrives damaged, courts have been willing to make an inference that the carrier had failed in its Article III(2) obligation. This was well explained by Lord Pearson in *The Maltasian*,[154] as follows:

> The convenient first step is to ascertain what is the *prima facie* obligation under Art III(2) … It is not an obligation to achieve the desired result, ie, the arrival of the goods in an undamaged condition at their destination. It is an obligation to carry out certain operations properly and carefully. The fact that goods, acknowledged in the bill of lading to have been received on board in apparent good order and condition, arrived at the destination in a damaged condition does not in itself constitute a breach of the obligation, though it may well be in many cases sufficient to raise an inference of a breach of the obligation. The cargo owner is not expected to know what happened on the voyage, and, if he shows that the goods arrived in a damaged condition and there is no evidence from the shipowner showing that the goods were duly cared for on the voyage, the court may well infer that the goods were not properly cared for on the voyage.

Accordingly, practically, the burden on the cargo claimant was to prove that the goods were damaged during transit, which the claimant would normally be able to prove by showing the state of the goods on loading (for which the bill of lading will be of great assistance and *prima facie* evidence to the cargo claimant) and their state on discharge. Then the burden, practically, shifts to the carrier to prove it had discharged Article III(2) functions properly and carefully or that it is entitled to rely on an Article IV(2) defence. But if the carrier manages to prove any of the excepted events in Article IV(2), then the burden shifts back to the cargo claimant to prove

---

[152] *Leesh River Tea Co Ltd v British India Steam Navigation Co Ltd (The Chyebassa)* [1967] 2 QB 250 at 271, [1966] 3 All ER 593, [1966] 3 WLR 642, [1966] 2 Lloyd's Rep 193 (UK CA).

[153] *Volcafe Ltd and others v Compania Sud Americana De Vapores SA (t/a CSAV)* [2018] UKSC 61, [2019] AC 358, [2019] 2 All ER 81, [2018] 3 WLR 2087, [2019] 1 All ER (Comm) 397, [2019] 1 Lloyd's Rep 21, [2018] All ER (D) 16 (Dec) (UK SC).

[154] *Albacora SRL v Westcott & Laurance Line Ltd (The Maltasian)* [1966] 2 Lloyd's Rep 53 (UK HL).

the negligence of the carrier. The duty of the carrier is similar to that of a bailee for reward.

Although a clean bill of lading will be of great assistance in proving damage during transit if the goods are discharged damaged, the burden to prove the state of the goods at the time of discharge is on the cargo claimant. This was well demonstrated by the case of *Vaynar Suppiah & Sons v KMA Abdul Rahim & Anor,*[155] decided by the Singapore Court of Appeal. In this case, many packages of clothing material were shipped from Karachi[156] to Singapore on board two ships, namely the Lars and the Jens, owned by the same shipowner under a few clean bills of lading. Upon delivery, the consignee (indorsee of the bills) complained that the goods had been damaged. For the goods carried by the Lars, the complaint was that the goods were damaged by seawater while in transit. For the goods carried by the Jens, the complaint was that the goods were damaged by rainwater while on lighterage. To prove the damage, its nature and extent, the only evidence essentially adduced by the consignee were some reports of experts, none of whom were called to give evidence. The court held that whilst the carriers would be estopped from challenging the order and condition of goods when shipped, the burden was still on the consignee to prove that they arrived damaged and the extent of the damage. The court pointed out that the estoppel is in respect of the external condition of the goods and not the internal condition. The reports, in the absence of the expert giving evidence before the court, was inadmissible, being hearsay evidence. In so holding, the court first pointed out that it did not fall within the Singapore Evidence Act Section 32(1)(b) exception, i.e. the witness 'attendance cannot be procured without an amount of delay or expense which under the circumstances of the case appears to the court unreasonable'. Second, the Section 32(1)(b) was not intended to be available to expert witnesses. Accordingly, the claim was disallowed. The UK Supreme Court in the recent landmark case of *Volcafe v CSAV*[157] held the legal burden in both Articles III(2) and IV(2) to be otherwise.

The origin of the Section 32(1)(b) is in the materially identical Section 32(2) of the Indian Evidence Act 1872, which model has been adopted in many Commonwealth counties, including in Malaysia. In Malaysia, an identical provision is found in Section 32(1)(b) of the Evidence Act 1950. The position in England and Wales is different. Hearsay evidence is admissible by virtue of Section 1 of the Civil Evidence Act 1995, subject to procedural safeguards in Sections 2 and 3 of the Act and Civil Procedure Rules (CPR) Rules 33.1 - 33.6. However, the weight to be attributed to the hearsay is a matter for the court to determine, depending on the circumstances.[158]

---

155 [1972-1974] 1 SLR 239 (SG CA).

156 In Pakistan.

157 *Volcafe Ltd and others v Compania Sud Americana De Vapores SA (t/a CSAV)* [2018] UKSC 61, [2019] AC 358, [2019] 2 All ER 81, [2018] 3 WLR 2087, [2019] 1 All ER (Comm) 397, [2019] 1 Lloyd's Rep 21, [2018] All ER (D) 16 (Dec) (UK SC).

158 Section 4 of the Act.

Subsequent to *Vaynar Suppiah*, the Evidence Act in Singapore was amended[159] by the addition of Section 32B(1)[160] that will allow Section 32(1) to be available also to expert witnesses. There is no equivalent amendment in Indian or Malaysia,[161] hence the observation made on this point, in this case, is still relevant to Indian and Malaysia.[162] The position in England and Wales is again different. CPR Rule 35.5 provides that expert evidence is normally given in a written report unless the court otherwise directs.[163] As cargo claims will more often fall into multi-track, the court will direct attendance of the export witness when desirable. Apart from this, provision is made for the report to be checked by various mechanisms.[164]

It must be noted that whether The Hague or Hague-Visby Rules will apply during lighterage will depend on the terms of the bill. If the bill stated that the goods will be so discharged into lighters, then the Rules will likely not apply for the lighterage phase.[165] However, if the bill did not state that the goods will be so discharged or that merely gave liberty to the carrier to so discharge, then likely the lighterage phase will be subject to the Rules.[166]

9.5.1 *Volcafe v CSAV [2018] UKSC 61*

In this case, coffee beans were carried from Buenaventura[167] to Bremen[168] on LCL/FCL[169] basis in unventilated containers over a period under a few bills of ladings. The carrier was responsible for stuffing the cargo into the containers and did so. The Hague Rules applied by incorporation of the same into the bill of lading. The bill rendered itself subject to English law and jurisdiction.

A coffee bean is a hygroscopic substance that will emit moisture when transferred from a warmer place to a cooler place, as it was in this case. The moisture, when carried on unventilated containers as in this case, will inevitably cause condensation on the walls of the container. The condensation will cause damage to the coffee beans. Such damage by condensation will be mitigated by lining the container's internal

---

[159] In 2012.

[160] The Section 32B(1) reads as follows: "Subject to this section, section 32 applies to statements of opinion as they apply to statements of fact."

[161] And India.

[162] And India.

[163] The court will not ordinarily direct an expert to attend a hearing in small claims tracks and fast tracks.

[164] Such as written questions to the expert (CPR Rule 35.6), court's direction to a party to provide further information to the expert (CPR Rule 35. 9), single joint expert report (CRP Rules 35.7 and 35.8), discussion between experts and a subsequent report by them to the court (CPR Rule 35.12, 35 PD 9).

[165] See *Captain v Far Eastern Shipping Co* [1979] 1 Lloyd's Rep 595 (Canada SC).

[166] See *Mayhew Foods Ltd v Overseas Containers Ltd* [1984] 1 Lloyd's Rep 317 (EW HC).

[167] In Colombia.

[168] In Germany.

[169] 'Less than container load'/'full container load'.

walls and roof with card or paper in order that the card or paper will absorb the moisture, which is a common practice. The carrier so lined the walls and roof. However, the cargo arrived damaged by water from condensation. The cargo owners[170] sued the shipowners as carriers for breach of Article III(2) obligation and for breach of carrier's duties as bailees, with the conventional proof that goods loaded in good state, arrived in damaged condition. The cargo owners also pleaded that the carrier was negligent in not using sufficient or adequate paper. The carrier proved that it had lined the walls and roofs but did not provide the details of the lining such as how thick the paper used was, how many layers were employed and what was the thickness and layers required in this case. Nor were the cargo owners able to adduce any evidence of them.

The carrier relied on Article IV(m) exception, namely inherent vice of the goods. But the question was whether the cargo damage was attributable to the inherent vice of the goods or negligence of the carrier. Following this, the question that the court had to answer was whether the carrier had to prove no negligence on its part in order to successfully rely on Article IV(m). In other words, the question was *whether* as a matter of law the burden was on the cargo owners to prove that the cargo was damaged by negligence rather than by inherent vice was on the cargo owner *or* was it on the carrier to prove that it was not negligence in order to rely on the inherent vice exception. The difference between bearing the legal burden and relying on *res ipsa loquitur* merely to shift the evidentiary burden must be observed. *Res ipsa loquitur* does not shift the legal burden, but it only imposes the evidentiary burden on the party who has the knowledge of the facts to speak up, maintaining the legal burden on the party wishing the court to accept a fact. The difference was well said by Sri Walter Phillimore in the Privy Council case of *Dwarkanath Raimohan Chaudhuri and Another v The Rivers Steam Navigation Company Limited*[171] as follows:

> [T]he defendant Company should call the material witnesses who were on the spot ... But this provision of the law of evidence does not discharge the plaintiffs from proving .... It may be for the Company to lay the materials before the court; but it remains for the plaintiffs to satisfy the court that the true inference from these materials is that the servants of the defendant Company have not shown due care, skill and nerve.[172]

However, the position in those Commonwealth countries, including Singapore[173] and Malaysia,[174] with an Evidence Act modelled on the Indian Evidence Act 1872 is

[170] Holder of the bills of lading.

[171] [1917] UKPC 108 (PC on appeal from India).

[172] Although the decision in this case as to who bore the legal burden was overruled by a subsequent Privy Council in *Port Swettenham Authority v Tw Wu and Company (M) Sdn Bhd* [1978] 2 MLJ 137 (PC on appeal from Malaysia), that did not affect the observation made (by the former Privy Council) as to the difference between legal burden and *res ipsa loquitur*, which will be relevant in the context of English law.

[173] Singapore Evidence Act.

[174] Malaysian Evidence Act 1950.

somewhat different. Section 106 of the Indian Evidence Act 1872[175] directly places the burden (i.e. legal burden) of proving facts especially within one party's knowledge on that party, as observed by the subsequent Privy Council in *Port Swettenham Authority v Tw Wu and Company (M) Sdn Bhd.*[176]

The Supreme Court in the present case, *Volcafe*, did not doubt that the carrier was a bailee for reward, subject to terms of the bailment, that is, the bill of lading in this case, and turned to the question of burden of proof for purposes associated with Article IV(2)(m) of the Hague Rules, which will be common for all Article IV(2)(c)-(q). The carrier argued that once it had proved that damage was caused by an exception, in this case, the inherent vice, the burden was on the cargo owners to prove that it was attributable to the negligence of the carrier. The Court of Appeal, following the popular pre-Hague Rules case of *The Glendarroch,*[177] agreed with the carrier's argument and held in favour of the carrier. In *The Glendarroch*, the Court of Appeal held that the burden of proving that an excepted peril had been occasioned by the carrier's negligence lay on the cargo owner. Lopes LJ, in that case, said this as follows:

> Where a peril of the sea is set up it is sufficient for the defendant to prove the peril relied on, and he need not go on to shew that that was really not caused by him; but if the plaintiff says that it was, then he must set it up in his replication and must prove it.

The Supreme Court in the present case, *Volcafe*, did not doubt that the carrier was a bailee for reward, subject to terms of the bailment, that is, the bill of lading in this case, and turned to the question of burden of proof for purposes associated with Article IV(2)(m) of the Hague Rules, which will be common for all Article IV(2)(c)-(q). The carrier argued that once it had proved that damage was caused by an exception, in this case, the inherent vice, the burden was on the cargo owners to prove that it was attributable to the negligence of the carrier. The Court of Appeal, following the popular pre-Hague Rules case of *The Glendarroch,*[178] agreed with the carrier's argument and held in favour of the carrier. In *The Glendarroch*, the Court of Appeal held that the burden of proving that an excepted peril had been occasioned by the carrier's negligence lay on the cargo owner. Lopes LJ, in that case, said this as follows:

In order to arrive at the above conclusion, the court held or observed a number of important matters. First, on the question of exhaustiveness of the rules. The court held that the Hague Rules "are not exhaustive of all matters relating to the legal responsibility of carriers for the cargo". The court also held that in general "the Rules do not deal with questions of evidence or the mode of proving a breach of the prescribed standard or the application of an exception". Having held this, the court pointed out that "they are part of the law of evidence and the rules of procedure,

[175] Materially identically reproduced in Section 108 of the Singapore Evidence Act and Section 106 of the Malaysian Evidence Act 1950.

[176] [1978] 2 MLJ 137 (PC on appeal from Malaysia).

[177] *The Glendarroch* [1894] P 226, [1891-4] All ER Rep 484 (EW CA).

[178] *The Glendarroch* [1894] P 226, [1891-4] All ER Rep 484 (EW CA).

which are liable to vary from one jurisdiction to another". These observations will readily apply also to the Hague-Visby Rules cases.

Second, the court observed that "the principle that the custodian of goods has a legal responsibility to justify their loss or redelivery in damaged condition is common to civil law jurisdictions as well" by reference to Scotland, France, Belgium, the Netherlands, Italy, Germany, Norway and Spain.

Third, and importantly, the court observed that at common law the burden was on the bailee for reward to disprove negligence and that the Hague-Rules do not deal with or change this position. The court held that:

> [N]othing in the Hague Rules alters the status of a contract of carriage by sea as a species of bailment for reward on terms.

The duty of a bailee for reward, in general, was well said by Cockburn CJ in *Reeve v Palmer*[179] as follows:

> The jury have found that he lost it: and I am of opinion that that must be taken to mean, in the absence of any explanation, that he lost it for want of that due and proper care, which it was his duty to apply to the keeping of it, unless it is qualified by circumstances shewing that the loss of the deed could not have been prevented by the application of ordinary care.

This was adopted in the context of carriage of goods by sea by cases such as *Joseph Travers & Sons Ltd v Cooper*,[180] where Lord Loreburn said as follows:

> I cannot think it is good law that in such circumstances he should be permitted to saddle upon the parties who have not broken their contract the duty of explaining how things went wrong. It is for him to explain the loss himself, and if he cannot satisfy the court that it occurred from some cause independent of his own wrong-doing he must make that loss good.

In the same case, Lord Halsbury said this point as follows:

> It appears to me that here there was a bailment made to a particular person, a bailment for hire and reward, and the bailee was bound to shew that he took reasonable and proper care for the due security and proper delivery of that bailment; the proof of that rested upon him.

Atkin LJ in *The Ruapehu*[181] followed the same school of thought. In deciding the above point, the Supreme Court in the present case, *Volcafe*, found itself supported by, and endorsed, a number of precedents. The court agreed with the ratio of Wright J in the early Hague-Rules case of *Gosse Millard v Canadian Government Merchant Marine Ltd.*[182] In that case, Wright J held that the carrier liable for damage as a result of an outturn which was not explained, because "because the burden of disproving negligence lay on him". The Supreme Court also endorsed the statement of Wright J, which was as follows:

---

[179] (1858) 5 CBNS 84 at 90, 141 ER 33, 175 ER 620 (EW Court of Exchequer Chamber).

[180] [1915] 1 KB 73, [1914-15] All ER Rep 104 (EW CA).

[181] *Ruapehu (Owners) v R and H Green and Silley Weir Ltd (The Ruapehu)* (1925) 21 Ll L Rep 310 at 315 (EW CA), affirmed by the House of Lords in [1927] AC 523, 27 Ll L Rep 385, [1927] All ER Rep 564 (UK HL).

[182] [1927] 2 KB 432, 43 LT 544 (EW HC).

I do not think that the terms of article III put the preliminary onus on the owner of the goods to give affirmative evidence that the carrier has been negligent. It is enough if the owner of the goods proves either that the goods have not been delivered, or have been delivered damaged. The carrier is a bailee and it is for him to show that he has taken reasonable care of the goods while they have been in his custody (which includes the custody of his servants or agents on his behalf) and to bring himself, if there be loss or damage, within the specified immunities. It is, I think, the general rule applicable in English law to the position of bailees that the bailee is bound to restore the subject of the bailment in the same condition as that in which he received it, and it is for him to explain or to offer valid excuse if he has not done so. It is for him to prove that reasonable care had been exercised.

The court endorsed the statement of Scrutton LJ in *Silver and Layton v Ocean Steamship Co Ltd*[183] in which Scrutton LJ agreed with Wright J's observation that the Hague Rules had made no difference to the incidence of the burden of proof in cases of bailment for carriage. The court approved the following statement of Hobhouse J in *The Torenia*[184]:

The relationship between the present parties is contractual. It follows ... that the question of legal burden of proof has ultimately to be decided by construing the contract between them. ... In ascertaining the effect of the contract one must take into account the nature of the contract. The contract here is a contract in a bill of lading; it is a contract of carriage - that is to say, a species of a contract of bailment.

... Nor do the Hague Rules contradict this conclusion.[185]

The court was in favour of the position taken by Denning LJ in *Spurling (J) Ltd v Bradshaw,*[186] where his Lordship said:

[A] bailor, by pleading and presenting his case properly, can always put on the bailee the burden of proof. In the case of non-delivery, for instance, all he need plead is the contract and a failure to deliver on demand. That puts on the bailee the burden of proving either loss without his fault (which, of course, would be a complete answer at common law) or, if it was due to his fault, it was a fault from which he is excused by the exempting clause.

The court disagreed with Lord Pearce in *The Maltasian,*[187] where Lord Pearce doubted without giving reasons the correctness of Wright J's view that the burden of disproving negligence lay upon the carrier. With the above, the court in effect concluded and pronounced the rule as to the burden of proof associated with Article III(2) and Article IV(2)(c)–(q) to be that:

[W]here cargo was shipped in apparent good order and condition but is discharged damaged the carrier bears the burden of proving that that was not due to its breach of the obligation in article III.2 to take reasonable care.

---

[183] [1930] 1 KB 416 at 424-425, [1929] All ER Rep 611 (EW CA).s

[184] *Aktieselskabet de Danske Sukkerfabrikker v Bajamar Compania Naviera SA (The Torenia)* [1983] 2 Lloyd's Rep 210 at 216-217 (EW HC).

[185] Lord Hobhouse repeated this point in *Homburg Houtimport BV v Agrosin Private Ltd (The Starsin)* [2003] UKHL 12, [2003] 1 AC 715 at [138] (UK HL).

[186] [1956] 1 WLR 461 at 466, [1956] 2 All ER 121, [1956] 1 Lloyd's Rep 392 (EW CA).

[187] *Albacora SRL v Westcott & Laurance Line Ltd (The Maltasian)* [1966] 2 Lloyd's Rep 53 (UK HL).

In a nutshell, the court regarded Article III(2) as a codification of the bailor's substantive duty to take reasonable care of the goods entrusted with it. This means it does not deal with who bears the legal burden of proof, as it quite plainly is the case. Hence, the question of the legal burden is left to the local laws and procedure as to evidence. Under English law, as is the case with most jurisdictions, the legal burden is generally on the party who asserts a fact. However, in the case of bailment, the legal burden to disprove negligence is on the bailor, and that, as held by the court, remains unaffected by the Rules. Notably, the court is not resorting to the local laws to determine any question of the duties of a bailee that has been codified by the Rules but only for purposes of proving discharge or breach of those duties.

9.5.1.1 Pre-Volcafe Cases in England and Wales

Prior to *Volcafe*, the effect of *The Glendarroch* was mitigated to some extent by two avenues. One was the application of *res ipsa loquitur* principle to impose the evidentiary burden to establish the cause of the damage or loss as they will usually be especially within the knowledge of the carrier. The other is by the court making an inference of breach of Article III(2) breach from the fact that the goods received by the carrier in good condition were delivered damaged, in the absence of a valid explanation from the carrier.

In *The Torenia*[188] the ship's shell plating fractured during the voyage in expected weather, resulting in seawater ingress and sinking of the ship with a total loss of the cargo. The English High Court inferred that the ship was unseaworthy at the outset, so that peril of the sea exception in respect of seawater ingress was not available. In contrast, the English High Court refused to make such inference in *The Hellenic Dolphin*[189] where the possibilities were that the indent that led to seawater ingress might have been there before or after the start of the voyage.

9.5.2 Application of Volcafe in Malaysia and Singapore

The *Volcafe's* determination as to who bears the legal burden under Articles III(2) and IV(2)(c)–(q) is in the context of local laws of evidence and procedure in England, where there is no Evidence Act covering bailment. In applying this case to Commonwealth countries, including Singapore and Malaysia, with an Evidence Act modelled on the Indian Evidence Act 1872, regard must be had to the provisions of the Evidence

---

[188] *Aktieselskabet de Danske Sukkerfabrikker v Bajamar Compania Naviera SA (The Torenia)* [1983] 2 Lloyd's Rep 210 at 216-217 (EW HC).

[189] *The Hellenic Dolphin* [1978] 2 Lloyd's Rep 336 (EW HC).

Act.[190] This subject has been discussed in detail earlier as part of the consideration of the burden of proof in bailment cases in Malaysia[191] and Singapore.[192]

9.5.2.1 Pre-Volcafe Cases in Malaysia and Singapore

The convention applicable in Malaysia has been, since about 1950,[193] the Hague Rules.[194] The Hague-Visby Rules have not been ratified. In 1955, in *P Odernamall & Co v American President Lines Ltd and Penang Harbour Board (No 1),*[195] the Malaysian High Court followed *Gosse Millard*, holding "Even if I am wrong in concluding that the loss occurred in the ship then on the alternative possibility that the cause of the damage has not been explained I think that following the case of *Gosse Millard* … the shipowners are still liable". This will align the Malaysian position with *Volcafe*. Although the courts in these cases made no reference to the Malaysian Evidence Act 1950 or the Malaysian Contracts Act 1950, they would have arrived at the same decision had such a reference been made.[196]

In Singapore, the Hague-Visby Rules came into effect by the Carriage of Goods by Sea Act of 1972 (Cap. 30), now renamed as the Carriage of Goods by Sea Act (Cap. 33). Before 1972 Act, the Hague-Rules applied. *Gosse Millard* had been followed. In *Successors of Moine Comte & Co Ltd v East Asiatic Co Ltd,*[197] the Singapore High Court in 1954 held that "the burden of proof lay upon the [carriers] to show that they were not negligent in carrying and handling the cargo …: *Gosse Millard* …". Similarly, in *Yeo Goon Nyoh and another v Ocean Steamship Co Ltd,*[198] the Singapore High Court in 1967 held as follows:

> The plaintiffs sued the defendant claiming damages for breach of contract or duty and/or for negligence in and about the carriage of the plaintiffs goods on the defendant's vessel. The defendant denied any breach of duty or reasonable care on their part in the loading or carriage of the plaintiffs' goods by allowing the goods to come in contact with sea water. The defendant maintained that the plaintiffs must prove not only damage to the goods but that the damage was caused by sea water as specifically pleaded in the statement of claim. It was not in dispute that the goods were damaged. It was also not in dispute that they were shipped in apparent good order and condition.
>
> …

---

[190] Singapore Evidence Act; Malaysian Evidence Act 1950. In the case of Malaysia, reference must also be made to the Malaysian Contracts Acts 1950, chapter IX (Bailments), like India.

[191] See Chap. 4.3.

[192] See Chap. 4.3.

[193] About 1960 in case of Sabah and about 1961 in case of Sarawak.

[194] Except for the federal territory of Labuan. The Carriage of Goods by Sea (Amendment) Act 2020 has now been passed to amend the 1950 Act, which, when it comes into force in July 2021, is expected to bring home the Hague-Visby Rules (as amended by SDR Protocol).

[195] [1956] 1 MLJ 6 (MY HC).

[196] See Chap. 4.3.

[197] [1954] MLJ 113 (SG HC).

[198] [1965 – 1967] SLR(R) 783, [1967] 2 MLJ 290 (SG HC).

> … I am, nevertheless, of the opinion that all the plaintiffs need prove is damage and it is not fatal to their case if the damage was caused other than by sea water. To hold otherwise so it seems to me would be to flout the application of the provisions of the Carriage of Goods by Sea Act 1924 and the rules comprised in the schedule thereto to which of course the bill of lading was subject. Under Article III rule 2 it is enough if the owner of the goods proves either that the goods have not been delivered or have been delivered damaged.

The above decisions will align the Singapore position with *Volcafe*. However, the court made no reference to the Singapore Evidence Act. Despite this shortfall, had the court made such reference, the court would have arrived at the same decision.[199]

9.5.2.2 Non-Application of Evidence Act to Arbitral Proceedings in Malaysia and Singapore

It must be noted that the Evidence Acts do not apply in arbitral proceedings, as expressly declared in those Acts. Malaysian Evidence Act, Section 2 reads as follows:

> This Act shall apply to all judicial proceedings in or before any court, but not to affidavits presented to any court or officer nor to proceedings before an arbitrator.

Singapore Evidence Act, Section 2(1) reads as follows:

> Parts I, II and III [covering Sections 103 - 105] shall apply to all judicial proceedings in or before any court, but not to affidavits presented to any court or officer nor to proceedings before an arbitrator.

In the Indian Evidence Act, the same is provided for in Section 1. The non-application of the Evidence Acts to arbitral proceedings merely means the arbitral tribunal has the freedom and flexibility to determine how it will convince itself as to the facts. However, in practice, it is unlikely that the non-application will result in any substantial difference.

---

[199] See Chap. 4.3.

Chapter 10
Hague/Hague-Visby Rules: Carriers' Liability and Time Limitations

This chapter analyses the liability and time limitations in the Hague Rules, Hague-Visby Rules (pre-SDR protocol) and Hague-Visby Rules (as amdned by SDR Protocol). A brief comparison of the three Rules are undertaken and the availability of tonnage limitation is noted. In addition to the position in the UK (that has now subscribed to the third Rules), the position in Malaysia and Singapore are also considered, which have respectively subscribed to the first two Rules. The time limitation under Article III(6) and the time limitation for indemnity actions introduced in the Hague-Visby Rules by Article III(6)*bis* are considered at depth. The liability limitation schemes (package/gross weight limitations) under the three Rules are analysed in detail and a separate treatment for each set of Rules is given where necessary. Observation is made of the loss of protection in case of deviation.

10.1 Introduction

Carriers enjoy two types of limitation under the Hague/Hague-Visby Rules. One is a short time limitation (i.e. one year from the date of delivery or the date the goods should have been delivered)—Article III(6). The other is the liability (quantum) limitation—Article IV(5). At common law, no such limitations are available to the carrier, but contractually the liability can be excluded or limited and the time limit can be shortened.[1] Under the Rules, where they apply statutorily, parties cannot contract out of the Rules such that the shipper is put in a more disadvantageous position than that under the Rules. It limits liability but does not allow this minimum liability to

[1] Although at common law carriers may fix any short time limit for cargo claims, that is not possible in Commonwealth countries, including Malaysia, with a Contract Act modelled on the Indian Contract Act 1872, as Section 28(a) invalidates such clauses. In Malaysia, the corresponding provision is Section 29 of the Malaysian Contracts Act 1950.

A. Kasi, *The Law of Carriage of Goods by Sea*,
https://doi.org/10.1007/978-981-33-6793-7_10

be ousted. Hence, the Rules are said to strike a balance between the interests of the shipowner and cargo owners. The limitations under the Rules apply generally to any claim under bills of lading contract, including those in respect of Articles III(1) and III(2).[2]

The limitations under the Rules are not the only ones available to a shipowner. The other limitation available to the shipowner is 'tonnage' limitation. It is regulated, in the UK, by the Merchant Shipping Act 1995. Such a limitation scheme is available in many countries by similar Acts.

A brief introduction to the tonnage limitation is given below in this chapter. That is followed by a brief comparison of the limitation schemes in the Hague Rules, Hague-Visby Rules (pre-SDR protocol) and Hague-Visby Rules (as amdned by SDR Protocol). Then, a detailed study of the time limitation under the Rules is undertaken, followed by a visit to Article III6*bis* introduced in the Hague-Visby Rules to provide a special scheme of time limitation for indemnity actions. Then is considered at depth the liability limitation under the three Rules with different treatment given to the scheme under each Rule where relevant. Finally, a note is made about loss of the limitation in case of deviation. The position in Singapore and Malaysia are also considered, which jurisdictions have, respectively, subscribed to the Hague-Visby Rules (without SDR protocol) and the Hague Rules.

10.2 Tonnage Limitation Preserved

Other than the liability-limitation in the Hague and Hague-Visby Rules, another limitation available to the shipowner is the tonnage limitation.[3] The major international conventions providing for the tonnage limitation are: International Convention relating to the Limitation of the Liability of Owners of Sea-Going Ships of 1957, Convention on Limitation of Liability for Maritime Claim of 1976, and the said 1976 Convention as amended by the Protocol of 1996,[4] the limits whereof were increased by an amendment to the Protocol in 2012. 2012 Amendments to Protocol of 1996 to amend the Convention on Limitation of Liability for Maritime Claims 1976.

The UK adopts the 1976 Convention as amended by the 1996 Protocol amended in 2012.[5] Singapore also adopts the 1976 Convention as amended by the 1996 Protocol

[2] *Parsons Corp v CV Scheepvaartonderneming (Happy Ranger)* [2002] EWHC Civ 649, [2002] 2 All ER (Comm) 24, [2002] 2 Lloyd's Rep 357, [2002] All ER (D) 278 (May) (EW CA).

[3] The tonnage limitation is an option for the shipowner (or salvor) to invoke to limit its liability by applying for a limitation decree, whether by an action therefor or by counterclaim, pursuant to the applicable admiralty and procedure. In England and Wales, the relevant procedure is in CPR rule 61.11 and PD 61 para 10. In Singapore, it is in Order 70 rules 36-39 of the Rules of Court. In Malaysia, it is in Order 70 rules 35-38 of the Rules of Court 2012.

[4] 'Protocol of 1996 to amend the Convention on Limitation of Liability for Maritime Claims 1976'.

[5] By the UK Merchant Shipping Act 1995, Section 185 read together with Schedule 7. The Merchant Shipping Act 1995 (Amendment) Order 2016, para 3, gives effect to the limits increased by the 2012 amendment to the 1996 Protocol.

amended in 2012.[6] Peninsular Malaysia adopts the 1976 Convention as amended by the 1996 Protocol.[7] All these adoptions are with some modifications or reservations. The Malaysian states of Sabah and Sarawak adopt the 1957 Convention.[8] There are jurisdictions which have not adopted any of the conventions but have enacted their own scheme of tonnage limitation.

The liability-limit in the 1957 Convention is 1,000 francs per ton of the ship's net tonnage where the occurrence has given rise to property claims only.[9] If the occurrence has given rise to property and personal claims, then the limit is 3,100 francs per ton of the relevant tonnage, of which 2,100 francs is for personal claims and 1,000 francs for property claims.[10] If the occurrence has given rise only to personal claims, then the limit is 3,100 francs per ton of the relevant tonnage.[11] The liability-limit is an overall one for the aggregate of all claims arising on any distinct occasion, and all the successful claimants will share the overall limited-liability amount in proportion to their established claims.[12] The limitation is available to the ship,[13] the shipowner, charterer, manager, operator of the ship', their servants, master and crew.[14] The limitation is lost, generally, if the occurrence was caused by the 'actual fault or privity' of the one claiming the limitation.[15]

The 1976 Convention, in the original version, the 1996 amended version and the last amended 2012 version, provides for the amounts of liability-limit based on the gross tonnage of the ship in the units of Special Drawing Rights (SDR)[16] in the case of jurisdictions, like the UK, Singapore and Peninsular Malaysia, that are members of the International Monetary Fund (IMF)[17] and in units of francs[18] for non-members.[19]

---

[6] By the Singapore Merchant Shipping Act, Section 136 read together with the Schedule.

[7] By the Malaysian Merchant Shipping Ordinance 1952, Section 360 read together with Sixteenth Schedule.

[8] By Part III of the 1960 Sarawak Regulations (Malaysia). For Sabah, the said 1960 Sarawak Regulations (Malaysia) are incorporated by reference in the 1961 Sabah Regulations, reg. 3.

[9] 1957 Convention, Article 3. A 'franc' is a unit consisting of 65.5 milligrams of gold of millesimal fineness 900. In the case of steamships or other mechanically propelled ships, the relevant tonnage by which the liability is limited is the net tonnage plus the amount deducted from the gross tonnage on account of engine room space for the purpose of ascertaining the net tonnage. If a ship's relevant tonnage, for the purpose of the liability-limit, is lower than 300 tons, then the relevant tonnage is deemed to be 300 tons.

[10] 1957 Convention, Article 3(1)(c).

[11] 1957 Convention, Article 3(1)(b).

[12] 1957 Convention, Article 2(1).

[13] Seagoing ships: 1957 Convention, Article 1(1).

[14] 1957 Convention, Article 6(1) and (2).

[15] Seagoing ships: 1957 Convention, Article 1(1).

[16] As defined by the International Monetary Fund (IMF), comprising a basket of five major currencies, namely: US dollar, Euro, British Pound and Japanese Yen. Daily exchange rates to convert the SDR units to numerous currencies are published by the IMF. At the beginning of 2021, the exchange rate was about £1.06 or USD1.45 per SDR.

[17] The 1976 Convention as amended by the 1996 Protocol, Article 8.1.

[18] A 'franc' is a unit consisting of 65.5 milligrams of gold of millesimal fineness 900.

[19] The 1976 Convention as amended by the 1996 Protocol, Articles 8.2 and 8.3.

The amounts of the liability-limits in the 1976 Convention, in the original version, is lower than that in the 1976 Convention as amended by the 1996 Protocol, the limits whereof were further increased by the 2012 amendment.

Under the 1976 Convention as amended by the 1996 Protocol, the claims in respect of which the limitation is available include those for 'loss of life or personal injury or loss of or damage to property … occurring on board or in direct [connection] with the operation of the ship or with salvage operations, and consequential loss resulting therefrom',[20] and 'loss resulting from delay in the carriage by sea of cargo, passengers or their luggage'.[21] However, the right to limit will be lost where the claimant proves that 'the loss resulted from his personal act or omission, committed with the intent to cause such loss, or recklessly and with knowledge that such loss would probably result'.[22] Where the shipowner or salvor has a counterclaim against the claimant, the limitation will work on the net liability of the shipowner or salvor after setting of the claimant's liability in the counterclaim.[23]

The amounts of liability-limit, for non-passenger claims,[24] in the 1976 Convention as amended by the 1996 Protocol with the limits increased by the 2012 amendment, by virtue of Article 6.1 thereof, are as follows:

1. The limits of liability for claims other than those mentioned in Article 7, arising on any distinct occasion, shall be calculated as follows:

(a) in respect of claims for loss of life or personal injury,

(i) 3.02 million Units of Account for a ship with a tonnage not exceeding 2,000 tons,[25]

(ii) for a ship with a tonnage in excess thereof, the following amount in addition to that mentioned in (i):

for each ton from 2,001 to 30,000 tons, 1,208 Units of Account;
for each ton from 30,001 to 70,000 tons, 906 Units of Account; and
for each ton in excess of 70,000 tons, 604 Units of Account,

(b) in respect of any other claims,

(i) 1.51 million Units of Account for a ship with a tonnage not exceeding 2,000 tons,[26]

---

20 The 1976 Convention as amended by the 1996 Protocol, Article 2.1(a).

21 The 1976 Convention as amended by the 1996 Protocol, Article 2.1(b).

22 The 1976 Convention as amended by the 1996 Protocol, Article 4.

23 The 1976 Convention as amended by the 1996 Protocol, Article 5.

24 The limitation in respect of passenger claims is provided by Article 7 of the 1976 Convention.

25 The UK Merchant Shipping Act 1995, Schedule 7, Part II, para 5 reduces this limit to 1,000,000 units of SDR in case of ships with a gross tonnage less than 300 tons. The Singapore Merchant Shipping Act, Section 137, sets this limit at 166,667 units of SDR.

26 The UK Merchant Shipping Act 1995, Schedule 7, Part II, para 5 reduces this limit to 500,000 units of SDR in case of ships with a gross tonnage less than 300 tons. The Singapore Merchant Shipping Act, Section 137, sets this limit at 83,333 units of SDR.

(ii) for a ship with a tonnage in excess thereof, the following amount in addition to that mentioned in (i):

for each ton from 2,001 to 30,000 tons, 604 Units of Account;

for each ton from 30,001 to 70,000 tons, 453 Units of Account; and

for each ton in excess of 70,000 tons, 302 Units of Account.

If the non-passenger claims for loss of life or personal injury is not fully paid within the limited amount in Article 6.1.(a), then the outstanding claim sum takes a second turn within Article 6.1(b). This is provided for by Article 6.2, which reads as follows:

2. Where the amount calculated in accordance with paragraph 1(a) is insufficient to pay the claims mentioned therein in full, the amount calculated in accordance with paragraph 1(b) shall be available for payment of the unpaid balance of claims under paragraph 1(a) and such unpaid balance shall rank rateably with claims mentioned under paragraph 1(b).

The reference to tonnage is to 'gross tonnage' of the ship.[27] All the claimants get a share from the relevant limited-liability amount, provided in Article 6, in proportion to their established claims.[28] The liability-limit is available to shipowners, which by definition covers also charterers, managers and operators of sea-going ships,[29] and to salvors, and to all those for whose acts, defaults and faults the shipowner or the salvor is responsible, and to the ship herself.[30]

The Hague and Hague-Visby Rules, in Article VIII, expressly preserve any liability-limitation available to carriers under domestic statutory laws. This includes tonnage limitation. Article VIII is materially the same in both the Rules. The said Article reads as follows, with those words in brackets below only found in the Hague Rules and those in the square bracket only found in the Hague-Visby Rules:

> The provisions of (this Convention) [these Rules] shall not affect the rights and obligations of the carrier under any statute for the time being in force relating to the limitation of the liability of owners of (sea-going) vessels.

In *The Benarty*,[31] the English Court of Appeal clarified that seeking to limit liability by tonnage limitation under the Indonesian law before an Indonesian court, by virtue of an exclusive jurisdiction clause pointing to Indonesia, rather than under

---

[27] The 1976 Convention as amended by the 1996 Protocol, Article 6.5.

[28] See The 1976 Convention as amended by the 1996 Protocol, Articles 6.1 and 12.1.

[29] The UK Merchant Shipping Act 1995, Schedule 7, Part II, para 2 extends the right to limit liability to ships that are not sea-going. A similar extension is made by the Malaysian Shipping Ordinance 1952, Sixteenth Schedule, Part II, para 2.

[30] The 1976 Convention as amended by the 1996 Protocol, Article 1.

[31] *RA Lister & Co Ltd v EG Thomson (Shipping) Ltd (The Benarty) (No. 2)* [1985] QB 325, [1984] 3 All ER 961, [1984] 3 WLR 1082, [1984] 2 Lloyd's Rep 244 (EW CA).

the Hague-Visby Rules limitation regime that would otherwise apply, does not contravene Article III(8) of the Rules. Hence, a shipowner is entitled to limit liability under the tonnage limitation when it is lower than the one under the Rules.[32]

The relationship between the Hague /Hague-Visby Rules limitation and the tonnage limitation must rightly be understood. A shipowner may limit its liability under both the regimes as two layers of limitation. The Rules limitation caps the amount for which the cargo claimant may obtain judgment or award for. This limitation is for the particular claim brought by the cargo interest against the shipowner or carrier. Tonnage limitation caps the amount that may be recovered to satisfy the judgment or award. This limitation is an overall limitation for the aggregate of all claims that are brought by any number of claimants against a shipowner arising on any distinct occasion.[33] All the successful claimants share the overall limited-liability amount in proportion to their established claims, i.e. the judgment or award that they hold.[34] Hence, when both limitation regimes are applied, the shipowner would enjoy two layers of limitation, first under the Rules and then under the tonnage limitation regime.

10.3 Comparison Between Schemes in the Rules: A Glimpse

While Article III(6) (one-year time limitation) in both the Hague and Hague-Visby Rules[35] are substantially the same, the Article IV(5) (liability limitation) is materially different in the two Rules. The former provides for 'package limitation' and the latter provides for 'package' and 'weight' limitation, whichever the higher. The 'package' limitation provided by the two Rules are very different from one another. A further change came with the Hague-Visby Rules as amended by the SDR Protocol, by which the unit of compensation was changed to Special Drawing Rights (SDR).[36] The 'package' limitation amount in the Hague Rules of 1924 is £100 gold value[37] per package or unit. It is 10,000 francs[38] in the Hague-Visby Rules as at 1968, and 666.67 SDR units in the Hague-Visby Rules as amended by the SDR Protocol of 1979. Similarly, the weight limitation in the Hague-Visby Rules as at 1968 was originally for 30 francs, which was changed to two SDR units by the 1979 SDR Protocol amendment.

---

[32] The court pointed out that *The Morviken* [1983] 1 AC 565 (HL) analysis is not relevant in cases where a shipowner seeks to limit liability under the tonnage limitation.

[33] The 1976 Convention as amended by the 1996 Protocol, Articles 6 and 9.

[34] See the 1976 Convention as amended by the 1996 Protocol, Article 12.

[35] As amdned by/pre SDR Protocol.

[36] . See Article IV(5)(d) of the Hague-Visby Rules as amended by SDR Protocol.

[37] Article IX of the Hague Rules.

[38] 'Franc' is defined as 65.5 milligrammes of gold of millesimal fineness 900—Article IV(5)(d) of the Hague-Visby Rules as at 1968.

Whether the scheme of limitation under the Hague or Hague-Visby Rules will better favour the carrier or the cargo claimant will depend on the case. At present, the package limitation under the Hague Rules will give a higher amount than the package limitation under the Hague-Visby Rules. However, this does not necessarily make the Hague-Visby Rules preferable for carriers because the weight limitation under the Hague-Visby Rules may give a larger sum for the particular cargo than even the package limitation under the Hague Rules. For instance, if a very heavy cargo like a heavy vehicle is carried, the weight limitation under the Hague-Visby Rules may far exceed any package limitation under the Hague Rules.

A benefit of the 'weight' limitation to the carrier is that liability related to bulk cargo is limited thereby, which is not available under 'package' limitation scheme.[39] Under the Hague-Rules, a carrier will stand without any liability limitation when it carries bulk cargo. A contrary view as to the applicability of the Hague Rules Article IV(5) limitation to the bulk cargo was expressed in *The Aramis*,[40] where the English High Court suggested that for bulk cargo the unit would be the 'freight unit' or 'customary freight unit'. However, this was later ruled out by the English Court of Appeal in *The Aqasia*.[41]

The Hague-Visby Rules (as amdned by SDR Protocol) limitation regime is applicable in the UK. Singapore has adopted the Hague-Visby Rules (without SDR Protocol) and brought into effect its own scheme of liability limitation by Carriage of Goods by Sea (Singapore Currency Equivalents) Order.[42] For Malaysia, it is the Hague Rules regime, but modified for Sabah and Sarawak with MYR850-limitation per package or unit by the 1960 Sarawak Regulations and 1961 Sabah Regulations, that must be read subject to Article IX of the Hague Rules.

10.4 Article III(6) and III(6)*bis*: Time Limitation

In this sub-chapter, Article III(6), that is materially similar in the Hague and Hague-Visby Rules and the Article III(6)*bis* that was introduced in the Hague-Visby Rules to provide a special scheme of time extension for indemnity actions will be considered.

---

[39] *Sea Tank Shipping AS (formerly known as Tank Invest AS) v Vinnlustodin HF and Another (The Aqasia)* [2018] EWCA Civ 276, [2018] 3 All ER 981, [2018] 2 All ER (Comm) 191, [2018] Bus LR 992, [2018] 1 Lloyd's Rep 530 (EW CA).

[40] *The Aramis (HC)* [1987] 2 Lloyd's Rep 58 (EW HC). The decision in this case was reversed by the Court of Appeal in *The Aramis (HC)* [1989] 1 Lloyd's Rep 213 (EW CA).

[41] *Sea Tank Shipping AS (formerly known as Tank Invest AS) v Vinnlustodin HF and Another (The Aqasia)* [2018] EWCA Civ 276, [2018] 3 All ER 981, [2018] 2 All ER (Comm) 191, [2018] Bus LR 992, [2018] 1 Lloyd's Rep 530 (EW CA).

[42] Dealt with later in Chap. 10.5.2.2.

10.4.1 Article III(6)

Article III(6) of the Hague Rules and Hague Visby Rules, that essentially provides the one-year time limit for cargo claims under bills of lading or any other shipping document to which the Rules apply, differs from one another. Article III(6) of the Hague Rules reads as follows:

> Unless notice of loss or damage and the general nature of such loss or damage be given in writing to the carrier or his agent at the port of discharge before or at the time of the removal of the goods into the custody of the person entitled to delivery thereof under the contract of carriage, or, if the loss or damage be not apparent, within three days, such removal shall be *prima facie* evidence of the delivery by the carrier of the goods as described in the bill of lading.
>
> The notice in writing need not be given if the state of the goods has at the time of their receipt been the subject of joint survey or inspection.
>
> In any event the carrier and the ship shall be discharged from all liability in respect of loss or damage unless suit is brought within one year after <u>delivery of **the goods**</u> or the date <u>when **the goods** should have been delivered</u>. In the case of any actual or apprehended loss or damage the carrier and the receiver shall give all reasonable facilities to each other for inspecting and tallying the goods. [emphasis added]

Article III(6) of the Hague-Visby Rules reads as follows:

> Unless notice of loss or damage and the general nature of such loss or damage be given in writing to the carrier or his agent at the port of discharge before or at the time of the removal of the goods into the custody of the person entitled to delivery thereof under the contract of carriage, or, if the loss or damage be not apparent, within three days, such removal shall be *prima facie* evidence of the delivery by the carrier of the goods as described in the bill of lading.
>
> The notice in writing need not be given if the state of the goods has, at the time of their receipt, been the subject of joint survey or inspection.
>
> Subject to paragraph 6bis the carrier and the ship shall in any event be discharged from all liability **whatsoever** <u>in respect of the goods</u>, unless suit is brought within one year of <u>**their** delivery</u> or of the date <u>when **they** should have been delivered</u>. This period may, however, be extended if the parties so agree after the cause of action has arisen. In the case of any actual or apprehended loss or damage the carrier and the receiver shall give all reasonable facilities to each other for inspecting and tallying the goods. [emphasis added]

The only substantive difference in the Article between the two Rules is the addition of the word 'whatsoever' in the last paragraph. There are three aspects to Article III(6), namely, first, procedure when goods arrive damaged or partly lost; second, effect of flouting the complaint procedure; third, the one-year time limitation.

Under the Hague-Visby Rules, only a claim 'in respect of goods' is caught by the one-year time limitation. Claims for economic loss are not subject to the time limitation, as demonstrated by *The Marinor*.[43] In this case, the ship was under a time charterparty to carry sulphuric acid from Canada to the USA. Hague-Visby Rules

[43] *Noranda Inc v Barton (Time Charter) Ltd (The Marinor)* [1996] 1 Lloyd's Rep 301 (EW HC).

were incorporated into the charterparty by a clause paramount. In four consecutive voyages, the ship discharged the cargo in contaminated condition. As a result, the charterers decided to charter another ship for further voyages and to do a test voyage, as a last chance, with *The Marinor,* to Tampa where the cargo could be disposed of as a fertiliser even if contaminated. The test voyage also resulted in discharge of the cargo contaminated. The charterer claimed for the loss resulting both from the new charter and from the contamination to the cargo in the test voyage. A question arose as to Article III(6). It was held that the former claim (loss from the new charter) was economic loss and not caught by the Article III(6) time limitation, but the latter claim (loss from contamination of the cargo) was 'in respect of goods and hence caught by Article III(6) time limitation. Under the Hague-Rules, it is likely that the same will be the position, although the words 'in respect of good' are not there, as the reference is made to delivery of the goods or the date when they should be delivered.

10.4.1.1 Procedure When Goods Arrive Damaged or Partly Lost

If the goods are found damaged or lost on arrival, immediate notice must be given to the carrier or its agent. If the damage or loss is not apparent at that time, then within three days of the removal of the goods into the custody of the receiver, who will normally be the bill of lading holder. However, no notice need be given where there is a joint inspection, as then both parties will have the record of the condition and quantity of the goods received by the receiver. Parties shall cooperate in facilitating inspection when there is an actual or apprehended loss or damage. The 'loss' referred to here can only mean short delivery, that is a partial loss, as there will be no delivery in case of total loss or misdelivery of the goods. The 'loss' referred to here in connection with the 'loss or damage' complaint procedure is not related to claims for economic loss as in such case, *prima facie* evidence of delivery of the goods as described in the bill of lading has no relevance.

10.4.1.2 Effect of Flouting the Complaint-Procedure

If the receiver fails to do so, that is not fatal to a cargo claim, but it operates as a *prima facie* evidence of receipt by the receiver of the goods as described in the bill of lading.[44] In practice, this may not make much difference as in any event the burden is on the cargo claimant to prove that the goods arrived in damaged condition or were short delivered. Usually, the cargo claimant will be able to establish this by reference to the goods as stated in the bill of lading and a survey made of the goods upon its receipt of the goods.

[44] This provision does not attach to the obligation of the parties to cooperate to facilitate inspection by each other in case of actual or apprehended loss or damage, and it does not also apply in respect of cases where there was a joint inspection.

10.4.1.3 The One-Year Time Limitation

Most importantly, the time limit for the cargo claimant to bring a suit against the carrier is one year from the date of delivery or the date when they should have been delivered.

Time Counts from Delivery, not from Discharge

The date counts from 'delivery' or when 'delivery' should have been given to the cargo interest and not from the date of 'discharge'. 'Delivery' to the cargo interest has two parts to it, one the offer to deliver by the carrier and the other the acceptance of it by the receiver. Suppose that the carrier offers to give delivery, but the cargo interest refuses to take delivery, there is no delivery. However, then the time will start count based on the date when the goods should have been delivered, which will likely be the same day that the carrier offered to deliver.

If goods are delivered in a port other than the port of discharge in the bill of lading and accepted by the receiver, then the date of delivery is when it was actually delivered rather than the date it should have been delivered in the originally agreed port.[45]

Application to Misdelivery and Non-delivery

When goods are delivered after discharge from the ship, the delivery will not be within the period covered by the Rules, which is from the start of loading to the end of discharge.[46] In fact, 'delivery' of the goods, unlike discharge, is not an obligation of the carrier under the Rules, although there cannot be any doubt that it will be a fundamental obligation of the carrier under the carriage contract. Despite that, the English High Court in *The Alhani*,[47] did not doubt that the Article III(6) applied where the misdelivery was committed within the responsibility period covered by the Rules, i.e. between loading and discharge. In this case, a cargo of bunker fuel was *discharged and delivered* by ship-to-ship transfer without production of the bill of lading. Upon a claim by the holder of the bill against the carrier for misdelivery, the English High Court held that '[Article III(6)] of the Hague Rules does apply to misdelivery claims, at least where the misdelivery occurs during the period of the Hague Rules period of responsibility' as it was in this case where the discharge and delivery happened simultaneously.

But a question arises as to whether Article III(6) limitation applies in respect of misdelivery when that happens after discharge. The Malaysian Federal Court in

[45] *Trafigura Beheer BV v Golden Stavraetos Maritime Inc (The Sonia)* [2003] EWCA Civ 664, [2003] All ER (D) 192 (May), [2003] 4 All ER 746, [2003] 1 WLR 2340, [2003] 2 All ER (Comm) 347, [2003] 2 Lloyd's Rep 201 (EW CA). *Minmetals South-East Asia Corp Pte Ltd v Nakhoda Logistics Sdn Bhd* [2019] 3 CLJ 19, [2018] 6 MLJ 152 (MY CA).

[46] Article II read with Article I(e); *Pyrene Co Ltd v Scindia Navigation Co Ltd* [1954] 2 QB 402, [1954] 2 All ER 158, [1954] 2 WLR 1005, [1954] 1 Lloyd's Rep 321 (EW HC).

[47] *Deep Sea Maritime Ltd v Monjasa A/S (The Alhani)* [2018] EWHC 1495 (Comm), [2018] 2 Lloyd's Rep 563, [2018] Bus LR 1552, [2018] All ER (D) 103 (Jun) (EW HC).

Peninsular & Oriental Steam Navigation Co Ltd & Ors v Rambler Cycle Co Ltd[48] ruled out the application of the time limitation in the Hague Rules to a case of misdelivery, when it happened after discharge. In this case, cycles were shipped from the UK to Singapore under five bills of lading, subject to the Hague Rules. The bills of ladings were indorsed to and held by the bank. Goods were misdelivered by the shipowner to another without production of the bill upon a letter of indemnity. The bank took action one year after the misdelivery. The shipowner relied on Article III(6) one-year time limit, that the court rejected. The court found for the bank. This case was approved and followed by a subsequent Malaysian Federal Court in *The Lung Yung & Thai Yung, Owners & Ors v Sadit Timber Sdn Bhd & Ors*[49] and by the Malaysian Court of Appeal in *Minmetals South-East Asia Corp Pte Ltd v Nakhoda Logistics Sdn Bhd*.[50] In the latter case, the court additionally went on to say that 'delivery' in Article III(6) meant delivery to the right person and as no delivery was made to the right person (i.e. lawful holder of the bill), the time did not start the count. This will not be correct as Article III(6) particularly when read in the full context provides for the time to start count from the date of delivery '*or the date when the goods should have been delivered*'. The court further said that delivery is always after discharge, hence not within the period covered by the Rules. This will normally be so, but not necessarily, as there are cases where discharge and delivery happen together and are performed by the consignee such as in free-out arrangements. The position taken by the Malaysian Federal Court would be supported by *The MSC Amsterdam*,[51] where the English Court of Appeal held that the carrier was not entitled to the benefit of Hague Rules Artcile IV(5) liability limitation where the goods were misdelivered after discharge.

However, a contrary position was taken by the NSW Court of Appeal in *The Zhi Jiang Kou*,[52] where it held that the Hague Rules Article III(6) time limitation applied to the case of misdelivery after discharge.[53] The arguments in support of application of the time limitation in the Rules to cases of misdelivery after discharge, as identified in *The Alhani* include these three. First, the Rules were intended to enable the shipowner to "close its books" after the time limit. Second, if the time

---

[48] [1964] 30 MLJ 443 (MY FC).

[49] [1984] 1 MLJ 29 (MY FC).

[50] [2019] 3 CLJ 19, [2018] 6 MLJ 152 (MY CA). See Arun Kasi, 'A Critical Analysis of the Court of Appeal Decision on Misdelivery in Minmetals South-East Asia Corp Pte Ltd v Nakhoda Logistics Sdn Bhd', *The Law Review*, [2020] LR 105. This article was referred to in *Punjab National Bank v Malayan Banking Berhad* [2020] 1 LNS 232, [2020] 5 MLJ 732 (MY CA).

[51] *Mediterranean Shipping Co SA v Trafigura Beheer BV and Another (The MSC Amsterdam)* [2007] EWCA Civ 794, [2008] 1 All ER (Comm) 385, [2007] 2 Lloyd's Rep 622, [2007] All ER (D) 444 (Jul) (EW CA).

[52] *PS Chellaram & Co Ltd v China Ocean Shipping Co (The Zhi Jiang Kou)* [1991] 1 Lloyd's Rep 493 (NSW SC).

[53] *Port Jackson Stevedoring Pty Ltd v Salmond & Spraggon (Australia) Pty Ltd (The New York Star)* [1981] 1 WLR 138, [1980-84] LRC (Comm) 105, [1980] 3 All ER 257, [1980] 2 Lloyd's Rep 317 (PC on appeal from NSW)—see Chap. 4.3 for the fact of the case—might lend some support to this proposition.

limitation in the Rules did not apply to events after discharge, then the carriers would be able to contractually put a shorter time limit for misdelivery after discharge, which will be prejudicial to the cargo interest.

The above visited arguments for and against application of the time limitation in cases of misdelivery after discharge must be common also in respect of the Article IV(5) liability limitation, while it cannot be doubted that the liability limitation would apply to cases of misdelivery where that happens simultaneously with discharge.[54]

Added to that, the Hague-Visby Rules, in Article III(6) discharges the carrier and shipper from all liability 'whatsoever' 'in respect of the goods'. In the case of the Hague Rules, word 'whatsoever' is not there, but the words 'in respect of the goods' is there. Arguments have been advanced based on the addition of the word 'whatsoever', as seen in*The Alhani*, that the intention of the Hague-Visby Rules, even if not of the Hague Rules, is to make available the time limitation including in cases of misdelivery after discharge.

It will be possible for carriers to overcome the effect of *Peninsular and Oriental Steam Navigation* by inserting specific time and liability-limitation clauses in the bill or by extending the Hague or Hague Visby Limitation regimes to misdelivery and post-discharge delivery by specific clause. A one-year limit clause appearing in the bill of lading was upheld by the Privy Council in *The New York Star*[55] to bar an out-of-time misdelivery-action by the cargo interest against the stevedore covered by a Himalaya clause. Similarly, in *The Zhi Jiang Kou*,[56] the bill stipulated a nine-month time limitation for any action. An action for misdelivery was taken after the nine months. The NSW Court of Appeal noted, in the context of the misdelivery claim, the contractual time-limitation operated independently of any Hague-Rules time limitation, and held that the action was time-barred. However, in Malaysia, such contractual provision, insofar as time limitation is concerned, will be invalidated by Section 29 of the Contracts Act 1950,[57] which reads as follows:

> *Every agreement*, by which any party thereto is restricted absolutely from enforcing his rights under or in respect of any contract, by the usual legal proceedings in the ordinary tribunals, or *which limits the time within which he may thus enforce his rights, is void to that extent.* [emphasis added]

For the UK and Singapore, there is no equivalent provision of law as the above. However, it may still be possible to test an argument against such time limitation premised on public policy grounds.

---

[54] See *Deep Sea Maritime Ltd v Monjasa A/S (The Alhani)* [2018] EWHC 1495 (Comm), [2018] 2 Lloyd's Rep 563, [2018] Bus LR 1552, [2018] All ER (D) 103 (Jun) (EW HC). The limitations are widely worded in Articles III(6) as well as IV(5) to apply 'in any event', hence they must include all events within the period covered by the Rules, i.e. until completion of discharge.

[55] *Port Jackson Stevedoring Pty Ltd v Salmond & Spraggon (Australia) Pty Ltd (The New York Star)* [1981] 1 WLR 138, [1980-84] LRC (Comm) 105, [1980] 3 All ER 257, [1980] 2 Lloyd's Rep 317 (PC on appeal from NSW)—see Chap. 4.3 for the fact of the case.

[56] *PS Chellaram & Co Ltd v China Ocean Shipping Co (The Zhi Jiang Kou)* [1991] 1 Lloyd's Rep 493 (NSW SC).

[57] Without the *Exceptions* stated in the section, which are not relevant in the context here. This section is materially identical to Section 28(a) of the Indian Contract Act 1872.

The discussion made above in respect of application of the time-limitation to claims for misdelivery after discharge will also be relevant to claims for damage to or loss of goods after discharge but before delivery.

Limitation extinguishes cause of action, not merely bars it

Unlike the application of limitation in ordinary cases, which does not extinguish a claim but merely provides a defence only,[58] the limitation here extinguishes the claim. *Aries Tanker Corpn v Total Transport Ltd (The Aries)* [1977] 1 All ER 398, [1977] 1 WLR 185 (UK HL) This is the effect of the words 'the carrier and the ship are *discharged* from all liability'.

The limitation is only in respect of a cargo claim instituted by cargo interest, but not in respect of any claim by the carrier against the cargo interest such as for freight. Accordingly, a carrier is at liberty to take action against the cargo interest even after a year from delivery.

If a carrier brings an action against the cargo interest after a year from delivery, the cargo interest will not be able to bring a 'counterclaim' against the carrier, as the cargo interest will be caught by the limitation.[59] In *The Aries*,[60] the shipowner sued the voyage charterer for short paid freight after one year of delivery. The charterparty was subject to the Hague Rules. According to the charterer, there was a short delivery and the chartered deducted an amount for that against the payment of freight. A year after delivery, the carrier sued the cargo interest for the short-paid freight. In defence, the cargo interest counterclaimed for the short delivery, which if successful will set off the claim. The House of Lords debarred the cargo interest from setting up the counterclaims as it was time-barred.[61] Another popular reason for the decision was that no set-off was available against freight. The effect of this rule has been confined to its strict limits. Arguably, this rule first pronounced in 1977 should now be reviewed in an environment where the risk in maritime adventures has significantly come down with advancement in technology. In *Globalink Transportation and Logistics Worldwide LLP v DHL Project & Chartering Limited*.[62] In this case, the English High Court well held that *The Aries*' 'no-set off against freight' rule did not apply to freight forwarding contracts where the freight forwarder agreed only to 'arrange' for the carriage of goods.

---

[58] *Ronex Properties Ltd v John Laing Construction Ltd* [1983] 1 QB 398, [1982] 3 WLR 875, [1982] 3 All ER 961 (EW CA).

[59] Counterclaims are in effect claims on their own and the defendant bringing a counterclaim is treated as the plaintiff for purposes of counterclaim.

[60] *Aries Tanker Corpn v Total Transport Ltd (The Aries)* [1977] 1 All ER 398, [1977] 1 WLR 185 (UK HL). This is a popular case for the rule that 'no set off against freight'.

[61] There was another reason for the decision including that no set off was available against freight.

[62] [2019] EWHC 225 (Comm), [2019] 2 All ER (Comm) 393, [2019] All ER (D) 131 (Mar) (EW HC).

The time-limitation against making a counterclaim does not debar a defendant from making a pure 'defence', as the time limit is only for a claim including a counterclaim. In *The Fiona*,[63] a cargo of fuel oil caused an explosion. The shipowners[64] sued the cargo owners for shipping dangerous cargo without the informed consent of the shipowners. In defence, the cargo owner pleaded that the dominant cause of the loss was unseaworthiness of the ship contrary to Article III(1). The English Court of Appeal held that Article III(6) limitation did not debar the cargo owner from defending itself with Article III(1).

Significance of Limitation: Right Claimant, Respondent, Jurisdiction, Mode and Procedure

Once the time limit has set in, the claimant will not be allowed to join a new defendant or to substitute the defendant with another against whom the time limit has set in. This is because, for all practical purposes, joining a defendant or substituting an existing defendant with another is as good as bringing an action against the right defendant.[65] Disallowing a claimant from joining or substituting defendants after the time limit has set in is a general principle and not something peculiar to shipping law. However, the principle has a significant effect in shipping law for two reasons, namely the time limit is as short as one year from delivery or supposed delivery date and it may be complex to rightly identify the carrier in the bill of lading particularly when issued by a charterer with a demise clause or issued by a shipowner or with conflicting clauses as has happened in many cases.[66]

In *The Jay Bola*,[67] the ex-shipowner, who was the owner of the ship some three months before the issuance of the bill of lading, was sued within the time limit. Subsequently, the cargo claimant substituted the defendant with the current shipowner who issued the bill, by leave of the court, however after the one-year time limit. Upon the application of the current shipowner, the court set aside the leave as any action against the current shipowner was time-barred. In *Davies v Elsby Brothers Ltd*,[68] Devlin LJ formulated the test, known as 'litigation finger test', to differentiate between cases of mere misnomer and substitution, as follows:

> If it can, it can be corrected without the addition of a party: the entity remains the same. If it cannot, if it refers to an entity which is not the intended defendant … then the only way of putting the matter right is to substitute another entity … Therefore the question is: Is it a mere misnomer or is it not?
>
> [T]he intention which the framer of the document has in mind when he brings it into existence is not material. … The test must be: How would a reasonable person receiving the document

[63] *Mediterranean Freight Services Ltd v BP Oil International Ltd (The Fiona)* [1994] 2 Lloyd's Rep 506 (EW CA).

[64] The carrier, in this case.

[65] Which is barred after the one-year period in the case of cargo claims.

[66] For a discussion on complexity of identifying the carrier, see Section 4.2.

[67] *Zalnalabdin Payabi and Baker Rasti Lari v Armstel Shipping Corporation and Panthai Shipping Ltd (The Jay Bola)* [1992] 2 Lloyd's Rep 62 (EW HC).

[68] [1960] 3 All ER 672 at 675–676, [1961] 1 WLR 170 (EW CA).

take it? If, in all the circumstances of the case and looking at the document as a whole, he would say to himself: "Of course it must mean me, but they have got my name wrong". Then there is a case of mere misnomer. If, on the other hand, he would say: "I cannot tell from the document itself whether they mean me or not and I shall have to make inquiries", then it seems to me that one is getting beyond the realm of misnomer. [emphasis added]

The test will equally apply in the context of Article III(6). It will be helpful to visit two more cases below to better understand the difference between misnomer and substitution. In *In re Nos 55 & 57, Holmes Road, Kentish Town*; *Beardmore Motors Ltd v Birch Bros (Properties) Ltd*[69] some tenants sought to sue their landlord and issued an action against "Birch Bros. Ltd". However, the landlord was "Birch Bros. (Properties) Ltd", a company related to "Birch Bros. Ltd". Both companies existed and the tenants knew of the same and that the landlord was Birch Bros. (Properties) Ltd. Harman J held that naming the wrong company as the respondent, in this case, was not a mere misnomer and accordingly refused leave to amend the name of the respondent in the action.

In contrast to *Holmes Road* case, in *Whittam v WJ Daniel & Co Ltd,*[70] an employee issued a writ against "W. J. Daniels and Company (a firm)" as his employer in connection with an accident. However, the employer was "W. J. Daniel & Co. Ltd". The firm had ceased to be in existence by the time of the writ. The English Court of Appeal adopted the 'litigation finger test' and held that it was merely a misnomer that can be corrected even after the time limit had set it. In applying the test to the case at hand, Donovan LJ said as follows:

[T]here could have been no doubt in the mind of the defendants when they got the writ that it was they whom the plaintiff intended to sue and that she had simply got the name wrong.

Although a cargo claimant may misidentify the carrier and sue a wrong defendant, the latter may in certain cases be estopped from denying that it was the carrier, hence the claim may be saved. This happened in *The Henrik Sif*.[71] In this case, a bill of lading was issued in the stationary of the time charterer. However, the bill contained a demise clause making the shipowner the carrier. Acting in the mistaken belief, the cargo interest corresponded with the charterers before instituting the action. The charterer went into the merits of the claim and also gave an extension of time to institute the action. The time charterer did not alert the cargo interest as to the mistake made by the cargo interest in identifying the carrier. The cargo interest instituted the action within the extended time allowed by the charterer. In defence, the charterer said that it was not the carrier and hence the action was bad, by when the one-year time limit to bring an action against the shipowner as the carrier had set it. The English High Court held that the charterer had assumed responsibility and was estopped by acquiescence, silence or inaction from raising the defence that it was not the carrier. The basis of the estoppel was the duty to speak, which the court described as follows:

[69] [1958] 2 All ER 311, [1959] Ch 298, [1958] 2 WLR 975 (EW HC).

[70] [1961] 3 All ER 796 at 799, [1962] 1 QB 271, [1961] 3 WLR 1123 (EW CA).

[71] *Pacol Ltd and Others v Trade Lines Ltd and R/I Sif IV (The Henrik Sif)* [1982] 1 Lloyd's Rep 456 at 465 (EW HC).

[T]he duty necessary to found an estoppel by silence or acquiescence arises where "a reasonable man would expect' the person against whom the estoppel is raised "acting honestly and responsibly" to bring the true facts to the attention of the other party known by him to be under a mistake as to their respective rights and obligations.

In *The Stolt Loyalty*,[72] the ship was demise-chartered. The bill of lading had a demise clause that made the demise charterer the carrier. Both the demise charter and the shipowner were insured for protection and indemnity by the same P&I Club,[73] which gave an undertaking to the cargo interest. The cargo interest wrote to the club for an extension of time to file the action from the 'owners'. The club replied granting the extension on behalf of the 'shipowners'. Subsequently, the cargo interest sued both the shipowner and the demise charterer within the extended time. The shipowner defended by saying that it was not the contractual carrier. The demise charterer defended by saying that the time limit had set it and the extension given was on behalf of the shipowner and not the demise charterer. The English High Court found that 'owners' was a generic term used in the shipping industry capable of referring both to the shipowner and demise charterers. The court further found that 'shipowners' too was a generic term in the industry that may refer both to the shipowners and demise charters. Accordingly, the extension was treated as being given by the demise charterer and hence the action was not time-barred. In the alternative, the court said that in any event the demise charterer would be estopped, following *The Henrik Sif*. The court added that the estoppel was founded on unconscionable behaviour of the party estopped, in the following words:

[W]hether you call it ... estoppel by acquiescence or estoppel by encouragement is really immaterial—requires a very much broader approach which is directed rather at ascertaining whether, in particular individual circumstances, it would be unconscionable for a party to be permitted to deny that which, knowingly, or unknowingly, he has allowed or encouraged another to assume to his detriment than to enquiring whether the circumstances can be fitted within the confines of some preconceived formula serving as a universal yardstick for every form of unconscionable behavior.

In contrast to that, in *The August Leonhardt*,[74] the P&I Club gave an extension of time conditional on the charterer giving a similar extension. The Plaintiff mistook that the P&I Club would secure the extension from the charterers. The Plaintiff had only itself to blame for the consequences. The English High Court held that the charterers were not estopped from raising the time limitation point.

The position of the law discussed above will also apply where the claim is by a wrong claimant. It will not be allowed to substitute or add another after the time limit has set in,[75] though this will not bar a mere correction of a misnomer.

It must be noted that in England and Wales, amendment and changes to parties after the period of limitation has expired is regulated by Civil Procedure Rules (CPR)

---

[72] *The Stolt Loyalty* [1993] 2 Lloyd's Rep 281 (EW HC).

[73] 'Protection and Indemnity Club'.

[74] *K Lokumal & Sons (London) Ltd v Lotte Shipping Co Pte Ltd (The August Leonhardt)* [1984] 1 Lloyd's Rep 322 (EW HC).

[75] *Transworld Oil (USA) Inc v Minos Compania Naviera SA (The Leni)* [1992] 2 Lloyd's Rep 48 (EW HC).

Rules 17.4 and 19.5. However, both the rules are limited to cases where the limitation is set by the UK Limitation Act 1980, UK Foreign Limitation Periods Act 1984 or any other enactment allowing such amendment or change. As the one-year time limit is not from any of the three enactments named in the CPR, but from Article III(6) of the Hague-Visby Rules incorporated by the UK Carriage of Goods by Sea Act 1971, the CPR rules will not apply to cargo claims. Thus, any amendment or change to parties in cargo claims will be governed by common law, discussed above.

In Singapore and Malaysia, amendments or changes to parties after the relevant period of limitation is governed by Order 20 rules 5(2) and 5(3) of the Rules of Court,[76] which is identical in both the jurisdictions. They apply also to cargo claims to which the Hague or Hague Visby Rules Article III(6) one-year time limit applies.

In *Colgate-Palmolive (Asia) Ltd v Swedish East Asia Co Ltd,*[77] a Malaysian case, the bill of lading prominently displayed a call name of Malaya Indonesia Line. However, the bill was actually issued Swedish East Asia Co Ltd, which a scrutiny of the bill would have revealed.[78] The claimant issued the writ against "Malaya Indonesia Line". There was no legal entity by this name, however, this was a call name used by three shipowners including Swedish East Asia Co Ltd. After the time limit had set in, the claimant substituted the defendant with the name of Swedish East Asia Co Ltd by leave of the court. The amended writ was served on an agent, who was the agent both for the Malaya Indonesia Line and Swedish East Asia Co Ltd. Unlike *The Jay Bola,*[79] the defendant did not apply to set aside the leave to substitute, instead pleaded the time limitation in the defence based on the date of the amendment to the writ. The High Court accepted the relevant date for purposes of time limitation, insofar as Swedish East Asia Co Ltd was concerned, was the date of the amendment and not the date of the writ. Accordingly, the High Court court allowed the defence and dismissed the action. The claimant appealed against the decision to the Federal Court,[80] which upheld the decision of the High Court. The Federal Court held that, after the time limitation, correction of a mere misnomer would be allowed, but not a substitution. The court relied on *Davies v Elsby Brothers Ltd,*[81] not a 'shipping' related case, that sets out the general principle and test in relation to amendments to parties after the time limit has set in.

In *The Pacific Wisdom,*[82] the Singapore Court of Appeal set out the three-point test for allowing the amendment, in an admiralty action, once time has set in. The test was this: three conditions were satisfied: (i) the mistake was a genuine mistake,

---

[76] In Malaysia, called the 'Rules of Court 2012'.

[77] [1967] 1 MLJ 115 (MY FC).

[78] In fact, the agent of the Malaya Indonesia Line and Swedish East Asia Co Ltd alerted the claimant of the fact that the shipowner concerned was the latter, even prior to issue of the writ, but which the claimant disregarded.

[79] *Zalnalabdin Payabi and Baker Rasti Lari v Armstel Shipping Corporation and Panthai Shipping Ltd (The Jay Bola)* [1992] 2 Lloyd's Rep 62 (EW HC).

[80] Apex court.

[81] [1960] 3 All ER 672 at 675–676, [1961] 1 WLR 170 (EW CA).

[82] *The Pacific Wisdom* [1998] 3 SLR 705 (SG CA).

(ii) it was not misleading or such as to cause reasonable doubt as to the identity of the party intending to sue or be sued, and (iii) it was just to allow the amendment. In relation to the second limb of the test, the court further pointed out that a distinction had to be made between the identity of the person intended to sue, and the name of that party, only in the latter of which an amendment may be allowed.

In *The Kota Pahlawan,*[83] the Singapore Court of Appeal dealt with an appeal concerning an application to change the plaintiff.[84] In this case, automotive spare parts carried from Singapore to Jakarta[85] under a bill of lading. The shipper was a Singapore company. The bill was issued to order of a bank. Party to notify was an Indonesian company. The Hague-Visby Rules were applicable.[86] The shipper requested Article III(6) one-year time limit to be extended by four months, which the carrier agreed. Within the extended time, an action *in rem* was filed in the name of "Owner of the Cargo ...". The plaintiff requested security by bank guarantee in the name of the shipper in order not to arrest the ship, which the carrier accordingly furnished. The carrier did not file an appearance,[87] hence the plaintiff secured default judgement. The carrier successfully applied to set aside the default judgment on grounds[88] that the plaintiff was not the indorsee of the bill of lading. At this point, the plaintiff applied to amend the writ,[89] seeking to name the indorsee of the bill as the plaintiff, while time limitation had already set in.

From the fact that the shipper's address was given as the plaintiff's address and that the security was requested and given in favour of the shipper, the court decided that the true identity of the plaintiff in the original writ was the shipper rather than owners of the cargo.[90] The court found that the amendment sought now was to change the identity of the plaintiff, and not merely to correct the name of any plaintiff where the mistake was a genuine one and not misleading as to the identity of the plaintiff. Accordingly, the court held that the amendment did not fall within Order 20 rules 5(2) and 5(3) of the Singapore Rules of the Supreme Court 1970[91] and refused the amendment.

The Singapore Court of Appeal in *The Kusu Island*[92] dealt with the question of time limitation when that was contractual and the amendment sought was to add *res* belonging to the same owner. In this case, a cargo of cotton sheets was carried from

---

[83] *The Kota Pahlawan* [1982–1983] 1 SLR 88 (SG CA).

[84] Called the 'claimant' in England and Wales.

[85] In Indonesia.

[86] By Singapore Carriage of Goods by Sea Act 1972 (Cap 30) now renamed as Carriage of Goods by Sea Act (Cap 33)).

[87] Equivalent to the 'acknowledgement of service' in England and Wales.

[88] Among others.

[89] Equivalent to the 'claim form' in England and Wales.

[90] Which could in effect mean the indorsee of the bill.

[91] The Singapore Rules of the Supreme Court 1970 is the predecessor to the current Singapore Rules of Court. The Order 20 rules 5(2) and 5(3) in the 1970 Rules are identical to those in the current Rules by the same reference.

[92] *The Kusu Island* [1989] 1 SLR 119 (SG CA).

Karachi[93] to Singapore under two bills of lading on board the vessel Brani Island. The bills provided Singapore laws to be the governing law. The bills also stipulated one-year time limitation to bring any suit and incorporated the Hague Rules.[94] The cargo arrived damaged and the cargo owner took an admiralty action *in rem* within the one-year limitation period against the owners of The Brani Island. After the one-year limitation period, the cargo owner applied *ex parte*[95] to amend the writ[96] change the description of the defendant as the owners of The Brani Island, The Senang Island and The Kusu Island. The last two are sister ships of The Brani Island. The registrar allowed the application. Subsequently, the cargo owner arrested The Kusu Island and the shipowner entered an unconditional appearance[97] and applied to strike out the amendment made.

First, the court dealt with the question of whether the addition of a *res* in an action in-rem was equivalent to an addition of a defendant, even when the owner of all the *res* was the same person. In an action *in-rem*, if the defendant does not enter appearance (or enters conditional appearance), then the liability is only on the *res* and limited to the *res*. If the owner enters an unconditional appearance and thereby submits to the jurisdiction of the court, the liability is also on the owner and it is not limited to the value of the *res* against the owner. Accordingly, when issued, the writ is only against the *res*, despite being described as the owners of the *res*. Thus, the court answered the question in the affirmation. Second, the court considered the question of whether *res* may be added, by an amendment to the description of the defendant, after the contractual limitation period. The court answered this question in the negative, as the amendment sought was not a mere correction to the name of the res-defendant, but to add to it. Accordingly, the court struck out the amendment and set aside the service of the same on The Kusu Island.

In *The Virginia Rhea*,[98] the Singapore Court of Appeal dealt with an application to amend the claim by inserting a new cause of action after the time had set in. In this case, a cargo claimant sued within the allowed time the carrier in respect of four bills of ladings, numbered KKS 1, KKS 3, KKS 31 and KKS 32. Subsequently, after the time had set in, the claimant sought to amend the claim by adding one more bill, number KKS 33. The court disallowed the application[99] as the addition of a new bill was an addition of a new cause of action not arising 'out of the same facts or substantially the same facts as a cause of action in respect of which relief has already been claimed'. In this case, the facts about the bill KKS 33 could not be inferred

---

93 In Pakistan.

94 This too provided for the one-year time limit by Article III(6).

95 Without notice.

96 Equivalent to the 'claim form' in England and Wales.

97 'Unconditional appearance' is equivalent to the 'acknowledgement of service' in England and Wales with the option of intent 'to contest jurisdiction' selected.

98 *China Steel Corporation & Anor v The Owners of Virginia Rhea (The Virginia Thea)* [1985] 2 MLJ 1 (MY CA).

99 Under Order 20 rr. 5(2) and 5(5) of the Singapore Rules of the Supreme Court 1970—these rules are the same as those in the present Singapore Rules of Court [identical to the Malaysian Rules of Court 2012].

from the original claim in any way. The court stressed that for an amendment to be allowed after time had set in, two conditions must be satisfied. First, it was a genuine mistake. Second, the mistake did not cause any misleading or doubt as to cause any reasonable doubt as to what the litigation was about in fact in the mind of the other party.

The suit must be instituted in the right jurisdiction. If a suit is dismissed or struck out by a court because it did not have the jurisdiction, the claimant will not subsequently be allowed to re-institute the action in the right jurisdiction after the one-year time limit has passed.[100] Accordingly, attention must be paid to any exclusive jurisdiction clause, as a breach of it may result in the action being struck out or dismissed as not being a 'competent' suit, i.e. no suit.[101] After such dismissal or striking out, the claimant will not be allowed to re-institute the action in the right jurisdiction once the one-year time limit has passed.

The time limit to bring a 'suit' refers to the substantive suit. Hence, the issuance of a writ *in rem* merely to arrest the ship is not a suit, unless the substantive dispute was intended to be tried by those proceedings. In *The Nordglimt*,[102] the English High Court held that a claimant who had instituted an action within the time limit in the right jurisdiction, in that case in Belgium, may subsequently get issued after the one-year period a writ *in rem* merely to arrest the ship anywhere else, in that case in England.

In cargo claims to which the one-year time limit applies procedural compliance is important. For any reason, if the suit is struck out, the claimant will not be able to re-institute an action if the one year has passed. In *The Finnrose*,[103] the original action was struck out for want of prosecution and the claimant was not subsequently allowed to re-institute the action. Similarly, if a case is struck out because the claimant did not appear, the claimant will not be able to re-institute the action but will be able to apply to set aside the order striking out the action and to have it reinstated.[104]

However, where the right claimant has sued the right defendant in the right jurisdiction and there is no procedural flaw like want of prosecution, the courts have allowed the claimant to amend the cause of action after the one-year period. In *The*

---

[100] *The Havhelt* [1993] 1 Lloyd's Rep 523 (EW HC).

[101] Saville J in *The Havhelt* [1993] 1 Lloyd's Rep 523 (QB) said this point as: "Mr. Havelock-Allan's first submission was that the present proceedings were not a 'suit' within the meaning of Article III, r. 6 of the Hague Rules—the plaintiffs having proceeded in the wrong Court. In other words, the present suit was not a competent suit. As a matter of English law it seems to me that Mr. Havelock-Allan's submission is correct and that, looking at it as an English lawyer, in the face of the exclusive jurisdiction clause to which I have referred, the proceedings here are not competent proceedings and so they do not amount to a suit within the meaning of Article III, r. 6 of the Hague Rules". This principle was accepted and followed in *Deep Sea Maritime Ltd v Monjasa A/S (The Alhani)* [2018] EWHC 1495 (Comm) (EW HC).

[102] *The Nordglimt* [1987] 2 Lloyd's Rep 470 (EW HC).

[103] *Fort Sterling Ltd and Another v South Atlantic Cargo Shipping NV and Others (The Finnrose)* [1994] 1 Lloyd's Rep 559 (EW HC).

[104] Depending on and subject to the procedural rules of the jurisdiction.

Pionier[105] the claimant first pleaded its case based on a bill of lading. Then it amended it to be one based on a charterparty. It was then allowed to amend the pleadings again to go back to the case based on the bill of lading.

Applies to in rem and in personam actions

The Article protects both the 'carrier and the ship'. Covering the 'ship' here seems to refer to *in rem* action. Even without such express coverage of the 'ship', the time limitation will apply to *in rem* actions. See Sections 20(2)(g) and (h) and Section 21(4) of the UK Senior Courts Act 1981. Accordingly, the express coverage of the 'ship' here does not really add anything to the coverage of the 'carrier'.

Application of Limitation to deviation and quasi-deviation cases

The subject of application of Hague/Hague-VisbyRules time-limitation to cases of deviation and quasi-deviation has been discussed at length earlier and is also discussed below.

Shortening of the One-Year Time Limit

While under the Hague-Visby Rules the time limitation may be extended by agreement of the parties at any time, but not shortened where the Rules statutorily apply.[106] Although such provision for an extension is not provided for in the Hague Rules, there is nothing to prohibit such an extension as it will not contravene Article III(8) being in favour of the cargo interest. If the application of the Rules is only by voluntary incorporation, then there is nothing in the Rules to prohibit the shortening of the time limitation. However, such shortening may be caught by public policy in general contract law and hence invalid. In fact, in a number of the Commonwealth countries, where there is a Contract Act modeled on the Indian Contract Act 1872, the Act will expressly debar such shortening. For instance, in Malaysia, Section 29 of the Contracts Act 1950, which is identical to Section 28(a) of the Indian Contract Act 1987, provides[107] for this rule as follows:

> **29. Agreements in restraint of legal proceedings void**
>
> Every agreement, by which any party thereto is restricted absolutely from enforcing his rights under or in respect of any contract, by the usual legal proceedings in the ordinary tribunals, or which limits the time within which he may thus enforce his rights, is void to that extent.

However, the Section 29 will be of no application where the one-year time limit applies statutorily. In *Chong Fui Shipping & Forwarding Sdn Bhd v Steel Industries (Sabah) Sdn Bhd,*[108] a clause in the bill of lading repeated the one-year time limit.

---

[105] *Continental Fertilizer Co Ltd v Pionier Shipping CV (The Pionier)* [1995] 1 Lloyd's Rep 223 (EW HC).

[106] *Unicoopjapan and Marubeni-Iida Company Ltd v Ion Shipping Company (The Ion)* [1971] 1 Lloyd's Rep 541 (EW HC); *Shun Cheong Steam Navigation Co Ltd v Wo Fong Trading Co* [1979] 2 MLJ 254 (MY FC): The invalidity of the clause does not in any way affect the liability-limitation in Article IV(5), to which extent the carrier will be liable.

[107] Without the *Exceptions*, which are not relevant in the context here.

[108] [2016] 5 MLJ 46 (MY CA).

The cargo claimant challenged the validity of the clause relying on Section 29 of the Malaysian Contracts Act 1950. The Malaysian Court of Appeal disagreed with the cargo claimant, as the one-year time limit was a mere repetition of the relevant legislative provision.[109]

Although the one-year time limit may seem to be a harsh one against the cargo interest, there is also a benefit to the cargo interest, namely, the carrier will not be able to shorten it by any contractual provision. This is one of the mischiefs intended to be remedied by the one-year time limit. Before the Hague Rules, it was not uncommon to find a 'notice-of-claim' clause in bills of lading that will take away the right of the suit unless the notice was given within a short time frame stipulated in the bill.[110] Similarly, there were also provisions that stipulated a short time frame of less than one year to bring a cargo action. This point was said in *The Leni*[111] as follows:

> [O]bjectives which Article III, r 6 sought to achieve ... to provide carriers with some protection against stale and therefore unverifiable claims; ... to prevent carriers from relying on 'notice-of-claim' provisions as an absolute bar to proceedings or from inserting clauses in their bills of lading requiring proceedings to be issued within short periods of less than one year.

Application to Arbitral Proceedings

Application of Article III(6) time limit to arbitral proceedings depends on whether the Rules apply statutorily or voluntarily. Where they apply statutorily, Article 31 of the Vienna Convention on the Law of Treaties[112] will require a construction of the Rules in line with its purpose and objective. Likely such a construction, as opposed to a literal construction, will lead to the 'suit' referred to in Article III(6) to be purposively interpreted to include arbitral proceedings. In addition to this, domestic legislation may more directly extend the application of statutory time limits prescribed for litigation to arbitration. In Britain, Section 13 of the Arbitration Act 1996 provides for this by rendering Limitation Acts applicable to arbitral proceedings as they apply to legal proceedings and defining the Limitation Acts as including any enactment relating to the limitation of actions, which will include the UK Carriage of Goods by Sea Act 1971 and, *through* that, Article III(6) of the Rules. In the case of Malaysia, the Limitation Act 1953 provides for this in Section 30(1).[113] In Singapore, the question of application of Article III(6) time-limit to arbitral proceedings is a little

---

[109] This was a Sabah case, to which the 1960 Sarawak Regulations was applicable through the 1961 Sabah Regulations.

[110] e.g. in *Unicoopjapan and Marubeni-Iida Company Ltd v Ion Shipping Company (The Ion)* [1971] 1 Lloyd's Rep 541 (EW HC), the bill of lading incorporated Centrocon charter which stipulated a three-month time limit to institute arbitral proceedings.

[111] *Transworld Oil (USA) Inc v Minos Compania Naviera SA (The Leni)* [1992] 2 Lloyd's Rep 48 (EW HC), speech of by Diamond QC sitting as the deputy judge.

[112] In force in the UK since 1980.

[113] Section 30(1): "This Act and any other written law relating to the limitation of actions shall apply to arbitrations as they apply to actions." The time limitation in Article III(6) of the Hague Rules will come within the ambit of 'other written law' in the Section 30 *vis-a-vis* the Carriage of Goods by Sea Act 1950.

more complex one. Section 3 of the Singapore Limitation Act provides the "Act shall not apply to any action *or arbitration* for which a period of limitation is prescribed by any other written law". This is to facilitate the application of any other time limit stipulated by any specific law, such as Article III(6) made part of the Singapore law by the Carriage of Goods by Sea Act. However, the Act does not expressly say that the other time limit provided for court actions will also apply to arbitral proceedings. Despite this shortfall, a purposive interpretation[114] of the Section 3 and Article III(6) will lead to the conclusion that Article III(6) time-limit also applies to arbitral proceedings.[115]

However, if the Rules apply only voluntarily, then different considerations apply. As a matter of construction of the contract in line with commercial reality, likely the court will include arbitral proceedings in the definition of 'suit'. However, in those Commonwealth jurisdictions, including Malaysia, with a Contract Act modelled on the Indian Contract Act 1872, the Act may invalidate any limitation period in contracts that provides for a limitation period shorter than that in the limitation statute which is normally six years. In Malaysia, Section 29 of the Contracts Act 1950, and in India Section 28(a) of the Contract Act 1872, will render any such shortening of statutory limitation period invalid.

Where the Rules apply voluntarily and there is no statute to render the shorter period invalid, as in the UK and Singapore, the domestic legislation may, however, authorise the courts to extend the time limit. In Britain, Section 12 of the Arbitration Act 1996 confers such power on the court.[116] In Singapore, Section 10 of the Arbitration Act confers such power on the court in case of domestic arbitrations.[117] In Malaysia, Section 45 of the Arbitration Act 2005 confers such power. It must be noted that, in all those statutes, such extensions are limited to cases where the Rules apply voluntarily but not statutorily.[118]

What happens if the action is brought before a court within the time limit when there is an arbitration agreement and by the time an objection is taken by the defendant, the one-year time limit has set in? This requires a conceptual visit to the New York Convention of 1958[119] and UNCITRAL[120] Model Law 1985

---

[114] Required by Section 9A of the Singapore Interpretation Act.

[115] In Singapore, the Arbitration Act (for domestic arbitration) and the International Arbitration Act do not provide for extension of time-limits provided in statutes to arbitral proceedings, other than for the limits provided by the Limitation Act and Foreign Limitation Periods Act 2012—see Section 11 of the Arbitration Act and Section 8A of the International Arbitration Act.

[116] A *dictum* in *Nea Agrex SA v Baltic Shipping Co Ltd and Intershipping Charter Co (The Agios Lazaros)* [1976] QB 933, [1976] 2 All ER 842 (EW CA) will support this proposition, while another *dictum* in *Rolimpex (Ch E) Ltd v Avra Shipping Co Ltd (The Angeliki)* [1973] 2 Lloyd's Rep 226 (EW HC) will contradict it.

[117] Such power is absent in the Singapore International Arbitration Act.

[118] The Court of Appeal in *Kenya Railways v Antares Co Pte Ltd (The Antares)* [1987] 1 Lloyd's Rep 424 held accordingly when dealing with Section 27 of the Arbitration Act 1950, the predecessor to Section 13 of the 1996 Act.

[119] Convention on the Recognition and Enforcement of Foreign Arbitral Awards (New York, 1958).

[120] United Nations Commission on International Trade Law.

(amended in 2006)[121] before delving into domestic legislation. Article II(3) of the 1958 Convention provides as follows:

> 3. The court of a Contracting State, when seized of an action in a matter in respect of which the parties have made an agreement within the meaning of this article, shall, at the request of one of the parties, *refer the parties to arbitration*, unless it finds that the said agreement is null and void, inoperative or incapable of being performed. [emphasis added]

In the same line, the Model Law, in Article 8(1), provides as follows:

> (1) A court before which an action is brought in a matter which is the subject of an arbitration agreement shall, if a party so requests not later than when submitting his first statement on the substance of the dispute, refer the parties to arbitration unless it finds that the agreement is null and void, inoperative or incapable of being performed.

Whilst the number of signatories to the 1958 Convention is about 160, the number of countries among them that have adopted[122] the Model Law is about 80. They are divided in the relief granted to a defendant sued in court when there is an arbitration agreement. In some countries, following the Model Law, the action is merely stayed, perpetually, so that parties may resort to arbitration. In other countries, the action is struck out. Examples of jurisdictions where the action will merely be *stayed* perpetually for reference to arbitration include the UK,[123] India,[124] Singapore[125] and Malaysia.[126]. On the other hand, examples of jurisdictions where the action will be *struck out*[127] as opposed to merely being stayed perpetually include Sri Lanka,[128] Thailand,[129] Switzerland[130] and Germany.[131] However, the effect, in both systems, for all practical purposes may be the same.

In the former group of countries, technically, the action is to be referred by the court to arbitration, although actually the court will merely stay leaving it to the parties to carry it submit to arbitration. Accordingly, it can arguably be treated that time stopped running when the action was instituted at the court so that the claim

121 UNCITRAL Model Law on International Commercial Arbitration 1985, amended in 2006.

122 On a voluntary basis.

123 UK Arbitration Act 1996, Sections. 9 and 86.

124 Indian Arbitration and Conciliation Act 1996, Section 8(1).

125 Singapore Arbitration Act, Section 6(1); Singapore International Arbitration Act, Section 6(1).

126 Malaysian Arbitration Act 2005, Section 10(1).

127 On ground that court lacked the jurisdiction to hear the case at the instance of objection by the defendant.

128 Section 5 of the Sri Lankan Arbitration Act 1995 provides "[w]here a party to an arbitration agreement institutes legal proceedings in a court … the Court shall have no jurisdiction to hear and determine such matter if the other party objects to the court exercising jurisdiction in respect of such matter".

129 Section 14 of the Arbitration Act B.E. 2545 (2002) of Thailand provides "… [u]pon the court having completed the inquiry and found that there are no grounds for rendering the arbitration agreement void or unenforceable or impossible to perform, the court shall issue an order striking the case".

130 Article 7 of the Swiss Private International Law 1987.

131 Section 1032 of the German Code of Civil Procedure.

will not be time-barred when it is taken to arbitration even after the one-year period. For an argument to be effectively taken in this line, the order of the court must be for more than a mere stay, such as the imposition of a condition that the matter is referred by one of the parties to arbitration within a certain time frame. Without such a condition, it will be hard to argue that the court played any role in the reference to arbitration, and the claimant will be left at his will to institute arbitral proceedings when he likes. If the court did not thus play a role in the reference to arbitration, it is unlikely that an arbitral proceeding instituted after the one-year period will be considered to be within time.

In the latter group of counties, as the domestic law declares the court to be without jurisdiction and hence requires the court to compulsorily strike out the action, upon request by the defendant, it is likely that the claimant will not be able to institute arbitral proceedings outside the one-year time limit even where the court action was brought within the one-year limit.

10.4.2 Article III(6)bis

Article III(6)*bis*, that is only in the Hague-Visby Rules, but not in the Hague Rules, provides as follows:

> An action for indemnity against a third person may be brought even after the expiration of the year provided for in the preceding paragraph if brought within the time allowed by the law of the Court seized of the case. However, the time allowed shall be not less than three months, commencing from the day when the person bringing such action for indemnity has settled the claim or has been served with process in the action against himself.

The above amendment will be a welcome one. It is not uncommon that a carrier who is sued by a cargo interest subject to the Rules may have a claim against another carrier also subject to the Rules. For instance, an intermediate carrier such as a freight forwarder may issue its own bill of lading to a cargo interest. The intermediate carrier will then take a bill of lading from the shipowner. Here there are two carriage contracts in respect of the same shipment, to both of which the Rules apply. If the intermediate carrier is sued by the cargo interest for damage to goods during transit, the intermediate carrier will have a claim for indemnity from the shipowner at the time of the damage. Under the Hague Rules, the intermediate carrier will almost have to immediately take third-party proceedings,[132] called an additional claim for contribution or indemnity from another party in England and Wales,[133] against the shipowner if the shipowner is subject to the same jurisdiction or else to institute an action against the shipowner in the appropriate jurisdiction. If the action against the intermediate carrier is issued within the time limit but served after the time limit, then the intermediate carrier would have lost its right to take indemnity action against the shipowner. Added to this, if the cargo interest loses its case against the intermediate

[132] Order 16 of the Malaysian Rules of Court 2012/Singapore Rules of Court.

[133] CPR Rule 20.6.

carrier, and the intermediate carrier accordingly loses its case against the shipowner, the intermediate carrier will be liable for the costs of the shipowner as well as its own cost in the indemnity claim made against the shipowner. This will put the carriers who were not the shipowners at the material time in a dilemma. This mischief was redressed by the Hague-Visby Rules by Article III(6)*bis*. However, countries such as Malaysia that have still subscribed only to the Hague Rules, do not enjoy Article III(6)*bis* advantage.

Under Article III(6)*bis,* the time to bring indemnity action is extended. In the case of England and Wales, it is two years. UK Limitation Act 1980, Section 10. In Singapore, there is a materially identical provision in Section 6 of the Singapore Limitation Act, has a materially identical provision. Arguments have been advanced that Section 39 of the UK Act (and Section 3 of the Singapore Act) excludes application of the Act to Hague-Visby Rules cases. However, the argument does not seem persuasive as the Hague-Visby Rules does not itself prescribe any limitation period for the indemnity actions dealt with in Article III(6) *bis*. If there is no specific time provided under the law in which the indemnity action is brought, then the Article seems to extends the time to the regular time limit in that jurisdiction, which will in many jurisdictions be six years from the date of cause of action, i.e. possibly meaning the day the indemnity claimant was served the principal claim papers. *See Sabarudin bin Othman & Anor v Malayan Banking Bhd and another appeal* [2018] MLJU 304 (MY CA). If the time limit is over by the time the main action is completed, which is possible in countries where the litigation or arbitration process is very time consuming, then the Rules seemingly extend the time to institute the indemnity action, to three months after settling the claim under the main action. However, the Article lacks clarity. It grants the three months extension after the claim was settled or the process was served. It does not have the usual 'whichever is later' or 'whichever is earlier'. It is likely that a court will read this ambiguity in favour of the claimant in the indemnity action and, in most cases, it will be at least three months after the claim was settled. However, this leaves the time limit quite open where the claimant in the indemnity action, i.e. the losing party in the main action, delays and drags settlement of the claim.

It must be noted that it is possible that of the two contracts, one may be governed by the Hague Rules and the other by the Hague-Visby Rules. Thus if the main claim is under the Hague Rules, that is no bar to an indemnity claim brought within Article III(6)*bis* extended time limit where the Hague-Visby Rules apply to the indemnity action.[134]

[134] *The Xingcheng v The Andros* [1988] LRC (Comm) 139, [1987] 1 WLR 1213, [1987] 2 Lloyd's Rep 210 (PC on appeal from Hong Kong).

10.5 Article IV(5): Liability-Limitation

One may wonder the purpose of or policy behind the liability-limitation. First, before the Hague Rules, carriers were able to freely exclude liability contractually, particularly when a shipper usually did not have the bargaining power against the carrier. When the Rules took away the contractual freedom, it had to strike a balance between the interests of the carrier and the shipper. Second, arguably, without liability-limitation, the cost of the P&I cover for carriers will be higher, in turn, the cost of carriage of goods by sea would be more expensive. An analogy can be drawn to the jurisprudence whereby the threshold for finding a doctor negligent is significantly high, as otherwise, the cost of indemnity insurance for doctors will be higher, resulting in an increased cost of medical service to the public.[135]

10.5.1 Hague Rules

Article IV(5) of the Hague Rules reads as follows:

> 5. Neither the carrier nor the ship shall in any event be or become liable for any loss or damage to or in connection with goods in an amount exceeding *£100 per package or unit*, or the *equivalent of that sum in other currency*, unless the nature and value of such goods have been declared by the shipper before shipment and inserted in the bill of lading.
>
> This declaration if embodied in the bill of lading shall be prima facie evidence, but shall not be binding or conclusive on the carrier.
>
> By agreement between the carrier, master or agent of the carrier and the shipper another maximum amount than that mentioned in this paragraph may be fixed, provided that such maximum shall not be less than the figure abovenamed.
>
> Neither the carrier nor the ship shall be responsible in any event for loss or damage to or in connection with goods if the nature or value thereof has been knowingly misstated by the shipper in the bill of lading. [emphasis added]

This must be read with Article IX of the Hague Rules, which reads as follows:

> The *monetary units* mentioned in these Rules are to be taken to be *gold value*. [emphasis added]

It is the above rules that apply[136] in Malaysia by virtue of the Carriage of Goods Act 1950. There are four paragraphs in Article IV(5). Each will be looked at on its own right below. To the question of application of the limitation to cases of

---

[135] *Dr V Thuraisingam v Sanmarkanganapathy* [2015] 8 CLJ 248 (MY CA); See also *Bolam v Friern Hospital Management Committee* [1957] 2 All ER 118, [1957] 1 WLR 582 (EW HC); *Bolitho v City and Hackney Health Authority* [1998] AC 232, [1997] 4 All ER 771, [1997] 3 WLR 1151, [1998] 3 LRC 355 (UK HL).

[136] Largely. See Chap. 1.3.6.2 for a detailed discussion of the application of the Hague Rules in different parts of Malaysia and the exception in the case of Labuan.

misdelivery where that happens after discharge, *Mediterranean Shipping Co SA v Trafigura Beheer BV and Another (The MSC Amsterdam)* [2007] EWCA Civ 794, [2008] 1 All ER (Comm) 385, [2007] 2 Lloyd's Rep 622, [2007] All ER (D) 444 (Jul) (EW CA): Carrier is not entitled to the Hague Rules Article IV(5) liability limitation when goods are misdelivered after discharge. the discussion made earlier as to application of the time-limitation to cases of misdelivery after discharge will be relevant See chap. 10.4.1.3 'Application to Misdelivery and Non-delivery'. The possible arguments shown there with the words 'whatsoever' and 'in respect of goods' will be relevant by analogy also in the context of liability limitation under Article IV(5) by virtue of the words 'in any event' and 'loss or damage to or in connection with the goods' in Article IV(5). However, it cannot be doubted that where goods are damaged or lost after discharge but before delivery, the Article IV(5) liability limitation will not be available as a matter of statute, although it may be made available as a matter of contract.[137]

10.5.1.1 First Paragraph of Article IV(5)

The first paragraph provides for the package limitation. The limitation is in respect of any loss or damage to or in connection with the goods. It applies in any event. The limit, per package or unit, is £100 or the equivalent amount in any other currency. However, the package limitation does not apply where the value of the cargo is stated in the bill of lading.

'Loss or damage to or in connection with goods'

First, 'loss or damage to or in connection with goods' is wide enough to cover also claims for pure economic loss in addition to claims for loss of or damage to goods.

'In any event'

Second, the words 'in any event' has been literally interpreted to afford wide protection to the carrier even when the breach committed by the carrier is a very serious one, such as deviation or fundamental in nature. In *The Kapitan Petko Voivoda*,[138] the contract provided for carriage 'under deck only' but the goods were carried on deck and damaged. In a claim by the cargo owner, the English Court of Appeal held that, despite this serious breach, the carrier was entitled to rely on the liability-limitation regime in the Hague Rules Article IV(5) because it was applicable 'in any event'.

A similar decision was reached by the Singapore Court of Appeal in *Parker Distributors (Singapore) Pte Ltd v A/S D/S Svenborg & Anor.*[139] In this case, the contract was to carry 17 packages of Parker writing instruments in a strong room or

---

[137] Article II read with Article I(e).

[138] *Daewoo Heavy Industries Ltd v Klipriver Shipping Ltd (The Kapitan Petko Voivoda)* [2003] EWCA Civ 451, [2003] 1 All ER (Comm) 801, [2003] 2 Lloyd's Rep 1, [2003] All ER (D) 46 (Apr) (EW CA).

[139] [1982–1983] 1 SLR 153 (SG CA).

locker room. The carrier failed to carry in such a room and five packages were lost and three damaged. In the bill of lading, the value of the goods was not declared. The applicable law was US Carriage of Goods by Sea Act 1936, which has largely adopted the Hague Rules.[140] Section 4(5) of the Act was materially similar to Article IV(5) of the Hague Rules, except that the amount of the liability-limitation is set at USD500.[141] The consignee made a claim for the loss in a sum of more than USD86,000. The carrier sought to limit the liability to the statutory regime. The consignee argued that the breach was a fundamental one or deviation so that the carrier should not be entitled to rely on the statutory liability-limitation. However, the court disagreed and emphasised the words 'in any event' in the section and held that the liability-limitation was available to the carrier.

Despite the appellate courts having favoured a *literal* reading of the words 'in any event', the doors for judicial ingenuity to refuse the liability-limitation to the carrier in cases of a serious breach is not closed. It is arguable that an agreement, such as to carry under deck or in a strong room, can be treated as a collateral contract separate from the main carriage contract but embodied in the bill of lading that will be passed on with the bill.

'£100'

Third, there has been uncertainty as to what is the value referred to by the '£100'. At a look, it may appear that it can be interpreted in two ways. One is to interpret it to mean barely £100. Another is to interpret it as meaning the value of gold that could be purchased for £100 in 1924, when the Rules were made, thus allowing inflammation factor.[142] The second line of interpretation accords with the purposive construction of the rules, as it is most unlikely that the Rules intended to fix an amount in perpetuity without allowing inflation factor. It was adopted in *The Rosa S*,[143] where the English High Court held the gold value of the £100 to be £6,630.50 in 1984. Similarly, in *The Nadezhda Krupskaya,*[144] the New South Wales Court of Appeal held the limit to be more than AUD11,000 in 1989, departing from the previous Australian authorities that had held the £100 merely to mean AUS200 at the face exchange rate. The Malaysian Federal Court, in *Shun Cheong Steam Navigation Co Ltd v Wo Fong Trading Co,*[145] similarly agreed that the £100 in the Hague Rules[146]

---

140 Although the USA is not a signatory to the Hague or Hague-Visby Rules.

141 Section 4(5): "Neither the carrier nor the ship shall in any event be or become liable for any loss or damage to or in connection with the transportation of goods in an amount exceeding $500 per package lawful money of the United States or in case of goods not shipped in packages per customary weight unit or the equivalent of that sum in other currency, unless the nature and value of such goods have been declared by the shipper before shipment and inserted in the bill of lading".

142 See Limitation Sum—Gold Value—Hague Rules, Article IV Rule 5, (1989) 6 MLAANZ Journal Part 2 at pp. 64–65.

143 *The Rosa S* [1988] 2 Lloyd's Rep 574 (EW HC).

144 *Brown Boveri (Australia) Pty Limited v Baltic Shipping Company (The Nadezhda Krupskaya)* [1989] 1 Lloyd's Rep 518 (NSW CA).

145 [1979] 2 MLJ 254 (MY FC).

146 Applicable in Malaysia.

referred to the gold value of £100, in the context of Peninsular Malaysia. However, it appears from the judgment that the court did not manipulate the £100 gold value to the current date, but instead awarded only £100 as the maximum amount when the value of the lost package of medicine was about MYR25,000, which was far more than £100 at the relevant date. On this score, this decision will not represent a good approach to be followed. Similarly, in *Sebor (Sarawak) Trading Sdn Bhd & Anor v Syarikat Cheap Hin Toy Manufacture Sdn Bhd*,[147] the Malaysian Court of Appeal said *obiter* that a clause in the bill of lading limiting the liability of the carrier to £100 per package or unit was in line with Article IV(5),[148] without reference to gold value and manipulation. This decision again will not represent the right approach to be followed.[149]

For the states of Sabah[150] and Sarawak[151] in Malaysia, the £100 is modified by reg. 7 of the 1960 Sarawak Regulations,[152] a delegated legislation, as MYR850.[153]. The Hague Rules in the schedule to the 1960 Regulations includes Article IX. This means that the MYR850 limit in reg. 7 must manipulated by reference to gold value of RM850 at a certain date. Is that certain date 1924 (date of the Hague Rules) or 1960 (date of the Regulations)? This is a complex question. If the Minister who made the Regulations had taken into account the inflation/manipulated the 1924 gold value to 1961, then the certain date will be 1960. Otherwise, it will be 1924. There is unlikely to be available any evidence of how the Minister arrived at the MYR850 translation. In the absence of such evidence, the exercise of the powers by the Minister in fixing the MYR850, hence its validity, must be challengeable by judicial review. If such a challenge succeeds, that will nullify the reg. 7 that has effected the modification, so that the £100 gold value in Article IV(5) read together with Article IX will apply at all times.[154]

In Singapore, in the case of *Sarathi Co v Owners of Vishva Prathiba; Port of Bombay India,*[155] decided by the High Court before *The Rosa S*, the court did not

---

[147] [2003] 2 MLJ 486, [2003] 3 AMR 354, [2003] 2 CLJ 381 (MY CA).

[148] Arun Kasi, 'Excluding Liability for Misdelivery and Non-Delivery under Bills of Lading: An Analysis under Laws of Malaysia, Singapore and England & Wales', *The Law Review* [2020] LR143. This article was referred to in *Punjab National Bank v Malayan Banking Berhad* [2020] 1 LNS 232, [2020] 5 MLJ 732 (MY CA).

[149] See Arun Kasi, 'The Dancing Liability-Limit in Hague Rules and Validity of MYR850 Limit for East Malaysia', *Malaysian Law Journal*, [2021] 1 MLJ cxciv, where a discussion of this subject first appeared.

[150] Merchant Shipping (Applied Subsidiary Legislation) Regulations 1961 (1961 Sarawak Regulations).

[151] Merchant Shipping (Implementation of Conventions Relating to Carriage of Goods by Sea and to Liability of Shipowners and Others) Regulations 1960 (1960 Sabah Regulations).

[152] Applicable also in Sabah through the 1961 Sabah Regulations.

[153] See Chap. 1.3.6.2

[154] This discussion substantially first appeared in Arun Kasi, 'The Dancing Liability-Limit in Hague Rules and Validity of MYR850 Limit for East Malaysia', *Malaysian Law Journal* [2021] 1 MLJ cxciv.

[155] [1980] 2 MLJ 265 (Singapore HC).

treat the £100 as anything more than its face value. Subsequently, the approach in Singapore was corrected in case of *The Thomaseverett*,[156] where the High Court adopted the approach laid down in *The Rosa S*. In this case, the gold value of £100 was manipulated SGD9,398 in 1982.

The risk of uncertainty had led to a practice of the merchants adopting a 'gold clause' in the shipping document that will expressly fix the package limitation such as £200 per package or unit. However, such a 'gold clause' will only be possible where the Hague Rules did not apply statutorily, where the limitation fixed by the clause will be less than the limitation under the Hague Rules, as it almost always be.

'Per package or unit'

Fourth, '*per* package or unit' will necessarily mean that the limitation in relation to the goods lost or damaged. Hence, if 15 packages are shipped and only three of them are damaged or lost, the limitation amount will be the gold value of £300, and not £1,500, in 1924. However, in the case of a claim for economic losses such as the one resulting from delay or delivery in a different port, the limit will be based on the entire cargo, which in the above example will be the gold value of £1,500 in 1924.

'Package or unit'

Fifth, questions had arisen as to what the 'package or unit' refers to, in relation to bulk cargo and containerised cargo. In *The Aqasia*,[157] '2000 tons of cargo of fish oil in bulk' was shipped. The carrier argued that the 'unit' covered the bulk cargo and, in this case, it meant 'ton', the unit of measurement by which the quantity shipped was stated. The English Court of Appeal rejected this argument and held that the Hague Rules liability-limitation does not apply to bulk cargo.

A package will refer to goods that are packaged, such as a carton of 12 coffee jars. Here the package is the carton. A unit will refer to goods that are countable but not packaged, such as where machines or vehicles are shipped, e.g. 10 units of car or 4 units of vertical form-fill-seal machines. There is no liability-limitation for bulk cargo in the Hague Rule, a shortfall redressed in the Hague-Visby Rules.

In relation to containerised cargo, the English Court of Appeal in *The River Gurara*[158] held the packages inside the container to be the packages, and not the containers, for purposes of the liability-limitation under the Hague Rules. In this case, the number of packages inside the container was stated in the bill. There is a small, but not substantial, scope for argument that *The River Gurara* does not apply where the number of packages is not stated in the bill. The proposition that, whether the number of packages is stated or not, the container is not the package will be

---

[156] *Owners of Cargo Lately Laden on Board the Ship or Vessel Thomaseverett v Owners of and Other Persons Interested in the Ship or Vessel Thomaseverett (The Thomaseverett)* [1992] 2 SLR 1068 (SG HC).

[157] *Tank Shipping AS (formerly known as Tank Invest AS) v Vinnlustodin HF and Another (The Aqasia)* [2018] EWCA Civ 276, [2018] 3 All ER 981, [2018] 2 All ER (Comm) 191, [2018] Bus LR 992, [2018] 1 Lloyd's Rep 530 (EW CA).

[158] *The River Gurara* [1997] 4 All ER 498 (EW CA).

supported by a US case, *The Aegis Spirit*,[159] where the US court held that the cartons inside the container were the packages and not the container itself.[160] In contrast to them, the Malaysian Court of Appeal in *Sebor (Sarawak) Trading Sdn Bhd & Anor v Syarikat Cheap Hin Toy Manufacture Sdn Bhd*[161] treated the containers to be the package without reference to the authorities on this point and full deliberation. This case does not represent the good law to be followed and has been severely criticised.[162]

'Unless ... value ... declared'

Sixth, the limitation is ousted if the value is declared by the shipper and inserted in the bill of lading. The rationale behind this was stated in the Malaysian Federal Court[163] case *Shun Cheong Steam Navigation Co Ltd v Wo Fong Trading Co.*[164] The court said:

> The declaration, from the nature of things, must first come from the shipper. It serves as notice to the carrier of need for additional care in the carriage of the goods in question and must therefore be made before a higher liability can be fixed on the carrier

10.5.1.2 Second Paragraph of Article IV(5)

However, the declared value does not mean that it is the agreed value. It only operates as a *prima facie* evidence of the value of the goods so that the burden to prove otherwise is on the carrier. This can be quite burdensome on the carrier where the goods shipped are not of the common commodity. For instance, if sugar is shipped, the value can easily be determined. However, if a custom-made machine is shipped, it may be difficult for the carrier to establish its value to rebut the *prima facie* value declared in the bill. However, in practice, the cargo interest is likely to produce some evidence of its value like sale and purchase agreement, invoices, etc., failing which possibly an adverse inference may be drawn against it. In those Commonwealth countries, including Singapore and Malaysia, with an Evidence Act modelled on the Indian Evidence Act 1872, this will be facilitated by the presumptions allowed in the Act such as by Section 114 (illustration (g)) of the Indian Act.[165]

---

[159] *The Aegis Spirit* [1977] 1 Lloyd's Rep 93 (US District Court, Washington).

[160] See earlier Chap. 7.2.4.3 for the relevant speech of Beeks DJ in this case.

[161] [2003] 2 MLJ 486, [2003] 3 AMR 354, [2003] 2 CLJ 381 (MY CA).

[162] Arun Kasi, 'Excluding Liability for Misdelivery and Non-Delivery under Bills of Lading: An Analysis under Laws of Malaysia, Singapore and England & Wales', *The Law Review* [2020] LR 143. This article was referred to in *Punjab National Bank v Malayan Banking Berhad* [2020] 1 LNS 232, [2020] 5 MLJ 732 (MY CA).

[163] The apex court.

[164] [1979] 2 MLJ 254 (MY FC).

[165] Section 114 (*illustration* (g)) of the Malaysian Evidence Act 1950; Section 116 (*illustration* (g)) of the Singapore Evidence Act.

10.5.1.3 Third Paragraph of Article IV(5)

This expressly allows the parties to fix another maximum amount, but which shall not be less than Article IV(5) amount. However, this applies only in cases of packaged goods, because Article IV(5) is only about packaged goods. If parties were to fix any ceiling liability amount for bulk cargo, that will fall foul of Article III(8) for lessening the otherwise full liability of the carrier in respect of bulk cargo under the Hague Rules, and hence be rendered invalid.

10.5.1.4 Fourth Paragraph of Article IV(5)

While the shipper has the comfort of declaring the value in the bill of lading and thereby ousting out of the liability-limitation regime, the fourth paragraph ensures the shipper does not abuse it by overstating the value. If it 'knowingly' overstates the value, then the carrier is not liable for the loss. There is uncertainty as to whether it means the cargo interest loses all its right for any damages at all or is merely barred from claiming any damages in excess of the package limitation under the Rules. The Australian court in *Frank Hammond Pty Ltd v Huddard Parker Ltd and the Australian Shipping Board*[166] was of the view, *obiter*, that it meant the second line of thought above, i.e. a mere bar to any claim in excess of the package limitation. However, a literal reading would suggest the first line of thought, i.e. complete forfeiture of all right to damages.

It is a little hard to ascertain the purpose of the Article by a mere surface reading, as it is possible that the makers of the Rules intended to impose a penalty where the nature or value was 'knowingly' misstated. It is also possible that they merely intended a partial penalty by removing any claim in excess of the package limitation amount to the amount of true value of the goods. For two reasons, the second possibility whereby the basic package limitation under the Rules survives despite the misstatement is a more potent one. First, if the right to damages is forfeited in entirety, that will mean that the carrier is completely discharged from its fundamental obligations under the carriage of contract. Second, it may affect a subsequent buyer and holder of the bill of lading, who has purchased the goods in transit in good faith. This argument will support the proposition in the Australian case *Frank Hammond*.

10.5.2 Hague-Visby Rules

Article IV(5)(a) and (d) in the Hague-Visby Rules, as made in 1968, respectively provides as follows:

> (a) Unless the nature and value of such goods have been declared by the shipper before shipment and inserted in the bill of lading, neither the carrier nor the ship shall in any event

---

[166] [1956] VLR 496 (Victoria Supreme Court).

be or become liable for any loss or damage to or in connection with the goods in an amount exceeding the equivalent of 10,000 francs per package or unit or 30 francs per kilo of gross weight of the goods lost or damaged, whichever is the higher.

(d) A franc means a unit consisting of 65.5 milligrammes of gold of millesimal fineness 900. The date of conversion of the sum awarded into national currencies shall be governed by the law of the Court seized of the case. [underlining added]

Article IV(5) in the Hague-Visby Rules, as amended in 1979, provides as follows:[167]

(a) Unless the nature and value of such goods have been declared by the shipper before shipment and inserted in the bill of lading, neither the carrier nor the ship shall in any event be or become liable for any loss or damage to or in connection with the goods in an amount exceeding 666.67 units of account per package or unit or 2 units of account per kilogramme of gross weight of the goods lost or damaged, whichever is the higher.

(b) The total amount recoverable shall be calculated by reference to the value of such goods at the place and time at which the goods are discharged from the ship in accordance with the contract or should have been so discharged.

The value of the goods shall be fixed according to the commodity exchange price, or, if there be no such price, according to the current market price, or, if there be no commodity exchange price or current market price, by reference to the normal value of goods of the same kind and quality.

(c) Where a container, pallet or similar article of transport is used to consolidate goods, the number of packages or units enumerated in the bill of lading as packed in such article of transport shall be deemed the number of packages or units for the purpose of this paragraph as far as these packages or units are concerned. Except as aforesaid such article of transport shall be considered the package or unit.

(d) The unit of account mentioned in this Article is the special drawing right as defined by the International Monetary Fund. The amounts mentioned in sub-paragraph (a) of this paragraph shall be converted into national currency on the basis of the value of that currency on a date to be determined by the law of the Court seized of the case.

The value of the national currency, in terms of the Special Drawing Right, of a State which is a member of the International Monetary Fund, shall be calculated in accordance with the method of valuation applied by the International Monetary Fund in effect at the date in question for its operations and transactions. The value of the national currency, in terms of the Special Drawing Right, of a State which is not a member of the International Monetary Fund, shall be calculated in a manner determined by that State.

Nevertheless, a State which is not a member of the International Monetary Fund and whose law does not permit the application of the provisions of the preceding sentences may, at the time of ratification of the Protocol of 1979 or accession thereto or at any time thereafter, declare that the limits of liability provided for in this Convention to be applied in its territory shall be fixed as follows:

(i) in respect of the amount of 666.67 units of account mentioned in sub-paragraph (a) of paragraph 5 of this Article, 10,000 monetary units;

[167] No changes to Article IV(5)(b), (c), (e), (f), (g) and (h). The changes are only to Article IV(5)(a) and (d).

(ii) in respect of the amount of 2 units of account mentioned in sub-paragraph (a) of paragraph 5 of this Article, 30 monetary units.

> The monetary unit referred to in the preceding sentence corresponds to 65.5 milligrammes of gold of millesimal fineness 900'. The conversion of the amounts specified in that sentence into the national currency shall be made according to the law of the State concerned.
>
> The calculation and the conversion mentioned in the preceding sentences shall be made in such a manner as to express in the national currency of the State as far as possible the same real value for the amounts in sub-paragraph (a) of paragraph 5 of this Article as is expressed there in units of account.
>
> States shall communicate to the depositary the manner of calculation or the result of the conversion as the case may be, when depositing an instrument of ratification of the Protocol of 1979 or of accession thereto and whenever there is a change in either.
>
> Neither the carrier nor the ship shall be entitled to the benefit of the limitation of liability provided for in this paragraph if it is proved that the damage resulted from an act or omission of the carrier done with intent to cause damage, or recklessly and with knowledge that damage would probably result.
>
> The declaration mentioned in sub-paragraph (a) of this paragraph, if embodied in the bill of lading, shall be *prima facie* evidence, but shall not be binding or conclusive on the carrier.
>
> By agreement between the carrier, master or agent of the carrier and the shipper other maximum amounts than those mentioned in sub-paragraph (a) of this paragraph may be fixed, provided that no maximum amount so fixed shall be less than the appropriate maximum mentioned in that sub-paragraph.
>
> Neither the carrier nor the ship shall be responsible in any event for loss or damage to, or in connection with, goods if the nature or value thereof has been knowingly mis-stated by the shipper in the bill of lading. [underlining added]

It is the Hague-Visby Rules, as amended by SDR Protocol in 1979, that applies in the UK.[168] For Singapore, it is the Hague-Visby Rules, as made in 1968,[169] with the scheme of liability-limitation and unit of currency as provided by Carriage of Goods by Sea (Singapore Currency Equivalents) Order, which in paragraph 2 states the modified scheme by reference to Article IV(5)(a) as follows:

> 2. For the purposes of paragraph 5 of Article IV of the Rules and of Article IV bis of the Rules set out in the Schedule to the Act, $1,563.65 cents and $4.69 cents are hereby specified as the amounts which shall be taken as equivalent to 10,000 gold francs and 30 gold francs, respectively. [underlining added]

By coming with a modified scheme in a fixed sum, Singapore will have to amend the sum from time to time to allow inflation factor appropriately. This need will not be there when the SDR Protocol is adopted, as the Special Drawing Rights

---

168 The UK Carriage of Goods by Sea Act 1971.

169 Singapore Carriage of Goods by Sea Act. Section 3(8) facilitates the liability limit to be set by the Ministerial order: "The Minister may, from time to time by order published in the Gazette, specify the respective amounts which, for the purposes of paragraph 5 of Article IV and of Article IV bis of the Rules, are to be taken as equivalent to the sums expressed in francs which are mentioned in paragraph 5(a) of Article IV".

fixed on a daily basis by the International Monetary Fund will allow for the flexibility. The discussion made earlier, in connection with the Hague Rules, concerning liability limitation for misdelivery after discharge and damage to or loss of goods after discharge but before delivery will be applicable also under the Hague-Visby Rules. See chap. 10.5.1.

10.5.2.1 General Observation on Article IV(5)

Those parts above underlined (with single or double lines) are the amendments made in 1979, called SDR Protocol.[170] The double-lined amendments are what were not adopted by the UK into the Rules incorporated via Schedule to the Carriage of Goods by Sea Act 1971. It must be noted that not all jurisdictions that have subscribed to the Hague-Visby Rules have adopted SDR Protocol.[171] Accordingly, to determine the applicable Rules, one must look at the Rules subscribed to by the relevant jurisdiction which may be the Hague Rules, the Hague-Visby Rules as of 1968 or the Hague-Visby Rules as amended by the SDR Protocol of 1979. In addition to that, one must also look at the domestic legislation to determine the exact parts of the Rules adopted into, or excluded from, the legislation of the jurisdiction. In essence, what the SDR Protocol has done was to replace the liability-limitation provided in 'francs' to Special Drawing Rights (SDR).[172] All further references in this chapter to the Hague-Visby Rules, insofar as this Article is concerned, will be to the Hague-Visby Rules as amended by the SDR Protocol.

10.5.2.2 Article IV(5)(a) and IV(5)(D): Package and Gross Weight Limitations

Under the Hague-Visby Rules—Article IV(5)(a) read with Article IV(5)(d)—there are two types of liability-limitation. One is based on the number of packages. Another is based on gross weight.[173] The one based on packages is limited to 666.67 units of account per package—the corresponding Singapore limit under the domestic legislation is SDG1,563.65.[174] The one based on gross weight is limited to 2 units of account per kilogramme—the corresponding Singapore limit under the domestic legislation is SGD4.69.[175] Whichever is higher applies, hence the option favours the

---

[170] Protocol amending the International Convention for the Unification of Certain Rules of Law relating to Bills of Lading, 25 August 1924, as amended by the Protocol of 23 February 1968.

[171] However, the number of countries that have subscribed to the Hague-Visby Rules as of 1968 but not subscribed to the SDR Protocol of 1979 is very small.

[172] Unlike gold value, it is easy to convert SDR to any local currency, as there is a daily exchange rate published by International Monetary Fund (IMF) available at its website https://www.imf.org/.

[173] There is no equivalent provision in the Hague Rules.

[174] Carriage of Goods by Sea (Singapore Currency Equivalents) Order.

[175] Carriage of Goods by Sea (Singapore Currency Equivalents) Order.

cargo claimant. The unit of account referred to in the Rules is the SDR.[176] Because of the availability of gross weight limitation, the liability-limitation regime also applies to bulk cargo, unlike the position under the Hague Rules.

Attention must be paid to the wording of Article IV(5)(a) when the scope of coverage is stated in general, followed by package limitation and gross weight limitation being described. The general scope is stated as '*any loss or damage* to or *in connection with the goods*', which is wide enough to cover also pure economic loss.[177] For package limitation, it is described as 'per package or unit' as it was in the Hague Rules. However, for gross weight limitation, it is described as 'per kilogramme of gross weight *of the goods lost or damaged*'. This addition of the words 'goods lost or damaged', which was not there in the Hague Rules for package limitation, has been held, in *The Limnos*,[178] to attach only to the gross weight limitation. Based on this analysis, it was held in this case that the gross weight limitation will only apply where the goods had been 'lost or damaged' meaning physical loss or damage and it will be based on the quantity of the goods thus lost or damaged.[179] It follows that in cases of bulk cargo shipment, for which the only possible limitation is the gross weight limitation under the Hague-Visby Rules, the limitation will not apply where the claim is one for pure economic loss, hence no limitation in such cases.

10.5.2.3 Article IV(5)(B): Mechanism for Assessing Value

Article IV(5)(b) is, in essence, about the mechanism for calculating the value of the goods. The value will be the one at the place and time of discharge or that they should have been discharged. The value will be fixed based, in order of priority, on commodity exchange price, current market price or normal value of the goods of the same kind and quality, as available. There is no equivalent provision to this in the Hague Rules.

This mechanism of assessment will be relevant where the claim is for goods are lost or short-delivered. In the case of damage to goods, the mechanism will not be relevant unless the claim involves a need to ascertain the value the goods. The mechanism will not be relevant where the claim is for delayed delivery.

Where the claim is for delay in delivery, the common law principle enunciated in *The Heron II*[180] will continue to apply, where the goods were intended for resale by the cargo interest. The principle will be applicable whether the case is under Hague or Hague-Visby Rules. In this case, a cargo of sugar was delivered late at Basra.

---

[176] The SDR unit does not apply in Singapore, which has its own scheme.

[177] Such as the one resulting from delay or delivery in a different port.

[178] *Serena Navigation Ltd v Dera Commercial Establishment (The Limnos)* [2008] EWHC 1036 (Comm), [2008] 2 All ER (Comm) 1005 (EW HC).

[179] *Serena Navigation Ltd v Dera Commercial Establishment (The Limnos)* [2008] EWHC 1036 (Comm), [2008] 2 All ER (Comm) 1005 (EW HC).

[180] *C Czarnikow Ltd v Koufos (The Heron II)* [1969] 1 AC 350 (UK HL).

The cargo was purchased by the cargo interest for resale and this was reasonably contemplatable by the shipowner as not unlikely[181] as there was a market for sugar in Basra. The House of Lords allowed damages assessed by the difference in value between the agreed time of delivery and the actual time of delivery, by when the value had dropped. If the cargo interest had sub-sold the goods, that sub-sale price will not normally be relevant to determine the value at the time when the goods should have been delivered or were actually delivered. However, it may be relevant where there is no market for the goods and the sub-sale was concluded around the time when the goods should have been delivered or were actually delivered.[182]

A more complex question arises where the goods are delivered late and they were meant for own use. In such a case, the damages sustained by the cargo interest can be substantial, irrespective of any change in the value between the agreed delivery time and the actual delivery time. The actual loss will be too remote to claim unless the carrier has actual (or ought to have had) knowledge that it was for own use. The *Hadley v Baxendale*[183] and *Victoria Laundry v Newman Industries*[184] common law principles will be applicable also under Hague/Hague-Visby Rules. In *Hadley v Baxendale*, the English Court of Exchequer refused to allow claim for loss of profits of a mill owner resulting from prolonged non-operation of the mill due to delay in delivery by the road-carrier of the mill's shaft. This was because a carrier could not contemplate, at the time the carriage contract was entered into, that the mill will stop operating by reason of any delay. In *Victoria Laundry*, the English Court of Appeal held that, where the carrier knew that the boilers were to be delivered for own use of the shipper, the carrier was liable for loss of profits that would be made on regular contracts by use of the boilers but not for profits that would be made on lucrative contacts. No doubt, when damages are assessed by common law principles in case of delay, not covered by Article IV(5)(b), any award will be subject to Article IV(5)(a) liability limitation.

10.5.2.4 Article IV(5)(C): Containerised Cargo

Article IV(5)(c) has two effects. One is that if the number of packages or units inside the container has been stated in the bill of lading as packed inside the container, the 'package or unit' will refer to that number and not the container. The other is that if it is not so stated, then the container will itself become the package. While the first effect is advantageous to cargo interests, but unlikely the second one. There is no equivalent provision to this in the Hague Rules. However, even without such a provision, a similar effect as the first one had been achieved under the Hague Rules as

---

[181] See *Hadley v Baxendale* (1854) 9 Ex D 341, [1843–60] All ER Rep 461 (EW Court of Exchequer Chamber).

[182] *The Arpad* [1934] All ER Rep 326, [1934] P 189, 152 LT 521 (EW CA).

[183] (1854) 9 Ex D 341, [1843–60] All ER Rep 461 (EW Court of Exchequer Chamber).

[184] *Victoria Laundry (Windsor) Ltd v Newman Industries Ltd* [1949] 2 KB 528, [1949] 1 All ER 997, 213 LT 18 (EW CA).

a matter of construction of 'package'.[185] Under the Hague Rules, even when the bill of lading does not state the number of packages or units, the court is still at liberty to construe 'package' to mean the actual packages inside the container.[186] This liberty is lost under the Hague-Visby Rules.

The requirement in the Hague-Visby Rules to declare the number of 'packages' inside the container in the bill can have consequences more than what it appears to have at a surface level reading. In *El Greco (Australia) Pty Ltd v Mediterranean Shipping Co SA*,[187] the Australian Federal Court held that merely stating the number of 'contents' inside the container will not suffice, but the number of 'packages' must be stated. This was the effect of the words of the Article that reads 'the number of packages or units enumerated in the bill of lading *as packed* in such an article of transport'. In this case, the contents of the container were stated in the bill as '200,945 pieces, posters and prints'. Actually, they were packed into about 2,000 packages, which was not stated. Accordingly, the court held that the number of packages was not stated in the bill, hence the container was treated as the package.[188] However, it would have been different if there were no packages inside the container, but the posters were merely stuffed as pieces, in which case the pieces would have at least arguably constituted the number of 'units' to attract the package limitation based on the units. This happened in *The Maersk Tangier*.[189] In this case, unpackaged tuna loins were stuffed into containers and shipped. The number of loins was stated in the sea waybill. The English Court of Appeal held that this number constituted the 'units' for purposes of package limitation.

10.5.2.5 Article IV(5)(E): Loss of Liability-Limitation

The carrier will lose the benefits of the liability-limitation, but not time limitation, when the 'damage resulted from an act or omission of the *carrier*' and it was 'done':

(i) with intent to cause damage; or
(ii) recklessly and with knowledge that damage would probably result.

---

[185] *Tank Shipping AS (formerly known as Tank Invest AS) v Vinnlustodin HF and Another (The Aqasia)* [2018] EWCA Civ 276, [2018] 3 All ER 981, [2018] 2 All ER (Comm) 191, [2018] Bus LR 992, [2018] 1 Lloyd's Rep 530 (EW CA); *Owners of Cargo lately on board River Gurara v Nigerian National Shipping Line Ltd (The River Gurara)* [1998] 1 Lloyd's Rep 225 at 228, [1998] QB 610, [1997] 4 All ER 498, [1997] 3 WLR 1128 (EW CA).

[186] As there is no requirement to state the number of packages in the bill.

[187] [2004] 2 Lloyd's Rep 537, [2004] FCAFC 202 (Australia FC).

[188] Despite that, the gross weight limitation option was available to the cargo claimant, that came to AUD38,250.

[189] *Kyokuyo Co Ltd v AP Møller-Maersk A/S (trading as 'Maersk Line') (The Maersk Tangier)* [2018] EWCA Civ 778, [2018] 3 All ER 1009, [2018] 2 All ER (Comm) 503, [2018] 2 Lloyd's Rep 59, [2018] All ER (D) 90 (Apr) (EW CA).

The act or omission must be of the carrier. It has been held that the 'carrier' here refers to a senior person in the management of the carrier-company. What constitutes 'carrier' for this purpose has been discussed in detail earlier.[190]

Once it is established that the act or omission was that of the carrier, the next question is as to the mental state of the person who represented the carrier. The intention in him must either be to cause damage or it must be done recklessly and with knowledge that damage would probably result. This is a very high threshold that will not ordinarily be met. In *Goldman v Thai Airways International Ltd*,[191] in dealing with a similar mental element required under the Warsaw Convention, the English Court of Appeal stressed that both recklessness and the knowledge that damage would probably result must be proved. In that case, although the pilot was reckless, he did not have the requisite knowledge of probable damage. Hence, the liability-limitation was not lost. Added to the high threshold, the burden of proof is on the cargo claimant, rendering the Article of little utility, if any.

10.5.2.6 Article IV(5)(F)—(H)

They are the same as the last three paragraphs of Article IV(5) in the Hague Rules, discussed in detail above.

10.6 Loss of Protection in Case of Deviation

This is a subject that is not so well settled. It has been discussed in detail earlier as part of the consideration of the consequences of deviation under the Hague and Hague-Visby Rules.[192]

---

[190] See Chap. 9.4.2.2.

[191] [1983] 1 WLR 1186, [1983] 3 All ER 693 (EW CA).

[192] See Chap. 7.2.5.

Chapter 11
Shipper's Obligation for Dangerous Goods

This chapter discusses the subject of shipping dangerous cargo at common law and under the Hague/Hague-Visby Rules. The common law absolute obligation of the shipper to inform the shipowner of any dangerous nature of the cargo is considered. This is followed by an analysis of the position under the Rules—Article IV(6). This includes the right of the carrier to abandon the cargo without liability and the liability of the shipper to compensate the carrier for losses consequent upon the shipment of the dangerous cargo. Then, the Article IV(3) general defence available to the shipper when a loss ensues without any act/fault/neglect of the shipper and its relationship to Article IV(6) is examined. Finally, the question of transfer of the shipper's liability to a subsequent transferee of the bill of lading is addressed.

11.1 Introduction

At common law the shipper has a duty to notify the shipowner of any dangerous characteristics of the cargo.[1] This is an absolute duty. It is not only for bills of lading, but also for all shipping-contracts including sea waybills, ship's delivery orders and charterparties.[2] It is a defence to a claim of breach of this duty that the shipowner knew or ought to have known of it.[3]

The Rules, in cases to which it applies, imposes a similar duty, but in somewhat different terms by Article IV(6). It allows the carrier to discharge the dangerous cargo or to render it innocuous without liability and hold the shipper liable when the carrier did not consent to carry the cargo with knowledge of its nature and character. It is the obligation of the shipper that it does not load dangerous cargo without securing the

[1] *Brass v Maitland* (1856) 26 LJ QB 49, (1856) 119 ER 940 (EW HC).

[2] Voyage and time charters.

[3] *The Athanasia Comninos and Georges Chr Lemos* [1990] 1 Lloyd's Rep 277 (EW HC).

A. Kasi, *The Law of Carriage of Goods by Sea*,
https://doi.org/10.1007/978-981-33-6793-7_11

consent of the carrier given with knowledge of nature and character.[4] Whether the liability for breach of the obligation extends to a transferee of the bill does not seem to have been authoritatively answered, whilst it is unlikely that it was intended by the Rules to so extend. The Rules apply statutorily to bills of lading, subject to the conditions set out there.[5] However, it can be made applicable to any shipping-contract by a voluntary incorporation.[6]

In deciding the question of dangerousness of a cargo, a court may make reference to the International Maritime Dangerous Goods Code (IMDG Code).[7] The Code was developed by the Maritime Safety Committee (MSC) of the International Maritime Organization (IMO). It classifies and lists numerous dangerous goods. It also deals with their documentation, packing, marking, labelling, placarding, warning, stowing, segregating.

In this chapter, first, the duty under the common law is visited, and then the duty and liability under the Rules. It must be noted that the common law duty co-exists with the Rules. But, in cases to which the Rules apply, if there is an inconsistency between the common law duty and the Article IV(6) duty, then the latter will prevail.

11.2 Duty Under Common Law

At common law, the duty on the shipper to notify the shipowner of any dangerous characteristics of the cargo is an absolute one.[8] Hence, it is no defence for the shipper to say that it did not know of the danger or that it could not have been known to it by the exercise of any due diligence. The duty is not one merely for shipping-contracts by bills of lading but also charterparties and other shipping documents.

It is a defence to the shipper if the shipowner knew or ought to have known of the dangerous characteristics so that there was no necessity to inform the shipowner of the dangerous characteristics. In turn, it is an important question whether the damage was caused by the characteristics that the shipowner knew or ought to have known[9] or by some other factor such as a defect in the cargo or failure by the consignor to properly pack or treat the cargo. Only in the former case, the shipper is relieved from liability.

---

[4] See Article IV(6) of the Hague/Hague-Visby Rules; *Effort Shipping Co Ltd v Linden Management SA (The Giannis NK)* [1998] AC 605, [1998] 1 Lloyd's Rep 337, [1998] All ER (D) 10, [1998] 1 All ER 495, [1998] 2 WLR 206, [1998] 4 LRC 97 (UK HL).

[5] Dealt with in detail in Chap. 8.

[6] Clause paramount.

[7] The Code has been recognised by the UK Merchant Shipping (Reporting Requirements for Ships Carrying Dangerous or Polluting Goods) Regulations 1995 and the UK Merchant Shipping Regulations (Dangerous Goods and Marine Pollutants) 1997 in regulating carriage of dangerous goods.

[8] *Brass v Maitland* (1856) 26 LJ QB 49, (1856) 119 ER 940 (EW HC).

[9] E.g. common characteristics.

In *The Athanasia Comninos and Georges Chr Lemos*,[10] a cargo of coal was carried under charterparty. Methane emission from the coal resulted in an explosion. This was an inherent risk in the carriage of coal that the shipowner knew or ought to have known. However, the shipowner argued that this particular cargo of coal had a higher rate of methane emission than ordinary coal. The English High Court rejected this argument as the risk was of the same kind though the degree of risk may be different. Accordingly, the court held that the shipper was not liable.

It can be a fine question in many cases whether the damage was caused by the inherent characteristics of the cargo that the shipowner knew or ought to have known or by some other cause. If the damage was caused by a *defect* in the cargo rather than the *inherent characteristics* of the cargo, then the shipper will be liable if it did not inform the shipowner of the danger posed by the defect.[11] In *The Amphion*,[12] a cargo of bagged fishmeal carried under charterparty caught fire and damaged the ship. It was an inherent characteristic of fish meat to catch fire, if not treated with antioxidant. Ordinarily, a consignor would treat a cargo of fishmeal with antioxidant, which was not done in this case. Such a treatment would have significantly reduced the risk of the cargo catching fire. The English High Court held that the cause of the damage was not the inherent characteristics of the cargo, but it was the failure of the shipper to have it treated with antioxidant. Hence, the court held the shipper liable for the damage.

At common law, the duty is only in respect of cargo that is physically dangerous but also legally dangerous. In *Mitchell, Cotts & Co v Steel Bros & Co Ltd*,[13] a cargo of rice caused a delay in discharge as a result of difficulties in the shipper securing the necessary permissions during wartime. The English High Court held that the cargo was legally dangerous and hence the shipper liable for the loss caused by the delay.

To the contrary, in *The Darya Radhe*,[14] the English High Court said that cargo was not legally dangerous merely because it caused a delay in discharge, in the absence of some legal barrier to carriage or discharge of the cargo. In this case, a cargo of soybean meal pellets was shipped. There were rats in the cargo. The rats did not pose a threat to the ship or any other cargo. There was also no likelihood of any quarantine or dumping order because of the presence of the rats. Accordingly, the court held that the cargo was neither physically nor legally dangerous.

It is likely that a court will regard a cargo to be legally dangerous only if there will be a legal prohibition in relation to carriage or discharge as opposed to a mere delay. It is doubtful if the approach in *Mitchell, Cotts & Co* will be followed except perhaps

---

[10] *The Athanasia Comninos and Georges Chr Lemos* [1990] 1 Lloyd's Rep 277 (EW HC).

[11] See *Mediterranean Freight Services Ltd v BP Oil International Ltd (The Fiona)* [1994] 2 Lloyd's Rep 506 (EW CA).

[12] *General Feeds Inc v Burnham Shipping Corpn (The Amphion)* [1991] 2 Lloyd's Rep 101 (EW HC).

[13] [1916] 2 KB 610, [1916–17] All ER Rep 578 (EW HC).

[14] *Bunge SA v Adm Do Brasil Ltd (The Darya Radhe)* [2009] EWHC 845 (Comm), [2010] 1 All ER (Comm) 784, [2009] 2 Lloyd's Rep 175, [2009] All ER (D) 174 (Apr) (EW HC).

in the case of a very substantial delay caused by legal requirements associated with the carriage or discharge of the cargo.

11.3 Duty Under Article IV(6)

Article IV(6) of the Rules[15] reads as follows:

> 6. Goods of an inflammable, explosive or dangerous nature to the shipment whereof the carrier, master or agent of the *carrier has not consented with knowledge* of their nature and character, may at any time before discharge be *landed at any place, or destroyed or rendered innocuous* by the carrier without compensation and the *shipper of such goods shall be liable for all damages and expenses* directly or indirectly arising out of or resulting from such shipment. If any such goods *shipped with such knowledge and consent* shall become a danger to the ship or cargo, they may in like manner be *landed at any place, or destroyed or rendered innocuous by the carrier without liability* on the part of the carrier *except to general average*, if any. [emphasis added]

There are two parts to Article IV(6). One is where the carrier has accepted the cargo without knowledge of the dangerous nature and character of the cargo. Another is where it accepts the cargo with such knowledge. Each part is, in turn, analysed separately below.

In *The Giannis NK*,[16] Lord Lloyd said that the words 'dangerous nature' in the Article carried a broad meaning. First, they are not confined to goods of an inflammable or explosive nature or the like. Second, goods may be dangerous within the meaning of this Article if they are dangerous to other goods, even though they are not dangerous to the vessel itself. In this case, Lord Steyn broke down this Article into three components as follows:

> Article 4, r 6 is a very specific provision. It falls into three parts. The first part allows the carrier to land, destroy or render innocuous goods of a dangerous nature to the shipment of which the carrier has not consented. The carrier may exercise this liberty without incurring any liability to pay compensation.
>
> The second part makes the shipper liable for all expenses directly or indirectly arising from such shipment. The words which I have emphasized seem to be a reference back to a shipment as described in the first part.
>
> The third part concerns shipment of goods to which the carrier has consented with knowledge of their nature and character but which become a danger to the ship or cargo. Again, the carrier is allowed to land, destroy or render innocuous the goods without incurring any liability 'except to general average, if any'. In such cases, however, the shipper is not liable in damages to the carrier.

---

[15] The Hague/Hague-Visby Rules.

[16] *Effort Shipping Co Ltd v Linden Management SA (The Giannis NK)* [1998] AC 605, [1998] 1 Lloyd's Rep 337, [1998] All ER (D) 10, [1998] 1 All ER 495, [1998] 2 WLR 206, [1998] 4 LRC 97 (UK HL).

11.3.1 Part 1 of Article IV(6)

The Article does not expressly say that the shipper has to notify the carrier of the dangerous nature and characteristics of the cargo, as does common law. However, it essentially means it, unless the carrier by any other means knew it already, by providing that the cargo may be destroyed without compensation and that the shipper will be liable for all damages and expenses arising from the shipment, where dangerous cargo is shipped without the carrier's knowledge of the nature and characteristics of the cargo.

Indeed, the reference to the carrier in this Article seems indeed to mean the shipowner. For instance, the dangerous cargo will be landed at any place, destroyed or rendered innocuous by the shipowner rather than a contractual carrier (if the two are different entities). Similarly, the reference to the 'carrier, master or agent of the carrier' also seems to refer to the shipowner, master or agent of the shipowner (which for this purpose may be the contractual carrier, if it is a different entity).

In *The Giannis NK*,[17] a cargo of groundnuts was shipped. Unknown to the shipper, the cargo was infected by khapra beetles. As a result, the cargo was condemned at the discharge port and ordered to be dumped into the sea, which the shipowner had to carry out. The House of Lords found the shipper liable under Article IV(6), holding that the liability under this Article was strict and that it covered both physically dangerous and legally dangerous cargo.

In *The Kapitan Sakharov*,[18] a dangerous cargo, without notice to the carrier, was carried on deck. The cargo exploded and, as a result, the ship suffered damage. The heat got transferred to an under-deck cargo, which was a highly volatile and flammable one. This resulted in a second explosion of the under-deck cargo, which the ship was not fit to carry and the carriage of which rendered the ship unseaworthy at the outset of the voyage. As a consequence of the heat-transfer, there was an explosion in the under-deck cargo, resulting in the ship sinking. The English Court of Appeal held that the on-deck cargo owners were liable only for the damage caused by the first explosion, but not the second one, as the 'effective cause'—which was also called 'most effective', 'dominant', and 'proximate' cause—of the second explosion was the unseaworthiness of the ship rather than the first explosion.

11.3.2 Part 2 of Article IV(6)

The second part to the Article permits the carrier to land at any place, destroy or render innocuous the cargo even when carried by informed consent of the carrier

[17] *Effort Shipping Co Ltd v Linden Management SA (The Giannis NK)* [1998] AC 605, [1998] 1 Lloyd's Rep 337, [1998] All ER (D) 10, [1998] 1 All ER 495, [1998] 2 WLR 206, [1998] 4 LRC 97 (UK HL).

[18] *Northern Shipping Co v Deutsche Seereederei GmbH and Others (The Kapitan Sakharov)* [2000] 2 Lloyd's Rep 255, [2000] All ER (D) 281 (EW CA).

when the cargo becomes a danger to the ship or cargo. The Article, in such a case, relieves the carrier from liability for loss of the cargo as between the carrier and the shipper/lawful holder of the bill of lading. The relief is limited to the loss of the cargo of the particular shipper who shipped the dangerous cargo under the particular bill of lading. It does not affect other cargo, as each bill of lading is an independent contract. In the event the carrier had to destroy other cargoes, the carrier will be liable for them unless the incident falls under an excepted peril of the sea and the carrier was not negligent. The carrier's liability for the other cargoes may also be founded in Article III(1) as acceptance of the dangerous cargo from a shipper may render the ship unseaworthy at the outset of the voyage unless the danger was not one that could be discovered then by any exercise of due diligence.

11.3.3 Article IV(3) Defence to Shipper

Article IV(3) avails a general defence available to the shipper, which is as follows:

> 3. The shipper shall not be responsible for loss or damage sustained by the carrier or the ship arising or resulting from any cause without the act, fault or neglect of the shipper, his agents or his servants.

In *The Giannis NK*,[19] the House of Lords held that Article IV(3) did not qualify the duty in Article IV(6). Lord Steyn described Article IV(6) as a 'free-standing provision'. Article IV(3) exempts the shipper from liability only where the damage was caused without any 'act', among others, of the shipper. Shipping a dangerous cargo is an *act* of the shipper, that will disentitle the shipper to Article IV(3) defence, as opposed to where the damage is caused by an *act of God or enemy* which is not within the *control* of the shipper. Article IV(3) provides as follows:

> The shipper shall not be responsible for loss or damage sustained by the carrier or the ship arising or resulting from any cause without the act, fault or neglect of the shipper, his agents or his servants.

It is not doubted that the defence available to the shipper will also be available to a subsequent holder of the bill, where the latter is sued by the carrier as the transferee of the liabilities under Section 3(1) of the UK Carriage of Goods by Sea Act 1992, that puts the latter "subject to the same liabilities under that contract as if he had been a party to that contract".[20]

---

[19] *Effort Shipping Co Ltd v Linden Management SA (The Giannis NK)* [1998] AC 605, [1998] 1 Lloyd's Rep 337, [1998] All ER (D) 10, [1998] 1 All ER 495, [1998] 2 WLR 206, [1998] 4 LRC 97 (UK HL).

[20] See the Chap. 2.2.10.3 for a brief discussion of transfer of liabilities under Section 3(1) of the UK 1992 Act.

11.4 Transfer of Shipper's Liability to Bill of Lading Holder

The transfer of shipper's liabilities under the bill of lading to the holder of the bill is, at present, governed by Section 3(1) of the Carriage of Goods by Sea Act 1992 in the UK, and identically by Section 3(1) of the Bills of Lading Act in Singapore, which subject has been covered earlier.[21] In essence, the liabilities will be transferred to the holder of the bill when it takes or demands delivery, makes a claim thereunder, took delivery before it held the bill. The transfer of liabilities to the holder does not exonerate the original shipper.[22] Hence, both the shipper and the holder of the bill (or the one who took before coming to hold the bill)[23] will be liable. While there is no doubt that liabilities such as that to pay freight will be thus transferred, it remains arguable whether the liability arising from the shipment of dangerous cargo is also transferred, because this liability is arguably imposed personally on the 'shipper'. In *The Giannis NK*,[24] Lord Lloyds and Lord Steyn seem to have assumed this liability too will be transferred to the holder of the bill once the Section 3(1) of Act is triggered. Despite that, this point remains an arguable one.

For Malaysia,[25] the transfer of the shipper's liability is still governed by Section 2 of the UK Bills of Lading Act 1855 and any common law regime in England on the subject. The Section 2 reads as follows:

> 2. Nothing herein contained shall prejudice or affect any right of stoppage *in transitu*, or any right to claim freight against the original shipper or *owner*, or any *liability of the consignee or endorsee* by reason or in consequence of his being such consignee or endorsee, or of *his receipt of the goods* by reason or in consequence of such consignment or endorsement. [emphasis added]

Apart from the above, by the principle of mutuality[26] recognised at the common law, the scheme of transfer of liabilities in Malaysia must be similar to that under the 1992 Act.

Insofar as the loss of the dangerous cargo because it is landed at any place, destroyed or rendered innocuous due to the danger is concerned, it is clear that the carrier is relieved from liability and hence a shipper or holder of the bill of lading will have no claim against the carrier for this.[27] This is so irrespective of whether the danger was known to the carrier or not. This position will be the same

---

[21] See Chap. 2.2.10.3.

[22] Section 3(3) of the UK Carriage of Goods by Sea Act 1992/Singapore Bills of Lading Act—discussed in Chap. 2.2.10.3.

[23] E.g. having furnished an indemnity-undertaking to the carrier.

[24] *Effort Shipping Co Ltd v Linden Management SA (The Giannis NK)* [1998] AC 605, [1998] 1 Lloyd's Rep 337, [1998] All ER (D) 10, [1998] 1 All ER 495, [1998] 2 WLR 206, [1998] 4 LRC 97 (UK HL).

[25] Save for the states/territories of Penang, Malacca, Sabah, Sarawak and Labuan. See Chap. 1.3.6.2.

[26] Discussed in Chap. 2.2.10.7.

[27] Article IV(6).

for jurisdictions like Malaysia[28] that subscribes to the old UK 1855 Act regime and to those like Singapore that subscribes to the new UK 1992 regime, as it ensues from Article III(6) of the Rules, which is the same both in the Hague and Hague-Visby Rules.

[28] Save for the states/territories of Penang, Malacca, Sabah, Sarawak and Labuan. See Chap. 1.3.6.2.

Part III
Charterparties

Chapter 12
Charterparty: Introduction

This chapter introduced charterparties in general. It covers demise charter, time charter and voyage charter. It also notes other variants of charters like trip and slot charters. Having thus introduced, it visits a few matters that are common to charterparties, particularly time and voyage charters. They include some common terms found in charterparties, questions of title to bunkers when the charterer did not pay the bunkers supplier at the time of redelivery of the ship with the bunkers, sale of the ship in midst of the charter term. Then, a detailed treatment is given to cancelling date and the shipowner's obligation as to the approach voyage. This is followed by a consideration of frustration. Finally, a visit is made to the dispute resolution mechanisms in charterparty cases. The section includes a brief discussion the popular arbitration clauses such as London Maritime Arbitrators Association (LMAA), Society of Maritime Arbitrators (SMA) and Singapore Chamber of Maritime Arbitration (SCMA) clauses. It also considers, briefly, appeals and applications arising from arbitration to the court under the UK Arbitration Act 1996 and the system in countries that have adopted the United Nations Commission on International Trade Law Model Law on International Commercial Arbitration (UNCITRAL Model Law), e.g. Singapore and Malaysia.

12.1 Introduction

A charterparty is an agreement between a shipowner and a charterer, whereby the shipowner allows the charterer to use the ship on certain terms. In the same way how a charterparty can be entered into between a shipowner and a charterer, it can also be entered into between a charterer and sub-charterer. In such a case, the principal charterer is called the head-charterer. It can similarly go down the line with sub-charterer and sub-sub-charterer, and so forth. There are essentially three types of charterparty, namely, demise charter, time charter and voyage charter. There are also some other types of charterparty such as a trip charter and slot charter.

A. Kasi, *The Law of Carriage of Goods by Sea*,
https://doi.org/10.1007/978-981-33-6793-7_12

A charterparty, unlike a bill of lading, is not a shipping document in the sense of being the receipt for the cargo, but it is merely an agreement. Accordingly, when the cargo is carried pursuant to a charterparty, a bill of lading will be issued to acknowledge receipt/shipment of the cargo that will be transferable in the usual way.[1] However, the bill of lading, in such case, will not perform the function of carriage contract as between the shipowner and the charterer.[2] But the bill will perform such function when in the hands of someone other than the charterer.[3] It follows that, unlike bills of lading, there is no question of transferability in the case of charterparty.[4] A bill of lading will usually be largely regulated by statutes incorporating the Hague or Hague-Visby Rules, but in the case of a charterparty, the regulation is almost solely by agreement of parties, which may voluntarily incorporate the Hague or Hague-Visby Rules. Such incorporation clauses are called 'clause paramount'. The agreement usually will be in one of the standard forms, with desired modifications. The popular forms are those made by Baltic and International Maritime Council (BIMCO) and Association of Ship Brokers & Agents (USA) Inc (ASBA). Charterparties are also sometime entered into with fixtures, [5] which may or may not be followed by a charterparty in one of the standard forms. A fixture is a commercial note of a concluded charter-agreement, whereby the ship is 'fixed' with the charter.[6] Such fixtures may also incorporate one of the standard forms by reference.[7] Sometimes, the fixture will include an expression 'clean fixed'. This means that the parties have considered that they have concluded a binding charterparty.[8] Where parties have not expressly agreed on some matter, the court may find an implied term and there are a number of such terms that the courts have regularly implied.

In this chapter, the three types of charterparty are introduced together with some other variants of charterparty. Then, some common terms found in charterparties are discussed. That is followed by a visit to title to bunkers, sale of the ship in midst of the charter term and the shipowner's obligations related to approach voyage and cancelling date. Finally, a brief visit is made to the operation of doctrine of frustration in charterparty cases and dispute resolution mechanisms in charterparty cases, namely popular arbitration clauses and appeals and application therefrom under the

---

[1] See Chapter 2.2.10.

[2] Because the charterparty will perform the function of the shipping contract between the shipowner and the charterer.

[3] See Chapter 4.2.1.

[4] Although there is nothing to prevent a charterparty being assigned and novated to a new charterer by agreement of all the parties (the shipowner, the current charterer and the new charterer), as will usually happen when the ship is sold in the midst of the charter term.

[5] *Freight Connect (S) Pte Ltd v Paragon Shipping Pte Ltd* [2015] SGCA 37, [2015] 5 SLR 178 (SA CA).

[6] *The Rainbow Spring* [2003] SGCA 31, [2003] 3 SLR 362 (SG CA).

[7] *Freight Connect (S) Pte Ltd v Paragon Shipping Pte Ltd* [2015] SGCA 37, [2015] 5 SLR 178 (SA CA).

[8] *Granit SA v Benship International Inc* [1994] 1 Lloyd's Rep 526 (EW HC); *Transgrain Shipping BV v Global Transporte Oceanico SA (The Mexico 1) (HC)* [1988] 2 Lloyd's Rep 149 (EW HC); *The Rainbow Spring* [2003] SGCA 31, [2003] 3 SLR 362 (SG CA).

UK Arbitration Act 1996 and the arbitration statues based on the UNCITRAL Model Law by particular reference to Singapore and Malaysia.

12.2 Types of Charterparty

The three types of charterparties, a variant of hybrid charterparty called 'trip charter' and slot charter, and the signification of the classification, will be considered below. That will be followed by a consideration of the standard forms of charterparties.

12.2.1 Demise Charter

A demise charter, also called a 'bareboat' charter, is one whereby the shipowner gives the entire control and management of the ship to the charterer for a certain period of time in return for a hire. This means the crew including the master will be employed by the charterer. Of course, the cost of the fuel will be on the charterer. The control over employment of the ship and navigation of the ship will be in the hands of the charterer, under whose employment the master is retained.

The hire will be paid on a daily rate from delivery of the ship by the shipowner to the redelivery of the ship by the charterer. Usually the hire will be paid for every two weeks in advance by two weeks. At the time of delivery, the charterer will pay the shipowner for the bunkers in the ship. At the time of redelivery, the shipowner will pay the charterer for the bunkers in the ship. Bills of lading to shippers or consignors will be issued by the demise charterer without any involvement of the shipowner, as it will be the charterer and its master responsible for the receipt, carriage and discharge of the cargo. A cargo claim, for which liability is incurred by the demise charterer, can be brought against the ship *in rem* and the ship can be arrested.[9]

12.2.2 Time Charter

In a time-charter, the ship will be made available for use by the charterer for a certain period of time in return for a hire on a daily rate. However, this will not pass the control and management of the ship to the charterer. The crew including the master will be under the employment of the shipowner. It does not matter that the charterparty says that the crew will be deemed to the employee of the charterer. The cost of the ship management company, insurance and maintaining the class will be on the shipowner. The cost of the fuel and port charges will be on the charterer, as well as the cost of loading, stowing and discharge. The control over navigation of the ship will remain

[9] UK Senior Courts Act 1981, Section 21(4)(b)(i).

with the shipowner. The charter will be entitled to make orders to the shipowner (or his master) as to employment of the ship, e.g. ordering the ship to proceed to a particular port.

The hire will be paid on a daily basis from delivery[10] of the ship to redelivery[11] of the ship. Usually the hire will be paid for every two weeks in advance by two weeks. Payment for the bunkers on delivery and redelivery will be the same as in the case of demise charter.

It is not common for time charters to require the shipowner to incorporate the terms of the charter into the bills of lading that the shipowner would issue to the shippers or consignors. In a time-charter, the performance and speed of the ship matters. If the ship is slow, that will affect the utility of the ship to the charterer. Hence, it is usual to find a warranty as to speed in time charters. In addition to that, there will also usually be a clause requiring the shipowner to prosecute the voyage with utmost dispatch during the charter. Even if not expressed, such a clause should ordinarily be implied as such an obligation is important part of consideration given by the shipowner. If the ship is temporarily not available for employment by the charterer during the time charter, then the hire for that period will be suspended, which is called 'off-hire'.

Ship is not liable *in rem* and cannot be arrested for liability incurred by the time charterer. However, usually, as the bill of lading will be issued by or on behalf of the shipowner, a cargo claimant will be able to take action *in rem* against the ship and arrest the ship, as the liability in such case will be directly incurred by the shipowner under the bill of lading.

12.2.3 Voyage Charter

A voyage charter is one under which the shipowner undertakes to perform a voyage for the charterer in return for a freight as opposed to a hire. The freight may be calculated as a lump sum or on a rate based on the quantity loaded. There will be a laytime in the voyage charter, i.e. time limit within which the charterer must load and discharge. If the charterer exceeds the laytime, then the charterer will be liable for demurrage, i.e. compensation on a daily rate. There is no such thing as laytime or demurrage in time charter, as he time-charterer would simply pay the hire on from the date of delivery to the date of redelivery.

The control and management of the ship remains with the shipowner. The crew including the master remains under the employment of the shipowner. The control over navigation of the ship remains with the shipowner. There will be no option for charter to give orders as to employment of the ship where the ports are named in the charter. However, if the charter does not name the ports but give an option for the charterer to nominate them within a given range, then, the charterer may give orders as to employment of the ship limited to such nomination.

[10] Putting her at the disposal of the charterer.

[11] Putting her back at the disposal of the shipowner.

It is common for voyage charters to require the shipowner to issue charterparty bills of lading to the shippers or consignors, i.e. a bill of lading incorporating the terms of the bill of lading. It is usual for the voyage charter to allow two liens in favour of the shipowner, namely a lien on the cargo and a lien on the sub-freight. The former lien allows the shipowner to retain the cargo when the freight due to it is not paid. The latter lien allows the shipowner to intercept sub-freights due to the charterer.

Ship is not liable *in rem* and cannot be arrested for liability incurred by the time charterer. However, usually, as the bill of lading will be issued by or on behalf of the shipowner, a cargo claimant will be able to take action *in rem* against the ship and arrest the ship, as the liability in such case will be directly incurred by the shipowner under the bill of lading.

12.2.4 Trip Charter and Importance of Classification

There are also other types of charters like trip charter, which is a hybrid of time charter and voyage charter. This happens when a charter that has some of the characteristics of a voyage charter is made in the form of a time charter. The same is true when a charter having some characteristics of a time charter is made in the form of a voyage charter, for instance, in the case of consecutive voyages.[12] Despite being labelled as 'trip' charter, it is necessary to classify it as either time charter or voyage charter, because the legal consequences differ depending on the classification.

For instance, the UK Law Reform (Frustrated Contracts) Act 1943[13] applies to time charters but not to voyage charters. A trip charter having the characteristics of a voyage charter made in the form of a time charter has been classified as a time charter.[14] The classification is also important as there is no set-off against freight[15] but a set-off may be claimed against hire.

Another type of charterparty is what is called 'slot charter'. This is a variant of voyage charterparty on a share basis, whereby the shipowner gives a slot of the ship in a voyage to the charterer. This usually happens with container ships.

---

[12] As it happened in *Suisse Atlantique Société d'Armement Maritime SA v Rotterdamsche Kolen Centrale NV* [1967] 1 AC 361 (UK HL).

[13] In Singapore, there is a materially identical Act, namely, Frustrated Contracts Act. There is no such separate Act in Malaysia, like India, but the Contracts Act 1950 deals with frustration of contracts.

[14] *Ocean Tramp Tankers Corpn v V/O Sovfracht (The Eugenia)* [1964] 2 QB 226, [1964] 1 All ER 161, [1964] 2 WLR 114, [1963] 2 Lloyd's Rep 381 (EW CA).

[15] *Aries Tanker Corpn v Total Transport Ltd (The Aries)* [1977] 1 WLR 185 (UK HL).

12.2.5 Standard Forms of Charterparty

Whichever the type of charter, usually the charterparty is entered into by one of the standard forms, with necessary modifications. New York Produce Exchange (NYPE)[16] and BIMCO BALTIME forms[17] are popular for time charters for dry cargo. BIMCO GENCON forms are popular for voyage charters. For voyage charter to carry fuel oil, forms such as EXXONVOY and BEEPEEVOY, and to carry gas, forms such as ASBATANKVOY and now ASBAGASVOY are common, while SHELLTIME and BPTIME for time charter to carry fuel oil. In the case of demise and time charters, usually the hire will be payable in advance.

A charterparty is not a shipping document in the sense how bills of lading, seaway bills or ship's delivery orders are shipping documents. An important characteristic of those documents is that they acknowledge receipt of the goods by the shipowner or the shipment. A charterparty is merely an agreement to carry the goods but does not in itself acknowledge receipt of the goods or the shipment. Hence, when goods are carried following a charterparty, there will be issued a bill of lading. However, as between the shipowner and the charterer, the bill of lading does not have the function of 'agreement' but has the function of receipt of goods.[18] Sometimes, a charterparty is also loosely called a 'shipping documents' as there is no hard and fast definition of 'shipping documents'.

12.3 Some Common Terms in Charterparties

There are certain terms quite commonly found in charterparties. Some of such terms will be discussed in this section, namely clause paramount, risk allocation in deck cargo and exclusion clauses. At the end of this section, a discussion will be made of construction of competing clauses found in charterparties, for instance where there is a conflict between a typed clause and a pre-printed clause, etc.

---

[16] The NYPE forms are a joint work of Association of Shipbrokers and Agents (ASBA), BIMCO and the Singapore Maritime Foundation (SMF), copyrighted by ASBA. The latest version is NYPE 2015. The previous editions were 1946 and 1993 versions.

[17] The latest version is BIMCO BALTIME 1939 (revised 2001).

[18] *Rodocanachi, Sons & Co v Milburn Bros* (1886) 18 QBD 67 (EW CA); *President of India v Metcalfe Shipping Co Ltd (The Dunelmia)* [1970] 1 QB 289, [1969] 3 All ER 1549, [1969] 3 WLR 1120 (EW CA). See Chapter 2.2.10.8 for more detailed discussion of this.

12.3.1 Clause Paramount

The Hague/Hague-Visby Rules statutorily apply only to bills of lading but not to any other shipping documents[19] or charterparties. In the case of such other shipping documents or charterparties, it is very common to find a clause paramount, that will voluntarily incorporate, by reference, the Hague or Hague-Visby Rules or a statute giving effect to one of these Rules.

Difficulties have arisen from poorly drafted or complex clause paramount. In *The Agios Lazaros*,[20] it was a voyage charter in a BIMCO GENCON form to carry a cargo from Preveza (in Greece) to Rotterdam/Hamburg, entered into on 5 January 1972. To it, a typed clause was added, saying:

> 31. New Jason clause, both to blame collision clause, P and I bunkering clause and Chamber of Shipping War Risks clauses Nos. 1 and 2 and also *Paramount clause* are deemed to be *incorporated* in this charterparty" [emphasis added].

The clause did not say which Rules were incorporated by the clause paramount. The English Court of Appeal had to decide if the fate of the clause paramount. The court said that it should strive to give effect to this incorporation, rather than render it meaningless, by making all reasonable implications, and held that the clause meant incorporation of the Hague Rules. At the time the charterparty was entered into, there were two conventions in existence, namely, the Hague Rules of 1924 and the Hague-Visby Rules of 1968. Greece had not subscribed to any of them, while the UK had subscribed to the Hague Rules.[21] In coming to this conclusion, the court had in mind that the charterparty had a connection to the English law as it provided for arbitration in London presumably under English law. If the facts were to appear today, then likely it will be the Hague-Visby Rules as amended by SDR Protocol applicable in London imported by the clause paramount, as noted, by *dicta*, in *The Superior Pescadores*.[22] In this case, a bill of lading, for carriage from Antwerp in Belgium in 2008, contained a clause paramount which read as follows:

> The Hague Rules contained in the International Convention … dated Brussels the 25th August 1924 as enacted in the country of shipment shall apply to this contract.

By 2008, the Rules in force in Belgium was the Hague-Visby Rules. The English Court of Appeal held that the Rules imported by the clause paramount was the Hague-Visby Rules.

---

[19] Like sea waybills and ship's delivery orders.

[20] *Nea Agrex SA v Baltic Shipping Co Ltd and Intershipping Charter Co (The Agios Lazaros)* [1976] QB 933, [1976] 2 All ER 842, [1976] 2 WLR 925, [1976] 2 Lloyd's Rep 47 (EW CA).

[21] At that time, the UK Carriage of Goods by Sea Act 1971 did not come into force, which came into force only on 23 June 1977 by virtue of SI 1977 No 981. The Rules adopted by the UK at that time was the Hague Rules by virtue of the UK Carriage of Goods by Sea Act 1924.

[22] *Yemgas Fzco v Superior Pescadores SA Panama (The Superior Pescadores)* [2016] EWCA Civ 101, [2016] 2 All ER (Comm) 104, [2016] 1 Lloyd's Rep 561 (EW CA).

Another issue with clause paramount in charterparties is that the imported Rules will need to be manipulated if it is to have an effective meaning in the context of charterparty. An example of a judicial manipulation can be seen in *Adamastos Shipping Co Ltd v Anglo-Saxon Petroleum Co Ltd*.[23] In this case, the clause paramount in the charterparty read:

> This *bill of lading* shall have effect subject to the provisions of the United States Carriage of Goods by Sea Act 1936. [emphasis added]

This case was, on appeal, decided by the House of Lords that had to resolve a few issues. First, the reference to "This bill of lading" while it was a charterparty. The House held that the reference to "This bill of lading" was to the charterparty. Second was the issue of Section 5 of the US Carriage of Goods by Sea Act 1936, which is materially identical to Article V of the Hague/Hague-Visby Rules, expressly excluding application of the Act to charterparties. The House gave effect to the commercial intention of the parties by holding that this section did not bar contractual incorporation of the Act, insofar as other provisions of the Act were concerned, into the charterparty. Third was the issue of Section 13 of the Act that rendered the Act applicable only to shipments from or to US ports in foreign trade, which was not the case in this case. The House again held, giving effect to the commercial intention of the parties, that this did not bar the contractual incorporation of the other provisions of the Act into the charterparty.[24]

12.3.2 Allocation of Risk in Deck Cargo

Both in time and voyage charter, usually the charterer charters the whole vessel and has the liberty to fill the cargo carrying capacity of the ship. However, when the charterer, in its economic interest, loads cargo on deck, the usual higher risk associated with deck cargo is involved. In such cases, it is common for shipowners to contractually allocate the risk associated with deck cargo to the charterer. The common clause will say that the deck cargo is carried at 'charterer's risk'.[25] It may also take the form of a clear exclusion clause that says all liability of the shipowner for loss or damage to cargo 'howsoever caused' is excluded.[26]

---

[23] [1959] AC 133, [1958] 1 All ER 725, [1958] 2 WLR 688, [1958] 1 Lloyd's Rep 73 (UK HL).

[24] Another issue was as to meaning of 'loss or damage' in Section 4 of the Act, which is materially identical to Article IV of the Hague/Hague-Visby Rules. It was the charterer's argument that the shipowner could not rely on the Section 4 defences because the claim was for economic loss consequent upon the ship broking down on her first ballast voyage to the loading port and the 'loss or damage' referred to in the section is loss or damage to the cargo. The House rejected this argument and afforded to the shipowners the benefit of the Section 4 defences.

[25] Eg. *Exercise Shipping Co Ltd v Bay Maritime Lines Ltd (The Fantasy)* [1992] 1 Lloyd's Rep 235 (EW CA).

[26] *Kuwait Maritime Transport Co v Rickmers Linie KG (The Danah)* [1993] 1 Lloyd's Rep 351 (EW HC).

Generally, exclusion clauses will be interpreted narrowly and general exclusion clauses have been not to cover liability for negligence.[27] However, when it is about allocation of risk between the shipowner and charterer in the matter of deck cargo, courts may interpret it more widely so that even a general exclusion clause have been held to cover liability for negligence. In *The Imvros*,[28] the exclusion clause read:

> Charterers are permitted to load cargo on the vessel's deck...provided always that the permissible loads...are not exceeded...The vessel is not to be held responsible for any loss of or damage to the cargo carried on deck whatsoever and howsoever caused.

The responsibility for loading and stowing was on the charterers under the supervision of the master, with an unamended cl. 8(a) of the NYPE 1993 form, which is largely similar to the same numbered clause in the NYPE 2015 form. Clause 8(a), in material part, reads[29] as follows:

> [T]he Charterers shall perform all cargo handling, including but not limited to loading, stowing, trimming, lashing, securing, dunnaging, unlashing, discharging, and tallying, at their risk and expense, under the supervision of the Master.

The charterparty provided that the crew was to be treated as servants of the charterer. The crew was negligent in lashing the deck cargo rendering the ship unseaworthy in the sense of being uncargoworthy. The question before the English High Court was whether the exclusion clause excepted liability also for the unseaworthiness. The court answered the question in the positive. This case decision has been subject of criticism as the shipowner's duty to provide a seaworthy and cargoworthy ship had been undermined, and there is scope for argument on this point.[30] The Singapore Court of Appeal in *Sunlight Mercantile Pte Ltd and Another v Ever Lucky Shipping Ltd*[31] refused to follow *The Imvros*. In *The Socol 3*,[32] the ship was time-chartered under NYPE 1993 form. Clause 13(b) of the form, which is similar to the same numbered clause in the NYPE 2015 form (save for the reference to the 'Vessel' in the 1993 form was materially changed to the 'deck cargo' in the 2015 form),[33] contained an indemnity clause reading:

> In the event of deck cargo being carried, the owners are to be and are hereby indemnified by the charterers for any loss and/or damage and/or liability of whatsoever nature caused to the *Vessel* as a result of the carriage of deck cargo and which would not have arisen had deck cargo not been loaded. [emphasis added]

---

[27] See Chapter 7.2.3.

[28] *Transocean Liners Reederei GmbH v Euxine Shipping Co Ltd (The Imvros)* [1999] 1 All ER (Comm) 724, [1999]1 Lloyd's Rep 848 (EW HC).

[29] The part is the same in both the 1993 and 2015 forms.

[30] See *Belships v Canadian Forest Products Ltd* (1999) 45 Lloyd's Alert Service (Canadian CA).

[31] [2003] SGCA 47, 2004] 1 SLR 171 (SG CA).

[32] *Onego Shipping & Chartering BV v JSC Arcadia Shipping (The Socol 3)* [2010] EWHC 777, [2010] 2 Lloyd's Rep 221 (EW HC).

[33] This is a matter for parties adopting the NYPE 2015 to consider if they wish to refer to the Vessel or the deck cargo in this context.

Clause 8(a) of the form,[34] that required the cargo to be loaded under the master's supervision was not modified to impose 'responsibility' on the shipowners. Timber was loaded on deck and fell overboard during the voyage. This was attributable to (i) inadequate stowage; (ii) inadequate lashing equipment and care about lashing during the voyage; and (iii) (c) instability of the ship, known only to the shipowners. The charterer made a claim for the loss against the shipowners, who relied on the above clause. The court held that the clause did not protect the shipowners from liability for the loss because the loss was effectively caused by shipowner's negligence and unseaworthiness rather than carriage of deck cargo.[35] A clause providing for 'shipper's risk', as opposed to 'charterer's risk', has been more narrowly construed.[36]

It is common that standard deck cargo clauses are modified to allocate some responsibilities/risks on to the shipowner. For instance, in *The Fantasy*,[37] the clause required the crew to check and protect the deck cargo during voyage. In *The Visurgis*,[38] it placed the responsibility for lashing on the crew. However, *The Imvros* suggests that if a clause in the charterparty says the crew is the servant of the charterer, then the responsibility placed on the crew will not render the shipowner liable. *The Imvros* has been subject of criticism and contrary views are arguable. A contrary view could be supported with cases such *The Aquacharm*,[39] where the English High Court held that cl. 9 of the BIMCO BALTIME 1939 form, putting the master at the disposal of the charterer as regards employment, agency and other arrangements, does not mean that the master is to be treated as a servant of the charterer, when the shipowner is sued for negligence of the master. Clause 9 in the BIMCO BALTIME 1939 form (revised 2001) reads, in relevant part, as follows:

> The Master shall be under the orders of the Charterers as regards employment, agency, or other arrangements.

When a particular responsibility is allocated to charterer, such as loading and stowing, the effect is twofold. First, the shipowner is not liable for any loss that the charterer suffers a loss in connection with the allocated responsibility. Second, if the shipowner suffers a loss in connection with the allocated responsibility, the shipowner may claim that loss from the charterer.

---

[34] Largely similar to the same numbered clause in the NYPE 2015 form.

[35] The court pointed out: "[88] … cl 13(b) only applies to loss, damage or liability which is effectively caused by the carriage of deck cargo and not to loss, damage or liability effectively caused by negligence or breach of the obligation of seaworthiness."

[36] *Kuwait Maritime Transport Co v Rickmers Linie KG (The Danah)* [1993] 1 Lloyd's Rep 351 (EW HC).

[37] *Exercise Shipping Co Ltd v Bay Maritime Lines Ltd (The Fantasy)* [1992] 1 Lloyd's Rep 235 (EW CA).

[38] *The Visurgis* [1999] 1 Lloyd's Rep 218 (EW HC).

[39] *Actis Co Ltd v Sanko Steamship Co Ltd (The Aquacharm) (HC)* [1980] 2 Lloyd's Rep 237 (EW HC).

12.3.3 Exceptions Clauses

Usually, a wide exceptions clause will be found where there is no clause paramount, e.g. BIMCO BALTIME 1939 form.[40] If a clause paramount is there, any exceptions clause is likely to be narrow, e.g. NYPE 1946/1993/2015 forms. The exceptions clause in the BIMCO BALTIME 1939 form (revised 2001) reads as follows:

> 12. The Owners shall only be responsible for *delay* in delivery of the Vessel or for delay during the currency of the Charter and for *loss or damage to goods* onboard, if such delay or loss has been caused by *want to due diligence* on the part of the *Owners or their Manager* in making the Vessel *seaworthy* and fitted for the voyage or any other *personal act or omission or default of the Owners or their Manager*. The Owners shall not be responsible in any other case or for damage or delay whatsoever and howsoever caused even if caused by the neglect of default of their servants. [emphasis added]

There appears to be two portions in this clause. In the first portion, it covers the (i) delay in approach voyage and in prosecuting the charter voyage; and (ii) loss or damage to cargo on board. Liability for them is excepted unless (i) the delay or loss was occasioned by want of due diligence to make the ship seaworthy on part of the shipowner/manager; or (ii) any personal act, omission or default of the shipowners/managers. In the second portion, it covers any delay or damage caused by the neglect or default of servants of the shipowner/manager.

In *The Brabant*,[41] the English High Court construed the clause quite widely and held that the shipowner was entitled to the exception under the clause when there was *personally* no want of due diligence on part of the shipowner. This meant if a contract was negligence, the shipowner will be relieved of liability as long as the shipowner had appointed a competent contractor. This mitigates, in cases to which the exceptions clause apply, the effect of *The Muncaster Castle*,[42] where the House of Lords held that the Article III(1) duty of due diligence to make the ship seaworthy is a non-delegable one.[43] However, there can be a scope to argue contrary to *The Brabant,* because the word 'personal' does not appear when reference is made to the duty of due diligence to make the ship seaworthy, but it appears only in reference to any other act, omission or default of the shipowner or manager.

In *The TFL Prosperity*,[44] the shipowner misdescribed the high of the main deck to the charterer. The charterer instituted the action against the shipowner for economic loss resulting from the misdescription. The shipowner relied on the cl. 12 exception. The House of Lords narrowly construed the clause and held that exception in the second portion, i.e. relief from liability for neglect and default of servants, was only

---

[40] (Revised 2001).

[41] *Gesellschaft Burgerlichen Rechts and Others v Stockholms Rederiaktiebolag Svea* [1967] 1 QB 588, [1966] 1 All ER 961, [1966] 2 WLR 909 (EW HC).

[42] *Riverstone Meat Co Pty Ltd v Lancashire Shipping Company Ltd (The Muncaster Castle)* [1961] AC 807 (UK HL).

[43] See Chapter 9.2.1.

[44] *Tor Line AB v Alltrans Group of Canada (The TFL Prosperity)* [1984] 1 Lloyd's Rep 123 (UK HL).

for loss or damage to *goods*. Although the second portion does not make any reference to 'goods', the House read this into this portion by reference to the first portion which covers only the loss or damage to goods. Accordingly, the shipowner was not able to rely on the exception.

It must be observed that an exception clause cannot be treated as an indemnity clause, as demonstrated by the case of *The C Joyce*.[45] In this case, an exceptions clause in a voyage charterparty excluded liability of the shipowner for cargo claims, as between the shipowner and the charterer, except where the claim arose due to unseaworthiness of the ship. Cargo claims arose from the bill of lading holders against the shipowner. The shipowner settled them and made a claim for indemnity against the charterer. There was no indemnity clause in the charterparty and the English High Court was not willing to imply one. The shipowners attempted to rely on the exceptions clause for the indemnity. The court refused the claim, as the exceptions clause merely provided a defence to the shipowner in a suit of the charterer but not a cause of action against the charterer. However, had this been a time charter, the court might have implied an indemnity clause for the shipowner to claim on.[46]

A question as to exceptions clause arose in a peculiar context in *Classic Maritime Inc v Limbungan Makmur Sdn Bhd*.[47] This case involved a long term contract of affreightment to regularly carry iron ore pellets from a Canadian mine to Malaysia. It had an exceptions clause, cl. 32, that read as follows:

> **32. Exceptions**
>
> Neither the Vessel, her Master or Owners, *nor the Charterers*, Shippers or Receivers *shall be Responsible for* loss or damage to, or *failure to supply, load*, discharge or deliver the cargo *resulting From*: Act of God, act of war, act of public enemies, pirates or assailing thieves; arrest or restraint of princes, rulers or people; embargoes; seizure under legal process ...; floods; frosts; fogs; fires; epidemics; quarantine; Intervention of sanitary, customs or other constituted authorities; Blockades; Blockages; riots; insurrections; civil commotions; political disturbances; earthquakes; Landslips; explosions; collisions; strandings, and accidents of navigation; *accidents at the mine or Production facility* or to machinery or to loading equipment; accidents at the Receivers' works, Port, wharf or facility; or any other causes beyond the Owners', Charterers', Shippers' or Receivers' Control; always provided that any such events directly affect the performance of either party under This Charter Party. If any time is lost due to such events or causes such time shall not count as Laytime or demurrage (unless the Vessel is already on demurrage in which case only half time to count).

There was a dam burst in the mine halting production for some time and the charterer did not supply cargo over that period of time, which would have covered five shipments had supply been made. The shipowner claimed damages for breach of the contract of affreightment in respect of the five shipments. The charterer argued

---

[45] *Ben Shipping Co (Pte) Ltd v An-Board Bainne (The C Joyce)* [1986] 2 Lloyd's Rep 285 (EW HC).

[46] *Triad Shipping Co v Stellar Chartering & Brokerage Inc (The Island Archon)* [1995] 1 All ER 595, [1994] 2 Lloyd's Rep 227 (EW CA).

[47] [2019] EWCA Civ 1102, [2019] 4 All ER 1145, [2019] 2 All ER (Comm) 592, [2019] Bus LR 2854, [2020] 1 Lloyd's Rep 178, [2019] 6 WLUK 422, [2019] 1 CLC 982, [2019] CLY 2229 (EW CA).

that the cl. 32 was a *force majeure* clause. However, even if the accident did not happen, it was probable that the charterer would not have been able and willing to supply cargoes for the shipments in question. The English Court of Appeal found that the cl. 32 was not a *force majeure* clause and does not automatically come into operation upon a provided event happening. Accordingly, in order for the charterer to rely on the clause, the charterer must prove that it did not supply the cargo due as a result of the accident, which it failed to prove. This was so despite that the accident made it impossible to supply the cargo. Accordingly, the charterer was held liable in damages to the shipowner.

12.3.4 Construction of Competing Clauses

When there are competing clauses, a typed clause will take precedence over the pre-printed clause. In *Adamastos Shipping Co Ltd v Anglo-Saxon Petroleum Co Ltd,*[48] it was held that the typed clause paramount, added to the BIMCO BALTIME 1939 form (which form does not have a standard pre-printed clause paramount) , took precedence over the pre-printed exceptions clauses.

If a charterparty incorporates Inter-Club Agreement (ICA)[49] and also contains a clause paramount, if there is a conflict between the terms of the ICA and the Hague or Hague-Visby Rules incorporated by the clause paramount, the ICA terms have been held to prevail. In *The Strathnewton,*[50] the conflict was between the Hague Rules one-year time limitation and the ICA two-year time limitation. The English Court of Appeal held the ICA limitation to prevail and be applicable.

12.4 Title to Bunkers

In the case of time and voyage charters, when the vessel is redelivered, the shipowner will pay the charterer for the bunkers remaining in the ship. However, a problem may arise when the charterer has not paid the bunkers supplier and the supplier has retained title to the bunkers until payment. The general rule is that *nemo dat quod non habet*, that is, 'no one gives what he does not have.' This in effect means that one who does not have the title cannot pass the same to another. This rule has been statutorily codified in UK and many commonwealth counties, including Singapore[51]

---

[48] [1959] AC 133, [1958] 1 All ER 725, [1958] 2 WLR 688, [1958] 1 Lloyd's Rep 73 (UK HL).

[49] ICA is an agreement between the Protection and Indemnity (P&I) Clubs in the International Group (IG) as to apportionment of liability for cargo claims between shipowners and charterers. See Chapter 17 for more details of ICA.

[50] *D/S A/S Idaho v Peninsular and Oriental Steam Navigation Co (The Strathnewton)* [1983] 1 Lloyd's Rep 219 (EW CA).

[51] In Singapore, it is in Section 21 of the Sale of Goods Act.

and Malaysia.[52] In the UK, the general rule is in Section 21 of the Sale of Goods Act 1979. One of the exceptions to the general rule is a sale is by the purchaser in possession to a bona fine buyer. The exception is in Section 25(1) in the UK 1979 Act.[53] Accordingly, as the charterer will be a buyer in possession, the title will pass to the shipowner as long as the shipowner pays for it in good faith.

In light of the above, it is unnecessary to consider whether any conversion is committed by the charterer or the shipowner against the bunkers supplier when the bunkers are sold by the charterer to the shipowner while the title is retained by the unpaid bunkers supplier. The answer must be in the negative as conversion is about right to possession and not about right to property. As long as there is no interference to one's possessory rights, there is no conversion. In this case, although the title is retained by the bunkers supplier, the charterer has rightfully the right to possess the bunkers, until the bunkers supplier has exercised the option to call back the possession for non-payment. Accordingly, there is no conversion committed, i.e. no interreference to anyone's possessory right, when the bunkers are passed by the charterer lawfully possessing them to the shipowner.[54]

The English High Court in *Angara Maritime Ltd v Oceanconnect UK Ltd*[55] assumed that, when the charterer had not paid for the bunkers the title in which was retained by the bunkers supplier but sells it to the shipowner upon redelivery, a conversion would have been committed but for Section 25(1) of the UK Sale of Goods Act 1979.[56] This assumption is not sustainable, as Section 25(1) is about passing of property and conversion is about passing of possession. But the overall decision that the title passed to the shipowner by virtue of Section 25(1) is sound.

12.5 Sale of Ship While Serving Charter

If the ship is sold by the shipowner to a new owner while she is serving a charter, usually, an assignment and novation agreement or deed will be made between the outgoing owner, incoming owner and the charterer. However, if such an arrangement is not made, then the question arises as to the relationship between the parties.

When a demise charter is given, the possessory right over the ship is passed to the charterer. However, no such right passes in the case of a time or voyage charter.

In the case of a demise charter, because the possessory right is held by the charterer, it will likely be able to enforce it against the new owner who has acquired the proprietary right from the original shipowner. In such case, as the possessory right

---

[52] In Malaysia, it is in Section 27 of the Sale of Goods Act 1957.

[53] In Singapore, Section 25 of the Sale of Goods Act; in Malaysia, Section 30(2) of the Sale of Goods Act 1957.

[54] See Chapter 4.5 for a detailed discussion of this.

[55] [2010] EWHC 619, [2011] 1 Lloyd's Rep 61 (EW HC).

[56] Materially identical to Section 25 of the Singapore Sale of Goods Act, and quite materially similar to Section 30(2) of the Malaysian Sale of Goods Act 1957.

is subject to compliance by the charterer with the charterparty particularly payment of the hire, it will be incumbent upon the charterer to enter into, or at least to offer to enter into, the assignment and novation arrangements.

In the case of time and voyage charters, enforcing any right of the charterer against the new owner will be difficult. The charter will not neither have any possessory right nor any contractual right against the new owner.

Swiss Bank Corp v Lloyds Bank Ltd[57] suggests the charterer may hold the new owner liable on two bases. One, for tort of inducing breach of contract, if there is no provision in the sale agreement for the charter to continue. The other, for breach of constructive trust, if there is a provision in the sale agreement for the charter to continue. Whichever the base is relied upon by the charterer, it will be incumbent upon the charterer to enter into, or at least to offer to enter into, the assignment and novation arrangements to facilitate the charter continuing with the new owner.

12.6 Cancelling Date and Approach Voyage

This section will deal with cancelling date (a contractual option for the charterer to cancel the charterparty if the ship is not delivered/offered ready to load by a certain date) and approach voyage (an implied obligation of the shipowner to prosecute with reasonable dispatch to the place of delivery/loading).

12.6.1 Cancelling Date

The charterparty will state when the ship will be delivered (in the case of time charterparty) or be ready to load (in the case of voyage charterparty) , though this statement may not be so specific in some cases. The charterparty, whether time or voyage, will also usually state the cancelling date, after which the charterer will have a contractual option to cancel if the ship is not delivered/ready to load.

In the case of time charters under NYPE 2015 form, cl. 3 states the cancelling date, which also serves as the latest delivery date because there is no separate delivery date.[58] The clause reads as follows:

> If required by the Charterers, time on hire shall not commence before ___ … and should the Vessel not have been delivered on or before ___ … at the port or place …, the Charterers shall have the option of cancelling this Charter Party at any time but not later than the day of the Vessel's notice of delivery.

---

[57] [1979] Ch 548 (EW HC).

[58] Cl. 3 also provides for the earliest date, before the cancelling date, that the ship may be delivered so that the charterer will not be liable for hire, if the ship is delivered before the earliest date, for the period until the earliest date.

In the case of BIMCO BALTIME 1939 form (revised 2001), box 16 states the delivery date and box 22 states the cancelling date. In the case of voyage charters under BIMCO GENCON 1994 form, box 9 states the about 'expected ready to load' date and box 21 states the 'cancelling date'. There may be a time limit fixed to the right to exercise the cancelling option. For example, ASBATANKVOY form, in cl. 5, limits the time to 24 hours after the end of the cancelling date. The clause 5, in relevant part reads as follows:

> … Charterer shall have the option of cancelling this Charter by giving Owner notice of such cancellation within twenty-four (24) hours after such cancellation date; otherwise this Charter to remain in full force and effect.

Once the ship is in the position to come on hire in a time charterparty[59] or ready for delivery to load in a voyage charterparty,[60] the shipowner will give notice of delivery/readiness to load. From about this point in time, the hire or laytime starts.

The right to cancel is a contractual option and it is not necessary, to exercise the option, that the shipowner has committed any breach. Similarly, it is irrelevant that that the charterer itself was not ready to take delivery/load even if the shipowner had performed by the cancelling date.[61] Equally, the right to cancel is not affected by the fact that the late delivery/readiness to load has not caused any loss or prejudice to the charterer.[62] However, subsequent to cancellation, to claim damages, it is necessary that there is a breach by the shipowner.[63] Examples of breach would be failure to comply with the approach-voyage obligation and, in the case of a time-charterparty, failure to deliver in time. However, it is unlikely to be a breach, on its own, if the ship was not offered ready to load by the expected date under a voyage-charterparty, where that was not by any fault of the shipowner.

In *The Ailsa Craig*,[64] the charterer had to nominate the delivery port in Ghana/Nigeria range. The ship was to commence her approach voyage from Piraeus. The deviation point on the approach voyage was Las Palmas, by when the charterer will have to notify the nomination. Until the cancelling date, the ship was still in Piraeus. The charterer exercised the cancellation option, that was upheld by the English Court of Appeal. It was no bar that that charterer had not nominated the delivery port as the deviation point had not been reached. If the shipowner's failure to deliver/offer ready to load is attributable to the charterer, then the charterer will not have the option of cancelling.[65]

---

[59] NYPE 2015 form, cl. 2(d).

[60] BIMCO Gencon 1994 form, cl. 6(3).

[61] *Compania de Naviera Nedelka SA of Panama v Tradax International SA of Panama City RP (The Tres Flores)* [1974] QB 264, [1973] 3 All ER 967, [1973] 3 WLR 545 (EW CA).

[62] See *Koufos v C Czarnikow Ltd (The Heron II)* [1969] 1 AC 350, [1967] 3 All ER 686, [1967] 3 WLR 1491 (UK HL).

[63] *Marbienes Compania Naviera SA v Ferrostaal AG (The Democritos)* [1976] 2 Lloyd's Rep 149 (EW CA).

[64] *Mansel Oil Ltd v Troon Storage Tankers SA (The Ailsa Craig)* [2009] EWCA Civ 425, [2009] 2 Lloyd's Rep 371 (EW CA).

[65] *Armement Adolf Deppe v John Robinson & Co Ltd* [1917] 2 KB 204 (EW CA).

What is usually required, in the case of voyage charters, is that the ship is 'ready to load'. 'Loading' here necessarily means that the cargo holds must be receive to cargo that is permitted by the charterparty. Issues have arisen on the question of readiness of the ship to load. This will be discussed on its own right in the next subsection with a visit to a few relevant cases.[66]

Until the option to cancel is exercised, the contract is alive, so that the shipowner's obligation to perform the approach voyage will be there. When there is no express time-limit, as will usually be the case, the option to cancel must be exercised within a reasonable time, though there is no obligation to given advance notice of such intention.[67] If the reasonable time has passed, then the charterer must give reasonable notice to reinstate time.[68]

If the charterer cancels before it had the right to cancel, that will amount to an anticipatory breach. In that case, the options available to the shipowner will be either to reject the anticipatory breach so that the charterparty will be alive or accept the anticipatory breach so that the charterparty will come to an end and hold the charterer liable in damages.[69] If the shipowner continues the charterparty, then the charterer will have the cancellation option at the right time if the ship is not delivered/offered ready for loading by the cancelling date.[70]

Operation of doctrine of frustration will not be affected by the right to cancel. This is demonstrated by *Bank Line v Capel (Arthur) & Co.*[71] In this case, the cancelling date was on 30 April 1915. The ship was not delivered by then. Subsequently, the ship was requisitioned by the British government during the First World War. Subsequently, the shipowner sold the ship to a new owner and got the ship released from the requisition in favour of the new owner in September 1915. The charterer never exercised the right to cancel. Now the charterer claimed that the charterparty was alive as the charter had never opted to cancel and that thus the shipowner had breached the charterparty by the sale. The shipowner argued that the charterparty was frustrated and thus came to an end. The House of Lords held in favour of the shipowner.

12.6.1.1. Readiness to Load/Discharge

Issues have arisen on the question of readiness of the ship to load and discharge the cargo. Those cases about readiness to discharge involve the same principles as that applicable to readiness to load. Hence, cases on both readiness for loading and discharge will be discussed here.

---

66 See Chapter 12.6.1.1.

67 *Moel Tryvan Ship Co Ltd v Andrew Weir & Co* [1910] 2 KB 844 (EW CA).

68 As in the case of any other contract.

69 *Maredelanto Compania Naviera SA v Bergbau-Handel GmbH (The Mihalis Angelos)* [1970] EWCA Civ 4, [1970] 3 WLR 601, [1971] 1 QB 164 (EW CA). See also *Cheikh Boutros Selim El-Khoury and Others v Ceylon Shipping Lines Ltd (The Madeleine)* [1967] 2 Lloyd's Rep 224 (EW HC).

70 *Fercometal SARL v Mediterranean Shipping Co SA (The Simona)* [1989] AC 788 (UK HL).

71 [1919] AC 435, [1918-19] All ER Rep 504 (UK HL).

In *Armement Adolf Deppe v John Robinson & Co Ltd*,[72] cargo was carried under a port charter. Under a port charter, as opposed to a berth charter, the shipowner's obligation is to offer the ship at the port rather than a berth. The ship reached the port and lay at the usual waiting area of the port while waiting for a berth to commence discharge operation. The ship did not take in stevedores while waiting as the charterer had no intention to receive the cargo until the ship berthed. The shipowner claimed that laytime started once the ship arrived at the waiting area. The charterer argued the ship was not ready to discharge until she berthed and took in stevedores and opened the hatches, hence laytime started only at the berth. The English Court of Appeal found in favour of the shipowner, holding that the ship was ready to discharge in a business and mercantile sense when she reached the waiting area and it was not necessary for the shipowner to incur unnecessary expense of taking in stevedores while waiting for berth as the charterer had no intention of receiving the cargo until the ship berthed. In coming to this conclusion, the court observed that it had been earlier held by the Court of Appeal in *Leonis Steamship Company Limited v Rank Limited Rank* ,[73] that laytime in a port charter could start at the waiting area. In *J Glynn & Sons Ltd v Consorzio Approvvigionamenti Fra Meccanici Ed Affini*,[74] Greer J said that 'ready' here:

> … does not mean that she is to be when she gives notice in a position to start the discharge immediately the minute after the notice has been given. What it means is ready in a *commercial sense*… that is to say, in such a position that the tackle can be got ready for use as soon as the receivers are in the ordinary course to do their part of the discharge… The hatches were not off, but matters of that sort do not prevent a vessel being readily put in order to commence her discharge… means having the tackle ready to be put into operation. [emphasis added]

In *Grampian Steamship Co Ltd v Carver & Co*, [75] the charterparty was to carry cotton-seed, wheat, beans, maize or other grain. The charterparty required the shipowner to provide the mats required for the carriage. When the ship arrived, the mates were not laid but ready to be laid. The English High Court held that it was sufficient, to render the ship ready to load within the scope of the charterparty, that the mats were ready to be laid if required.

In *Noemijulia Steamship Co Ltd v Minister of Food*, [76] the cargoes permitted to be loaded were wheat, maize, rye, and/or any other lawful merchandise—in bulk or bags. The obligation to load was on the shipowner. Due to a fire accident, the derricks were broken. However, that did not affect the loading as the charterer largely intended to load bulk cargo. There were some bagged cargoes, but it was possible to load them by other means without using the derricks. The charterer claimed that the ship was not ready to load, which the shipowner challenged. The English Court of Appeal found for the shipowner, holding that the ship was ready in a business sense. The

[72] [1917] 2 KB 204 (EW CA).

[73] [1908] 1 KB 499 (EW CA).

[74] (1920) 4 Ll L Rep 183 at 184 (EW HC).

[75] (1893) 9 TLR 210 (EW HC).

[76] (1950) 84 Ll L Rep 354 (EW CA).

court stressed that for the ship to be ready to load, the loading gear need not be placed at the disposal of the charterer. All that was required was that the shipowner was able to load any permitted cargo and it was for the shipowner to decide how it would carry out the loading operation. It must be observed that in this case the loading operation was to be carried on by the shipowner, although usually that will be on the charterers.

In *The Demosthenes V (No. 1)*,[77] the charterparty required the shipowner to provide, minimum, six vacuators for discharge. These were to be brought in from shore at the discharge port. On arrival at the discharge port, before berthing, notice of readiness was given by the shipowner. The charterer rejected this for reason that the vacuators were on not on board when the notice was given. The issue was taken before the English High Court, which found for the shipowner, holding that the ship, as a ship, was ready. In arriving at the conclusion, the court distinguished the ship from equipment that had to be brought in from the shore.

In *Sun Shipping Co Ltd v Watson & Youell Shipping Agency Ltd*, [78] the English High Court held that the ship was not ready to load grain when only some of the required shifting boards were fitted. In *Vaughan v Campbell, Heatley & Co*, [79] the charter was to carry wheat and/or flour in bags or other lawful merchandise. The cargo holds were not lined as usually required for wheat. Thus, the charterer cancelled, which the shipowners challenged. The English Court of Appeal found in favour of the shipowners, holding that the ship was ready to load. The court said that the charterparty required the ship to be *ready* to load but not *fit* to load. The court also said that because any cargo may be loaded, the lining was not a requirement since many cargoes would not require such lining. This does not seem to represent the right law. The court had, in construing the charterparty, undermined the commercial intention of the parties, which was, objectively, in essence to load wheat or flour. Again, the court distinguishing 'readiness' to load from 'fitness' to load is contrary to commercial realty. 'Loading' must always relate to a cargo. If the ship is not fit to load that cargo, then it would be too unreal to say that the ship is ready to load that cargo.

12.6.2 Approach Voyage

An approach voyage is the one that the shipowner performs, before the charter term commences, to deliver the ship to the charterer (or offer her ready to load)) pursuant to the charterparty. The BIMCO GENCON 1994 form, in cl. 1, says:

> … The said Vessel shall, as soon as her prior commitments have been completed, proceed to the loading port(s) … or so near thereto as she may safely get and lie always afloat …

---

[77] *Gerani Compania Naviera SA v General Organisation for Supply Goods (The Demosthenes V) (No. 1)* [1982] 1 Lloyd's Rep 275 (EW HC).

[78] (1926) 24 Ll L Rep 28 (EW HC).

[79] (1855) 2 TLR 33 (EW CA).

There is no equivalent clause in the NYPE or BIMCO BALTIME forms. Irrespective of any express provision, it is always an implied term at common law in all charterparties, whether time charter[80] or voyage charter,[81] that the shipowner will perform the approach voyage with reasonable dispatch.[82] This obligation has two parts. First, the shipowner must reasonably timely commence the approach voyage so that the ship will arrive at the delivery/loading place by the agreed delivery/expected ready to load time. Second, once the approach voyage has commenced, to prosecute it with reasonable dispatch to arrive at the delivery/loading place by the agreed delivery/expected ready to load time. It must be noted that, for purposes of the approach voyage, the target time is the agreed delivery/expected ready to load date (if one is specified) rather than the cancelling date.

The obligation to *commence* the approach-voyage in reasonably safe time is an absolute one, hence it is no defence that the shipowner is not at fault for the delay in *commencing* the approach voyage. It is not a breach of the approach-voyage obligation if, *during* the approach voyage *after* it had commenced, delay occurs in prosecution of the approach voyage, which delay is not attributable to the shipowner, such as accident during the approach voyage.

The severity of the 'absolute' duty is demonstrated by *The Pacific Voyager*.[83] In this case, the disponent owners agreed, by a SHELLVOY 5 form on 5 January, to let the ship on a voyage charter to the charterers for a voyage to commence in Rotterdam. At the time the charterparty was entered into, the ship was laden with cargo under a previous charter. No expected time of arrival (ETA) was specified in the charterparty. Instead, the expected date of arrival at the discharge port under the previous charter was specified as 25 January at Antifer. The cancelling date was 4 February. Due to rapid water ingress on 12 January when passing Suez Canal, the ship had to be drydocked, resulting in missing the cancelling date. The charterer cancelled on 6 February and claimed damaged for failing to timely commence the approach voyage. The disponent shipowner argued that there was no obligation as to approach voyage as there was no ETA at the loading port. The English Court of Appeal held that when there is no ETA at the loading port, the obligation to commence the approach would be a reasonable time. In this case, given that the ETA at the last discharge port was specified as 25 January, the court held, the reasonable time to commence the approach voyage was on or about 28 January. As the disponent shipowner did not so commence, it was held liable to the charterer in damages. It must be noted that there is nothing to stop the parties from contractually modifying the absoluteness of the duty.

---

80 *Marbienes Compania Naviera SA v Ferrostaal AG (The Democritos)* [1976] 2 Lloyd's Rep 149 (EW CA).

81 *MacAndrew v Chapple* (1866) LR 1 CP 643 (EW Court of Common Pleas); *Freeman v Taylor* (1831) 8 Bing 124 (US District Court).

82 *Monroe Brothers Ltd v Ryan* [1935] 2 KB 28 (EW CA); *Mitsui OSK. Lines Ltd v Garnac Grain Co Inc (The Myrtos)* [1984] 2 Lloyd's Rep 449 (EW HC).

83 *CSSA Chartering and Shipping Services SA v Mitsui OSK Lines Ltd (The Pacific Voyager)* [2018] All ER (D) 32 (Nov) (EW CA).

In the case of failure to commence the approach voyage at the right time, the breach occurs at the time when the shipowner should have commenced the approached voyage but did not. The duty to commence the approach voyage at the appropriate time and to prosecute the approach voyage with reasonable dispatch is an obligation of the shipowner *in addition to and independent of* the obligation of the shipowner to deliver/offer ready to load by the agreed time. This means that the charterer may have a relief against the shipowner for two different and independent causes. One, failure of the shipowner to commence the approach voyage at the right time/prosecute the approach voyage with reasonable dispatch. Another, failure of the shipowner to deliver/offer ready to load by the agreed time. For the former breach, the charterer may be able to terminate the charterparty without waiting for the cancelling date.

The implied term as to the approach voyage is treated as an innominate term. Hence, for breach of the implied term, the charterer may terminate only if the consequences are so serious as to 'frustrate the commercial purposes of the contract.[84] Otherwise, the relief will be limited to damages. The significance of the obligation to commence the approach voyage in reasonably safe time is that the charterer may terminate the charterparty before the agreed date of delivery/expected ready to load date, where consequences of the breach are serious.

This principles relating to the approach-voyage obligation, as distinct from the obligation to deliver/offer ready to load, was well demonstrated by *The Baleares*.[85] In this case, a voyage charterparty was entered into on 12 January 1987,[86] whereby the ship was to be made available at Bethioua port in Algeria to load refrigerated LPG. At the time the charterparty was entered into the ship was serving a previous charter.[87] The current charterparty provided 'expected ready 31 January 1987' and 'cancelling 5 February 1987'. There was a delay in the previous charter with the result that the ship arrived Taragona in Spain under that charter to discharge only on 4 February 1987 and completed the discharge on 7 February 1987. It would take about a day more to sail from Tragona to Bethioua. In the meantime, the charterer in this case cancelled the charterparty on 6 February 1987. The market price of refrigerated LPG had gone up by end of January 1987 with the result that the charterer would lose on its contracts with its buyers. The charterer claimed the loss. The English Court of Appeal held that the breach of the approach-voyage obligation had occurred by at least 20 January 1987, as it was clear by this date that the ship would not be made available for loading timely under the charterparty. As the cargo's market price increase happened after this date, the consequent loss by the increase was attributable to the breach, hence the shipowner must compensate the charterer for the same. However, had the case been based on the failure of the shipowner to deliver on 5 January 1987, then the charterer would not have recovered the loss as the market price increase had already happened before this date. It was no defence to the shipowners that the delay happened in the previous charter without fault of the shipowner.

---

84 *Universal Cargo Carriers Corp v Citati* [1957] 2 QB 401 (EW HC).

85 *Geogas SA v Trammo Gas Ltd (The Baleares)* [1993] 1 Lloyd's Rep 215 (EW CA).

86 In ASBATANKVOY form.

87 Which fact was noted in the charterparty entered into on 12 January 1987 as "now trading".

The 'expected ready to load' or 'expected to arrive' representations have another significance, namely as a representation of fact that the shipowner genuinely and reasonably held that belief. If the belief was not so held, then the charterer may be entitled to relief for misrepresentation from the time the charterparty was entered into. The relief may include a right to terminate. The availability of a claim for misrepresentation is independent of any claim available for breach of the approach-voyage obligation and obligation to delivery/offer ready to load. The same is true of other representations in the charterparty such as the current position of the ship.[88]

12.7 Frustration

A contract will be frustrated only where there is a fundamental change of circumstances altering the entire commercial basis of the contract, such as sinking of the ship under a charter.[89] Where the contract makes a provision in respect of the event that frustrates, then the contract will not be frustrated but the rights and liabilities of the parties will be regulated by that provision.[90] Usually, a *force majeure* clause will make such provision.

12.7.1 Consequences of Frustration

If a contract is frustrated, it comes to an end and the parties are discharged from obligation to give further performance under the contract. At common law, advance payments made under a contract subsequently frustrated were not generally recoverable, even if the other party had not done the work to the extent that will justify the advance payment. The harsh effect of frustration was modified by the UK Law Reform (Frustrated Contracts) Act 1943. This Act does not apply to voyage charterparties but applies to other types of charterparty including time charterparty. Section 1(2) of the Act requires advance payments to be returned, subject to a discretion in the hands of the court to allow any part of it, or the whole sum of it, to be retained by the party to whom it was paid to cover the expenses incurred by him in pursuit of performing the contract. If a party, in pursuit of performing the contract, has conferred a valuable benefit on the other, then the court may, under Section 1(3), order the party who benefited to pay a suitable sum to the other party. Section 2(4) gives a further power to the court to sever the part of the contract affected by frustration and save the remaining contract. The Section 1(2) and (3) of the Act read as follows:

---

[88] Eg. Box 8 of the BIMCO Gencon 1994 form; box 13 of the BALTIME 1939 form (revised 2001).

[89] *Compania Naviera General SA v Kerametal Ltd (The Lorna I)* [1983] 1 Lloyd's Rep 373 (EW CA).

[90] See *Bank Line v Capel (Arthur) & Co* [1919] AC 435, [1918-19] All ER Rep 504 (UK HL).

(2) All sums paid or payable to any party in pursuance of the contract before the time when the parties were so discharged (in this Act referred to as "the time of discharge") shall, in the case of sums so paid, be recoverable from him as money received by him for the use of the party by whom the sums were paid, and, in the case of sums so payable, cease to be so payable:

Provided that, if the party to whom the sums were so paid or payable incurred expenses before the time of discharge in, or for the purpose of, the performance of the contract, the court may, if it considers it just to do so having regard to all the circumstances of the case, allow him to retain or, as the case may be, recover the whole or any part of the sums so paid or payable, not being an amount in excess of the expenses so incurred.

(3) Where any party to the contract has, by reason of anything done by any other party thereto in, or for the purpose of, the performance of the contract, obtained a valuable benefit (other than a payment of money to which the last foregoing subsection applies) before the time of discharge, there shall be recoverable from him by the said other party such sum (if any), not exceeding the value of the said benefit to the party obtaining it, as the court considers just, having regard to all the circumstances of the case and, in particular,—

(a) the amount of any expenses incurred before the time of discharge by the benefited party in, or for the purpose of, the performance of the contract, including any sums paid or payable by him to any other party in pursuance of the contract and retained or recoverable by that party under the last foregoing subsection, and

(b) the effect, in relation to the said benefit, of the circumstances giving rise to the frustration of the contract.

Section 2(4) of the Act reads as follows:

(4) Where it appears to the court that a part of any contract to which this Act applies can properly be severed from the remainder of the contract, being a part wholly performed before the time of discharge, or so performed except for the payment in respect of that part of the contract of sums which are or can be ascertained under the contract, the court shall treat that part of the contract as if it were a separate contract and had not been frustrated and shall treat the foregoing section of this Act as only applicable to the remainder of that contract.

Singapore has a similar statute, namely, Frustrated Contracts Act, of which Section 2(2) and (3) and Section 2(4) are materially equivalent respectively to Section 1(2) and 1(3) of the UK 1943 Act. Those Commonwealth countries, including Malaysia,[91] that has adopted the Indian Contract Act 1872 model for their Contract Act, has provisions that will mitigate the harsh effect of the common law on this point. The 1872 Act renders, by Sections 56 (para 2) and 65, a contract the performance of which has become impossible void and requires any party that has obtained a benefit to restore it or compensate for it. Sections 56 (para 2) and 65 provide as follows:[92]

56 (para 2) Contract to do act afterwards becoming impossible or unlawful

A contract to do an act which, after the contract is made, becomes impossible, or by reason of some event which the promisor could not prevent, unlawful, becomes void when the act becomes impossible or unlawful.

---

[91] Malaysian Contracts Act 1950.

[92] Sections 57(2) and 66, respectively, of the Malaysian Contracts Act 1950 identically provide.

> **65 Obligation of person who has received advantage under void agreement, or contract that becomes void**
>
> When an agreement is discovered to be void, or when a contract becomes void, any person who has received any advantage under the agreement or contract is bound to restore it, or to make compensation for it, to the person from whom he received it.

12.7.2 Self-induced Frustration

Self-induced frustration is no frustration. The classic case for this point is *Maritime National Fish Ltd v Ocean Trawlers Ltd.*[93] In this case, the shipowner owned five trawlers and had agreed to let one to the charterer. In the midst of the charter period, a law was implemented requiring a licence to be obtained for the use of trawlers. The shipowner applied for five licences but was granted only three which it then applied to its three trawlers other than the one that let to the charterer. The Privy Council held that this was not a frustration, as it was self-induced.[94]

12.7.3 Judging Frustration

Determining if an event has frustrated a charterparty can be a complex one, as demonstrated by the following cases. In *The Eugenia*,[95] the ship was let on a voyage charter from Genoa to India. This would ordinarily take 108 days via Suez Canal. Subsequent to the parties entering into the charterparty, the Suez Canal was closed. This would require the voyage to be carried out via the Cape, which will take extra 30 days, hence a total voyage time of 138 days. At the time the parties entered into the charterparty, the risk of the Suez Canal being closed was present. The English Court of Appeal held that there was no frustration.[96] In arriving at this decision, the court was influenced by the ratio of the difference, which was 108:138. The greater the number for the voyage via the Cape, the greater would be the chances for there to be a frustration.

In *Bank Line v Capel (Arthur) & Co*,[97] the ship was on a time charter of one year. She was requisitioned by the government. At the time of requisition, the duration of requisition was indefinite. Subsequently, the duration transpired to a short one for four months only. The House of Lords held that the frustration must be determined

[93] [1935] AC 524, [1935] All ER Rep 86, 153 LT 425 (PC on appeal from Canada).

[94] See *J Lauritzen AS v Wijsmuller BV (The Super Servant Two)* [1990] 1 Lloyd's Rep 1 (EW CA) for a similar self-induced frustration that was held to be no frustration.

[95] *Ocean Tramp Tankers Corpn v V/O Sovfracht (The Eugenia)* [1964] 2 QB 226, [1964] 1 All ER 161, [1964] 2 WLR 114, [1963] 2 Lloyd's Rep 381 (EW CA).

[96] See *Tsakiroglou & Co Ltd v Noblee Thorl GmbH* [1962] AC 93, [1961] 2 All ER 179, [1961] 2 WLR 633, [1961] 1 Lloyd's Rep 329 (UK HL) for a similar decision.

[97] [1919] AC 435, [1918-19] All ER Rep 504 (UK HL).

as at the time of the relevant event without taking into account subsequent events. In this case, as the duration was indefinite at the time of the requisition, the House held that the charterparty was frustrated. Comparatively, in *FA Tamplin Steamship Co Ltd v Anglo-Mexican Petroleum Products Co Ltd*,[98] House of Lords held that there was no frustration, where the charter was for five year and the ship was requisitioned after about three years, which requisition was expected to be for a short period only. Again comparatively, in *WJ Tatem Ltd v Gamboa*,[99] the ship was chartered for 30 days from 1 July for 250 per day. The charterparty provided for obligation to pay hire to continue until redelivery. The hire was three times higher than the market rate, given the parties knew that the purpose of the charter was to evacuate civilian refugees from Santander to French Bay. On 14 July, the ship was seized by a nationalist. She was released and redelivered in September. The shipowner claimed hire until redelivery in September. The charterer argued that the charterparty was frustrated. The English High Court agreed with the argument of the charterer and held that the charterparty was frustrated.

In *The Sea Angel*,[100] a tanker carrying light crude oil grounded in the port of Karachi, which caused a major pollution. The owners of the tanker employed salvers to salve, which included removal of the oil from the tanker to another storage tanker. For this, the salvers chartered The Sea Angel from her head-charterers for 20 days. By about 13 days, the removal of the oil was completed, and the salvers gave a definite notice to redeliver The Sea Angel in 3 days. However, the port authorities wrongfully detained her by refusing to give 'No Demand Certificate'. The objective of the port authority was to detain The Sea Angel as security for the expenses connected with the pollution. This was something, though wrong, that could be expected in case of pollution. The Sea Angel was subsequently released by the port authority upon court order after about 3 months. Thereafter, The Sea Angel was redelivered, which was on the 108th day after she was chartered. The salvors argued that the charterparty was frustrated as a result of the indefinite detention by the port authorities, which was indeed unproportionate to the original charter period. The English Court of Appeal rejected the argument and held that the charterparty was not frustrated. In coming to the decision, the court said that a multi-factorial approach must to taken to determine frustration. The factor to consider included the terms of the contract, its matrix or context, knowledge of the parties, their expectations, assumptions and contemplations, at the time of the contract, particularly about risk, the nature of the supervening event. The factors leaned in favour of the shipowner, as the ship was chartered specifically for the salvage operation and the risk in of the detention, even if wrongful, was not something that was beyond foreseeability.

---

[98] [1916] 2 AC 397 (UK HL).

[99] [1939] 1 KB 132, [1938] 3 All ER 135 (EW HC).

[100] *Edwinton Commercial Corp v Tsavliris Russ (Worldwide Salvage and Towage) Ltd (The Sea Angel)* [2007] EWCA Civ 547, [2007] 2 All ER (Comm) 634, [2007] 2 Lloyd's Rep 517 (EW CA).

12.8 Dispute Resolution

It is common that standard charterparty forms will provide for disputes to be resolved by arbitration. An application or appeal against the arbitral award to the court will be pursuant to the laws of the seat of arbitration. In the case of England and Wales and N. Ireland, an application to challenge on grounds of substantive jurisdiction or serious irregularity is available and dealt with under Sections 67, 68, 70 and 71 of the UK Arbitration Act 1996. An appeal on point of law, subject to parties' agreement or court's leave, is available and dealt with under Sections 69, 70 and 71. The procedure is in Civil Procedure Rules (CPR) Part 62.[101]

In the case of an application to challenge on grounds of substantive jurisdiction, the court's powers are to "(a) confirm the award, (b) vary the award, or (c) set aside the award in whole or in part."[102] In the case of an application to challenge on grounds of serious irregularity, the court's power are to "(a) remit the award to the tribunal, in whole or in part, for reconsideration, (b) set the award aside in whole or in part, or (c) declare the award to be of no effect, in whole or in part."[103] In an appeal on question of law, the court's powers are to "(a) confirm the award, (b) vary the award, (c) remit the award to the tribunal, in whole or in part, for reconsideration in the light of the court's determination, or (d) set aside the award in whole or in part.[104]

The UK is not a model law country, i.e. it has not adopted the UNCITRAL[105] Model Law on International Arbitration.[106] More than 80 countries/110 jurisdictions have substantially adopted the model law, including Singapore and Malaysia. Under the model law, there is no appeal available, but an application can be made, on narrow grounds, to set aside the award or a challenge to enforcement of the award can be taken. The model provisions are, respectively, in Articles 34 and 36.[107]

The NYPE 2015 form, in cl. 54, gives four options for arbitration. First, in New York under the rules of Society of Maritime Arbitrators (SMA) subject to US maritime law. Second, London under the rules of London Maritime Arbitrators Association (LMAA) subject to English laws. Third, in Singapore under the rules of Singapore Chamber of Maritime Arbitration (SCMA), subject to Singapore or English as the parties may chose. Last, arbitration as mutually agreed by the parties.

---

[101] In Malaysia and Singapore, it is in Order 69 of the respective Rules of Court.

[102] UK Arbitration Act 1996, Section 67

[103] UK Arbitration Act 1996, Section 68

[104] Arbitration Act 1996, Section 69.

[105] 'United Nations Commission on International Trade Law'.

[106] UNCITRAL Model Law on International Commercial Arbitration 1985, amended in 2006.

[107] In Malaysia, Sections 37 and 39 of the Arbitration Act 2005, amended in 2006. In Singapore, the model law is included in the first schedule to the Singapore International Arbitration Act, and additionally Section 31 of the Act makes provision for challenge to an award at the enforcement stage.

BIMCO BALTIME 1939 form (revised 2001), in cl. 22, makes similar provision except for Singapore option. BIMCO GENCON 1994, cl. 19, form is similar in terms to cl. 22 of the BALTIME 1939 form.[108]

Where parties have designated arbitration in a certain place/subject to certain rules, but did not expressly provide for the applicable law, the gap has to be filled by rules of conflict of laws. A court may find that it was implied that the law at the place of arbitration is the law applicable to the substantive dispute and also to the arbitration agreement. However, this depends on the factual matrix of the case. *Enka Insaat Ve Sanayi AS v OOO Insurance Company Chubb*[109] has some guiding principles on this, where the UK Supreme Court said as follows:

> There are still cases in which an arbitration clause providing for arbitration in London by, for example, English maritime arbitrators, or by London brokers, or by a local association or exchange, may in combination with other factors be regarded as conveying an implied choice of law. An example is *Egon Oldendorff v Libera Corpn (No 2)*,[110] where an arbitration clause in a charterparty made between Japanese owners and German charterers provided for arbitration in London by arbitrators appointed by the London Maritime Arbitrators' Association. Also relevant to Clarke J's decision that the parties intended English law to govern the charterparty were: (1) the fact that it was made on a well-known standard form containing clauses with well-known meanings in English law; and (2) that having agreed a "neutral" forum, the parties intended that forum to apply a "neutral" law, namely English law and not German or Japanese law. In such cases that implied choice of law will equally apply to the arbitration agreement: see *Habas Sinai Ve Tibbi Gazlar Istihsal v VSC Steel Co Ltd*.[111]

[108] (Revised 2001).

[109] [2020] UKSC 38 at [114] (UK SC).

[110] [1996] 1 Lloyd's Rep 380 (EW HC).

[111] [2013] EWHC 4071 (Comm), [2014] 1 Lloyd's Rep 479 at [102] (EW HC).

Chapter 13
Voyage Charter: Freight and Lien

This chapter analyses freight and lien in voyage charterparties. The distinction between freight and hire is observed. The different bases of freight calculation such as on a lump sum, deadweight and quantity loaded or discharged are introduced. Then, the concept of 'earning of freight' is analysed at depth. This is followed by a consideration of the circumstances in which the shipowner may hold both the charterer and the bill of lading holder liable for the freight and cesser clauses by which the liability of the charterer to pay freight is cut off and passed on to the bill of lading holder. Finally, the shipowner's lien in common law and contract on cargo, sub-freight and sub-hire for outstanding freight and other charges are examined.

13.1 Introduction

The reward paid to the shipowner in a voyage charterparty is 'freight'. It is different from reward by 'hire' paid to a shipowner in a time charterparty. At a look, although freight appears to be a just a contractual reward, it indeed more than that. There are some peculiar common law protections available to freight. For instance, there is no set-off against the freight. Once the freight is earned, it must be paid even if the voyage is not completed for any reason, and so forth. This requires a study of freight, in its own right, which is undertaken in this chapter.

In this chapter, first the difference between a freight and hire is set out, then the various bases of freight-calculation are looked at. That is followed by a study of an important concept peculiar to freights, i.e. earning of freight. Thereafter, considered are the practice of incorporating charterparty terms into bills of lading with the result of rendering also the holder of the bill liable for freight and the practice of including a cesser clause to cut-off charterer's liability when the liability is taken over by the holder of the bill of lading. Finally, liens at common law and by contract terms are analysed.

A. Kasi, *The Law of Carriage of Goods by Sea*,
https://doi.org/10.1007/978-981-33-6793-7_13

13.2 Freight v. Hire

The consideration paid by the charterer to the shipowner, in the case of a voyage charterparty and bill of lading, is freight, i.e. a reward for *carriage of goods from the loading port to the discharge port.* Comparatively, the consideration paid by the charterer to the shipowner, in the case of a time charterparty and demise charterparty, is hire, i.e. reward for *allowing use of the ship for a period of time.*[1] Thus, in the case of a voyage charterparty, it is a contract of *carriage*. In the case of a time charterparty, it is a contract for *hire.*

13.3 Bases of Freight Calculation

The freight can be calculated on a few *bases*. One is a *lump sum* for carrying the goods on a particular voyage. Another is by a rate per *deadweight* of the ship—this will be the case where the shipowner has the option of providing one of its ships with different deadweights within a range. Yet another is by a rate per *quantity* of cargo loaded or discharged. In the case of a charterparty with a lump sum freight, should the ship prove incapable of loading the minimum guaranteed quantity, the charterer, if it proceeds to load, will be entitled to a rebate on the lump sum as damages.

The effect of clauses providing for computation of freight based on quantity of cargo loaded where payment was to be made without discount upon discharge was considered by the English Court of Appeal in *The Metula.*[2] In this case, the cargo was carried under EXXONVOY 1969 form. The charterparty provided that the freight was to be computed on quantity of cargo loaded and the payment was to be made without discount upon discharge. During the voyage, the ship ran aground, resulting in about one third of the cargo being lost and the balance transshipped to the destination port and discharged. The shipowner claimed full freight based on the quantity of cargo loaded. The charterer argued that the clause was to protect the shipowner in case of discrepancy between quantity of cargo loaded and discharged and in case of loss as a result of inherent vice and the like, but not loss due to an accident. The court did not favour this argument and found for the shipowner.

In the case of a quantity-based freight, it is usual that an obligation will be imposed on the charterer to load 'a full and complete cargo'. Alternatively, the obligation can be for the charterer to load a minimum quantity with the maximum capacity specified, i.e. a range. If the charterer loads below the minimum quantity, the charterer will be liable to pay the freight for the shortfall, called deadfreight. This means the charterer will have to pay the freight as if the minimum quantity was loaded. Although it would be expected that the rule of *de minimis* will apply in the case of a trivial shortfall in the quantity loaded, this was held by the English Court of Appeal not to be the case

---

[1] See *Thomas v Harrowing Steamship Co* [1913] 2 KB 171 (EW CA), speech of Kennedy LJ.

[2] *Shell International Petroleum Co Ltd v Seabridge Shipping (The Metula)* [1978] 2 Lloyd's Rep 5 (EW CA).

in *The Vrontados, Margaronis Navigation Agency Ltd v Henry W Peabody & Co of London Ltd (The Vrontados) (CA)* [1965] 2 QB 430 (EW CA). where the full and complete cargo to be loaded would be 12,600 tons but the quantity loaded was 12 tons short. However, this must be a matter of construction, in line with the commercial intention of the parties, of the charterparty in each case.

Difficulties may arise if the charterer is ready to load the full and complete cargo and the ship has the capacity to carry that quantity, but she is prevented from receiving the full quantity for reasons such as draft restrictions in the port of loading. This happened in *The Archimidis*[3] and the English Court of Appeal held that it did not relieve the charterer from the obligation to load full and complete cargo, failing which it must pay deadfreight. The court found that the charterer could have loaded the full and complete cargo by ship-to-ship transfer at anchorage. However, this is a matter of construction of the 'full and complete cargo' clause, per the commercial intention of the parties, in each case. The 'full and complete cargo' can mean one of the two things. One is full cargo to the *carrying* capacity of the ship. Another is full cargo that the ship can *receive* at the intended port of loading. In order to determine the commercial intention of the parties, the court may consider if any party had undertaken the responsibility for the port of loading.

There may appear to be a conflict where the shipowner gives a warranty as to the cargo carrying capacity of the ship, called deadweight, and at the same time the charterer is obliged to load full and complete cargo. Indeed, there is no conflict. The warranty is the shipowner's assurance that the ship can *minimum* load the stated quantity but that does not mean that the obligation of the charterer is only to load that quantity. Rather, the relevant obligation of the charterer is the one to load 'full and complete cargo', which in fact refers to the *maximum* quantity that the ship can carry. In *Steamship Heathfield Co v Rodenacher*,[4] the ship was "guaranteed by owners to carry 2,600 tons deadweight. Along with that, there was the 'full and complete cargo' clause. The full capacity was 2,950 tons and the charterer loaded 2,673 tons. The English Court of Appeal held the charterer liable for the shortfall (deadfreight) between 2,950 tons and 2,673 tons.

However, it will be different if it was not a warranty of cargo carrying capacity but a description of the capacity. If it is a description, then it will be justified to construe the 'full and complete cargo' clause to refer to described capacity. But if the ship indeed cannot carry the described quantity, then naturally the obligation of the charterer can only be to load whatever the maximum quantity the ship can carry within the limit of the described quantity. This is illustrated by *Rotherfield Steamship Co Ltd v Tweedie, Reid & Co.*[5] In this case, the ship was described to be 'of the capacity of 4,250 tons' and the charterer was obliged to load full and complete cargo. Only 3,947 tons could be loaded as the remaining capacity was used for bunkers. The shipowner claimed

---

[3] *AIC Limited v Marine Pilot Limited (The Archimidis)* [2008] EWCA Civ 175, [2008] 2 All ER (Comm) 545, [2008] 1 Lloyd's Rep 597 (EW CA).

[4] (1986) 2 Com Cas 55 (EW CA).

[5] (1897) 2 Com Cas 84, 13 TLR 183 (EW HC).

freight based on full 4,250 tons, which the English High Court turned down and found the charterer had only to pay freight for 3,947 tons.

If a contract for carriage is there but no quantum of freight has been agreed between the parties for the voyage in question, then[6] the quantum will be determined by *quantum meruit*. Where the parties materially modify the charterparty by conduct, then although there is a charterparty, i.e. modified charterparty, between the parties, the quantum may no longer be the agreed one. In such cases, the freight payable will be a *quantum meruit* one. Such material modification may happen where the charterer loads a cargo materially different from that agreed[7] or requires the ship to proceed to a different port.[8]

In case the shipowner performs only a part of the voyage, where the freight is not earned in advance, the shipowner is not entitled to any pro rata freight.[9] Of course, if the charterer prevents the shipowner from completing the voyage, then the charterer has to be responsible for the consequent loss to the shipowner.[10] However, the freight agreement will be modified if the charterer voluntarily accepts the goods at a point before or different from that of the contracted discharge port. In the result, the charterer will have to pay the freight on pro rata or *quantum meruit* basis, depending on the circumstances of the case.[11] But the right for such a freight will not be available where the charterer accepts the cargo at an intermediate port on a 'without prejudice' basis.[12] In *St Enoch Shiping v Phosphate Mining,*[13] the English High Court refused to find any agreement to modify the original freight agreement where the consignees merely took their own goods when they were landed at a different port. Rowlatt J emphasised:

> The consignee must accept the goods in such a way as to imply that he and the shipowner agree that the goods have been carried far enough and that the shorter transit shall be substituted for that named in the original contract.

---

[6] Only then. In *Ocean Projects Inc v Ultratech Pte Ltd* [1994] 2 SLR 369 (SG CA), there was no contract between the disponent shipowner and the cargo interest, as the disponent shipowner carried the goods by an agreement between it and a freight forwarder. Hence, the shipowner was not able to claim *quantum meruit* freight from the cargo interest, when the freight forwarder went into liquidation and the freight was not paid. For more detailed facts of this case, see chapter 4.2.1.1 'Freight Forwarder's Bill'/chapter 13.7.1.

[7] *Stevens v Bromley* & Sons [1919] 2 KB 722, 88 LJKB 1147, 14 Asp MLC 455, 24 Com Cas 254, 121 LT 354, 35 TLR 594 (EW CA).

[8] *Batis Maritime Corporation v Petroleos Del Mediterraneo SA (The Batis)* [1990] 1 Lloyd's Rep 345 (EW HC).

[9] *Hopper v Burness* (1876) 1 CPD 137, 45 LJQB 377, 3 Asp MLC 149 (EW HC); *Hunter v Prinsep* (1808) 10 East 378, 103 ER 818 (EW Court of King's Bench): the question is if there was a 'new bargain'.

[10] See chapter 13.1.5.

[11] *Ellis Shipping Corporation v Voest Alpine Intertrading (The Lefthero)* [1991] 2 Lloyd's Rep 599 (EW HC).

[12] *Ellis Shipping Corporation v Voest Alpine Intertrading (The Lefthero)* [1991] 2 Lloyd's Rep 599 (EW HC).

[13] [1916] 2 KB 624 at 627 (EW HC).

A back freight, on *quantum meruit* basis, may be chargeable by the shipowner where the shipowner had to carry back the goods to the loading port. This happened in the case of *Cargo ex Argos.*[14] In this case, petroleum was carried from London to Le Havre, but the ship could not discharge the cargo. This was because the port authorities refused to allow the discharge of petroleum or any other flammable material, because there were munitions in the port at that time. Attempts of the master to discharge the cargo in any other nearby port failed. Hence, the ship carried back the cargo to London. The Privy Council held that the shipowner can claim freight, for the return voyage, on a *quantum meruit* basis.

13.4 Earning of Freight

The concept of earning here is something peculiar to freights. Earning of freight has some serious consequences such as no set-off against the earned freight and liability to pay even if the voyage is not completed for any reason. An analysis of this concept follows.

13.4.1 Concept of Freight Earned and No Set-Off

At common law, the implied term is that the freight is earned and payable upon right and true delivery.[15] In the event of a part delivery, freight only on the part is earned and payable.[16] But if cargo is delivered damaged, then full freight is payable. If the damage is so extensive that the goods are no longer the goods of the original description, then the delivery will no longer to treated as delivery of the goods.[17]

However, the common law position is frequently modified by the express terms of the charterparty, so that the freight or majority of it is earned and payable in advance. Some charterparties expressly state that the full amount of the freight, or part of it, is earned upon right and true delivery.

Charterparties may provide different times when the freight is *earned* by the shipowner. The provision can be for the freight to be earned upon receipt of the goods by the shipowner, loading,[18] issuance of the bill of lading, sailing or final

[14] *Brown v Gaudet (Cargo ex Argos)* (1873) LR 5 PC 134, 42 LJ Adm 1, 1 Asp MLC 519, 21 WR 420, 28 LT 77, [1861–73] All ER Rep Ext 1057 (PC).

[15] *Black v Rose* (1864) 2 Moo PCCNS 277, 10 Jur NS 1009, 2 Mar LC 89 (PC on appeal from Ceylon); *Paynter v James* (1867) LR 2 CP 348, 2 Mar LC 450 (EW Court of Common Pleas).

[16] *Ritchie v Atkinson* (1808) 10 East 295, 103 ER 787 (EW Court of King's Bench).

[17] *Asfar v Blundell* [1896] 1 QB 123 (EW CA); *Montedison SpA v Icroma SpA (The Caspian Sea)* [1979] 3 All ER 378, [1980] 1 WLR 48, [1980] 1 Lloyd's Rep 91 (EW HC).

[18] Eg. *China Offshore Oil (Singapore) International Pte Ltd v Giant Shipping Ltd (The Posidon)* [2001] 1 Lloyd's Rep 697 (EW HC); *Pentonville Shipping Ltd v Transfield Shipping Inc (The Johnny K)* [2006] EWHC 134 (Comm), [2006] 1 Lloyd's Rep 666 (EW HC); *AIC Limited v Marine Pilot*

sailing, arrival at the discharge port, before breaking bulk or delivery of the goods.[19] Charterparties also provide for a part of the freight to be earned at a time and the balance at a different time. It is common for charterparties to provide 80% earned upon loading and the balance 20% earned upon right and true delivery. Splits of 95:5 are also common.

In *Roelandts v Harison,*[20] the English Court of Exchequer made a distinction between freight earned on sailing and on final sailing. The court held that 'sailing' meant when the ship is fully fit for sea and breaks ground, and 'final sailing' meant leaving the port and being at sea. In this case, the ship passed the dock gates under tow and grounded in the canal connecting the dock and the open sea. The charterparty provided for a part of the freight to be earned upon final sailing. The court found that the ship had not done her final sailing, hence the freight was not earned.

In *D'Amico Shipping Italia SpA v Endofa DMCC,*[21] the English High Court made a distinction between freight payable 'on breaking bulk' and 'before breaking bulk'. If the freight is payable on breaking bulk, then it is to be paid once the discharge has commenced. If the freight is payable before breaking bulk, then it is to be paid once the ship has been tendered to the charterer for discharge.

The fact that the freight is earned at a particular time does not mean that it is necessarily payable at that time. The charterparty may provide a different time when the freight or any portion of it is *payable.* For example, a charterparty may provide that the freight is earned upon loading but is payable 80% in advance and 20% upon discharge. It is common that the charterparties will have a clause providing the freight is 'deemed earned' at a particular time. In *The Karin Vatis,*[22] the clause read 'freight deemed earned as cargo loaded ... 95% to be paid within three banking days after signed bills of lading ... vessel and/or cargo lost or not lost ... Balance of freight to be settled within 20 days after completion of discharge ...' The 95% was paid upon loading, and shortly after sailing, the ship sank. The shipowner claimed the balance 5% freight. The English Court of Appeal found in favour of the shipowner, as the entire freight was earned after loading, though the 5% was payable after discharge.

It is not compulsory that the word 'earned' or the words 'deemed earned' is used in order for the freight to become earned at a particular time. This is a matter of construction. Where the freight is calculated by the intake quantity and rendered payable upon discharge, the courts have treated the freight as earned upon loading, although the word 'earned' or the words 'deemed earned' are not there in the charterparty, as was the case in *The Aries* and *The Metula.*

Limited (The Archimidis) [2008] EWCA Civ 175, [2008] 2 All ER (Comm) 545, [2008] 1 Lloyd's Rep 597 (EW CA).

[19] These are examples only and charterparties may provide for the freight to be earned at other points of time.

[20] (1854) 23 LJ Ex 169, 9 Exch 444, (1854) 156 ER 189 (EW Court of Exchequer Chamber).

[21] [2016] EWHC 2223 (Comm) (EW HC).

[22] *Vagres Compania Maritima SA v Nissho-Iwai American Corporation (The Karin Vatis)* [1988] 2 Lloyd's Rep 330 (EW CA).

A mere reference to the place of loading in the clause providing for payment of the freight does not, by itself, mean that the freight is to be paid upon loading. In *Krall v Burnett*,[23] the cargo was shipped in London for Rouen. The charterparty provided 'freight payable in London'. The freight was not paid and the ship was lost in the voyage. The shipowner claimed the freight arguing that the reference to London in the payment clause meant payment upon loading. The English High Court rejected this argument. In the absence of the charterparty specifying when the freight was payable, it is payable upon right and true delivery.

13.4.1.1 Load Port Obligation Modified by 'Near' Clause

Where the freight is earned upon loading, the obligation of the shipowner is to put the ship at the disposal of the charterer for loading and it does not matter whether the charterer actually loads or not.[24] However, if the charterparty contains a 'near' clause, as does the BIMCO GENCON 1994 form in cl. 1, the obligation of the shipowner will only be to offer the ship at a nearby port if the originally designated load port is not safely accessible. The clause, in the said form, reads:

> … the Vessel shall proceed to the discharging port or place(s) ... on signing Bills of Lading, or so near thereto as she may safely get and lie always afloat, and there deliver the cargo …

The 'near' clause is discussed further later.[25]

13.4.1.2 No Freight Earned after Ship and Cargo Lost

If the ship and the cargo are lost before the time stipulated for earning of the freight, then no freight will be earned. In *Smith Hill & Co v Pyman Bell & Co*,[26] the charterparty provided for the freight to be paid 'if required'. The ship was lost, until when no such 'requirement' was made. The English Court of Appeal held that no requirement can be made after the ship was lost. This case must be distinguished from *Oriental Steamship v Tylor*.[27] In this case, a part of the freight was payable 'on signing bills of lading'. After the cargoes were loaded and the ship broke ground, she sank. By then, no bill of lading was signed. The English Court of Appeal held that the charterer had an implied duty to present the bills of lading for signing within a reasonable time although the voyage was no longer there. As the charterer breached this duty, they were liable in damages to the shipowner, which was the amount of the freight payable upon signing of the bills. The rationale behind issuance of bills of lading even when the ship and the cargo were no longer there was that the bill performed

---

[23] (1877) 25 WR 305 (EW HC).

[24] *Robinson v Knights* (1873) LR 8 CP 465 (EW Court of Common Pleas).

[25] See chapter 13.4.2.1.

[26] [1891] 1 QB 742, 60 LJQB 621 (EW CA).

[27] [1893] 2 QB 518, 63 LJQB 128, [1891–94] All ER Rep Ext 1551 (EW CA).

the function of receipt of the cargo and evidenced shipment and it was necessary for claims purposes including insurance claims. When the freight was payable within a period after certain event, it had been held that the freight is not earned until end of the period, and if the ship and the cargo is lost before the end, then no freight was earned. In *Lorna I*,[28] the 'freight non-returnable, cargo and/or vessel lost or not lost, to be paid ... 75% within give ... days after master signed bills of lading and the balance after right and true delivery'. The ship was lost within the five-day period after the master signed the bills. The English Court of Appeal held that the freight was not earned.[29]

13.4.1.3 Effect of Freight Earned

The significance of the freight becoming 'earned' is that, irrespective of anything happening subsequently, the freight must be paid.[30] This is so even if the shipowner does not perform the carriage after the freight was earned or the cargo is delivered damaged or even not delivered. No set-off for losses suffered by the charterer is available against the freight-claim. The classic case for this special rule is *The Aries*,[31] decided by the House of Lords. This is not the case where it originated, but the rule was already there[32] and the House in this case merely endorsed the rule. The reason for the rule is said to be avoid cargo interests delaying payment of freight on grounds of claims for damages. This reason may not be so convincing. However, the House upheld it in the interests of commercial certainty. The rule is something that is not found or accepted in many other jurisdictions.

The extent of the concept can be seen in cases such as *The Dominique*.[33] In this case, 95% of the freight was payable within five days of signing the bills of lading and it was deemed earned on signing of the bills of lading, discountless and non-returnable, vessel and/or cargo lost or not lost. After the cargo was loaded and the bills of lading signed, the ship commenced her voyage and called at an intermediate port for bunkering. She was arrested at the intermediate port by creditors and the shipowners were not able to put up security and it was likely that there would be a judicial sale of the ship. In the circumstances, the charterers rightfully terminated the

---

[28] *Compania Naviera General SA v Kerametal Ltd (The Lorna I)* [1983] 1 Lloyd's Rep 373 (EW CA).

[29] See *Asfar v Blundell* [1896] 1 QB 123 (EW CA).

[30] See *Allison v Bristol Marine Insurance Co* (1876) 1 App Cas 209, 3 Asp MLC 178, [1874–80] All ER Rep 781 (UK HL).

[31] *Aries Tanker Corpn v Total Transport Ltd (The Aries)* [1977] 1 All ER 398, [1977] 1 WLR 185, [1976] 2 Lloyd's Rep 256 (UK HL).

[32] *Dakin v Oxley* (1864) 15 CBNS 646, 33 LJCP 115, (1864) 143 ER 938 (EW Court of Common Pleas); *Henriksens Rederi A/S V Thz Rolimpex (The Brede)* [1973] 2 Lloyd's Rep 333 (EW CA). The rule was also in practice in Singapore, as seen from *Skibs A/S Trolla And Skibs A/S Tautra v United Enterprises & Shipping (Pte) Ltd (The Tarva)* [1973] 2 Lloyd's Rep 385 (SG HC).

[33] *Colonial Bank v European Grain & Shipping Ltd (The Dominique)* [1989] 1 Lloyd's Rep 431 (UK HL).

charter. The 95% freight was not paid at that time. The shipowner's bank, to whom the freight was assigned, claimed payment of the freight, which the charterer refused to pay. The House of Lords found in favour of the shipowner's bank as the freight was earned, i.e. unconditionally earned, at the time the bills of ladings were signed. The bank made no claim in respect of the balance 5% freight payable upon delivery.

Once the freight is earned, if there is a breach by the shipowner, then the remedy available to the cargo owner is to make a separate claim, by way of counterclaim or crossclaim, for damages but not a set-off. Thus, in a charterparty where the freight is deemed earned on loading and payable on true and right delivery and the ship does not complete the voyage for any reason, the charterer must pay the freight as it is already earned. In such a case, the courts have, by construction, replaced the contractual time for payment with a reasonable time.[34] But if the ship did not complete the voyage (or short delivers) by reason of breach by the shipowner, the charterer can claim back the freight paid or payable on the non-delivered goods as damages.[35] In such a case, the freight will be part of the value of the cargo and hence included in the damages-claim by the charterer.[36] If the court first finds in favour of the shipowner in the freight-claim, there is nothing to stop the court from granting a stay of execution pending disposal of the charterer's counterclaim.

Although it may appear that no significant imbalance ensues from the rule, that is not so, as demonstrated by *The Aries*.[37] In this case, the cargo was carried under a voyage charterparty that incorporated the one-year time limitation in the Hague Rules.[38] The freight was payable based on the intake quantity upon discharge. The cargo was short delivered. The charterer paid the freight after deducting the value of the short-delivered cargo. The shipowner made a claim, more than a year after the delivery, for the freight that was deducted. The charterer was not able to make a counterclaim for the short-delivery as the one-year has passed but put forward a defence of set-off. The House of Lords upheld a summary judgement given in favour of the shipowner, holding that the freight was payable based on the intake quantity and no set-off was available against it.

13.4.2 Freight Payable Upon Delivery

Where the common law implied term is not modified or the terms of the charterparty provides for any part of the freight to be earned upon delivery, usually 'right and

---

[34] *Vagres Compania Maritima SA v Nissho-Iwai American Corporation (The Karin Vatis)* [1988] 2 Lloyd's Rep 330 (EW CA).

[35] See *Great Indian Peninsula Rly v Turnbull* (1885) 5 Asp MLC 465, Cab & El 595, 33 WR 874, 53 LT 325, 1 TLR 570 (EW HC).

[36] See *Great Indian Peninsula Rly v Turnbull* (1885) 5 Asp MLC 465, Cab & El 595, 33 WR 874, 53 LT 325, 1 TLR 570 (EW HC).

[37] *Aries Tanker Corpn v Total Transport Ltd (The Aries)* [1977] 1 All ER 398, [1977] 1 WLR 185 (UK HL).

[38] Article III(6).

true delivery', no freight is earned if there is no *delivery*. It does not matter that the shipowner is not at fault or responsible for the non-delivery. If the cargo is destroyed by an excepted peril, the shipowner is not liable for the loss, but still the shipowner cannot claim the freight.

At a look, the words 'right and true delivery' may appear to suggest that if the cargo is not delivered in quality and condition as loaded, then the freight is not payable. But that is not so. Lord Lindley in *Williams & Co v Canton Insurance*[39] said about 'right and true delivery' as follows:

> [R]ight and true delivery … does not mean the cargo shipped, but the cargo which the shipowner undertakes to deliver.

In continuation, Lord Lindley also said that:

> [N]on-delivery of some of [the cargo] affords no defence to a claim for a lump sum freight, although such non-delivery, if wrongful, will give rise to a cross claim.

It is quite hard to reconcile the above two propositions of Lord Linley. Later, the effect of 'right and true delivery' was considered in by Kennedy LJ in *Thomas v Harrowing Steamship Co,*[40] who said:

> [W]hat the shipowner has to deliver is not in all circumstances the quantity of cargo shipped, but all which was shipped and of which delivery was not prevented by any of the excepted perils.

Kennedy LJ felt that if the ship did not arrive or the ship arrived with no cargo, then the freight would not be earned. He also expressed, *obiter*, that if part of the cargo was lost by fault of the shipowner and a short delivery is made, that would still be good as right and true delivery. It is hard to fit this last proposition within Lord Linley's definition of 'right and true delivery'. Nor will it fit within the natural and commercial meaning of the words 'right and true delivery'. It will be a contradiction in terms to allow short delivery by fault of shipowner within *right and true* delivery. The commercial intention behind those words can only, at best, be that the shipowner must delivery all which was shipped and of which delivery was not prevented by any of the excepted perils, i.e. what the shipowner undertook to deliver. A similar conclusion was reached by the Singapore High Court in *The Tarva,*[41] where the court held that the words 'right and true delivery' did not mean delivery of the entire cargo shipped. If the quantity delivered is relatively so small that it will not be commercially considered delivery at all, then that cannot constitute right and true delivery.

If the ship does not arrive due to some accident but the goods, or the saved portion of them, are delivered by the shipowner at the destination port, then that would constitute right and true delivery. The clause is about *delivery of goods* and

---

[39] [1901] AC 462 (UK HL).

[40] [1913] 2 KB 171 (EW CA), affirmed by the House of Lords in [1915] AC 58 (UK HL).

[41] *Skibs A/S Trolla And Skibs v United Enterprises & Shipping (Pte) Ltd (The Tarva)* [1983] 2 Lloyd's Rep 385 (SG HC).

not *arrival of the ship*,[42] as illustrated by *Thomas v Harrowing Steamship Co.*[43] In this case, the ship met an accident, an excepted peril, just before reaching the port of discharge and about two-thirds of the cargo was washed ashore and were collected by the shipowner at the beach and delivered. The House of Lords held this to constitute true and right delivery.

Determining when the freight is earned can be difficult where there is no specific 'deemed earned' clause and the freight is rendered payable within a period of time. In *Duthie v Hilton,*[44] cement was carried from London to Sydney. Freight was payable 'within three days of arrival and before delivery of any portion of the goods'. The ship arrived at Sydney but was scuttled, within the three days, before delivery could be made. The cement hardened and lost its character as cement. It was not disputed that this was a case of total loss of the cargo. The shipowner argued that the freight was earned when the ship arrived. The English High Court rejected the argument and held that the freight would be earned only if the ship was ready to deliver throughout the period of the three days.[45]

What is meant by 'delivery of goods' here is delivery of the contracted goods. If the goods are so damaged that they are no longer the contracted goods, i.e. the merchantable character or commercial identity is lost, the delivery is not considered to be delivery of the goods. In *Asfar v Blundell,*[46] a cargo of dates was carried. The freight was payable upon right delivery. In the course of the voyage, the ship sank. Some dates were recovered and delivered, but not in a merchantable condition and they were sold for some other purpose for £12,400. The shipowner had insured against loss of freight and made a claim against the insurer for lost freight. In order for a claim of loss of freight to succeed, the fright must have first been earned. The English Court of Appeal held that the freight was not earned in this case as the character of the goods was so changed that it was no longer the contracted goods. A similar decision was arrived at in *The Caspian Sea.*[47] In this case, the ship carried 'Bachaquero Crude', which is usually paraffin free. The freight was payable upon delivery. The delivered cargo was contaminated with paraffin and the charterer refused to pay the freight. The shipowners instituted arbitration and the arbitral tribunal stated a case for the opinion of the English High Court. The court held as follows. If 'Bachaquero Crude' meant paraffin free crude, then paraffin-contaminated crude delivered would not constitute delivery and hence the freight would not be earned. However, if it meant crude from Bachaquero region which in its natural state contains no paraffin, then the arbitrators must consider the degree of the contamination to determine whether the crude had lost its character as Bachaquero crude. Only if it had lost the character, then the

---

[42] See *Hunter v Prinsep* (1808) 10 East 378, 103 ER 818 (EW Court of King's Bench).

[43] See *Thomas v Harrowing Steamship Co* [1913] 2 KB 171 (EW CA), speech of Kennedy LJ.

[44] (1868) 4 CP 138 (EW HC).

[45] See *Compania Naviera General SA v Kerametal Ltd (The Lorna I)* [1983] 1 Lloyd's Rep 373 (EW CA).

[46] [1896] 1 QB 123 (EW CA).

[47] *Montedison SpA v Icroma SpA (The Caspian Sea)* [1979] 3 All ER 378, [1980] 1 WLR 48, [1980] 1 Lloyd's Rep 91 (EW HC).

delivery would no longer be considered delivery of the contracted goods and the freight would not be earned.

13.4.2.1 Delivery Obligation Modified by 'Near' Clause

When freight is payable upon right and true delivery, the freight will be earned when the goods are delivered at the *destination* port. However, the obligation can be modified when there is a 'near' clause, which is quite common to be found in voyage charterparties. The clause will allow the shipowner to deliver at a nearby port or place where the originally designated delivery port is not safely accessible. In BIMCO GENCON 1994, the clause—cl. 1—reads as follows:

> … the Vessel shall proceed to the discharging port or place(s) ... on signing Bills of Lading, or so near thereto as she may safely get and lie always afloat, and there deliver the cargo.

At a look, the clause does not say that the near clause may be invoked only if the originally designated port is not safely accessible, but it means that because it says 'so near thereto as she may safely get'. This, in essence, implies that the clause is of use only if the originally designated port is not safely accessible. Where the clause is invokable, the courts have restrictively so construed the clause that delivery may only be made at a port or place 'near' the originally designated port. If no such port or place is available nearby, then the clause will not be of assistance to the shipowner. The courts have also restricted the clause to cases where the inaccessibility of the originally designated port was not foreseeable at the time the charterparty was entered into.

In *The Athamas*,[48] the voyage charterparty, which had a 'near' clause, was to carry and deliver the cargo at two ports in Vietnam, namely Saigon and Phnom Penh. The ship discharged at Saigon the portion of the cargo, the larger portion, due for Saigon in May 1959. However, thereafter she could not proceed to Phnom Penh, which was 250 nautical miles away, as the local pilotage authority refused its services on grounds of low-water season, which refusal was unexpected. Had the ship waited for the pilotage service, it would have taken three months. But if the waiting period would only have been a short period, then the clause would not have been available for reliance by the shipowner. The English Court of Appeal held that the shipowner could rely on the 'near' clause. In similar factual matrix, a contrary decision was reached by the English Court of Appeal in the previous case of *Metcalfe v Britannia Ironworks*,[49] where the sea froze up for three months. This was because the freezing up of the river was foreseeable when the charterparty was entered into.[50] In this case, the parties had even provided for the freezing up by adding an ice-clause.

---

[48] *SS Athamas (Owners) v Dig Vijay Cement Co Ltd (The Athamas)* [1963] 1 Lloyd's Rep 287, 107 Sol Jo 315 [1963] (EW CA).

[49] (1877) 2 QBD 423 (EW CA).

[50] Cf *Dahl v Nelson, Donkin & Co* (1881) 6 App Cas 38 at 44–45, 50 LJ Ch 411, [1881–85] All ER Rep 572 (UK HL), speech of Lord Blackburn.

The authorities show that a 'near' clause is one for the court to construe in the factual matrix of each case, where the court will consider if it was reasonable in the circumstances for the shipowner to invoke the clause and deliver at the nearby port or place.

13.4.3 Case of Cargo Ex Galam/Voyage Interrupted by Charterer

In *Cargo ex Galam,*[51] a ship was voyage-chartered to carry a cargo from the island of Terceira in North Atlantic Ocean to various ports including Hamburg. The owners had given a *respondentia* bond[52] to its creditors. At Hamburg, the cargo was arrested by the holders of the bond and removed to London by order of court. The freight was not paid. The Privy Council held the shipowner was entitled to a possessory lien over the cargo for full freight and general average (which was incurred when the ship was stranded in Scilly during the voyage), because the shipowner's performance of the charter was prevented by default of the cargo owners. The board further held that the shipowner's lien was in preference to the rights of the bond holders because the shipowner has rendered services in the nature of salvage.

A few things must be observed about this case. The decision is not directly about freight being earned, but about possessory lien. At common law, there are two types of liens, namely, specific liens and general liens. Specific lien accrues where the owner of the goods parts with the possession of the goods to a service provider who provides services in relation to the goods and the service provider is in possession of the goods and the payment for the service is due but not paid, eg. car repairers. General lien is where the owner of the goods is indebted to another for any reason and secures the debt with the goods, eg. pledge. In the context of freight and general average, the lien is a specific one. In order for the lien to be exercisable in respect of full freight, the freight must have been earned and have become payable but not paid. Hence, the Privy Council in effect had treated the freight as earned.

The correctness of the decision is arguable. The concept of earning the freight is a strict one. The freight can only be earned as per the contractual arrangement. If the shipowner is prevented by the charterer from completing the contractual voyage and delivering the goods at the destination port, the shipowner had lost the opportunity of earning the freight. The action must be the losses consequent on breach of the charterparty, i.e. freight for the part of the voyage completed and the loss of profit in respect of the uncompleted portion of the voyage. When the Privy Council allowed lien for *full* freight, it did not take into account that the shipowner would be over-enriched by charging the full freight when it had not incurred the cost and expenses

---

[51] *The Galam (Cargo ex)* (1863) Brown & Lush 167, 2 Moo PCCNS 216, (1863) 33 LJ Adm 91 (PC).

[52] A bond by which cargo to be discharged is given in security for a loan.

in respect of the uncompleted portion of the voyage. It will be hard to justify any extension of the strict concept of freight earned in this direction.

13.4.4 Applicability of Principles to Bills of Lading

The principles discussed of freight in charterparty is also appliable in the context of bills of lading.

13.5 Obligation of B/L Holder to Pay Charter-Freight

The obligation to pay the freight under the charterparty is on the charterer. However, because the terms of the charterparty are frequently incorporated into the bill of lading, also the holder of the bill may become liable for the freight directly to the shipowner.[53] This will not be the case where the shipowner has issued 'freight prepaid' bill,[54] which will estop the shipowner from claiming the freight from the holder of the bill where the freight under the bill was indeed paid to the charterer, as it will usually be the case. But if the bill is not a 'freight prepaid' one, then the holder of the bill will be liable to the shipowner for freight. A difficult question is what if, under such a bill, the holder pays the charterer and subsequently faces a claim by the shipowner for the freight. The answer depends on whether the charterer collected the freight as agent for the shipowner. The English High Court in *The Constanza M*[55] took the position that the charterer was not the agent of the shipowner when collecting the freight. To the contrary, the English High Court in *Wehner v Dene Steam Shipping Co*[56] found the charterer to be the agent of the shipowner when collecting the freight. This is a question that must be answered on the factual matrix of each case by established principles of apparent or ostensible authority. A more difficult question is where the holder of the bill sets off accounts between itself and the charterer when paying the freight to the charterer. *The Spiros C*[57] will lend some support to the proposition that it will be considered the full freight was paid, so that the shipowner cannot claim any freight from the holder of the bill where the charterer is treated as the agent of the shipowner.

---

[53] This means the shipowner has two persons to hold liable for the freight, i.e. the charterer and the bill of lading holder.

[54] 'Freight prepaid' statement is more common with time charters than voyage charters.

[55] *Compania Comercial y Naviera San Martin SA v China National Foreign Trade Transportation Corporation (The Constanza M) (HC)* [1980] 1 Lloyd's Rep 505 (EW HC).

[56] [1905] 2 KB 92 (EW HC).

[57] *Tradigrain SA and Others v King Diamond Marine Ltd (The Spiros C)* [2000] All ER (D) 979, [2000] 2 Lloyd's Rep 319 (EW CA).

Should a bill oblige the holder to pay freight but does not state the amount of the freight, then the liability of the holder will be to pay on *quantum meruit* basis.[58] There is nothing to change this position where a charterer is in picture between the shipowner and the holder of the bill.[59]

Where the bill is annotated 'freight prepaid' and at the same time incorporates the charterparty, although the incorporation will enable the shipowner to claim the freight from the holder of the bill, the 'freight prepaid' annotation will estop the shipowner from making such a claim. In order for the annotation to estop, the holder must have relied on it to its detriment. Hence, where the annotation is mistakenly made and the holder of the bill is aware of the mistake, there will be no estoppel, as held in *The Indian Reliance.*[60]

Where the bill is annotated 'freight prepaid' and there is no charterparty-incorporation clause, it was held in *Cho Yang Shipping Co Ltd v Coral (UK) Ltd,*[61] there would be no need for the holder of the bill to rely on any estoppel. This was because the annotation would, in such a case, mean that the holder has not undertaken to pay any freight to the shipowner but rather perhaps only to the charterer. However, the difficulty with this line of argument is that the bill is still a contract, statutorily, between the shipowner and the holder. The annotation is not that the holder has not undertaken to pay any freight to the shipowner but rather than the freight was paid. If that is untrue to the knowledge of the holder, its effect can be questionable where the holder has not relied on it to its detriment.

13.6 'Cesser' Clause

Where a bill of lading incorporates the charterparty and the bill is not a 'freight prepaid' bill, both the charterer and the holder of the bill are liable directly to the shipowner. However, the charterer may wish to be relieved of liability once the holder of the bill has undertaken the liability to the shipowner. This will be achieved by what is known as a 'cesser' clause, whereby the charterer will quit from liability once the holder of the bill has come in to take the liability. Courts have restrictively interpreted 'cesser' clauses so that the charterer is not relieved of liability until effectively the holder of the bill has become liable.

First, as demonstrated by *The Silva Plana.*[62] In this case, there was a shipowner, a head-charterer and a sub-charterer. The sub-charterparty had a cesser clause whereby

[58] *Dommett v Beckford* (1833) 5 B & Ad 521.

[59] As thought in *Ngo Chew Hong Edible Oil Pte Ltd v Scindia Steam Navigation Co Ltd (The Jalamohan)* [1988] 1 Lloyd's Rep 443 (EW HC).

[60] *India Steamship Co v Louis Dreyfus Sugar Ltd (The Indian Reliance)* [1997] 1 Lloyd's Rep 52 (EW HC).

[61] [1997] 2 Lloyd's Rep 641 (EW CA).

[62] *Oriental Maritime Pte Ltd v Ministry of Food, Government of the People's Republic of Bangladesh (The Silva Plana, Bahamastars and Magic Sky)* [1989] 2 Lloyd's Rep 371 (EW HC).

the liability of the sub-charterer to the head-charterer would be terminated once the bill of lading is issued by the shipowner to the holder of the bill. The English High Court held that the cesser clause was not effective because the bill of lading did not render the holder liable to the head-charterer but only to the shipowner. This in effect means that there is no consideration for the promise of the head-charter to release the sub-charterer unless the bill of lading holder becomes liable to the head-charterer in return. In those commonwealth jurisdictions, including Singapore and Malaysia, where a Contract Act modelled on the Indian Contract Act 1987 is in place, the requirement of consideration for cesser clause will be no different.[63]

Second, it is not sufficient that the shipowner, in return for relinquishing its rights against the charterer, acquires merely paper rights. In *The Aegis Brittanic,*[64] the bill of lading conferred on the shipowner the rights against the holder of the bill, but the courts at the port of discharge would not give effect to the conferment. Accordingly, the English Court of Appeal held the cesser clause was ineffective. Hence, the consideration must be an effective one.

Third, the courts have gone further to impose an additional requirement that, in order for the 'cesser' clause to be effective, the bill must incorporate the lien clause from the charterparty into the bill of lading, as held in *The Aegis Brittanic.*[65]

13.7 Lien

If freight is not paid when due, the shipowner may have a lien over the cargo or sub-freight. The source of the lien can be common law or contractual terms. The two are different. At common law, a lien is available only over cargo but not freight. Hence, any lien over freight must be founded on contract.

The common law lien in the context of carriage of goods by sea is a specific lien,[66] that arises because the owner of the goods has parted with the possession of the goods to a service provider who provides services in relation to the goods and the service provider is in possession of the goods and the payment has become due but not paid. The right to lien comes to an end when the person entitled to it lets go the possession of the goods.[67] Examples of persons who would have this lien include sea carriers, air carriers, land carriers, and other service providers like repairers. When the lien is exercised, the service provider retains possession of the goods pending payment, i.e. the interest that the service provider acquires is a possessory right over the goods.

---

[63] See Sections 2(d) and 10 (para 1) of the Indian Contract Act 1872/Malaysian Contracts Act 1950.

[64] *Action SA v Britannic Shipping Corpn Ltd (The Aegis Britannic)* [1987] 1 Lloyd's Rep 119 (EW CA).

[65] *Action SA v Britannic Shipping Corpn Ltd (The Aegis Britannic)* [1987] 1 Lloyd's Rep 119 (EW CA).

[66] As opposed to general lien. See chapter 13.4.3.

[67] Cl. 21 of the ASBATANKVOY form states "the lien shall continue after delivery of the cargo". However, the effectiveness of this clause is dubious as it may not be legally possible for the shipowner to have a lien when it has lost the possession.

Common law has recognised a lien only for those payments which would be due under the common law even in the absence of a specific agreement to pay it. For example, in a contract for repair of car, the common law obligation of the car owner, even in the absence of a specific agreement, is to pay the cost of the repair, hence for this cost, there will be a lien. Coming to carriage of goods by sea, the common law obligations of the cargo interest is to pay the freight on delivery and any general average. Hence, a lien will be for the freight and general average[68] (if any). A claim for detention, arguably, must fall within this category, as it is a common law obligation of the cargo interest arising from the contract of carriage, although the popular view is to the contrary. Dues for deadfreight and demurrage will not entitle the shipowner to a lien, as they are purely contractual in nature. In the same vein, a shipowner may not exercise any lien at common law for freight contractually payable in advance but may exercise the lien where the freight remains unpaid at the point of delivery.[69]

It is common for charterparties to contain wide lien clause that will include freight, deadfreight, demurrage, claims for damages and for all other amounts due under the charterparty including costs of recovering same. For example, cl. 8 of the BIMCO GENCON 1994 form provides for this as follows:

> The Owners shall have a lien on the cargo and on all sub-freights payable in respect of the cargo, for freight, deadfreight, demurrage, claims for damages and for all other amounts due under this Charter Party including costs of recovering same.

A lien for freight, whether under common law or contract, will only be exercisable if the freight is both earned and has become payable, except where the performance of the voyage was prevented by the charterer as in *Cargo ex Galam.*[70] Common law lien will, generally, bind any person entitled to or having an interest in the goods,[71] whereas contractual lien will only be as between the contracting parties. However, as often the terms of the voyage charterparty are incorporated into the bills of lading, the contractual right for lien in the charterparty will also fall into the bill of lading. For the purpose of exercise of a lien by the shipowner to which it is contractually entitled by the bill of lading, it does not matter that the holder of the bill has not

---

[68] *Hingston v Wendt* (1876) 1 QB 367 (EW HC).

[69] See *Kirchner v Venus* (1859) 12 Moo PC 361, 14 ER 948. 7 WR 455, 5 Jur NS 395 (PC); *Allison v Bristol Marine Insurance Co* (1876) 1 App Cas 209[1874–80] All ER Rep 781 (UK HL).

[70] *The Galam (Cargo ex)* (1863) Brown & Lush 167, 2 Moo PCCNS 216, (1863) 33 LJ Adm 91 (PC). See chapter 13.4.3 for a detailed discussion of this case.

[71] *The Exeter Carrier Case* (1743) 2 Ld Raym 867. Note the general rule that a lien at common law can only be created by the owner of the goods or by his express or implied authority: see Buxton v Baughan (1834) 6 C & P 674, 172 ER 1414 (EW Court of Exchequer); Pennington v Reliance Motors Ltd [1923] 1 KB 127 (EW HC). A bareboat charterer or a mortgagee in possession of the ship will usually have such authority to create lien at least in the ordinary course of trading: See Williams v Allsup (1861) 10 CB NS 417, 142 ER 514 (EW Court of Common Pleas): mortgagee of a ship may validly create a lien in favour of repairer for repairs performed to keep he seaworthy; see also Green v All Motors Ltd [1917] 1 KB 625 (EW CA); Ablemarle Supply Co Ltd v Hind [1928] 1 KB 307 (EW CA), involving repairers' lien over car under hire-purchase against the financier-owner, held in favour of the repairer.

become liable under the bill within Section 3 of the UK Carriage of Goods by Sea Act 1992.[72]

Questions may arise as to whether the shipowner may lien the cargo belonging to the holder of the bill of lading, upon the request of the charterer, where the freight was payable by the holder of the bill to the charterer. It is likely in such case the shipowner may not exercise any lien over the cargo, as no freight is due to it and the charterer does not have the possession to exercise any lien, unless there is contractual provision allowing exercise of a contractual lien in this manner.

If a shipowner wrongfully refuses to deliver by a purported exercise of a lien, that is not available, and that results in a cargo claim, such as where a shipowner refuses to deliver to the holder of a 'freight prepaid' bill of lading for freight due from the charterer to the shipowner, the Protection and Indemnity (P&I) insurance will not cover the claim. Such a wrongful holding of the cargo, despite breach on part of the charterer to pay the freight, may also constitute a breach of the shipowner's contractual obligation to the charter to deliver the cargo.[73]

13.7.1 Conditions for Lien: Contractual Link/Completion of Carriage

In order for there to be a lien by contract, the contract must be between the person seeking to exercise the lien and the cargo interest. When a bill of lading is transferred from one to another, there will of course be such a contract by statute.[74] However, this may not be very straightforward in the context of carriage of goods by sea, as demonstrated by by *Ocean Projects Inc v Ultratech Pte Ltd*.[75] However, to claim a common law lien, although there need not be such a contractual link between the carrier and the cargo interest, the carrier must have performed the contract of carriage under which the cargo was carried by the carrier, as demonstrated again by the same case.

In this case, the buyers contracted with a freight forwarder to ship the buyer's cargo from Houston[76] to Damai.[77] In turn, the freight forwarders contracted with a disponent shipowner for the carriage. The buyers paid the freight to the freight forwarder. The freight forwarder returned a clean bill of lading issued to the buyer's

[72] *Miramar Maritime Corpn v Holborn Oil Trading Ltd (The Miramar)* [1984] AC 676, [1984] 2 All ER 326, [1983] 2 Lloyd's Rep 319 at 324 (EW HC).

[73] *Steelwood Carriers Inc of Monrovia, Liberia v Evimeria Cia Naviera SA of Panama (The Agios Giorgis)* [1976] 2 Lloyd's Rep 192 (EW HC). Cf *Aegnoussiotis Shipping Corpn of Monrovia v A/S Kristian Jebsens Rederi of Bergen (The Aegnoussiotis)* [1977] 1 Lloyd's Rep 268 (EW HC).

[74] Section 2(1) of the UK Carriage of Goods by Sea Act 1992/UK Bills of Lading Act 1855 (now repealed). See chapter 2.2.10.1.

[75] [1994] 2 SLR 369 (SG CA).

[76] In the USA.

[77] In Malaysia.

bank, noting 'freight prepaid', issued by someone other than the disponent shipowner. Subsequently, the disponent shipowner issued another bill also to the buyer's bank. This bill was claused and noted freight was not paid. This bill, as usual, also conferred on it the right of lien on cargo for the freight. The buyer did not come forward to pay the freight once again. The disponent shipowner discharged the cargo in Singapore without completing the voyage and claimed its right of lien under its bill of lading. In turn, the respondent claimed damages for breach of contract based on the bill given by the freight forwarder. The freight forwarder has gone into liquidation.

The Singapore Court of Appeal found that the freight forwarder was the principal contracting party *vis-a-vis* the buyer and the disponent owner.[78] One contract of carriage between the buyer and the freight forwarder, and another between the freight forwarder and the disponent shipowner. Thus, the court held that the disponent shipowner would not be able to rely on the lien clause in its bill of lading[79] against the buyer. Although a private carrier who carries a cargo of a cargo-owner to the destination intended by him will be entitled to a lien even without any direct contract between them, that did not help the disponent shipowner here because it did not complete the voyage to Damai.

13.7.2 Manner of Exercising Lien and Sale of Cargo

All that the common law lien gives the shipowner is the right to hold the goods, i.e. possessory rights. It is usually exercised by discharging the cargo into a bonded warehouse at the destination port. However, the lien may be exercised by the ship waiting outside the discharge port, where it is not practicable to discharge into bonded warehouse.[80]

Once the lien is exercised, any sale thereafter of the liened goods is not regulated by the laws relating to lien but are regulated by the civil procedure appliable at the place of discharge. However, if the contractual terms provide for sale of the goods following exercise of the lien, the shipowner may sell accordingly. In the absence of such contractual provisions, any sale will be according to the civil procedure. Notably, such a sale provision is not commonly found in charterparties, including in the BIMCO GENCON 1994 form. In England and Wales, the relevant civil procedure is in Civil Procedure Rules (CPR) Part 25.1(1)(c)(v), which provides:

> (1) The court may grant the following interim remedies - ... (c) an order - ... (v) for the sale of relevant property which is of a perishable nature or which for any other good reason it is desirable to sell quickly; ...

---

[78] Prior to making the final decision, the court made an interim order for release of the cargo to the respondents subject to the respondent furnishing a banker's guarantee for any lien claim.

[79] I.e. Contract between the disponent shipowner and the freight forwarder.

[80] *Santiren Shipping Ltd v Unimarine SA (The Chrysovalandou Dyo)* [1981] 1 All ER 340, [1981] 1 Lloyd's Rep 159 (EW HC).

This rule was invoked in *The Moscow Stars*[81] to order the sale of liened cargo after the ship had been drifting off Curacoa Island for nine months and there was no other practical way of realising the benefits of the lien.[82] In Singapore and Malaysia, Order 29 rule 4(1) of the respective Rules of Court facilitates the same, which reads as follows:

Sale of perishable property (O. 29, r. 4)

> 4. (1) The Court may, on the application of any party to a cause or matter, make an order for the sale by such person, in such manner and on such terms, if any, as may be specified in the order of any movable property which is the subject matter of the cause or matter or as to which any question arises therein and which is of a perishable nature or likely to deteriorate if kept or which for any other good reason it is desirable to sell forthwith.

In the case of Malaysia, the above rule should be read with paragraph 6 of the Schedule to the Courts of Judicature Act 1964, which reads as follows:

> Power to provide for the interim preservation of property the subject matter of any cause or matter by sale … in any manner whatsoever.

In *The Daphne L*,[83] the cargo was carried under a voyage charterparty, which allowed lien on cargo for all freight, deadfreight and demurrage. The cargo interest was not able to present the bill of lading at the destination port to receive the cargo. This resulted in a delay of 130 days before discharge. The Singapore Court of Appeal upheld the right of the shipowner to lien the cargo for the demurrage and to recover the demurrage from the proceeds of the judicial sale of the cargo.

In cases where an arbitration clause is in place between the shipowner and the cargo interest, that does not prevent the shipowner from applying to the court for an order for sale out of necessity and urgency according to the applicable civil procedural rules. Section 44(3) of the UK Arbitration Act 1996, which is materially identical to Section 12A(1)(4) Singapore International Arbitration Act, provides as follows:

> If the case is one of urgency, the [court] may, on the application of a party or proposed party to the arbitral proceedings, make such orders as [it] thinks necessary for the purpose of preserving evidence or assets.

In the case of Singapore, in addition to the above, Section 12(1)(d) of the Singapore International Arbitration Act empowers the arbitral tribunal to make an order for "the preservation, interim custody or *sale* of any property which is or forms part of the subject-matter of the dispute". [emphasis added]

---

[81] *Dainford Navigation Inc v PDVSA Petroleo SA (The Moscow Stars)* [2017] EWHC 2150 (Comm), [2017] 1 Lloyd's Rep 409 (EW HC).

[82] See *Castleton Commodities Shipping Co Pte Ltd v Silver Rock Investments (The Clipper Monarch)* [2015] EWHC 2584 (Comm), [2016] 1 Ll L Rep 1 (EW HC) for another instance of order for sale of cargo liened by the shipowner, where the ship was waiting outside the Chinese territorial waters with the liened cargo.

[83] *Feoso (Singapore) Pte Ltd v Faith Maritime Co Ltd (The Daphne L)* [2003] SGCA 34 (SG CA).

Coming to Malaysia, there is no provision at the moment in the Arbitration Act 2005[84] enabling an application to be made to the court for sale, although there was such a provision in Section 11(1)(f) which was removed by an amendment to the Act in 2018. At the same time, there is nothing to stop a shipowner, before arbitration proceedings are commenced, from going to the court by way of *ex parte* (i.e. without notice) application for sale in view of urgency. An arbitration clause does not take away the jurisdiction of the court[85] but merely enables a defendant from asking the proceedings to be stayed for reference to the arbitration, in an *inter partes* proceedings.[86] The Act contains an express provision empowering the arbitral tribunal to make an interim order to "provide a means of preserving assets out of which a subsequent award may be satisfied". This provision may be used for making an application to the arbitral tribunal for sale when there is an agency of necessity, where arbitration proceedings are already in place.[87]

In all the above instances, it must be noted that a sale is allowed only in case of necessity, also called agency of necessity. A sale, in the absence of necessity, will only be possible if it is contractually provided for, binding the cargo interest.

The cost of exercising the lien can be charged to the cargo interest. Although it was once held that the cost could not be recovered from the cargo interest in a mid-19th century case affirmed by the House of Lords, *Somes v British Empire Shipping Co*,[88] the position was tactfully reversed by the English Court of Appeal in 2013 by *The Lehmann Timber*.[89] In this case, the court said that the lien had to be exercised by the shipowner because of the breach by the charterer of its obligation to discharge the cargo upon due payment of the freight. Hence, the cost of exercising the lien was the loss consequent upon this breach by the charterer for which the charterer was liable to compensate the shipowner for. The decision was affirmed by the House of Lords. However, this issue is unlikely to arise in practice with the charterparties commonly providing for recovery of costs of exercise of lien, whether it is common law lien or contractual lien. For example, cl. 8 of the BIMCO GENCON 1994 form provides for this.

---

[84] As last amended in 2018.

[85] See Arun Kasi, *Arbitration: Stay of Court Proceedings and Anti-Suit Injunctions*, Malaysia, CLJ Publication, 2014.

[86] Section 10 of the Malaysian Arbitration Act 2005.

[87] See *Dainford Navigation Inc v PDVSA Petroleo SA (The Moscow Stars)* [2017] EWHC 2150 (Comm), [2017] 1 Lloyd's Rep 409 (EW HC).

[88] (1858) El Bl & El 353, 120 ER 540 (EW Court of Exchequer Chamber), affirmed by the House of Lords in (1860) 8 HL Cas 338, [1843–60] All ER Rep 844 (UK HL).

[89] *Metall Market OOO v Vitorio Shipping Co Ltd (The Lehmann Timber)* [2013] EWCA Civ 650, [2014] QB 760 (EW CA).

13.7.3 Lien on Sub-freight

There is no common law lien on sub-freight. Hence, this lien will be available only if provided contractually. It is common find this provision in voyage charterparties. For instance, cl. 8 of the BIMCO GENCON 1994 form provides for this as follows:

> The Owners shall have a lien on the *cargo* and on all *sub-freights* payable in respect of the cargo, for freight, deadfreight, demurrage, claims for damages and for all other amounts due under this Charter Party including costs of recovering same. [emphasis added]

The manner of exercising this lien is by giving notice to the person bound to pay the sub-freight,[90] who may be the holder of the bill of lading or a sub-charterer. This is called [91] intercepting freight. The lien will be on the sub-freight limited to the portion of it that is unpaid and in the hands of the holder of the bill of lading or sub-charterer. This was demonstrated by the case of *The Spiros C*.[92] In this case, the shipowner had given the ship on a time-charter and there was a clause in the time charterparty allowing the shipowner to intercept sub-freight when the hire was not paid to the shipowner. The ship was given by the time charterers to a voyage charterer, i.e. sub-charter. The shipowner issued bill of lading to the sub-charterer incorporating the terms of the sub-charterparty. Accordingly, a connection was established between the sub-charterers and the shipowners on terms of the sub-charterparty. The sub-charterer had already paid the freight to the head-charterer less deductions on accounts between the sub-charterer and the head-charterer, which accounts were outside the scope of the sub-charterparty. The question was whether the shipowner can claim those deducted amounts. The English Court of Appeal held that the shipowner could not make the claim, as there was no freight payable as between the sub-charterer and the head-charterer. The lien could only be exercised on the freight that is unpaid in the accounts between the sub-charterer and the head-charterer.

In *Cascade Shipping Inc v Eka Jaya Agencies (Pte) Ltd*,[93] a ship was on time charter. The charterparty included a demise clause which authorised the charterer to issue bills of lading as agents for the shipowner. It also included a lien clause which gave the shipowner a lien on sub-freight. The charterer had an agent who issued bills and collected freight. The charterer defaulted in payment of hire. The shipowner gave notice to the charterer's agents that the shipowner had exercised the lien and accordingly asked the agent to pay, to the shipowner, any freight they have collected and were holding as well as the freight that they will collect in the future. The Singapore Court of Appeal summarily dismissed[94] the claim of the shipowner

---

[90] *Dry Bulk Handy Holding Inc and Another v Fayette International Holdings Ltd and Another (The Bulk Chile)* [2013] EWCA Civ 184, [2013] 2 Lloyd's Rep 38.

[91] *Dry Bulk Handy Holding Inc and Another v Fayette International Holdings Ltd and Another (The Bulk Chile)* [2013] EWCA Civ 184, [2013] 2 Lloyd's Rep 38.

[92] *Tradigrain SA and Others v King Diamond Marine Ltd (The Spiros C)* [2000] All ER (D) 979, [2000] 2 Lloyd's Rep 319 (EW CA).

[93] [1993] 1 SLR 980 (SG CA).

[94] At the instance of an application by the shipowner for summary judgment.

holding that the exercise of the lien must be by giving notice to the shippers asking them to pay any freight, not paid yet, to the shipowners. It could not be exercised by giving notice to the charterer or its agent to on-pay any freight collected or to be collected.

The next question is whether a bill of lading holder is obliged to pay the shipowner any unpaid freight upon the notice. The right of the shipowner to intercept the sub-freight is a contractual right between the shipowner and the charterer, which will not bind the bill of lading holder being a third party.[95] The contractual lien does not create any *in rem* right over the freight. Hence, the notice will not bind the bill of lading holder. But it will bind the bill of lading holder where the terms of the charterparty are incorporated in the bill of lading, as will often be the case.

If it was not a bill of lading holder but a sub-charterer only,[96] then the notice will not bind the sub-charterer. If the terms of the head-charterparty has been incorporated into the sub-charterparty, still the notice will not bind as the incorporation will not benefit the shipowner as it is a third party to the sub-charterparty. Sec. 1(1) of UK Contracts (Rights of Third Parties) Act 1999 will not confer any rights on the shipowner because exclusion of contracts of carriage by Section 6(5)(a) of the UK Act.

However, the English High Court in *The Western Moscow*[97] overcame the limitations in effectiveness of the notice where there is no contractual nexus between the shipowner and the bill of lading holder or sub-charterer incorporating the lien clause between the shipowner and the charterer or head-charterer. It was so overcome by finding that the contractual lien creates an equitable assignment, by way of charge, of the sub-freight in favour of the shipowner. In so finding, the judge said "If the right is only some form of sui generis contractual right it is one of restricted use. It would give the owners no direct claim against the sub-charterer". Having so found, Christopher Clark J limited the effect of the lien by saying the lien gives:

> ... only a right to have the charterers restrained from receiving the sub-charter hire or ordered to direct its payment to the owners or to a blocked account.

It is difficult to justify the finding of Christopher Clark J that freight, generally, creates an equitable assignment by way of charge. In any event, should there be such a charge, it must be registered pursuant to the companies laws where the charterer or the head-charterer is a company, as it will usually be, and the companies laws of the jurisdiction where the company is incorporated requires the same. In the England and Wales, Section 859A of the Companies Act 2006 will require such registration within 21 days of creation of the charge, i.e. the date of the charterparty. If this is not done, the charge is not invalid against the company bound by the charge, i.e. the charterer or the head-charterer, except against a liquidator, administrator or creditor. In Malaysia, a similar provision is made by Section 352 of the Companies Act 2006,

---

[95] Doctrine of privity of contract.

[96] To whom no bill of lading has been issued by the shipowner, hence no contractual nexus between them.

[97] *Western Bulk Shipowning III A/S v Carbofer Maritime Trading ApS (The Western Moscow)* [2012] EWHC 1224 (Comm), [2012] 2 All ER (Comm) 1140, [2012] 2 Lloyd's Rep 163 (EW HC).

with a 30-day timeframe for registration. In Singapore, by s. 131 of the Companies Act, a provision similar to that in Malaysia is in place.

When the obligation of the bill of lading holder or the sub-charterer to pay the shipowner is not clear, the safer approach will be for the bill of lading holder or the sub-charterer to interplead[98] and secure a court's order in this respect, which can be one for a payment into court. The bill of lading holder or sub-charterer must be mindful of running the risk of being in breach of its contract with the charterer or the head-charterer by paying the freight to the shipowner.

13.7.4 Lien on Sub-hire

A provision in a charterparty giving the shipowner a lien over 'sub-freight' has been strictly interpreted, in *The Cebu (No. 2)*,[99] not to cover sub-hire. It will be a sub-hire rather than sub-freight where a head time charterer grants a sub time charter. Hence, if there is an intention to intercept sub-hire, a lien on sub-hire that must be expressly stipulated, as was the case in *The Western Moscow.*[100] In this case, the head-charterparty was in NYPE 1946 form, the cl. 18 provided for the lien over cargoes and all sub-freights. The clause was modified with an addition of 'hire and sub-hire', hence read:

> That the owners shall have a lien upon all cargoes, and *all* sub-freights, <u>hire and sub-hire</u> for any amounts due under this Charter, including General Average contributions. [emphasis and underlining added]

Christopher Clark J held that the shipowners had a lien not only on the sub-freight but 'it was to extend to all sub-freight down the line'. A clause similar to the cl. 18 of the 1946 form is found in cl. 23 of the NYPE 1993 form with an additional coverage of all sub-hire. In cl. 23 of the NYPE 2015 form inclusion of deadfreight and demurrange is expressly stated, although in the absence of if, they would still be included by the words 'for any amounts due under this Charter' in the 1946 and 1993 forms. Clause 23 (para 1) of the NYPE 2015 form reads as follows:

> The Owners shall have a lien upon all cargoes, sub-hires and sub-freights (*including deadfreight and demurrage*) belonging or due to the Charterers or any sub-charterers, *for any amounts due under this Charter Party*, including general average contributions, and the Charterers shall have a lien on the Vessel for all monies paid in advance and not earned, and any overpaid hire or excess deposit to be returned at once. [emphasis added]

---

[98] In England and Wales, under CPR 35. In Malaysia and Singapore, under Order 17 of the respective Rules of Court.

[99] *Itex Itagrani Export SA v Care Shipping Corp (The Cebu) (No. 2)* [1990] 2 Lloyd's Rep 316 (EW HC).

[100] *Western Bulk Shipowning III A/S v Carbofer Maritime Trading ApS (The Western Moscow)* [2012] EWHC 1224 (Comm), [2012] 2 All ER (Comm) 1140, [2012] 2 Lloyd's Rep 163 (EW HC).

Chapter 14
Voyage Charter: Laytime and Demurrage

This chapter covers laytime and demurrage in voyage charterparties. The various laytime definitions such as weather working day, etc and the charterer's obligations arising from the laytime clause are considered. The question of when laytime starts and the associated matters such as notice of readiness (NOR), 'arrived ship', readiness of the ship to load/discharge, pre-conditions and manner and timing for issuance of notice of readiness are analysed in detail. That is followed by an examination of circumstances when the laytime will be suspended, namely, by laytime exceptions and fault of the shipowner. Finally, a study demurrage (contractual rate of compensation when the laytime is exceeded) and damages for detention (at common law) and termination for breach of the laytime are undertaken.

14.1 Introduction

A basic characteristic of the voyage charter is that the charter is for a voyage. This naturally requires that the loading and discharge operations, usually carried out by the charterer, to be done within a certain time. At common law the operations must be carried out within a *reasonable time frame*, if no specific time frame has been agreed. In practice, almost always a specific time frame will be agreed. This is called *laytime*. If the applicable time frame, whether a reasonable time frame or laytime, is exceed, at common law the charterer will be liable to the shipowner in damages for *detention* at the market rate, if no rate of compensation has been agreed. Again, almost always, a specific rate of compensation will be agreed. This is called *demurrage*. It is also common for voyage charterparties to allow a reward by the shipowner to the charterer if the charterer completes the loading or discharge ahead of laytime. The reward is called *dispatch,* which is usually at half the daily laytime rate. Alternatively, a charterparty may also allow the laytime for loading and discharge to be counted together, so that the saving in any one laytime can be used for the other. This is described a *total laytime for loading and discharging*. The converse is *separate*

A. Kasi, *The Law of Carriage of Goods by Sea*,
https://doi.org/10.1007/978-981-33-6793-7_14

laytime for loading and discharge. Generally, unless the charterparty allows the total laytime, the laytime will be computed on 'separate' basis. BIMCO GENCON 1994 form[1] has the option of selecting separate or total laytime.

It is not compulsory that a voyage charter is for the whole ship. It is possible that a voyage charter blocks only a portion of the ship and the shipowner may then carry cargo for others in the same voyage. Such carriage for other may be merely under a bill of lading or another concurrent voyage charter.[2]

This chapter will cover laytime definitions, charterer's obligation in relation to laytime, study of when the laytime commences and when it is suspended. That is followed by the remedies available to the shipowner when laytime is exceeded, namely the rights of termination and demurrage.

14.2 Laytime Definitions

Laytime can be defined in different ways in a charterparty, in terms of calculation of the laytime as well as more detailed definition such exclusion of weekends from it or admitting only weather working days within it. A study of them will be the subject of this sub-chapter.

14.2.1 Calculation of Laytime

There are a few different ways how the period of laytime is usually defined in charterparties. The period may be stated by number of days. Laytime may alternatively be stated by the rate of loading or discharge. It may even be stated by number of hours, which is quite common in tanker voyage charters.

When the laytime is to be computed in number of days, there are two ways the days may be defined, expressly or impliedly. One is 'calendar' day. Another is 'conventional' day. A calendar day goes by calendar days. A conventional day means 24 hours from the start of the loading/discharge operation to end of it. If a charterer starts loading at 2 pm on Monday and finishes it at 1 pm on Tuesday, the charterer has used two calendar days, but only one conventional day. If the charterer starts loading at 10 am on Monday and finishes it at 11 am on Tuesday, then the calendar/conventional days used are two. If a charterparty merely says 'days ', then it is thought to refer to the calendar days, but however this is as matter of construction and it may well refer to conventional days. For example, in *Leonis Steamship Company Limited v Rank Limited*,[3] the charterparty provided that the laytime would commence 12 hours after the notice of readiness was given. The English Court of Appeal held that the 'days'

[1] Box 16 and cl. 6(a) and (b).

[2] E.g. *Stolt Tankers v Landmark* [2002] 1 Lloyd's Rep 786 (EW HC).

[3] [1908] 1 KB 499 (EW CA).

provided for laytime in the charterparty was 'conventional' days. The same must be true of BIMCO GENCON 1994 form, which provides, in cl. 16(c), in relevant part, as follows:

> Laytime for loading and discharging shall commence at 13.00 hours, if notice of readiness is given up to and including 12.00 hours, and at 06.00 hours next working day if notice given during the office hours after 12.00 hours.

14.2.2 Weather Day and Working Day Qualifications

It is common that laytime period will be qualified with 'weather permitting' or 'weather working days'. 'Weather permitting' day will mean that a day is to count as part of laytime only if weather permits. 'weather working day' will mean that it is both a weather permitting and working day. BIMCO GENCON 1994 form, in cl. 6(a)/(b), defines laytime as weather permitting days/hours, Sundays and holidays excepted. Clause 6(a)/(b) reads as follows:

> **(a)* Separate laytime for loading and discharging**
>
> The cargo shall be loaded within the number of running days/hours as indicated in …, weather permitting, Sundays and holidays excepted, unless used, in which event time used shall count. The cargo shall be discharged within the number of running days/hours as indicated in …, weather permitting, Sundays and holidays excepted, unless used, in which event time used shall count.
>
> **(b)* Total laytime for loading and discharging**
>
> The cargo shall be loaded and discharged within the number of total running days/hours as indicated in …, weather permitting, Sundays and holidays excepted, unless used, in which event time used shall count.

A working day within limited working hours only, such as a Saturday in certain places, was held by the House of Lords in *Reardon Smith Line Ltd v Ministry of Agriculture, Fisheries and Food*[4] to be a 'working day' for the purposes here.

Where the laytime is defined as weather permitting days, if weather does not permit doing the relevant work on a day and, at the same time, working is prevented by other factors like strike, the charterer is still entitled to exclusion of the day.[5] If a ship, under port charter, is waiting for berth and it is not a weather day at berth, then the charterer is entitled to the exclusion of the day, although no working was prevented on day as the ship did not reach berth yet, as held by the English Court of Appeal in *The Vorras*.[6]

---

[4] [1963] AC 691 (UK HL).

[5] *Reardon Smith Line Ltd v Ministry of Agriculture, Fisheries and Food* [1963] AC 691 (UK HL).

[6] *Dow Chemical (Nederland) BV v BP Tanker Co Ltd (The Vorras)* [1983] 1 Lloyd's Rep 579 (EW CA).

14.3 Charterer's Obligations

The charterer has no obligation to save any part of laytime. In *The Vrontados*,[7] the loading was almost completed by end of the year. But the charterer delayed completion of the final one percent, because the charterer wanted a bill of lading showing shipment in January, in order to comply with its agreement with the buyers. The English High Court held that the charterer was entitled to do so as long as it was within the laytime, which it was in this case.[8]

This point was further demonstrated by *Hudson v Ede*.[9] In this case, in the midst of loading operation, the river by which cargo was brought to the ship was frozen for two months. A 'detention by ice' clause in the charterparty suspended laytime because the river was frozen. However, the shipowner argued had the charterer loaded with due diligence, it would have completed the loading before the river was frozen. The court rejected the argument and upheld the laytime suspension as the charterer had no duty to load with any due diligence beyond that of loading within the laytime subject to any laytime exceptions.

If a charterer does not load, the charterer will be liable in damages to the shipowner for the breach. In *Freight Connect (S) Pte Ltd v Paragon Shipping Pte Ltd*,[10] a head charterer let the ship to a sub-charterer, back-to-back, at a profit of USD6,000 on the freight. Daily detention charges for any time lost was agreed at the rate of USD25,000. Freight was deemed earned upon loading. It was a port charter with a cancelling date of 20 August. The ship arrived at the port and the head charterer gave the notice of readiness on 20 August and a berth was secured for 23 August. However, the sub-charterer did not provide the required documents to the port authority, hence the ship could not berth. The sub-charterer arranged for the cargo to be shipped on board another ship and notified the head charterer of the same. The Singapore Court of Appeal found the sub-charterer to be in breach of the charterparty. The court held that the head charterer was not entitled to the freight as it was not earned yet, but only to USD6,000 as loss of profit and the detention charges at the agreed rate. The court refused to consider the head-charterer's claim that the sub-charterer should indemnity the head-charterer for any claim that may be brought by the shipowner against the head-charterer, while no such action was yet brought.

---

[7] *Margaronis Navigation Agency Ltd v Henry W Peabody & Co of London Ltd (The Vrontados) (HC)* [1965] 1 QB 300, [1964] 2 All ER 296 (EW HC).

[8] Another similar decision was reached in *Total Transport Corporation v Arcadia Petroleum Ltd (The Eurus)* [1996] 2 Lloyd's Rep 408 (EW HC).

[9] (1868) LR 2 QB 566 (EW HC), affirmed by the Court of Appeal in (1868) LR 3 QB 412 (EW CA).

[10] [2015] SGCA 37, [2015] 5 SLR 178 (SG CA).

14.4 Starting of Laytime

It can be a complex question when laytime starts. It depends on the terms of the charterparty. Almost always, the laytime will be tied to notice of readiness (NOR). Laytime will start when the notice of readiness is issued or in a certain time after the notice was issued. BIMCO GENCON 1994 form starts the laytime at 1 pm if notice was given before 12 pm. If notice is given after 12 pm, it starts the laytime at 6 am next working day. The form, in cl. 6(c) (para 1), provides for this as follows:

> Laytime for loading and discharging shall commence at 13.00 hours, if notice of readiness is given up to and including 12.00 hours, and at 06.00 hours next working day if notice given during office hours after 12.00 hours. …

ExxonMobil Voy 2005[11] form provides that the laytime will start six hours after the notice is given or the ship arrived at the berth, whichever is early. The requirement of notice of readiness is customary and implied insofar as loading is concerned, though it may not be so in respect discharging.[12] However, usually, the charterparty will require such a notice of readiness for both loading and discharging. This takes us to the question of when the notice of readiness may be issued, that is considered below.

14.4.1 Notice of Readiness

For the notice of readiness (NOR) to be issued, the ship must first become an 'arrived ship', i.e. complete the approach/carrying voyage and reach the place designated in the charterparty. Second, the ship must be ready to load/discharge. Third, the ship has complied with any other pre-conditions stipulated in the charterparty to issue the notice. The notice must be issued in the manner required by the charterparty and within the time frame permitted by the charterparty.

If a ship issues the notice, when it has actually not *arrived* or is not *ready to load* or the *pre-conditions for notice* required by the charterparty are not met, then the notice is invalid. The time to test the readiness is the time the notice is issued. Accordingly, the ship cannot issue a notice first and then become ready before actually the charterer is ready to load.[13] In *The Tres Flores*,[14] the ship arrived at the port waiting for a berth. The ship gave a notice of readiness. However, the ship's cargo holds needed fumigation before cargo could be loaded. Fumigation would take only a short while and could be, and was in fact, completed before a berth was available. The English Court of Appeal held the notice to be invalid as the ship was not ready at the time the

---

[11] Cl. 13.

[12] *Houlder v General SN Co* (1862) 3 F&F 170.

[13] *Christensen v Hindustan Steel* [1971] 1 Lloyd's Rep 395 (EW HC).

[14] *Compania de Naviera Nedelka SA v Tradax International SA of Panama City RP (The Tres Flores) [1974] QB 264,* [1973] 2 Lloyd's Rep 247, [1973] 3 All ER 967, [1973] 3 WLR 545 (EW CA).

notice was given. The court distinguished this from *preliminary routine matters* like removal of hatch covers that would not render a ship unready for loading/discharging.

A difficulty will arise if the notice is issued while waiting at port and, after a long wait, it is found upon reaching berth that the ship was not indeed ready due to want of some minor repairs. This may cause an injustice to the shipowner, as a long wait can be wasted for a minor repair. This effect can be mitigated by the charterparty expressly providing that if the ship is found not ready upon berthing, the laytime will not be affected save for the time that will be required for repairing. A provision to this effect is found in BIMCO GENCON 1994 form at para 6(c) (para 2), which provides as follows:

> **(c) Commencement of laytime (loading and discharging)**
>
> ...
>
> If the loading/discharging berth is not available on the Vessel's arrival at or off the port of loading/discharging, the Vessel shall be entitled to give notice of readiness ... whether in free pratique or not, whether customs cleared or not. Laytime or time on demurrage shall then count as if she were in berth and in all respects ready for loading/discharging *provided that the Master warrants that she is in fact ready in all respects.* Time used in moving from the place of waiting to the loading/ discharging berth shall not count as laytime. *If, after inspection, the Vessel is found not to be ready in all respects to load/discharge* time lost after the discovery thereof until the Vessel is again ready to load/discharge shall not count as laytime. *Time used before commencement of laytime shall count.* [emphasis added]

With such provision and comfort, the English High Court in *The Linardos*[15] held that it is implied that the ship must give the notice in good faith. It is common that charterparties will require the ship to issue notice of expected arrival, which is not the notice of readiness, a few hours before the expected arrival, such as 24, 48 or 72 hours, so that the charterer can get ready for loading or discharge.

14.4.1.1 Estoppels and Waivers

If a notice is invalid but the charterer accepts it without protest and the ship relies on it to its detriment, the charterer will be estopped from later raising the irregularity to invalidate the notice. This scenario is demonstrated by *The Shackleford.*[16] In this case, the charterparty required the ship to obtain customs clearance before issuing the notice. However, the ship issued the notice before obtaining the clearance and the charterer did not protest but accepted the notice. In consequence of this, the ship did not seek to obtain the customs clearance at the earliest possible time after the notice. The ship would have done so had the notice not been accepted. Accordingly, the ship suffered a detriment relying on the acceptance. Hence, the English Court of Appeal held that the charter was estopped from pleading the irregularity and thus the invalidity of the notice.

---

[15] *Cobelfret NV v Cyclades Shipping Co Ltd (The Linardos)* [1994] 1 Lloyd's Rep 28 (EW HC).

[16] *Surrey Shipping Co Ltd v Compagnie Continentale (France) SA (The Shackleford)* [1978] 1 WLR 1080, [1978] 2 Lloyd's Rep 154 (EW CA).

If a charterer accepts an invalid notice, the charterer may be taken to have waived its rights to object. 'Waiver' is a voluntary relinquishment or surrender of some known right or privilege. Accordingly, if the facts constituting the invalidity of the notice were not known to the charterer, there can be no waiver, as held by the English Court of Appeal in *The Mexico 1*.[17] In this case, the ship gave the notice, while the charterer's cargo was inaccessible as it was overstowed by another cargo. This meant that the ship was not ready to discharge the cargo at the time the notice was given. However, being unaware of this, the charterer accepted the notice. The court held that this did not waive the charterer's right to object to the notice as the charterer was unaware of the facts rendering the notice invalid. In *The Northgate*,[18] the charterparty allowed the notice to be given to the terminal. The ship gave a notice that was invalid, but the terminal, with knowledge of the facts rendering the notice, accepted the notice without protest. The question before the court was whether the authority given to the terminal to accept the notice included an authority to waive the irregularity. The court answered this question in the affirmative, so that the irregularity was waived.

Prior to *The Mexico 1*, the contrary was held by the English High in *The Helle Skou*.[19] In this case, the charterparty required the cargo holds to be free from odor before the notice of readiness was issued. The ship issued the notice while the holds had odor. Upon commencing the loading operation, the charterer came to know this and sought to have the notice invalid. The court disallowed the charterer from raising the issue as the notice was already accepted, albeit without knowledge of the irregularity. This authority does not represent the good law, while *The Mexico 1* does.

The question of waiver arose in a different way in *The Happy Day*.[20] In this case, it was a berth charter with a 'wibon' (whether in berth or not) clause. A berth charter means that the ship becomes an arrived ship and may give the notice of readiness only when she had berthed. However, the 'wibon' clause will allow the ship to be considered arrived and to give the notice upon arrival at the port if there was a congestion preventing her from berthing. The ship arrived at the port and there was no congestion, but the ship gave the notice before reaching the berth. Hence, the notice was invalid. However, the charterer allowed the cargo to be discharged after the ship berthed. It was the argument of the charterer that the laytime never started because no valid notice of readiness was given. The English Court of Appeal refused the argument and held that the laytime started when the discharge commenced. The court supported its decision on grounds that the charterer had waived its right for a notice of readiness by allowing the discharge without protest. Had the charterer not done so, the shipowner would have given a second notice at the berth. This

[17] *Transgrain Shipping BV v Global Transporte Oceanico SA (The Mexico 1) (CA)* [1990] 1 Lloyd's Rep 507 (EW CA).

[18] *Ocean Pride Maritime Ltd Partnership v Qingdao Ocean Shipping Co (The Northgate)* [2007] EWHC 2796 (Comm), [2008] 2 All ER (Comm) 330 (EW HC).

[19] *Sofial SA v Ove Skou Rederi (The Helle Skou)* [1976] 2 Lloyd's Rep 205 (EW HC).

[20] *Glencore Grain Ltd v Flacker Shipping Ltd (The Happy Day)* [2002] EWCA Civ 1068, [2002] 2 All ER (Comm) 896, [2002] All ER (D) 219 (Jul), [2002] 2 Lloyd's Rep 487 (EW CA).

decision, a welcome one, reversed the decision of the High Court in the same case and previous decisions in other cases[21] that held that commencing the loading or discharge operation was not a waiver of any irregularity in the notice.

14.4.2 Arrived Ship

The question when a ship becomes an arrived ship can be a complex one in some cases. There are, basically, two types of charters.[22] One is a port charter, in which the ship is considered 'arrived' upon reaching the waiting area within the port limits. The other is berth charter, in which the ship becomes an arrived ship only when she reaches the berth. It may not always be a straightforward question to answer if a given charter is a port charter or berth charter. Further, whether it is basically a port charter or berth charter, various qualifications are usually written into charterparties that will allow a ship to become an arrived ship before reaching the port or the berth. BIMCO GENCON 1994 form[23] is in the nature of berth charter with qualifications, as it allows the ship to give the notice at port only if a berth is not available upon arrival at the port.

In *The Merida*,[24] the charterparty provided the 'vessel to load at one good and safe port/one good and safe charterers' berths Xingang …' The reference was made both to safe port and safe charterer's berth. The English High Court held this to be a berth charter. Hence, 20 days delay in berthing was on the shipowners. The 'contractual destination' of the loading or discharge point plays an important part in determining whether it is a port or berth charter. Lord Brandon delivering the judgement of the House of Lords in *The Kyzikos*[25] said this as follows:

> The characteristics of a port charterparty are … the contractual destination of the chartered ship is a named port. … By contrast, the characteristics of a berth charterparty are … the contractual destination of the chartered ship is a berth designated by the charterers within a named port.

In *Freight Connect (S) Pte Ltd v Paragon Shipping Pte Ltd*,[26] there was a first fixture that described the loading point as 'loading port: 1 safe berth or port owner's berth Nanwei port'. The vessel did not arrive under the first fixture and the parties agreed

---

[21] E.g. *Pteroti Cia Nav SA v National Coal Board* [1958] 1 QB 469 (EW HC); *Glencore Grain Ltd v Goldbeam Shipping Inc; Goldbeam Shipping Inc v Navios International Inc (The Mass Glory)* [2002] EWHC 27 (Comm), [2002] 2 Lloyd's Rep 244 (EW HC).

[22] It is not compulsory that the destination point stipulated in the charterparty is a port or berth. It can also be other places like a sea mooring buoy or customary anchorage.

[23] Cl. 6(c) (para 2).

[24] *Novologistics SARL v Five Ocean Corp (The Merida)* [2009] EWHC 3046 (Comm), [2010] 1 Lloyd's Rep 274 (EW HC).

[25] *Bulk Transport Group Shipping Co Ltd v Seacrystal Shipping Ltd (The Kyzikos)* [1989] AC 1264, [1988] 3 All ER 745, [1989] 1 Lloyd's Rep 1 (UK HL).

[26] [2015] SGCA 37, [2015] 5 SLR 178 (SG CA).

on a second fixture, replacing the first one, in which the loading point was described as 'port of loading: Nanwei port'. It was a common ground between the parties that the first fixture was a berth charter, but they disagreed as to the type of the second fixture. The Singapore Court of Appeal held the second one to be a port charter. In coming to the conclusion, the court particularly observed that the first fixture had the words 'owner's berth' which was missing in the second fixture and that the contractual destination in the second fixture was a port rather than berth.

In *Stag Line Ltd v Board of Trade*,[27] the charterparty provided that the loading was to be at 'one or two ports [East] Canada/Newfoundland, place or places as ordered by charterer'. The English Court of Appeal found this to be a berth charter, as the charterer would nominate both the port and the place, meaning the berth. Upon the ship's arrival at the port, the ship gave the notice while the charterer nominated a particular loading place (i.e. berth). As this was a berth charter and the ship had not berthed at the time the notice was given, the notice was invalid.

The difference between the two types of charter can be narrower that what it appears to be, following the decision of the House of Lords in *The Johanna Oldendorff.*[28] In this case, it was held that even under a port charter the ship will become arrived only if she reached a berth where a berth was immediately available. Only if a berth was not immediately available and the ship had to wait within the port limits for a berth, then she would be considered arrived upon reaching the port and could thereupon give the notice of readiness. Once the notice is given and the laytime starts, the laytime will continue to count also during the shifting time from the port's waiting area to the berth. If a berth was available upon the ship reaching the port, then the shifting time would have been on the shipowner.

14.4.2.1 Port Charter, Port Limits and 'Wipon' Clause

It is often said that the ship becomes an arrived ship when the ship is 'immediately and effectively at the disposal of the charterer'. This phrase may lack clarity in practical context. *The Johanna Oldendorff,*[29] decided by the House of Lords, has offered some guidelines about what it means and when a ship becomes an arrived ship in a port charter. The ship will become an arrived ship when the ship is within the 'port limits', if no berth is immediately available. That takes one to the question of what the 'port limit' is. If there is a law regulating the port limit, then the port limit as according to what is set by the law. If there is no such law, then a good indication of the port limit is the area within which a port authority exercises its various powers to regulate the movements and conduct of ships. This list was, however, not exhaustive. The House also noted that the powers relating to pilotage and other matters may well extend

[27] [1950] 2 KB 194 (EW CA).

[28] *Oldendorff (E L) & Co GmbH v Tradax Export SA (The Johanna Oldendorff)* [1974] AC 479, [1973] 3 All ER 148 (UK HL).

[29] *Oldendorff (E L) & Co GmbH v Tradax Export SA (The Johanna Oldendorff)* [1974] AC 479, [1973] 3 All ER 148 (UK HL).

beyond the port limits. The House seemed to suggest that the usual waiting place may not be decisive in answering the question of port limit, although it is indicative of the port limit, as it was in this case, where the ship was in the usual waiting area 17 nautical miles away from the dock. The waiting area was within the port's legal and commercial limits. The House found that the ship was within the port limit.

Two years after *The Johanna Oldendorff* was decided, the House of Lords decided *The Maratha Envoy*.[30] In this later case the ship, a large one, was asked to wait some 25 nautical miles away, which was outside the legal and commercial limits of the port. This was the customary place where large ships were asked to wait. No berth was immediately available. The House found that the ship was lying outside the port limits and hence did not become an arrived ship under the port charter. There was a 'wibon' clause ('whether in berth or not' clause). This was redundant as with or without the clause the obligation of the shipowner to reach the port and, if a berth is immediately available, to proceed to berth.[31] If a berth is not immediately available, then the ship may give the notice upon arrival at the waiting area within the port. However, if there was a 'wipon' ('whether in port or not') clause or a 'time lost' clause (time lost in waiting for berth to count as laytime), that would have made a difference when the ship would not enter the port area due to congestion. A 'wipon' clause can be an important one for the shipowner where a particular port usually requires the ship to wait outside the port limits.

In the more recent case, *The Arundel Castle*,[32] the charterparty allowed the notice of readiness to be given upon the 'vessel's arrival at load/discharge ports within the *port limits*'. The charterer relied on Admiralty chart to say that the ship was outside the port limit as delineated in the chart when she gave the notice of readiness. The shipowner argued that, although the place where the ship waited when she gave the notice was outside the area delineated in the chart, that was the customary place where ships were asked to wait. The arbitrators, with whom the English High Court agreed, rejected the argument that the customary place where ships were asked to wait were determinative of the port limit, where the Admiralty chart provided otherwise.

14.4.2.2 Customary-Anchorage Charter

A near alternative to port charter is one where the ship is required to proceed to the 'customary anchorage'. The key difference between a port charter and a customary-anchorage charter is that in the later it does not matter whether the customary waiting area is within or outside the port limits. The customary-anchorage destination has an effect similar to 'wipon' clause. The customary-anchorage destination can be more

---

[30] *Federal Commerce and Navigation Co Ltd v Tradax Export SA (The Maratha Envoy)* [1978] AC 1, [1977] 2 All ER 849 (UK HL).

[31] See also *Federal Commerce and Navigation Co Ltd v Tradax Export SA (The Maratha Envoy)* [1978] AC 1, [1977] 2 All ER 849 (UK HL).

[32] *Navalmar UK Ltd v Kale Maden Hammaddeler Sanayi Ve Ticart AS (The Arundel Castle)* [2017] EWHC 116 (Comm), [2017] 2 All ER (Comm) 1033, [2017] 1 Lloyd's Rep 370 (EW HC).

favourable to the shipowner, as likely there is no need to proceed to berth, even if one is available, to become an arrived ship.[33] Customary-anchorage charter is usually seen in tanker charterparties.

14.4.2.3 Berth Charter, 'Wibon', 'Time Lost' and 'Reachable on Arrival' Clauses

In the case of a berth charter, the ship will become an arrived ship only upon the ship berthing. This may cause a lot of hardship on the shipowner where a berth is not available due to congestion. Hence, the shipowners developed a practice of included clauses like 'wibon' ('whether in berth or not') or 'time lost' ('time lost to count *as laytime*') clause, so that the ship will become arrived when the ship is unable to berth due to congestion. However, this does not change the character of the charter as a berth charter, and the wibon or time lost clause is invokable only if a berth could not be reached due to congestion.

'wibon' and 'time lost' clauses

Courts have narrowly interpreted such clauses to permit the notice to be given before berthing only where berthing is prevented by congestion and not by other causes such as bad weather. In *The Kyzikos*,[34] it was a berth charter with 'wibon' and 'time lost' clauses. The berth, although available, was not reachable due to fog and resultant closure of the pilot station. The ship gave the notice of readiness and it was the claim of the shipowner that laytime had started and that demurrage was due. The House of Lords rejected the claim of the shipowner and held that the ship did not become an arrived ship while waiting to reach a berth because the clauses were limited to cases where the ship could not berth due to congestion only. In *Suck AG v Glencore International AG*,[35] it was a berth charter with 'wibon' clause. A berth was not available. However, even if it was available, it would not have been reachable due to bad weather. The ship gave notice of readiness upon reaching the port while waiting to reach a berth. The English High Court held that the 'wibon' clause became operative and laytime commenced while waiting and that it was sufficient that the unavailability of berth was one of the reasons for inability to berth.

There is a significant difference between the 'wibon' clause and 'time lost' clause. The 'wibon' clause merely renders the ship an arrived one allows the ship to give notice of readiness and start the laytime whether the ship is berth or not. After this, the shifting time is on the charterer and takes up laytime. But the 'time lost' clause operates automatically by treating the waiting time, and only the *waiting time*, as laytime. A 'time lost' clause itself, in the absence of being coupled with a 'wibon'

---

[33] There are a few LMAA awards that recognise this proposition. See *Feoso (Singapore) Pte Ltd v Faith Maritime Co Ltd (The Daphne L)* [2003] SGCA 34, [2003] SLR 556 (SG CA).

[34] *Bulk Transport Group Shipping Co Ltd v Seacrystal Shipping Ltd (The Kyzikos)* [1989] AC 1264, [1988] 3 All ER 745, [1989] 1 Lloyd's Rep 1 (UK HL).

[35] [2011] EWHC 1361 (Comm), [2011] 2 Lloyd's Rep 278 (EW HC).

clause, does not render the ship an arrived one and does not permit issuing notice of readiness. The time taken for shifting from the waiting place to the berth is on the shipowner.

A 'time lost' clause operates independently of notice of readiness and laytime. It is not necessary for the ship to become arrived, notice of readiness to be given or laytime to have commenced for the 'time lost' clause to operate.[36]

In order for 'time lost' clause to operate the time must be lost due to 'waiting'. In *The Agios Stylianos*,[37] a ship was carrying cement under a voyage charterparty with a 'time lost' clause and vehicles under another charterparty. The English High Court held that only the 'time lost in waiting for a cement berth' can be claimed from the charterer in cement-charterparty. In *The Massalia (No. 2)*,[38] a berth charter had a 'time lost' clause. The ship waited at the port for a berth to discharge and claimed the waiting time to be counted as laytime. However, the cargo of the charterer was overstowed, hence the ship was not ready to discharge the cargo yet until she berthed and discharged the other cargo. The English High Court held that the waiting time was to be counted as laytime and that demurrage was due. It must be observed that, in this case, the time was lost because of the waiting and not by the fact of overstowed cargo.

Both the 'wibon' and 'time lost' clause render the time in issue to count as laytime. A consequence of this is that the charterer will then be entitled to laytime definition and exceptions that would be available if the ship was at the berth. In line with this, BIMCO GENCON 1994 form[39] expressly provides that, while waiting, laytime should count 'as if she were in berth'. This is demonstrated by *Carboex SA v Louis Dreyfus Commodities Suisse SA*.[40] In this case, a 'wibon' clause in a berth charter started the laytime clock while the ship was waiting for a berth due to congestion. There was a laytime exception for congestion following strike, which happened in this case. Hence, it was held, although the laytime was started by the 'wibon' clause, it was suspended by the laytime exception clause. A similar decision was arrived at by the House of Lords in *The Darrah*.[41] In this case, 'time lost in waiting for berth [was] to count *as laytime*'. It was held that the charterer was entitled to rely on

---

[36] *North River Freighters Ltd v HE President of India (North River)* [1956] 1 QB 333 (EW CA); *Ionian Navigation Company Inc v Atlantic Shipping Company SA (The Loucas N)* [1971] 1 Lloyd's Rep 215 (EW CA); *Aldebaran Compania Maritime SA, Panama v Aussenhandel AG Zurich (The Darrah)* [1977] AC 157, [1976] 2 All ER 963 (UK HL); *Freight Connect (S) Pte Ltd v Paragon Shipping Pte Ltd* [2015] SGCA 37, [2015] 5 SLR 178 (SG CA).

[37] *Agios Stylianous Compania Naviera SA v Maritime Associates International Ltd Lagos (The Agios Stylianos)* [1975] 1 Lloyd's Rep 426 (EW HC).

[38] *Government of Ceylon v Societe Franco-Tunisienne D'armement-Tunis (The Massalia) (No. 2)* [1960] 2 Lloyd's Rep 352 (EW HC).

[39] Cl. 6(c) (para 2).

[40] [2011] EWHC 1165 (Comm), [2011] 2 Lloyd's Rep 177 (EW HC).

[41] *Aldebaran Compania Maritime SA, Panama v Aussenhandel AG Zurich (The Darrah)* [1977] AC 157, [1976] 2 All ER 963 (UK HL).

laytime definition and exceptions in relation to the 'time lost' clause as the lost time was to count as laytime.[42]

A complex combination of clauses was found in *The Stainless Emperor*,[43] resulting in quite an anomalous result. In this case, 'time lost' was to be counted as '*used* laytime'. The laytime definition excluded Fridays and holidays from laytime, '*unless used*'. The English High Court held that since the time lost was to be considered as used laytime, Fridays and holidays were not excluded. This is arguably too literal construction of the clause that may not accord with the commercial intention associated with those clauses.

While usually a charterparty will provide that time lost is to count as 'laytime', the fixture in *Freight Connect (S) Pte Ltd v Paragon Shipping Pte Ltd*[44] provided for agreed 'detention charges' for time lost. In such a case, it is questionable whether the laytime definition and exceptions will apply to the detention charges, which point did not fall to be decided in this case.

'reachable on arrival' and 'always accessible' clauses

Some berth charterparties will have a clause requiring the charterer to nominate a berth 'reachable on arrival' at the port. For example, cl. 9 of the Asbatankvoy form requires this as follows:

> **9. SAFE BERTHING-SHIFTING.**
>
> The vessel shall load and discharge at any safe place or wharf, or alongside vessels or lighters reachable on her arrival, which shall be designated and procured by the Charterer, provided the Vessel can proceed thereto, lie at, and depart therefrom always safely afloat, any lighterage being at the expense, risk and peril of the Charterer. …

If the charterer fails to do so it will be liable in damages for detention, which may most of the time be same as the demurrage, unless the market rates have differed since the charterparty was entered into. But this does not render the ship an arrived one, hence no notice of readiness can be given and the laytime clock will not start at this point. When a reachable berth is nominated, the shifting time from the waiting place to the berth will be on the charterer. The charterer's liability will be only for the time lost while waiting for the berth-nomination. The key difference between this clause and the 'time lost' clause is that this clause is wider than the 'time lost' clause in that it is not limited to unavailability of berth due to congestion. This clause imposes an absolute obligation. Hence, it does not matter that the failure to nominate was not the fault of the charterer but attributable to congestion, weather, etc. This was demonstrated by *The Fjordaas*.[45] In this case, the charterer was not able to

---

[42] The House of Lords overruled *The Radnor* [1955] 2 Lloyd's Rep 668 (EW CA). *The Radnor* treated 'time lost' that did not admit laytime definition and exceptions when dealing with 'time lost' clauses.

[43] *Huyton SA v Inter Operators SA (The Stainless Emperor)* [1994] 1 Lloyd's Rep 298 (EW HC).

[44] [2015] SGCA 37, [2015] 5 SLR 178 (SG CA).

[45] *Moerland (Arnt J) K/S v Kuwait Petroleum Corpn (The Fjordaas)* [1988] 2 All ER 714, [1988] 1 Lloyd's Rep 336 (EW HC).

nominate an available berth, first due to restrictions against night navigation at the port, followed by bad weather and then by strike. The charterer was found in breach of the nomination clause, hence liable to compensate the shipowner.

Hence, a 'reachable on arrival' clause is more favourable to the shipowner than a 'time lost' clause. In one way, 'wibon' clause can be more favourable to the shipowner as it will enable the shipowner to issue the notice of readiness and start the laytime clock so that shifting time will be on the charterer. In another way, the 'wibon' clause will be less favourable because it is limited to berth-unavailability due to congestion only.

Another similar clause will be one that requires the charterer to nominate a berth that is 'always accessible'. This clause is wider than the 'reachable on arrival' clause. With an 'always accessible', the port nominated must be one that can both be reached on arrival and left upon completion of loading/discharge. Hence, with an 'always accessible' clause if weather does not permit the ship leaving after loading or discharge, the charterer is liable for detention. Comparatively, with a 'reachable on arrival' clause, the charterer's responsibility is limited to the berth being accessible on arrival only.[46]

Unlike 'time lost' and 'wibon' clauses, the laytime clock is not started with a 'reachable on arrival' or 'always accessible' clause. The time lost is not counted as laytime. The liability of the charterer is to pay detention as opposed to demurrage. Hence, the charterer will not be entitled to laytime definition and exceptions.[47]

In a port charter, a 'reachable on arrival' clause will be of no use when the ship entered the port, since the ship could give the notice of readiness and start the laytime clock.[48] However, in *The President Brand*,[49] the English High Court found that a shipowner who had to wait outside the port limits until a berth was available could claim damages for detention for the waiting period until she could enter the port and give the notice of readiness. However, the correctness of the decision on this point is dubious in view of later decision by the House of Lords in *The Johanna Oldendorff*.[50]

Generally, a 'reachable on arrival' clause will not be of use once the laytime regime has started. However, a peculiar combination of clauses may render 'reachable on arrival' clause relevant even after the laytime regime has started, as demonstrated

[46] *Seatrade Group NV v Hakan Agro DMCC (The Aconcagua Bay)* [2018] EWHC 654 (Comm), [2018] 2 All ER (Comm) 843 (EW HC).

[47] *Inca Compania Naviera SA and Commercial and Maritime Enterprises Evanghelos P Nomikos SA v Mofinol Inc (The President Brand)* [1967] 2 Lloyd's Rep 338 (EW HC); *Nereide SpA di Navigazione v Bulk Oil International (The Laura Prima)* [1982] 1 Lloyd's Rep 1 (UK HL).

[48] *Shipping Developments Corpn v v/o Sojuzneftexport (The Delian Spirit)* [1972] 1 QB 103, [1971] 2 WLR 1434, [1971] 1 Lloyd's Rep 506 (EW CA).

[49] *Inca Compania Naviera SA and Commercial and Maritime Enterprises Evanghelos P Nomikos SA v Mofinol Inc (The President Brand)* [1967] 2 Lloyd's Rep 338 (EW HC).

[50] *Oldendorff (E L) & Co GmbH v Tradax Export SA (The Johanna Oldendorff)* [1974] AC 479, [1973] 3 All ER 148 (UK HL). See Chapter 14.4.2.1 for a discussion of this case.

by *The Laura Prima*.[51] In this case, it was a port charter in Exxonvoy form, which provided, in cl. 6, for the notice of readiness to be issued upon arrival at the port, 'berth or no berth'. There was a laytime exception for delay beyond control of the charterer. The form, in another clause, namely cl. 9, obliged the charterer to nominate a berth reachable on arrival. The ship arrived at the port, but there was congestion so that the charterer was not able to so nominate a berth. The ship gave the notice of readiness and started the laytime clock. The shipowner claimed demurrage, which the charterer refused to pay. The charterer relied on the laytime exception of delay beyond control which should cover congestion. The shipowner relied on the 'reachable on arrival' clause to say that for whatsoever reason if the charterer did not nominate an available berth upon the ship's arrival at the port, the charterer was liable to compensate the shipowner. The House of Lords found that the 'reachable on arrival' clause takes precedence over the laytime exceptions and found for the shipowner.[52]

14.4.2.4 Charterer's Obligation to Facilitate Arrival/Provide Cargo

The charterer has an implied obligation to do what it has to do on its part to facilitate the ship becoming arrived.[53] If the charterer breaches this obligation and as a result the ship would not become arrived, the ship is not allowed to give the notice of readiness, nor will laytime start. But the charterer will be liable in damages to the shipowner for breach of this obligation, that preventing starting the laytime clock, which may most of the time be same as the demurrage, unless the market rates have differed since the charterparty was entered into. This obligation includes a duty to make available cargo for loading, where that is exceptionally required for the ship to become arrived. In such case, the obligation is an absolute one and it is no defence for the charterer to say that it had taken reasonable steps to make the cargo available, but unsuccessfully. Otherwise than for this, the charterer has no obligation to have the cargo ready for loading at any point, as the obligation of the charterer is only to complete loading of the cargo by end of the laytime, failing which the charterer will be liable to pay demurrage. This happened in *The Aello*.[54] In this case, it was a port charter. The ship was not allowed to reach the commercial area of the port because cargo was not ready. The House of Lords held that the ship did not become arrived,[55] but the charterer was liable in damages to the shipowner for breach of the implied

[51] *Nereide SpA di Navigazione v Bulk Oil International (The Laura Prima)* [1982] 1 Lloyd's Rep 1 (UK HL).

[52] The compensation payable by the charter, rightly, will be damages for detention, which may most of the time be same as the demurrage, unless the market rates have differed since the charterparty was entered into.

[53] *Sunbeam Shipping Co Ltd v President of India (The Atlantic Sunbeam)* [1973] 1 Lloyd's Rep 482 (EW HC): the charterer had a duty to secure 'jetty challan' for the ship to enter the port, where that was a requirement of the port authority.

[54] *Sociedad Financiera De Bienes Raices Sa v Agrimpex Hungarian Trading Company for Agricultural Products [Appeal in The Aello]* [1961] AC 135, [1960] 3 WLR 145 (UK HL).

[55] It follows that the ship could not issue notice of readiness.

obligation to make available cargo as that was required for the ship to be allowed entry into the port and become arrived. The amount of damages was same as that of demurrage.

While the obligation to reasonably facilitate performance by the other party is implied in the English law, this has been substantially codified in those Commonwealth countries, including Malaysia,[56] that has a Contract Act modelled on the Indian Contract Act 1872. Section 67 of the Indian Contract Act 1872 provides for this as follows:[57]

> **67. Effect of neglect of promisee to afford promisor reasonable facilities for performance.**
>
> If any promisee neglects or refuses to afford the promisor reasonable facilities for the performance of his promise, the promisor is excused by the neglect or refusal as to any non-performance caused thereby.

The obligation, where applicable, will be relevant both to port charters and berth charters, where the ship is prevented from arriving at the port or the berth, respectively, because of unavailability of cargo or other failure on part of the charterer or consignee to facilitate.

14.4.3 Ready to Load/Discharge

What was studied earlier[58] about 'readiness to load' in the context of the contractual right of the charter to cancel if the ship is not ready to load by the cancelling date is applicable also in the context of readiness to load or discharge for purposes of giving the notice of readiness.

If the cargo is not ready for discharge because it is overstowed by other cargo, then the ship may not give notice of readiness. This happened in *The Mexico 1*[59] in which the English Court of Appeal found the notice to be invalid because the charterer's cargo was inaccessible, at the time the notice was given, as it was overstowed by another cargo.

14.4.4 Pre-conditions for Notice

It is a common pre-condition that the ship has obtained 'free pratique' before the notice is issued. Free pratique is heath clearance for the ship and the crew at the

---

[56] Malaysian Contracts Act 1950.

[57] Section 68 of the Malaysian Contracts Act 1950 identically provides.

[58] See Chapter 12.6.1.

[59] *Transgrain Shipping BV v Global Transporte Oceanico SA (The Mexico 1) (CA)* [1990] 1 Lloyd's Rep 507 (EW CA).

port. BIMCO GENCON 1994 form[60] expressly provides that free pratique is not a pre-condition to issue the notice. Contrary to that, SHELLVOY 5 form[61] allows the notice to be issued without free pratique but requires it to be obtained within six hours of issuance of the notice. If it is not obtained, the notice is invalid.

14.4.5 Manner and Timing of Issuance of Notice

The notice must be given in the manner and within the time frame stipulated in the charterparty, if any. The words 'laydays' and 'laycan' are used in connection with this time frame. 'Laydays' means the earliest date when the notice of readiness can be given. Ordinarily, the deadline to give the notice is by the 'cancelling date', although it may be given after this date if the charterer has not exercised the option to cancel yet. For example, 'laydays 1 June 2020 cancelling 10 June 2020' will mean that the earliest date is 1 June and the latest date is 10 June (but the notice can be given after this date if the charterer did not cancel). This can be expressed in terms of 'laycan' as 'laycan 1 June 2020/10 June 2020).

Asbatankvoy does not allow laytime to commence before the commencement date, except with sanction of the charterer.[62] Clause 5 of the Asbatankvoy form provides this as follows:

> **5. LAYDAYS.**
>
> Laytime shall not commence before the date stipulated in … except with the Charterer's sanction. Should the Vessel not be ready to load by 4:00 o'clock P.M. (local time) on the cancelling date stipulated in Part I, the Charterer shall have the option of cancelling this Charter by giving Owner notice of such cancellation within twenty-four (24) hours after such cancellation date; otherwise this Charter to remain in full force and effect.

Although the ship has arrived, is ready and has complied with all pre-conditions for issuance of the notice, it may become defective because is it not given in the manner or within the time frame stipulated in the charterparty. In *The Agamemnon*,[63] the notice was given at a place other than that stipulated in the charterparty. The notice was held to be ineffective. In *The Petr Schmidt*,[64] the charterparty required tender of the notice during office hours, which is common in general cargo charterparties. The ship gave the notice out of the office hours. It was held that the notice was deemed given at the beginning of the next office hour and refused the charterer's argument that the notice was invalid. In the case of oil tankers, it is common that notice may

---

[60] Cl. 6(3) (para 2).

[61] Cl. 22.

[62] *Tidebrook Maritime Corp v Vitol SA of Geneva (The Front Commander)* [2006] 2 Lloyd's Rep 251 (EW CA), speech of Rix JL: where the charterer requires early notice of readiness, the charter sanctions early commencement of laytime.

[63] *TA Shipping Ltd v Comet Shipping Ltd (The Agamemnon)* [1998] 1 Lloyd's Rep 675 (EW HC).

[64] *Galaxy Energy International Ltd v Novorossiysk Shipping Co (The Petr Schmidt)* [1997] 1 Lloyd's Rep 284 (EW HC), affirmed by the Court of Appeal in [1998] 2 Lloyd's Rep 1 (EW CA).

be permitted to be given at any time, as the oil terminals usually operate 24 hours a day.

If the notice is given earlier than it may be given under the charterparty, then the charterer has an option either to waive its right to insist on agreed time for notice and accepts the early notice or treat it as given only at earliest time when it may be given under the charterparty. If the charter accepts the early notice and commences loading, the laytime will start running earlier.[65] There is no specific format or mode by which the notice must be issued. In *The Eagle Valencia*,[66] the English Court of Appeal held that a notice by email was good. But this will not be so if the charterparty expressly lists the modes of giving notice which does not include 'email'.[67] If the notice is given later than the cancelling date, that will still be good as long as the charterer has not exercised the option to cancel prior to the notice.

14.5 Suspension of Laytime

Laytime, once it has started, may be suspended in two ways. One is pursuant to a laytime exception, such as one for strikes. Another is fault of or delay attributable to the shipowner. This sub-chapter will discuss these two bases of suspension.

14.5.1 Laytime Exceptions

Once laytime starts running, it may be interrupted and suspended by laytime exceptions provided in the charterparty. Examples of exceptions are 'unavoidable hinderances delaying loading/discharge', 'strikes,[68] frost or other unavoidable accidents preventing loading/discharge', etc.

In *Grant v Coverdale*,[69] there was a laytime exception for frost. The cargo was brought through a canal to be loaded into the ship at dock. In the midst of loading, the canal was subjected to frost and the balance cargo could not be brought. The House of Lords held that the frost exception did not apply as the cargo could be brought by other means although at too high expense. The House observed that in order for the laytime exception to operate, the 'loading' had to be prevented and that in this

[65] See *Tidebrook Maritime Corp v Vitol SA of Geneva (The Front Commander)* [2006] EWCA Civ 944, [2006] 2 All ER (Comm) 813, [2006] 2 Lloyd's Rep 251 (EW CA); *Total Transport Corporation v Arcadia Petroleum Ltd (The Eurus)* [1996] 2 Lloyd's Rep 408 (EW HC).

[66] [2010] EWCA Civ 713, [2010] 2 Lloyd's Rep 257 (EW CA).

[67] See *Trafigura Beheer BV v Ravennavi SpA (The Port Russel)* [2013] EWHC 490 (Comm), [2013] 2 Lloyd's Rep 57 (EW HC).

[68] Cl. 16 of Gencon 1994 form has detailed provision dealing with strikes.

[69] *Grant & Co v Coverdale, Todd & Co* (1884) 9 App Cas 470, 53 LJQB 462 (UK HL).

case the 'loading' was not prevented as there was no frost at the dock, but merely the cargo could not be brought to the loading point because of frost in the canal.

Somewhat a contrary decision was arrived at in *Hudson v Ede*,[70] where the court allowed 'detention by ice' laytime exception where, in the midst of loading operation, the river by which cargo was brought to the ship was frozen. The only difference between *Grant* and *Hudson* was that in *Grant* there were other ways of bringing the cargo though that would be too expensive and in *Hudson* there was no such other way. However, *Grant* found that loading was not prevented because frost was not at dock where the ship was will not align with *Hudson*. Laytime exceptions are a matter of construction in each case.

In *The Radauti*,[71] there was a laytime exception that was for 'unavoidable hinderances delaying the discharge of the cargo'. The English Court of Appeal held that this covered also congestion by which an arrived ship was prevented from berthing, where the time waiting for berth was to count as laytime. It did not make a difference whether the congestion was foreseeable or not. Hence, although the waiting time was to count as laytime by the charterparty terms, the shipowner did not benefit from it because of the laytime exception.

Where the laytime has started while the ship is waiting for berth, BIMCO GENCON 1994 form[72] excepts the shifting time in subsequently 'moving from the place of waiting to the loading/discharging berth' from laytime.

14.5.1.1 Laytime Exception Applicable to One Cargo but Not Others

The charterparty may provide a laytime exception where the cargo is prevented from being loaded. The question of whether this exception applies may depends on what the cargo is, as one type of cargo may be prevented but not another. In *Bunge y Born Ltda Sociedad Anonima Commercial Financiera y Industrial of Buenos Aires v HA Brightman & Co*,[73] the charterparty was to carry 'wheat and/or maize and/or rye'. A laytime exception was as follows:

> If the cargo cannot be loaded by reason of .... a strike or lock-out of any class of workmen essential to the loading of the cargo, or by reason of obstruction or stoppages beyond the control of the charterers on the railways, or in the docks, or other loading places .... the time for loading .... shall not count during the continuance of such causes.

The charterers intended to load wheat. First, there was an obstruction in bringing wheat to the port as the cargo was to be bought by rail to the port and a railway workers strike was going on. The House of Lords found that this obstruction was

---

[70] (1868) LR 2 QB 566 (EW HC), affirmed by the Court of Appeal in (1868) LR 3 QB 412 (EW CA).

[71] *Navrom v Callitsis Ship Management SA (The Radauti)* [1988] 2 Lloyd's Rep 416 (EW CA).

[72] Cl. 6(c) (para 2): "... Time used in moving from the place of waiting to the loading/ discharging berth shall not count as laytime. ..."

[73] [1925] AC 799, [1925] All ER Rep 607 (UK HL).

not covered by the laytime exception as the cargo was not prevented from being loaded but only prevented from being brought to the port. Second, export of wheat was banned. The House held that a ban of export of contracted cargo would fall within the laytime exception. However, it found that the exception did not apply in this case because there were other cargoes, namely maize or rye, can be loaded under the charterparty. But the House held that the charterer was entitled to a reasonable time, with laytime suspended, for it to arrange any of the other cargoes to be loaded. The laytime suspension allowed by the court is something that may arguably a little difficult to justify based on the current jurisprudence, as the charterparty did not provide for any laytime exception to cover the time in switching between cargoes when one of them could not be loaded, unless such a term was found to be necessarily implied.

The question of laytime exception and its relationship to cargo again came up before the House of Lords in *Reardon Smith Line Ltd v Ministry of Agriculture, Fisheries and Food*.[74] In this case, the charterparty was for carriage of 'a full and complete cargo … of wheat in bulk … and/or barley in bulk and/or flour in sacks'. It also provided that if barley or flour was loaded, there would be an increase in the freight. Wheat could not be loaded and this was covered by a laytime exception. However, there was no difficulty if barley/flour were to be loaded, in which case the laytime exception would not apply. The House of Lords found that the basic contracted cargo was wheat. The charterer was not obliged to exercise the option to load barley/flour, hence was entitled to the laytime exception. The difference between *Bunge* and *Reardon* was that in the former the charterer could load any of the cargoes and in the later the basic cargo was wheat only, but the charterer may load other cargoes only at an increased freight.

14.5.2 Loss of Laytime Attributable to Shipowner

Once the laytime has commenced, if loading is prevented or slowed down due to fault of the shipowner, then laytime for that period will be suspended. In *The Fontevivo*,[75] while the ship was in the midst of discharging, the crew sailed away for fear of war risks and then returned to the port of discharge after three days. The English High Court found that the loss of the loading time was attributable to the shipowner, hence laytime for this period was suspended. This will be so even if the fault is not actionable because of an exclusion clause in the charterparty, as held *The Union Amsterdam*.[76] If the delay was caused by independent contractors such as stevedores, courts have held that that was not the fault of the shipowner, hence laytime would

[74] [1963] AC 691 (UK HL).

[75] *Gem Shipping Co of Monrovia v Babanaft (Lebanon) SARL (The Fontevivo)* [1975] 1 Lloyd's Rep 339 (EW HC).

[76] *Blue Anchor Line Ltd v Alfred C Toepfer International GmbH (The Union Amsterdam)* [1982] 2 Lloyd's Rep 432 (EW HC).

not be suspended. This is so even if the charterparty provides that the stevedores appointed by the charterer were to be considered as servants of the shipowner, as held in *The Sinoe*.[77] In *William Alenxander & Sons v Aktieselskabet Dampskibet Hansa*,[78] discharge was joint responsibility of the charterer and the shipowner. A delay was caused by manpower shortage at the port. The House of Lords held that it was not the fault of the shipowner, hence laytime was not suspended.

If the shipowner removes the ship temporarily for other purposes, after the laytime has started, the laytime will be suspended for the period of interruption. In *Stolt Tankers v Landmark*,[79] the laytime started, under a port charter, at anchorage off Mumbai. Knowing that a berth would not be available for 15 days, the ship left to another port to discharge a cargo belonging to another charterer, carried concurrently with the charterer in this case. Although there was no loss of loading time to the charterer, the English High Court held that the laytime was suspended. However, had the ship idly waited at the anchorage, then laytime would run. Similarly, in *Re Ropner Shipping Co Ltd & Cleeves Wester Valley Anthracite Colliers Ltd*,[80] the ship left to take bunkers, while the charterer did not have the cargo to start loading. The English Court of Appeal held that demurrage was interrupted. The same would be true if it was laytime.

However, laytime will not be interrupted if the ship has to do something for safe loading, carriage or discharge of the cargo. In *Houlder v Weir*,[81] the English High Court held that demurrage was not interrupted where the ship had to take ballast for safe discharge. The decision would have been the same had it been about laytime.

14.6 Termination and Demurrage

The charterer's principal obligation to load or discharge within the laytime is an innominate term. When the charterer has breached this, by exceeding the laytime, there are two consequences. One is that the charterer is liable for demurrage. Another is that shipowner can become entitled to terminate the charterparty.

14.6.1 Termination

It is only quite rarely that a shipowner will be entitled to terminate, as this is an innominate term. To terminate, the delay must be so serious as to 'frustrate the

[77] *Overseas Transportation Co v Mineralimportexport (The Sinoe)* [1971] 1 Lloyd's Rep 514 (EW HC), affirmed by the Court of Appeal in [1972] 1 Lloyd's Rep 201 (EW CA).

[78] [1920] AC 88 (UK HL).

[79] [2002] 1 Lloyd's Rep 786 (EW HC).

[80] [1927] 1 KB 879 (EW CA).

[81] [1905] 2 QB 267 (EW HC).

commercial purpose of the contract'.[82] An unreasonably long delay will be such a serious delay.[83] Ordinarily, the shipowner must allow the ship to go into demurrage.[84]

A shipowner may avail itself of the concept of anticipatory breach to terminate in anticipation where it is unavoidable that there will be such a delay. This happened in *Universal Cargo Carriers Corp v Citati.*[85] In this case, the ship waited for six days and no cargo was provided. By then the charterer was 'completely disabled from finding a cargo and thus from performing his obligation under the charter'. While three more days only were left for laytime to finish, the charterer terminated the charterparty and gave the ship to another. The English High Court found held that the shipowner was entitled to do so.

Sometimes, the charterparty may expressly provide for termination in the event of default in payment by the charterer. BIMCO GENCON 1994 form, in cl. 7, allows the shipowner to terminate the charterparty if demurrage is not paid within 96 hours of notice following invoice provided the ship is in or at the loading port. This makes sense as it may not be practical to terminate once the ship has sailed off the loading port with the cargo which may belong to third parties to whom the shipowner has issued bills of lading. However, in such case the security in the hands of the shipowner is the lien,[86] which is provided in cl. 8 of the BIMCO GENCON 1994 form.

14.6.2 Demurrage

Demurrage is the compensation payable at a pre-agreed rate for when laytime is exceeded in loading or discharging. Demurrage is payable for the time taken in excess of the laytime. A ship will go on demurrage once the laytime finished. In order for demurrage to be payable, the laytime must have started and finished. If the laytime never started, there can be no demurrage, although there can be a claim for damages for detention where the charterer, in breach of the charterparty, prevented the laytime from starting.

In *The Daphne L* ,[87] the ship carried heavy crude oil under a voyage charterparty with a laytime and demurrage clause, and a bill of lading was issued. At the destination port, the cargo owner was not able to produce the bill of lading to receive the cargo. The shipowner obtained a court order for sale of the cargo by the Sheriff. This caused a delay of 130 days beyond laytime before discharge. The Singapore Court of Appeal held that the shipowner was entitled to demurrage.

The classical question in relation to demurrage is whether laytime definition and exceptions will apply once the ship is on demurrage to suspend the demurrage. The

---

[82] *Universal Cargo Carriers Corp v Citati* [1957] 2 QB 401 (EW HC).

[83] *Inverkip SS Co v Bunge* [1917] 2 KB 193 (EW CA).

[84] *Wilson & Coventry Ltd v Otto Thoresen Linie* [1910] 2 KB 405 (EW HC).

[85] *Universal Cargo Carriers Corp v Citati* [1957] 2 QB 401 (EW HC).

[86] See Chapter 13.7.

[87] [2003] SGCA 34 (SG CA).

general answer to this question is 'no'. This follows the popular saying that 'once on demurrage, always on demurrage'. This was demonstrated by *The Dias.*[88] In this case, the charterparty provided that the time spent in fumigating the cargo will not count as laytime. However, the charterer fumigated when the ship had already gone on demurrage. The House of Lords held that the charterer was not entitled to the laytime definition excluding the fumigation time, hence had to pay demurrage for this time.

It must be borne in mind that 'demurrage' is a contractual creation. Hence, there is nothing to expressly provide that laytime exceptions will apply to demurrage. But, in the absence of such express provisions, court will not infer that.[89] General exception clauses have been held not to apply in relation to demurrage. This was demonstrated by *The Kalliopi A.*[90] In this case, the charterparty excluded liability for 'unavoidable hindrances' were excepted for both sides. Demurrage was incurred because a berth was not available. The charterer claimed that the general exception clause excluded liability for the demurrage as the unavailability of berth was an unavoidable hindrance. The Court of Appeal rejected the argument holding a general exception clause does not interfere with the liability for demurrage.

However, where the delay resulting in demurrage was caused by the fault of the shipowner, then the liability for demurrage for that period is excepted.[91] This is so even if the fault is not actionable against the shipowner by virtue of an exclusion clause protecting the shipowner, as one may not benefit from his own fault. This is shown by *The Union Amsterdam.* [92] In this case, demurrage was incurred because the ship was grounded by negligence of the shipowner. Although liability for negligent navigation and management of the ship was excluded by Section 4(2)(a) of the US Carriage of Goods by Sea Act 1936, applicable in this case,[93] the English High Court held that the fault excepted the charterer's liability for demurrage for the period of delay caused by the grounding. This decision is consistent with the commercial reality whereby it must be an implied term that the charterer is not liable for demurrage if the delay was caused by the shipowner's fault, irrespective of whether it is actionable or not.

When the charterer fails to complete the loading or unloading operation within the laytime, the charterer commits a breach of the charterparty. Hence, the charterer may be liable, apart from having to pay the demurrage, for damages, if any damage suffered by the shipowner other than the lost time. This happened in *The Eternal*

---

[88] *Dias Cia Naviera SA v Louis Dreyfus Corpn (The Dias)* [1978] 1 All ER 724, [1978] 1 WLR 261 (UK HL).

[89] *Dias Cia Naviera SA v Louis Dreyfus Corpn (The Dias)* [1978] 1 All ER 724; *Nippon Yusen Kaisha v Marocaine de L'Industrie du Raffinage (The Tsukuba Maru)* [1979] 1 Lloyd's Rep 459.

[90] *Rich (Marc) & Co Ltd v Tourloti Cia Naviera SA (The Kalliopi A)* [1988] 2 Lloyd's Rep 101 (UK CA).

[91] *DGC Commodities Corp v Sea Metropolitan SA (The Andra)* [2012] EWHC 1984 (Comm), [2012] 2 Lloyd's Rep 587 (EW HC).

[92] *Blue Anchor Line Ltd v Alfred C Toepfer International GmbH (The Union Amsterdam)* [1982] 2 Lloyd's Rep 432 (EW HC).

[93] Which is identical to Article IV(2) of the Hague/Hague-Visby Rules.

Bliss.[94] In this case, the voyage charterer delayed discharge of a cargo of soybean. The delay resulted in the soybean developing moulding and caking and cargo claims were brought by holders of the bills of lading. The shipowner, having settled the claims in a sum of about USD1.1 million, instituted arbitral proceedings against the charterers for to cover this as damages, in addition to demurrage. An application was made to the English High Court under Section 45 of the UK Arbitration Act 1996 to determine a preliminary question. The question was whether the shipowner may claim damages in addition to demurrage when the charterer exceeded the laytime, which resulted in losses to the shipowner other than loss of use of the ship for the certain period. The court answered the question in the affirmative. The court pointed out that demurrage is the agreed rate of compensation only for one type of loss, namely, loss of use of the ship for the period covered by demurrage. It does not affect the parties' rights and liabilities in respect of other types of losses.

14.6.2.1 Contractual Time Limits for Demurrage Claims

Some charterparties may have a special time limit for the shipowner to submit demurrage claim to the charterer. For example, SHELLVOY 5[95] requires a demurrage claim to be submitted 'fully and correctly' documented within 90 days after it is due, failing which the form provides that the claim 'shall be extinguished'. It is not compulsory that the claim and the document are all together submitted, but they can be submitted in parts, as long as all are submitted by the 90 days.[96] In *The Eagle Valencia*,[97] the charterparty was under the SHELLVOY 5 form. There were two notices of readiness issued. The first one was invalid as the require free pratique was not obtained, but the second one was valid. The shipowner submitted the claim within 30 days based on the first notice. The charterer rejected the claim on the basis of invalidity of the first notice, however, after the 90-day limit had expired. The shipowner then submitted another claim based on the second notice. The English Court of Appeal held that the claim was time-barred. A claim will escape the time limit if it is for damages for detention.

When the claim was submitted within the time-limit, but with partial documentation, in one case[98] the court held that the entire claim was barred, but in another[99] the court held only the part of the claim in respect of which the claim was documentation

[94] *K Line PTE Ltd v Priminds Shipping (HK) Co Ltd (The Eternal Bliss)* [2020] EWHC 2373 (Comm), [2020] 9 WLUK 40 (EW HC).

[95] Part II, cl. 15(c)

[96] *National Shipping Co of Saudi Arabia v BP Oil Supply Co (The Abqaiq)* [2011] EWCA Civ 1127, [2012] 1 Lloyd's Rep 18 (EW CA).

[97] [2010] EWCA Civ 713, [2010] 2 Lloyd's Rep 257 (EW CA).

[98] *Waterfront Shipping Company Ltd V Trafigura AG (The Sabrewing)* [2007] EWHC 2482 (Comm), [2008] 1 Lloyd's Rep 286 (EW HC).

[99] *The Petroleum Oil and Gas Corporation of South Africa (Pty) Ltd v Fr8 Singapore Pte Ltd (The Eternity)* [2009] 1 Lloyd's Rep 107 (EW HC).

was not provided to be time-barred. Notably, there is no such time-limit in BIMCO GENCON 1994 form.

In Commonwealth countries, including Malaysia,[100] with a Contract Act modelled on the Indian Contract Act 1872, such contractual time limit would be invalid. The relevant section in the Indian Contract Act 1872 is Section 28, which reads as follows:

> **Agreements in restraint of legal proceedings, void.**
>
> Every agreement,–
>
> (a) by which any party thereto is restricted absolutely from enforcing his rights under or in respect of any contract, by the usual legal proceedings in the ordinary tribunals, or which limits the time within which he may thus enforce his rights; or
>
> (b) which extinguishes the rights of any party thereto, or discharges any party thereto, from any liability, under or in respect of any contract on the expiry of a specified period so as to restrict any party from enforcing his rights, is void to the extent.

Section 29 of the Malaysian Contracts Act 1950 provides in identical terms to Section 28(a) of the Indian Act. There is no Contract Act in Singapore and the position will be that as in the English common law.

14.6.3 Detention Distinguished from Demurrage

There can be various instances whereby a ship will suffer a delay by breach of an express or implied term of the charterparty, which is not about laytime and demurrage. Laytime definitions and exceptions are not applicable to detention claims. In those cases, the shipowner's claim will be for damages for detention. The damage may likely be assessed at the same rate as demurrage.[101] Some examples of instances of detention follow, in addition to those already visited earlier in this chapter.

If loading finishes before expiry of the allowed laytime, the laytime comes to an end. Thereafter, if the ship is delayed by the charterer due to documentation or other reasons, then the charterer will be liable in damages for detention even if is within the period allowed for laytime in the charterparty.[102] The same thing is true, where the charterparty provides that the laytime comes to an end when the hoses are disconnected.

Clause 11 of Asbatankvoy form provides "Laytime shall continue until the hoses have been disconnected." For demurrage purpose, the cl. 8 of the form provides "Charterer shall pay demurrage per running hour and pro rata … for all time that loading and discharging and used laytime as elsewhere herein provided *exceeds the allowed laytime* …" Reading the two clauses together, if the loading/discharge is

---

[100] Malaysian Contracts Act 1950.

[101] *Emeraldian Ltd Partnership v Wellmix Shipping Ltd (The Vine)* [2010] EWHC 1411 (Comm), [2011] 1 Lloyd's Rep 301 (EW HC).

[102] *Nolisement (Owners) v Bunge and Born* [1916-17] All ER Rep 734, [1917] 1 KB 160 (EW CA).

completed before the *allowed* laytime, the laytime comes to an end. However, if the loading/discharge exceeds the *allowed* laytime, then the ship goes on demurrage.

In *The Timna,*[103] the ship carried grain to multiple ports in the region of Holland, Belgium and Germany. The names of the port had to be nominated by the charterer. After discharge at the first port, the charterer did not nominate a second port, resulting in the master going to a port upriver and giving notice of readiness. Thereafter the charterer nominated another port. The shipowner claimed both demurrage and damages for detention. The English Court of Appeal held that the notice was invalid and the laytime did not start at the upriver port. Hence, no demurrage. However, the court ordered damages for detention for the delay caused by the breach of the charterer to timely nominate the second discharge port.

In *The Vine,*[104] the charterers nominated an unsafe port, which resulted in delay in the ship berthing. Until the ship berthed laytime did not start. However, the English High Court held, that the shipowners were entitled to damages for detention resulting from the breach of the charterer's obligation to nominate a safe port. The damages awarded was at the demurrage rate.

In *Chandris v Isbrandtsen-Moller Co Inc* ,[105] the charterer loaded dangerous cargo in breach of the charterparty but with knowledge of the shipowner. These dangerous goods caused delay at the discharge point, as the dangerous cargo had to be unloaded into barges in the river. The English High Court held that the shipowner was not entitled to any demurrage but was entitled to damages for detention in respect of the delay. The damages awarded were at the demurrage rate. Indeed, if there is no laytime/demurrage clause, then the shipowner will be entitled to damages for detention when the laytime/reasonable time for loading or discharging has been exceeded.

---

[103] *Zim Israel Navigation Co Ltd v Tradax Export SA (The Timna)* [1971] 2 Lloyd's Rep 91 (EW CA).

[104] *Emeraldian Ltd Partnership v Wellmix Shipping Ltd (The Vine)* [2010] EWHC 1411 (Comm), [2011] 1 Lloyd's Rep 301 (EW HC).

[105] [1951] 1 KB 240, [1950] 1 All ER 768 (EW HC).

Chapter 15
Time Charter: Orders and Indemnity

This chapter discusses orders and indemnities in time charterparties. Time charterers usually have wide liberty to give *orders* to the ship as to employment. This liberty is balanced by liability of the charterer to *indemnity* provided for in the charterparty. A distinction is made between legitimate and illegitimate orders. Similarly, a distinction is made between claims for indemnity for loss consequent upon legitimate orders and claims for breach for loss consequent upon illegitimate orders. Then, limitations to indemnity claims are observed. This is followed by a consideration of the common types of orders, namely, about issuing of bills of lading, cargoes to be loaded, ports to call and delivery against indemnity.

15.1 Introduction

In a time-charter, the charterer will usually have a wide liberty to give orders to the ship as to her employment, e.g. ordering the ship to proceed to a particular port, load a particular cargo and issue bills of ladings to shippers of consignors of cargoes. In voyage charters, a charterer may not have such liberties or, if it has, they will usually be limited, as the charter will likely be a for a specified voyage. Such limited liberties will be there where the voyage charter allows the charterer to nominate ports or cargoes within a specified range. In the case of a demise charter, there will be no such orders because the ship will be under the control and management of the ship and the crew including the master will be under the employment of the charterer.

This chapter considers the distinctions between legitimate and illegitimate orders, claims for breach of charter and claims in indemnity, limitations to indemnity claim and the common types of orders, namely orders as to issuance of bills of lading, cargoes to be loaded and ports to trade between.

A. Kasi, *The Law of Carriage of Goods by Sea*,
https://doi.org/10.1007/978-981-33-6793-7_15

15.2 Legitimate v. Illegitimate Orders

An order given may be legitimate or illegitimate. It will be legitimate when it is given pursuant to the charterparty, e.g. ordering the ship to proceed to a port within the agreed range. It will be illegitimate when it is given in breach of the charterparty, e.g. ordering to proceed to a port outside the agreed range.

If it is an illegitimate order, the shipowner is not obliged to comply with the order. However, in practice, it may be difficult for a shipowner to immediately determine if the order is legitimate or illegitimate. If the shipowner determines that it is an illegitimate order and refuses to comply, it may take a risk. If subsequently a court or arbitrator decides that it was a legitimate order, the shipowner will be liable to the charterer. The refusal by the shipowner to comply with a legitimate order may even justify termination of the charter by the charterer. Accordingly, a shipowner may opt to comply with the order even if it thinks it is illegitimate. Then, the shipowner may hold the charterer liable for the breach of the charter in giving the illegitimate order. Usually, by opting to comply with the order, the shipowner would not be taken to have waived its rights to pursue a claim for breach or other remedies under the charter.

If a shipowner reasonably needs time to verify the legitimacy of the order, then the delay will not be taken as a breach of the charter by the shipowner. Hence, the off-hire clause would not be triggered by this. However, this will only happen in peculiar circumstances such as that demonstrated by *The Houda*.[1] In this case, the ship was under time-charterparty. The charterer was Kuwait Petroleum Corporation, who were giving orders from Kuwait. Four months into the charterparty, Kuwait was invaded by Iraq and the charterer's management was moved to London. Subsequently, the ship received an order from brokers claiming to act for the charterer to proceed to the Red Sea. The shipowners put the order on hold to verify the authenticity of the order, that took some significant time. The charterer claimed off-hire for the delay-period. The English Court of Appeal refused the claim. The court was guided by how a man of reasonable prudence would have acted in the circumstances. The court said that it was not for the court decide whether on the facts the owners had reasonable grounds to pause but in a war situation a shipowner may have a right, or indeed a duty, to pause in order to seek further information about the source and validity of any orders received.

15.3 Breach v. Indemnity Claims

Other than a claim for breach of charter, another potential claim that the shipowner may have when it incurred loss as a result of complying with an order is a claim in indemnity. This is different from a claim for damages in two aspects.

[1] *Kuwait Petroleum Corpn v I and D Oil Carriers Ltd (The Houda)* [1994] 2 Lloyd's Rep 541 (EW CA).

First, for an indemnity-claim, there must be a contractual provision for it. It may be express or implied. BIMCO BALTIME 1939 form[2] has an express indemnity clause. Clause 9 of the form provides for this as follows:

> … The Charterers shall indemnify the Owners against all consequences or liabilities arising from the Master, officers or Agents signing Bills of Lading or other documents or otherwise complying with such orders, as well as from any irregularity in the Vessel's papers or for overcarrying goods.

NYPE 2015 form[3] (for time charter) does not have an express indemnity clause, but it has been held that such a provision is implied.[4] The reason for implying a provision for indemnity in time charters is that the wide liberty of the charterer to give orders to the shipowner must be met with an indemnity for losses that the shipowner suffers as a result of complying with the orders. This is colloquially said to be *quid pro quo,* i.e. something for something.[5] The rationale behind this was well said by the English Court of Appeal in *The Island Archon*[6] as follows:

> [T]he implication is justified … first by 'business efficacy' in the sense that if the charterer requires to have the vessel at his disposal, and to be free to choose voyages and cargoes and bill of lading terms also, then the owner must be expected to grant such freedom only if he is entitled to be indemnified against loss and liability resulting from it, subject always to the express terms of the charterparty …; and secondly by the legal principle underlying the 'lawful request'cases …

The 'lawful request' principle mentioned above refers to cases such as *Sheffield Corp v Barclays*,[7] in which the House of Lords explained the principle as follows:

> [W]hen an act is done by one person at the request of another which act is not in itself manifestly tortious … and such act turns out to be injurious … the person doing it is entitled to an indemnity from him who requested …

Second, an indemnity is for losses suffered by the shipowner as a result of complying with the orders given by the charterer. It does not matter whether the order is legitimate or illegitimate. Accordingly, when the order is legitimate and hence no claim for breach is available, a claim for indemnity will still be available where there is an express or implied contractual provision for indemnity.

---

[2] (Revised 2001).

[3] And the previous versions: 1946 and 1993 versions.

[4] *Triad Shipping Co v Stellar Chartering & Brokerage Inc (The Island Archon)* [1994] 2 Lloyd's Rep 227, [1995] 1 All ER 595 (EW CA).

[5] *Triad Shipping Co v Stellar Chartering and& Brokerage Inc (The Island Archon)* [1994] 2 Lloyd's Rep 227, [1995] 1 All ER 595 (EW CA).

[6] *Triad Shipping Co v Stellar Chartering & Brokerage Inc (The Island Archon)* [1995] 1 All ER 595 at 608, [1994] 2 Lloyd's Rep 227 (EW CA), speech of Evans LJ.

[7] [1905] AC 392, [1905] UKHL 556, 43 SLR 556 (UK HL).

15.4 Limitations to Indemnity Claim

There are some limitations to indemnity claims. First, an indemnity claim is only for loss suffered as a result of an order as to employment of the ship but not navigation of the ship. Second, the proximate cause of the loss must be the order and not something else. Third, indemnity is not available where, at the time of entering into the charterparty, the risk of the loss was foreseeable and the shipowner had voluntarily taken the risk. Each of the limitations will be visited below.

15.4.1 Employment V Navigation Orders

A charterer may give orders only as to employment of the ship but not as to navigational matters.[8] The distinction between the two may not always be clear. This can be demonstrated with *The Hill Harmony*.[9] In this case, a time charterer ordered the ship to take the shorter of the two available routes. The master ignored the order and took the longer route as he had earlier experienced difficulties with the shorter route. As a result, the voyage took 10 extra days and 200 extra tonnes of bunkers. The charterer claimed that the order as to the route was one as to employment and the shipowner wrongfully refused to comply with it, hence the shipowner was liable for the loss of the extra days and bunkers. The shipowner argued that the order was one as to navigation, hence not within the power of the charterer to give and the shipowner was not liable for the loss of the extra days and bunkers. The High Court and the Court of Appeal held that it was an order as to navigation. However, the House of Lords reversed the decision, holding the order to be one as to employment, hence the shipowner breached the charter by refusing to comply with the order and liable for the consequent losses. At the same time the House observed that the master would be entitled to refuse the order if that posed a navigational risk that the master should not take. It follows that an indemnity will only be available if the order is one about employment but not when it is about navigation.[10]

15.4.2 Proximate Causation

In order for a shipowner to claim damages consequent upon an illegitimate order or indemnity on a legitimate or illegitimate order, the order must be the proximate cause

---

[8] *Weir v Union Steamship* [1900] AC 525 (UK HL); *Newa Line v Erechthion Shipping Co SA* [1987] 2 Lloyd's Rep 180 at p 185 (EW HC).

[9] *Whistler International Ltd v Kawasaki Kisen Kaisha Ltd (The Hill Harmony)* [2001] 1 Lloyd's Rep 147, (1999) LMCLQ 461 (UK HL).

[10] *Weir v Union Steamship* [1900] AC 525 (UK HL); *Newa Line v Erechthion Shipping Co SA* [1987] 2 Lloyd's Rep 180 at p 185 (EW HC).

of the loss. In *The Berge Sund*,[11] the cargo holds of the ship became contaminated. It was not attributable to the fault of the carrier or the shipowner. The charterer ordered cleaning of the holds. It was held that no indemnity for loss arising from the cleaning was available to the shipowner. In this case, the proximate cause of the loss was not the order but the contaminated holds that needed cleaning, although the decision of the court was rather based on interpretation of off-hire clause in the charterparty.

15.4.3 Voluntarily Assumed Risk

No indemnity will be available if the shipowner voluntarily assumed the risk of the loss at the time of entering into the charterparty. This was reiterated in *The Island Archon*.[12] In this case, the charterer ordered the ship to discharge at an Iraqi port. There was a problem in Iraqi ports at that time, whereby short-lading certificates were issued even where the cargo was discharged in full quantity, as a result, shipowners suffered false cargo claims. The English Court of Appeal held that if the shipowner had agreed to trade at Iraqi ports, knowing this problem was there when the charterparty was entered into, then the shipowner could not claim in indemnity. However, in this case, at the time the charterparty was entered into, this problem was not there. Hence, the court held that the shipowner was entitled to claim in indemnity. In *The Athanasia Comninos*,[13] the charter was to carry coal. The ship suffered an explosion during the carriage as a result of methane emissions from the coal, which was not the fault of the charterer. The risk of explosion by methane emissions from coal was inherent. The shipowner claimed indemnity from the charterer. The English High Court refused the indemnity-claim, as the risk was known or ought to have been known when the charterparty was entered into and the shipowner voluntarily assumed the risk entering into the charterparty. The shipowner argued that this particular cargo of coal had a higher rate of methane emission than ordinary coal. The court rejected this argument as the risk was of the same kind though the degree of risk may be different. In *The Kitsa*,[14] the ship was ordered, within the scope of the charter, to load at a warm water port where she remained for more than 20 days. As a result, marine growth developed on the ship's hull, that required bottom cleaning. This resulted in loss of time, for which the shipowner claimed indemnity. The English High Court refused the claim, holding that the risk was a known one that the shipowner had taken by entering into the charterparty that permitted trading at those ports. Similarly, when a shipowner agrees to carry deck cargo, under a charter, the shipowner had been held to voluntarily

---

[11] *Sig Bergesen DY & Co and Others V Mobil Shipping and Transportation Co (The Berge Sund)* [1993] 2 Lloyd's Rep 453 (EW CA).

[12] *Triad Shipping Co v Stellar Chartering & Brokerage Inc (The Island Archon)* [1994] 2 Lloyd's Rep 227, [1995] 1 All ER 595 (EW CA).

[13] *The Athanasia Comninos and Georges Chr Lemos* [1990] 1 Lloyd's Rep 277 (EW HC).

[14] *Action Navigation Inc v Bottiglieri di Navigation SpA (The Kitsa)* [2005] EWHC 177 (Comm), [2005] 1 Lloyd's Rep 432 (EW HC).

take the risk inherent in carriage of deck cargo, with the result the shipowner could not claim indemnity for loss suffered consequent on deck carriage.[15]

15.5 Common Types of Order

There are four common types of order that a charter will give. First, about issuing bills of lading. Second, about trading ports. Third, about cargoes to be loaded. Fourth, about delivery. Each of them will be visited in turn below.

Any order that the charterer gives must be within the scope of the charterparty. If not, that will be a breach by the charterer. If there is a breach, the options available to the shipowner is either to comply with the order and claim damages for any loss suffered as a result of the compliance or to refuse to comply with the order. If the order is issued within the scope of the charterparty, then the shipowner must ordinarily comply with it but will be entitled to indemnity for any loss suffered as a result of the compliance if there is a contractual provision for indemnity.

15.5.1 Orders About Issuing Bills of Lading

It is common that voyage charterparties will provide for issuance of 'charterparty bills of lading', meaning bills that incorporate the terms of the charterparty. In such cases, the charterer can only order the shipowner to issue bills which are charterparty bills. However, a provision for charterparty bill does not permit the shipowner to clause the bill with details of current claims against the charterer.[16]

A provision for 'charterparty bill' is not common with time charters. In time charters, the common requirement will be that the master (on behalf of the shipowner) must sign the bill 'as presented'. This gives a wide liberty to the charterer about the form of the bill. In *The Nanfri,*[17] the shipowners, due to some disputes with the time-charterer on hire-payment, purported to revoke the charterer's authority to issue bills of lading and also asked the master not to sign any 'freight prepaid' bill presented by the charterer. This was contrary to the terms of the charterparty. The House of Lords held that the conduct of the shipowners amounted to a breach, wiping the charterer out of almost the entire benefit of the charterparty, the consequences of which were so serious as to entitle the charterers to terminate the charterparty.

---

[15] *Seals (LD) NV v Mitsui Osk Lines Ltd (The Darya Tara)* [1997] 1 Lloyd's Rep 42 (EW HC): the shipowner incurred the cost of re-stowing the deck cargo but failed in its indemnity claim against the charterer for the cost.

[16] See *The Helenus and Motagua* [1982] 2 Lloyd's Rep 261 (EW HC).

[17] *Federal Commerce and Navigation Ltd v Molena Alpha Inc and others (The Nanfri, The Benfri, The Lorfri)* [1979] AC 757, [1979] 1 All ER 307, [1978] QB 949, [1979] 1 Lloyds Rep 201, [1978] 3 WLR 991 (UK HL).

However, the wide liberty of the charterer does not mean that the shipowner must sign a bill that is contrary to the terms of the charterparty, such as imposing greater liability on the shipowner to the holder of the bill than that undertaken to the charterer. In such cases, the charter presenting the bill will be in breach of the charterparty so that the shipowner can refuse to sign the bill or claim in damages (apart from any indemnity claim contractually available) for any loss suffered if it signs the bill.[18]

Clause 31(b) of the NYPE 2015 form provides that the issuance of the bills of lading will be "without prejudice" to the charter. The clause reads as follows:

> (b) All bills of lading or waybills shall be without prejudice to this Charter Party and the Charterers shall indemnify the Owners against all consequences or liabilities which may arise from any inconsistency between this Charter Party and any bills of lading or waybills signed by the Charterers or their agents or by the Master at their request.

This must mean that the shipowner signing the bill is not be taken a waiver of any of its right to claim for breach or indemnity. Even in the absence of such a clause, likely the position will ordinarily be the same. Clause 31(c) states that any bill for deck cargo must declare that they are at the charterer's, shipper's and receiver's risk. The clause reads as follows:

> (c) Bills of lading covering deck cargo shall be claused: "Shipped on deck at the Charterers', Shippers' and Receivers' risk, expense and responsibility, without liability on the part of the Vessel or her Owners for any loss, damage, expense or delay howsoever caused."

The liberty as to 'form' does not permit the charterer to present a bill that is in accurate in 'contents', such as the description, quantity, condition and order of goods, leading marks and date of shipment. In *The Boukadoura*,[19] the bill presented did not show the right quantity and the shipowner insisted on the right quantity to be stated before it signs the bill. This resulted in some loss of time, for which the charterer was held responsible.

However, had the reason for inaccurate quantity first stated in the bill was because the master issued the mate's receipt with such wrong quantity, then the fault and responsibility for the consequences will fall on the shipowner. In such a case, the shipowner would have no recourse in any indemnity against the shipowner. This is because the cause of the loss to the shipowner would be the master's negligence rather than the bill presented by the charterer. In *The Nogar Marin*,[20] the master issued a clean mate's receipt for coils that were rusty. This was followed by the charterer presenting a clean bill that was signed and delivered to the cargo interest, which resulted in a cargo claim by the holder of the bill against the shipowner. The shipowner sought indemnity from the charterers. The English Court of Appeal refused the indemnity claim as the bill merely followed the inaccurate mate's receipt.

---

[18] *Telfair Shipping Corporation v Inersea Carriers SA (The Caroline P)* [1985] 1 WLR 553, [1985] 1 All ER 243, [1984] 2 Lloyd's Rep 466 (EW HC).

[19] *Boukadoura Maritime Corpn v Marocaine de l'Industrie et du Raffinage SA (The Boukadoura)* [1989] 1 Lloyd's Rep 393 (EW HC).

[20] *Naviera Mogor SA v Société Metallurgique de Normandie (The Nogar Marin)* [1988] 1 Lloyd's Rep 412 (EW CA).

It is common that, in time-charters, the charterer will be allowed to sign the bill on behalf of the shipowner. In such cases, if the charterer signs the bill contrary to the mate's receipt and thereby renders the shipowner liable to the holder of the bill, the charterer must be liable both in breach and, if there is an express or implied indemnity provision as will usually be, in indemnity.[21] Clause 31(a) of the NYPE 2015 form[22] requires the bills presented to conform with the mate's receipt and authorises the charterer[23] to sign bills in conformity with the mate's receipt. The clause reads as follows:

> (a) The Master shall sign bills of lading or waybills for cargo as presented in conformity with mates' receipts. However, the Charterers or their agents may sign bills of lading or waybills on behalf of the Master, with the Owners'/Master's prior written authority, always in conformity with mates' receipts.

Even in the absence of such clause, a charterer must be liable where it signs an inaccurate bill on behalf of the shipowner contrary to an accurate mate's receipt and thereby renders the shipowner liable to the holder of the bill.

15.5.2 Orders About Cargoes to Be Loaded

The charterer may load the cargo permitted by the charterparty. If the charterer loads a cargo that is not permitted, the charterer would commit a breach.[24] If the charterer loads a permitted cargo but there is a special risk associated with it, then the charterer must inform the shipowner of the same, unless the risk is one that the shipowner knows or ought to know. Even if the terms of the charterparty does not say so, this will be an implied obligation. An inherent risk in the cargo need not be informed to the shipowner, as the shipowner ought to know that.[25] The risk referred to here includes physical loss or damage to the cargo, any other cargo and the ship as well as the economic loss, as demonstrated by *Mitchell, Cotts & Co v Steel Bros & Co Ltd*.[26] In this case, a cargo of rice caused a delay in discharge at Piraeus as a result of difficulties in the shipper obtaining the necessary permissions during wartime. The risk was known to the charterer. However, even if the charterer were not aware of

---

[21] See *Oceanfocus Shipping Ltd v Hyundai Merchant Marine Co Ltd (The Hawk)* [1999] 1 Lloyd's Rep 176 (EW HC). In this case, the NYPE form required the bills presented to conform with the mate's receipt and expressly authorised the charterer to sign the bills in conformity with the mate's receipt.

[22] NYPE 1993 form, cl. 30(a); NYPE 1946 form, cl. 8.

[23] Subject to prior written authorisation by the shipowner.

[24] *Chandris v Isbrandtsen-Moller Co Inc* [1951] 1 KB 240, [1950] 2 All ER 618, (1950) 84 Lloyd's Rep 347 (EW CA).

[25] *The Athanasia Comninos and Georges Chr Lemos* [1990] 1 Lloyd's Rep 277 (EW HC).

[26] [1916] 2 KB 610 (EW HC).

it, that would not, likely, have made a difference, as the implied duty to notify the shipowner of special risks is an absolute one.[27]

When a beach in respect of the cargo to be loaded is committed or is anticipated to be committed by the charterer, the shipowner may either refuse to allow such cargo to be loaded or allow it to be loaded and subsequently hold the charterer liable in damages should a loss arise from that. Even if there is no breach, the shipowner may recover loss or damage arising from the cargo loaded, if there is an express or implied indemnity in the charterparty.

15.5.3 Orders About Ports to Call

A voyage charter will likely specifically state the loading and discharge ports, although sometimes it may provide a range of ports for the charterer to nominate. A time charter will likely state the permitted geographical range of trading ports any of which the charterer may nominate.

In the case of a voyage charter, if the charterer orders the ship to proceed to any port other than the permitted port or ports, then the charterer would commit breach. The shipowner may refuse to comply with it or comply with it and claim *quantum meruit* freight for the difference, if any, between the contracted voyage and the ordered voyage.

Similarly, in the case of a time charter, if the charterer orders the ship to proceed to any port outside the permitted range, then the charterer would commit breach. Then, the shipowner may refuse to comply with it or may comply with it and claim damages for any loss incurred as a result of the illegitimate order. An order will be in breach of the charter not only where it is to proceed to a port outside the permitted range but also where it would mean the ship cannot be redelivered at the agreed place and time pursuant to the charterparty.

Of course, irrespective of any breach, a shipowner will be entitled to indemnity for any loss suffered as a result of an order to proceed to any port, where there is an express or implied indemnity provision, as will usually be in the case of time charters.

15.5.3.1 Safe Port and Berth Warranties

When a charterparty gives the liberty to the charterer to nominate the port, the liberty will be balanced by a warranty as to safety of the port. Usually, it will be express. In the absence of an express warranty, it will usually be implied when nomination is available to the charterer. However, such a warranty will not be implied where the

[27] See Chapter 7.6.2.

shipowner has voluntarily taken the risk of unsafe port at the time of entering into the charterparty, e.g. including ports in known war zone within the permitted range.[28]

Where there is no nomination available to the charterer, as with voyage charters usually, there is nothing to stop the parties from expressly providing for the safe port warranty.[29] But if none is expressed, it is unlikely that a court will imply such a term because there no nomination is available to the charterer. Safe port warranty clauses are also found in demise charterparty to ensure that the charterer, although in complete control of the ship, does not take her to unsafe ports.

A safe port warranty clause in a charterparty may be rendered ineffective in certain circumstances where the risk in question is exhaustively dealt with by some other specific provision of the charterparty. In *The Evia (No. 2)*,[30] the House of Lords held that a war risks clause in BIMCO BALTIME 1939 form rendered ineffective an express safe port warranty clause.[31] In *The Chemical Venture*,[32] the English High Court held that the war risks clause in SHELLTIME 3 form was not a 'complete code' to render the express warranty clause ineffective.

A safe port warranty impliedly includes a safe berth warranty, but not vice versa.[33] In *The Reborn*,[34] the ship was chartered for a voyage from Chekka port in Lebanon to Algiers under an amended BIMCO GENCON form. While the loading port was specified in the charterparty, it allowed the charterer to nominate the loading berth. The charterer accordingly nominated a particular berth, which the ship complied with. At the berth, ship's hull was damaged by an underwater projection. There was no safe port warranty in the charterparty, as will usually be the case with voyage charters. There was no express safe berth warranty. There were clauses dealing with port, which provided that the shipowner guaranteed the ship's compliance with the port's specifications, the shipowner would perform the necessary investigation on the specified port or take the risk associated with the port. A clause dealt with berth, that provided that the berth nominated by the charterer must comply with the 27-feet saltwater draft. The question before the court was whether there a safe berth warranty should be implied against the charterer. The court refused to so imply. The court held

[28] See *Atkins International HA v Islamic Republic of Iran Shipping Lines (The APJ Priti)* [1987] 2 Lloyd's Rep 37 (EW CA).

[29] *STX Pan Ocean Co Ltd v Ugland Bulk Transport AS (The Livanita) [2007] All ER (D) 43 (Jun)*, [2007] EWHC 1317 (Comm), [2008] 1 Lloyd's Rep 86 (EW HC); *AIC Limited v Marine Pilot Limited (The Archimidis)* [2008] EWCA Civ 175, [2008] 2 All ER (Comm) 545, [2008] 1 Lloyd's Rep 597 (EW CA).

[30] *Kodros Shipping Corp v Empresa Cubana de Fletes (The Evia) (No. 2)* [1983] 1 AC 736, [1982] 2 Lloyd's Rep 307 (UK HL).

[31] Cl. 20.

[32] *Pearl Carriers Inc v Japan Line Ltd (The Chemical Venture)* [1993] 1 Lloyd's Rep 508 (EW HC).

[33] See *Mediterranean Salvage & Towage Ltd v Seamar Trading & Commerce Inc (The Reborn)* [2008] EWHC 1875 (Comm) (EW HC), affirmed by the Court of Appeal in [2009] EWCA Civ 531, [2009] 2 Lloyd's Rep 639 (EW CA).

[34] *Mediterranean Salvage & Towage Ltd v Seamar Trading & Commerce Inc (The Reborn)* [2008] EWHC 1875 (Comm) (EW HC), affirmed by the Court of Appeal in [2009] EWCA Civ 531, [2009] 2 Lloyd's Rep 639.

that the right of the charterer to nominate the berth did not mean, by itself, that a safe berth warranty would be implied. The court took into account the provisions as to port and berth in the charterparty, that put the responsibility on the shipowner save that the charterer must comply with the saltwater draft condition in nominating the port.

There are lighter versions of the safe port/berth undertaking such as an obligation to exercise due diligence only to ensure that the port/berth will be safe. In *Dow-Europe v Novoklav Inc*,[35] there was such an obligation and the charterer authorised the port authority to nominate the berth. The port nominated, by want of due diligence, a berth that was unsafe. The English High Court held that the charterer had failed in its duty, as it was responsible for the actions of the port authority whom it had authorised.

If the charterer makes a nomination in breach of the warranty (or fails to exercise the due diligence where that is what was undertaken), the shipowner may either accept it and comply with it or refuse it and ask for a new nomination. If the shipowner accepts and complies with it and suffers a loss as a result, the shipowner may hold the charterer liable for the loss. The loss that the charterer is liable for includes both physical damage/loss and economic loss such as loss of time.[36] If the shipowner accepts the order, the shipowner may not subsequently change its mind and ask for a new nomination.[37]

However, the shipowner would lose its right to claim the damages, if the shipowner had waived the right or abandoned the safe port warranty or undertaking. This happened in *The Chemical Venture*,[38] where the charterer nominated a port that was unsafe due to wartime and the shipowner agreed subject to bonus payment for taking the risk. The court held that by this conduct, the shipowner had abandoned the safe port warranty.

Another situation where the shipowner would lose its right for the damages is when the conduct of the shipowner in accepting the nomination is such that the causal link between the nomination and the loss is broken and the cause of the loss is rather the shipowner's compliance with the nomination. This will happen where the shipowner so deliberately allows the ship to run into danger that it throws its ship away. The threshold to find that a shipowner acted so unreasonably in complying with the nomination to break the causal link is very high.[39]

Irrespective of whether there is a breach of the warranty or undertaking, the shipowner may be able to claim any loss resulting from the nomination under

---

[35] [1988] 1 Lloyd's Rep 206 (EW HC).

[36] See *Emeraldian Ltd Partnership v Wellmix Shipping Ltd (The Vine)* [2010] EWHC 1411 (Comm), [2011] 1 Lloyd's Rep 301 (EW HC).

[37] *Motor Oil Hellas (Corinth) Refineries SA v Shipping Corpn of India (The Kanchenjunga)* [1990] 1 Lloyd's Rep 391 (UK HL).

[38] *Pearl Carriers Inc v Japan Line Ltd (The Chemical Venture)* [1993] 1 Lloyd's Rep 508 (EW HC).

[39] *Motor Oil Hellas (Corinth) Refineries SA v Shipping Corpn of India (The Kanchenjunga)* [1990] 1 Lloyd's Rep 391 (UK HL); *Compania Naviera Maropan SA v Bowaters Lloyd Pulp and Paper Mills Ltd (The Stork)* [1955] 2 QB 68 at 104,[1955] 2 All ER 241,[1955] 2 WLR 998 (EW CA), *dicta* of Morris LJ.

indemnity, if there is one expressed or implied,[40] subject to limitations applicable to indemnities such as voluntarily assumed risk.[41]

In deciding the question of safety of a port, a court may make reference the International Ship and Port Facility Security Code (ISPS Code), given effect to by the International Convention for the Safety of Life at Sea of 1974 (SOLAS).[42] A classification of a port at security-level 3 (the lowest) in the ISPS Code may be indicative of an unsafe port. However, this depends on the factual matrix of each case.

15.5.3.2 When Must the Port Be Safe?

The time at which the 'safe port' is tested is the time of the nomination of the port by the charterer.[43] At this time, the port must be prospectively safe.[44] This means within what can be reasonably foreseen at the time of the nomination, the port will be safe at the anticipated time of the ship's arrival at the port and remain so until the anticipated time of the ship's return from there.

In *The Lucille*,[45] the Iran-Iraq war outbroke subsequent to the charterparty was entered into but before the nomination of Basra port in Iraq was made. The outbreak of the war made the port unsafe at the time of nomination. However, the ship proceeded to the port. Subsequent to the nomination, as the ship was proceedings, the Shatt al Arab waterway was closed, trapping the ship. She shipowner claimed from the charterer the losses consequent upon the trapping. In defence, the charterer argued that it was not responsible for the loss resulting from the trapping as closure of the waterway happened after the nomination. The English Court of Appeal refused this argument, holding that the cause of the loss was intrinsically linked to the nomination by the charterer of Basra port which was unsafe at the time of nomination.

---

[40] *Vardinoyannis v The Egyptian General Petroleum Corporation (The Evaggelos Theta)* [1971] 2 Lloyd's Rep 200 (EW HC).

[41] See Chapter 15.4.3.

[42] As amended from time to time.

[43] *Kodros Shipping Corp v Empresa Cubana de Fletes (The Evia) (No. 2)* [1983] 1 AC 736, [1982] 2 Lloyd's Rep 307 (UK HL).

[44] *Gard Marine and Energy Ltd v China National Chartering Co Ltd; China National Chartering Co Ltd v Gard Marine and Energy Ltd; Daiichi Chuo Kisen Kaisha v Gard Marine and Energy Ltd (The Ocean Victory)* [2017] UKSC 35, [2018] 1 All ER 832, [2018] 1 All ER (Comm) 1, [2017] 1 WLR 1793 (UK SC).

[45] *Uni-Ocean Lines Pte Ltd v C-Trade SA (The Lucille)* [1984] 1 Lloyd's Rep 387 (EW CA).

15.5.3.3 What if Port Becomes Unsafe Subsequent to Nomination?

If a port was prospectively safe at the time of nomination and subsequently turns unsafe before the ship arrives there, the charterer must re-nominate.[46] If not expressed, this will be an implied duty on the charterer. This may be classified as a secondary duty. If the charterer fails to re-nominate when it should, then the charterer will be in breach.

However, such a breach will be avoided if the charterparty has a 'near' clause and there is a safe port within the scope of the clause. In such as case, if the shipowner fails to invoke the 'near' clause, then any loss would likely be caused by the shipowner's failure to invoke the clause rather than the charterer's failure to re-nominate so that the shipowner may not be able to claim the losses from the charterer. If the shipowner invokes the 'near' clause, the charterer will no longer be liable on the safe port warranty as far as the 'near' port is concerned. If there is neither a safe port within the agreed range nor a safe 'near' port, then the charterparty will be frustrated.

15.5.3.4 What Is 'Safe Port'?

The classical definition of 'safe port' was given by Sellars LJ in *The Eastern City*,[47] which was as follows:

> [I]n the relevant period of time … the particular ship *can reach it, use it, and return from it* without, in the absence of some *abnormal occurrence*, being exposed to *danger* which cannot be avoided by good navigation or seamanship. [emphasis added]

The 'danger' referred to by Sellars J encompasses both physical danger and political danger.[48] The concept of 'safe port' is a relative one. The two points for comparison are the time when the charterparty was entered into and the time when the order was made. Only if the port became less safe when the order was made than when the charterparty was entered into, the safe port warranty would be breached. In *The Product Star*,[49] the time charterer ordered, in 1987, the ship to proceed to Ruwais in UAE that the shipowner considered to be dangerous due the Iran-Iraq war at that time. Ruwais was within the permitted range of ports in the charterparty and the same conditions and risks were prevailing at the time the charterparty was entered into, which risk the shipowner voluntarily took. Accordingly, the English Court of Appeal held that relatively the port was not an unsafe port and the shipowners were in breach by refusing to proceed to that port.

---

[46] *Kodros Shipping Corp v Empresa Cubana de Fletes (The Evia) (No. 2)* [1983] 1 AC 736, [1982] 2 Lloyd's Rep 307 (UK HL).

[47] *Leeds Shipping Co Ltd v Société Française Bunge (The Eastern City)* [1958] 2 Lloyd's Rep 127 at 131 (EW CA).

[48] *Kodros Shipping Corp v Empresa Cubana de Fletes (The Evia) (No. 2)* [1983] 1 AC 736, [1982] 2 Lloyd's Rep 307 (UK HL).

[49] *Product Star Shipping Ltd (The Product Star) (No. 2)* [1993] 1 Lloyd's Rep 397 (EW CA).

Physical Danger

Some examples of physical danger rendering the port an unsafe one follow. In *The Eastern City*, [50] the port was unsafe because it was liable to sudden strong winds that could drag the anchor. In *The Houston City*,[51] the port was unsafe because of inadequate fendering there. In *The Marinicki*,[52] the port did not have a system of checking and removing obstacles in the dredged channel to the port and for giving warnings to ships coming into the port. The English High Court held that this rendered the port unsafe. A port does not become unsafe merely because it is liable to bad weather, if there is sufficient system to safely warn, sufficient tugs, pilots and sea room for manoeuvring.[53]

In *The Ocean Victory*, [54] the ship was discharging cargo at the port of Kashima in Japan under a time-charter that had a safe port warranty. At that time, meteorological warnings of 'long waves' were received that rendered it unsafe to remain at the port. Hence, the ship terminated the discharge operation and attempted to leave the port through Kashima Fairway, which was the only way out of the port. The Kashima Fairway encountered gale force winds at the same time, that resulted in the ship breaking up and becoming a total loss. The port, in its 35 years of history, had previously experienced long waves and gale force winds but not at the same time save for this incident. Either one of them happening would not render the port unsafe. But what rendered the port unsafe in this case was the both happening at the same time, which was unprecedented and unforeseeable. Accordingly, at the time the port was nominated there was nothing that rendered the port prospectively unsafe, hence the UK Supreme Court held that the safe port warranty was not breached.

Political Danger

In *The Saga Cob*,[55] the ship was ordered to proceed to an Ethiopian port around end of August 1988. While anchored about four or five miles off the port, the ship was attacked by guerrillas around early Sept 1988. Prior to this, another ship, *The Omo Wonz*, was subjected to attack by guerrillas about end of May 1988 around the port. The question before the English Court of Appeal was whether the port was prospectively unsafe, in political terms, at the time the order was given. The English Court of Appeal answered the question in the negative holding that the risk of attack was not a normal characteristic of the port. The court said that *The Omo Wonz* incident

---

[50] *Leeds Shipping Co Ltd v Société Française Bunge (The Eastern City)* [1958] 2 Lloyd's Rep 127 (EW CA).

[51] *Reardon-Smith Line v Australian Wheat Board (The Houston City)* [1956] AC 266 (UK HL).

[52] *Maintop Shipping Co Ltd v Bulkindo Lines Pte Ltd (The Marinicki)* [2003] EWHC 1894 (Admlty), [2003] 2 Lloyd's Rep 655 (EW HC).

[53] *Islander Shipping Enterprises SA v Empresa Maritima Del Estado SA (The Khian Sea)* [1979] 1 Lloyd's Rep 545 (EW CA).

[54] *Gard Marine and Energy Ltd v China National Chartering Co Ltd; China National Chartering Co Ltd v Gard Marine and Energy Ltd; Daiichi Chuo Kisen Kaisha v Gard Marine and Energy Ltd (The Ocean Victory)* [2017] UKSC 35, [2018] 1 All ER 832, [2018] 1 All ER (Comm) 1, [2017] 1 WLR 1793 (UK SC).

[55] *Penta Shipping (K/S) A/S v Ethiopian Shipping Lines Corpn (The Saga Cob)* [1991] 2 Lloyd's Rep 398 (EW CA).

did not render the risk of the attack a normal characteristics or port unsafe because the incident was attributable to want of security system and far distance from from the escort frigate. In coming to the conclusion, the court took into account the fact that subsequent to the attack in this case, there was no further attach until early 1990. The court making reference to events after the incident in question has rightly been subject of criticism, as the question is one of prospective safety at the time the order was given.[56]

15.5.4 Orders for Delivery Against Indemnity-Undertaking

This is yet another type of order that charterers give the shipowners. The order will be to ask the shipowner to deliver the cargo without presentation of the bill but against an undertaking for indemnity from the charterer/shipper.

However, this type of orders runs contrary to the fundamental obligation of the issuer of the bill to the holder of the bill (or the named consignee of a straight bill in possession of the bill) to delivery the goods against the presentation of the bill. Any delivery otherwise than against the bill of lading is a misdelivery, hence a tort of conversion against the holder of the bill or the named consignee of a straight bill in possession of the bill).

In *The Sormovskiy 3068*,[57] the charterparty *authorised* the shipowner to deliver against an indemnity-undertaking. The terms of the charterparty were incorporated into the bill of lading issued by the shipowner. The English High Court held that despite this arrangement, the shipowner will be liable for misdelivery if it delivers goods otherwise than against the bill. The same would be the position even if the charterparty *required* the shipowner to deliver against an indemnity-undertaking.[58]

A shipowner is not bound to take such an order, that will put the shipowner in possible liability for misdelivery, as held in cases such as *The Sagona*[59] and *The Houda*.[60] This must be so even if the charterparty authorises or requires the shipowner to deliver against such an undertaking.[61] It must be so even if the bill incorporates the charterparty that so authorises or requires. In fact, if such a bill were to be read as allowing delivery otherwise than against presentation of the bill, that would divest

---

[56] *Pearl Carriers Inc v Japan Line Ltd (The Chemical Venture)* [1993] 1 Lloyd's Rep 508 (EW HC).

[57] *Sucre Export SA v Northern Shipping Ltd (The Sormovskiy 3068)* [1994] 2 Lloyd's Rep 266 (EW HC).

[58] *Aegean Sea Traders Corpn v Repsol Petroleo SA (The Aegean Sea)* [1998] 2 Lloyd's Rep 39, [1998] All ER (D) 135 (EW HC); *The Dolphina* [2012] 1 Lloyd's Rep 304, [2011] SGHC 273 (SG HC).

[59] *Hansen-Tangens Rederi III A/S v Total Transport Corpn (The Sagona)* [1984] 1 Lloyd's Rep 194 (EW HC).

[60] *Kuwait Petroleum Corpn v I and D Oil Carriers Ltd (The Houda)* [1994] 2 Lloyd's Rep 541 (EW CA).

[61] Cf *The Epic* [2000] 3 SLR 735 (SG CA). This case does not appear to be decided on sound principles, as commented in Chapter 4.5.2.

the bill of the very characteristics required of a bill, namely, a document conferring construction possession on the holder. It must be noted that Protection and Indemnity (P&I) insurance does not cover liability for misdelivery.

However, if the shipowner takes the order and delivers without presentation of the bill but against an indemnity-undertaking, then the shipowner would be able to enforce the indemnity-undertaking. An indemnity-undertaking is not illegal or unenforceable although the order for delivery without bill is contrary to the law.[62] In *The Laemthong Glory (No. 2)*,[63] the receiver gave an indemnity-undertaking. The undertaking was, as it will usually be, both for indemnity and to provide security if the ship is arrested upon a cargo claim by the person rightly entitled to delivery. Upon the indemnity-undertaking, that the chartered required the shipowner to deliver, which the shipowner did. The indemnity was addressed as 'you, your servants and agents', but the security was addressed only to the charterer. Subsequently, the shipowner faced a cargo claim and claimed the indemnity and security, by way of specific performance, directly from the receiver. The English Court of Appeal found in favour of the shipowner on both counts.

In this case, the indemnity-undertaking can be interpreted as given to the shipowner because of the words 'your … agents'. However, the security-undertaking could only be taken as binding in favour of the shipowner by virtue of Section 1(1)(b) of the UK Contracts (Rights of Third Parties) Act 1999,[64] materially identical to Section 2(1)(b) of the Singapore Contracts (Rights of Third Parties) Act. It reads as follows:

> (1) Subject to the provisions of this Act, a person who is not a party to a contract (… third party …) may in his own right enforce a term of the contract if—
>
> …
>
> (b) subject to subsection (2), the term purports to confer a benefit on him.

The indemnity-point would have been decided in the same even if the words 'your … agents' were not there, by virtue of the Act. There is no corresponding statutory provision in Malaysia, like a number of other Commonwealth countries. Hence, by virtue of doctrine of privity of contract, if such a claim for indemnity and security had arisen under the Malaysian law, neither count would have been allowed. This is because the undertaking, including the one to indemnify with the words 'your … agents', was to the charterer, hence the shipowner as a third party would not be able to rely on it. Of course, the shipowner could make a claim against the charterer, and in turn, the charterer can pull in the receiver who gave the indemnity.[65] Upon

---

[62] *Oldendorff GmbH & Co KG v Sea Powerful II Special Maritime Enterprises (The Zagora)* [2016] EWHC 3212, [2017] 1 Lloyd's Rep 194 (EW HC).

[63] *Laemthong International Lines Co Ltd v Artis (The Laemthong Glory) (No 2)* [2005] EWCA Civ 519, [2005] 2 All ER (Comm) 167, [2005] 1 Lloyd's Rep 688 (EW CA).

[64] Applicable in England and Wales and N. Ireland.

[65] Likely under Order 16 of the Malaysian Rules of Court 2012 (Third Party and Similar Proceedings).

the charterer's claim against the receiver, the receiver would have to give both the indemnity and security.

In *The Songa Winds*,[66] the charterers issued a letter of indemnity, upon which the disponent shipowner delivered the cargo. Subsequently, in a claim by the disponent shipowner based on the letter of indemnity, the charterer attempted to rely on a time-limit clause in the voyage charterparty. The English Court of Appeal held that the letter of indemnity was an independent agreement, in the factual matrix of the case as will usually be the case, and was not barred by the time-limit clause in the charterparty.

When a ship is arrested, as a result of misdelivery upon an undertaking, and the shipowner furnishes security to have the ship released, the shipowner can still require the undertaker to provide the security to replace the shipowner's security.[67]

---

[66] *Navig8 Chemicals Pool Inc v Glencore Agriculture BV (The Songa Winds)* [2018] All ER (D) 115 (Aug) (EW CA).

[67] *Farenco Shipping Co Ltd v Daebo Shipping Co Ltd (Dampskibsselskabet Norden A/S, third party) (Deiulemar Shipping SpA, fourth party) (The Bremen Max)* [2009] 1 All ER (Comm) 423, [2008] EWHC 2755 (Comm), [2009] 1 Lloyd's Rep 81 (EW HC).

Chapter 16
Time Charter: Withdrawal, Off-Hire and Redelivery

This chapter analyses the events from delivery of the ship to the charterer to the redelivery to the shipowner. In that course, the obligation of the charterer to pay hire, the contractual right of withdrawal for non-payment of hire and the limitation imposed by anti-technicality clause are considered. The contractual right to suspend performance for default in hire-payment is also noted. The circumstances in which the shipowner may terminate for breach of charterer's obligation to pay hire are looked at. The off-hire clause is analysed at depth and detailed examination of off-hire events and off-hire period calculation in NYPE forms and BIMCO BALTIME 1939 forms is undertaken. Then, obligation of the charterer as to redelivery is considered in detail. This includes a detailed treatment of the time widow by which redelivery is to be given, consequences of early and late redelivery.

16.1 Introduction

In a time-charter, the obligation of the shipowner is to allow the use of the ship, equipped with crew and a few other services, by the charterer. In return, the charterer pays the hire, usually fixed on daily basis and payable in advance. If the charter defaults in proper payment of the hire, a possible remedy that may be available at law to the shipowner is termination of the charterparty, but not always available. Another option that will usually be contractually available to the shipowner is to withdraw the ship form service to the charterer.

However, the obligation to pay hire may sometimes be suspended such as when the ship goes on repair. This is called 'off-hire'. Again, it will be contractually provided when the ship will go 'off-hire'.

Second to the obligation of the charterer to pay hire, another important obligation of the charterer is to timely redeliver the ship at the designated location. A charterer may come into difficulty with this obligation, for example, where the last voyage that the charterer orders takes longer than expected.

A. Kasi, *The Law of Carriage of Goods by Sea*,
https://doi.org/10.1007/978-981-33-6793-7_16

If the hire is not paid promptly and in correct amount, that will be a breach by the charterer. However, that does not mean that the shipowner can terminate the charterparty as the obligation to pay hire has been classified as an innominate term. When the charterer fails to pay the hire promptly, this may put a great financial pressure on the shipowner in meeting its various obligations such as to the financiers, crew, insurers, ship management company, etc. Accordingly, the common practice has been to include a 'withdrawal' clause in the agreement.

The withdrawal class will allow the charterer to contractually withdraw the ship from the charter service and thereby terminate the agreement. Such a withdrawal is based on breach by the charterer but an exercise by the shipowner of a contractual option. Hence, a withdrawal, on its own, does not entail in the consequences that a termination for breach would entail, such as liability for damages.

All these: termination and withdrawal, off-hire and redelivery are, in order, the subject of this chapter.

16.2 Termination and Withdrawal

This sub-chapter will visit the charterer's obligation to pay hire, and the shipowners rights of termination and withdrawal when the hire is not paid as per the charterparty.

16.2.1 Obligation to Pay Hire

The time-charterparty will usually stipulate advance payment of hire for a certain period. For example, every 15 days' hire to be paid in advance by 15 days. This will mean the hire for the first day of the month to the fifteenth day of the month will be paid on the first day of the month. Clause 11(a) of the NYPE 2015 form provides for 15 days' advance payment as follows:

> **(a) Payment**
>
> Payment of Hire shall be made *without deductions due to Charterers' bank charges* so as to be received by the Owners or their designated payee into the bank account … *in funds available to the Owners on the due date* … [emphasis added]

When a hire is due on a day, the charterer has until the midnight to pay the hire. If money is transferred to the shipowner's account, the money must be in the shipowner's account by the midnight in clear funds. If not, there will be a default. The BALTIME 1939 (revised 2001) form expressly requires payment of hire in 'cash' without discount every 30 days in advance in the manner prescribed by the charterparty. Clause 6(2) (para 2) of the form states this requirement as follows:

> Payment of hire shall be made *in cash*, in the currency stated in Box 20, without discount, *every 30 days, in advance*, and *in the manner prescribed* in Box 20. [emphasis added]

'Cash' here does not mean hard cash, but that the money must be received by the shipowners in its designated account in cleared funds on the due date, as in the case of the NYPE 2015 form. This can be done via transfer of funds though banks, whether online or not.

In *The Chikuma*,[1] the charterparty required hire payment in cash. The charterer made a transfer of the full hire amount, but if the amount was to be credited in the shipowner's account on the same day, a bank charge of USD100 would be deducted. The House of Lords found this to be short of the charterer's obligation to pay the full hire in time.

If the hire payment falls due on a bank holiday, then it can be made on the holiday if online instant transfers make that possible, which is normally the case. In those days when such transfers were not possible, the charterer would have to pay on the last banking day before the due date to avoid being in default.[2] Bank holiday is no excuse for not ensure the hire payment is in the account of the shipowner on the designated day. However, if there is any fault in the banking system of the shipowner or its account that the money was not received into the account, then the charterer cannot be considered to be in default as it had offered the payment which was not received by the shipowner for a reason attributable to the shipowner. In those Commonwealth countries, including Malaysia,[3] with a Contract Act modelled on the Indian Contract Act 1872, the obligation on a party will be discharged by offering to perform. Section 37 of the Indian Act, in relevant part, provides for this as follows[4]:

> The parties to a contract must either perform, or offer to perform, their respective promises, unless the performance is dispensed with or excused under this Act, or of any other law.

Charterparties may allow the charterer to pay an approximate sum of hire in respect of the last hire-payment under the charterparty, since it may not be practical to calculate the exact amount in advance, and then make a daily payment in the event the redelivery runs beyond the period for which the payment was made. An example of such a provision is cl. 11(a) of NYPE 2015 form. However, the 'approximate'-allowance given to the charterer does not permit it to pay less than for the estimated days. In *The Chrysovalandou Dyo*,[5] the charterer made the last hire payment covering up to 10 September while the estimated redelivery date was 13 September. The English High Court found the charterer to be in default and a clause in the charterparty allowing the charterer to pay an 'approximate' amount for the last hire did not allow the charterer to pay for less days than that estimated. Hence, the shipowner was entitled to withdraw.

---

[1] *Awilco A/S v Fulvia SpA di Navigazione (The Chikuma)* [1981] 1 All ER 652, [1981] 1 WLR 314 (UK HL).

[2] *Mardorf Peach & Co Ltd v Attica Sea Carriers Corpn of Liberia (The Laconia)* [1977] AC 850, [1977] 1 All ER 545 (UK HL).

[3] Malaysian Contracts Act 1950.

[4] Identically reproduced in Section 38(1) of the Malaysian Contracts Act 1950.

[5] *Santiren Shipping Ltd v Unimarine SA (The Chrysovalandou Dyo)* [1981] 1 Lloyd's Rep 159, [1981] 1 Lloyd's Rep 159 (EW HC).

16.2.1.1 Equitable Set-Off Against Hire

The relief of equitable set-off is available to the charterer.[6] Thus, the charterer may deduct cross-claim that will fall within the narrow scope of equitable set-off. In order for a cross-claim to fall within the scope, there must be a close proximity between the primary claim and the close cross-claim. In the context of payment of hire under a time charterparty, such a close proximity will be there where the cross-claim is about the use of the ship for which the hire is payable. The set-off will be available in respect of speed and consumption claims[7] and claims arising from loading less cargo than that permitted and required.[8] Similarly, if a charterer has made a hire-payment in advance and subsequently the ship goes off-hire, the charterer will be entitled to set-off the payment made in respect of the off-hire period from the next hire-payment. But it will not be available for cargo claims or bunker misappropriation claims.[9] In *The Aditya Vaibhav*,[10] the English High Court held that a set-off was not available in respect of a bunker reimbursement claim. Similarly, in *The Li Hai*,[11] it was held that a bunker cancellation fee incurred by the charterer was not available for equitable set-off against hire.

A charterer must be cautious in exercising the right of equitable set-off in quantifying the cross-claim. A wrongful or over claim of set-off may result in the charterer being in default of hire-payment. In *The Nanfri*,[12] a special case was stated by an arbitral tribunal asking a question whether a charterer may make deductions for equitable set-off arising from speed-claim without the consent of the shipowner. The House of Lords answered the question in the affirmative. At the Court of Appeal,[13] Lord Denning added that insofar as the quantification of the equitable set-off claim is made by reasonable assessment and in good faith, the shipowner would not have

---

[6] *Federal Commerce and Navigation Ltd v Molena Alpha Inc and others (The Nanfri, The Benfri, The Lorfri)* [1979] AC 757, [1979] 1 All ER 307, [1978] QB 949, [1979] 1 Lloyds Rep 201, [1978] 3 WLR 991 (UK HL).

[7] *Santiren Shipping Ltd v Unimarine SA (The Chrysovalandou Dyo)* [1981] 1 All ER 340, [1981] 1 Lloyd's Rep 159 (EW HC); *Federal Commerce and Navigation Ltd v Molena Alpha Inc and others (The Nanfri, The Benfri, The Lorfri)* [1979] AC 757, [1979] 1 All ER 307, [1978] QB 949, [1979] 1 Lloyds Rep 201, [1978] 3 WLR 991 (UK HL).

[8] *Compania Sud Americana de Vapores v Shipmair BV (The Teno)* [1977] 2 Lloyd's Rep 289 (EW HC).

[9] *Leon Corporation v Atlantic Lines and Navigation Co Inc (The Leon)* [1985] 2 Lloyd's Rep 470 (EW HC).

[10] *Century Textiles and Industry Ltd v Tomoe Shipping Co (Singapore) Pte Ltd (The Aditya Vaibhav)* [1991] 1 Lloyd's Rep 573 (EW HC).

[11] *Western Bulk Carriers K/S v Li Hai Maritime Inc (The Li Hai)* [2005] EWHC 735 (Comm), [2005] 2 Lloyd's Rep 389 (EW HC). See also *Schelde Delta Shipping BV v Astarte Shipping Ltd (The Pamela)* [1995] 2 Lloyd's Rep 249 (EW HC).

[12] *Federal Commerce and Navigation Ltd v Molena Alpha Inc and others (The Nanfri, The Benfri, The Lorfri)* [1979] AC 757, [1979] 1 All ER 307, [1978] QB 949, [1979] 1 Lloyds Rep 201, [1978] 3 WLR 991 (UK HL).

[13] Reported in [1978] QB 927, [1978] 3 All ER 1066, [1978] 3 WLR 309, [1978] 2 Lloyd's Rep (EW CA).

the right to withdraw even if it is subsequently found to be an over-assessment by a court or an arbitral tribunal. Goff LJ differed on this point, who was of the view that the charterer acts 'at his peril', when assessment and deducting.

The better approach will be the one taken by Goff LJ. If a charterer makes a deduction, it must absolutely take the risk of it going wrong later resulting in the charterer being in default of payment obligation, as how a shipowner would take the risk when making withdrawal.[14] However, in a few subsequent cases decided by the English High Court, the view of Lord Denning has been followed.[15] The position may be reconsidered by the court in the future.

16.2.1.2 Contractually allowed Deductions

In the absence of an equitable set-off being available, the charterer may avail any contractual provisions allowing deductions from the hire-payment. Such provisions are usually made in respect of claims such as for disbursements to the ship advanced by the charterer,[16] advance hire paid in respect of an off-hire period,[17] and fuel consumed and expenses incurred during the off-hire period.[18] Some of them may overlap with, or be a repetition of, the equitable set-off rights.

16.2.2 Termination

If the hire is not paid promptly and in correct amount, that will be a breach by the charterer. However, that does not mean that the shipowner can terminate the charterparty as the obligation to pay hire has been classified as an innominate term,[19] unless it is expressly stated to be a condition. A general 'time of essence' clause will not make a difference. The consequence of this is that the shipowner will not be entitled to terminate the charterparty for failure to pay hire timely or in full, unless that constitutes a repudiatory breach. This will happen only exceptionally, for

[14] *Western Bulk Carriers K/S v Li Hai Maritime Inc (The Li Hai)* [2005] EWHC 735 (Comm), [2005] 2 Lloyd's Rep 389 (EW HC). See also *Schelde Delta Shipping BV v Astarte Shipping Ltd (The Pamela)* [1995] 2 Lloyd's Rep 249 (EW HC).

[15] *SL Sethia Liners Ltd v Naviagro Maritime Corpn (The Kostas Melas)* [1981] 1 Lloyd's Rep 18 (EW HC); *Santiren Shipping Ltd v Unimarine SA (The Chrysovalandou Dyo)* [1981] 1 All ER 340, [1981] 1 Lloyd's Rep 159 (EW HC); *Owneast Shipping Ltd v Qatar Navigation QSC* [2010] EWHC 1663 (Comm), [2011] 1 Lloyd's Rep 350 (EW HC).

[16] E.g. NYPE 2015 form, cl. 11(f); NYPE 1993 form, cl. 11(c); NYPE 1946 form, cl. 5.

[17] E.g. NYPE 2015 form, cl. 17; *Tradax Export SA v Dorada Compania Naviera SA (The Lutetian)* [1982] 2 Lloyd's Rep 140, [1982] Com LR 130 (EW HC); *Western Bulk Carriers K/S v Li Hai Maritime Inc (The Li Hai)* [2005] EWHC 735 (Comm), [2005] 2 Lloyd's Rep 389 (EW HC).

[18] E.g. NYPE 2015 form, cl. 17; NYPE 1993 form, cl. 17; NYPE 1946 form, cl. 15.

[19] *Spar Shipping AS v Grand China Logistics Holding (Group) Co Ltd* [2016] EWCA Civ 982, [2016] 2 Lloyd's Rep 447 (EW CA).

example, where the failure to properly pay evinces an intention not to properly pay the hire in the future, as it was the case in *Spar Shipping AS v Grand China Logistics Holding (Group) Co Ltd.*[20] In this case, the charterers had been making late/short payments over a period of five months. The English Court of Appeal found this to be sufficiently serious to entitle the shipowner to terminate the charterparty.

16.2.3 Withdrawal

When the charterer fails to pay the hire promptly, this may put a great financial pressure on the shipowner in meeting its various obligations such as to the financiers, crew, insurers, ship management company, etc. Accordingly, the common practice has been to include a 'withdrawal' clause in the charterparty.

The 'withdrawal' clauses will allow the charterer to contractually withdraw the ship from the charter service and thereby terminate the agreement if any hire payment, even a single payment, is not made timely or in full. Such a withdrawal is not based on breach by the charterer but an exercise by the shipowner of a contractual option. As a contractually provided option, its details such as when it may be exercised and what the consequences are governed by the terms of the contract only. Hence, a withdrawal, on its own, does not entail in the consequences that a termination for breach would entail, such as liability for damages.[21] However, there is nothing to stop a contractual provision allowing certain damages. This is, for example, the case with NYPE 2015 form, by cl. 11(c), which provides as follows:

> **(c) Withdrawal**
>
> Failure by the Charterers to pay hire due in full within three (3) Banking Days of their receiving a notice from Owners under Sub-clause 11(b) above shall entitle the Owners, without prejudice to any other rights or claims the Owners may have against the Charterers:
>
> (i) to withdraw the Vessel from the service of the Charterers;
>
> (ii) to damages, if they withdraw the Vessel, for the loss of the remainder of the Charter Party.

In contrast to 'withdrawal', if the failure to pay freight is so serious as to entitle the shipowner to terminate the charterparty for breach by the charterer, then the shipowner will automatically be entitled to damages upon termination. However, in practice, this difference is eliminated as popular time-charterparty forms like NYPE 2015[22] allow the shipowner to claim damages for loss of reminder of the charter-party upon withdrawal. It is not compulsory that the shipowner refuses the short/late tendered payment or that it immediately withdraws upon such payment but must do so

---

[20] [2016] EWCA Civ 982, [2016] 2 Lloyd's Rep 447 (EW CA).

[21] *Spar Shipping AS v Grand China Logistics Holding (Group) Co Ltd* [2016] EWCA Civ 982, [2016] 2 Lloyd's Rep 447 (EW CA).

[22] Cl. 11(c)(ii).

promptly. In *The Mihalios Xilas*,[23] the shipowner accepted a short payment and then decided to withdraw after four days. The House of Lords held that the shipowner had a reasonable time after the short payment to exercise the withdrawal-right and that the four days was reasonable. Having rightfully withdraw, the shipowner had to return the part of the payment in excess of the four days' hire. Similarly, in *The Laconia*,[24] the shipowners withdrew following a late payment received by the shipowner's agent without protest. Immediately after that the shipowner instructed the agent to return the payment. The charterer argued that the shipowner's agent had accepted the payment, hence the withdrawal-right had been waived. The House of Lords disagreed with the charterer and allowed the withdrawal. However, if the shipowner had failed to act promptly, that might have constituted a temporary waiver.[25]

Similarly, if a shipowner has habitually been accepting late payments from a charterer without any protest, the shipowner might have temporarily waived its right to insist on timely payment and accordingly temporarily waived also the consequent right to withdraw. The right may be put back upon the shipowner giving a reasonable notice to the charterer that it will insist on timely payment in the future.[26] If the shipowner affirms the charterparty subsequent to the short/late payment, then the right to withdraw for that default will be lost.[27]

Although the standard option to withdraw is only in respect of failure to pay hire timely and in full, there is nothing to stop extending it to other breaches. In *The Tropwind (No. 1)*,[28] the withdrawal option was extended to allow withdrawal 'for any other breach of charter'. The English High Court construed this too narrowly to exclude a breach by late payment of additional insurance premium. Contrary to this, in the subsequent case, *The Ahtos*,[29] the English Court of Appeal refused to follow *The Tropwind* and held that the such extension would encompass any breach. *The Tropwind* approach was too unrealistic and *The Athos* approach should be preferred.

---

[23] *China National Foreign Trade Transportation Corporation v Evlogia Shipping Co SA of Panama (The Mihalios Xilas)* [1979] 2 All ER 1044, [1979] 1 WLR 1018 (UK HL).

[24] *Mardorf Peach & Co Ltd v Attica Sea Carriers Corpn of Liberia (The Laconia)* [1977] AC 850, [1977] 1 All ER 545 (UK HL).

[25] *More OG Romsdal Fylkesbatar AS v The demise charters of the Ship Jotunheim* [2005] 1 Lloyd's Rep 181 (EW HC); *Parbulk II A/S Heritage Maritime SA (The Mahakam)* [2011] EWHC 2917 (Comm), [2012] 2 All ER (Comm) 418 (EW HC).

[26] *Tenax Steamship Co Ltd v Reinante Transoceania Navegacion SA (The Brimnes)* [1975] QB 929, [1974] 3 All ER 88, [1974] 3 WLR 613 (EW HC).

[27] *White Rosebay Shipping SA v Hong Kong Chain Glory Shipping Ltd (The Fortune Plum)* [2013] EWHC 1355 (Comm), [2013] 2 All EW (Comm) 449 (EW HC); *Primera Maritime (Hellas) Ltd v Jiangsu Eastern Heavy Industry Co Ltd* [2013] EWHC 3066 (Comm), [2014] 1 Lloyd's Rep 255 (EW HC).

[28] *Tropwood AG v Jade Enterprises Ltd (The Tropwind) (No.1)* [1977] 1 Lloyd's Rep 397 (EW HC).

[29] *Telfair Shipping Corporation v Athos Shipping Co SA, Solidor Shipping Co Ltd, Horizon Finance Corporation and AN Cominos (The Athos)* [1983] 1 Lloyd's Rep 127 (EW CA).

16.2.3.1 Anti-technicality Clause

The Laconia demonstrates the drastic nature of the withdrawal-right. In this case, the hire was due on Sunday in 1970. At that time there was no online banking and it was not possible to make a payment on Sunday. The charterer made the payment on Monday. The shipowner exercised the contractual option to withdraw. The House of Lords held that the shipowner was entitled to do so.

In such a situation what a charterer must do is to make the payment on the last banking day before the Sunday. The difficulty will be if it is a sudden holiday declared on a day. However, the times of such difficulties are gone now with the current age of online payment transfers.

The right to withdraw, thus being a drastic contractual relief available to the shipowner, has subsequently been commonly balanced with a 'grace period' clause known an 'anti-technicality' clause, that will mitigate *The Laconia*-like effects. The anti-technicality clause will require the shipowner to give an unambiguous ultimatum notice before exercising the right to withdraw. For example, cl. 11(b) of the NYPE 2015 form requires the charterer to give three banking days' notice in writing to the charterer to rectify the default in payment. Only if the charterer fails to so rectify, then the shipowner may exercise the right to withdraw.[30] Clause 11(b) reads as follows:

> **(b) Grace Period**
>
> Where there is failure to make punctual payment of hire due, the Charterers shall be given by the Owners three (3) Banking Days (as recognized at the agreed place of payment and the place of currency of the Charter Party) written notice to rectify the failure, and when so rectified within those three (3) Banking Days following the Owners' notice, the payment shall stand as punctual.

Clause 11(b) is referred to in the cl. 11(c) as a precondition for exercise of the right of withdrawal by the cl. 11(c). The anti-technicality clause is strictly construed. Any failure by the shipowner to strictly comply with it will deprive the shipowner of its right to withdraw on account of the hire-default in question. This was demonstrated by *The Li Hai*.[31] In this case, the required anti-technicality notice did not state the outstanding hire claimed clearly and did not contain an unambiguously ultimatum. The English High Court held the notice to be defective, thus the shipowner was not entitled to withdraw.

In *The Endurance 1*,[32] the charterparty was in SHELLTIME 4 form, whose anti-technicality clause[33] required seven days' notice before withdrawal. The shipowner gave a notice shorter than this and withdrew the ship. The Singapore Court of Appeal held the notice to be defective and the withdrawal to be in breach of the charterparty.

---

[30] Cl. 11(c) read with cl. 11(b).

[31] *Western Bulk Carriers K/S v Li Hai Maritime Inc (The Li Hai)* [2005] EWHC 735 (Comm), [2005] 2 Lloyd's Rep 389 (EW HC). See also *Schelde Delta Shipping BV v Astarte Shipping Ltd (The Pamela)* [1995] 2 Lloyd's Rep 249 (EW HC).

[32] [1999] 1 SLR 661 (SG CA).

[33] Cl. 9(a).

The strict compliance requirement not only attaches to the form and content of the notice but also to the time when it is given and the manner how it is given. If the notice is given before the right to withdraw accrued, the notice has been held invalid and of no effect. In *The Afovos,*[34] the notice was given at 4.40 pm on the day when the hire was due. When a hire is due on a day, the charterer has until midnight to pay the hire. Accordingly, the notice was pre-matured. In *The Pamela,*[35] the notice was sent by telex at 11.41 pm on the day when the hire was due. It was only read on the next business day. The English High Court held that the notice was good as it was not read at the night it was sent. This does not seem to be a right approach as the notice is given at the time it is given irrespective of whether it is read. The anti-technicality clause requires the shipowner to *give* the notice and it does not matter when it is read. Taking this a little further, if a pre-matured notice is given on the late night of day when the hire is due but is ante-dated next day, then perhaps the notice may be upheld for reason that the notice, by itself, was meant and considered to be given only on the next day.

In *Owneast Shipping Ltd v Qatar Navigation QSC,*[36] the NYPE 1946 form, which does not have an anti-technicality clause in the standard form, was modified by addition of a clause 62 to include an anti-technicality clause requiring notice to be given to the charterer before withdrawal in respect of 'any failure to make punctual and regular payment ... for any reason *where there is absence of intention to fail to make payment*'.[37] This meant if the charterer had the intention not to pay, then no anti-technicality notice was required and a withdrawal can be made without any such notice in advance. The charterer computed a deduction from the hire in bad faith and recklessly missed to make the payment even with a wrongful deduction. The English High Court held that there was an *intention* to fail to make the payment because of the deductions made in *bad faith.* But for such deduction, the court said that the notice would be required even if the reason for missing was that the charterer was *reckless*, which is short of *intentionally* failing to pay.

16.2.3.2 Consequences of Withdrawal

A shipowner must exercise its right to withdraw only sparingly, as it can have adverse consequences on the shipowner, even when rightly exercised. The shipowner might have issued bills of lading to the shippers. Irrespective of any withdrawal, the shipowner has to perform the bill of lading contracts. If freight is not paid, the shipowner can collect the freight on account of the hire. However, if freight is pre-paid, as will usually be the case, then the shipowner must honour it. The shipowner

---

[34] *Afovos Shipping Co SA v Pagnan and Lli (The Afovos)* [1983] 1 All ER 449, [1983] 1 WLR 195, [1983] 1 Lloyd's Rep 335 (UK HL).

[35] *Schelde Delta Shipping BV v Astarte Shipping Ltd (The Pamela)* [1995] 2 Lloyd's Rep 249 (EW HC).

[36] [2010] EWHC 1663 (Comm), [2011] 1 Lloyd's Rep 350 (EW HC).

[37] Such a requirement is not found in the standard NYPE 1946/1993/2015 forms.

cannot claim hire from the charterer, as the charterparty is no longer alive after the withdrawal. In *The Alev*[38] the shipowner secured the agreement of the cargo interest to contribute by putting pressure that otherwise the shipowner would not complete the voyage. The English High Court found the agreement to contribute to be vitiated by duress and hence unenforceable by the shipowner. In *The Bulk Chile,*[39] the shipowner completed the voyage upon the request of the sub-charterer. The English Court of Appeal held the sub-charterers liable for *quantum meruit* reward to the shipowner.

Clause 11(c)(ii) of NYPE 2015 permits damages only for loss of the reminder of charterparty, but not for other losses consequent upon withdrawal such as performing the bill of lading contracts. However, even in the absence of a contractual provision, the UK Supreme Court in *The Kos*[40] held such other consequent losses to be recoverable, while prior to this it was thought that such losses were not recoverable.[41] In this case, while the cargo was being loaded, the shipowner withdrew. Then, it took about three days for the shipowner to unload the cargo and free the ship at the loading port. There was no doubt that the shipowner was entitled to hire until the time of withdrawal, but the question was whether the shipowner was entitled to compensation for the three days spent on unloading the cargo. The court held that the shipowner was entitled to recover compensation for the unloading operation which included the detention of the ship and bunkers used for three days and the cost of issuing bank guarantee to release the ship from the arrest by the charterer. One of the bases of recovery was bailment. The shipowner in possession of the cargo, as a bailee, even after the carriage contract was terminated, was entitled to reasonable expenses for discharge of its duties as bailee.[42]

Another risk in exercising the withdrawal-option is that if it is later found that the withdrawal was not rightfully made, then the shipowner will be liable in damages to charterer, as happened in *The Li Hai.*[43] The quantum of damages will be the difference between the market hire and the contract hire for the balance period, provided the market hire at the time is higher than the contract hire. The question arose in a more complex scenario in In *The Endurance 1.*[44] In this case, the charterparty was for a year with an option to renew for another year and the daily hire rate was

[38] *Vantage Navigation Corp v Suhail and Saud Bahvan Building Materials (The Alev)* [1989] 1 Lloyd's Rep 138 (EW HC).

[39] *Dry Bulk Handy Holding Inc and Another v Fayette International Holdings Ltd and Another (The Bulk Chile)* [2013] EWCA Civ 184, [2013] 2 All ER (Comm) 295, [2013] 1 WLR 3440 (EW CA).

[40] *ENE Kos 1 Ltd v Petroleo Brasileiro SA (No 2) (The Kos)* [2012] UKSC 17, [2012] 2 AC 164 (UK SC).

[41] Dicta of Lord Denning in *Tropwood AG of Zug v Jade Enterprises Ltd (The Tropwind) (No. 2)* [1982] 1 Lloyd's Rep 232 at 237 (EW CA).

[42] *China-Pacific SA v Food Corpn of India (The Winson)* [1982] AC 939, [1981] 3 All ER 688 (UK HL).

[43] *Western Bulk Carriers K/S v Li Hai Maritime Inc (The Li Hai)* [2005] EWHC 735 (Comm), [2005] 2 Lloyd's Rep 389 (EW HC). See also *Schelde Delta Shipping BV v Astarte Shipping Ltd (The Pamela)* [1995] 2 Lloyd's Rep 249 (EW HC).

[44] [1999] 1 SLR 661 (SG CA).

USD2,000. The charter, back-to-back, sub-let the ship to a sub-charterer on similar terms with a daily hire rate of USD2,800. Indeed, the ship was directly delivered by the shipowner to the sub-charterer, on the instruction of the charterer. The shipowner was aware at all material times that the charterer entered into the charterparty to let her on sub-charter. In about a month after commencement of the charter, the shipowner wrongfully withdrew.[45] The Singapore Court of Appeal refused to assess damages by reference to the market rate of hire at the time of withdrawal, which was higher than USD2,800 daily, but awarded damages at the rate of USD800 per day for the remaining 11 months, namely, the difference between the hire rate under the head charter and the sub-charter. The court also refused to take into account the option to renew. The rightness of the court's refusal to award damages for loss of the opportunity or chance of renewal can be questionable.

If the shipowner affirms the charterparty after the short/late payment, it will lose the right to withdraw for reason of that payment. If the shipowner were to withdraw subsequent to such affirmation, that will be a wrongful withdrawal rendering the shipowner liable in damages to the charterer.[46] The withdrawal may also go wrong where the hire was short-paid because the charterer had rightly deducted some set-off against hire.[47]

16.2.4 Suspending Performance

In the standard time-charterparty forms, there is no midway relief for the shipowner to withhold or suspend any service if there is a payment default or other breach by the charterer. However, there is no barrier to contractually making a provision for such a midway relief.

Such provisions are found in cl. 11(d) of the NYPE 2015 form, which reads as follows:

> **(d) Suspension**
>
> At any time while hire is outstanding, the Owners shall, without prejudice to the liberty to withdraw, be entitled to *withhold the performance of any and all obligations hereunder and shall have no responsibility whatsoever for any consequences thereo*f, and Charterers hereby indemnify the Owners for all legitimate and justifiable actions taken to secure their interests, and hire shall continue to accrue and any extra expenses resulting from such withholding shall be for the Charterers' account. [emphasis added]

---

[45] The charterparty was in the SHELLTIME 4 form, whose anti-technicality clause—cl. 9(a)—required seven day's notice before withdrawal. The shipowner did not comply with it.

[46] *White Rosebay Shipping SA v Hong Kong Chain Glory Shipping Ltd (The Fortune Plum)* [2013] EWHC 1355 (Comm), [2013] 2 All EW (Comm) 449 (EW HC); *Primera Maritime (Hellas) Ltd v Jiangsu Eastern Heavy Industry Co Ltd* [2013] EWHC 3066 (Comm), [2014] 1 Lloyd's Rep 255 (EW HC).

[47] *Federal Commerce and Navigation Ltd v Molena Alpha Inc and others (The Nanfri, The Benfri, The Lorfri)* [1979] AC 757, [1979] 1 All ER 307, [1978] QB 949, [1979] 1 Lloyds Rep 201, [1978] 3 WLR 991 (UK HL).

It allows the shipowner to suspend any service, without liability, if the hire is in arrears. Unlike withdrawal, it appears that there is no requirement to give anti-technicality notice before suspension.[48] During the suspension, the hire continues to run.

An example of such a suspension could be the shipowner refusing to sign bills of lading presented by the charterer as happened in *The Nanfri*,[49] although this case was not about invocation of a right to suspend. The practical effect of suspension can be drastic to the charterer as it may not be able to operate as it would during the suspension. If a suspension were to be made wrongfully, that would be a repudiatory breach entitling the charterer to terminate the charterparty and claim damages, as happened in *The Nanfri*. Even if the charterer did not elect to terminate, it would still be entitled to damages for the breach. Accordingly, the right to suspend must be exercised sparingly like the right to withdraw.[50]

A similar right to suspend is found in BIMCO SUPPLYTIME 2017 form in cl. 12(f)(ii). The predecessors to this form is the BIMCO SUPPLYTIME 89 form which has a similar provision in cl. 10(e)(4) and the BIMCO SUPPLYTIME 2005 which had a similar provision in cl. 12(f)(i). The wording in these three forms are somewhat different from each other. In *The Greatship Dhriti*,[51] the English High Court dealt with the 1989 form and held that no anti-technicality notice was required before exercising the right to suspend, unlike in the case of exercising the right to withdraw. However, the court opined that the wording in the 2005 form is not clear. The clause referred to by the court was cl. 12(f)(i), which in relevant part read as follows:

> Where there is a failure to pay Hire by the due date, the Owners *shall notify* the Charterers in writing of such failure *and further may also suspend* the performance of any or all of their obligations … [emphasis added]

It appears that that the 2005 form indeed required the anti-technicality notice to be issued as a pre-condition to the exercise of right to suspend. In contrast to it, the 1989 form in cl. 10(e) provides:

> [I]n default of payment … the Owners *may* require the Charterers to make payment … within 5 banking days … failing which the Owners shall have the right to withdraw. … While payment remains due the Owners shall be entitled to suspend …

It is clear in the 1989 form that no anti-technicality notice is required for suspension. Comparatively, in the 2017 form, it is provided in cl. 12(f) as follows:

---

[48] See *Greatship (India) Ltd v Oceanografia SA de CV (The Greatship Dhriti)* [2012] EWHC 3468 (Comm), [2013] 1 All ER (Comm) 1244, [2013] 2 Lloyd's Rep 359, [2012] All ER (D) 38 (Dec) (EW HC).

[49] *Federal Commerce and Navigation Ltd v Molena Alpha Inc and others (The Nanfri, The Benfri, The Lorfri)* [1979] AC 757, [1979] 1 All ER 307, [1978] QB 949, [1979] 1 Lloyds Rep 201, [1978] 3 WLR 991 (UK HL).

[50] See Chapter 16.2.3.2.

[51] *Greatship (India) Ltd v Oceanografia SA de CV (The Greatship Dhriti)* [2012] EWHC 3468 (Comm), [2013] 1 All ER (Comm) 1244, [2013] 2 Lloyd's Rep 359, [2012] All ER (D) 38 (Dec) (EW HC).

> (i) Where there is a failure to make punctual payment of hire or other sums due … the Owners *shall* promptly notify the Charterers … and require payment within five (5) days.
>
> (ii) At any time while hire or other sums due … remain outstanding the Owners shall be entitled to suspend …

In the 2017 form, the anti-technicality notice is not made a condition precedent to the exercise of right to suspend. Although it is required to be issued when there is a payment-default on part of the charterer, the right of the shipowner to suspend is not put on hold until the notice period expires. Indeed, even if the notice is not issued, that would merely be a breach by the shipowner but not affect the shipowner's right to suspend.

The position is similar in the NYPE 2015 form. In this form, the anti-technicality notice requirement is provided in cl. 11(b) and the right to suspend in cl. 11(d). These clauses read as follows:

> (b) Where there is a failure to make punctual payment of hire due, the Charterers shall be given by the Owners three (3) Banking Days … written notice …
>
> …
>
> (d) At any time while hire is outstanding, the Owners shall … be entitled to withhold the performance of any and all obligations …

Clause 11(d) is not tied to the anti-technicality notice, unlike the right to withdraw in cl. 11(c). Hence, no anti-technicality notice would be required for suspension.

16.3 Off-Hire

Charterparties will usually provide for suspension of hire in certain circumstances. This is called 'off-hire',[52] which is sometime also called 'suspension of hire'.[53] The charterer does not pay hire for the off-hire period. This is a contractual relief and hence its details are governed as per the terms of the Charterparty. The NYPE 2015 form provides for this in cl. 17. This clause additionally allows the bunkers consumed during the off-hire period to be placed on owner's account and to be deducted from the hire. Off-hire period is not added to extend the original period of charterparty, in the absence of a specific clause giving the option to so add to the charterer,[54] as it is in cl. 52(c) of the NYPE 2015 form.

Usually, there will be two elements in an 'off-hire' clause. First, the clause will list the events that *can* trigger off-hire. This may include a saving event, namely,

---

[52] E.g. NYPE 2015 form, cl. 17; NYPE 1993 form, cl. 17; NYPE 1946 form, cl. 15.

[53] E.g. BIMCO BALTIME 1939 form (revised 2001), cl. 11.

[54] E.g. *Hong Kong Fir Shipping Co Ltd v Kawasaki Kisen Kaisha Ltd* [1962] 2 QB 26, [1961] 2 Lloyd's Rep 478 (EW CA); *Petroleo Brasileiro SA v Kriti Akti Shipping Co SA (The Kriti Akti)* [2004] EWCA Civ 116, [2004] 1 Lloyd's Rep 712 (EW CA).

any other cause *preventing the full working of the vessel.* This is the wording for the saving event in the NYPE 2015 form.[55] In the case of BIMCO BALTIME 1939 form (revised 2001), the wording essentially is that the event *hinders or prevents the working of the vessel and continuing for more than 24 consecutive hours such that the vessel is unable to perform the service immediately required*,[56] although this is not provided as a saving item but rather as a qualification attaching to each of the specific events listed in the clause. Second, in order for a ship to go off-hire, the clause may require that time is actually lost by the event. In such a case, if no loss of time to the charterer despite the event, then no off-hire. If there is a loss of time, then that is the period of off-hire. This type of clause is called 'net' clause. Alternatively, the clause may not require time to be lost but instead count the time from the start of the event to its end.[57] This type of clause is called 'period' clause. Both NYPE 2015 and the BIMCO BALTIME 1939[58] forms provide 'net' clause. The NYPE form provides this as 'the payment of hire and overtime, if any, shall cease 'for the time thereby lost'.[59] The BALTIME form provides this as 'no hire shall be paid in respect of any time lost thereby during the period'.[60] Third, other than the suspension of the hire, the clause may also provide for other matters following the off-hire. For example, the NYPE 2015 form provides, in cl. 17, that 'all bunkers used by the Vessel while off-hire shall be for the owner's account'. The first two elements are considered in detail below.

16.3.1 Triggering Event

An 'off-hire' is not prevented because the shipowner's liability for the triggering event is excluded or limited, as the liability exclusion/limitation protection to the shipowner is different from suspension of the obligation of the charterer's obligation for hire.[61] Similarly, fault of or breach by the shipowner is not required in connection with the triggering event. In the event the shipowner has breached the charterparty in connection with the triggering event, the charterer will additionally have any remedies

---

[55] Cl. 17.

[56] Cl. 11(a).

[57] E.g. The added cl. 57 in the amended NYPE 1993 form charterparty in *TS Lines Ltd v Delphis NV; Delphis NV v Ulrike F Kai Freese GmbH & Co KG (The TS Singapore)* [2009] EWHC 678 (Comm), [2010] 1 All ER (Comm) 434, [2009] 2 Lloyd's Rep 54 (EW HC). SeeChapter 16.3.1.1, sub-heading 'Other off-hire' clauses'.

[58] (Revised 2001).

[59] E.g. NYPE 2015 form, cl. 17; NYPE 1993 form, cl. 17; NYPE 1946 form, cl. 15.

[60] E.g. BIMCO BALTIME 1939 form (revised 2001), cl. 11

[61] *Ocean Glory Compania Naviera SA v A/S PV Christensen (The Loanna)* [1985] 2 Lloyd's Rep 164 at 167 (EW HC), speech of Staughton J.

available for the breach subject to any exclusion or limitation clause.[62] Similarly, off-hire is not prevented even if it was caused by the charterer's fault or breach. But in such a case, the shipowner will be able to recover from the charterer the losses including the loss of hire as damages.[63] In *The Darya Tara*,[64] deck cargo was carried at charterer's or shipper's risk. The deck carriage necessitated re-stowing, hence loss of time, which fell within the off-hire clause. The shipowner sought to recover the lost hire as damages and was unsuccessful as there was no breach by the charterer on loading the deck cargo (although it was to be carried at the charterer's risk). The triggering events in the contexts of NYPE 2015 form and BIMCO BALTIME 1939 form (revised 2001) are considered below.

16.3.1.1 NYPE 'Off-Hire' Clause

The NYPE 2015 form, in cl. 17, lists 10 triggering events, which are as follows:

(i) deficiency/default/strike of officers or ratings;
(ii) deficiency of stores;
(iii) fire;
(iv) breakdown of, or damage to hull, machinery or equipment;
(v) grounding;
(vi) detention by the arrest of the Vessel, (unless such arrest is caused by events for which the Charterers, their sub-charterers, servants, agents or sub-contractors are responsible);
(vii) detention by Port State control or other competent authority for Vessel deficiencies;
(viii) detention by average accidents to the Vessel or cargo, unless resulting from inherent vice, quality or defect of the cargo;
(ix) drydocking for the purpose of examination, cleaning and/or painting of underwater parts and/or repair;
(x) by any other similar cause pre*venting the full working of the Vessel.*

In *The Rijn*,[65] the English High Court quite narrowly construed the off-hire events list so that the ship will go off-hire only if the event was caused fortuitously but not if it was the result of ordinary use of the ship by the charterer. In this case, the time charterparty was in the NYPE 1946 form. In the 1946 form, the off-hire events are listed in cl. 15. The difference between off-hire events list in the 1946 form and the

---

[62] See *Actis Co Ltd v Sanko Steamship Co Ltd (The Aquacharm) (HC)* [1980] 2 Lloyd's Rep 237 (EW HC), affirmed by the Court of Appeal in [1982] 1 All ER 390, [1982] 1 WLR 119, [1982] 1 Lloyd's Rep 7 (EW CA); *Eastern Mediterranean Maritime (Liechtenstein) Ltd v Unimarine SA (The Marika M)* [1981] 2 Lloyd's Rep 622 (EW HC).

[63] See *Lensen Shipping Ltd v Anglo-Soviet Co* (1935) 52 Ll L Rep 141 (EW CA).

[64] *Seals (LD) NV v Mitsui Osk Lines Ltd (The Darya Tara)* [1997] 1 Lloyd's Rep 42 (EW HC).

[65] *Santa Martha Baay Scheepvaart and Handelsmaatschappij NV v Scanbulk A/S (The Rijn)* [1981] 2 Lloyd's Rep 267 (EW HC).

2015 form is that items six and seven above are not there in the 1946 form, the word 'similar' is not there in the last item of the events list in the 1946 form which reads more widely as '*any other cause* preventing the full working of the vessel' and the first item simply reads as 'deficiency of men' only. The ship was waiting too long at a warm water port to load, which resulted in marine growth on the ship's hull and consequent loss of time in cleaning. The court held that this was not covered within the scope of cl. 15, namely damage to hull or other cause preventing the full working of the vessel, because the cause of the marine growth was a natural consequence of trading at that port and not fortuitous. However, the court took a wider approach to the off-hire events list in *The Doric Pride*.[66] In this case, the ship was chartered to carry grain from US Gulf to South Korea. The charterers then nominated a US port for loading. It was the first time for the ship to call at a US port and hence she was detained as per the US laws for anti-terrorism clearance. This will happen to any hip calling at a US port for the first time. The relevant off-hire clause was that any detention by authorities will result in off-hire subject to an exclusion of detention by reason of cargo carried or calling port of trading under this charter. The court construed the off-hire exclusion provision narrowly so that the detention did not fall within the exclusion, hence the ship went off-hire for reason of detention by authorities. This was because the charter was to carry cargo from a US port and the detention would have happened with any US port that the charterer may nominate, hence the detention was not because of the particular US port nominated by the charterer. Again, a wider approach was recently taken by the UK Supreme Court in *The Global Santosh*.[67] In this case, the ship was arrested by the sub-charterer. The relevant off-hire clause read as follows:

> Should the vessel be … arrested … by any legal process … the payment of hire shall be suspended … unless such … arrest is occasioned by any personal act or omission or default of the Charterers or *their agents*." [emphasis added]

The court construed the words 'their agents' in the above clause fairly narrowly and held that the sub-charterer would not be treated as agents of the charterer for the purposes here,[68] hence the head charterer was entitled to the benefit of off-hire for detention by arrest. However, if the NYPE 2015 form were used here, then the head charterer would not be entitled to the off-hire benefit as the sixth item of the list expressly excludes from off-hire arrest by sub-charterer. It does not matter whether the sub-charterer is treated as an agent of the head charterer or not.

In *The Saldanha*,[69] the English High Court considered if capture of the ship by Somali pirates would fall within any of the off-hire events in the NYPE 1946 form.

---

[66] *Hyundai Merchant Marine Co Ltd v Furness Withy (Australia) Pty (The Doric Pride)* [2006] EWCA Civ 599, [2006] 2 All ER (Comm) 188 (EW CA).

[67] *NYK Bulkship (Atlantic) NV v Cargill International SA (The Global Santosh)* [2016] UKSC 20, [2016] 1 Lloyd's Rep 629, [2016] 4 All ER 298 (UK SC).

[68] Although the sub-charterers would be the agent of the head-charterer when discharging the cargo.

[69] *Cosco Bulk Carrier Co Ltd v Team-Up Owning Co Ltd (The Saldanha)* [2010] EWHC 1340 (Comm), [2011] 1 Lloyd's Rep 187 (EW HC).

The court answered this question in the negative. The court held that it did not fall within 'the detention by average accidents' event, as there was no accident. The court held that even if the crew had failed to adopt established anti-piracy precautions or was otherwise negligence in connection with the pirates capturing the ship, that would not fall within the 'deficiency of men' event. However, the court opined that if there was a refusal by the master or crew to perform their duties resulting in the piracy, then it could fall within the 'deficiency of men' event. The court also held that the piracy would not fall within 'any other cause' by construing this in line with *ejusdem generis* rule.[70]

Other causes preventing full working of the vessel

The question of whether the ship was prevented from full working more often arose under the NYPE 1946 form than under the NYPE 1993 or 2015 forms. In the case of the 1946 form, often reliance had to be placed on the 'other cause preventing full working of the vessel' item which was frequently amended with insertion of the 'whatsoever' after 'other cause'. Reliance on this saving item was necessary because the specific items listed in cl. 15, unlike cl. 17 of the 2015 form, were very limited and the charterer might not find any suitable specific item.

The utility of this requirement can be limited where a specific listed event has happened because, in such a case, off-hire can only be claimed if time is thereby lost. When time is so lost, that means the event has prevented full working of the ship. Next, the utility of the requirement is likely limited even with the saving item of 'other cause' or 'other similar cause' preventing the full working of the vessel, because *ejusdem generis* rule will limit the 'other cause' to the like of the specific list.[71] But there will be utility of the requirement where the words 'other cause' is modified, as frequently happens, as 'other cause *whatsoever*'. This is because this modified version allows any cause preventing the full working of the ship to put the ship into off-hire. It will be necessary to ask the question whether the ship was prevented from full working only where the 'other cause *whatsoever*' item is relied on.

Some scholars have considered whether the words 'preventing full working of the vessel' attaches to all the items in the list or only to the 'other cause' and argued that it attaches to all items. However, this analysis is not necessary as the words 'preventing full working of vessel' will have a utility only if it attaches to 'other cause whatsoever'.

The application of the *ejusdem generis* rule to the last item in the 1946 form was demonstrated by *The Laconian Confidence*.[72] The ship was detained by the port authorities for presence of residue sweepings. The port authorities, unexpectedly,

[70] General words that follow specific words in a list must be construed as referring only to the types of things identified by the specific words.

[71] *Andre & Cie SA v Orient Shipping Rotterdam BV (The Laconian Confidence)* [1997] 1 Lloyd's Rep 139 (EW HC).

[72] *Andre & Cie SA v Orient Shipping Rotterdam BV (The Laconian Confidence)* [1997] 1 Lloyd's Rep 139 (EW HC).

took 18 days to authorise disposal of the residue at a designated ocean position and detained the ship for these 18 days after discharge, although the authorisation could have been within a few hours after discharge. The charterer argued that the ship went off-hire under the last item: 'any other cause preventing the full working of the vessel'. The English High Court found that, by reason of the *ejusdem generis* rule, the last would only include physical causes as those listed above the last time, hence held that the ship did not go off-hire. However, the court said had 'whatsoever' been added to the last item, then *ejusdem generis* rule would have been excluded so that the ship would go off-hire when her full working is prevented by legal causes. Although the court treated the items in the list to be physical matters, indeed the 'deficiency' of men and stores could refer to legal deficiencies. If this case were to happen under NYPE 2015 form, the court will have to consider the seventh item, namely detention by reason of the vessel's deficiency. This will possibly include legal deficiency of the vessel. However, in this case there was no deficiency on part of the vessel but only inefficiency or bureaucracy of part of the port authority. Hence, the ship will not go off-hire. The last item too will not help the charterer for reasons stated in the *The Laconian Confidence*. More so, with the addition of 'similar' in the last item in the case of NYPE 2015 form. Even if 'whatsoever' were to be added that would not make a difference due to the presence of 'similar'. But it might make a difference if the word 'similar' is taken out and the word 'whatsoever' is added. The charterparty may expressly exclude from the off-hire list any detention resulting from calling ports of trading, as was the case in *The Doric Pride*,[73] where the relevant off-hire clause provided as follows.

> Should the vessel be ... detained ... by any authority ... the payment of hire shall be suspended ... unless such ... detention ... is occasioned ... by reason of cargo carried or calling port of trading under this charter.

With such a clause as above, the ship will not go off-hire when unreasonably detained by the port authority. Some courts have adopted a narrow approach to the words 'other cause *whatsoever* preventing the full working of the vessel', while other courts have adopted a wider approach.

The following two three cases will demonstrate the narrow approach. In *The Berge Sund*,[74] the English Court of Appeal held that cleaning required of cargo holds, whether ordinary or extraordinary, does not prevent the vessel from being in full working, hence does not trigger off-hire under the 'any other cause preventing the efficient working of the vessel' clause. However, if a specific item in connection with time spent on necessary cleaning of cargo holds is added the off-hire events list, then a court will find this to trigger off-hire. If the cleaning was necessary because of fault of the shipowner, then the charterer may be able to claim from the shipowner damages including for the hire lost.

---

[73] *Hyundai Merchant Marine Co Ltd v Furness Withy (Australia) Pty (The Doric Pride)* [2006] EWCA Civ 599, [2006] 2 All ER (Comm) 188, [2006] 2 Lloyd's Rep 175 (EW CA).

[74] *Sig Bergesen DY & Co and Others V Mobil Shipping and Transportation Co (The Berge Sund)* [1993] 2 Lloyd's Rep 453 (EW CA).

In *The Aquacharm*,[75] the time-charter was under NYPE 1946 form with cl. 15 unamended. The master over-loaded cargo, contrary to the charterer's order. This necessitated discharge of some of the cargo into lighter to comply with draught requirements for passing Panama Canal and hence loss of time of about nine days and cost of lightening. The English Court of Appeal disallowed the owner's claim for the cost of lightening. As to the charterer's off-hire claim, the court disallowed the same holding that the lightening did not fall with the 'other cause' clause.

In *The Roachbank*,[76] the form concerned was NYPE 1946, the cl. 15 whereof was amended with addition of the word 'whatsoever' to 'other cause'. In this case, the ship took 293 Vietnamese refugees sighted in a pitiful condition at the sea crammed into a small boat. In line with the seafarer's tradition and the UK Maritime Conventions Act 1911, the master received them into the ship and proceeded to the discharge port in Taiwan. The port authority refused to allow the ship to enter the port because of the presence of Vietnamese refugees, but subsequently allowed after a loss of many days. The English High Court held this not to fall within the 'other cause whatsoever' off-hire event,[77] holding:

> [F]or the clause to be capable of applying at all, the charterers have to show that the vessel in herself or as a vessel was not "fully efficient in all respects" ... Only if she is not "fully efficient and able to render to the charterers the service then required" ... is it necessary to consider whether she is prevented from being so by a relevant clause.

A wider approach was demonstrated by *The Apollo*,[78] which involved NYPE 1946 form with amended cl. 15 by addition of the words 'whatsoever' to 'other cause'. In this case, at Naples, two crew members were suspected of typhus and were hospitalised there. The ship subsequently sailed to Lower Buchanan to load. As a result of the typhus suspect, the port authority here delayed issuance of free pratique for about two days. The English High Court held that this was an off-hire event under the 'other cause whatsoever' clause.

Other 'off-hire' clauses

In *The TS Singapore*,[79] the form used was NYPE 1993 form with modifications. Clause 17 of the 1993 form is identical to cl. 17 of the 2015 form in material parts. An added clause, cl. 57, provided as follows:[80]

> Any time lost ... putting back whilst on voyage ... due to an accident ... the hire shall be suspended from the time of inefficiency ... until the vessel is again efficient in the same or equivalent position ... and the voyage resumed therefrom.

---

[75] *Actis Co Ltd v Sanko Steamship Co Ltd (The Aquacharm) (CA)* [1982] 1 All ER 390, [1982] 1 WLR 119, [1982] 1 Lloyd's Rep 7 (EW CA).

[76] *Venezolana (CA) de Navegacion SA v Bank Line Ltd (The Roachbank)* [1987] 2 Lloyd's Rep 498 (EW HC).

[77] Upheld by the Court of Appeal in [1988] 2 Lloyd's Rep 337 (EW CA).

[78] *Sidermar SpA v Apollo Corporation (The Apollo)* [1978] 1 Lloyd's Rep 200 (EW HC).

[79] *TS Lines Ltd v Delphis NV; Delphis NV v Ulrike F Kai Freese GmbH & Co KG (The TS Singapore)* [2009] EWHC 678 (Comm), [2009] 2 Lloyd's Rep 54 [2010] 1 All ER (Comm) 434 (EW HC).

[80] 'Period' clause.

Another added clause, cl. 81, provided that if the vessel was off-hire for a period of 20 consecutive days the charterers had an option to re-deliver the vessel when next cargo free. The ship, shortly after departing from the loading place at Yokohama, met an accident by hitting a breakwater on 7 September. This held up the ship at Yokohama until 22 September, when she was required by the classification society to sail to Hong Kong and discharge the cargo there. The route from Yokohama to Hong Kong and Shanghai was a common one for a day and half sailing from Yokohama. It was not in dispute that the ship went off hire on 7 September. On 28 September, the charterer counted more than 20 consecutive days and notified termination according to cl. 81. The shipowner contented that there had not been 20 consecutive days because the ship came back efficient on 22 September for one and a half day when sailing on the common route. The English High Court held that the ship had not come back efficient on 22 September because she was sailing at the disposal of the classification society and not the charterer and she was not on the charter voyage. In *The Eleni P, Eleni Shipping Ltd v Transgrain Shipping BV (The Eleni P)* [2019] EWHC 910 (Comm), [2019] 1 CLC 655 (EW HC) the time charterparty was on an amended NYPE 1946 form. An additional typewritten clause, cl. 49, provided "[should] the vessel be [captured] or seized or detained or arrested by any authority or by any legal process … the payment of hire shall be suspended …". Another additional typewritten clause, cl. 101, read "[charterers] are allowed to transit Gulf of Aden any time, all extra war risk premium and/or kidnap and ransom as quoted by vessel's [underwriters], if any, will be reimbursed by [charterers]. … In case vessel should be threatened/kidnapped by reason of piracy, payment of hire shall be suspended." The ship was captured by pirates, after transiting Gulf of Aden, in Arabian Sea for seven months. The charterers claim off-hire for the seven months, that the shipowners contested. The arbitral tribunal held that the word 'capture' in cl. 49 was to be read disjunctively from 'arrested by any authority or by any legal process', hence the off-hire event in cl. 49 was triggered. The arbitral tribunal also held that the hire would be suspended also under cl. 101 as the ship was captured as an immediate consequence of transiting the Gulf of Aden. On appeal to the High Court, 1939 form (revised in 2001). The court disagreed with the interpretation by the arbitral tribunal of cl 46 and held that the word 'capture' therein was to be read conjunctively so that it was not triggered when the ship was captured by pirates rather than by any authority or legal process. However, the High Court agreed with the arbitral tribunal on its interpretation of cl. 101 and accordingly off-hire was triggered.

16.3.1.2 BALTIME 'Off-Hire' Clause

The BIMCO BALTIME 1939 form (revised in 2001) off-hire event list is narrower than that in the NYPE 2015 form. The BALTIME form[81] off-hire events (called 'suspension of hire'), in cl. 11(a), are as follows:

---

[81] 1939 form (revised in 2001).

(i) drydocking or other necessary measures to maintain the efficiency of the Vessel;
(ii) deficiency of men;
(iii) deficiency of Owners' stores;
(iv) breakdown of machinery, damage to hull or other accident

either hindering or preventing the working of the Vessel and continuing for more than twenty-four consecutive hours … in which the Vessel is unable to perform the service immediately required.

The discussion made[82] in respect of the corresponding items in the NYPE forms are largely relevant here. Unlike in the case of NYPE 2015 form, there is no off-hire provision for fire, grounding, detention by arrest, detention by competent authority and detention by average accidents. Notably, there is no 'other cause' or 'other similar cause' event here, which anyway has been narrowly construed in the context of the NYPE 1946/1993/2015 forms, as will be seen below.[83] The utility of the words 'hindering or preventing the working of the vessel' must have a limited utility only, for reasons explained below[84] as part of discussion of the utility of the words 'preventing the full working of the vessel' in the NYPE 1946/1993/2015 forms.

16.3.2 Calculating 'Off-Hire' Period

There are two common ways of calculating the off-hire period. The off-hire clause in a charterparty usually will adopt either one of them. One is 'net' clause and another is 'period' clause.[85]

In a net clause, the actual time lost by the triggering event is the off-hire period. In a period clause, the off-hire period is from the onset of the triggering event to its end, even if time was not actually lost (or only less time than this period was lost) to the charterer. The 'net' clause is usually a fairer method than the 'period' clause. Both NYPE and BIMCO BALTIME[86] forms provide 'net' clause. The NYPE 1946/1993/2015 forms[87] provide for this as "in the event of loss of time … the payment of hire … shall cease for the time thereby lost".[88] The BALTIME 1939 form (revised 2001) provides for this as "In the event of [off-hire events] … no hire shall be paid in respect of any time lost thereby during the period'.[89] A clause that might look like a period clause in the opening words might indeed be a net clause,

---

[82] See Sects. 16.3.1.1 and 16.3.2.

[83] See Chapter 16.3.2.

[84] See Chapter 16.3.2.

[85] See Chapter 16.3.

[86] BIMCO BALTIME 1939 form (revised 2001).

[87] 1946, 1993 and 2015 versions.

[88] Cl. 17 in the 2015 version; cl. 15 in the 1946 version.

[89] Cl. 11 in the 2001 revised version.

as it is in the case of SHELLTIME 4 form.[90] The off-hire clause, cl. 21, of this form reads as follows:

> … the vessel shall be off-hire from the commencement of such loss of time until she is again ready and in an efficient state to resume her service from a position not less favourable to Charterers than that at which such loss of time commenced; *provided, however, that any service given or distance made good by the vessel whilst off-hire shall be taken into account in assessing the amount to be deducted from hire.* [emphasis added]

Off-hire period has been construed narrowly by the courts, so that it covers only the time directly lost by the off-hire event but not any consequential loss of time.[91] This was demonstrated by the following two cases. In *The Marika M*,[92] the time charterparty was in NYPE 1946 form. The ship was scheduled to berth on 18 July. But she grounded on 17 July, thus unable to proceed to berth on 18 July. She refloated on 27 July, but no berth was available after this until 6 August. The charterer claimed off-hire until 6 August. The shipowner argued that off-hire was only until 27 July. The English High Court agreed with the shipowner, holding that consequential loss of time cannot be claimed. In this case, it was a net clause in cl. 15 of the NYPE 1946 form. It would not have been different had it been a period clause.

In *The Athena*,[93] the time charterparty was in NYPE 1946 form, with the usual net clause in the off-hire clause, cl. 15 with a slight modification by addition of default of master to the list of events. The ship originally carried a cargo of wheat cargo to a Syrian port. However, the cargo was not discharged there as the receivers refused. Then the charterers order the ship to proceed to a Libyan port, where the bills of lading would be switched to a new receiver at Libya. However, the shipowner required the master to wait in international waters off Libya and have the bills switched while there. She waited there for about 11 days before proceeding to the Libyan port. The charterer claimed off-hire for the 11 days. The shipowner argued that no time was indeed lost because even if the ship had straight proceeded to the Libyan port, she would not have been able to berth any earlier. The English Court of Appeal agreed with the charterers and held that the ship was off-hire for the 11 days, holding that the enquiry should be as to whether time was lost in the service immediately required of the vessel as opposed to the chartered service as a whole or the entire maritime adventure.[94] Again, in this case, it was a net clause in cl. 15 of the NYPE 1946 form and it would not have been different had it been a period clause.

---

[90] Issued 1984, amended in 2003.

[91] *Vogemann v Zanzibar* [1902] 7 Com Cas 254 (EW CA).

[92] *Eastern Mediterranean Maritime (Liechtenstein) Ltd v Unimarine SA (The Marika M)* [1981] 2 Lloyd's Rep 622 (EW HC).

[93] *Minerva Navigation Inc v Oceana Shipping AG (The Athena)* [2013] EWCA Civ 1723 (EW CA).

[94] In so holding, the Court of Appeal disagreed with *Forestships International Ltd v Armonia Shipping and Finance Corporation (The Ira)* [1995] 1 Lloyd's Rep 103 (EW HC), where the court took into account facts that occurred after the off-hire event.

The effect of a period clause was demonstrated by *The Westfalia*.[95] In this case, the off-hire clause in the time charterparty covered engine breakdown and had a 'period' clause. It read as follows:

> In the event of loss of time from deficiency of men or stores, breakdown of machinery, *want of repairs, or damage*, whereby the *working of the vessel is stopped* for more than 48 consecutive working hours, the payment of hire shall cease *until she be again in an efficient state to resume her service*. [emphasis added]

The ship's high-pressure engine broke down during the voyage and the ship was towed to the discharged port. The tow was assisted and a little expedited (by about one and a half days) with the ships low-pressure engine. The charterer claimed off-hire for the entire tow period, although only a portion of the period was the actual time lost, since it would have taken some less time even if the ship ordinarily sailed with its high-pressure engine to the discharge port. The shipowner argued that only the actual time lost must count as off-hire period. The House of Lords, by majority, held that the entire tow period was off-hire because of the period clause, but once the ship commenced, the hire period recommenced as the engine's inefficiency did not prevent the working of the ship in relation to discharging the cargo.

16.4 Redelivery

The hire obligation starts upon delivery by the shipowner of the ship to the charterer and it stops upon redelivery of the ship by the charterer to the shipowner. Although, it is said that the ship is delivered/redelivered, indeed there is no delivery/redelivery physically as the ship is always under the management of the shipowner during the time charter period.[96] Hence, what the 'delivery' or 'redelivery' means here is putting the ship at the disposal of the charterer or shipowner. Being at the disposal of the charterer means the ship is obliged to comply with legitimate order of the charterer.[97] Comparatively, in the case of demise charter, the ship will be physically delivered/redelivered.

The consequences of the shipowner defaulting in its obligation to deliver within the allowed time frame has been dealt earlier.[98] Usually, the redelivery obligation of the charterer is not provided in terms of a specific date and time but it is provided in terms of a time frame, as it will be hard to say in advance the exact date of redelivery given the uncertainties at sea and port particularly associated with the last voyage.

---

[95] *Hogarth v Alexander Miller Bros & Co (The Westfalia)* [1891] AC 48 (UK HL).

[96] *Skibsaktieselskapet Snefonn, Skibsaksjeselskapet Bergehus and Sig Bergesen DY & Co v Kawasaki Kisen Kaisha Ltd (The Berge Tasta)* [1975] 1 Lloyd's Rep 422 at 424 (EW HC), speech of Donaldson J.

[97] See Chapter 15.

[98] See Chapter 12.6.

The redelivery clause will also state the geographical location where the ship will be redelivered.[99] Should the ship be redelivered out of the allowed area, the shipowner will be entitled to damages to run a ballast voyage to the nearest contractual redelivery point.[100] The ship must be redelivered in the agreed condition. The NYPE 2015 form, in cl. 4, describes the agreed condition for redelivery as 'in like good order and condition, ordinary wear and tear excepted',[101] while the BIMCO BALTIME 1939 form (revised 2001), in cl. 7, describes it as 'in the same good order as when delivered to the Charterers (fair wear and tear excepted)'.[102] Should the ship not be redelivered in the right condition, the shipowner has no option to refuse to accept but may only claim damages for losses suffered as a result of the breach,[103] usually the cost of repair and time lost.

This sub-chapter will visit the consequences the charterer failing to redeliver within the allowed widow of time or at the designated place. The default may happen because the ship is redelivered in advance or later than the window. The earliest day of the window is also called the 'earliest terminal date' and the latest date the 'final terminal date'.

16.4.1 Redelivery Window

The period of charterparty, which will determine the redelivery time, may be stated in various ways, such as 'about 12 months', '12 months, 10 days more or less in charterer's option', 'minimum 12 months maximum 14 months', or 'about 90 days to maximum 100 days', so forth. Sometimes, the redelivery window may be directly stated, e.g. 'minimum 1 June 2020/maximum 30 June 2020', so forth. In all these examples, there is a margin in the delivery time, as there will usually be. Only if the charterparty does not provide such a margin, the courts will imply one, unless the intention of the parties was clearly otherwise.[104] The redelivery time may also be

---

[99] E.g. NYPE 2015 form, cl. 4; BIMCO BALTIME 1939 form (revised 2001), cl. 7.

[100] *Santa Martha Baay Scheepvaart and Handelsmaatschappij NV v Scanbulk A/S (The Rijn)* [1981] 2 Lloyd's Rep 267 (EW HC).

[101] NYPE 2015 form, cl. 4(a): "The Vessel shall be redelivered to the Owners in like good order and condition, ordinary wear and tear excepted, at ___ (state port or place)"

[102] BIMCO BALTIME 1939 form (revised 2001), cl. 7: "**Re-delivery**. The Vessel shall be re-delivered on the expiration of the Charter in the same good order as when delivered to the Charterers (fair wear and tear excepted) at an ice- free port in the Charterers' option at the place or within the range stated in Box 21, between 9 a.m. and 6 p.m., and 9 a.m. and 2 p.m. on Saturday, but the day of redelivery shall not be a Sunday or legal Holiday. …"

[103] *Attica Sea Carriers Corpn v Ferrostaal Poseidon Bulk Reederei GmbH (The Puerto Buitrago)* [1976] 1 Lloyd's Rep 250 (EW CA).

[104] *Almas Shipping Corp of Monrovia v Mantovani (The Dione)* [1975] 1 Lloyd's Rep 114 (EW CA).

stated on a 'without guarantee' basis, as it was in *The Lendoudis Evangelos II.*[105] In this case, the period of charterparty was stated as 'duration about 70/80 days without guarantee'. The charterer redelivered in 103 day. The arbitral tribunal found that the estimate of the trip-duration made by the charterer was not reasonable, although it did not find any want of good faith in making the objection. Hence, the award was for the shipowner in damages for late delivery. On appeal to the English High Court, the decision of the arbitral tribunal was reversed. The court found for the charterer, holding that the charterer's obligation was only to make in good faith their estimate of the duration of the trip and it did not matter whether the estimate was reasonable or not.

The charterparty may provide an option to the charterer to add any off-hire period to the period of charterparty,[106] e.g. cl. 52(c) of the NYPE 2015 form. This clause reads as follows:

> **(c) Off-hire**
>
> The Charterers to have the option of adding any time the Vessel is off-hire to the Charter period. Such option shall be declared in writing not less than one (1) month before the expected date of redelivery, or latest one (1) week after the event if such event occurs less than one (1) month before the expected date of redelivery.

In the absence of such an option, the off-hire period may not be added to the charter period. In addition to stating the redelivery date window, usually, a charterparty will require the charterer to give advance notice of expected date of redelivery. This notice-requirement may comprise a set of notices in certain number of days in advance. They may also comprise notices of estimated delivery and notices of firm delivery. They may also include the intended port of redelivery first and the confirmed port of redelivery later. An example of such a clause in *The Zenovia*[107] read as follows:

> Charterers are to give Owners not less than 30 days followed by 20/15/10/7 days notice of approximate redelivery date and intended port thereafter 5/3/2/1 days definite notice of redelivery and port'.

In this case, the redelivery window was stated as 'minimum 20 September 2007/maximum 22 November 2007'. On 5 October, the charterer gave the first notice of approximate redelivery as 'on or about 04 Nov 2007'. On 15 October, the charterer changed it to 'about Nov 20th'. The shipowners claimed that the charterer might not change the date and that the charterer had thereby breached the charterparty. Hence, on 2 November, the shipowner terminated the charterparty. The English High Court held the termination to be wrongful and that the charters might change the date.

---

[105] *Continental Pacific Shipping Ltd v Deemand Shipping Co Ltd (The Lendoudis Evangelos II)* [1997] 1 Lloyd's Rep 404 (EW HC).

[106] E.g. *Petroleo Brasileiro SA v Kriti Akti Shipping Co SA (The Kriti Akti)* [2004] EWCA Civ 116, [2004] 1 Lloyd's Rep 712 (EW CA).

[107] *IMT Shipping and Chartering GmbH v Changsung Shipping Company Limited (The Zenovia)* [2009] EWHC 739 (Comm), [2009] 2 All ER (Comm) 177 (EW HC).

16.4.2 Early Redelivery

If the charterer redelivers before the earliest terminal date, that will constitute a repudiatory breach of the charterparty and the shipowner, if it accepts, will be entitled to damages.[108] The crucial question here is about assessment of damages. The basic principle of assessment of damages for breaches of contract applies, i.e. to put the innocent party in the position that he would be in had the contract been performed. However, application of the principle and assessment has not been an easy task in cases of early or late delivery under charterparties.

If there is a ready market at the time of the early redelivery, whereby the ship can be employed under a similar fixture for the balance period under the original charterparty, then the damages may be assessed by the difference between original charter hire and the current market hire. This means that if the new charter hire is equal to or more than the original charter hire, then there is no loss. However, this is only the starting point. If market changes subsequently but before the hearing the subsequent changes will be taken into account. In *The Golden Victory,*[109] the ship was under a time charter for seven year. The charterparty gave the charterer an option to cancel the charterparty if war broke out between certain countries including the UK, US and Iraq. The charterer, in breach of the charterparty, redelivered in about three years. In about a year after that, the Gulf War broke out. The question before the arbitral tribunal and subsequently the court was whether the damages were to be assessed for four years (i.e. the full balance under the charterparty) or for a year only (i.e. until the war broke out). The House of Lords held that the true loss was only the loss for a year until the war broke out, hence awarded the loss only for this period.

The 2008 collapse of the shipping market brought before arbitral tribunals and court numerous claims by shipowners against charterers who redelivered before the earliest terminal date with years more to run under the original charterparty. In these cases, there was no market at the time of redelivery, but a market emerged subsequently by 2010. In *The Kildare,*[110] the time charter was for 5 years entered into in December 2007, but the charterer redelivered in January 2019. The market revived in February 2010. The shipowner claimed damages on the highest basis that there was no market at the time of redelivery. The charterer argued that the market revival in 2010 must be taken into account. The English High Court held, in line with the principle of assessment of damages in contract cases, the market revival must be taken into account.

But some subsequent events will be irrelevant to assess damages in line with the principle that the innocent party must be put in the same position as if the contract

[108] *Clea Shipping Corporation v Bulk Oil International Ltd (The Alaskan Trader) (No. 2)* [1983] 2 Lloyd's Rep 645 (EW HC).

[109] *Golden Strait Corporation v Nippon Yusen Kubishka Kaisha (The Golden Victory)* [2007] UKHL 12, [2007] 2 Lloyd's Rep 164, [2007] 2 WLR 691, [2007] Bus LR 997, [2007] 2 AC 353 (EW HL).

[110] *Zodiac Maritime Agencies Limited v Fortescue Metals Group Limited (The Kildare)* [2010] EWHC 903, [2011] 2 Lloyd's Rep 360 (EW HC).

was performed. In *The New Flamenco*,[111] the ship was to be redelivered in 2009 but the charterer, in breach of the charterparty, redelivered in 2007. About this time, the shipowner sold the ship for about USD24 million. Had the ship been redelivered in 2009 and sold, the market value would only have been about USD7 million, i.e. a drop of about USD17 million. The charterer argued that this has overshot any loss that the charterer suffered by reason of the early redelivery, hence no damages were payable. The UK Supreme Court rejected the argument and awarded damages by the difference in the market rate in 2007 when the ship was redelivered and the charter rate for the balance period. Similarly, in *Rimpacific Navigation Inc v Daehan Shipbuilding Co*,[112] the court refused to take into account the fact and value of sale of a ship by the shipowner in assessing damages against the charterer for early delivery.

In *Star Reefers Pool Inc v JFC Group Co Ltd*,[113] there was a ready market and the shipowner claimed the difference between the original charter rate and the new rate based on the market for similar fixture. However, in actual fact, the shipowner traded on sport market, hence earned more than the market rate for a similar fixture to the original charterparty. The English High Court held that the charterer did not have to bring into account the additional profit made by trading on spot market. Indeed, any additional earning is the result of the extra efforts/risk taken by the shipowner in trading on spot market, hence it should not be brought into assessment of damages for breach of the original time charterparty.

The earning or potential earning will be taken into account only up to the remining period under the original charterparty.[114] However, exceptional circumstances arose in *The Elbrus*[115] whereby the earning made after the original charter period was relevant for purposes of assessment in line with the principles of assessing damages in contract cases. In this case, the charter was at the rate of USD10,800 per day. The earliest terminal date was 13 May. The charterer, in breach of the charterparty, redelivered on 4 April, i.e. 39 days ahead. The shipowner secured another fixture with a laycan of 1 May/20 May at the rate of USD18,100 per day. The ship had to be drydocked before she could be delivered to the new charter. The repudiatory breach allowed sufficient time to drydock the ship before delivery to the new charterer within the laycan. But for the breach by the original charterer, the shipowner would not have been able to meet the new charter terms, which would yield a far higher profit than any loss resulting from the breach. As the market had softened after this, the new charter deal might not have materialised but for the breach. In the peculiar factual matrix of the case, the arbitral tribunal and the English High Court, on appeal against the arbitral award, held that the higher earnings secured by the shipowner, even beyond the original charter period, had to be taken into account in assessing the damages.

---

[111] *Fulton Shipping Inc of Panama v Globalia Business Travel SAU (formerly TravelPlan SAU) of Spain (The New Flamenco)* [2017] UKSC 43, [2018] 1 All ER 45, [2017] 1 WLR 2581, [2018] 1 All ER (Comm) 95, [2017] 2 Lloyd's Rep 177, 173 ConLR 20, (2017) Times, 12 July (UK SC).

[112] [2011] EWHC 2618 (Comm) (EW HC).

[113] [2011] EWHC 2204 (Comm) (EW HC).

[114] *Rheinoel GmbH v Huron Liberian Co (The Concordia C)* [1985] 2 Lloyd's Rep 55 at 58; *Sib International SRL v Metallgesellschaft Corporation (The Noel Bay)* [1989] 1 Lloyd's Rep 361 (EW CA).

[115] *Dalwood Marine Co v Nordana Line A/S (The Elbrus)* [2009] EWHC 3394 (Comm), [2010] 2 All ER (Comm) 802 (EW HC).

In *The North Prince*,[116] a head charterer let the ship to a sub-charter until 'minimum 27 June 2009'. The sub-charterer redelivered early, in breach of the charterparty, on 5 January 2009. The head charterer redelivered the ship to the shipowner on 5 June 2009, i.e. 22 days before the earliest terminal date of the sub-charterparty. Between redelivery by the sub-charterer and the redelivery by the head charterer, the ship was continuously trading. The arbitral tribunal assessed damaged, from 5 January to 5 June, by the difference between the actual earning and the sub-charterparty hire, although there was a ready market at the time of the redelivery by the sub-charterer. It also allowed damages, based on market value, from 5 June to 27 June, i.e. the earliest terminal date. The charterer objected to the damages awarded for 5 June–27 June because the ship was already redelivered by the head charterer to the shipowner. On appeal by the charterer, the English High Court found this to be the correct method of assessment and dismissed the appeal.

16.4.3 Late Redelivery

Late redelivery, i.e. redelivery after the final terminal date, will normally be connected to the last voyage order of the charterer. The last voyage order will be a legitimate order if it will, by a reasonable estimate, allow redelivery by the final terminal date. Otherwise, it will be an illegitimate order. If it is a legitimate order, the shipowner must comply with it. If it is an illegitimate order, the shipowner may either refuse to comply or accept it and claim damages at the charter-hire or market rate for any extra days it may take to complete, called 'period of overlap'. Even if the order is legitimate but the time is overrun before redelivery, the shipowner will be entitled to the overlap-period damages at the charter-hire or market rate.[117]

The fact that it is a legitimate order does not prevent a claim for the damages, unless the charterparty excludes the liability for such damages in the event of a legitimate order. In *The Peonia*,[118] the charterparty provided the period of charter as follows:

> … about minimum ten months' maximum twelve months' time charter, exact duration in charterers' option. *Charterers have further option to complete last voyage.* [emphasis added]

The hire clause provided as follows:

> *Hire to continue until the hour of the day of her re-delivery* in like good order and condition, ordinary wear and tear excepted, to the owners unless lost, on dropping outward sea pilot Singapore/Japan range, including Indonesia, charterer's option, United States West Coast/Vancouver range and time day/night Sundays and holidays included, actual range and port always to be in charterer's option. [emphasis added]

The final terminal date was on or about 11 June 1988. In the beginning of May 1988, the charterers ordered the last voyage, which was expected to take at least 19 July to

[116] *Glory Wealth Shipping Pte Limited v North China Shipping Limited (The North Prince)* [2010] EWHC 1692 (Comm), [2011] 1 All ER (Comm) 641 (EW HC).

[117] See *Timber Shipping Co SA v London & Overseas Freighters Ltd (The London Explorer)* [1972] AC 1, [1971] 2 WLR 1360, [1971] 2 All ER 599 (UK HL).

[118] *Hyundai Merchant Marine Co Ltd v Gesuri Chartering Co Ltd (The Peonia)* [1991] 1 Lloyd's Rep 100 (EW CA).

complete, hence the order was illegitimate. The English Court of Appeal held that the charterparty allowed the final terminal date to be exceeded, without the charterer being in breach, upon a legitimate last voyage order, in which case only hire but not damages at the prevailing market rate would be payable. However, the court held that that did not help the charterer in this case as this was an illegitimate order. The English High Court in *The Black Falcon*[119] arrived at a similar conclusion where the relevant clause read 'charterers having option to complete last round voyage under performance prior to delivery'.

Comparatively, SHELLTIME 3 form has been construed differently. Clause 3 of the form states the charter-period. Clause 18 of the form provides as follows:

> Notwithstanding the provisions of clause 3 hereof, should the vessel be upon a voyage at the expiry of the period of this charter, Charterers shall have the use of the vessel at the same rate and conditions for such extended time as may be necessary for the completion of the round voyage on which she is engaged and her return to a port of redelivery as provided by this charter.

The English Court of Appeal in The World Symphony and The World Renown[120] held that this clause limited what the shipowner can recover for the overlap-period, even if the last voyage order was an illegitimate one which the shipowner complied with, to the charter-hire only. Clauses similar to clauses 3 and 18 of the SHELLTIME 3 form are found respectively in clauses 4 and 19 of the latest SHELLTIME 4 form.

The legitimacy of the order is determined not at the time the order is made but at the time it is performed by the shipowner, as held by the House of Lords in *The Gregos.*[121] In this case, the charterer ordered the ship to proceed from Matanzas to Palua to load iron for Italy, which would be the last voyage. At the time the order was given, it could be reasonably expected that the ship would be timely redelivered after the last voyage. However, after discharge at at Matanzas, another ship grounded around Palua, which would obstruct navigation around there. Hence, it could not be expected that performing the last voyage order would take the ship, by two to four days, beyond the final terminal date. Hence, the House held this to be an illegitimate order. The House was of the view that the redelivery obligation was an innominate term, hence the shipowner might not *terminate* the charterparty for a short delay, while it was entitled to *refuse to perform* any illegitimate order and ask to replace it with a legitimate order. Similarly, the Court of Appeal in *The Paragon*[122] found the obligation of the charterer to give legitimate order for the last voyage to be an innominate term, so that an illegitimate order may not be treated as a repudiatory breach by the charterer. It follows that the shipowner may not terminate the charterparty for this but may ask for a legitimate order.

---

[119] *Shipping Corpn of India Ltd v Nsb Niederelbe Schiffahrtsgesellschaft Mbh & Co (The Black Falcon)* [1991] 1 Lloyd's Rep 77 (EW HC).

[120] Chiswell Shipping Ltd and Liberian Jaguar Transports Inc v National Iranian Tanker Co (The World Symphony and The World Renown) [1992] 2 Lloyd's Rep 115 (EW CA). This case was followed in Petroleo Brasileiro SA v Kriti Akti Shipping Co SA (The Kriti Akti) [2004] EWCA Civ 116, [2004] 1 Lloyd's Rep 712 (EW CA).

[121] *Torvald Klaveness A/S V Arni Maritime Corporation (The Gregos)* [1995] 1 Lloyd's Rep 1 (UK HL).

[122] *Lansat Shipping Co Ltd v Glencore Grain BV (The Paragon)* [2009] EWCA Civ 855, [2001] 1 All ER (Comm) 459, [2009] 2 Lloyd's Rep 688 (EW CA).

Damages awarded to the shipowner will be at the rate of the charter-hire or prevailing market rate, whichever is higher.[123] The damages will limited to that only and not extend to consequential losses such as loss of next charterparty, as held by the House of Lords in *The Achilleas*.[124] In this case, the shipowner had fixed next charterparty at the rate of USD39,500 per day. The last charterer re-delivered nine days late. As a result, the shipowner was not able to deliver to the follow-on charterer within the laycan and had to renegotiate and reduce the hire to USD31,500 as by then the market had softened. The shipowner claimed the loss made in the follow-on charterparty, which the House refused, holding that the charterer may only claim damages for the nine-day delay.

To mitigate the effect of this decision, parties may expressly provide that the charterer will be liable for any loss made in the next charterparty as a result of late redelivery, insofar as this does not turn out to be a penalty clause.

What will be a 'penalty' clause in this context was demonstrated by *The Paragon*.[125] In this case the clause provided that if redelivery is made after the final terminal date, then the charterer would pay the prevailing market hire, if that is more than the charter hire, for the period of overlap and additionally for the last 30 days before the final terminal date. The English Court of Appeal struck down this clause holding it is a penalty clause. While there was nothing wrong to ask for the prevailing market hire, if that is more than the charter hire, for the overlap-period, it was a penalty to ask for this increased hire for the last 30 days before the final terminal date.

While in English contract law, which is followed in Singapore, a penalty clause is invalid, that is no so in those Commonwealth countries, including Malaysia,[126] with a Contract Act modelled on the Indian Contract Act 1872. Section 74 of the Act allows a penalty clause, contrary to the position under the English common law. However, the Section 74 limit the effect of the clause, whether it is a penalty or liquidated damages clause, by providing that the court may award only a reasonable sum as compensation subject to a ceiling limit of the stipulated penalty/liquidated damages amount. The Section 74 reads as follows:[127]

> **74. Compensation for breach of contract where penalty stipulated for**
>
> When a contract has been broken, if a sum is named in the contract as the amount to be paid in case of such breach, or if the contract contains any other stipulation by way of penalty, the party complaining of the breach is entitled, whether or not actual damage or loss is proved to have been caused thereby, to receive from the party who has broken the contract reasonable compensation not exceeding the amount so named or, as the case may be, the penalty stipulated for.

---

[123] *Hyundai Merchant Marine Co Ltd v Gesuri Chartering Co Ltd (The Peonia)* [1991] 1 Lloyd's Rep 100 (EW CA): a case that involved legitimate last voyage order.

[124] *Transfield Inc v Mercator Shipping Inc (The Achilleas)* [2008] UKHL 28, [2008] 2 Lloyd's Rep 275 (UK HL).

[125] *Lansat Shipping Co Ltd v Glencore Grain BV (The Paragon)* [2009] EWCA Civ 855, [2001] 1 All ER (Comm) 459, [2009] 2 Lloyd's Rep 688 (EW CA).

[126] Malaysian Contracts Act 1950.

[127] In Malaysia, Section 75 of the Contracts Act 1950.

Chapter 17
Time Charter: Apportionment of Cargo-Claims Liability

This chapter visits the contractual apportionment of liability for cargo claims between the shipowner and the charterer. The Inter-Club Agreement, which is commonly incorporated into time charterparties to regulate the apportionment is briefly considered. That is followed by a short discussion of the apportionment where in cases where there is no special contractual provision regulating the apportionment. In this course, particular reference is made to the NYPE 2015 form.

17.1 Introduction

In the case of time charters, it is usual that the time charterer will enter into contracts to carry cargo for various shippers and usually the bills of ladings for the carriage will be issued by the shipowner. In such situations, if a cargo claim arises from the carriage, then a question of apportionment of liability between the shipowner and the charterer will arise. It is not necessary that the shipowner is responsible for any cargo claim, as some claims may arise out of operations carried on by the charterer, for example, loading, stowing, discharge, etc.

There are basically two ways by which the liability for the cargo claims will be apportioned. One is by adopting a standard form for apportionment, i.e. Inter-Club Agreement (ICA). In the absence of any specific agreement, a construction of the charterparty will tell who takes what liability. These two methods are considered in this chapter.

17.2 Inter-Club Agreement

This is an agreement between the Protection and Indemnity (P&I) Clubs in International Group (IG). It obliges the Clubs to *recommend* to their members, which

A. Kasi, *The Law of Carriage of Goods by Sea*,
https://doi.org/10.1007/978-981-33-6793-7_17

will include the shipowners and charterers, to adopt the apportionment of liabilities set out in the agreement in relation to *cargo claims* arising from or connected to time charterparties in the NYPE or Asbatime forms. The current version of the agreement is called Inter-Club New York Produce Exchange Agreement 1996 (as amended September 2011), abbreviated as ICA. It is common practice to incorporate the agreement into time charterparties and render it contractually binding between the shipowner and the time-charterer as to apportionment of liability.

The ICA imposes liability for loss arising from unseaworthiness, including uncargoworthiness, fully on the shipowner. The test of unseaworthiness is same as that applicable in bill of lading cases. It is sufficient, like bill of lading cases,[1] if unseaworthiness is 'a' cause. In *The Kamilla*,[2] about one percent of a cargo of lentil, carried under a time-charterparty that incorporated the ICA, was damaged by seawater ingress due to ship's unseaworthiness. The cargo was discharged in Bejaia in Algeria, where the authorities condemned the entire cargo. The action of the authorities was foreseeable. The shipowner was held fully liable for the loss.

Clause 27 of the NYPE 1993/2015 forms[3] incorporates the ICA. Clause 8 of the form imposes the responsibility for "all cargo handling, including … loading, stowing, trimming, lashing, securing, dunnaging, unlashing, discharging, and tallying, at their risk and expense, under the supervision of the Master." The ICA imposes the entire liability for loss occurring from any of these responsibilities on the charterer. However, if the clause is modified with addition of "and responsibility" after "the supervision", then the liability is apportioned 50:50 between the charterer and the shipowner. It is quite common that the cl. 8 will be modified with such addition.

Short-delivery is apportioned 50:50. The same is true of delay and all other cargo claims, save where the claim arose out of act or neglect of one of the parties,[4] in which case the party responsible for the act or neglect takes the liability entirely. In *The Yangtze Xing Hua*,[5] the trip charterers ordered the ship with cargo to wait off the discharge port, due to payment issues between the charterer and the consignee. This resulted in the cargo being overheated and consequent cargo claim. The loss resulting from the cargo claim was held to fall fully on the charterer as the overheating happened by the 'act' of the charterer in ordering the waiting.

---

[1] See Chapter 7.2.3.7.

[2] *Kamilla Hans-Peter Eckhoff KG v AC Oerssleff's EFTF A/B (The Kamilla)* [2006] EWHC 509, [2006] 2 Lloyd's Rep 238 (EW HC).

[3] Cl. 27: "**Cargo Claims**. Cargo claims as between the Owners and the Charterers shall be settled in accordance with the Inter-Club NYPE Agreement 1996 (as amended 1 September 2011), or any subsequent modification or replacement thereof."

[4] Or its servants/sub-contractors.

[5] *Transgrain Shipping (Singapore) Pte Ltd v Yangtze Navigation (Hong Kong) Co Ltd (The Yangtze Xing Hua)* [2016] EWHC 3132, [2017] 1 Lloyd's Rep 212 (EW HC), affirmed by the Court of Appeal in [2017] EWCA Civ 2107, [2018] 1 Lloyd's Rep 330, [2018] 2 All ER (Comm) 99 (EW CA).

Customs dues, fines and reasonable cost of defending cargo claims are all part of the liability to be apportioned.[6] The claim under the terms of the incorporated ICA may only be made after the cargo claim is paid.[7] For a claim under the incorporated ICA terms, written notice of the claim must be given to by the claiming party to the responding party within two years of the date of delivery of the cargo or the date that the cargo should have been delivered.[8]

If the claiming party has given security to the cargo claimant, the claiming party may require the responding party to provide security to the claiming party.[9] In such case, the responding party may require the claiming party to give reciprocating security to the responding party. To claim security, it does not matter whether a right to apportionment has arisen. In the case of a conflict between the Rules incorporated by virtue of a clause paramount and the terms of the ICA, the terms of the ICA will prevail.

17.3 No Special Clauses Relating to Cargo Claims

If the charterparty does not expressly allocate the task of loading, stowing, trimming and discharge on any party, then the task will be on the shipowner, by an implied term at common law.[10] However, practically, the charterparty will usually allocate expressly this task to the charterer.

Issues have arisen as to construction and effect of contractual provisions allocating these tasks. One such provision is the cl. 8 of the NYPE 1993/2015 forms, which provide "Charterers shall perform all … loading, stowing, trimming, … discharging … *under the supervision of the Master*".[11] This shifts the obligation for, and thus the liability in conneciton with, these tasks onto the charterer that would otherwise be on the shipowner at common law.[12] However, the words "under the supervision of the Master" may shift back the liability onto the shipowner in certain rare circumstances where the cause of the loss was the Master's supervision. In *The Imvros*,[13] the defective stowage by the charterer rendered the ship uncargoworthy but not otherwise unseaworthy. The English High Court held that this was not sufficient to trigger the shift-back of the responsibility to the shipowner under the cl. 8 of the NYPE 1993 form, which clause is largely similar to that in the NYPE 2015 form. In *Compania*

[6] ICA, cl. 3.

[7] ICA, cl. 4.

[8] ICA, cl. 6. If the Hamburg Rules are applicable, then the time limit is three years.

[9] ICA, cl. 9.

[10] *Filikos Shipping Corpn of Monrovia v Shipmair BV (The Filikos)* [1983] 1 Lloyd's Rep 9 (EW CA).

[11] [emphasis added].

[12] *Court Line Ltd v Canadian Transport Co Ltd* [1940] AC 934 (UK HL).

[13] *Transocean Liners Reederei GmbH v Euxine Shipping Co Ltd (The Imvros)* [1999] 1 All ER (Comm) 724, [1999] 1 Lloyd's Rep 848 (EW HC).

Sud American Vapores v MS ER Hamburg Schiffarhtsgesellschaft mbH & Co KG,[14] the English High Court held that even where the defective loading, etc. by the charterer rendered the ship unseaworthy, that did not shift back the responsibility to the shipowner under the cl. 8. However, it appears that the minimum meaning that the words 'under the supervision of the Master' must be that the Master, and thus the shipowner, is responsible to ensure that the ship is seaworthy before commencing the voyage.

In practice, the cl. 8 is often modified with an addition of 'and responsibility' This will clearly shift the liability in connection with loading etc. onto the shipowner, while the cost of the operation is on the charterer, as held in *The Argonaut*.[15] However, *The Clipper San Luis*[16] placed limitation on this by saying that the responsibility will thus be shifted back, even with a so modified cl. 8, to the shipowner only if the charterer had appointed a reasonably competent stevedores to perform those tasks. It appears that the court's approach was that if the charterer failed to appoint such reasonably competent stevedores then the cause of the loss is linked to the incompetent appointment rather than the loading etc.operation itself. A consequence of the responsibility being placed on the shipowner with such a modified cl. 8 is that if the loading etc.is defective so that a re-loading etc. or transshipment becomes necessary, the cost of the re-loading etc./transshipment will be on the shipowner, while course the cost of the initial loading etc. is on the charterer.

---

[14] [2006] EWHC 483 (Comm) (EW HC).

[15] *MSC Mediterranean Shipping Co SA v Alianca Bay Shipping Co Ltd (The Argonaut)* [1985] 2 Lloyd's Rep 216 (EW HC).

[16] *Macieo Shipping Ltd v Clipper Shipping Lines Ltd (The Clipper Sao Luis)* [2000] 1 Lloyd's Rep 645 (EW HC).

Appendix A
Hague Rules of 1924[1]

Article I

In this Convention the following words are employed with the meanings set out below:

(a) "Carrier" includes the owner or the charterer who enters into a contract of carriage with a shipper.
(b) "Contract of carriage" applies only to contracts of carriage covered by a bill of lading or any similar document of title, in so far as such document relates to the carriage of goods by sea, including any bill of lading or any similar document as aforesaid issued under or pursuant to a charter party from the moment at which such bill of lading or similar document of title regulates the relations between a carrier and a holder of the same.
(c) "Goods" includes goods, wares, merchandise and articles of every kind whatsoever except live animals and cargo which by the contract of carriage in stated as being carried on deck and is so carried.
(d) "Ship" means any vessel used for the carriage of goods by sea.
(e) "Carriage of goods" covers the period from the time when the goods are loaded on to the time they are discharged from the ship.

Article II

Subject to the provisions of Article VI, under every contract of carriage of goods by sea the carrier, in relation to the loading, handling, stowage, carriage, custody, care and discharge of such goods, shall be subject to the responsibilities and liabilities, and entitled to the rights and immunities hereinafter set forth.

[1] The International Convention for the Unification of Certain Rules of Law relating to Bills of Lading of 1924.

A. Kasi, *The Law of Carriage of Goods by Sea*,
https://doi.org/10.1007/978-981-33-6793-7

Article III

1. The carrier shall be bound before and at the beginning of the voyage to exercise due diligence to:

   (a) Make the ship seaworthy.
   (b) Properly man, equip and supply the ship.
   (c) Make the holds, refrigerating and cool chambers, and all other parts of the ship in which goods are carried, fit and safe for their reception, carriage and preservation.

2. Subject to the provisions of Article IV, the carrier shall properly and carefully load, handle, stow, carry, keep, care for, and discharge the goods carried.
3. After receiving the goods into his charge the carrier or the master or agent of the carrier shall, on demand of the shipper, issue to the shipper a bill of lading showing among other things:

   (a) The leading marks necessary for identification of the goods as the same are furnished in writing by the shipper before the loading of such goods starts, provided such marks are stamped or otherwise shown clearly upon the goods if uncovered, or on the cases or coverings in which such goods are contained, in such a manner as should ordinarily remain legible until the end of the voyage.
   (b) Either the number of packages or pieces, or the quantity, or weight, as the case may be, as furnished in writing by the shipper.
   (c) The apparent order and condition of the goods.
   Provided that no carrier, master or agent of the carrier shall be bound to state or show in the bill of lading any marks, number, quantity, or weight which he has reasonable ground for suspecting not accurately to represent the goods actually received, or which he has had no reasonable means of checking.

4. Such a bill of lading shall be prima facie evidence of the receipt by the carrier of the goods as therein described in accordance with paragraph 3(a), (b) and (c).
5. The shipper shall be deemed to have guaranteed to the carrier the accuracy at the time of shipment of the marks, number, quantity and weight, as furnished by him, and the shipper shall indemnity the carrier against all loss, damages and expenses arising or resulting from inaccuracies in such particulars. The right of the carrier to such indemnity shall in no way limit his responsibility and liability under the contract of carriage to any person other than the shipper.
6. Unless notice of loss or damage and the general nature of such loss or damage be given in writing to the carrier or his agent at the port of discharge before or at the time of the removal of the goods into the custody of the person entitled to delivery thereof under the contract of carriage , or, if the loss or damage be not apparent, within three days, such removal shall be prima facie evidence of the delivery by the carrier of the goods as described in the bill of lading.

If the loss or damage is not apparent, the notice must be given within three days of the delivery of the goods.

The notice in writing need not be given if the state of the goods has, at the time of their receipt, been the subject of joint survey or inspection.

In any event the carrier and the ship shall be discharged from all liability in respect of loss or damage unless suit is brought within one year after delivery of the goods or the date when the goods should have been delivered.

In the case of any actual or apprehended loss or damage the carrier and the receiver shall give all reasonable facilities to each other for inspecting and tallying the goods.

7 After the goods are loaded the bill of lading to be issued by the carrier, master, or agent of the carrier, to the shipper shall, if the shipper so demands, be a "shipped" bill of lading, provided that if the shipper shall have previously taken up any document of title to such goods, he shall surrender the same as against the issue of the "shipped" bill of lading, but at the option of the carrier such document of title may be noted at the port of shipment by the carrier, master, or agent with the name or names of the ship or ships upon which the goods have been shipped and the date or dates of shipment, and when so noted, if it shows the particulars mentioned in paragraph 3 of Article III, shall for the purpose of this Article be deemed to constitute a "shipped" bill of lading.

8. Any clause, covenant, or agreement in a contract of carriage relieving the carrier or the ship from liability for loss or damage to, or in connexion with, goods arising from negligence , fault, or failure in the duties and obligations provided in this Article or lessening such liability otherwise than as provided in this Convention, shall be null and void and of no effect. A benefit of insurance in favour of the carrier or similar clause shall be deemed to be a clause relieving the carrier from liability.

Article IV

1. Neither the carrier nor the ship shall be liable for loss or damage arising or resulting from unseaworthiness unless caused by want of due diligence on the part of the carrier to make the ship seaworthy and to secure that the ship is properly manned, equipped and supplied, and to make the holds, refrigerating and cool chambers and all other parts of the ship in which goods are carried fit and safe for their reception, carriage and preservation in accordance with the provisions of paragraph 1 of Article III. Whenever loss or damage has resulted from unseaworthiness the burden of proving the exercise of due diligence shall be on the carrier or other person claiming exemption under this Article.
2. Neither the carrier nor the ship shall be responsible for loss or damage arising or resulting from:

   (a) Act, neglect, or default of the master, mariner, pilot, or the servants of the carrier in the navigation or in the management of the ship.
   (b) Fire , unless caused by the actual fault or privity of the carrier.
   (c) Perils, dangers and accidents of the sea or other navigable waters.

(d) Act of God.
(e) Act of war.
(f) Act of public enemies.
(g) Arrest or restraint or princes, rulers or people, or seizure under legal process.
(h) Quarantine restrictions.
(i) Act or omission of the shipper or owner of the goods, his agent or representative.
(j) Strikes or lockouts or stoppage or restraint of labour from whatever cause, whether partial or general.
(k) Riots and civil commotions.
(l) Saving or attempting to save life or property at sea.
(m) Wastage in bulk or weight or any other loss or damage arising from inherent defect, quality or vice of the goods.
(n) Insufficiency of packing.
(o) Insufficiency or inadequacy of marks.
(p) Latent defects not discoverable by due diligence .
(q) Any other cause arising without the actual fault or privity of the carrier, or without the actual fault or neglect of the agents or servants of the carrier, but the burden of proof shall be on the person claiming the benefit of this exception to show that neither the actual fault or privity of the carrier nor the fault or neglect of the agents or servants of the carrier contributed to the loss or damage.

3. The shipper shall not be responsible for loss or damage sustained by the carrier or the ship arising or resulting from any cause without the act, fault or neglect of the shipper, his agents or his servants.
4. Any deviation in saving or attempting to save life or property at sea or any reasonable deviation shall not be deemed to be an infringement or breach of this Convention or of the contract of carriage , and the carrier shall not be liable for any loss or damage resulting therefrom.
5. Neither the carrier nor the ship shall in any event be or become liable for any loss or damage to or in connexion with goods in an amount exceeding 100 pounds sterling per package or unit, or the equivalent of that sum in other currency unless the nature and value of such goods have been declared by the shipper before shipment and inserted in the bill of lading.
   This declaration if embodied in the bill of lading shall be prima facie evidence, but shall not be binding or conclusive on the carrier.
   By agreement between the carrier, master or agent of the carrier and the shipper another maximum amount than that mentioned in this paragraph may be fixed, provided that such maximum shall not be less than the figure above named.
   Neither the carrier nor the ship shall be responsible in any event for loss or damage to, or in connexion with, goods if the nature or value thereof has been knowingly misstated by the shipper in the bill of lading.

6. Goods of an inflammable, explosive or dangerous nature to the shipment whereof the carrier, master or agent of the carrier has not consented with knowledge of their nature and character, may at any time before discharge be landed at any place, or destroyed or rendered innocuous by the carrier without compensation and the shipper of such goods shall be liable for all damage and expenses directly or indirectly arising out of or resulting from such shipment. If any such goods shipped with such knowledge and consent shall become a danger to the ship or cargo, they may in like manner be landed at any place, or destroyed or rendered innocuous by the carrier without liability on the part of the carrier except to general average , if any.

Article V

A carrier shall be at liberty to surrender in whole or in part all or any of his rights and immunities or to increase any of his responsibilities and obligations under this Convention, provided such surrender or increase shall be embodied in the bill of lading issued to the shipper.

The provisions of this Convention shall not be applicable to charter parties, but if bills of lading are issued in the case of a ship under a charter party they shall comply with the terms of this Convention. Nothing in these rules shall be held to prevent the insertion in a bill of lading of any lawful provision regarding general average .

Article VI

Notwithstanding the provisions of the preceding Articles, a carrier, master or agent of the carrier and a shipper shall in regard to any particular goods be at liberty to enter into any agreement in any terms as to the responsibility and liability of the carrier for such goods, and as to the rights and immunities of the carrier in respect of such goods, or his obligation as to seaworthiness , so far as this stipulation is not contrary to public policy, or the care or diligence of his servants or agents in regard to the loading, handling, stowage, carriage, custody, care and discharge of the goods carried by sea, provided that in this case no bill of lading has been or shall be issued and that the terms agreed shall be embodied in a receipt which shall be a non-negotiable document and shall be marked as such.

Any agreement so entered into shall have full legal effect.

Provided that this Article shall not apply to ordinary commercial shipments made in the ordinary course of trade, but only to other shipments where the character or condition of the property to be carried or the circumstances, terms and conditions under which the carriage is to be performed are such as reasonably to justify a special agreement.

Article VII

Nothing herein contained shall prevent a carrier or a shipper from entering into any agreement, stipulation, condition, reservation or exemption as to the responsibility and liability of the carrier or the ship for the loss or damage to, or in connexion with, the custody and care and handling of goods prior to the loading on, and subsequent to, the discharge from the ship on which the goods are carried by sea.

Article VIII

The provisions of this Convention shall not affect the rights and obligations of the carrier under any statute for the time being in force relating to the limitation of the liability of owners of sea-going vessels.

Article IX

The monetary units mentioned in this Convention are to be taken to be gold value.

Those contracting States in which the pound sterling is not a monetary unit reserve to themselves the right of translating the sums indicated in this Convention in terms of pound sterling into terms of their own monetary system in round figures.

The national laws may reserve to the debtor the right of discharging his debt in national currency according to the rate of exchange prevailing on the day of the arrival of the ship at the port of discharge of the goods concerned.

Article X

The provisions of this Convention shall apply to all bills of lading issued in any of the contracting States.

Article XI

After an interval of not more than two years from the day on which the Convention is signed, the Belgian Government shall place itself in communication with the Governments of the High Contracting Parties which 4/11/2020 Hague Rules (Brussels 1924) have declared themselves prepared to ratify the Convention, with a view to deciding whether it shall be put into force. The ratifications shall be deposited at Brussels at a date to be fixed by agreement among the said Governments. The first deposit of ratifications shall be recorded in a *procès-verbal* signed by the representatives of the Powers which take part therein and by the Belgian Minister of Foreign Affairs.

The subsequent deposit of ratifications shall be made by means of a written notification, addressed to the Belgian Government and accompanied by the instrument of ratification.

A duly certified copy of the procès-verbal relating to the first deposit of ratifications, of the notifications referred to in the previous paragraph, and also of the instruments of ratification accompanying them, shall be immediately sent by the Belgian Government through the diplomatic channel to the Powers who have signed this Convention or who have acceded to it. In the cases contemplated in the preceding paragraph, the said Government shall inform them at the same time of the date on which it received the notification.

Article XII

Non-signatory States may accede to the present Convention whether or not they have been represented at the International Conference at Brussels.

A State which desires to accede shall notify its intention in writing to the Belgian Government, forwarding to it the document of accession, which shall be deposited in the archives of the said Government.

The Belgian Government shall immediately forward to all the States which have signed or acceded to the Convention a duly certified copy of the notification and of the act of accession, mentioning the date on which it received the notification.

Article XIII

The High Contracting Parties may at the time of signature, ratification or accession declare that their acceptance of the present Convention does not include any or all of the self-governing dominions, or of the colonies, overseas possessions, protectorates or territories under their sovereignty or authority, and they may subsequently accede separately on behalf of any self-governing dominion, colony, overseas possession, protectorate or territory excluded in their declaration. They may also denounce the Convention separately in accordance with its provisions in respect of any self-governing dominion, or any colony, overseas possession, protectorate or territory under their sovereignty or authority.

Article XIV

The present Convention shall take effect, in the case of the States which have taken part in the first deposit of ratifications, one year after the date of the protocol recording such deposit.

As respects the States which ratify subsequently or which accede, and also in cases in which the Convention is subsequently put into effect in accordance with Article 13, it shall take effect six months after the 4/11/2020 Hague Rules (Brussels 1924) notifications specified in paragraph 2 of Article 11 and paragraph 2 of Article 12 have been received by the Belgian Government.

Article XV

In the event of one of the contracting States wishing to denounce the present Convention, the denunciation shall be notified in writing to the Belgian Government, which shall immediately communicate a duly certified copy of the notification to all the other States, informing them of the date on which it was received.

The denunciation shall only operate in respect of the State which made the notification, and on the expiry of one year after the notification has reached the Belgian Government.

Article XVI

Any one of the contracting States shall have the right to call for a fresh conference with a view to considering possible amendments.

A State which would exercise this right should notify its intention to the other States through the Belgian Government, which would make arrangements for convening the Conference.

DONE at Brussels, in a single copy, August 25th, 1924.

PROTOCOL OF SIGNATURE

At the time of signing the International Convention for the Unification of Certain Rules of Law relating to Bills of Lading the Plenipotentiaries whose signatures appear below have adopted this Protocol, which will have the same force and the same value as if its provisions were inserted in the text of the Convention to which it relates.

The High Contracting Parties may give effect to this Convention either by giving it the force of law or by including in their national legislation in a form appropriate to that legislation the rules adopted under this Convention.

They may reserve the right:

1. To prescribe that in the cases referred to in paragraph 2(c) to (p) of Article 4 the holder of a bill of lading shall be entitled to establish responsibility for loss or damage arising from the personal fault of the carrier or the fault of his servants which are not covered by paragraph (a).
2. To apply Article 6 in so far as the national coasting trade is concerned to all classes of goods without taking account of the restriction set out in the last paragraph of that Article.

DONE at Brussels, in single copy, August 25th, 1924.

Appendix B
Hague-Visby Rules of 1968[2]

Article I

In this Convention the following words are employed with the meanings set out below:

(a) "Carrier" includes the owner or the charterer who enters into a contract of carriage with a shipper.
(b) "Contract of carriage" applies only to contracts of carriage covered by a bill of lading or any similar document of title, in so far as such document relates to the carriage of goods by sea, including any bill of lading or any similar document as aforesaid issued under or pursuant to a charter party from the moment at which such bill of lading or similar document of title regulates the relations between a carrier and a holder of the same.
(c) "Goods" includes goods, wares, merchandise and articles of every kind whatsoever except live animals and cargo which by the contract of carriage in stated as being carried on deck and is so carried.
(d) "Ship" means any vessel used for the carriage of goods by sea.
(e) "Carriage of goods" covers the period from the time when the goods are loaded on to the time they are discharged from the ship.

Article II

Subject to the provisions of Article VI, under every contract of carriage of goods by sea the carrier, in relation to the loading, handling, stowage, carriage, custody, care and discharge of such goods, shall be subject to the responsibilities and liabilities, and entitled to the rights and immunities hereinafter set forth.

[2] The International Convention for the Unification of Certain Rules of Law relating to Bills of Lading of 1924, amended by Brussels Protocol of 1968.

A. Kasi, *The Law of Carriage of Goods by Sea*,
https://doi.org/10.1007/978-981-33-6793-7

Article III

1. The carrier shall be bound before and at the beginning of the voyage to exercise due diligence to:

   (a) Make the ship seaworthy.
   (b) Properly man, equip and supply the ship.
   (c) Make the holds, refrigerating and cool chambers, and all other parts of the ship in which goods are carried, fit and safe for their reception, carriage and preservation.

2. Subject to the provisions of Article IV, the carrier shall properly and carefully load, handle, stow, carry, keep, care for, and discharge the goods carried.
3. After receiving the goods into his charge the carrier or the master or agent of the carrier shall, on demand of the shipper, issue to the shipper a bill of lading showing among other things:

   (a) The leading marks necessary for identification of the goods as the same are furnished in writing by the shipper before the loading of such goods starts, provided such marks are stamped or otherwise shown clearly upon the goods if uncovered, or on the cases or coverings in which such goods are contained, in such a manner as should ordinarily remain legible until the end of the voyage.
   (b) Either the number of packages or pieces, or the quantity, or weight, as the case may be, as furnished in writing by the shipper.
   (c) The apparent order and condition of the goods.
   Provided that no carrier, master or agent of the carrier shall be bound to state or show in the bill of lading any marks, number, quantity, or weight which he has reasonable ground for suspecting not accurately to represent the goods actually received, or which he has had no reasonable means of checking.

4. Such a bill of lading shall be prima facie evidence of the receipt by the carrier of the goods as therein described in accordance with paragraph 3(a), (b) and (c). However, proof to the contrary shall not be admissible when the bill of lading has been transferred to a third party acting in good faith
5. The shipper shall be deemed to have guaranteed to the carrier the accuracy at the time of shipment of the marks, number, quantity and weight, as furnished by him, and the shipper shall indemnity the carrier against all loss, damages and expenses arising or resulting from inaccuracies in such particulars. The right of the carrier to such indemnity shall in no way limit his responsibility and liability under the contract of carriage to any person other than the shipper.
6. Unless notice of loss or damage and the general nature of such loss or damage be given in writing to the carrier or his agent at the port of discharge before or at the time of the removal of the goods into the custody of the person entitled to delivery thereof under the contract of carriage , or, if the loss or damage be

not apparent, within three days, such removal shall be prima facie evidence of the delivery by the carrier of the goods as described in the bill of lading.

If the loss or damage is not apparent, the notice must be given within three days of the delivery of the goods.

The notice in writing need not be given if the state of the goods has, at the time of their receipt, been the subject of joint survey or inspection.

Subject to paragraph 6bis the carrier and the ship shall in any event be discharged from all liability whatsoever in respect of the goods, unless suit is brought within one year of their delivery or of the date when they should have been delivered. This period may, however, be extended if the parties so agree after the cause of action has arisen.

In the case of any actual or apprehended loss or damage the carrier and the receiver shall give all reasonable facilities to each other for inspecting and tallying the goods.

6*bis*. An action for indemnity against a third person may be brought even after the expiration of the year provided for in the preceding paragraph if brought within the time allowed by the law of the Court seized of the case. However, the time allowed shall be not less than three months, commencing from the day when the person bringing such action for indemnity has settled the claim or has been served with process in the action against himself.

7. After the goods are loaded the bill of lading to be issued by the carrier, master, or agent of the carrier, to the shipper shall, if the shipper so demands, be a "shipped" bill of lading, provided that if the shipper shall have previously taken up any document of title to such goods, he shall surrender the same as against the issue of the "shipped" bill of lading, but at the option of the carrier such document of title may be noted at the port of shipment by the carrier, master, or agent with the name or names of the ship or ships upon which the goods have been shipped and the date or dates of shipment, and when so noted, if it shows the particulars mentioned in paragraph 3 of Article III, shall for the purpose of this Article be deemed to constitute a "shipped" bill of lading.
8. Any clause, covenant, or agreement in a contract of carriage relieving the carrier or the ship from liability for loss or damage to, or in connexion with, goods arising from negligence , fault, or failure in the duties and obligations provided in this Article or lessening such liability otherwise than as provided in this Convention, shall be null and void and of no effect. A benefit of insurance in favour of the carrier or similar clause shall be deemed to be a clause relieving the carrier from liability.

Article IV

1. Neither the carrier nor the ship shall be liable for loss or damage arising or resulting from unseaworthiness unless caused by want of due diligence on the part of the carrier to make the ship seaworthy and to secure that the ship is properly manned, equipped and supplied, and to make the holds, refrigerating and cool chambers and all other parts of the ship in which goods are carried fit

and safe for their reception, carriage and preservation in accordance with the provisions of paragraph 1 of Article III. Whenever loss or damage has resulted from unseaworthiness the burden of proving the exercise of due diligence shall be on the carrier or other person claiming exemption under this Article.

2. Neither the carrier nor the ship shall be responsible for loss or damage arising or resulting from:

   (a) Act, neglect, or default of the master, mariner, pilot, or the servants of the carrier in the navigation or in the management of the ship.
   (b) Fire , unless caused by the actual fault or privity of the carrier.
   (c) Perils, dangers and accidents of the sea or other navigable waters.
   (d) Act of God.
   (e) Act of war.
   (f) Act of public enemies.
   (g) Arrest or restraint or princes, rulers or people, or seizure under legal process.
   (h) Quarantine restrictions.
   (i) Act or omission of the shipper or owner of the goods, his agent or representative.
   (j) Strikes or lockouts or stoppage or restraint of labour from whatever cause, whether partial or general.
   (k) Riots and civil commotions.
   (l) Saving or attempting to save life or property at sea.
   (m) Wastage in bulk or weight or any other loss or damage arising from inherent defect, quality or vice of the goods.
   (n) Insufficiency of packing.
   (o) Insufficiency or inadequacy of marks.
   (p) Latent defects not discoverable by due diligence .
   (q) Any other cause arising without the actual fault or privity of the carrier, or without the actual fault or neglect of the agents or servants of the carrier, but the burden of proof shall be on the person claiming the benefit of this exception to show that neither the actual fault or privity of the carrier nor the fault or neglect of the agents or servants of the carrier contributed to the loss or damage.

3. The shipper shall not be responsible for loss or damage sustained by the carrier or the ship arising or resulting from any cause without the act, fault or neglect of the shipper, his agents or his servants.
4. Any deviation in saving or attempting to save life or property at sea or any reasonable deviation shall not be deemed to be an infringement or breach of this Convention or of the contract of carriage , and the carrier shall not be liable for any loss or damage resulting therefrom.
5. (a) Unless the nature and value of such goods have been declared by the shipper before shipment and inserted in the Bill of Lading, neither the carrier nor the ship shall in any event be or become liable for any loss or damage to or in connection with the goods in an amount exceeding the equivalent of 10,000

francs per package or unit or 30 francs per kilo of gross weight of the goods lost or damaged, whichever is the higher.

(b) The total amount recoverable shall be calculated by reference to the value of such goods at the place and time at which the goods are discharged from the ship in accordance with the contract or should have been so discharged.

The value of the goods shall be fixed according to the commodity exchange price, or, if there be no such price, according to the current market price, or, if there be no commodity exchange price or current market price, by reference to the normal value of goods of the same kind and quality.

(c) Where a container, pallet or similar article of transport is used to consolidate goods, the number of packages or units enumerated in the Bill of Lading as packed in such article of transport shall be deemed the number of packages or units for the purpose of this paragraph as far as these packages or units are concerned. Except as aforesaid such article of transport shall be considered the package or unit.

(d) A franc means a unit consisting of 65.5 milligrammes of gold of millesimal fineness 900'. The date of conversion of the sum awarded into national currencies shall be governed by the law of the Court seized of the case.

(e) Neither the carrier nor the ship shall be entitled to the benefit of the limitation of liability provided for in this paragraph if it is proved that the damage resulted from an act or omission of the carrier done with intent to cause damage, or recklessly and with knowledge that damage would probably result.

(f) The declaration mentioned in sub-paragraph (a) of this paragraph, if embodied in the Bill of Lading, shall be prima facie evidenceBill of ladingprima facie evidence rule, but shall not be binding or conclusive on the carrier.

(g) By agreement between the carrier, master or agent of the carrier and the shipper other maximum amounts than those mentioned in sub-paragraph (a) of this paragraph may be fixed, provided that no maximum amount so fixed shall be less than the appropriate maximum mentioned in that sub-paragraph.

(h) Neither the carrier nor the ship shall be responsible in any event for loss or damage to, or in connection with, goods if the nature or value thereof has been knowingly mis-stated by the shipper in the Bill of Lading.

6. Goods of an inflammable, explosive or dangerous nature to the shipment whereof the carrier, master or agent of the carrier has not consented with knowledge of their nature and character, may at any time before discharge be landed at any place, or destroyed or rendered innocuous by the carrier without compensation and the shipper of such goods shall be liable for all damage and expenses directly or indirectly arising out of or resulting from such shipment. If any such goods shipped with such knowledge and consent shall become a danger to the ship or cargo, they may in like manner be landed at any place, or destroyed or rendered innocuous by the carrier without liability on the part of the carrier except to general average , if any.

Article IV *bis*

1. The defences and limits of liability provided for in this Convention shall apply in any action against the carrier in respect of loss or damage to goods covered by a contract of carriage whether the action be founded in contract or in tort.
2. If such an action is brought against a servant or agent of the carrier (such servant or agent not being an independent contractor), such servant or agent shall be entitled to avail himself of the defences and limits of liability which the carrier is entitled to invoke under this Convention.
3. The aggregate of the amounts recoverable from the carrier, and such servants and agents, shall in no case exceed the limit provided for in this Convention.
4. Nevertheless, a servant or agent of the carrier shall not be entitled to avail himself of the provisions of this Article, if it is proved that the damage resulted from an act or omission of the servant or agent done with intent to cause damage or recklessly and with knowledge that damage would probably result.

Article V

A carrier shall be at liberty to surrender in whole or in part all or any of his rights and immunities or to increase any of his responsibilities and obligations under this Convention, provided such surrender or increase shall be embodied in the bill of lading issued to the shipper.

The provisions of this Convention shall not be applicable to charter parties, but if bills of lading are issued in the case of a ship under a charter party they shall comply with the terms of this Convention. Nothing in these rules shall be held to prevent the insertion in a bill of lading of any lawful provision regarding general average .

Article VI

Notwithstanding the provisions of the preceding Articles, a carrier, master or agent of the carrier and a shipper shall in regard to any particular goods be at liberty to enter into any agreement in any terms as to the responsibility and liability of the carrier for such goods, and as to the rights and immunities of the carrier in respect of such goods, or his obligation as to seaworthiness , so far as this stipulation is not contrary to public policy, or the care or diligence of his servants or agents in regard to the loading, handling, stowage, carriage, custody, care and discharge of the goods carried by sea, provided that in this case no bill of lading has been or shall be issued and that the terms agreed shall be embodied in a receipt which shall be a non-negotiable document and shall be marked as such.

Any agreement so entered into shall have full legal effect.

Provided that this Article shall not apply to ordinary commercial shipments made in the ordinary course of trade, but only to other shipments where the character or condition of the property to be carried or the circumstances, terms and conditions under which the carriage is to be performed are such as reasonably to justify a special agreement.

Article VII

Nothing herein contained shall prevent a carrier or a shipper from entering into any agreement, stipulation, condition, reservation or exemption as to the responsibility and liability of the carrier or the ship for the loss or damage to, or in connexion with, the custody and care and handling of goods prior to the loading on, and subsequent to, the discharge from the ship on which the goods are carried by sea.

Article VIII

The provisions of this Convention shall not affect the rights and obligations of the carrier under any statute for the time being in force relating to the limitation of the liability of owners of sea-going vessels.

Article IX

This Convention shall not affect the provisions of any international Convention or national law governing liability for nuclear damage.

Article X

The provisions of this Convention shall apply to every Bill of Lading relating to the carriage of goods between ports in two different States if:

(a) the Bill of Lading is issued in a Contracting State,
or
(b) the carriage is from a port in a Contracting State,
or
(c) the contract contained in or evidenced by the Bill of Lading provides that the rules of this Convention or legislation of any State giving effect to them are to govern the contract

whatever may be the nationality of the ship, the carrier, the shipper, the consignee, or any other interested person.

Each Contracting State shall apply the provisions of this Convention to the Bills of Lading mentioned above.

This Article shall not prevent a Contracting State from applying the rules of this Convention to Bills of Lading not included in the preceding paragraphs.

Article XI

After an interval of not more than two years from the day on which the Convention is signed, the Belgian Government shall place itself in communication with the Governments of the High Contracting Parties which 4/11/2020 Hague Rules (Brussels 1924) have declared themselves prepared to ratify the Convention, with a view to deciding whether it shall be put into force. The ratifications shall be deposited at Brussels at a date to be fixed by agreement among the said Governments. The first deposit of ratifications shall be recorded in a *procès-verbal* signed by the representatives of the Powers which take part therein and by the Belgian Minister of Foreign Affairs.

The subsequent deposit of ratifications shall be made by means of a written notification, addressed to the Belgian Government and accompanied by the instrument of ratification.

A duly certified copy of the procès-verbal relating to the first deposit of ratifications, of the notifications referred to in the previous paragraph, and also of the instruments of ratification accompanying them, shall be immediately sent by the Belgian Government through the diplomatic channel to the Powers who have signed this Convention or who have acceded to it. In the cases contemplated in the preceding paragraph, the said Government shall inform them at the same time of the date on which it received the notification.

Article XII

Non-signatory States may accede to the present Convention whether or not they have been represented at the International Conference at Brussels.

A State which desires to accede shall notify its intention in writing to the Belgian Government, forwarding to it the document of accession, which shall be deposited in the archives of the said Government.

The Belgian Government shall immediately forward to all the States which have signed or acceded to the Convention a duly certified copy of the notification and of the act of accession, mentioning the date on which it received the notification.

Article XIII

The High Contracting Parties may at the time of signature, ratification or accession declare that their acceptance of the present Convention does not include any or all of the self-governing dominions, or of the colonies, overseas possessions, protectorates or territories under their sovereignty or authority, and they may subsequently accede separately on behalf of any self-governing dominion, colony, overseas possession, protectorate or territory excluded in their declaration. They may also denounce the Convention separately in accordance with its provisions in respect of any self-governing dominion, or any colony, overseas possession, protectorate or territory under their sovereignty or authority.

Article XIV

The present Convention shall take effect, in the case of the States which have taken part in the first deposit of ratifications, one year after the date of the protocol recording such deposit.

As respects the States which ratify subsequently or which accede, and also in cases in which the Convention is subsequently put into effect in accordance with Article 13, it shall take effect six months after the 4/11/2020 Hague Rules (Brussels 1924) notifications specified in paragraph 2 of Article 11 and paragraph 2 of Article 12 have been received by the Belgian Government.

Article XV

In the event of one of the contracting States wishing to denounce the present Convention, the denunciation shall be notified in writing to the Belgian Government, which shall immediately communicate a duly certified copy of the notification to all the other States, informing them of the date on which it was received.

The denunciation shall only operate in respect of the State which made the notification, and on the expiry of one year after the notification has reached the Belgian Government.

Article XVI

Any one of the contracting States shall have the right to call for a fresh conference with a view to considering possible amendments.

A State which would exercise this right should notify its intention to the other States through the Belgian Government, which would make arrangements for convening the Conference.

DONE at Brussels, in a single copy, August 25th, 1924.

Appendix C
Hague-Visby Rules as amended by SDR Protocol of 1979[3]

Article I

In this Convention the following words are employed with the meanings set out below:

(a) "Carrier" includes the owner or the charterer who enters into a contract of carriage with a shipper.
(b) "Contract of carriage " applies only to contracts of carriage covered by a bill of lading or any similar document of title , in so far as such document relates to the carriage of goods by sea, including any bill of lading or any similar document as aforesaid issued under or pursuant to a charter party from the moment at which such bill of lading or similar document of title regulates the relations between a carrier and a holder of the same.
(c) "Goods" includes goods, wares, merchandise and articles of every kind whatsoever except live animals and cargo which by the contract of carriage in stated as being carried on deck and is so carried.
(d) "Ship" means any vessel used for the carriage of goods by sea.
(e) "Carriage of goods" covers the period from the time when the goods are loaded on to the time they are discharged from the ship.

Article II

Subject to the provisions of Article VI, under every contract of carriage of goods by sea the carrier, in relation to the loading, handling, stowage, carriage, custody, care and discharge of such goods, shall be subject to the responsibilities and liabilities, and entitled to the rights and immunities hereinafter set forth.

[3] Protocol amending the International Convention for the Unification of Certain Rules of Law relating to Bills of Lading of 25 August 1924, amended by Brussels Protocol of 1968, and further amended by the Brussels Protocol of 1979.

A. Kasi, *The Law of Carriage of Goods by Sea*,
https://doi.org/10.1007/978-981-33-6793-7

Article III

1. The carrier shall be bound before and at the beginning of the voyage to exercise due diligence to:

   (a) Make the ship seaworthy.
   (b) Properly man, equip and supply the ship.
   (c) Make the holds, refrigerating and cool chambers, and all other parts of the ship in which goods are carried, fit and safe for their reception, carriage and preservation.

2. Subject to the provisions of Article IV, the carrier shall properly and carefully load, handle, stow, carry, keep, care for, and discharge the goods carried.
3. After receiving the goods into his charge the carrier or the master or agent of the carrier shall, on demand of the shipper, issue to the shipper a bill of lading showing among other things:

   (a) The leading marks necessary for identification of the goods as the same are furnished in writing by the shipper before the loading of such goods starts, provided such marks are stamped or otherwise shown clearly upon the goods if uncovered, or on the cases or coverings in which such goods are contained, in such a manner as should ordinarily remain legible until the end of the voyage.
   (b) Either the number of packages or pieces, or the quantity, or weight, as the case may be, as furnished in writing by the shipper.
   (c) The apparent order and condition of the goods.
   Provided that no carrier, master or agent of the carrier shall be bound to state or show in the bill of lading any marks, number, quantity, or weight which he has reasonable ground for suspecting not accurately to represent the goods actually received, or which he has had no reasonable means of checking.

4. Such a bill of lading shall be prima facie evidence of the receipt by the carrier of the goods as therein described in accordance with paragraph 3(a), (b) and (c). However, proof to the contrary shall not be admissible when the bill of lading has been transferred to a third party acting in good faith
5. The shipper shall be deemed to have guaranteed to the carrier the accuracy at the time of shipment of the marks, number, quantity and weight, as furnished by him, and the shipper shall indemnity the carrier against all loss, damages and expenses arising or resulting from inaccuracies in such particulars. The right of the carrier to such indemnity shall in no way limit his responsibility and liability under the contract of carriage to any person other than the shipper.
6. Unless notice of loss or damage and the general nature of such loss or damage be given in writing to the carrier or his agent at the port of discharge before or at the time of the removal of the goods into the custody of the person entitled to delivery thereof under the contract of carriage , or, if the loss or damage be

not apparent, within three days, such removal shall be prima facie evidence of the delivery by the carrier of the goods as described in the bill of lading.
If the loss or damage is not apparent, the notice must be given within three days of the delivery of the goods.
The notice in writing need not be given if the state of the goods has, at the time of their receipt, been the subject of joint survey or inspection.
Subject to paragraph 6bis the carrier and the ship shall in any event be discharged from all liability whatsoever in respect of the goods, unless suit is brought within one year of their delivery or of the date when they should have been delivered. This period may, however, be extended if the parties so agree after the cause of action has arisen.
In the case of any actual or apprehended loss or damage the carrier and the receiver shall give all reasonable facilities to each other for inspecting and tallying the goods.
6*bis*. An action for indemnity against a third person may be brought even after the expiration of the year provided for in the preceding paragraph if brought within the time allowed by the law of the Court seized of the case. However, the time allowed shall be not less than three months, commencing from the day when the person bringing such action for indemnity has settled the claim or has been served with process in the action against himself.

7. After the goods are loaded the bill of lading to be issued by the carrier, master, or agent of the carrier, to the shipper shall, if the shipper so demands, be a "shipped" bill of lading, provided that if the shipper shall have previously taken up any document of title to such goods, he shall surrender the same as against the issue of the "shipped" bill of lading, but at the option of the carrier such document of title may be noted at the port of shipment by the carrier, master, or agent with the name or names of the ship or ships upon which the goods have been shipped and the date or dates of shipment, and when so noted, if it shows the particulars mentioned in paragraph 3 of Article III, shall for the purpose of this Article be deemed to constitute a "shipped" bill of lading.
8. Any clause, covenant, or agreement in a contract of carriage relieving the carrier or the ship from liability for loss or damage to, or in connexion with, goods arising from negligence , fault, or failure in the duties and obligations provided in this Article or lessening such liability otherwise than as provided in this Convention, shall be null and void and of no effect. A benefit of insurance in favour of the carrier or similar clause shall be deemed to be a clause relieving the carrier from liability.

Article IV

1. Neither the carrier nor the ship shall be liable for loss or damage arising or resulting from unseaworthiness unless caused by want of due diligence on the part of the carrier to make the ship seaworthy and to secure that the ship is properly manned, equipped and supplied, and to make the holds, refrigerating and cool chambers and all other parts of the ship in which goods are carried fit

and safe for their reception, carriage and preservation in accordance with the provisions of paragraph 1 of Article III. Whenever loss or damage has resulted from unseaworthiness the burden of proving the exercise of due diligence shall be on the carrier or other person claiming exemption under this Article.

2. Neither the carrier nor the ship shall be responsible for loss or damage arising or resulting from:

    (a) Act, neglect, or default of the master, mariner, pilot, or the servants of the carrier in the navigation or in the management of the ship.
    (b) Fire , unless caused by the actual fault or privity of the carrier.
    (c) Perils, dangers and accidents of the sea or other navigable waters.
    (d) Act of God.
    (e) Act of war.
    (f) Act of public enemies.
    (g) Arrest or restraint or princes, rulers or people, or seizure under legal process.
    (h) Quarantine restrictions.
    (i) Act or omission of the shipper or owner of the goods, his agent or representative.
    (j) Strikes or lockouts or stoppage or restraint of labour from whatever cause, whether partial or general.
    (k) Riots and civil commotions.
    (l) Saving or attempting to save life or property at sea.
    (m) Wastage in bulk or weight or any other loss or damage arising from inherent defect, quality or vice of the goods.
    (n) Insufficiency of packing.
    (o) Insufficiency or inadequacy of marks.
    (p) Latent defects not discoverable by due diligence .
    (q) Any other cause arising without the actual fault or privity of the carrier, or without the actual fault or neglect of the agents or servants of the carrier, but the burden of proof shall be on the person claiming the benefit of this exception to show that neither the actual fault or privity of the carrier nor the fault or neglect of the agents or servants of the carrier contributed to the loss or damage.

3. The shipper shall not be responsible for loss or damage sustained by the carrier or the ship arising or resulting from any cause without the act, fault or neglect of the shipper, his agents or his servants.
4. Any deviation in saving or attempting to save life or property at sea or any reasonable deviation shall not be deemed to be an infringement or breach of this Convention or of the contract of carriage , and the carrier shall not be liable for any loss or damage resulting therefrom.
5. (a) Unless the nature and value of such goods have been declared by the shipper before shipment and inserted in the bill of lading, neither the carrier nor the ship shall in any event be or become liable for any loss or damage to or in connection with the goods in an amount exceeding 666.67 units of account per package or

unit or 2 units of account per kilogramme of gross weight of the goods lost or damaged, whichever is the higher.

(b) The total amount recoverable shall be calculated by reference to the value of such goods at the place and time at which the goods are discharged from the ship in accordance with the contract or should have been so discharged.The value of the goods shall be fixed according to the commodity exchange price, or, if there be no such price, according to the current market price, or, if there be no commodity exchange price or current market price, by reference to the normal value of goods of the same kind and quality.

(c) Where a container, pallet or similar article of transport is used to consolidate goods, the number of packages or units enumerated in the Bill of Lading as packed in such article of transport shall be deemed the number of packages or units for the purpose of this paragraph as far as these packages or units are concerned. Except as aforesaid such article of transport shall be considered the package or unit.

(d) The unit of account mentioned in this Article is the Special Drawing Right-Special Drawing Rights (SDR) as defined by the International Monetary Fund. The amounts mentioned in sub-paragraph (a) of this paragraph shall be converted into national currency on the basis of the value of that currency on a date to be determined by the law of the Court seized of the case.

The value of the national currency, in terms of the Special Drawing RightSpecial Drawing Rights (SDR), of a State which is a member of the International Monetary Fund, shall be calculated in accordance with the method of valuation applied by the International Monetary Fund in effect at the date in question for its operations and transactions. The value of the national currency, in terms of the Special Drawing RightSpecial Drawing Rights (SDR), of a State which is not a member of the International Monetary Fund, shall be calculated in a manner determined by that State.

Nevertheless, a State which is not a member of the International Monetary Fund and whose law does not permit the application of the provisions of the preceding sentences may, at the time of ratification of the Protocol of 1979 or accession thereto or at any time thereafter, declare that the limits of liability provided for in this Convention to be applied in its territory shall be fixed as follows:

(i) in respect of the amount of 666.67 units of account mentioned in sub-paragraph (a) of paragraph 5 of this Article, 10,000 monetary units;
(ii) in respect of the amount of 2 units of account mentioned in sub-paragraph (a) of paragraph 5 of this Article, 30 monetary units.

The monetary unit referred to in the preceding sentence corresponds to 65.5 milligrammes of gold of millesimal fineness 900'. The conversion of the amounts specified in that sentence into the national currency shall be made according to the law of the State concerned.

The calculation and the conversion mentioned in the preceding sentences shall be made in such a manner as to express in the national currency of the State

as far as possible the same real value for the amounts in sub-paragraph (a) of paragraph 5 of this Article as is expressed there in units of account.
States shall communicate to the depositary the manner of calculation or the result of the conversion as the case may be, when depositing an instrument of ratification of the Protocol of 1979 or of accession thereto and whenever there is a change in either.
(e) Neither the carrier nor the ship shall be entitled to the benefit of the limitation of liability provided for in this paragraph if it is proved that the damage resulted from an act or omission of the carrier done with intent to cause damage, or recklessly and with knowledge that damage would probably result.
(f) The declaration mentioned in sub-paragraph (a) of this paragraph, if embodied in the Bill of Lading, shall be prima facie evidenceBill of ladingprima facie evidence rule, but shall not be binding or conclusive on the carrier.
(g) By agreement between the carrier, master or agent of the carrier and the shipper other maximum amounts than those mentioned in sub-paragraph (a) of this paragraph may be fixed, provided that no maximum amount so fixed shall be less than the appropriate maximum mentioned in that sub-paragraph.
(h) Neither the carrier nor the ship shall be responsible in any event for loss or damage to, or in connection with, goods if the nature or value thereof has been knowingly mis-stated by the shipper in the Bill of Lading.

6. Goods of an inflammable, explosive or dangerous nature to the shipment whereof the carrier, master or agent of the carrier has not consented with knowledge of their nature and character, may at any time before discharge be landed at any place, or destroyed or rendered innocuous by the carrier without compensation and the shipper of such goods shall be liable for all damage and expenses directly or indirectly arising out of or resulting from such shipment. If any such goods shipped with such knowledge and consent shall become a danger to the ship or cargo, they may in like manner be landed at any place, or destroyed or rendered innocuous by the carrier without liability on the part of the carrier except to general average , if any.

Article IV *bis*

1. The defences and limits of liability provided for in this Convention shall apply in any action against the carrier in respect of loss or damage to goods covered by a contract of carriage whether the action be founded in contract or in tort.
2. If such an action is brought against a servant or agent of the carrier (such servant or agent not being an independent contractor), such servant or agent shall be entitled to avail himself of the defences and limits of liability which the carrier is entitled to invoke under this Convention.
3. The aggregate of the amounts recoverable from the carrier, and such servants and agents, shall in no case exceed the limit provided for in this Convention.
4. Nevertheless, a servant or agent of the carrier shall not be entitled to avail himself of the provisions of this Article, if it is proved that the damage resulted from

an act or omission of the servant or agent done with intent to cause damage or recklessly and with knowledge that damage would probably result.

Article V

A carrier shall be at liberty to surrender in whole or in part all or any of his rights and immunities or to increase any of his responsibilities and obligations under this Convention, provided such surrender or increase shall be embodied in the bill of lading issued to the shipper.

The provisions of this Convention shall not be applicable to charter parties, but if bills of lading are issued in the case of a ship under a charter party they shall comply with the terms of this Convention. Nothing in these rules shall be held to prevent the insertion in a bill of lading of any lawful provision regarding general average .

Article VI

Notwithstanding the provisions of the preceding Articles, a carrier, master or agent of the carrier and a shipper shall in regard to any particular goods be at liberty to enter into any agreement in any terms as to the responsibility and liability of the carrier for such goods, and as to the rights and immunities of the carrier in respect of such goods, or his obligation as to seaworthiness , so far as this stipulation is not contrary to public policy, or the care or diligence of his servants or agents in regard to the loading, handling, stowage, carriage, custody, care and discharge of the goods carried by sea, provided that in this case no bill of lading has been or shall be issued and that the terms agreed shall be embodied in a receipt which shall be a non-negotiable document and shall be marked as such.

Any agreement so entered into shall have full legal effect.

Provided that this Article shall not apply to ordinary commercial shipments made in the ordinary course of trade, but only to other shipments where the character or condition of the property to be carried or the circumstances, terms and conditions under which the carriage is to be performed are such as reasonably to justify a special agreement.

Article VII

Nothing herein contained shall prevent a carrier or a shipper from entering into any agreement, stipulation, condition, reservation or exemption as to the responsibility and liability of the carrier or the ship for the loss or damage to, or in connexion with, the custody and care and handling of goods prior to the loading on, and subsequent to, the discharge from the ship on which the goods are carried by sea.

Article VIII

The provisions of this Convention shall not affect the rights and obligations of the carrier under any statute for the time being in force relating to the limitation of the liability of owners of sea-going vessels.

Article IX

This Convention shall not affect the provisions of any international Convention or national law governing liability for nuclear damage.

Article X

The provisions of this Convention shall apply to every Bill of Lading relating to the carriage of goods between ports in two different States if:

(a) the Bill of Lading is issued in a Contracting State,
or
(b) the carriage is from a port in a Contracting State,
or
(c) the contract contained in or evidenced by the Bill of Lading provides that the rules of this Convention or legislation of any State giving effect to them are to govern the contract

whatever may be the nationality of the ship, the carrier, the shipper, the consignee, or any other interested person.

Each Contracting State shall apply the provisions of this Convention to the Bills of Lading mentioned above.

This Article shall not prevent a Contracting State from applying the rules of this Convention to Bills of Lading not included in the preceding paragraphs.

Article XI

After an interval of not more than two years from the day on which the Convention is signed, the Belgian Government shall place itself in communication with the Governments of the High Contracting Parties which 4/11/2020 Hague Rules (Brussels 1924) have declared themselves prepared to ratify the Convention, with a view to deciding whether it shall be put into force. The ratifications shall be deposited at Brussels at a date to be fixed by agreement among the said Governments. The first deposit of ratifications shall be recorded in a *procès-verbal* signed by the representatives of the Powers which take part therein and by the Belgian Minister of Foreign Affairs.

The subsequent deposit of ratifications shall be made by means of a written notification, addressed to the Belgian Government and accompanied by the instrument of ratification.

A duly certified copy of the procès-verbal relating to the first deposit of ratifications, of the notifications referred to in the previous paragraph, and also of the instruments of ratification accompanying them, shall be immediately sent by the Belgian Government through the diplomatic channel to the Powers who have signed this Convention or who have acceded to it. In the cases contemplated in the preceding paragraph, the said Government shall inform them at the same time of the date on which it received the notification.

Article XII

Non-signatory States may accede to the present Convention whether or not they have been represented at the International Conference at Brussels.

A State which desires to accede shall notify its intention in writing to the Belgian Government, forwarding to it the document of accession, which shall be deposited in the archives of the said Government.

The Belgian Government shall immediately forward to all the States which have signed or acceded to the Convention a duly certified copy of the notification and of the act of accession, mentioning the date on which it received the notification.

Article XIII

The High Contracting Parties may at the time of signature, ratification or accession declare that their acceptance of the present Convention does not include any or all of the self-governing dominions, or of the colonies, overseas possessions, protectorates or territories under their sovereignty or authority, and they may subsequently accede separately on behalf of any self-governing dominion, colony, overseas possession, protectorate or territory excluded in their declaration. They may also denounce the Convention separately in accordance with its provisions in respect of any self-governing dominion, or any colony, overseas possession, protectorate or territory under their sovereignty or authority.

Article XIV

The present Convention shall take effect, in the case of the States which have taken part in the first deposit of ratifications, one year after the date of the protocol recording such deposit.

As respects the States which ratify subsequently or which accede, and also in cases in which the Convention is subsequently put into effect in accordance with Article 13, it shall take effect six months after the 4/11/2020 Hague Rules (Brussels 1924) notifications specified in paragraph 2 of Article 11 and paragraph 2 of Article 12 have been received by the Belgian Government.

Article XV

In the event of one of the contracting States wishing to denounce the present Convention, the denunciation shall be notified in writing to the Belgian Government, which shall immediately communicate a duly certified copy of the notification to all the other States, informing them of the date on which it was received.

The denunciation shall only operate in respect of the State which made the notification, and on the expiry of one year after the notification has reached the Belgian Government.

Article XVI

Any one of the contracting States shall have the right to call for a fresh conference with a view to considering possible amendments.

A State which would exercise this right should notify its intention to the other States through the Belgian Government, which would make arrangements for convening the Conference.

DONE at Brussels, in a single copy, August 25th, 1924.

Appendix D
Hague Rules, Hague-Visby Rules, Hague-Visby Rules as amended by SDR Protocol (Compared)

Hague Rules of 1924 [4]

Hague-Visby Rules of 1968 [5]

Hague-Visby Rules, as amended by SDR Protocol in 1979 [6]

(The first ten substantive Articles only)

Comparison colour coding notes:

Black	: Hague Rules, Hague-Visby Rules, Hague-Visby Rules with SDR Protocol
Dimmed black	: Hague Rules; removed in Hague-Visby Rules
Blue	: Hague-Visby Rules
Dimmed blue	: Hague-Visby Rules; removed in Hague-Visby Rules with SDR Protocol
Red	: Hague-Visby Rules with SDR Protocol

Flow of amendment:

Black & Dimmed black	: Hague Rules
Dimmed black	: Removed in Hague-Visby Rules
Blue & Dimmed blue	: Introduced in Hague-Visby Rules
Dimmed blue	: Removed in Hague-Visby Rules with SDR Protocol
Red	: Introduced in Hague-Visby Rules with SDR Protocol

[4] The International Convention for the Unification of Certain Rules of Law relating to Bills of Lading of 1924.

[5] The International Convention for the Unification of Certain Rules of Law relating to Bills of Lading of 1924, amended by Brussels Protocol of 1968.

[6] Protocol amending the International Convention for the Unification of Certain Rules of Law relating to Bills of Lading of 25 August 1924, amended by Brussels Protocol of 1968, and further amended by the Brussels Protocol of 1979.

A. Kasi, *The Law of Carriage of Goods by Sea*,
https://doi.org/10.1007/978-981-33-6793-7

Article I

In this Convention the following words are employed with the meanings set out below:

(a) "Carrier" includes the owner or the charterer who enters into a contract of carriage with a shipper.
(b) "Contract of carriage " applies only to contracts of carriage covered by a bill of lading or any similar document of title , in so far as such document relates to the carriage of goods by sea, including any bill of lading or any similar document as aforesaid issued under or pursuant to a charter party from the moment at which such bill of lading or similar document of title regulates the relations between a carrier and a holder of the same.
(c) "Goods" includes goods, wares, merchandise and articles of every kind whatsoever except live animals and cargo which by the contract of carriage in stated as being carried on deck and is so carried.
(d) "Ship" means any vessel used for the carriage of goods by sea.
(e) "Carriage of goods" covers the period from the time when the goods are loaded on to the time they are discharged from the ship.

Article II

Subject to the provisions of Article VI, under every contract of carriage of goods by sea the carrier, in relation to the loading, handling, stowage, carriage, custody, care and discharge of such goods, shall be subject to the responsibilities and liabilities, and entitled to the rights and immunities hereinafter set forth.

Article III

1. The carrier shall be bound before and at the beginning of the voyage to exercise due diligence to:

    (a) Make the ship seaworthy.
    (b) Properly man, equip and supply the ship.
    (c) Make the holds, refrigerating and cool chambers, and all other parts of the ship in which goods are carried, fit and safe for their reception, carriage and preservation.

2. Subject to the provisions of Article IV, the carrier shall properly and carefully load, handle, stow, carry, keep, care for, and discharge the goods carried.
3. After receiving the goods into his charge the carrier or the master or agent of the carrier shall, on demand of the shipper, issue to the shipper a bill of lading showing among other things:

    (a) The leading marks necessary for identification of the goods as the same are furnished in writing by the shipper before the loading of such goods starts, provided such marks are stamped or otherwise shown clearly upon the goods if uncovered, or on the cases or coverings in which such goods are contained, in such a manner as should ordinarily remain legible until the end of the voyage.

(b) Either the number of packages or pieces, or the quantity, or weight, as the case may be, as furnished in writing by the shipper.

(c) The apparent order and condition of the goods.

Provided that no carrier, master or agent of the carrier shall be bound to state or show in the bill of lading any marks, number, quantity, or weight which he has reasonable ground for suspecting not accurately to represent the goods actually received, or which he has had no reasonable means of checking.

4. Such a bill of lading shall be prima facie evidence of the receipt by the carrier of the goods as therein described in accordance with paragraph 3(a), (b) and (c).

4. Such a bill of lading shall be prima facie evidence of the receipt by the carrier of the goods as therein described in accordance with paragraph 3(a), (b) and (c). However, proof to the contrary shall not be admissible when the bill of lading has been transferred to a third party acting in good faith.

5. The shipper shall be deemed to have guaranteed to the carrier the accuracy at the time of shipment of the marks, number, quantity and weight, as furnished by him, and the shipper shall indemnity the carrier against all loss, damages and expenses arising or resulting from inaccuracies in such particulars. The right of the carrier to such indemnity shall in no way limit his responsibility and liability under the contract of carriage to any person other than the shipper.

6. Unless notice of loss or damage and the general nature of such loss or damage be given in writing to the carrier or his agent at the port of discharge before or at the time of the removal of the goods into the custody of the person entitled to delivery thereof under the contract of carriage , or, if the loss or damage be not apparent, within three days, such removal shall be prima facie evidence of the delivery by the carrier of the goods as described in the bill of lading.
If the loss or damage is not apparent, the notice must be given within three days of the delivery of the goods.
The notice in writing need not be given if the state of the goods has, at the time of their receipt, been the subject of joint survey or inspection.
In any event the carrier and the ship shall be discharged from all liability in respect of loss or damage unless suit is brought within one year after delivery of the goods or the date when the goods should have been delivered.
Subject to paragraph 6bis the carrier and the ship shall in any event be discharged from all liability whatsoever in respect of the goods, unless suit is brought within one year of their delivery or of the date when they should have been delivered. This period may, however, be extended if the parties so agree after the cause of action has arisen.
In the case of any actual or apprehended loss or damage the carrier and the receiver shall give all reasonable facilities to each other for inspecting and tallying the goods.

6*bis*. An action for indemnity against a third person may be brought even after the expiration of the year provided for in the preceding paragraph if brought within the time allowed by the law of the Court seized of the case. However, the time allowed shall be not less than three months, commencing from the day when the person bringing such action for indemnity has settled the claim or has been served with process in the action against himself.

7. After the goods are loaded the bill of lading to be issued by the carrier, master, or agent of the carrier, to the shipper shall, if the shipper so demands, be a "shipped" bill of lading, provided that if the shipper shall have previously taken up any document of title to such goods, he shall surrender the same as against the issue of the "shipped" bill of lading, but at the option of the carrier such document of title may be noted at the port of shipment by the carrier, master, or agent with the name or names of the ship or ships upon which the goods have been shipped and the date or dates of shipment, and when so noted, if it shows the particulars mentioned in paragraph 3 of Article III, shall for the purpose of this Article be deemed to constitute a "shipped" bill of lading.
8. Any clause, covenant, or agreement in a contract of carriage relieving the carrier or the ship from liability for loss or damage to, or in connexion with, goods arising from negligence , fault, or failure in the duties and obligations provided in this Article or lessening such liability otherwise than as provided in this Convention, shall be null and void and of no effect. A benefit of insurance in favour of the carrier or similar clause shall be deemed to be a clause relieving the carrier from liability.

Article IV

1. Neither the carrier nor the ship shall be liable for loss or damage arising or resulting from unseaworthiness unless caused by want of due diligence on the part of the carrier to make the ship seaworthy and to secure that the ship is properly manned, equipped and supplied, and to make the holds, refrigerating and cool chambers and all other parts of the ship in which goods are carried fit and safe for their reception, carriage and preservation in accordance with the provisions of paragraph 1 of Article III. Whenever loss or damage has resulted from unseaworthiness the burden of proving the exercise of due diligence shall be on the carrier or other person claiming exemption under this Article.
2. Neither the carrier nor the ship shall be responsible for loss or damage arising or resulting from:

   (a) Act, neglect, or default of the master, mariner, pilot, or the servants of the carrier in the navigation or in the management of the ship.
   (b) Fire , unless caused by the actual fault or privity of the carrier.
   (c) Perils, dangers and accidents of the sea or other navigable waters.
   (d) Act of God.
   (e) Act of war.
   (f) Act of public enemies.

(g) Arrest or restraint or princes, rulers or people, or seizure under legal process.
(h) Quarantine restrictions.
(i) Act or omission of the shipper or owner of the goods, his agent or representative.
(j) Strikes or lockouts or stoppage or restraint of labour from whatever cause, whether partial or general.
(k) Riots and civil commotions.
(l) Saving or attempting to save life or property at sea.
(m) Wastage in bulk or weight or any other loss or damage arising from inherent defect, quality or vice of the goods.
(n) Insufficiency of packing.
(o) Insufficiency or inadequacy of marks.
(p) Latent defects not discoverable by due diligence .
(q) Any other cause arising without the actual fault or privity of the carrier, or without the actual fault or neglect of the agents or servants of the carrier, but the burden of proof shall be on the person claiming the benefit of this exception to show that neither the actual fault or privity of the carrier nor the fault or neglect of the agents or servants of the carrier contributed to the loss or damage.

3. The shipper shall not be responsible for loss or damage sustained by the carrier or the ship arising or resulting from any cause without the act, fault or neglect of the shipper, his agents or his servants.
4. Any deviation in saving or attempting to save life or property at sea or any reasonable deviation shall not be deemed to be an infringement or breach of this Convention or of the contract of carriage , and the carrier shall not be liable for any loss or damage resulting therefrom.

5. Neither the carrier nor the ship shall in any event be or become liable for any loss or damage to or in connexion with goods in an amount exceeding 100 pounds sterling per package or unit, or the equivalent of that sum in other currency unless the nature and value of such goods have been declared by the shipper before shipment and inserted in the bill of lading.

This declaration if embodied in the bill of lading shall be prima facie evidence, but shall not be binding or conclusive on the carrier.

By agreement between the carrier, master or agent of the carrier and the shipper another maximum amount than that mentioned in this paragraph may be fixed, provided that such maximum shall not be less than the figure above named.

Neither the carrier nor the ship shall be responsible in any event for loss or damage to, or in connexion with, goods if the nature or value thereof has been knowingly misstated by the shipper in the bill of lading.

5. (a) Unless the nature and value of such goods have been declared by the shipper before shipment and inserted in the Bill of Lading, neither the carrier nor the ship shall in any event be or become liable for any loss or damage to or in connection with the goods in an amount exceeding the equivalent of 10,000 francs per package or unit or 30 francs per kilo of gross weight of the goods lost or damaged, whichever is the higher.

(a) Unless the nature and value of such goods have been declared by the shipper before shipment and inserted in the bill of lading, neither the carrier nor the ship shall in any event be or become liable for any loss or damage to or in connection with the goods in an amount exceeding 666.67 units of account per package or unit or 2 units of account per kilogramme of gross weight of the goods lost or damaged, whichever is the higher.

(b) The total amount recoverable shall be calculated by reference to the value of such goods at the place and time at which the goods are discharged from the ship in accordance with the contract or should have been so discharged.

The value of the goods shall be fixed according to the commodity exchange price, or, if there be no such price, according to the current market price, or, if there be no commodity exchange price or current market price, by reference to the normal value of goods of the same kind and quality.

(c) Where a container, pallet or similar article of transport is used to consolidate goods, the number of packages or units enumerated in the Bill of Lading as packed in such article of transport shall be deemed the number of packages or units for the purpose of this paragraph as far as these packages or units are concerned. Except as aforesaid such article of transport shall be considered the package or unit.

(d) A franc means a unit consisting of 65.5 milligrammes of gold of millesimal fineness 900'. The date of conversion of the sum awarded into national currencies shall be governed by the law of the Court seized of the case.

(d) The unit of account mentioned in this Article is the Special Drawing Right as defined by the International Monetary Fund. The amounts mentioned in sub-paragraph (a) of this paragraph shall be converted into national currency on the basis of the value of that currency on a date to be determined by the law of the Court seized of the case.

The value of the national currency, in terms of the Special Drawing Right, of a State which is a member of the International Monetary Fund, shall be calculated in accordance with the method of valuation applied by the International Monetary Fund in effect at the date in question for its operations and transactions. The value of the national currency, in terms of the Special Drawing Right, of a State which is not a member of the International Monetary Fund, shall be calculated in a manner determined by that State.

Nevertheless, a State which is not a member of the International Monetary Fund and whose law does not permit the application of the provisions of the preceding sentences may, at the time of ratification of the Protocol of 1979 or accession thereto or at any time thereafter, declare that the limits of liability provided for in this Convention to be applied in its territory shall be fixed as follows:

(i) in respect of the amount of 666.67 units of account mentioned in sub-paragraph (a) of paragraph 5 of this Article, 10,000 monetary units;
(ii) in respect of the amount of 2 units of account mentioned in sub-paragraph (a) of paragraph 5 of this Article, 30 monetary units.

The monetary unit referred to in the preceding sentence corresponds to 65.5 milligrammes of gold of millesimal fineness 900′. The conversion of the amounts specified in that sentence into the national currency shall be made according to the law of the State concerned.

The calculation and the conversion mentioned in the preceding sentences shall be made in such a manner as to express in the national currency of the State as far as possible the same real value for the amounts in sub-paragraph (a) of paragraph 5 of this Article as is expressed there in units of account.

States shall communicate to the depositary the manner of calculation or the result of the conversion as the case may be, when depositing an instrument of ratification of the Protocol of 1979 or of accession thereto and whenever there is a change in either.

(e) Neither the carrier nor the ship shall be entitled to the benefit of the limitation of liability provided for in this paragraph if it is proved that the damage resulted from an act or omission of the carrier done with intent to cause damage, or recklessly and with knowledge that damage would probably result.

(f) The declaration mentioned in sub-paragraph (a) of this paragraph, if embodied in the Bill of Lading, shall be prima facie evidence, but shall not be binding or conclusive on the carrier.

(g) By agreement between the carrier, master or agent of the carrier and the shipper other maximum amounts than those mentioned in sub-paragraph (a) of this paragraph may be fixed, provided that no maximum amount so fixed shall be less than the appropriate maximum mentioned in that sub-paragraph.

(h) Neither the carrier nor the ship shall be responsible in any event for loss or damage to, or in connection with, goods if the nature or value thereof has been knowingly mis-stated by the shipper in the Bill of Lading.

6. Goods of an inflammable, explosive or dangerous nature to the shipment whereof the carrier, master or agent of the carrier has not consented with knowledge of their nature and character, may at any time before discharge be landed at any place, or destroyed or rendered innocuous by the carrier without compensation and the shipper of such goods shall be liable for all damage and expenses directly or indirectly arising out of or resulting from such shipment. If any such goods shipped with such knowledge and consent shall become a danger to the ship or cargo, they may in like manner be landed at any place, or destroyed or rendered innocuous by the carrier without liability on the part of the carrier except to general average , if any.

Article IV*bis*

1. The defences and limits of liability provided for in this Convention shall apply in any action against the carrier in respect of loss or damage to goods covered by a contract of carriage whether the action be founded in contract or in tort.
2. If such an action is brought against a servant or agent of the carrier (such servant or agent not being an independent contractor), such servant or agent shall be entitled to avail himself of the defences and limits of liability which the carrier is entitled to invoke under this Convention.
3. The aggregate of the amounts recoverable from the carrier, and such servants and agents, shall in no case exceed the limit provided for in this Convention.
4. Nevertheless, a servant or agent of the carrier shall not be entitled to avail himself of the provisions of this Article, if it is proved that the damage resulted from an act or omission of the servant or agent done with intent to cause damage or recklessly and with knowledge that damage would probably result.

Article V

A carrier shall be at liberty to surrender in whole or in part all or any of his rights and immunities or to increase any of his responsibilities and obligations under this Convention, provided such surrender or increase shall be embodied in the bill of lading issued to the shipper.

The provisions of this Convention shall not be applicable to charter parties, but if bills of lading are issued in the case of a ship under a charter party they shall comply with the terms of this Convention. Nothing in these rules shall be held to prevent the insertion in a bill of lading of any lawful provision regarding general average .

Article VI

Notwithstanding the provisions of the preceding Articles, a carrier, master or agent of the carrier and a shipper shall in regard to any particular goods be at liberty to enter into any agreement in any terms as to the responsibility and liability of the carrier for such goods, and as to the rights and immunities of the carrier in respect of such goods, or his obligation as to seaworthiness , so far as this stipulation is not contrary to public policy, or the care or diligence of his servants or agents in regard to the loading, handling, stowage, carriage, custody, care and discharge of the goods carried by sea, provided that in this case no bill of lading has been or shall be issued and that the terms agreed shall be embodied in a receipt which shall be a non-negotiable document and shall be marked as such.

Any agreement so entered into shall have full legal effect.

Provided that this Article shall not apply to ordinary commercial shipments made in the ordinary course of trade, but only to other shipments where the character or condition of the property to be carried or the circumstances, terms and conditions under which the carriage is to be performed are such as reasonably to justify a special agreement.

Article VII

Nothing herein contained shall prevent a carrier or a shipper from entering into any agreement, stipulation, condition, reservation or exemption as to the responsibility and liability of the carrier or the ship for the loss or damage to, or in connexion with, the custody and care and handling of goods prior to the loading on, and subsequent to, the discharge from the ship on which the goods are carried by sea.

Article VIII

The provisions of this Convention shall not affect the rights and obligations of the carrier under any statute for the time being in force relating to the limitation of the liability of owners of sea-going vessels.

Article IX

The monetary units mentioned in this Convention are to be taken to be gold value.

Those contracting States in which the pound sterling is not a monetary unit reserve to themselves the right of translating the sums indicated in this Convention in terms of pound sterling into terms of their own monetary system in round figures.

The national laws may reserve to the debtor the right of discharging his debt in national currency according to the rate of exchange prevailing on the day of the arrival of the ship at the port of discharge of the goods concerned.

This Convention shall not affect the provisions of any international Convention or national law governing liability for nuclear damage.

Article X

The provisions of this Convention shall apply to all bills of lading issued in any of the contracting States.

The provisions of this Convention shall apply to every Bill of Lading relating to the carriage of goods between ports in two different States if:

(a) the Bill of Lading is issued in a Contracting State,
or

(b) the carriage is from a port in a Contracting State,
or

(c) the contract contained in or evidenced by the Bill of Lading provides that the rules of this Convention or legislation of any State giving effect to them are to govern the contract

whatever may be the nationality of the ship, the carrier, the shipper, the consignee, or any other interested person.

Each Contracting State shall apply the provisions of this Convention to the Bills of Lading mentioned above.

This Article shall not prevent a Contracting State from applying the rules of this Convention to Bills of Lading not included in the preceding paragraphs.

Appendix E
Bills of Lading Act 1855 (UK)

18 & 19 Vict. Cap. 111
(Repealed)

Preamble

An Act to amend the Law relating to Bills of Lading.
14th August 1855
WHEREAS by the Custom of Merchants a Bill of Lading of Goods being transferable by Endorsement the Property in the Goods may thereby pass to the Endorsee, but nevertheless all Rights in respect of the Contract contained in the Bill of Lading continue in the original Shipper or Owner, and it is expedient that such Rights should pass with the Property: And whereas it frequently happens that the Goods in respect of which Bills of Lading purport to be signed have not been laden on board, and it is proper that such Bills of Lading in the Hands of a bona fide Holder for Value should not be questioned by the Master or other Person signing the same on the Ground of the Goods not having been laden as aforesaid:' Be it therefore enacted by the Queen's most Excellent Majesty, by and with the Advice and Consent of the Lords Spiritual and Temporal, and Commons, in this present Parliament assembled, and by the Authority of the same, as follows:

1. **Rights under Bills of Lading to vest in Consignee or Endorsee**
Every Consignee of Goods named in a Bill of Lading, and every Endorsee of a Bill of Lading to whom the Property in the Goods therein mentioned shall pass, upon or by reason of such Consignment or Endorsement, shall have transferred to and vested in him all Rights of Suit, and be subject to the same Liabilities in respect of such Goods as if the Contract contained in the Bill of Lading had been made with himself.
2. **Not to affect Right of Stoppage *in transitu* or Claims for Freight**
Nothing herein contained shall prejudice or affect any Right of Stoppage *in transitu*, or any Right to claim Freight against the original Shipper or Owner, or any Liability of the Consignee or Endorsee by reason or in consequence of

A. Kasi, *The Law of Carriage of Goods by Sea*,
https://doi.org/10.1007/978-981-33-6793-7

his being such Consignee or Endorsee, or of his Receipt of the Goods by reason or in consequence of such Consignment or Endorsement.

3. **Bill of Lading in Hands of Consignee, &c. conclusive Evidence of the Shipment as against Master, &c. Proviso**

Every Bill of Lading in the Hands of a Consignee or Endorsee for valuable Consideration representing Goods to have been shipped on board a Vessel shall be conclusive Evidence of such Shipment as against the Master or other Person signing the same, notwithstanding that such Goods or some Part thereof may not have been so shipped, unless such Holder of the Bill of Lading shall have had actual Notice at the Time of receiving the same that the Goods had not been in fact laden on board:

Provided, that the Master or other Person so signing may exonerate himself in respect of such Misrepresentation by showing that it was caused without any Default on his Part, and wholly by the Fraud of the Shipper, or of the Holder, or some Person under whom the Holder claims.

Appendix F
Carriage of Goods by Sea Act 1924 (UK)

14 & 15 Geo. 5 Cap. 22

Preamble

An Act to amend the law with respect to the carriage of goods by sea.

1st August 1924

WHEREAS at the International Conference on Maritime Law held at Brussels in October, 1922, the delegates at the Conference, including the delegates representing His Majesty, agreed unanimously to recommend their respective Governments to adopt as the basis of a convention a draft convention for the unification of certain rules relating to bills of lading :

And whereas at a meeting held at Brussels in October, 1923, the rules contained in the said draft convention were amended by the Committee appointed by the said Conference:

And whereas it is expedient that the said rules as so amended and as set out with modifications in the Schedule to this Act (in this Act referred to as "the Rules") should, subject to the provisions of this Act, be given the force of law with a view to establishing the responsibilities, liabilities, rights and immunities attaching to carriers under bills of lading:

Be it therefore enacted by the King's most Excellent Majesty, by and with the advice and consent of the Lords Spiritual and Temporal, and Commons, in this present Parliament assembled, and by the authority of the same, as follows:

1. **Application of Rules in Schedule**
   Subject to the provisions of this Act, the Rules shall have effect in relation to and in connection with the carriage of goods by sea in ships carrying goods from any port in Great Britain or Northern Ireland to any other port whether in or outside Great Britain or Northern Ireland.
2. **Absolute warranty of seaworthiness not to be implied in contracts to which Rules apply**

A. Kasi, *The Law of Carriage of Goods by Sea*,
https://doi.org/10.1007/978-981-33-6793-7

There shall not be implied in any contract for the carriage of goods by sea to which the Rules apply any absolute undertaking by the carrier of the goods to provide a seaworthy ship.

3. **Statement as to application of Rules to be included in bills of lading**
Every bill of lading, or similar document of title , issued in Great Britain or Northern Ireland which contains or is evidence of any contract to which the Rules apply shall contain an express statement that it is to have effect subject to the provisions of the said Rules as applied by this Act.

4. **Modification of Article VI of Rules in relation to coasting trade**
Article VI. of the Rules shall, in relation to the carriage of goods by sea in ships carrying goods from any port in Great Britain or Northern Ireland to any other port in Great Britain or Northern Ireland or to a port in the Irish Free State, have effect as though the said Article referred to goods of any class instead of to particular goods and as though the proviso to the second paragraph of the said Article were omitted.

5. **Modification of Rules 4 and 5 of Article III in relation to bulk cargoes**
Where under the custom of any trade the weight of any bulk cargo inserted in the bill of lading is a weight ascertained or accepted by a third party other than the carrier or the shipper and the fact that the weight is so ascertained or accepted is stated in the bill of lading, then, notwithstanding anything in the Rules, the bill of lading shall not be deemed to be prima facie evidence against the carrier of the receipt of goods of the weight so inserted in the bill of lading, and the accuracy thereof at the time of shipment shall not be deemed to have been guaranteed by the shipper.

6. **Short title, saving, and operation**

    (1) This Act may be cited as the Carriage of Goods by Sea Act, 1924.
    (2) Nothing in this Act shall affect the operation of sections four hundred and forty-six to four hundred and fifty, both inclusive, five hundred and two, and five hundred and three of the Merchant Shipping Act, 1894[1], as amended by any subsequent enactment, or the operation of any other enactment for the time being in force limiting the liability of the owners of seagoing vessels.
    (3) The Rules shall not by virtue of this Act apply to any contract for the carriage of goods by sea made before such day, not being earlier than the thirtieth day of June, nineteen hundred and twenty-four, as His Majesty may by Order in Council direct, nor to any bill of lading or similar document of title issued, whether before or after such day as aforesaid, in pursuance of any such contract as aforesaid.

SCHEDULE: Rules Relating to Bills of Lading

Article I

In these Rules the following words are employed, with the meanings set out below:—

(a) "Carrier" includes the owner or the charterer who enters into a contract of carriage with a shipper.
(b) "Contract of carriage" applies only to contracts of carriage covered by a bill of lading or any similar document of title, in so far as such document relates to the carriage of goods by sea, including any bill of lading or any similar document as aforesaid issued under or pursuant to a charter party from the moment at which such bill of lading or similar document of title regulates the relations between a carrier and a holder of the same.
(c) "Goods" includes goods, wares, merchandise, and articles of every kind whatsoever except live animals and cargo which by the contract of carriage is stated as being carried on deck and is so carried.
(d) "Ship" means any vessel used for the carriage of goods by sea.
(e) "Carriage of goods" covers the period from the time when the goods are loaded on to the time they are discharged from the ship.

Article II

Subject to the provisions of Article VI, under every contract of carriage of goods by sea the carrier, in relation to the loading, handling, stowage, carriage, custody, care and discharge of such goods, shall be subject to the responsibilities and liabilities, and entitled to the rights and immunities hereinafter set forth.

Article III

1. The carrier shall be bound before and at the beginning of the voyage to exercise due diligence to—

   (a) Make the ship seaworthy.
   (b) Properly man, equip and supply the ship.
   (c) Make the holds, refrigerating and cool chambers, and all other parts of the ship in which goods are carried, fit and safe for their reception, carriage and preservation.

2. Subject to the provisions of Article IV, the carrier shall properly and carefully load, handle, stow, carry, keep, care for, and discharge the goods carried.
3. After receiving the goods into his charge the carrier or the master or agent of the carrier shall, on demand of the shipper, issue to the shipper a bill of lading showing among other things—

   (a) The leading marks necessary for identification of the goods as the same are furnished in writing by the shipper before the loading of such goods starts, provided such marks are stamped or otherwise shown clearly upon the goods if uncovered, or on the cases or coverings in which such goods are contained, in such a manner as should ordinarily remain legible until the end of the voyage.
   (b) Either the number of packages or pieces, or the quantity, or weight, as the case may be, as furnished in writing by the shipper.

(c) The apparent order and condition of the goods.
Provided that no carrier, master or agent of the carrier shall be bound to state or show in the bill of lading any marks, number, quantity, or weight which he has reasonable ground for suspecting not accurately to represent the goods actually received, or which he has had no reasonable means of checking.

4. Such a bill of lading shall be prima facie evidence of the receipt by the carrier of the goods as therein described in accordance with paragraph 3 (a), (b), and (c).
5. The shipper shall be deemed to have guaranteed to the carrier the accuracy at the time of shipment of the marks, number, quantity, and weight, as furnished by him, and the shipper shall indemnify the carrier against all loss, damages, and expenses arising or resulting from inaccuracies in such particulars. The right of the carrier to such indemnity shall in no way limit his responsibility and liability under the contract of carriage to any person other than the shipper.
6. Unless notice of loss or damage and the general nature of such loss or damage be given in writing to the carrier or his agent at the port of discharge before or at the time of the removal of the goods into the custody of the person entitled to delivery thereof under the contract of carriage , or, if the loss or damage be not apparent, within three days, such removal shall be prima facie evidence of the delivery by the carrier of the goods as described in the bill of lading.
The notice in writing need not be given if the state of the goods has at the time of their receipt been the subject of joint survey or inspection.
In any event the carrier and the ship shall be discharged from all liability in respect of loss or damage unless suit is brought within one year after delivery of the goods or the date when the goods should have been delivered.
In the case of any actual or apprehended loss or damage the carrier and the receiver shall give all reasonable facilities to each other for inspecting and tallying the goods.
7. After the goods are loaded the bill of lading to be issued by the carrier, master or agent of the carrier, to the shipper shall, if the shipper so demands, be a "shipped" bill of lading, provided that if the shipper shall have previously taken up any document of title to such goods, he shall surrender the same as against the issue of the "shipped" bill of lading, but at the option of the carrier such document of title may be noted at the port of shipment by the carrier, master, or agent with the name or names of the ship or ships upon which the goods have been shipped and the date or dates of shipment, and when so noted the same shall for the purpose of this Article be deemed to constitute a "shipped" bill of lading.
8. Any clause, covenant or agreement in a contract of carriage relieving the carrier or the ship from liability for loss or damage to or in connection with goods arising from negligence , fault or failure in the duties and obligations provided in this Article or lessening such liability otherwise than as provided in these Rules, shall be null and void and of no effect.

A benefit of insurance or similar clause shall be deemed to be a clause relieving the carrier from liability.

Article IV

1. Neither the carrier nor the ship shall be liable for loss or damage arising or resulting from unseaworthiness unless caused by want of due diligence on the part of the carrier to make the ship seaworthy, and to secure that the ship is properly manned, equipped and supplied, and to make the holds, refrigerating and cool chambers and all other parts of the ship in which goods are carried fit and safe for their reception, carriage and preservation in accordance with the provisions of paragraph 1 of Article III.
   Whenever loss or damage has resulted from unseaworthiness, the burden of proving the exercise of due diligence shall be on the carrier or other person claiming exemption under this section.
2. Neither the carrier nor the ship shall be responsible for loss or damage arising or resulting from—

   (a) Act, neglect, or default of the master, mariner, pilot, or the servants of the carrier in the navigation or in the management of the ship.
   (b) Fire , unless caused by the actual fault or privity of the carrier.
   (c) Perils, dangers and accidents of the sea or other navigable waters.
   (d) Act of God.
   (e) Act of war.
   (f) Act of public enemies.
   (g) Arrest or restraint of princes, rulers or people, or seizure under legal process.
   (h) Quarantine restrictions.
   (i) Act or omission of the shipper or owner of the goods, his agent or representative.
   (j) Strikes or lockouts or stoppage or restraint of labour from whatever cause, whether partial or general.
   (k) Riots and civil commotions.
   (l) Saving or attempting to save life or property at sea.
   (m) Wastage in bulk or weight or any other loss or damage arising from inherent defect, quality or vice of the goods.
   (n) Insufficiency of packing.
   (o) Insufficiency or inadequacy of marks.
   (p) Latent defects not discoverable by due diligence .
   (q) Any other cause arising without the actual fault or privity of the carrier, or without the fault or neglect of the agents or servants of the carrier, but the burden of proof shall be on the person claiming the benefit of this exception to show that neither the actual fault or privity of the carrier nor the fault or neglect of the agents or servants of the carrier contributed to the loss or damage.

3. The shipper shall not be responsible for loss or damage sustained by the carrier or the ship arising or resulting from any cause without the act, fault or neglect of the shipper, his agents or his servants.
4. Any deviation in saving or attempting to save life or property at sea, or any reasonable deviation shall not be deemed to be an infringement or breach of these Rules or of the contract of carriage , and the carrier shall not be liable for any loss or damage resulting therefrom.
5. Neither the carrier nor the ship shall in any event be or become liable for any loss or damage to or in connection with goods in an amount exceeding 100 pounds sterling per package or unit, or the equivalent of that sum in other currency, unless the nature and value of such goods have been declared by the shipper before shipment and inserted in the bill of lading.
   This declaration if embodied in the bill of lading shall be *prima facie* evidence , but shall not be binding or conclusive on the carrier.
   By agreement between the carrier, master or agent of the carrier and the shipper another maximum amount than that mentioned in this paragraph may be fixed, provided that such maximum shall not be less than the figure above named.
   Neither the carrier nor the ship shall be responsible in any event for loss or damage to or in connection with goods if the nature or value thereof has been knowingly misstated by the shipper in the bill of lading.
6. Goods of an inflammable, explosive or dangerous nature to the shipment whereof the carrier, master or agent of the carrier, has not consented, with knowledge of their nature and character, may at any time before discharge be landed at any place or destroyed or rendered innocuous by the carrier without compensation, and the shipper of such goods shall be liable for all. damages and expenses directly or indirectly arising out of or resulting from such shipment.
   If any such goods shipped with such knowledge and consent shall become a danger to the ship or cargo, they may in like manner be landed at any place or destroyed or rendered innocuous by the carrier without liability on the part of the carrier except to general average , if any.

Article V

A carrier shall be at liberty to surrender in whole or in part all or any of his rights and immunities or to increase any of his responsibilities and liabilities under the Rules contained in any of these Articles, provided such surrender or increase shall be embodied in the bill of lading issued to the shipper.

The provisions of these Rules shall not be applicable to charterparties , but if bills of lading are issued in the case of a ship under a charterparty they shall comply with the terms of these Rules. Nothing in these Rules shall be held to prevent the insertion in a bill of lading of any lawful provision regarding general average .

Article VI

Notwithstanding the provisions of the preceding Articles, a carrier, master or agent of the carrier and a shipper shall in regard to any particular goods be at liberty to enter into any agreement in any terms as to the responsibility and liability of the carrier for such goods, and as to the rights and immunities of the carrier in respect of such goods, or his obligation as to seaworthiness , so far as this stipulation is not contrary to public policy, or the care or diligence of his servants or agents in regard to the loading, handling, stowage, carriage, custody, care, and discharge of the goods carried by sea, provided that in this case no bill of lading has been or shall be issued and that the terms agreed shall be embodied in a receipt which shall be a non-negotiable document and shall be marked as such.

Any agreement so entered into shall have full legal effect:

Provided that this Article shall not apply to ordinary commercial shipments made in the ordinary course of trade, but only to other shipments where the character or condition of the property to be carried or the circumstances, terms and conditions under which the carriage is to be performed, are such as reasonably to justify a special agreement.

Article VII

Nothing herein contained shall prevent a carrier or a shipper from entering into any agreement, stipulation, condition, reservation or exemption as to the responsibility and liability of the carrier or the ship for the loss or damage to or in connection with the custody and care and handling of goods prior to the loading on and subsequent to the discharge from the ship on which the goods are carried by sea.

Article VIII

The provisions of these Rules shall not affect the rights and obligations of the carrier under any statute for the time being in force relating to the limitation of the liability of owners of sea-going vessels.

Article IX

The monetary units mentioned in these Rules are to be taken to be gold value.

Appendix G
Carriage of Goods by Sea Act 1971 (UK)

Cap. 19

Preamble

An Act to amend the law with respect to the carriage of goods by sea.

8th April 1971

BE IT ENACTED by the Queen's most Excellent Majesty, by and with the advice and consent of the Lords Spiritual and Temporal, and Commons, in this present Parliament assembled, and by the authority of the same, as follows:

1. Application of Hague Rules as amended

   (1) In this Act, "the Rules" means the International Convention for the unification of certain rules of law relating to bills of lading signed at Brussels on 25th August 1924, as amended by the Protocol signed at Brussels on 23rd February 1968 [and by the Protocol signed at Brussels on 21st December 1979].

   (2) The provisions of the Rules, as set out in the Schedule to this Act, shall have the force of law.

   (3) Without prejudice to subsection (2) above, the said provisions shall have effect (and have the force of law) in relation to and in connection with the carriage of goods by sea in ships where the port of shipment is a port in the United Kingdom, whether or not the carriage is between ports in two different States within the meaning of Article X of the Rules.

   (4) Subject to subsection (6) below, nothing in this section shall be taken as applying anything in the Rules to any contract for the carriage of goods by sea, unless the contract expressly or by implication provides for the issue of a bill of lading or any similar document of title .

   (5) …

   (6) Without prejudice to Article X(c) of the Rules, the Rules shall have the force of law in relation to—

A. Kasi, *The Law of Carriage of Goods by Sea*,
https://doi.org/10.1007/978-981-33-6793-7

(a) any bill of lading if the contract contained in or evidenced by it expressly provides that the Rules shall govern the contract, and

(b) any receipt which is a non-negotiable document marked as such if the contract contained in or evidenced by it is a contract for the carriage of goods by sea which expressly provides that the Rules are to govern the contract as if the receipt were a bill of lading,

but subject, where paragraph (b) applies, to any necessary modifications and in particular with the omission in Article III of the Rules of the second sentence of paragraph 4 and of paragraph 7.

(7) If and so far as the contract contained in or evidenced by a bill of lading or receipt within paragraph (a) or (b) of subsection (6) above applies to deck cargo or live animals , the Rules as given the force of law by that subsection shall have effect as if Article I(c) did not exclude deck cargo and live animals .

In this subsection "deck cargo " means cargo which by the contract of carriage is stated as being carried on deck and is so carried.

1A Conversion of special drawing rights into sterling

(1) For the purposes of Article IV of the Rules the value on a particular day of one special drawing right shall be treated as equal to such a sum in sterling as the International Monetary Fund have fixed as being the equivalent of one special drawing right —

(a) for that day; or

(b) if no sum has been so fixed for that day, for the last day before that day for which a sum has been so fixed.

(2) A certificate given by or on behalf of the Treasury stating—

(a) that a particular sum in sterling has been fixed as aforesaid for a particular day; or

(b) that no sum has been so fixed for a particular day and that a particular sum in sterling has been so fixed for a day which is the last day for which a sum has been so fixed before the particular day,

shall be conclusive evidence of those matters for the purposes of subsection (1) above; and a document purporting to be such a certificate shall in any proceedings be received in evidence and, unless the contrary is proved, be deemed to be such a certificate.

(3) The Treasury may charge a reasonable fee for any certificate given in pursuance of subsection (2) above, and any fee received by the Treasury by virtue of this subsection shall be paid into the Consolidated Fund.

2 Contracting States, etc.

(1) If Her Majesty by Order in Council certifies to the following effect, that is to say, that for the purposes of the Rules—

(a) a State specified in the Order is a contracting State, or is a contracting State in respect of any place or territory so specified; or

(b) any place or territory specified in the Order forms part of a State so specified (whether a contracting State or not),

the Order shall, except so far as it has been superseded by a subsequent Order, be conclusive evidence of the matters so certified.

(2) An Order in Council under this section may be varied or revoked by a subsequent Order in Council.

3 Absolute warranty of seaworthiness not to be implied in contracts to which Rules apply

There shall not be implied in any contract for the carriage of goods by sea to which the Rules apply by virtue of this Act any absolute undertaking by the carrier of the goods to provide a seaworthy ship.

4 Application of Act to British possessions, etc.

(1) Her Majesty may by Order in Council direct that this Act shall extend, subject to such exceptions, adaptations and modifications as may be specified in the Order, to all or any of the following territories, that is—

(a) any colony (not being a colony for whose external relations a country other than the United Kingdom is responsible),

(b) any country outside Her Majesty's dominions in which Her Majesty has jurisdiction in right of Her Majesty's Government of the United Kingdom.

(2) An Order in Council under this section may contain such transitional and other consequential and incidental provisions as appear to Her Majesty to be expedient, including provisions amending or repealing any legislation about the carriage of goods by sea forming part of the law of any of the territories mentioned in paragraphs (a) and (b) above.

(3) An Order in Council under this section may be varied or revoked by a subsequent Order in Council.

5 Extension of application of Rules to carriage from ports in British possessions, etc

(1) Her Majesty may by Order in Council provide that section 1(3) of this Act shall have effect as if the reference therein to the United Kingdom included a reference to all or any of the following territories, that is—

(a) the Isle of Man;

(b) any of the Channel Islands specified in the Order;

(c) any colony specified in the Order (not being a colony for whose external relations a country other than the United Kingdom is responsible);

(d) …

(e) any country specified in the Order, being a country outside Her Majesty's dominions in which Her Majesty has jurisdiction in right of Her Majesty's Government of the United Kingdom.

(2) An Order in Council under this section may be varied or revoked by a subsequent Order in Council.

6 Supplemental

(1) This Act may be cited as the Carriage of Goods by Sea Act 1971.
(2) It is hereby declared that this Act extends to Northern Ireland.
(3) The following enactments shall be repealed, that is—

(a) the Carriage of Goods by Sea Act 1924,
(b) section 12(4)(a) of the Nuclear Installations Act 1965,
and without prejudice to section 38(1) of the Interpretation Act 1889, the reference to the said Act of 1924 in section 1(1)(i)(ii) of the Hovercraft Act 1968 shall include a reference to this Act.

(4) It is hereby declared that for the purposes of Article VIII of the Rules section 186 of the Merchant Shipping Act 1995 (which entirely exempts shipowners and others in certain circumstances for loss of, or damage to, goods) is a provision relating to limitation of liability.
(5) This Act shall come into force on such day as Her Majesty may by Order in Council appoint, and, for the purposes of the transition from the law in force immediately before the day appointed under this subsection to the provisions of this Act, the Order appointing the day may provide that those provisions shall have effect subject to such transitional provisions as may be contained in the Order.

SCHEDULE: The Hague Rules as amended by the Brussels Protocol 1968

Article I

In these Rules the following words are employed, with the meanings set out below:

(a) "Carrier" includes the owner or the charterer who enters into a contract of carriage with a shipper.
(b) "Contract of carriage" applies only to contracts of carriage covered by a bill of lading or any similar document of title, in so far as such document relates to the carriage of goods by sea, including any bill of lading or any similar document as aforesaid issued under or pursuant to a charter party from the moment at which such bill of lading or similar document of title regulates the relations between a carrier and a holder of the same.
(c) "Goods" includes goods, wares, merchandise, and articles of every kind whatsoever except live animals and cargo which by the contract of carriage is stated as being carried on deck and is so carried.
(d) "Ship" means any vessel used for the carriage of goods by sea.
(e) "Carriage of goods" covers the period from the time when the goods are loaded on to the time they are discharged from the ship.

Article II

Subject to the provisions of Article VI, under every contract of carriage of goods by sea the carrier, in relation to the loading, handling, stowage, carriage, custody, care and discharge of such goods, shall be subject to the responsibilities and liabilities, and entitled to the rights and immunities hereinafter set forth.

Article III

(1) The carrier shall be bound before and at the beginning of the voyage to exercise due diligence to—

  (a) Make the ship seaworthy.
  (b) Properly man, equip and supply the ship.
  (c) Make the holds, refrigerating and cool chambers, and all other parts of the ship in which goods are carried, fit and safe for their reception, carriage and preservation.

(2) Subject to the provisions of Article IV, the carrier shall properly and carefully load, handle, stow, carry, keep, care for, and discharge the goods carried.

(3) After receiving the goods into his charge the carrier or the master or agent of the carrier shall, on demand of the shipper, issue to the shipper a bill of lading showing among other things—

  (a) The leading marks necessary for identification of the goods as the same are furnished in writing by the shipper before the loading of such goods starts, provided such marks are stamped or otherwise shown clearly upon the goods if uncovered, or on the cases or coverings in which such goods are contained, in such a manner as should ordinarily remain legible until the end of the voyage.
  (b) Either the number of packages or pieces, or the quantity, or weight, as the case may be, as furnished in writing by the shipper.
  (c) The apparent order and condition of the goods.
  Provided that no carrier, master or agent of the carrier shall be bound to state or show in the bill of lading any marks, number, quantity, or weight which he has reasonable ground for suspecting not accurately to represent the goods actually received, or which he has had no reasonable means of checking.

(4) Such a bill of lading shall be prima facie evidence of the receipt by the carrier of the goods as therein described in accordance with paragraph 3(a), (b) and (c). However, proof to the contrary shall not be admissible when the bill of lading has been transferred to a third party acting in good faith.

(5) The shipper shall be deemed to have guaranteed to the carrier the accuracy at the time of shipment of the marks, number, quantity and weight, as furnished by him, and the shipper shall indemnify the carrier against all loss, damages and expenses arising or resulting from inaccuracies in such particulars. The

right of the carrier to such indemnity shall in no way limit his responsibility and liability under the contract of carriage to any person other than the shipper.

(6) Unless notice of loss or damage and the general nature of such loss or damage be given in writing to the carrier or his agent at the port of discharge before or at the time of the removal of the goods into the custody of the person entitled to delivery thereof under the contract of carriage , or, if the loss or damage be not apparent, within three days, such removal shall be prima facie evidence of the delivery by the carrier of the goods as described in the bill of lading.

The notice in writing need not be given if the state of the goods has, at the time of their receipt, been the subject of joint survey or inspection.

Subject to paragraph 6*bis* the carrier and the ship shall in any event be discharged from all liability whatsoever in respect of the goods, unless suit is brought within one year of their delivery or of the date when they should have been delivered. This period may, however, be extended if the parties so agree after the cause of action has arisen.

In the case of any actual or apprehended loss or damage the carrier and the receiver shall give all reasonable facilities to each other for inspecting and tallying the goods.

6*bis*. An action for indemnity against a third person may be brought even after the expiration of the year provided for in the preceding paragraph if brought within the time allowed by the law of the Court seized of the case. However, the time allowed shall be not less than three months, commencing from the day when the person bringing such action for indemnity has settled the claim or has been served with process in the action against himself.

(7) After the goods are loaded the bill of lading to be issued by the carrier, master, or agent of the carrier, to the shipper shall, if the shipper so demands, be a "shipped" bill of lading, provided that if the shipper shall have previously taken up any document of title to such goods, he shall surrender the same as against the issue of the "shipped" bill of lading, but at the option of the carrier such document of title may be noted at the port of shipment by the carrier, master, or agent with the name or names of the ship or ships upon which the goods have been shipped and the date or dates of shipment, and when so noted, if it shows the particulars mentioned in paragraph 3 of Article III, shall for the purpose of this article be deemed to constitute a "shipped" bill of lading.

(8) Any clause, covenant, or agreement in a contract of carriage relieving the carrier or the ship from liability for loss or damage to, or in connection with, goods arising from negligence , fault, or failure in the duties and obligations provided in this article or lessening such liability otherwise than as provided in these Rules, shall be null and void and of no effect.

A benefit of insurance in favour of the carrier or similar clause shall be deemed to be a clause relieving the carrier from liability.

Article IV

1. Neither the carrier nor the ship shall be liable for loss or damage arising or resulting from unseaworthiness unless caused by want of due diligence on the part of the carrier to make the ship seaworthy, and to secure that the ship is properly manned, equipped and supplied, and to make the holds, refrigerating and cool chambers and all other parts of the ship in which goods are carried fit and safe for their reception, carriage and preservation in accordance with the provisions of paragraph 1 of Article III.
   Whenever loss or damage has resulted from unseaworthiness the burden of proving the exercise of due diligence shall be on the carrier or other person claiming exemption under this article.
2. Neither the carrier nor the ship shall be responsible for loss or damage arising or resulting from—
   (a) Act, neglect, or default of the master, mariner, pilot, or the servants of the carrier in the navigation or in the management of the ship.
   (b) Fire , unless caused by the actual fault or privity of the carrier.
   (c) Perils, dangers and accidents of the sea or other navigable waters.
   (d) Act of God.
   (e) Act of war.
   (f) Act of public enemies.
   (g) Arrest or restraint of princes, rulers or people, or seizure under legal process.
   (h) Quarantine restrictions.
   (i) Act or omission of the shipper or owner of the goods, his agent or representative.
   (j) Strikes or lockouts or stoppage or restraint of labour from whatever cause, whether partial or general.
   (k) Riots and civil commotions.
   (l) Saving or attempting to save life or property at sea.
   (m) Wastage in bulk or weight or any other loss or damage arising from inherent defect, quality or vice of the goods.
   (n) Insufficiency of packing.
   (o) Insufficiency or inadequacy of marks.
   (p) Latent defects not discoverable by due diligence .
   (q) Any other cause arising without the actual fault or privity of the carrier, or without the fault or neglect of the agents or servants of the carrier, but the burden of proof shall be on the person claiming the benefit of this exception to show that neither the actual fault or privity of the carrier nor the fault or neglect of the agents or servants of the carrier contributed to the loss or damage.
3. The shipper shall not be responsible for loss or damage sustained by the carrier or the ship arising or resulting from any cause without the act, fault or neglect of the shipper, his agents or his servants.

4. Any deviation in saving or attempting to save life or property at sea or any reasonable deviation shall not be deemed to be an infringement or breach of these Rules or of the contract of carriage, and the carrier shall not be liable for any loss or damage resulting therefrom.
5. (a) Unless the nature and value of such goods have been declared by the shipper before shipment and inserted in the bill of lading, neither the carrier nor the ship shall in any event be or become liable for any loss or damage to or in connection with the goods in an amount exceeding [666.67 units of account] per package or unit or [2 units of account per kilogramme] of gross weight of the goods lost or damaged, whichever is the higher.
(b) The total amount recoverable shall be calculated by reference to the value of such goods at the place and time at which the goods are discharged from the ship in accordance with the contract or should have been so discharged.
The value of the goods shall be fixed according to the commodity exchange price, or, if there be no such price, according to the current market price, or, if there be no commodity exchange price or current market price, by reference to the normal value of goods of the same kind and quality.
(c) Where a container, pallet or similar article of transport is used to consolidate goods, the number of packages or units enumerated in the bill of lading as packed in such article of transport shall be deemed the number of packages or units for the purpose of this paragraph as far as these packages or units are concerned. Except as aforesaid such article of transport shall be considered the package or unit.
(d) The unit of account mentioned in this Article is the special drawing right as defined by the International Monetary Fund. The amounts mentioned in sub-paragraph (a) of this paragraph shall be converted into national currency on the basis of the value of that currency on a date to be determined by the law of the Court seized of the case.
(e) Neither the carrier nor the ship shall be entitled to the benefit of the limitation of liability provided for in this paragraph if it is proved that the damage resulted from an act or omission of the carrier done with intent to cause damage, or recklessly and with knowledge that damage would probably result.
(f) The declaration mentioned in sub-paragraph (a) of this paragraph, if embodied in the bill of lading, shall be prima facie evidence, but shall not be binding or conclusive on the carrier.
(g) By agreement between the carrier, master or agent of the carrier and the shipper other maximum amounts than those mentioned in sub-paragraph (a) of this paragraph may be fixed, provided that no maximum amount so fixed shall be less than the appropriate maximum mentioned in that sub-paragraph.
(h) Neither the carrier nor the ship shall be responsible in any event for loss or damage to, or in connection with, goods if the nature or value thereof has been knowingly mis-stated by the shipper in the bill of lading.
6. Goods of an inflammable, explosive or dangerous nature to the shipment whereof the carrier, master or agent of the carrier has not consented with knowledge of their nature and character, may at any time before discharge be landed at

any place, or destroyed or rendered innocuous by the carrier without compensation and the shipper of such goods shall be liable for all damages and expenses directly or indirectly arising out of or resulting from such shipment.
If any such goods shipped with such knowledge and consent shall become a danger to the ship or cargo, they may in like manner be landed at any place, or destroyed or rendered innocuous by the carrier without liability on the part of the carrier except to general average , if any.

Article IV *bis*

1. The defences and limits of liability provided for in these Rules shall apply in any action against the carrier in respect of loss or damage to goods covered by a contract of carriage whether the action be founded in contract or in tort.
2. If such an action is brought against a servant or agent of the carrier (such servant or agent not being an independent contractor), such servant or agent shall be entitled to avail himself of the defences and limits of liability which the carrier is entitled to invoke under these Rules.
3. The aggregate of the amounts recoverable from the carrier, and such servants and agents, shall in no case exceed the limit provided for in these Rules.
4. Nevertheless, a servant or agent of the carrier shall not be entitled to avail himself of the provisions of this article, if it is proved that the damage resulted from an act or omission of the servant or agent done with intent to cause damage or recklessly and with knowledge that damage would probably result.

Article V

A carrier shall be at liberty to surrender in whole or in part all or any of his rights and immunities or to increase any of his responsibilities and obligations under these Rules, provided such surrender or increase shall be embodied in the bill of lading issued to the shipper. The provisions of these Rules shall not be applicable to charter parties, but if bills of lading are issued in the case of a ship under a charter party they shall comply with the terms of these Rules. Nothing in these Rules shall be held to prevent the insertion in a bill of lading of any lawful provision regarding general average .

Article VI

Notwithstanding the provisions of the preceding articles, a carrier, master or agent of the carrier and a shipper shall in regard to any particular goods be at liberty to enter into any agreement in any terms as to the responsibility and liability of the carrier for such goods, and as to the rights and immunities of the carrier in respect of such goods, or his obligation as to seaworthiness , so far as this stipulation is not contrary to public policy, or the care or diligence of his servants or agents in regard to the loading, handling, stowage, carriage, custody, care and discharge of the goods carried by sea, provided that in this case no bill of lading has been or shall be issued and that the terms agreed shall be embodied in a receipt which shall be a non-negotiable document and shall be marked as such.

Any agreement so entered into shall have full legal effect.

Provided that this article shall not apply to ordinary commercial shipments made in the ordinary course of trade, but only to other shipments where the character or condition of the property to be carried or the circumstances, terms and conditions under which the carriage is to be performed are such as reasonably to justify a special agreement.

Article VII

Nothing herein contained shall prevent a carrier or a shipper from entering into any agreement, stipulation, condition, reservation or exemption as to the responsibility and liability of the carrier or the ship for the loss or damage to, or in connection with, the custody and care and handling of goods prior to the loading on, and subsequent to the discharge from, the ship on which the goods are carried by sea.

Article VIII

The provisions of these Rules shall not affect the rights and obligations of the carrier under any statute for the time being in force relating to the limitation of the liability of owners of sea-going vessels.

Article IX

These Rules shall not affect the provisions of any international Convention or national law governing liability for nuclear damage.

Article X

The provisions of these Rules shall apply to every bill of lading relating to the carriage of goods between ports in two different States if:

(a) the bill of lading is issued in a contracting State, or
(b) the carriage is from a port in a contracting State, or
(c) the contract contained in or evidenced by the bill of lading provides that these Rules or legislation of any State giving effect to them are to govern the contract,

whatever may be the nationality of the ship, the carrier, the shipper, the consignee, or any other interested person.

(The last two paragraphs of this article are not reproduced. They require contracting States to apply the Rules to bills of lading mentioned in the article and authorise them to apply the Rules to other bills of lading.)

(Articles 11 to 16 of the International Convention for the unification of certain rules of law relating to bills of lading signed at Brussels on 25th August 1924 are not reproduced. They deal with the coming into force of the Convention, procedure for ratification, accession and denunciation, and the right to call for a fresh conference to consider amendments to the Rules contained in the Convention.)

Appendix H
Carriage of Goods by Sea Act 1992 (UK)

Cap. 50

Preamble

An Act to replace the Bills of Lading Act 1855 with new provision with respect to bills of lading and certain other shipping documents .

16th July 1992

BE IT ENACTED by the Queen's most Excellent Majesty, by and with the advice and consent of the Lords Spiritual and Temporal, and Commons, in this present Parliament assembled, and by the authority of the same, as follows:

(1) **Shipping documents etc to which Act applies**

(1) This Act applies to the following documents, that is to say—
  (a) any bill of lading;
  (b) any sea waybill ; and
  (c) any ship's delivery order.

(2) References in this Act to a bill of lading—
  (a) do not include references to a document which is incapable of transfer either by indorsement or, as a bearer bill , by delivery without indorsement; but
  (b) subject to that, do include references to a received for shipment bill of lading.

(3) References in this Act to a sea waybill are references to any document which is not a bill of lading but—
  (a) is such a receipt for goods as contains or evidences a contract for the carriage of goods by sea; and
  (b) identifies the person to whom delivery of the goods is to be made by the carrier in accordance with that contract.

A. Kasi, *The Law of Carriage of Goods by Sea*,
https://doi.org/10.1007/978-981-33-6793-7

(4) References in this Act to a ship's delivery order are references to any document which is neither a bill of lading nor a sea waybill but contains an undertaking which—
 (a) is given under or for the purposes of a contract for the carriage by sea of the goods to which the document relates, or of goods which include those goods; and
 (b) is an undertaking by the carrier to a person identified in the document to deliver the goods to which the document relates to that person.

(5) The Secretary of State may by regulations make provision for the application of this Act to cases where [an electronic communications network] or any other information technology is used for effecting transactions corresponding to—
 (a) the issue of a document to which this Act applies;
 (b) the indorsement, delivery or other transfer of such a document; or
 (c) the doing of anything else in relation to such a document.

(6) Regulations under subsection (5) above may—
 (a) make such modifications of the following provisions of this Act as the Secretary of State considers appropriate in connection with the application of this Act to any case mentioned in that subsection; and
 (b) contain supplemental, incidental, consequential and transitional provision;
 and the power to make regulations under that subsection shall be exercisable by statutory instrument subject to annulment in pursuance of a resolution of either House of Parliament.

(2) **Rights under shipping documents**

(1) Subject to the following provisions of this section, a person who becomes-—
 (a) the lawful holder of a bill of lading;
 (b) the person who (without being an original party to the contract of carriage) is the person to whom delivery of the goods to which a sea waybill relates is to be made by the carrier in accordance with that contract; or
 (c) the person to whom delivery of the goods to which a ship's delivery order relates is to be made in accordance with the undertaking contained in the order,
 the other person shall be entitled to exercise those rights for the benefit of the person who sustained the loss or damage to the same extent as they could have been exercised if they had been vested in the person for whose benefit they are exercised.

(2) Where, when a person becomes the lawful holder of a bill of lading, possession of the bill no longer gives a right (as against the carrier) to

possession of the goods to which the bill relates, that person shall not have any rights transferred to him by virtue of subsection (1) above unless he becomes the holder of the bill—

(a) by virtue of a transaction effected in pursuance of any contractual or other arrangements made before the time when such a right to possession ceased to attach to possession of the bill; or

(b) as a result of the rejection to that person by another person of goods or documents delivered to the other person in pursuance of any such arrangements.

(3) The rights vested in any person by virtue of the operation of subsection (1) above in relation to a ship's delivery order—

(a) shall be so vested subject to the terms of the order; and

(b) where the goods to which the order relates form a part only of the goods to which the contract of carriage relates, shall be confined to rights in respect of the goods to which the order relates.

(4) Where, in the case of any document to which this Act applies—

(a) a person with any interest or right in or in relation to goods to which the document relates sustains loss or damage in consequence of a breach of the contract of carriage ; but

(b) subsection (1) above operates in relation to that document so that rights of suit in respect of that breach are vested in another person, the other person shall be entitled to exercise those rights for the benefit of the person who sustained the loss or damage to the same extent as they could have been exercised if they had been vested in the person for whose benefit they are exercised.

(5) Where rights are transferred by virtue of the operation of subsection (1) above in relation to any document, the transfer for which that subsection provides shall extinguish any entitlement to those rights which derives—

(a) where that document is a bill of lading, from a person's having been an original party to the contract of carriage ; or

(b) in the case of any document to which this Act applies, from the previous operation of that subsection in relation to that document; but the operation of that subsection shall be without prejudice to any rights which derive from a person's having been an original party to the contract contained in, or evidenced by, a sea waybill and, in relation to a ship's delivery order, shall be without prejudice to any rights deriving otherwise than from the previous operation of that subsection in relation to that order.

(3) Liabilities under shipping documents

(1) Where subsection (1) of section 2 of this Act operates in relation to any document to which this Act applies and the person in whom rights are vested by virtue of that subsection—

(a) takes or demands delivery from the carrier of any of the goods to which the document relates;

(b) makes a claim under the contract of carriage against the carrier in respect of any of those goods; or

(c) is a person who, at a time before those rights were vested in him, took or demanded delivery from the carrier of any of those goods, that person shall (by virtue of taking or demanding delivery or making the claim or, in a case falling within paragraph (c) above, of having the rights vested in him) become subject to the same liabilities under that contract as if he had been a party to that contract.

(2) Where the goods to which a ship's delivery order relates form a part only of the goods to which the contract of carriage relates, the liabilities to which any person is subject by virtue of the operation of this section in relation to that order shall exclude liabilities in respect of any goods to which the order does not relate.

(3) This section, so far as it imposes liabilities under any contract on any person, shall be without prejudice to the liabilities under the contract of any person as an original party to the contract.

(4) **Representations in bills of lading**

A bill of lading which—

(a) represents goods to have been shipped on board a vessel or to have been received for shipment on board a vessel; and

(b) has been signed by the master of the vessel or by a person who was not the master but had the express, implied or apparent authority of the carrier to sign bills of lading,

(c) shall, in favour of a person who has become the lawful holder of the bill, be conclusive evidence against the carrier of the shipment of the goods or, as the case may be, of their receipt for shipment.

(5) **Interpretation etc.**

(1) In this Act—

"bill of lading", "sea waybill " and "ship's delivery order" shall be construed in accordance with section 1 above;

"the contract of carriage "—

(a) in relation to a bill of lading or sea waybill , means the contract contained in or evidenced by that bill or waybill; and

(b) in relation to a ship's delivery order, means the contract under or for the purposes of which the undertaking contained in the order is given;

"holder", in relation to a bill of lading, shall be construed in accordance with subsection (2) below;

"information technology" includes any computer or other technology by means of which information or other matter may be recorded or communicated without being reduced to documentary form; ...

...

(2) References in this Act to the holder of a bill of lading are references to any of the following persons, that is to say—

(a) a person with possession of the bill who, by virtue of being the person identified in the bill, is the consignee of the goods to which the bill relates;

(b) a person with possession of the bill as a result of the completion, by delivery of the bill, of any indorsement of the bill or, in the case of a bearer bill, of any other transfer of the bill;

(c) a person with possession of the bill as a result of any transaction by virtue of which he would have become a holder falling within paragraph (a) or (b) above had not the transaction been effected at a time when possession of the bill no longer gave a right (as against the carrier) to possession of the goods to which the bill relates;

and a person shall be regarded for the purposes of this Act as having become the lawful holder of a bill of lading wherever he has become the holder of the bill in good faith.

(3) References in this Act to a person's being identified in a document include references to his being identified by a description which allows for the identity of the person in question to be varied, in accordance with the terms of the document, after its issue; and the reference in section 1(3)(b) of this Act to a document's identifying a person shall be construed accordingly.

(4) Without prejudice to sections 2(2) and 4 above, nothing in this Act shall preclude its operation in relation to a case where the goods to which a document relates—

(a) cease to exist after the issue of the document; or

(b) cannot be identified (whether because they are mixed with other goods or for any other reason);

and references in this Act to the goods to which a document relates shall be construed accordingly.

(5) The preceding provisions of this Act shall have effect without prejudice to the application, in relation to any case, of the rules (the Hague-Visby Rules) which for the time being have the force of law by virtue of section 1 of the Carriage of Goods by Sea Act 1971.

6 Short title, repeal, commencement and extent

(1) This Act may be cited as the Carriage of Goods by Sea Act 1992.

(2) …

(3) This Act shall come into force at the end of the period of two months beginning with the day on which it is passed; but nothing in this Act shall have effect in relation to any document issued before the coming into force of this Act.

(4) This Act extends to Northern Ireland.

Appendix I
Carriage of Goods by Sea Act 1936 (US)

Cap. 299

Preamble

AN ACT Relating to the carriage of goods by sea.

Be it enacted by the Senate and House of Representatives of the United States of America in Congress assembled.

Every bill of lading or similar document of title which is evidence of a contract for the carriage of goods by sea to or from ports of the United States, in foreign trade, shall have effect subject to the provisions of this Act.

Title I

Section 1. Terms defined

When used in this Act—

(a) The term 'carrier' includes the owner or the charterer who enters into a contract of carriage with a shipper.
(b) The term 'contract of carriage ' applies only to contracts of carriage covered by a bill of lading or any similar document of title , insofar as such document relates to the carriage of goods by sea, including any bill of lading or any similar document as aforesaid issued under or pursuant to a charter party from the moment at which such bill of lading or similar document of title regulates the relations between a carrier and a holder of the same.
(c) The term 'goods' includes goods, wares, merchandise, and articles of every kind, whatsoever, except live animals and cargo which by the contract of carriage is stated as being carried on deck and is so carried.
(d) The term 'ship' means any vessel used for the carriage of goods by sea.
(e) The term 'carriage of goods' covers the period from the time when the goods are loaded on to the time when they are discharged from the ship.

A. Kasi, *The Law of Carriage of Goods by Sea*,
https://doi.org/10.1007/978-981-33-6793-7

Section 2. Risks

Subject to the provisions of section 6, under every contract of carriage of goods by sea, the carrier in relation to the loading, handling, stowage, carriage, custody, care, and discharge of such goods, shall be subject to the responsibilities and liabilities and entitled to the rights and immunities hereinafter set forth.

Section 3. Responsibilities and liabilities

1. The carrier shall be bound, before and at the beginning of the voyage, to exercise due diligence to—
   (a) Make the ship seaworthy;
   (b) Properly man, equip, and supply the ship;
   (c) Make the holds, refrigerating and cooling chambers, and all other parts of the ship in which goods are carried, fit and safe for their reception, carriage, and preservation.
2. The carrier shall properly and carefully load, handle, stow, carry, keep, care for, and discharge the goods carried.
3 After receiving the goods into his charge the carrier, or the master or agent of the carrier, shall, on demand of the shipper, issue to the shipper a bill of lading showing among other things—
   (a) The leading marks necessary for identification of the goods as the same are furnished in writing by the shipper before the loading of such goods starts, provided such marks are stamped or otherwise shown clearly upon the goods if uncovered, or on the cases or coverings in which such goods are contained, in such a manner as should ordinarily remain legible until the end of the voyage.
   (b) Either the number of packages or pieces, or the quantity or weight, as the case may be, as furnished in writing by the shipper.
   (c) The apparent order and condition of the goods: Provided, That no carrier, master, or agent of the carrier, shall be bound to state or show in the bill of lading any marks, number, quantity, or weight which he has reasonable ground for suspecting not accurately to represent the goods actually received, or which he has had no reasonable means of checking.
4. Such a bill of lading shall be prima facie evidence of the receipt by the carrier of the goods as therein described in accordance with paragraphs (3)(a), (b), and (c), of this section: Provided, That nothing in this Act shall be construed as repealing or limiting the application of any part of the Act, as amended, entitled 'An Act relating to bills of lading in interstate and foreign commerce,' approved August 29, 1916, commonly known as the 'Pomerene Bills of Lading Act' [49 USCS §§ 80101 et seq.].
5. The shipper shall be deemed to have guaranteed to the carrier the accuracy at the time of shipment of the marks, number, quantity, and weight, as furnished by him; and the shipper shall indemnify the carrier against all loss, damages, and

expenses arising or resulting from inaccuracies in such particulars. The right of the carrier to such indemnity shall in no way limit his responsibility and liability under the contract of carriage to any person other than the shipper.

6. Unless notice of loss or damage and the general nature of such loss or damage be given in writing to the carrier or his agent at the port of discharge before or at the time of the removal of the goods into the custody of the person entitled to delivery thereof under the contract of carriage , such removal shall be prima facie evidence of the delivery by the carrier of the goods as described in the bill of lading. If the loss or damage is not apparent, the notice must be given within three days of the delivery.
   Said notice of loss or damage may be endorsed upon the receipt for the goods given by the person taking delivery thereof.
   The notice in writing need not be given if the state of the goods has at the time of their receipt been the subject of joint survey or inspection.
   In any event the carrier and the ship shall be discharged from all liability in respect of loss or damage unless suit is brought within one year after delivery of the goods or the date when the goods should have been delivered: Provided, That if a notice of loss or damage, either apparent or concealed, is not given as provided for in this section, that fact shall not affect or prejudice the right of the shipper to bring suit within one year after the delivery of the goods or the date when the goods should have been delivered.
   In the case of any actual or apprehended loss or damage the carrier and the receiver shall give all reasonable facilities to each other for inspecting and tallying the goods.
   After the goods are loaded the bill of lading to be issued by the carrier, master, or agent of the carrier to the shipper shall, if the shipper so demands, be a 'shipped' bill of lading: Provided, That if the shipper shall have previously taken up any document of title to such goods, he shall surrender the same as against the issue of the shipped" bill of lading, but at the option of the carrier such document of title may be noted at the port of shipment by the carrier, master, or agent with the name or names of the ship or ships upon which the goods have been shipped and the date or dates of shipment, and when so noted the same shall for the purpose of this section be deemed to constitute a 'shipped' bill of lading.
7. Any clause, covenant, or agreement in a contract of carriage relieving the carrier or the ship from liability for loss or damage to or in connection with the goods, arising from negligence , fault, or failure in the duties and obligations provided in this section, or lessening such liability otherwise than as provided in this Act, shall be null and void and of no effect. A benefit of insurance in favor of the carrier, or similar clause, shall be deemed to be a clause relieving the carrier from liability.

Section 4. Rights and immunities

1. Neither the carrier nor the ship shall be liable for loss or damage arising or resulting from unseaworthiness unless caused by want of due diligence on

the part of the carrier to make the ship seaworthy, and to secure that the ship is properly manned, equipped, and supplied, and to make the holds, refrigerating and cool chambers, and all other parts of the ship in which goods are carried fit and safe for their reception, carriage, and preservation in accordance with the provisions of paragraph (1) of section 3. Whenever loss or damage has resulted from unseaworthiness, the burden of proving the exercise of due diligence shall be on the carrier or other persons claiming exemption under this section.

2. Neither the carrier nor the ship shall be responsible for loss or damage arising or resulting from—

   (a) Act, neglect, or default of the master, mariner, pilot, or the servants of the carrier in the navigation or in the management of the ship;
   (b) Fire , unless caused by the actual fault or privity of the carrier;
   (c) Perils, dangers, and accidents of the sea or other navigable waters;
   (d) Act of God;
   (e) Act of war;
   (f) Act of public enemies;
   (g) Arrest or restraint of princes, rulers, or people, or seizure under legal process;
   (h) Quarantine restrictions;
   (i) Act or omission of the shipper or owner of the goods, his agent or representative;
   (j) Strikes or lockouts or stoppage or restraint of labor from whatever cause, whether partial or general: Provided, that nothing herein contained shall be construed to relieve a carrier from responsibility for the carrier's own acts;
   (k) Riots and civil commotions;
   (l) Saving or attempting to save life or property at sea;
   (m) Wastage in bulk or weight or any other loss or damage arising from inherent defect, quality, or vice of the goods;
   (n) Insufficiency of packing;
   (o) Insufficiency or inadequacy of marks;
   (p) Latent defects not discoverable by due diligence ; and
   (q) Any other cause arising without the actual fault and privity of the carrier and without the fault or neglect of the agents or servants of the carrier, but the burden of proof shall be on the person claiming the benefit of this exception to show that neither the actual fault or privity of the carrier nor the fault or neglect of the agents or servants of the carrier contributed to the loss or damage.

3. The shipper shall not be responsible for loss or damage sustained by the carrier or the ship arising or resulting from any cause without the act, fault, or neglect of the shipper, his agents, or his servants.
4. Any deviation in saving or attempting to save life or property at sea, or any reasonable deviation shall not be deemed to be an infringement or breach of this Act or of the contract of carriage , and the carrier shall not be liable for any

loss or damage resulting therefrom: Provided, however, That if the deviation is for the purpose of loading or unloading cargo or passengers it shall, prima facie, be regarded as unreasonable.

5. Neither the carrier nor the ship shall in any event be or become liable for any loss or damage to or in connection with the transportation of goods in an amount exceeding $500 per package lawful money of the United States, or in case of goods not shipped in packages, per customary freight unit, or the equivalent of that sum in other currency, unless the nature and value of such goods have been declared by the shipper before shipment and inserted in the bill of lading. This declaration, if embodied in the bill of lading, shall be prima facie evidence , but shall not be conclusive on the carrier.

   By agreement between the carrier, master, or agent of the carrier, and the shipper another maximum amount than that mentioned in this paragraph may be fixed: Provided, That such maximum shall not be less than the figure above named. In no event shall the carrier be liable for more than the amount of damage actually sustained.

   Neither the carrier nor the ship shall be responsible in any event for loss or damage to or in connection with the transportation of the goods if the nature or value thereof has been knowingly and fraudulently misstated by the shipper in the bill of lading.

6. Goods of an inflammable, explosive, or dangerous nature to the shipment whereof the carrier, master or agent of the carrier, has not consented with knowledge of their nature and character, may at any time before discharge be landed at any place or destroyed or rendered innocuous by the carrier without compensation, and the shipper of such goods shall be liable for all damages and expenses directly or indirectly arising out of or resulting from such shipment. If any such goods shipped with such knowledge and consent shall become a danger to the ship or cargo, they may in like manner be landed at any place, or destroyed or rendered innocuous by the carrier without liability on the part of the carrier except to general average , if any.

Section 5. Surrender of rights and immunities and increase of liabilities and responsibilities

A carrier shall be at liberty to surrender in whole or in part all or any of his rights and immunities or to increase any of his responsibilities and liabilities under this Act, provided such surrender or increase shall be embodied in the bill of lading issued to the shipper.

The provisions of this Act shall not be applicable to charter parties; but if bills of lading are issued in the case of a ship under a charter party, they shall comply with the terms of this Act. Nothing in this Act shall be held to prevent the insertion in a bill of lading of any lawful provision regarding general average .

Section 6. Special conditions

Notwithstanding the provisions of the preceding sections, a carrier, master or agent of the carrier, and a shipper shall, in regard to any particular goods be at liberty to enter into any agreement in any terms as to the responsibility and liability of the carrier for such goods, and as to the rights and immunities of the carrier in respect of such goods, or his obligation as to seaworthiness (so far as the stipulation regarding seaworthiness is not contrary to public policy), or the care or diligence of his servants or agents in regard to the loading, handling, stowage, carriage, custody, care, and discharge of the goods carried by sea: Provided, That in this case no bill of lading has been or shall be issued and that the terms agreed shall be embodied in a receipt which shall be a nonnegotiable document and shall be marked as such.

Any agreement so entered into shall have full legal effect: Provided, That this section shall not apply to ordinary commercial shipments made in the ordinary course of trade but only to other shipments where the character or condition of the property to be carried or the circumstances, terms, and conditions under which the carriage is to be performed are such as reasonably to justify a special agreement.

Section 7. Liability for goods prior to loading and after discharge from ship

Nothing contained in this Act shall prevent a carrier or a shipper from entering into any agreement, stipulation, condition, reservation, or exemption as to the responsibility and liability of the carrier or the ship for the loss or damage to or in connection with the custody and care and handling of goods prior to the loading on and subsequent to the discharge from the ship on which the goods are carried by sea.

Section 8. Rights and obligations of carrier under designated Acts

The provisions of this Act shall not affect the rights and obligations of the carrier under the provisions of the Shipping Act, 1916, or under the provisions of sections 4281 to 4289, inclusive, of the Revised Statutes of the United States [46 USCS §§ 30501 et seq.], or of any amendments thereto; or under the provisions of any other enactment for the time being in force relating to the limitation of the liability of the owners of seagoing vessels.

Title II

Section 9. Discrimination between competing shippers not permitted

Nothing contained in this Act shall be construed as permitting a common carrier by water to discriminate between competing shippers similarly placed in time and circumstances, either (a) with respect to their right to demand and receive bills of lading subject to the provisions of this Act; or (b) when issuing such bills of lading, either in the surrender of any of the carrier's rights and immunities or in the increase of any of the carrier's responsibilities and liabilities pursuant to section 5, title I, of this Act; or (c) in any other way prohibited by the Shipping Act, 1916, as amended.

Section 10. Through bills of lading issued by rail-road carriers

[Omitted–This section amended former 49 USCS Sect. 25.]

Section 11. Where cargo weight is ascertained or accepted by third party

Where under the customs of any trade the weight of any bulk cargo inserted in the bill of lading is a weight ascertained or accepted by a third party other than the carrier or the shipper, and the fact that the weight is so ascertained or accepted is stated in the bill of lading, then, notwithstanding anything in this Act, the bill of lading shall not be deemed to be prima facie evidence against the carrier of the receipt of goods of the weight so inserted in the bill of lading, and the accuracy thereof at the time of shipment shall not be deemed to have been guaranteed by the shipper.

Section 12. Existing provisions not affected

Nothing in this Act shall be construed as superseding any part of the Act entitled "An Act relating to navigation of vessels, bills of lading, and to certain obligations, duties, and rights in connection with the carriage of property", approved February 13, 1893 [46 USCS §§ 30701 et seq.], or of any other law which would be applicable in the absence of this Act, insofar as they relate to the duties, responsibilities, and liabilities of the ship or carrier prior to the time when the goods are loaded on or after the time they are discharged from the ship.

Section 13. Scope of Act

This Act shall apply to all contracts for carriage of goods by sea to or from ports of the United States in foreign trade. As used in this Act the term "United States" includes its districts, territories, and possessions: *Provided, however,* That the Philippine Legislature may by law exclude its application to transportation to or from ports of the Philippine Islands]. The term "foreign trade" means the transportation of goods between the ports of the United States and ports of foreign countries. Nothing in this Act shall be held to apply to contracts for carriage of goods by sea between any port of the United States or its possessions, and any other port of the United States or its possessions: *Provided, however,* That any bill of lading or similar document of title which is evidence of a contract for the carriage of goods by sea between such ports, containing an express statement that it shall be subject to the provisions of this Act, shall be subjected hereto as fully as if subject hereto by the express provisions of this Act: *Provided further,* That every bill of lading or similar document of title which is evidence of a contract for the carriage of goods by sea from ports of the United States, in foreign trade, shall contain a statement that it shall have effect subject to the provisions of this Act.

Section 14. Suspension of Title I by Presidential proclamation

Upon the certification of the Secretary of Transportation that the foreign commerce of the United States in its competition with that of foreign nations is prejudiced by the provisions, or any of them, of title I of this Act, or by the laws of any foreign country or countries relating to the carriage of goods by sea, the President of the United States may, from time to time, by proclamation, suspend any or all provisions of title I of this Act for such periods of time or indefinitely as may be designated in the proclamation. The President may at any time rescind such suspension of title I hereof, and any provisions thereof which may have been suspended shall thereby be reinstated and again apply to contracts thereafter made for the carriage of goods by sea. Any proclamation of suspension or rescission of any such suspension shall take effect on a date named therein, which date shall be not less than ten days from the issue of the proclamation.

Any contract for the carriage of goods by sea, subject to the provisions of this Act, effective during any period when title I hereof, or any part thereof, is suspended, shall be subject to all provisions of law now or hereafter applicable to that part of title I which may have thus been suspended.

Section 15. Effective data

This Act shall take effect ninety days after the date of its approval; but nothing in this Act shall apply during a period not to exceed one year following its approval to any contract for the carriage of goods by sea, made before the date on which this Act is approved, nor to any bill of lading or similar document of title issued, whether before or after such date of approval in pursuance of any such contract as aforesaid.

Section 16. Citation of Act

This Act may be cited as the "Carriage of Goods by Sea Act".

Approved, April 16, 1936.

Index

A

Agency, 13, 16, 17, 22, 90, 101–105, 111, 112, 118, 121, 168, 199, 253, 293, 380, 389, 401, 419, 420, 426

Arbitration, 8, 13, 17, 60, 61, 113–116, 138, 167, 169, 293, 342–346, 371–373, 377, 396, 397, 409, 418, 419, 446

Arrest, 135, 142, 240, 286, 288, 306, 338, 340, 374, 375, 382, 476, 481, 482, 486, 504, 512, 522, 533, 545, 555, 568

B

Bailment, 3, 11, 13, 16, 18, 49, 65, 66, 69, 101, 102, 121, 125–132, 134–139, 142, 145, 168, 171, 173, 188, 244, 269, 315, 317–319, 476

- burden of proof, 101, 127, 128, 130, 269, 317–319
- for reward, 276, 315, 316
- head bailee and sub-bailee, 125
- successors in title
- terms, 101, 136
- utility, 134, 135

Bill of lading, 6, 11, 18, 23–25, 30, 33, 34, 36, 43, 45, 52, 53, 55, 56, 59, 65, 66, 74, 90, 110, 113, 119, 134, 136, 138, 145–147, 155, 162, 169, 173, 174, 192, 193, 195, 246, 250, 342, 348, 412, 421

- apparent good order and condition, 22, 31, 179, 182, 194, 195, 312, 320
- bearer bill, 38, 61, 74, 120, 559
- claused, 31, 61
- clauses
  - contents not known, 179, 192
  - quantity or weight not known, 179, 180, 190, 191
  - Relta, 179, 180, 194
  - said to contain, 32, 179, 180
- clean, 31, 37, 88, 110, 132, 182, 184, 306, 307, 309, 312, 416
- collective through bill, 42, 48
- combined transport/multimodal transport, 40, 44, 125, 138, 145, 169, 173, 174, 192, 195
- conclusive evidence rule, 186
- constructive possession, 3, 6, 12, 16, 23, 25, 29, 32–35, 39, 41, 44, 47, 52, 54, 119, 154
- contract of carriage, 22, 23, 35, 36, 47, 55, 65, 68, 73, 76, 102, 111, 121, 166, 167, 187, 249, 259, 317, 328, 501, 502, 504, 509, 510, 519, 520, 522, 530, 531, 533, 543, 544, 546, 552, 554, 556, 560–562, 565, 567, 568
- document of title, 9, 23, 28, 29, 44, 51–53, 155, 187, 248–251, 501, 503, 509, 511, 519, 521, 530, 532, 542–544, 549, 552, 554, 565, 567, 571, 572
- electronic bill, 23, 72
- estoppel, 31, 179, 181, 182, 184–187, 336
- extinction of liability, 66
- extinction of rights, 65, 66
- false through bill, 42, 135
- history, 23, 25, 33, 54
- intermediate holders, 66
- issued by freight forwarder/NVOC, 23, 40–47, 102, 111, 135, 144, 145

A. Kasi, *The Law of Carriage of Goods by Sea*,
https://doi.org/10.1007/978-981-33-6793-7

negotiability/negotiable, 6, 23, 28, 31, 37, 38, 52, 54, 74, 75, 113, 138, 149, 169, 173, 192, 195, 250, 256, 257, 263, 505, 514, 525, 536, 550, 557, 570
parol evidence, 36
presumptions, 150, 179–181, 185–187
prima facie evidence rule, 31, 75, 183–186, 328, 329, 347, 354, 502, 510, 511, 520, 521, 531, 542, 544, 546, 553, 554, 566, 567, 569, 571
pure charterer's bill, 106, 107, 142
pure through bill, 47, 48
receipt function, 31, 47, 180
received for shipment bill, 23, 31, 36–39, 56, 181, 184, 187, 241, 249–251, 559
representations, 179–181, 184–187, 197, 562
shipowner's bill, 42, 103, 107, 108, 111–113
shipped bill, 23, 28, 31, 36, 42, 198, 251
spent bill, 67, 164
straight bill, 66, 74, 75, 120, 463
switch bill, 191
through bill, 23, 40, 46, 47, 106
to order bill, 23, 30, 56, 59, 65, 120, 146
transferability/transferable, 3, 6, 11, 12, 16, 23, 26, 28, 30, 32, 35–37, 39, 40, 42–48, 52, 54, 64, 72, 111, 120, 147, 372, 539
undertaking to deliver, 22, 28, 32, 39–41
Bolero, 71

C

Cargo claims, 3, 4, 7, 18, 40, 101, 102, 109, 143, 165, 176, 179, 216, 247, 263, 270, 285, 286, 313, 321, 328, 329, 333, 334, 337, 340, 373, 382, 383, 416, 446, 453, 455, 464, 470, 497–499
Cargoworthiness, 203–207, 211, 214–216, 218, 220–225, 237, 241, 269–271, 276, 282, 283, 498
contractual description of cargo holds, 220, 221
Carriage contract/contract of carriage, 3, 4, 7, 9, 11, 21–23, 28, 35, 36, 40, 41, 44, 46, 55, 56, 63, 67, 68, 70, 73, 82, 83, 88, 104, 110, 119, 121–123, 126, 142, 146, 172, 176, 184, 187, 189, 197, 200, 219, 220, 225, 229, 236, 238, 246, 248, 249, 253, 259, 265, 267, 276, 284, 306, 308, 316, 328, 345, 348, 357, 372, 400, 415–417, 476, 501–503, 509–512, 514, 519–521, 524, 530–532, 536, 543–545, 550, 552–554, 557, 560–562, 565–567
Charterparty, 8, 11, 21, 23, 26, 42, 43, 45, 56, 67, 68, 92, 93, 102, 105, 107, 109, 111–119, 136, 138, 147, 167, 187, 192, 194, 203, 220, 221, 224, 225, 228, 229, 234, 236, 241, 245, 247, 251, 293, 328, 329, 333, 341, 361–363, 371–373, 375–380, 382, 383, 385–392, 394–397, 399–405, 407, 410–415, 417–435, 437, 439–461, 463, 465, 467–474, 476–481, 484, 487, 488, 490–499, 546
allocation of risk, 378
always accessible clause, 435
anti-technicality clause, 467, 474, 475, 477
apportionment of cargo claims, 497
approach voyage, 371, 372, 385–387, 389–391
berth charter, 388, 429, 430, 434
BIMCO BALTIME, 376, 380, 383, 386, 390, 397, 451, 458, 467, 480, 481, 487, 489
BIMCO GENCON, 67, 376, 377, 386, 389, 405, 415, 419, 424, 425, 427, 428, 439, 441, 444, 447, 458
calculating off-hire period, 487
cancelling date, 371, 372, 385–387, 390, 391, 426, 439, 440
carrying voyage, 427
cesser clause, 399, 413, 414
competing clauses, 376, 383
deductions against hire, 468, 471
delivery, 21, 76, 102, 113, 147, 167, 220, 333, 376, 385, 386, 391, 392, 403, 407, 454, 463, 490–492
demise charter, 42, 371, 384, 400, 458
demurrage, 67, 116–119, 234, 418, 423, 424, 435, 437, 443–448
detention, 116, 395, 426, 435, 437, 441, 444, 446–448, 484
equitable set-off against hire, 470
free pratique, 428, 446
freight, 67, 80, 83, 105, 107, 116–118, 333, 372, 375, 399, 400, 402–405, 407, 411–413, 415, 418, 420–422, 430, 454, 472, 475
frustration, 371, 372, 387, 394, 395
hire-payment, 107, 454, 469

indemnity, 74, 147, 382, 449, 452–454, 457, 463, 465
inter-club agreement, 383, 497
laycan, 439, 496
laydays, 439
laytime, 116, 386, 423–427, 435, 437, 439–442, 444, 445, 447
calculating, 487
exceptions, 437, 440–442, 445, 447
starting, 427, 437, 444
lien
exercise, 105, 118, 420
near clause, 410
net clause, 488
notice of readiness, 389, 424, 426, 427, 434, 437
NYPE, 293, 422, 469, 472, 476, 479–481, 487, 489
off-hire/suspension, 450, 453, 479, 481, 484, 487, 488, 490
orders, 21, 102, 113, 116, 167, 219, 376, 395, 404, 414, 434, 449, 450, 452, 454, 456, 457, 461, 463, 470, 494, 495
employment, 293, 374, 449, 452
illegitimate, 450, 494, 495
legitimate, 449, 450, 494, 495
navigation, 136, 452, 495
overlap period, 494–496
period clause, 487, 488
permitted port, 457
port charter, 388, 426, 430, 431
reachable on arrival clause, 435
ready to load and discharge, 427
redelivery, 395, 469, 490–493, 495
delivery window, 490, 491
early delivery, 491, 492
late delivery, 386, 490, 491
repudiatory breach, 478, 491, 493, 495
safe berth, 430, 458, 459
safe port, 448, 457, 458, 460, 461
sale of ship, 384
standard forms, 11, 67, 372, 376, 397
suspending performance, 477
termination, 91, 105, 220, 443, 444, 467, 468, 471, 472
time charter, 105, 111, 113, 220, 247, 293, 328, 361, 371, 373, 375, 376, 385, 386, 392, 399, 400, 412, 420, 422, 449, 454, 461, 470, 481, 487, 488, 491–493
time lost clause, 433
title to bunkers, 371, 372
trip charter, 371, 373, 375
voyage charter, 67, 102, 111, 119, 215, 221, 222, 234, 333, 371, 375–377, 382, 385–387, 390–392, 394, 399, 400, 407, 410, 412, 415, 418, 420, 434, 454, 458, 465
weather permitting, 425
weather working day, 423–425
wibon clause, 432, 433
withdrawal, 468, 472–477
Choice of law, 101, 113, 115, 137–139, 172, 245, 246, 259–263, 397
Choice of law clause, 101, 115, 138, 139, 172, 245, 246, 260–263
circumventing, 260
Cif, 37, 79–84, 88
Circular indemnity clause, 45, 47, 102, 142, 165, 166, 173–175
Clause paramount, 8–11, 14, 68, 70, 187, 245, 248, 258, 260, 261, 329, 362, 372, 376, 377, 381, 383, 499
Combined transport/multimodal transport, 21, 40, 44, 45, 125, 135, 138, 145, 174, 195
Conflicting clauses, 108, 334
Containerised cargo, 31, 32, 44, 48, 192, 196, 222, 350, 351, 358
Contract of carriage/carriage contract
contract by agency, 101–103, 121
direct contract, 107, 417
implied contract, 121–123
statutory contract, 107, 137
Contractual action/action in contract, 30, 54, 141, 143, 150, 151, 200
Convention gap, 45, 50, 254
Conversion, 101, 102, 118, 125, 135, 143–145, 353, 354, 384, 463
assessment of damages for misdelivery, 158
detinue, 153, 154, 157, 158
misdelivery, 33, 49, 101, 102, 143–145, 149–152, 158, 164, 463
possessory right, 4, 11, 148–150, 152–156, 158, 250, 384
proprietary right, 52, 148, 152, 153, 156–158
Cost and freight, 79, 80, 82

D

Dangerous goods, 280, 361, 362, 448
common law, 64
Hague/Hague-Visby Rules, 3, 8, 49, 50, 75, 188, 353, 362

Deceit, 179, 180, 191, 197, 198, 200
Deck cargo, 9, 253, 259, 273, 280, 281, 365, 376, 378–380, 453–455, 481, 550
Deviation, 18, 56, 112, 121, 205, 220, 225–239, 276, 307, 321, 322, 341, 348, 359, 386, 504, 512, 522, 533, 546, 556, 568, 569
  defence of saving property/life at sea, 228, 229
  justification, 144, 204, 225, 227, 229, 230, 235, 238, 276
  liberty clauses, 225, 227, 230, 231
  quasi-deviation, 204, 205, 227, 238, 239, 267, 341
Due diligence, 131, 208, 210, 212–216, 222, 223, 225, 240, 241, 269–274, 276–282, 286, 288, 289, 301, 302, 310, 362, 366, 381, 426, 459, 502–504, 510–512, 520–522, 530, 532, 533, 543, 545, 553, 555, 566–568

E

Ejusdem generis, 483, 484
Evidence, 3, 7, 9, 11, 13, 16, 21, 26, 28, 30, 31, 35, 36, 39, 41, 47, 51, 67, 75, 76, 95, 112, 119, 127–133, 159, 179–188, 191, 193, 195, 226, 248, 257, 269, 279, 281, 293, 312–320, 328, 350, 352, 418, 540, 542, 550, 551, 559, 562, 565, 571
Exceptions clause/liability exclusion clause/liability limitation clause, 168, 243, 244, 381–383
Exclusion clauses, 4, 5, 160, 162, 168, 204, 206, 208, 213, 219, 228, 235, 241–243, 275, 376, 378, 379, 442, 445
  burden of proof, 243, 244
  negligence, 168, 208, 209, 219, 378, 379, 381
  perils of the sea, 228, 242

F

Fiost, 284
Fire, 122, 132, 134, 135, 162, 194, 209, 210, 214, 217, 218, 240, 271, 272, 280, 282, 286, 288, 297–299, 301, 302, 363, 382, 388, 481, 486, 503, 512, 522, 532, 545, 555, 568
Fob, 26, 79–85, 88, 93, 103, 106, 121–123, 127, 185, 197, 253
Free-in, free-out, 68, 69, 146, 188, 284, 306
Freight, 22, 27, 45, 46, 62, 63, 79, 80, 83, 90, 104–107, 110, 113, 114, 116–118, 126, 132, 137, 145, 220, 234, 236, 275, 300, 327, 333, 334, 345, 363, 367, 372, 374, 375, 399–417, 419–422, 426, 434, 435, 442, 457, 475, 539, 569
  deemed earned clause, 404, 406, 407, 409, 426
  set-off, 333, 375, 399, 403, 406, 407
Freight forwarder, 21, 40, 42, 43, 46, 47, 90, 102, 109–111, 125, 135, 143–145, 300, 333, 345, 402, 416, 417

G

General average, 62, 212, 213, 273, 279, 280, 364, 411, 415, 422, 505, 513, 514, 524, 525, 535, 536, 546, 557, 569

H

Hague/Hague-Visby Rules, 5, 7–10, 12, 15, 18, 37, 44, 45, 47–50, 54, 68–70, 74, 75, 123, 126–128, 138, 140–142, 160, 165, 169, 171, 172, 176, 179, 181, 186, 189–191, 194, 197, 200, 201, 204–208, 211, 212, 214, 216, 221–223, 225, 227, 229, 232, 236–240, 242, 243, 245–249, 252, 254–256, 258–267, 269–271, 274, 287, 294, 297, 300, 302, 316, 319, 321, 322, 326–328, 337, 338, 341, 345, 346, 351, 353, 355–359, 361, 368, 372, 376–378, 383, 509, 519, 563
  acts of god
  burden of proof, 128, 269, 276, 315, 317
  contractual application, 246
  defences, 138, 142, 169, 200, 210, 225, 227, 236, 238, 240, 265, 267, 269, 287, 308, 378
    actual fault or privity of carrier, 189, 210, 299
  due diligence, 216, 223, 277
  gross weight limitation, 321, 356
  inherent defect, 276
  insufficiency of packing, 216
  interpretation
  liability limitation, 12, 321, 322, 326, 347
  loss of liability limitation, 359
  loss of time limitation
  management of ship
  navigation of ship, 243, 293, 349

package limitation, 168, 222, 239, 247, 252, 261, 262, 326, 327, 350, 353, 356
statutory application, 245–247, 258
time limitation, 321, 322, 326–329, 339, 341, 342, 383, 407
Hamburg Rules, 5, 6, 8
Himalaya clause, 47, 102, 138, 142, 165, 166, 168–173, 266

I
Implied contract
on discharge, 123, 124
on loading, 103, 121–124
Implied terms at common law, 203, 270, 274
Incorporation clause, 8, 113, 115–117, 256, 372
Incoterms, 79–81, 83–86, 88
Indemnity-undertaking/undertaking to indemnify, 146, 147, 197, 367, 463, 464
Innominate terms, 84, 89, 220, 391, 443, 468, 471, 495
In personam action, 341
In rem action, 159, 286, 287, 341
Inter-Club Agreement (ICA), 247, 383, 497

J
Jurisdiction clause
circumventing, 260

L
Letter of credit/documentary credit, 4, 7, 37, 39, 43, 45, 48, 53, 60–62, 79, 86–96, 98, 180, 198, 253
fraud exception, 96, 98
Liens, 105–107, 110, 116–118, 220, 375, 399, 411, 414–422, 444
on cargo, 4, 110, 399, 416, 418
on sub-freight, 105, 107, 419, 420
Live animal, 9, 203, 253, 259, 273, 501, 509, 519, 530, 543, 550, 552, 565

M
Misrepresentation, 13, 16, 179, 180, 197, 199–202, 392, 540

N
Negligence, 3, 4, 11, 13, 16, 18, 49, 101, 102, 125, 128, 131, 132, 135, 137, 139–142, 145, 161, 168, 172, 173, 180, 188, 191, 193, 198, 208–212, 218, 235, 240, 243, 244, 246, 265, 271, 272, 276, 278, 280–282, 288, 292, 295, 297, 302–306, 308, 311, 312, 314–318, 320, 380, 445, 455, 483, 503, 511, 521, 532, 545, 554, 567
Negligent misstatement, 197, 199, 200
Non-delivery, 30, 101, 102, 104, 143–145, 150, 151, 158–160, 162, 170, 228, 231, 318, 349, 351, 408
Non-vehicle owning carrier, 21, 23, 40, 102, 300

P
Piracy, 213, 305, 483
Privity of contract, 11, 17, 30, 35, 41, 62, 166, 420, 464
Property
passing, 85
Protection and Indemnity (PI), 18, 37, 102, 336, 383, 416, 464, 497
Pure economic loss, 141, 347, 356

R
Res ipsa loquitur, 128, 314, 315, 318
Risk
passing, 4, 79, 84–86
Rotterdam rules, 5, 6, 8

S
Sale of goods, 3, 4, 7, 12, 13, 17, 34, 52, 77, 79, 84–86, 88, 153, 155, 383, 384
Sea waybill, 7, 15, 21, 22, 32, 46, 55, 59, 62, 65, 66, 73–76, 102, 113, 120, 138, 167, 169, 173, 176, 179, 192, 195, 203, 245, 252, 256, 257, 259, 273, 361, 376, 559–562
Seaworthiness, 12, 14, 203–208, 210, 211, 213–218, 220, 223, 225, 237, 241, 242, 263, 269–276, 278–283, 292, 302, 306, 307, 380, 505, 514, 525, 536, 542, 547, 551, 557, 570
absolute duty, 225
burden of proof, 203, 206, 217, 277, 282
causation, 203, 218, 219, 224, 225, 282
crew-competency, 207, 208
doctrine of stages, 203, 215, 217, 273, 274, 276
due diligence, 208, 215, 216, 223, 225, 270–273, 276–279, 281, 282, 301, 302,

503, 511, 512, 521, 532, 545, 555, 567, 568
legal fitness, 207, 208
standard, 203, 206, 208, 210, 211, 214, 215
Ship's delivery order, 7, 15, 21, 22, 25, 55, 59, 62, 63, 65, 66, 73, 75, 76, 79, 120, 164, 167, 176, 179, 203, 361, 376
Shipping document, 4, 7, 8, 21, 22, 63, 85, 102, 113–116, 120, 179, 180, 235, 246, 247, 255, 263, 302, 328, 350, 362, 372, 376, 377, 559–561
Special Drawing Rights (SDR), 5, 326, 354, 355, 534, 550

T
Third-party, 3, 7, 11, 13, 17, 19, 34, 35, 56, 102, 106, 111, 119, 121, 128, 138, 139, 147, 153, 165–168, 170, 171, 173–176, 186, 195, 246, 266, 306, 307, 309, 345, 420, 421, 444, 464, 510, 520, 531, 542, 553, 571
liabilities, 66, 106, 553, 571
representative action, 176
rights, 3, 7, 11
suit for benefit of, 175
Transshipment, 42, 46, 48, 50, 69, 102, 107, 126, 134–136, 139, 141, 142, 228, 252, 254, 255, 258, 500

U
UCP 500/600, 7, 37, 39, 40, 42, 43, 45, 47, 48, 53, 87–94, 96, 113
Unilateral contract, 36, 64, 87

W
Waiver, 90, 93, 428–430, 455, 473
Weather, 182, 211, 217, 228, 230, 302–305, 308, 318, 423–425, 433, 435, 436, 462

Y
York Antwerp Rules, 212

The manufacturer's authorised representative in the EU is Springer Nature Customer Service Centre GmbH, Europaplatz 3, 69115 Heidelberg, Germany. If you have any concerns regarding our products, please contact ProductSafety@springernature.com

Printed and bound by CPI Group (UK) Ltd, Croydon, CR0 4YY
30/09/2026
02225290-0019